THE GLEN CANYON COUNTRY

The Glen Canyon Country

A Personal Memoir

Don D. Fowler

THE UNIVERSITY OF UTAH PRESS | *Salt Lake City*

The Defiance House Man colophon is a registered trademark of the University of Utah Press. It is based upon a four-foot-tall, Ancient Puebloan pictograph (late PIII) near Glen Canyon, Utah.

Library of Congress Cataloging-in-Publication Data

Fowler, Don D., 1936–

The Glen Canyon country : a personal memoir/Don D. Fowler.

p. cm.

Includes bibliographical references and index.

ISBN 978-1-60781-127-5 (alk. paper)

ISBN 978-1-60781-134-3 (paper : alk. paper)

1. Glen Canyon (Utah and Ariz.)—History. 2. Glen Canyon (Utah and Ariz.)—Discovery and exploration. 3. Explorers—Glen Canyon (Utah and Ariz.)—Biography. 4. Glen Canyon (Utah and Ariz.)—Description and travel. 5. Glen Canyon (Utah and Ariz.)—Antiquities. 6. Fowler, Don D., 1936– 7. Fowler, Don D., 1936—Travel—Utah—Glen Canyon. 8. Archaeologists—Southwest, New—Biography. I. Title.

F832.G5F69 2010

979.2'51—dc22 2010045206

FRONTISPIECE. Floyd Sharrock descending from Fence Ruin site, Wilson Canyon, August 1959. Photograph by William Lipe. Archaeology Center Collection, 42Sa377-33. Courtesy of Special Collections, Marriott Library, University of Utah.

FOR

Catherine (Kay) Fowler

whose life has been intertwined with mine
ever since our early Glen Canyon Project student days—

AND FOR

Katie Lee

whose love of the Glen Canyon that was,
remains undiminished by time and circumstance.

CONTENTS

List of Illustrations ix
Foreword by W. L. Rusho xiii
Preface and Acknowledgments xvii

1. Prelude 1
2. The Glen Canyon Country and Its First Explorers, 1776–1856 11
3. Mapping and Defining the Glen Canyon Country 27
4. John Wesley Powell and the Canyon Country, 1867–1869 36
5. Powell and the Glen Canyon Country 53
6. Powell, the U.S. Geological Survey, and the Canyon Country 73
7. Laccoliths and Grand Staircases: The Work of C. E. Dutton and G. K. Gilbert 84
8. Glen Canyon Country Geology in the Twentieth Century 94
9. Colorado Canyon Railroad and Gold Fever: Stanton and Spencer 103
10. Romancing the Glen Canyon Country 118
11. Pack Trips and River Running: Exploring the Country for Fun 140
12. Harnessing the Colorado River 181
13. Early Archaeology in the Glen Canyon Country 200
14. The Enamored Explorers 232
15. The Glen Canyon Project: Beginnings 242
16. Implementing the Glen Canyon Project 259
17. The 1959 and 1960 Seasons 275
18. The 1961 and 1962 Seasons 294
19. The Museum of Northern Arizona and the Glen Canyon Project 316
20. Lives and Times of Sojourners in the Glen Canyon Country 327
21. Postlude: The Glen Canyon Country of the Imagination 349

Notes 359
Bibliography 377
Index 407

ILLUSTRATIONS

MAPS

Map 1. The Glen Canyon Country section of the Colorado Plateau xvi
Map 2. The Glen Canyon Country in the context of the Four Corners region 12
Map 3. Glen Canyon and major tributary canyons 253

FIGURES

Frontispiece. Floyd Sharrock descending from Fence Ruin in Slick Rock Canyon, August 1959 ii
1.1. Gates Roost site, Twenty Five Mile Canyon, September 1957 7
2.1. Aerial view of Glen Canyon below the confluence of the Colorado and San Juan rivers, August 1958 13
2.2. Satellite image of Lake Powell, 1970 14
2.3. Aerial view of Henry Mountains, 1962 15
2.4. Navajo Mountain and Bald Rock crescent, 1959 16
2.5. Aerial view of Rainbow Bridge, 1961 17
2.6. Aerial view of the east face of Kaiparowits Plateau, 1937 17
2.7. Section of Miera map, 1776 21
3.1. Portrait of John Strong Newberry 29
3.2. Steamboat *Explorer* on lower Colorado River, 1856 30
3.3. Sketch of lower San Juan River area, 1860 33
3.4. Section of Macomb map, 1860 34
4.1. Portrait of John Wesley Powell, ca. 1882 37
5.1. Launch of Powell's second river trip, 1871 57
5.2. A glen in Glen Canyon, July 1872 58
5.3. Powell's men's names in Music Temple, 1871–1872 59
5.4. Almon Harris Thompson, 1872 62
5.5. Refitting *Cañonita* at Dirty Devil River, July 1872 66

5.6. Mouth of Music Temple, Glen Canyon, July 1872 67
5.7. Chuarumpeak, Kaibab Paiute leader, 1872 69
5.8. Kaibab Paiute round dance, 1872 70
5.9. Thomas Moran and Justin E. Colburn, Kanab, Utah, 1872 71
5.10. Posed Kaibab Paiute Indians, August 1872 71
6.1. Portrait of Henry Gannett, 1890s 77
7.1. Portrait of Clarence Dutton, 1882 86
7.2. *Smithsonian Butte*, by W. H. Holmes, 1882 88
7.3. Portrait of Grove Karl Gilbert, 1910 89
8.1. Portrait of Herbert E. Gregory, 1901 95
8.2. Glen Canyon at Meskin Bar, 1922 96
8.3. Kane Spring Valley near Gunsight Pass, 1922 97
8.4. Gregory pack train descending into Moqui Canyon, 1927 98
9.1. Robert B. Stanton at rock art panel, upper Glen Canyon 104
9.2. Cass Hite, 1907 108
9.3. Stanton dredge, 1909 114
9.4. Remains of Warm Creek coal mine buildings, 1962 116
9.5. *Charles Spencer* steamboat, mouth of Warm Creek, 1912 116
10.1. Sipapu Bridge, Natural Bridges National Monument, 1925 119
10.2. Gothic Arch, Soda Gulch, 1944 120
10.3. Rainbow Bridge, 1921 121
11.1. Bert Loper at his cabin in Red Canyon, 1947 144
11.2. Dave Rust and Sarah Fraser in Glen Canyon, 1930 153
11.3. George Fraser, Sarah Fraser, and Bert Loper, 1930 157
11.4. Norm Nevills and Bill Woods at Mexican Hat, 1933 163
11.5. Nevills, Clover, and Jotter at Lee's Ferry, 1938 167
11.6. Nevills's boats at Hidden Passage, 1945 171
11.7. Georgie White river party, Grand Canyon, 1950s 179
12.1. Arthur Powell Davis, 1920s 187
12.2. USGS river party at Lee's Ferry, 1924 189
13.1. Wetherill trading post at Kayenta, Arizona, 1930s 203
13.2. Byron Cummings at Rainbow Bridge, 1936 204
13.3. Ida Wetherill and Malcolm Cummings at Keet Seel Ruin, 1909 206
13.4. Charles Bernheimer, Earl Morris, and Zeke Johnson, 1923 211
13.5. Julian Steward party at Lee's Ferry, 1932 219
13.6. Rainbow Bridge–Monument Valley Expedition directors, 1933 220
13.7. Rainbow Bridge–Monument Valley Expedition field crew, 1937 223
13.8. Rainbow Bridge–Monument Valley Expedition river crew, 1935 226
13.9. Rainbow Bridge–Monument Valley Expedition river crew, 1936 227
14.1. Harry Aleson repairing boat motor 233
14.2. Harry Aleson Glen Canyon river trip, 1940s 234
14.3. Dudy Thomas, Dick Sprang, and Mickey the cat, 1953 235

14.4. Mickey the cat at Anasazi Ruin, Glen Canyon, 1953 236
14.5. Dudy Thomas, Pard the dog, and Mickey the cat climbing Slick Rock Slope 236
14.6. "We Three" in Glen Canyon, 1953 238
15.1. Lobo Arch, Coyote Gulch, 1957 252
15.2. Frank Wright and C. Gregory Crampton in Glen Canyon, 1959 256
16.1. Jesse D. Jennings in Glen Canyon, 1958 260
16.2. University of Utah boats in Glen Canyon, 1958 261
16.3. Herbert Alexander, Norman Ritchie, and "Manure" on Kaiparowits Plateau, 1958 265
16.4. C. Melvin Aikens mapping on Kaiparowits Plateau, 1958 266
16.5. University of Utah river crew, Red Canyon, 1958 267
16.6. Bert Loper Cabin, Red Canyon, 1958 272
17.1. Loper Ruin excavations, 1959 276
17.2. "Fort Moki" at mouth of White Canyon 277
17.3. Don Fowler at mouth of Moqui Canyon, 1959 278
17.4. Don Fowler at lunch, Wilson Canyon, 1959 279
17.5. Cliffs and water opposite Music Temple, 1959 280
17.6. Cliffs and water below Meskin Bar, 1958 281
17.7. Section of rock art panel, Smith Fork Bar, 1959 282
17.8. Don Fowler and Dick Ross chalking petroglyphs, 1959 282
17.9. Keith Anderson and Tom Roth on Forgotten Canyon steps, 1959 284
17.10. Crumbling Kiva Ruin, Forgotten Canyon, 1959 285
17.11. Defiance House pictographs, 1959 286
17.12. Recording Defiance House, 1959 287
17.13. Camp Number 1 in Lake Canyon, 1960 288
17.14. Jesse D. Jennings and Richard Gould at Horsefly Hollow site, Lake Canyon, 1960 290
17.15. Falling Dune in Moqui Canyon, 1961 292
17.16. Wasp House site in Lake Canyon, 1960 293
18.1. "Fowler's Folly," Harris Wash, 1961 295
18.2. View to the south from Kaiparowits Plateau, 1958 298
18.3. View to the west from Kaiparowits Plateau, 1958 299
18.4. Excavation crew in Moqui Canyon, 1961 300
18.5. Excavation camp in Moqui Canyon, 1961 302
19.1. Bill and Nettie Adams on the San Juan River, 1959 319
19.2. Alexander (Lex) Lindsay Jr. at a site on Paiute Mesa, 1961 320
19.3. Museum of Northern Arizona excavation crew, West Canyon, 1959 321
19.4. Museum of Northern Arizona pack train in a slickrock area, Navajo Mountain, 1961 322
19.5. Museum of Northern Arizona pack train on Oak Canyon Trail, 1960 323
20.1. Creeping Dune Reservoir site, 1960 331
20.2. Prehistoric irrigation ditches, Beaver Creek, 1959 332
20.3. Aerial view of Escalante, Utah, 1937 338
20.4. Dance Hall Rock, near Forty-mile Spring 340
20.5. Top of Hole-in-the-Rock, 1959 342

20.6. Dugway across Colorado River from Hole-in-the-Rock 343
20.7. Lee's Ferry, ca. 1925 345
20.8. Hite Ferry, 1946 346
21.1. "Last Bucket of Concrete," Glen Canyon Dam, 1963 350
21.2. Glen Canyon Dam and Lake Powell, 1984 351
21.3. Crucified dummies for movie set on road to Kane Creek, 1963 352
21.4. Set for *The Greatest Story Ever Told*, 1963 353
21.5. Defiance House restored, 1970 354

TABLES

7.1. USGS consensus scheme of North American historical geology, 1880s 84
7.2. Consensus scheme of the geological history of the Plateau Province, 1960s 85
13.1. Pecos Classification 210
20.1. General Ancestral Puebloan chronology 329

FOREWORD

W. L. Rusho

GLEN CANYON, AS A CHANNEL OF THE Colorado River, was a magical place. Of course, as the present cradle for the bathtub-ringed Lake Powell, it is still often considered magical. Yet, as author Wallace Stegner has written, "Glen Canyon was for delight. . . . in gaining the lovely and the useable, we have given up the incomparable."

Lake Powell can indeed be beautiful—at least in several red rock locales—but the boaters who skim, or roar, across its reflecting blue surface are missing not only the depth of the canyon and the flowing river, but also many of the jewels of the former canyon, namely the historic artifacts and the Indian ruins and petroglyphs that were dotted along the cliffs and alcoves above the river. These relics of the past were not always obvious to a river boater, for many were located far up side canyons, in places only an intrepid hiker who knew what he or she was looking for could find.

Glen Canyon's pre–Lake Powell magnificence, what observant river runners of the 1950s and early 1960s came away with, lay in its towering rust-red domes, vertical cliffs, burning sun, constantly changing cool shadows, murmuring, swirling brown water, and deep, narrow slot canyons where colored sunlight bounced about in narrow rays, illuminating tiny rivulets, pools, and ferns. Alternating with dramatic cliffs were crescent-shaped shorelines where brilliant green vegetation provided a startling contrast to the bare orange strata of rock above. It was a veritable Kodachrome world—a wonderland for the eye or camera.

It was into this fairyland that Don Fowler and I arrived almost at the same time, around 1958, yet many miles and assignments far apart. I was given the job of public information officer for the Bureau of Reclamation at Glen Canyon Dam, then under construction, while Don was a student archaeologist for the University of Utah who had been assigned the task, along with several others, of "salvaging" the prehistory of Glen Canyon prior to its being flooded by Lake Powell.

Although I did not know Don at the time (we met years later), slowly, through experience, we grew to share a kindred spirit. We were being captured by the charm of Glen Canyon. For no matter how objectively one approached a study, or a job, in Glen Canyon, a few months or even years of exposure to its myriad charms—its stunning lighting, its almost hidden side canyons, dripping springs and pools, relics of both cliff-dwelling Indians and intrepid miners, and even hermits—was bound to leave an indelible mark on memory and feelings of nostalgia.

It took time and experience to gain full appreciation of Glen Canyon, for its magic was slow acting. Certainly many of those who caught only a glimpse of the canyon failed to appreciate its beauty. Padres Domínguez and Escalante, frustrated in their initial attempts to cross the river in 1776, saw only barren desolation. Ninety-three years later, the men who were part of John Wesley Powell's expedition, the first to boat through the canyon, were hungry and tired, their clothes in tatters, and they could only bemoan the slow river current carrying them to a takeout somewhere far downriver. For the Mormon colonists of 1880, Hole-in-the-Rock and the Colorado River were terrible obstacles that temporarily blocked their wagon trip to southeastern Utah. Engineers starting visiting Glen Canyon as early as 1916, looking for a place to build a dam to prevent the periodic floods that devastated croplands in California. When Hoover Dam was built in the early 1930s, the prospective dam in Glen Canyon was shelved but not forgotten. It was only about fifteen years after Hoover Dam was completed that a new proposal emerged for Glen Canyon Dam, planned to be the key component in the basinwide Colorado River Storage Project, and it was authorized in 1956.

Although it was the construction of dam that brought both me and Don Fowler to Glen Canyon, it would appear that we had totally different objectives. While I was charged with publicizing the dam and conveying its virtues to the press and to visitors, Don was engaged in collecting artifacts and learning as much as possible about ancient life in the canyon soon to be flooded.

On a lovely spring morning in 1958, I chanced to meet Professor C. Gregory Crampton, who was responsible for researching and documenting the written history of Glen Canyon. Greg was amazingly generous with his abundant information, and I almost instantly became an avid student. With his guidance, and what I could learn from books and letters from old-timers, I began to learn the canyon's history. Whenever I could find an excuse, I boated up the canyon, and twice boated down the canyon with Crampton, stopping frequently along the way to investigate historic sites. Glen Canyon, Greg wrote, is the most historic of all Colorado River canyons. Although the region was remote, with almost no roads, it was accessible to those filled with determination and a willingness to endure slow, laborious travel over, around, and through almost impassible red rock lands. And come they did—explorers, colonists, missionaries, miners, traders, and finally river runners—not prolific in number, of course, but all with some degree of adventure. In Glen Canyon, adventure was just a mirror image of experience.

So it must have been with the ancient Indians whom Don Fowler investigated so thoroughly. Although they left no written record, the long-departed Indians left telltale clues, in the form of artifacts, about their lifestyle, eventually allowing Don and his associates to piece together a cogent narrative of how they survived in this harsh land. It was, however, a tough assignment, for nothing was immediately apparent. How could the Indians have lived without agriculture and with few animals to hunt? After years of study, the archaeologists finally concluded that conditions were different a few hundred years ago, and that limited farming would have been possible in some of the side canyons. Also, the ingenuity of the canyon's former inhabitants was outstanding; they harvested a great variety of native plants for both food and textiles, they housed and clothed themselves, and they even seemed to have moments of leisure when they could carve petroglyphs into the sandstone.

Through his work, Don Fowler fell under the spell of Glen Canyon, as did I. Although Don left to pursue his doctorate degree at the University of Pittsburgh before the project was concluded in 1962, his fascination with Glen Canyon over the ensuring years only grew. He and his wife, Catherine, later spent several decades teaching at the University of Nevada—Reno and researching Great Basin archaeology. Yet all that time Don continued thinking about Glen Canyon and conducting exhaustive research of written Glen Canyon history. It was on these terms that our lives finally intersected. Don and I finally met in 2005, when I was filming a documentary DVD on Glen Canyon before Lake Powell, for which Don commented on his archaeology work. In each other, I believe, we instantly felt a bond: the charm of Glen Canyon that had touched both of us fifty years ago—and still holds us today.

Don's boss on the Glen Canyon Project was the late Dr. Jesse Jennings of the University of Utah, one of the most respected and thorough archaeologists ever to work in the American West. I once asked Don if he had any trouble getting along with Dr. Jennings, to which Don quickly replied, "I'm still alive, aren't I?" Jennings wrote a book of his experiences entitled *Accidental Archaeologist* that includes a chapter on the Glen Canyon Project. Hard-charging and demanding, as Jennings was known to be, he had to use tender words to reflect on Glen Canyon:

> On the personal side, learning the Glen and working in and near it for six or seven summers were a rich, emotionally charged period of my life. The vastness, the isolation, the stillness, the overwhelming beauty of the land, even (especially) the heat, the still starlit nights, the blue or brassy midday sky, all combined to make me constantly aware of my good fortune. . . . In retrospect, to coin a phrase—tension or not—I fear I loved every minute of it.

Certainly, Don Fowler and I feel the same about Glen Canyon. If anything, Jennings understated the emotions that one who has lived with the canyon has when reflecting on those marvelous scenes and experiences. Of course, someday, some year, the original canyon will return; dams and reservoirs—even the stored sediment—do not last forever. But the remains, the historic relics and the ancient artifacts, are gone, now either in an archaeology storage basement or vanished for eternity. But we do have the valuable reports, known as "anthropological papers," compiled by Don and his fellow researchers and published by the University of Utah, that provide a detailed glimpse into the lives of Glen Canyon's first residents.

Thankfully, and for prosperity, in this present book Don has given us not only his own personal story, but also his extensive knowledge of Glen Canyon's prehistory and history—the most complete view of human life in the canyon yet published. It is a compelling account—a well written, entertaining, and comprehensive interpretation of the different cultures and objectives of the various residents and visitors who experienced Glen Canyon in times past.

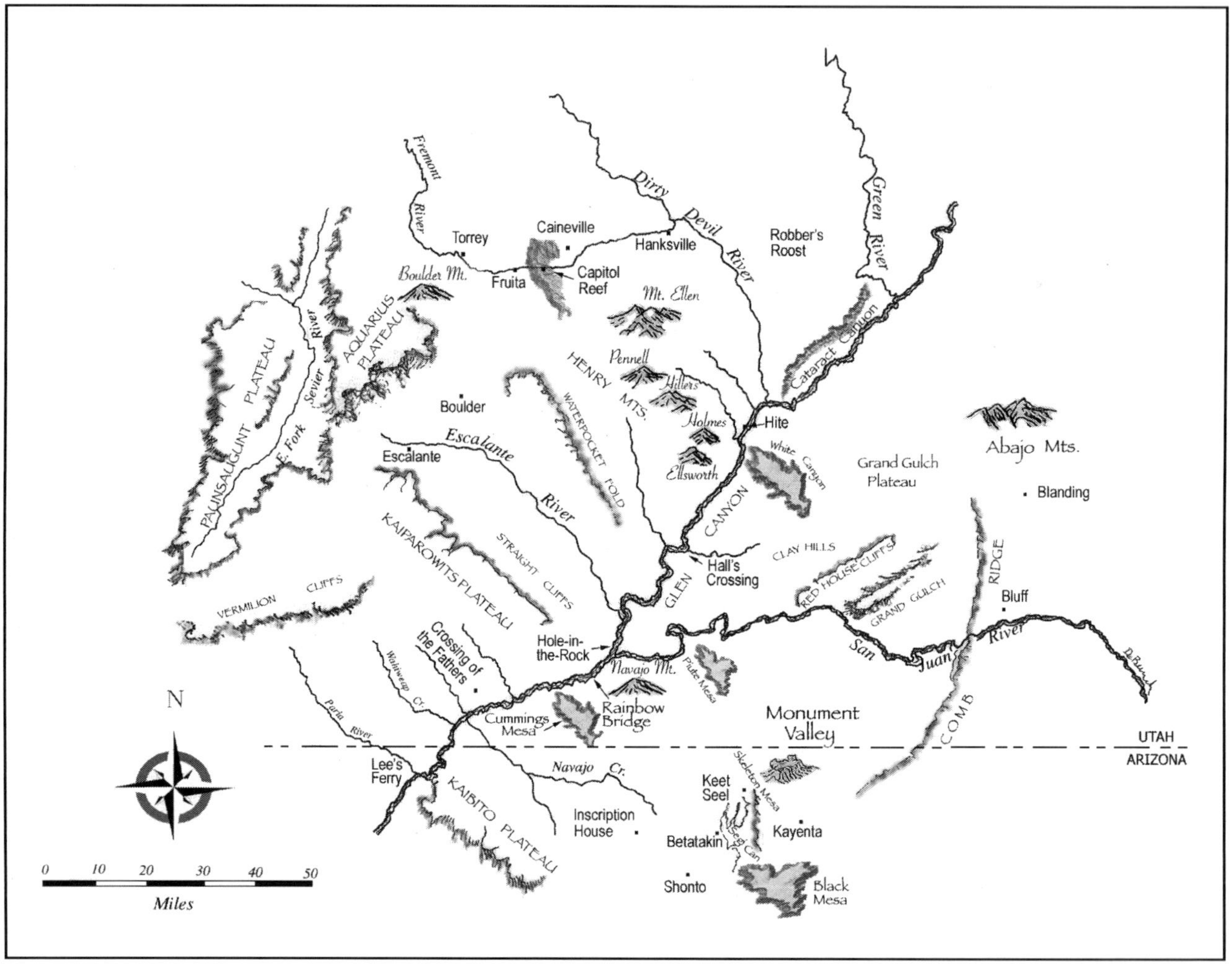

MAP 1. The Glen Canyon Country section of the Colorado Plateau. Map by Patricia DeBunch.

PREFACE AND ACKNOWLEDGMENTS

This book is about a place I call the Glen Canyon Country—an area in southern Utah and northern Arizona around which I have drawn a lopsided loop (Map 1). I was born on the edge of the Country, in Torrey, Utah, but was carried away to northern Utah and environs when I was three. I did not return until I was a junior at the University of Utah, in 1957, when I began what became a six-year involvement with the Country as shovel bum and later staff archaeologist on the Upper Colorado River Archaeological Salvage Project—better known as the Glen Canyon Project (GCP). The project set my career trajectory. I went on to be a practicing archaeologist over a forty-year career, and a historian of western exploration and American anthropology. I also met my wife, Catherine (Kay) Sweeney Fowler, as a result of the project, and we have enjoyed nearly fifty years together as colleagues, scholars, and keen students of the Great Basin and Southwest.

In the late 1980s, the late Norma Mikkelsen, whom I had known and admired since early GCP days, and who was at that time director of the University of Utah Press, suggested I write a book, perhaps semiautobiographical, about Glen Canyon and the country round about. It seemed an opportunity to bring together my archaeological and intellectual history interests. So I agreed, and started in. But, numerous other "more pressing" projects, books, papers, duties and responsibilities intervened, and I put the book aside until the late 1990s, when I was able to do a good deal of research and write drafts of chapters 1–6, 13, and 16–17. I worked on it intermittently thereafter in fits and starts (always those "more pressing" projects taking precedence) but in earnest since late 2008, when my sense of guilt and the gentle prodding of Reba Rauch at the University of Utah Press drove me on.

The book has two themes. One is the place itself, the Glen Canyon Country, and the lives of some of the people who sojourned there. The second, and central, theme is about others, including me, who came to the Country to explore it, to define it from various perspectives, chronicle what they did and saw, and produce "stories" (books, journals, maps, scientific reports, historical chronicles, literary works, and films) about what they encountered. In some instances—for example miners, would-be railroad developers, and some river runners—our concern is what others wrote about them and their sojourns in the Country. The main characters include explorers, geologists, topographers, archaeologists, biologists, river runners, tourists, novelists and essayists, filmmakers, and packers and guides. We also focus on the geologists, engineers, and bureaucrats who came to the canyons of the Colorado River to survey them and study their geology and topography so that they might build dams to "harness the wild" Colorado River.

My own six-year intermittent sojourn in the Glen Canyon Country was a direct result of the decisions of those geologists, engineers, and bureaucrats filtered through the political process and codified into law by the U.S. Congress. The law passed in 1956 authorizing the construction of dams in the Upper Colorado River Basin triggered a "salvage archaeology" project funded by the federal government and implemented by the University of Utah and the Museum of Northern Arizona. It was formally known as the Upper Colorado River Basin Archaeological Salvage Project, but more generally, the Glen Canyon Project (GCP). The background to the project, how it was implemented, and the results thereof are explained in chapters 15–20.

Those of us who were directly involved in the project from 1957 to 1963 were simply the latest of many who had come to the Glen Canyon Country to explore, and to try to understand and describe it from various perspectives. Thus, my perspective is both biographical and autobiographical: Who were those men and women (including me), and what did they do in—and what did they write about—the Country?

Others have written knowingly and perceptively about the Country, and the doings of people therein, among them James Aton, Bruce Berger, C. Gregory Crampton, Brad Dimock, Michael Ghiglieri, Katie Lee, Russell Martin, Robert McPherson, P. T. Reilly, W. L. (Bud) Rusho, Wallace Stegner, Gary Topping, Roy Webb, Donald Worster, and numerous others. I have drawn, with appreciation, from their works, as I have from Earle Spamer's wondrous Internet bibliography of the Grand Canyon and lower Colorado River.[1] For more than a decade or so, I have been privileged to be a member of Clio, an Internet list-serve devoted to the history and lore of river running, principally the Colorado and its tributaries, but also the Snake River and its tributaries, and now and then some others as well. I learned much from fellow Clions Brad Dimock, Al Holland, Eleanor Inskip, Dove Menkes, John O'Brien, Richard Quartaroli, Bud Rusho, Gus Scott, Earle Spamer, Scott Thybony, Roy Webb, and many more. Special thanks to Clion Don Lago, who kindly shared his own unpublished archival materials relating to John Wesley Powell and his men. Chapters 4 and 5 are richer because of his kindnesses.

Books are always a collaborative effort, that of the author of record and that of all the people who supply the author with encouragement, information, images, suggestions, moral support, and useful criticism. I have had many such collaborators for this book, as I have had for others in the past. In addition to those listed above, there are many more.

First, I owe a special debt to the indomitable Katie Lee, not only for her wry wisdom and passionate essays, poems, and songs about Glen Canyon, but for her personal interest in, and help with, the project over the past four years. *Gracias*, Katie, for your wisdom and passion and all you've done!

A special thanks to Marjorie Chan, professor of geology at the University of Utah, for her friendship, interest in the book and the Country, and help with the chapters on geology.

Many others have provided information and assistance over the years, including Bruce Berger, Brad Dimock, Barbara Ekker, Vance Fowler, Joel Janetski, Heidi Roberts, and Vaughan Short. At the American Museum of Natural History in New York, grateful thanks to David Hurst Thomas, Lorann Pendleton, and Chelsea Graham. At Northern Arizona University Cline Library Special Collections, heartfelt thanks to Colorado Plateau history maven Richard Quartaroli, and his associates Pipp Piatchek, Bradley Cope, and Jess Ryan Vogelsang. At the Museum of Northern Arizona, many thanks to Martha Clark, Kelley Hays-Gilpin, Tony Marinella, Michael O'Hara, Jonathan Pringle, and David R. Wilcox. At the University of Utah: Kirk Baddley at the Archives and Records Center; at the

University Archaeology Center, James F. O'Connell, Duncan Metcalfe, Jennifer Graves, and Shannon Arnold; at Special Collections, J. W. Marriott Library, Greg Thompson, Kristin Giacoletto, Lorraine Crouse, Paul Mogren, Stan Larson, Walter Jones, and especially river historian and archivist extraordinaire Roy Webb, whose help, knowledge, and critical eye made this a much better book.

At the Utah State Historical Society, numerous thanks to Michelle Elnicky, Melissa Ferguson, Doug Misner, and Greg Walz.

At the National Park Service Glen Canyon National Recreation Area office, Page, Arizona (later at the Salt Lake City Office), Norm Henderson; at Natural Bridges National Monument, Janet McVickar; at Arches National Park, Jim McChristal. At the Bureau of Reclamation office, Salt Lake City, Barry Worth, Sybil Brooks, and Ginger Reeve. At the Glen Canyon Institute, Salt Lake City, Rich Ingebretsen and his colleagues. At the National Anthropological Archives, Smithsonian Institution, Jake Homiak, Robert Leopold, Daisy Njoku, and Vertis Thomas. In Blanding, Utah, stalwart scholars Winston Hearst, Robert McPherson, and Ron MacDonald have been most helpful, as has Jim Aton in Cedar City.

I owe a collective thank-you to all my Glen Canyon Project colleagues. At Utah, especially C. Melvin Aikens, Carol Condie (Stout), the late David Dibble, William D. Lipe, Thomas R. Lynch, Florence C. Lister and the late Robert Lister, the late Norma Mikkelsen, the late Floyd Sharrock, and Dee Ann Story. At the Museum of Northern Arizona, David Breternitz, Alexander J. Lindsay, Jr. Paul Long, and Mary Anne Stein.

Special thanks to the staff of the University of Utah Press, former directors, the late Norma Mikkelsen and Jeff Grathwohl, current director Glenda Cotter, and especially Reba Rauch and Jessica Booth, without whose expertise this book would not have come into existence. Alexis Mills has done wonders as copy editor with good cheer and élan. Map 1 was compiled by Penny Hudson, and edited by the good folks at Gnomon, Inc., Sandra Atkinson, Mike Drews, and Eric Ingbar. Maps 2 and 3 were produced by Patricia DeBunch. My thanks to all for all their cartographic expertise.

A particular thanks to W. L. (Bud) Rusho, who started his career in the Glen Canyon Country about the same time I did, who has shared his wisdom and insights with me, and who graciously agreed to write the foreword for the book. His passion for the Country and its history is reflected in his own books and films. This book would be far poorer without his help, guidance, and advice.

In sum, my gratitude to all those listed and an assurance that remaining errors of fact and interpretation herein are my fault, not theirs.

A special thanks to some mentors and friends: the late Professor Jesse D. Jennings, who saw enough in me to turn me away from a possible career as an urban lounge lizard to that of a scholar-archaeologist; and Warren and Kathleen d'Azevedo, teachers and close friends since 1960, who brought Kay and me together at the University of Utah, and in 1964 brought us to the University of Nevada, Reno, where we have flourished among congenial colleagues for four decades and counting.

Lastly, this book is for Catherine (Kay) Sweeney Fowler, who came into my life because of the Glen Canyon Project and has been there ever since.

Don D. Fowler

> 1 <

PRELUDE

IN EARLY AUGUST OF 1957, I STOPPED BY the Anthropology Department at the University of Utah in Salt Lake City to see about registering for my senior year. I had just spent two months working as a produce clerk in a grocery store near Los Angeles but had been fired for inflating my previous experience on my job application (I never dreamed they'd actually check!). I had also unsuccessfully pursued an attractive coed of my acquaintance thither and yon across Southern California. Feeling somewhat chastened, I was told by Mildred Treacy, the department secretary, that "Dr. Jennings has been trying to find you for two months." She picked up the phone and announced my presence. Dr. Jesse D. Jennings emerged from his office and greeted me with a kindly "Where the hell have you been?" I mumbled something about my Southern California sojourn, but he dismissed that with a wave of one of the roll-your-own Bull Durham cigarettes for which he was famous in the local halls of academe. "Be here tomorrow," he commanded. "You're going to work in the lab."

The next day I was introduced to several thousand dull gray pot sherds from archaeological excavations of Fremont sites in central Utah and told to wash and number them. After that I was instructed to break a small piece off each one and look at the fresh break under a binocular microscope. While the sherds looked superficially alike, their makers had used different kinds of temper in the paste. Once I learned to recognize temper (more or less), I sorted the sherds into different piles. It was dreadfully soporific.

But I was now an archaeological lab assistant receiving the munificent wage of 85 cents an hour. It was much better (although duller) work than an earlier job I'd had as an orderly in the University Hospital, but not nearly as good as a job in a local grocery store (whose kindly owner told the LA store manager how much experience I'd *really* had). Nor was it as interesting as my various jobs in the summer of 1956 in Jackson Hole, Wyoming, which had simultaneously included bus boy, maitre d' in the steakhouse, dice-table shill, and part-time bartender, all at the famed Cowboy Bar. In the mornings I was a gas station attendant; the job description included huckstering elk horn souvenirs to gullible tourists. Still, I finally had a job in my chosen field of anthropology, although not quite what I'd envisioned, which was some sort of leisurely ethnographic study on a tropical isle or in a pleasant urban setting, such as San Francisco's Chinatown.

My presence in the Anthropology Department on that fateful day was due to the usual sorts of (often serendipitous) accidents that befall befuddled college students, coupled with the Kismet of my heritage. My various great-great- or great-grandparents had either followed Brigham Young to Utah or been converted in England or Denmark and then made their way to Zion, or its northern province, southern Idaho. The exception was great-grandfather James Fowler, a young English seaman from Swansea, Wales. He jumped ship in San Francisco and made his way to southern Idaho, where he met a sweet young Mormon girl, Anne Mariah Bennett, married her and settled down to a life of poverty-level dirt farming. A son, William Fowler, married Rose Christiansen, the strong-headed daughter of Danish converts; their oldest child was my father, Eldon Christian Fowler, born near Lago, Idaho, a place that apparently no longer exists, perhaps for good reason.

On my mother's side, my great-great-grandfather Isaac Behunin, according to family legend, was baptized a Mormon by Joseph Smith himself. True or not, Isaac was with the Mormons from the time they left New York State, had helped build the temple in Kirtland, Ohio, and may have been one of Smith's bodyguards for a time. After Isaac's first wife died, he married Elmina Taylor. One of their sons, Elijah Cutlar Behunin, was born at Council Bluffs, Iowa, in early 1847, as the Mormons prepared to followed Brigham Young westward to Zion later that year. The family headed west in 1849, and by 1854 they were helping settle Ephraim in central Utah.

In 1861 Brigham Young sent Isaac, his family, and numerous others to the "Dixie" area to explore and settle. In 1862 the family came to Springdale at the mouth of Zion Canyon and soon established the first farm inside the canyon proper. Isaac is generally credited with naming the place "Zion Canyon," as the audio and visual history displays in the Zion National Park Visitors Center attest daily.[1] In 1872 Isaac sold his holdings and moved to Mount Carmel, where he later died. Isaac was not a Mormon polygamist, perhaps because he had neither the money nor a position in the church hierarchy that warranted such status, but more likely because his wife, Elmina, wouldn't let him.

Elijah Cutlar Behunin married Tabatha Jane Earl, and in 1882 they settled in Caineville, in what would become Wayne County, Utah. Elijah later was involved in settling the Fruita area and was named presiding elder of the Fruita branch of the Torrey Ward of the Mormon Church in 1900. He and Tabatha Jane built a cabin outside Fruita in 1892. There they raised eleven children, including my grandmother, Amanda Monettie Behunin, or "Nettie," as she was known. The cabin, by the way, still exists as a stop-by exhibit in Capitol Reef National Park.

In 1931, when he was eighty-four years old, Elijah bought an automobile, probably a Model T Ford. He apparently drove it as fast as he could whenever he could. It was a long way from the covered wagon in which he had come to Utah in 1849. He and Tabatha Jane drove all the way to Zion National Park and told the park personnel about the family's early days in the canyon. They often drove west "over the mountain" to Richfield on business or to visit relatives. In the fall of 1933, on one such trip, Elijah was apparently motoring along at his usual high speed when he missed a curve and the car flipped onto its top, killing him and his passenger, a son-in-law.

I am also descended from the Noyes clan, who were early settlers in New England; several were Protestant ministers. Some of them, particularly

John Humphrey Noyes, were involved in the social experiment of "complex marriage" at Oneida, New York, from the 1840s until 1879.[2] However, Fred Franklyn Noyes, my great-grandfather, apparently was not part of all that. Sadly, perhaps, great-great-grandfather Isaac and both maternal great-grandfathers seem to have missed out on the mysteries of differing forms of "complex marriage." Fred Franklyn was born in Albany, New York, in 1847 and grew up in upstate New York. He may have been a Union Army drummer boy in the Civil War. He converted to Mormonism in 1865, and soon after found employment driving freight wagons from Missouri to Salt Lake City. There he met—and in January 1869, married—my great-grandmother, Hanner Mariah Williams, who was born in Salt Lake City in 1849.

Soon after, the newlyweds accompanied Hanner's parents to St. Thomas, Nevada, the short-lived "Muddy Mission" of 1865 to 1871, designed to control the lower reaches of the Virgin River drainage, grow cotton, and develop a port for goods coming up the Colorado River by steamboat.[3] In early 1871, the Noyes and Williams families moved to Parowan, where my grandfather, Fred Williams Noyes, was born in 1874. But they were soon on the move, living for short periods in Silver Reef, Kanab, and Escalante before settling for several years in Teasdale, then moving to Caineville by 1892. Fred Franklyn Noyes was one of the Wayne County incorporators in that year.[4] There, too, Fred Williams Noyes met and courted Nettie Behunin.

On March 15, 1897, Elijah Behunin, acting as "A Minister of the Gospel," married his daughter Amanda, age eighteen, to Fred Williams Noyes, age twenty-two. The couple remained in the Wayne County area. Fred W. sometimes worked as a mail carrier and on his father's farm, but also herded sheep in the Henry Mountains. In 1909 a devastating Fremont River flood destroyed the Noyes farm in Caineville. Fred W. and one or more brothers found work in the mines in Carbon County and Park City. Ultimately Fred and Nettie Noyes settled in a place originally called Poverty Flat and later Central, Poplar, and Bonita. But in late 1898, when a post office was established and a firm decision on a name had to be made, someone chose Torrey, apparently for Jay Linn Torrey (1852–1920).

Jay Linn had gone to Wyoming in the 1880s to manage a large cattle and cavalry horse ranch. It is said that he was the one who first proposed that cowboys and stockman—"Rough Riders," as he called them—be enlisted as cavalry troops for the Spanish-American War. He was commissioned as Colonel of the Second Regiment, U.S. Cavalry Volunteers. His troops trained in Wyoming, then headed for the Caribbean and the action, but suffered a disastrous train wreck in Florida. Neither Colonel Torrey nor his troops ever reached Cuba. Instead, Teddy Roosevelt and the First Regiment of "Rough Riders" got there and charged up San Juan Hill and on to glory. Despite the train wreck, Torrey was enough of a hero in 1898 to have a small-town post office in the recently created state of Utah named for him. He was also prominent enough to be mentioned as a possible running mate for William McKinley in his bid for the presidency in 1900, but the Republican Party chose Rough Rider Teddy Roosevelt instead. One wonders how American history, especially conservation of resources, might have played out if Torrey had been chosen instead of Roosevelt. In 1905 Torrey moved to Missouri, where he was active in business and civic affairs until his death in 1920.[5]

Fred and Nettie Noyes had six children, the youngest being my mother, Ruby. The family managed to acquire a lot in Torrey and moved a house onto it. There was a corral for milk cows, an orchard, and garden, enough for subsistence but not to earn a living, so Fred continued to work as a miner and sheepherder. Nettie became a nurse and midwife, tutored by her mother-in-law, Hanner Williams Noyes, who was a well-known midwife and caregiver throughout her adult life.[6]

In 1934 Eldon C. Fowler arrived in Torrey as a member of a Civilian Conservation Corps contingent. He soon met Ruby Noyes; she courted him assiduously, and they were married in March 1935. They had a son, Donald Dee Fowler, who was born at home in April 1936. My birth certificate lists my father's occupation as "weed eradicator," obviously one of the government make-work jobs available to young, unskilled men in the Depression years.

In 1939 the Fowler family moved to Nampa, then Caldwell, and then to Atlanta, Idaho, a mining town in the mountains north of Boise where Eldon found work in the mill. In early 1943, after the birth of brother Vance, we moved to northern Utah, finally settling in Ogden, where Eldon worked at the Army Supply Depot before being drafted into the army in late 1944. He was discharged in May 1945, and in early 1946 Eldon and Ruby divorced. For about a year Ruby made a living by running a small nursery school and playing piano in a local night club. In 1947 she married Reed Tippets, a nine-year army sergeant who had seen extensive combat duty in World War II. That easily qualified him to take in hand two errant boys, ages eleven and four, and turn them into semicivilized human beings, which he lovingly did, to our great benefit.

The education I received in the Ogden school system, I only later realized, was excellent, although I loathed most of it at the time. By high school I was busy with normal male teen extracurricular activities—smoking, drinking beer, trying to understand the mysteries called teen-aged girls, dragging Main (several miles along Washington Boulevard between drive-in burger joints), and learning the intricacies of eight ball and snooker at a local pool hall. I (barely) graduated from the venerable Ogden High School in 1954. The principal, Dr. Maurice Conroy, handed me my diploma and predicted I'd be on Skid Row in three years. I later came to think that he meant to spur me on to seek a somewhat better neighborhood, and perhaps he did.

Some of my wastrel friends, to my considerable mystification, suddenly began getting ready to go on their Mormon missions, abandoning all those shared delinquent pleasures of our youth, which I assumed would continue forever. A few, however, kept to the old ways and were well-established barflies the last time I checked in at "The Troc," about 1962; some, or their descendants, may still be there. Other friends, who'd kept their grades up, went off to Reed College, the University of Chicago, Stanford, and the University of Utah.

My family was in poor circumstances at the time due to serious illnesses, but my stepfather managed to find the tuition for my first quarter, and I registered at Weber Junior College (now Weber State University) in the fall of 1954. Thereafter, I was on my own. I was the first member of my various families ever to go to college. The day after classes began I got a job as an orderly at St. Benedict's Hospital, then run by kindly and extraordinarily competent Benedictine nuns instead of the faceless, avaricious HMOs of later days.

It was thus that I suddenly found myself in two congenial situations. Despite my mildly wayward ways, and so-so high school grades, I had read voraciously and widely (often beyond my full understanding) from my early years. Now, at the hospital, I encountered highly educated nuns, some with master's degrees, who could, and did, talk with me about topics ranging from medicine and philosophy to science, music, and art in lulls between carrying bedpans and taking temperatures. Sister Mercy, who had a master's degree in mathematics, knew much about Buddhism, Hinduism, and Islam as well as Christianity and Judaism, and we discussed comparative theology at length during the long evening shifts on the surgical ward. All of the nuns, and some of the doctors, took an interest in my education and motivated me to continue. One doctor even offered to put me through college and medical school if I'd become a gynecologist. I declined, but have occasionally wondered about the road not taken.

The other congenial situation was college. At first I had no idea what I wanted to do. I vaguely thought of engineering or medicine, but came to grief in chemistry—partly because of the instructor's off-putting lectures on "God and the molecule." But I soon encountered three English professors—Larry Evans, H. E. D. Redford, and Robert Mikkelsen—who encouraged me to write, to continue to read widely and critically, and to respect the wondrous facility of the English language. I also encountered Jennings Olsen, a remarkable, charismatic, and controversial individual (he loved the controversy part) who taught anthropology, psychology, philosophy, and comparative religion with verve and brilliance. He also sang opera, when asked, and lifted weights, without being asked.

I have since come to understand that practically all anthropologists "find" anthropology in college—few if any go to college with the intent of becoming one. I signed up for Olsen's Anthropology I class on the advice of a friend and had a quasi-epiphany. By the end of the second quarter I knew I wanted to be a professor. I took all the other classes I could from Olsen and from the three gurus in English. My stated intention to become a professor and an anthropologist (whatever *that* was) amused and bewildered my family, but they encouraged me nonetheless—after all, I was actually going to college and earning my own way.

In May 1955 I went to the University of Utah in Salt Lake City and called on Dr. Jesse David Jennings, the chair of the Anthropology Department. He allowed as how they might admit me if I thought I could cut it and overcome the deficiencies of my upbringing—to wit, my Mormon background. It was the first of many challenges Jennings gave me. On the recommendation of the Benedictine nuns, I got a job at University Hospital and started the fall term. I knew instantly I had found a home. With fellow students I plunged into the intellectual life of the university and the city, tempered by the usual partying. We explored the high culture of symphony, ballet, and theater (with which Salt Lake City was well endowed, then as now), the middlebrow coffee houses and bars offering poor to middlin' folk singers and good jazz, and the social underbelly of Salt Lake's ethnically mixed, honky tonk, jazz club, and pretend-Beatnik west side. I discovered Sam Weller's Zion's Book Store and was launched on a lifetime of acquisitive bibliophilia. I also discovered the university's Philosophy Department and reveled in courses with William Kent and Sterling McMurrin. I took all the classes I could from a remarkable political scientist, Francis Wormuth, whose course on the history of Western social thought became the basis for one I later taught for three decades and more. Courses on Max Weber and comparative religion from Thomas O'Dea, later awarded an endowed chair in the Comparative Religion Department at Columbia University, were brilliant.

In the spring of 1957 I took Professor Jennings's famous "tabletop archaeology" class—excavating one of the miniature sites he built in the lab for the course. I also took his North American archaeology course and a class in Old World prehistory taught by Robert Anderson. Those were my sole academic qualifications to be an archaeologist as of the summer of 1957—but then I did not intend to become one.

Toward the end of August 1957 James Gunnerson came in from the field. Jim was Utah State Archaeologist and curator of the nascent University of Utah Anthropology Museum. He had come to Utah after finishing coursework at Harvard and six years of fieldwork in the Great Plains. He began an active excavation program in Fremont sites in central Utah, in effect continuing an archaeological research program begun by others from Harvard in the 1920s and early 1930s (chapter 13). It was Jim who had dug up all those wretched gray pot sherds from the Old Woman and Snake Rock sites that I was washing and numbering. He had spent much of the summer in the Escalante River area surveying for archaeological sites and doing test excavations in a few of them (chapter 14).[7]

A few days after Gunnerson returned from the field, Dr. Jennings called me into his office and told me to acquire a sleeping bag and some work clothes and boots. I was going to the field with Jim and two others, and we would be out until the weather drove us in; I could resume classes in the winter term. Having studiously avoided "the outdoor scene" from earliest childhood (I resigned from the Boy Scouts after three weeks, and my family had long since quit asking me to go along on hunting trips), I had, in fact, never camped out. My intention had been to be a sparkling urban lounge lizard. But there it was: I was going to have to live in the dreaded outdoors, sans all real and imagined creature comforts. In fact, I would spend seventeen or so of the next sixty months camping in and near a place called Glen Canyon, returning, in effect, to the red rock country of my birth.

A few days later we were in Escalante, Utah. We headed south out of town on the Hole-in-the-Rock Road and finally dropped down into a shallow part of Coyote Gulch. Jim had already done some work at what was being called the Alvey site, and we did some more. A deep and complex site, it provided a wondrous introduction to dirt archaeology for a novice such as me.[8] Finishing up, we returned to Escalante. There we met Loyd (spelled with one "L") Gates, a garrulous and savvy local rancher and handyman. Loyd was in his fifties, had lived in Escalante all of his life, and knew the Escalante Desert, Boulder Mountain, Aquarius Plateau, and Kaiparowits Plateau country intimately. Loyd introduced us to our traveling companions—three mules. My compatriots, besides Jim Gunnerson, were Downey Raibourne and Dick Graham, the latter a student at Utah who had worked with Gunnerson on various projects. Raibourne was from Indiana University, a perennial archaeology graduate student who could never finish his doctorate—there was always another field project.

Gunnerson and Raibourne were archetypical "field men" (my gender usage reflects the male chauvinism of the time)—a personality type endemic to archaeology, geology, and biology. They tolerate their jobs in museums or universities, but live to be "in the field," camping out, doing science (as they conceive it), and being able to ignore confining social graces—"to fart with impunity," as Gunnerson put it. Jim Gunnerson was extraordinarily competent, knowledgeable, witty, full of puns and good humor, and taught me much of what I ever knew about the intricacies of field archaeology. Raibourne was a good field hand, and I learned from him as well. He also possessed a small machine for rolling cigarettes, which he filled with Bugle pipe tobacco; the machine fascinated Loyd, and Raibourne's manipulations thereof entertained us in the evenings.

Our camp was well supplied with food. Loyd approved, citing his favorite maxim: "Don't greasy-sack-it when you don't have to." In the West, a "greasy sack outfit" is a dirty camp with a meager food supply. Therefore, not "greasy-sackin-it" can be translated to mean "Live as high on the hog as you can," especially when your employer is providing the grub. Both Loyd and Jim were proficient in the mysteries of the Dutch oven, an art I failed to grasp despite repeated attempts. That deficiency often doomed me—and my fellow crew members—to a diet of Dinty Moore's stew, Spam, dehydrated potatoes, stewed tomatoes, and World War II surplus C-rations.

We began work on a site in a high alcove in Twenty Five Mile Gulch. After the site had been abandoned, the canyon's alluvial fill had flushed out. To gain access, Gunnerson had brought along a 35-foot sectional ladder, which the mules had skittishly carried with great verbal complaint several miles downcanyon from the trucks. The top of the ladder reached nearly to an alluvial remnant that marked the level of the canyon floor when the site was occupied, some 40 feet above the present

1.1. Gates Roost site, Twenty Five Mile Canyon, Escalante River drainage, September 1957. Richard Graham is in the alcove, Don Fowler is in the white shirt, and Downey Raiburn is on the ladder. Photograph by James Gunnerson. Archaeology Center Collection, 42KA178-29. Courtesy of Special Collections, Marriott Library, University of Utah.

streambed. By placing lag screws into the cliff face, we were able to climb to the top of the remnant and scramble up some hand- and toeholds that the Indians had cut up a steep slickrock slope. A rope anchored at the top of the steps provided something to cling to while climbing up and down (fig. 1.1).

At first we camped in a small alcove below the main shelter, but it started to rain and soon the creek began to rise. Gunnerson wisely moved us and the camp into the higher alcove, which conveniently had a spring, before the flash flood came. Loyd already had moved the mules onto the mesa top to graze. After several days, the rains ceased and the creek dropped.

We finished excavating the site, which Gunnerson had named Gates Roost, retrieved the mules, loaded up, and headed back upcanyon to the vehicles. Loyd, being a local, knew that it never rained in October in the Escalante country. He had therefore left his stock truck in the bottom of the wash. It was buried in sand and debris to nearly the top of the cab—and there it remained. Our jeep, parked high up on the side of the wash, had had its wheels lapped by water but otherwise was okay. Loyd shook his head at the arbitrary and capricious behavior of rain deities, got on one of the mules, and trailed the others the long distance back to Escalante. Thus did I learn my first two lessons about the Glen Canyon Country: be extremely wary of flash floods, and avoid the greasy sack whenever you can.

When we got back to Escalante, we were at first mystified by the major news story. It was mid-October 1957, and something called Sputnik was busily beeping its way around the world every several hours a day. We soon learned all about it, and I was later to give thanks for it because it provided my ticket to graduate school, as will be seen.

We next moved to a camp at the base of Gunsight Butte on the edge of Glen Canyon proper. I was awestruck by the Country, and remain so. Perhaps I could forego my urbanite lounge lizard aspirations, at least during the field season, if I got to do archaeology in country like that! We spent a couple of days at a site near Warm Creek, but it had little of interest. We finished by testing a site near Escalante at a place called Rattlesnake Point, but by then it was deer season, and after a couple of stray bullets whizzed overhead, we decamped for Salt Lake City.

We returned to find a new laboratory being readied for the Glen Canyon Project. During World War II, the venerable army base Fort Douglas, just uphill from the University of Utah, had expanded downslope with a series of "temporary" wooden buildings onto the eastern edge of the campus. After the war the buildings were handed over to the university (some continue to be "temporary" into the twenty-first century). The Anthropology Department was housed in Building 411, a former mess hall. Therein, Dr. Jennings had created a storage area and lab (using the old walk-in meat locker to protect valuable textiles), a small museum, some faculty offices, and a classroom. A two-story barracks across the street, Building 405, was now fitted out to be a processing lab, offices, and curation facility for the Glen Canyon Project.

The day after our return, Jennings called me into his office and rehearsed my numerous sins of omission, as reported by Gunnerson, during our recent field trip. He said that the following summer would be the first full field season for the Glen Canyon Project. My immediate job, in between numbering and sorting pot sherds, was to buy all the field equipment needed to send three field crews into the Glen Canyon Country, plus outfit an archaeological field school in Boulder, Utah. Under Jennings's stern guidance I was given a budget and bought shovels, trowels, cameras, film, cooking gear, compasses, data forms, canvas wall tents, jerry cans, etc.—the plethora of equipment and supplies needed to survive in remote field situations, one of which was to be on the Colorado River itself. Jennings personally saw to the purchase of four bright red jeeps and a green cab-over jeep truck, and the acquisition and modification of two motor boats for the river survey, of which more later.

Jennings also informed me that the Glen Canyon Project was scheduled to run for several years, and barring screw-ups on my part, he expected I'd be part of it. And so it came to be. My dreamed-of, nebulous career as an urban anthropologist vanished in a cloud of Jennings's Bull Durham smoke, which filled his cramped office in the back of the mess hall museum.

I went back to classes, the wretched pot sherds, and buying all that equipment. I was now an apprentice archaeologist, committed to some role in what would become the single biggest archaeological salvage project yet seen in the United States. It would engulf me for the next five years, while I also went to school full-time. I would come to know many of the side canyons and all the mainstem gravel terraces of Glen Canyon from Hite to the dam site, and I spent one summer atop the Kaiparowits Plateau—Zane Grey's Wild Horse Mesa—enjoying some of the grandest views in the country. In those years I made lifelong friends among those working for the University of Utah and the Museum of Northern Arizona, and during my last field season, in 1962, I courted my future wife, Catherine (Kay) Sweeney. In the Glen Canyon Country I met river runners, artists, photographers, geologists, ecologists, cowboys, ranchers, horse and mule wranglers, tourists, and federal bureaucrats. I watched the construction of Glen Canyon Bridge and the dam in amazement, and saw the Page, Arizona, company town come into existence.

I soon became a participant in the informal network of southwestern anthropologists, especially through the Pecos Conference, held annually in August, and I became fascinated with the Colorado Plateau and the ethnically diverse peoples who live, and had lived, there. I eventually became deeply involved in studying the life and work of John Wesley Powell, who was the first to run the Colorado River in 1869, who named Glen Canyon, and who is memorialized by the lake that drowned it.[9] I first learned about Powell when I read his reports in 1959 while making rubber latex molds of his and his men's names carved in the walls of Music Temple (chapters 4 and 5).

The photographer Eliot Porter called Glen Canyon "the place no one knew," but he knew some of it, and preserved images and thoughts about it in his wondrous book of the same name. I knew some of it too. In 1969 I was privileged to be part of a book celebrating Powell's 1869 trip, *Down the Colorado*, which contains more Porter photographs and his further thoughts on Glen Canyon.[10] To my great regret, I never met Porter nor some others deeply involved with Glen Canyon, although many years later I met David Brower. But I did meet, know, and come to respect many individuals whose lives, like mine, were dominated by the canyon, the river, the dam, and the surrounding country for greater or lesser periods of time. Many of them will appear as we progress.

This, then, is the background to the present story, or biography, in a loose sense, of a place, the Glen Canyon Country, where I and others sojourned at various times. My job, and that of the other archaeologists employed by the University of Utah and the Museum of Northern Arizona for the Glen Canyon Project, was to find and excavate archaeological sites. We then used what we found to piece together a story about the lives and ways of the ancient peoples who lived there now and then for millennia.

Others involved in the project, most notably Catherine Sweeney, did what is now called "ethnoarchaeology"—visiting places in the Glen Canyon Country with Native American elders to talk about where they and their families had lived in the late nineteenth and early twentieth centuries. Still others, especially the late C. Gregory Crampton, studied the histories of the Euro-Americans in the region, beginning with the Spanish in the 1760s. Biologists studied the ecology of Glen Canyon, and Maurice Cooley, a geologist, did a reconnaissance of Glen Canyon and summarized previous research.

But we were simply the latest archaeologists, ethnographers, historians, ecologists, and geologists to have studied the Glen Canyon Country in order to define it and write some of its many stories, aided by several highly competent river runners and overland packers. My tale thus begins with the first explorers and scholars who came to the Glen Canyon Country before us. Then came the Glen Canyon Project, and those of us involved in it produced some new or different definitions and stories, often adding to what was already known. Other scholars came after we moved on. They have filled in, corrected, and amplified some of the stories we and our predecessors we able to tell, so some of their work has become part of my story as well. This is as it should be; scholarship is an ongoing enterprise, always aiming to tell better and more accurate stories.

Three other groups are important to my story about the Glen Canyon Country. One includes the writers, poets, filmmakers, painters, and photographers who defined the Country from their many individual perspectives between about 1900 to 1960. A second includes the hydrologists, planners, engineers, administrators, and elected officials who wanted to *do something* with, and to, the Country—most notably build high dams across its central artery, beginning very early in the twentieth century. In the 1950s to early 1960s they managed to build three dams and had plans for many more. Making up the third group are the professional river runners and guides who led the artists, scientists, engineers—and tourists—through the Colorado canyons and across the plateaus, and helped them define and interpret what they saw. All these people defined the Country in various ways, according to what they were looking for.

Because Glen Canyon Dam did get built, I have a story to tell. Had it not (and many are those who wish it never had been), I might well have become the sparkling urban lounge lizard/anthropologist of my sophomoric dreams, or perhaps the skid row habitué envisioned by my high school principal. Far worse, I may never have met and married my spouse and colleague of forty-eight years and counting, Catherine Sweeney Fowler.

Instead, I became an archaeologist and a historian of western exploration, particularly of John Wesley Powell and his colleagues in the 1870s and 1880s, as well as a historian of my profession of anthropology. I did become a university professor—and I did marry Kay. She, too, became a university professor and an acknowledged expert on the Southern Paiute people of the Glen Canyon Country as well as other Indian peoples throughout the Great Basin and across North America. For us, our mutual sojourn in the Glen Canyon Country largely defined our subsequent lives.

Lastly, a word or two about the point of view adopted in this book. It is, I hope, simultaneously the biography of a place and of those who defined it and lived in it. I am aware that places, strictly speaking, don't have "biographies"—people and other sentient creatures do. Biographies usually follow the format of born, grew up, stood in lots of lines, went on some diets, maybe did something interesting, and died. Places, however, have biographies, too, because they are both *seen as* and *lived in* by people. "Seen as," a useful term offered by the philosopher Ludwig Wittgenstein, means defined, interpreted, or categorized from a particular point of view. Having defined, interpreted, and categorized a place, what did individuals or groups do there? It's the *seen as* combined with the *doing/living* therein that makes the biography of a place.

My story—my biography of a place, the Glen Canyon Country—is not strictly chronological. I begin with the physical place and how it has been defined by mapmakers, geologists, and archaeologists. This provides the stage, the historical place, in and across which many different peoples moved over many millennia. I then explore how the histories of those who were there over the millennia have variously been pieced together, interpreted, and defined by archaeologists, ethnographers, historians, and artists. I attempt to provide brief summaries of those histories, both the doing/living on the land and, where possible, how various groups interpreted the Glen Canyon Country and the places therein.

In 1963 the flood gates of Glen Canyon Dam were closed, and Lake Powell began to rise. The dam, the lake, and the Glen Canyon Country itself were *seen* and *seen as* in a plethora of new, yet sometimes old, ways. I touch on some of the resultant stories in the postlude, but there are many others—some already told, others waiting for another time.

› 2 ‹

THE GLEN CANYON COUNTRY AND ITS FIRST EXPLORERS, 1776–1856

THIS BOOK IS ABOUT THE GLEN CANYON Country (maps 1 and 2). The canyon proper is a sinuous 180-plus-mile chasm, variable in depth and width, through which the Colorado River once flowed (fig. 2.1). It is now filled, to greater or lesser depths, by Lake Powell (fig. 2.2). The Glen Canyon Country, as I shall call it, lies within a large, lopsided ellipse. Starting at Torrey, Utah, my birthplace, the boundary line moves clockwise along the Fremont River, down the Dirty Devil River, across the Colorado River, up Dark Canyon, around Elk Ridge and the Bears Ears (with a blip to include the Abajos), southward along Comb Ridge, along the west side of Black Mesa to about Tuba City, then northwestward along the Echo Cliffs, past the Gap to Lee's Ferry and the mouth of the Paria River, up the Paria to the Pink Cliffs and on to the headwaters of the Fremont River—thus enclosing the Pink Cliffs, the Table Cliff Plateau, and the Aquarius Plateau, including Boulder Mountain—then back to Torrey. Glen Canyon proper jaggedly slices through the heart of our ellipse from about two o'clock to eight o'clock.

Like all arbitrary lines, mine is elastic and permeable, and I shall sometimes slip beyond its bounds to talk about places relevant to my story, such as Monument Valley, Butler Wash, and tributaries of the San Juan River. Besides Glen Canyon proper and its tributaries, including the Escalante River and the San Juan River and its lower tributaries, the Country contains other major topographic features. These include the Henry Mountains (fig. 2.3), the Waterpocket Fold, the Red Rock Plateau east of the Colorado and north of the San Juan River to Dark Canyon, Natural Bridges, the Grand Gulch Plateau, Navajo Mountain and Rainbow Bridge (figs. 2.4, 2.5), the Kaibito Plateau, and the Kaiparowits Plateau (fig. 2.6). This, then, is the setting for my story.

Eliot Porter called Glen Canyon "the place no one knew,"[1] but in truth, many people, over many centuries, knew parts of Glen Canyon and the country around it in different ways, although no one individual knew all of it. When travel was by foot, horse, mule, or wagon, "knowing the country"

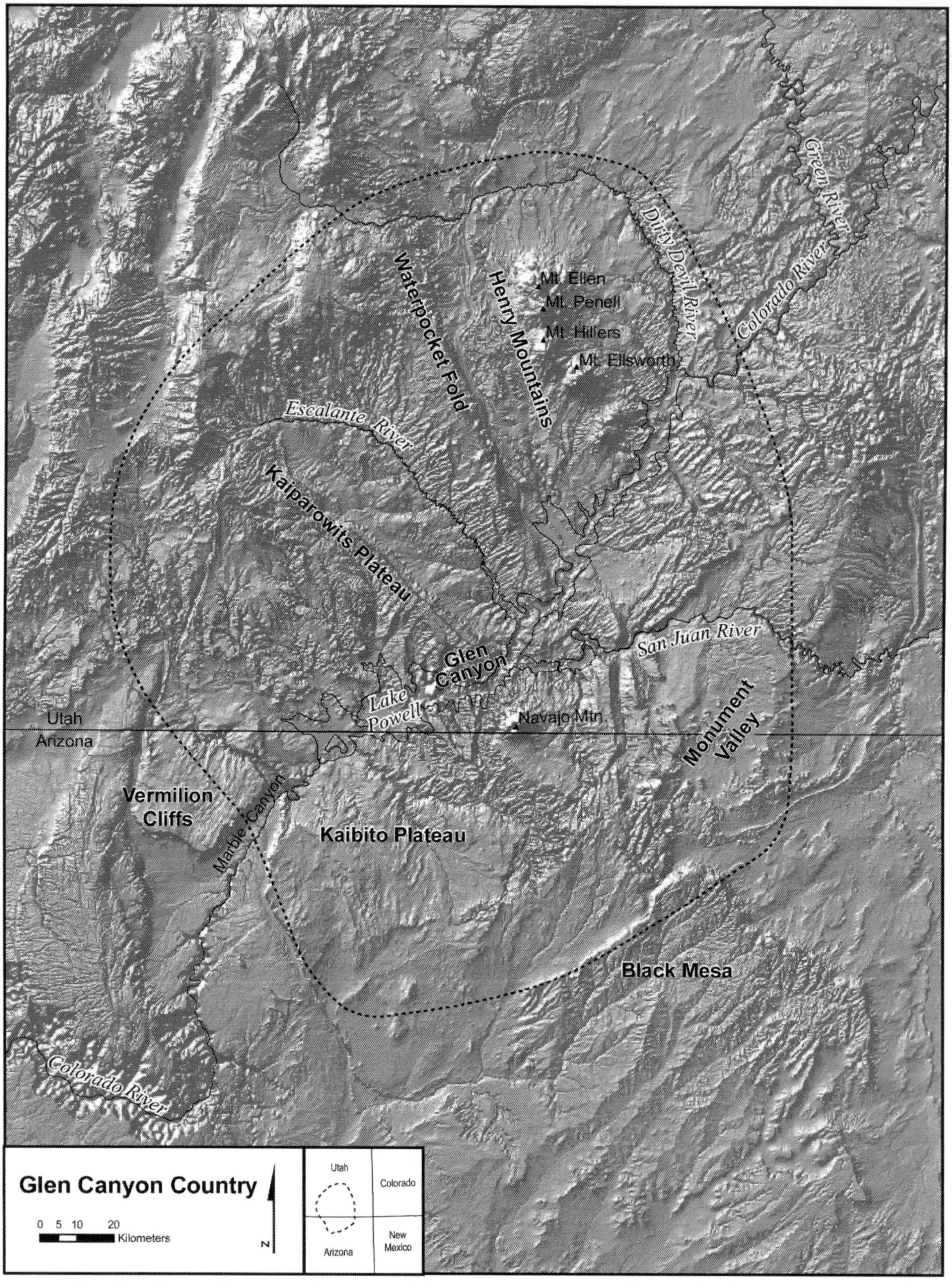

MAP 2. The Glen Canyon Country in the context of the Four Corners region of the Colorado Plateau. Map by Penny Hudson and Gnomon, Inc.

2.1. Aerial view of Glen Canyon looking downstream below the confluence with the San Juan River, August 1958. Cummings Mesa is on the left; Gunsight Butte and Leche-e Rock can be seen in the distance. Photographer unknown, NAU. PH.97.46.76.64. Courtesy of Cline Library, Northern Arizona University.

in unmapped areas usually meant finding one's way by landmarks and knowing where the water holes were and how to find feed for their animals; it sometimes also meant knowing where to hide to evade enemies. This sort of "knowing" is the cliché for every western novel and movie ever made: "We'll never catch 'em beyond the pass, Roy. They know that country like the backs of their hands."

But such knowing is also very real. Packers and guides who led scientists and tourists back and forth across the Country in the nineteenth and twentieth centuries "knew" it, or parts of it, very well indeed. Experienced Colorado River runners know every rapid and smooth water spot, and how each changes with different water levels, from Lodore Canyon on the Green River to the Grand Wash Cliffs at the foot of Grand Canyon. Native peoples knew, traversed, and lived in the Country off and on for 10,000 years, perhaps more.

To some of the nineteenth-century Euro-Americans who penetrated into the Glen Canyon Country and beyond, the entire region was a "trackless wilderness, a wasteland." For the Indians, Spaniards, Mexicans, and Anglos who could "read" the landscape, it was less forbidding, but always difficult. The geologist Charles Hunt, who studied the Henry Mountains in the 1930s, explains how his predecessor, Grove Karl Gilbert (chapter 7) found his away through the Country in the 1870s.

> How did Gilbert find his way across thousands of square miles of vacant, unmapped, rugged wilderness to reach the Henry Mountains, and how was he always able to complete a day of

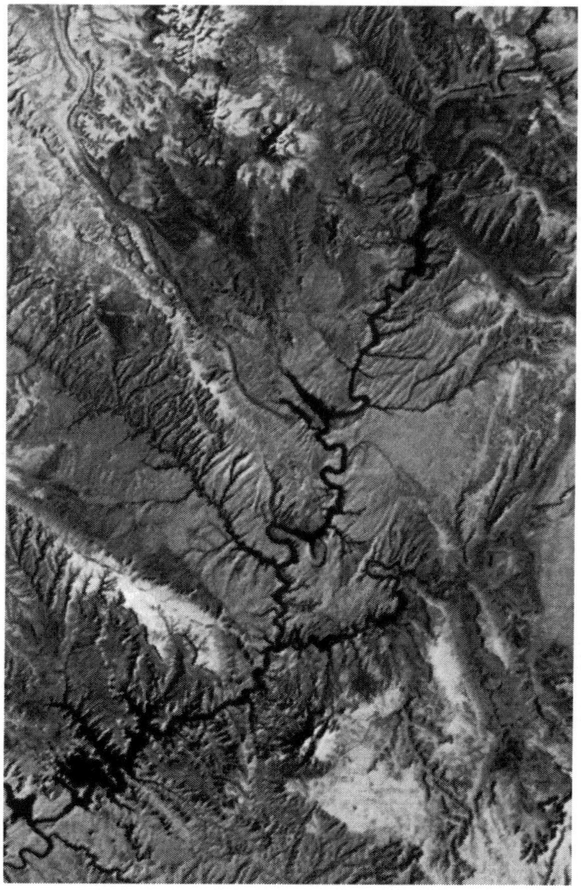

2.2. Satellite image of Lake Powell, 1970. Courtesy of the National Air and Space Administration.

> travel and end at a spring? He did so by following the prehistoric Indian trails. . . . To explorers like Gilbert, those Indian trails were as easy to follow as a modern freeway. They were the conspicuous routes through the otherwise trackless wilderness before there was grazing by livestock. Moreover, one can even find directional signs along the trails indicating whether one is approaching water or going away from it. The secondary trails of coyotes, foxes and rabbits diverge from the main trail away from water; they converge toward water. . . . That Gilbert knew these signs and could use them to his advantage is indicated by the ease with which he generally found satisfactory camp sites that provided the pasturage and water for his animals as well as his men. In two field seasons, only a couple of his camps proved unsatisfactory.[2]

THE SPANISH EXPLORERS, THE COLORADO RIVER, AND THE GLEN CANYON COUNTRY

The first non-native people to explore the Colorado River were with the Spanish expeditions. In 1539 Francisco de Ulloa reached the head of the Sea of Cortés (the Gulf of California) and surmised that a river entered the gulf from the north, although he did not actually see it. In 1540 two related expeditions, one led overland by Francisco Vásquez de Coronado, came into what is now Arizona and New Mexico looking in vain for "golden cities." It was thought that ships might be able to go up the river at the head of the Sea of Cortés to supply Coronado's expedition, on the mistaken assumption that said river might closely parallel the latter's route. This effort was under the command of Hernando de Alarcón, who encountered a "very mighty river, which ran with so great fury of a stream that we could hardly sail against it."[3] He was able to go upriver in small boats, about 100 miles beyond the mouth of the Gila River. Coronado's route was far to the east of the Lower Colorado, and there was no direct contact.

Melchior Díaz, sent by Coronado to make contact with Alarcón, finally reached the Colorado River near its confluence with the Gila to find that Alarcón had returned southward. Díaz explored the lower river area for a few days and named the river Río del Tizón, or Firebrand River, after a practice native peoples used to keep themselves warm. The name was often used over the next two centuries.

When Coronado reached and subjugated the Zuni pueblos in western New Mexico, he heard of the province of "Tusayan"—the Hopi villages to the northwest. He sent Pedro de Továr to investigate. The Hopis told him of a great river to the

2.3. Aerial view of the Henry Mountains, 1962. Photograph by A. E. Turner, P557-450-6867. Courtesy of the U.S. Bureau of Reclamation.

northwest. Továr reported back to Coronado, who sent Captain López de Cárdenas and a small party to investigate in the hope that the river would lead them to Alarcón. Cárdenas and his men finally reached the south rim of the Grand Canyon, becoming the first Europeans to see that grand spectacle. They tried to climb down to the river but could not, so they reported back to Coronado that it was a "useless piece of country." Coronado then turned to the east, seeking in vain for legendary golden cities. Finding none, in 1542 he returned in disgust, and some disgrace, to Mexico.[4]

The Spanish did not come again until 1598, this time to stay in the Rio Grande valley in what they called the Provincia de Nuevo México. They settled along the Rio Grande and gradually pushed their way up its tributaries. One of these, the Chama River valley, provided, as it had for millennia, a route northwestward from the Rio Grande drainage. Ancient trails led across the divide between the upper Chama and the drainage of the San Juan River to the country beyond. Spanish explorers probably had ventured into and beyond the San Juan Valley by the early 1760s, although there is no firm documentary evidence for such trips.

The first official foray into the San Juan Valley was in 1765, when the governor of the Province of New Mexico, Tomás Vélez Cachupín,

2.4. Aerial view of Navajo Mountain and Bald Rock Crescent, 1959. Photograph by David Dibble. Archaeology Center Collection, 42Sa00-50. Courtesy of Special Collections, Marriott Library, University of Utah.

commissioned Juan María Antonio Rivera to verify the existence of the Colorado (Grand) River and its only purported crossing. Rivera made two trips with small parties, the first in June–July 1765 and the second in October–November. The first trip was up the Chama and into the drainage of the San Juan River (which they named), and then northwest past the future sites of Durango and Bayfield, Colorado, to near the site of Dolores. They then turned southwest and came again to the San Juan River, but they mistook it for another stream and called it the Río Grande de Navajo. They then returned to Santa Fe, generally following their outbound route.[5]

Rivera made the second trip that fall, but his route of travel is contested because of the vagaries of his report. Some think he followed his earlier trail northwest to Dolores and then turned westward, passing east of present-day Monticello before reaching the Grand River at present-day Moab. Others think he stayed in present-day Colorado, going past the future sites of Dove Creek and Delta before reaching the confluence of the Gunnison and Uncompahgre rivers, where he turned back.[6] If he did make it to Moab, he found the crossing. If not, he heard about it from the Utes, who told him of a trail west of the crossing of the Grand River at Moab that led southward toward the lower

2.5. Aerial view of Rainbow Bridge looking downstream, May 1961. Photograph by E. A. Turner, P557-420-5989. Courtesy of the U.S. Bureau of Reclamation.

2.6. Aerial view of the east face of the Kaiparowits Plateau, 1937. Rainbow Bridge–Monument Valley Expedition Flight 3. Photograph by E. Beckwith, MS-122-2275. Courtesy of the Museum of Northern Arizona.

Colorado River. The also told him about an Indian group they called People of the Rock, los Timpanogas.[7] Rivera returned to Santa Fe and submitted his report, which records his naming of not only the San Juan, but also the La Plata, Animas, and Dolores rivers. This report was not generally known until 1975, and not closely analyzed and his routes determined in detail until 1992.[8] But Rivera's information was conveyed to the next official Spanish party to head up the Chama, cross into the San Juan drainage and go beyond—the Domínguez-Escalante expedition of 1776.

DOMÍNGUEZ AND ESCALANTE

The Spanish claimed that New Spain included most of what is now the western United States. They had known about what is now the state of California for centuries, but were only moved to colonize the area in the early 1760s in response to a geopolitical threat from the Russians pushing down the west coast from Alaska. The capitol of the Province of Alta California was established in Monterey in 1769. Soon after, the Spanish became concerned about finding an overland route from Santa Fe to Monterey. One attempt to do so was apparently Rivera's search in 1765 for a crossing of the Colorado River northwest of Santa Fe, which he did.

Eleven years later, in 1776, three Franciscan friars were sent to find routes to Monterey. One was Fray Francisco Hermenegildo Garcés (1738–80), who traveled south of the Grand Canyon. The other two were Fray Francisco Atanasio Domínguez (ca. 1740–ca. 1803–5) and Fray Silvestre Vélez de Escalante (ca. 1750–81), who were sent to find Rivera's crossing and continue on toward Monterey.

Father Garcés, born in Aragón, Spain, entered the Franciscan order at age fifteen. He was sent to Mexico in 1766 and the next year was assigned to San Xavier del Bac, the mission south of present-day Tucson, Arizona, graced by its wonderful eighteenth-century Spanish Baroque church. In 1774, Garcés had journeyed to California with the commander of the Tubac presidio, Juan Bautista de

Anza. In January 1776, Garcés again set out from San Xavier for California. He visited San Gabriel and the Central Valley, and then headed east across the Sierra Nevada and the Mojave Desert. After crossing the Colorado River, he followed a route parallel to the south rim of the Grand Canyon, visited the Havasupai, and finally arrived at Oraibi, the westernmost of the Hopi pueblos, on July 2, 1776. The Hopis were not pleased to see him and drove him out of the village on July 4, 1776, the same day other events of importance were taking place 2,000 miles to the east in the Old State House in Philadelphia.[9]

The Spanish had been in contact with the Hopis since 1540, and the route from Hopi to Zuni and eastward to Albuquerque and Santa Fe was well known and traveled. What Garcés had done was connect the Hopi end of the trail with California. In the decades following Garcés's trek, other Spaniards followed his route between Santa Fe and Albuquerque on one end, and San Gabriel and Los Angeles on the other. Garcés was able to send a letter by Indian courier to Escalante at Zuni before he headed back to San Xavier—a round trip of 1,700 miles, on foot and burro, in seven months. In 1780 Garcés and two others established a mission along the lower Colorado River among the Yuma Indians, who didn't like the missionaries any more than the Hopis had and killed them the next year.[10]

While Garcés was on his journey, Domínguez arrived in New Mexico on an official tour for the Franciscan order, the missionaries in Nuevo México. Born in Mexico City, Domínguez had joined the order in 1757 at the age of seventeen. Now, nearly twenty years later, he had been entrusted with a major inspection tour of the missions in Nuevo México. His assignment was to report on their condition and administration, which he did in great detail in a massive and rather critical report.[11] His second assignment was to seek an overland route from Santa Fe to Monterey. He appointed Escalante as his chief assistant and journal keeper. Escalante was born in Treceño, Spain, about 1750. He too had joined the Franciscans at age seventeen, and in 1774 he was assigned to the Nuevo México missions, first at Laguna Pueblo and later at Zuni.

The two friars assembled a group of "companions," including mapmaker Don Bernardo Miera y Pacheco, a retired captain of the militia from Santa Fe, and Andrés Muñiz, who had a working knowledge of the Ute language. Armed with the information from Rivera's report, the party started from Santa Fe on July 29, 1776.[12] Escalante had received Garcés's letter, but he and Domínguez apparently concluded that the more routes to California, the better. Besides, they might have opportunities to make new converts among the Indians they would encounter. "Harvesting souls" for the Church, after all, was the Franciscans' chief reason for being.

The good padres followed the usual route, going up the Chama Valley and across the divide into the San Juan drainage. They then skirted the north side of Mesa Verde, went northwest along the Dolores River, and then looped northeast around the Uncompahgre Plateau and Grand Mesa before turning northwest again. Having apparently misinterpreted Rivera's information about the Moab crossing, they did not find a place to cross the Grand (Colorado) River until they were near present-day Grand Valley. They then headed northwest across the Green River near present-day Jensen, Utah, and followed the Uinta (Duchesne) River generally west, eventually crossing the Wasatch Mountains into the Great Basin at Utah Lake. There they found the Timpanogats people the Utes had mentioned to Rivera, but they called them "Laguna" Indians.

From there they turned southward, passing through the sites of present-day Nephi and Levan, and then swung west into the desert, south through the site of present-day Milford, and on down into the Virgin River drainage.[13] By then it was mid-October, and the party was still several hundred miles from Monterey, as best they could calculate their position by astronomical observations. They already had decided to head back to Santa Fe by way of the Hopi country, and near present-day Toquerville, Utah, they turned southeast to try to find their way back.

They knew they would have to cross the Colorado River; the questions were "How?" and "Where?" On October 16, 1776, some Indian people told them they should not continue southward to cross the river because they would encounter the Grand Canyon. After traveling south along the Hurricane Cliffs, they finally were able to ascend them and head northeast. On October 22, they found themselves on the east side of the Kaibab Plateau at a camp of Southern Paiutes, ancestors of those John Wesley Powell would befriend and study nearly a century later (chapter 5). The mapmaker, Don Bernardo Miera, had been ill for some time. During the night, the Paiutes, according to their lights, "set about to cure him with chants and ceremonials which, if not overt idolatries (which they had to be), were wholly superstitious." When the priests found out the next day, they were deeply insulted by this breach of "evangelical and divine law." The diary goes on at some length about such untoward behavior: "For, if in our company, after having heard these idolatries repeatedly being refuted and condemned, they attend them, furnish occasion for them, and applaud them, what will they not do while wandering three or four months among the infidel Yutas and Navajos with no one to correct them or restrain them?"[14] Clearly the friars were in no mood for any ecumenical curing.

Despite their sacerdotal fit of pique, the Franciscans otherwise got on well with the Indians, who told them that the Colorado River was about 12 leagues away, and there was a ford where the water was only about waist deep. An Indian man agreed to guide them but then backed out, so they proceeded on their own. They finally reached the Colorado at its confluence with the Paria River and camped downstream near the present-day boat launching area at Lee's Ferry. But having finally reached the river, they felt trapped: "We were surrounded on all sides by mesas and big hogbacks [the Echo and Vermilion cliffs] impossible to climb." They called their camp San Benito de Salsipuedes. To eighteenth-century New Mexican Franciscans, a "San Benito" was a "garish white cassock with colored markings worn by errant brothers as a mark of punishment. *Salsipuedes* means 'get out if you can.'" The name clearly reflected the frustrations of the friars and their companions,[15] and it took on even more meaning later the same day. Two men were sent to swim across the river to see if they could find a way up the cliffs on the opposite shore:

> Two of those who knew how to swim well entered the river naked with their clothes upon their heads. It was so deep and wide that the swimmers, in spite of their prowess, were barely able to reach the other side, leaving in midstream their clothing, which they never saw again. And since they became so exhausted getting there, nude and barefoot, they were unable to walk far enough to do the said exploring, coming back across after having paused a while to catch their breath.[16]

The situation appeared critical. The party not only had to get themselves and their baggage across the river, but also the horse remuda, which they depended on for riding and pack horses as well as food. The next day,

> [a] wood raft was put together . . . and Padre Fray Silvestre with the servants tried to cross the river by means of it; but since the poles used for pushing it, even though more than five yards long, did not touch bottom a short distance away from the shore, it was held back by the waves raised by the contrary wind. And so it thrice came back to the shore it had

> left, without getting even as far as the river's middle. This, besides being deep and wide, here has quicksands on either bank, in the likes of which we could lose all or a better part of the horse herd.[17]

Later observers noted that had the men gone farther upstream, they could have crossed the river and found a way to climb out.[18] But they didn't. Rather, scouts were sent to find a way out of the canyon and a ford which better fit the description they had received from the Kaibab people.

After three days the men returned, saying they had spotted a way up onto the Paria Plateau, and that the country toward the east looked as if it might offer easier access to the river. The route out of Paria Canyon was a long and dangerous climb that finally brought them about 1,700 vertical feet above the river. The party then headed generally east across Wahweap and Warm creeks, and around the base of Gunsight Butte. After enduring days of rain, snow, and hail accompanied by thunder and lightening, on November 7, 1776, the weary party finally found its way down Padre Creek canyon. By cutting some steps in the slickrock, they were able to get the horses, "although without pack or rider," down into the canyon and onto the river bank. The saddles and gear were lowered down to the sand bar.

The ford was, in fact, quite easy. They "finished crossing the river about five in the afternoon, praising God our Lord and firing off some muskets in demonstration of the great joy we all felt in having overcome so great a problem, one which had caused us so much labor and delay."[19] The friars named the ford La Purísima Concepción de la Virgen Santísima, and in their honor, it was later called "Crossing of the Fathers." Having finally crossed Glen Canyon, Escalante described what they had seen of it:

> The river's ford is very good. . . . [But] in all that we saw around here no settlement can be established along [the] . . . banks, nor can one go even one day's march downstream or upstream along either side with the hope of the waters being of service to the people and the horse herd, because, besides the terrain being bad, the river flows through a very deep gorge. Everything else adjacent to the ford consists of very tall cliffs and precipices. Eight or ten leagues to the northeast of it rises a round mountain, high but small, which the Payuchis—who begin from here onward [that is their territory began on the left bank of the river]—call Tucane, meaning Black Mountain [Navajo Mountain], and the only one to be seen hereabouts. The river passes very close to it.[20]

This is the first known written description of Glen Canyon and Navajo Mountain.

Although the Domínguez-Escalante journals were not published until the mid-twentieth century, several manuscript copies were made, and these were consulted by various Spanish and other European and Anglo explorers in later years. Bernardino Miera's map thus became well known.[21] It shows the confluence of the San Juan and Colorado rivers, with Miera calling the former "Río de Nabajoó," following Rivera, and the latter "Río de los Zaguaganas." He named Navajo Mountain "El Cerro Azul" (fig. 2.7). Miera's map was used by the great European explorer Alexander von Humboldt to develop the map that accompanied his *Political Essay on the Kingdom of New Spain*, by Lt. Zebulon Pike in his report of his 1810 expedition into the Province of Nuevo México, and by Lewis and Clark to create their maps of 1810–20.[22] All of these were known to John Charles Frémont, who used them to produce maps during his western explorations in the 1840s and 1850s (see below).

Having finally crossed the Colorado River, the Domínguez-Escalante party headed south, following a "well beaten path" along the southern

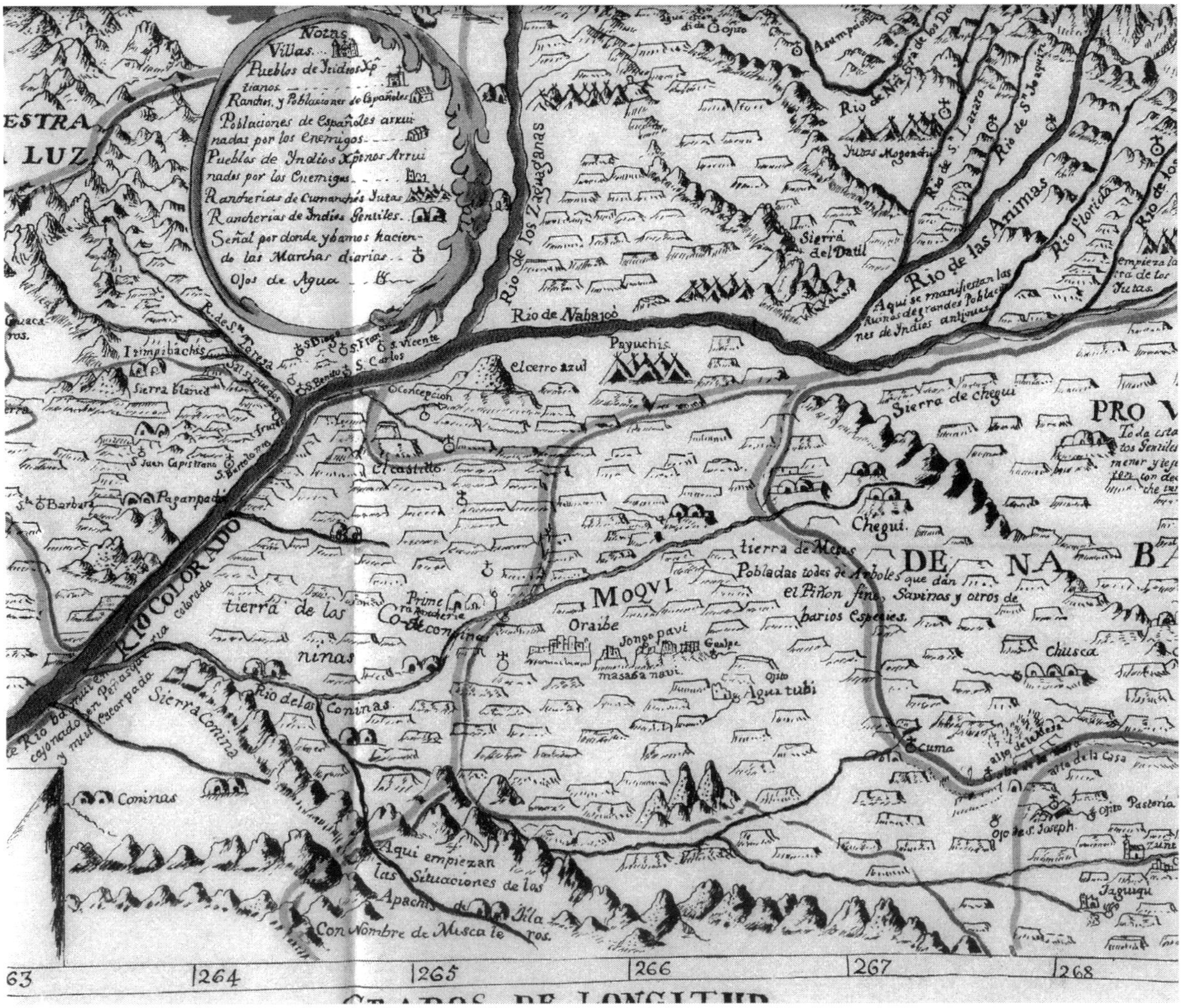

2.7. Section of map by Bernardo Miera y Pacheco, 1776, for the Domínguez-Escalante expedition. From Bolton 1950.

edge of the Rainbow Plateau and north of Navajo Canyon. On November 9, 1776, they encountered "some camps of the Payuchi Yutas," who spoke the same Southern Numic dialect as the people they had encountered on the other side of the Colorado. The Paiutes told the Spanish that they were friendly with the Havasupais who lived to the south, but were enemies of the Oraibi Hopis. Nevertheless, they directed the party to a well-established trail leading to Oraibi. Descending into upper Navajo Canyon, the trail included "a stairway . . . more than three yards wide long and two yards wide" made of "loose stones and sticks." The party followed the trail across the Kaibito Plateau to near Moenkopi and then on to the Hopi mesas. There they were civilly received and given food and lodging. They then traveled on to Zuni, and on January 2, 1777, they finally reached Santa Fe and submitted their report.[23]

Escalante remained in New Mexico for about two years, suffering declining health. He finally was sent to Mexico City for treatment but died on the way in Parral, Mexico, in April 1780. Domínguez's life took a different course. His critical report on the New Mexican Franciscan missions angered some higher-ups, and he suffered the usual fate of whistle-blowers. His report was buried "in the files" (it did not resurface until the twentieth century), and he was assigned to a series of hardship posts at obscure presidio missions until he died sometime between 1803 and 1805. His and Escalante's dream, often expressed in the diary, of bringing Catholicism to the Indian peoples of the Glen Canyon Country and areas to the north went unfulfilled.

THE OLD SPANISH TRAILS

As it turned out, some Indian people from the region did become Catholics in later years—not at Franciscan missions, but as slaves of their Spanish, and later Mexican, masters in New Mexico and California. Even before Mexico gained independence in 1821, there was a fair amount of commerce, including slave trading, between New Mexico and California. At first the route used was that of Escalante and Domínguez as far as Utah Lake, thence south to the Virgin River drainage, and southwestward to Las Vegas and on to California. Later an easier route was found crossing the Colorado at present-day Moab and the Green River at the site of Green River, Utah, thence across the Wasatch Plateau, into the Sevier River drainage, then southward up the Sevier Valley, across into the Parowan Valley, then southwest to Mountain Meadows, into the Virgin drainage, and on to Las Vegas and southern California. This came to be called the Spanish (or Old Spanish) Trail and was still in use into the 1850s.[24] After the Mormons came to the Great Basin in 1847, the portion of the trail from Utah Lake southwestward was sometimes called the Mormon Trail.

THE FUR TRAPPERS

Of course, other forces were at work in the mid-eighteenth century that would bring people into, or at least onto the edges of, the Glen Canyon Country. By the 1740s, the British and French were actively moving across the Great Plains and into the Rocky Mountains, expanding the fur trade that dominated the North American West for so many decades. By about 1820, the upper Green River had become a focal point for the trade, and some of the legendary annual rendezvous were held on Henry's Fork and other accessible places along the river. Various trading and trapping parties began moving south, exploring the Grand and the Green rivers and their tributaries.

In 1821 Mexico gained its independence from Spain. There were already "Yanquis," or Anglos—that is, citizens of the United States—resident in the Province of Nuevo México, especially in Taos and Santa Fe. With Mexican independence and the opening of the Santa Fe Trail, many more Yanquis arrived. Some quickly became trappers and moved into the Colorado drainage from Taos. They generally followed the Spanish Trail northwestward, but others headed southwest down the Gila River and its tributaries.

In 1826 James Ohio Pattie joined a group of about twenty trappers working out of Taos, New Mexico, including George Yount and Tom ("Pegleg") Smith. According to Pattie's rather garbled *Narrative*, published in 1831, the group went upstream from the confluence of the Gila and Colorado rivers. They may have traveled along the north rim of the Grand Canyon and then followed the Colorado River through the Glen Canyon Country, possibly making a side trip up the lower San Juan River, then onward past the confluence of the Grand and Green, up the Grand River to its headwaters, across the Rockies, and then south along the Rockies to Taos. Whether the trip was made at all, or as Pattie described it, has puzzled historians for more than a century.[25] (As an aside, Pegleg Smith received his name for reputedly amputating his own leg with a butcher knife during the winter of 1827 along the Green River.)

In 1827 fur trapper and trader Richard Campbell led a group of men to California. He possibly went by way of the Zuni and Hopi pueblos, northward across Glen Canyon at Crossing of the Fathers, and thence westward to the Virgin River and on to California, arriving in the fall. Whether Campbell took that route or the more southerly one down the Gila River and westward into California is unclear. However, the route across Glen Canyon was followed in 1829–30 by the Mexican trader Antonio Armijo, and there were likely various other, unrecorded trips along the same route.[26]

What is clear is that Anglo fur trappers were working out of Taos into the upper San Juan drainage and along various tributaries of the Colorado above the Glen Canyon Country after 1824. Much of what they did and where they went was unrecorded because they were usually trying to outwit the authorities who forbade them to trap in what was then Mexican territory without licenses. At the same time, from the early 1820s on, other trappers were moving into the Green and Grand drainages from the north and east. Like their counterparts from Taos, few left any records of where they had been and what they saw. One who did was Warren Ferris (1810–99).

Ferris, who was well read and had some experience as a surveyor, worked for the American Fur Company from 1830 to 1835. In 1833, he was along the upper Green River and then went north to winter near Flathead Lake, Montana. In 1834 he was again along the Green River, where he attended the annual rendezvous, and then "was sent southward to trade. He explored the White River, which flows into the Green from the east, and traded with the Ute Indians in the Green River area."[27] He apparently was also farther south and saw the confluence of the Grand and the Green rivers. He returned home to Buffalo, New York, in December 1835 and spent much of 1836 turning his diary into a book. He submitted the manuscript to a Philadelphia publisher, but it was rejected. In 1842 his brother, Charles Ferris, bought into a Buffalo magazine, the *Western Literary Messenger*, and began serially publishing brother Warren's manuscript. By that time Warren had moved to Texas, where he spent the rest of his life. Of particular interest are his descriptions of the Green River and the "Chanion [Canyon] of the Colorado," by which he meant Cataract Canyon.

> Green River, which takes its rise in the Wind [River] Mountains . . . flows south-east, south and finally south-west, four hundred miles to its junction with Grand River, where it becomes the Rio Colorado of the West, one of the most magnificent streams in the world, and descending the mountains, rolls its sublime volume away, many hundreds of miles through Upper and Lower California, until at last it reaches and empties into the gulf of that name. . . . The Colorado a short distance below the junction of Green and Grand rivers, enters the great chanion [canyon], which is a canal [*sic*] in many places more than a thousand feet deep, and bounded on either side by perpendicular walls of rock, that bid defiance to horsemen, who would descend to the river; in fact, they are seldom accessible to footmen. From the summit of the walls, a succession of rocky cedar-covered hills, and sandy plains, appear, losing themselves in the distance. This chanion confines the river between two and three hundred miles; and even to those, who have seen and for years been familiar with the mightiest production of nature, presents a scene from which they recoil with terror. Reader have you ever stood on the brink of the precipice, midway between the falls of Niagara and the Whirlpool, and looked down with terror upon the rushing waters beneath you? If so, fancy yourself there at this moment; but suppose the walls to be six hundred feet higher, and in the same proportion, more distant

> from each other. Let the foaming torrent beneath you vanish, and imagine a beautiful meadow, perfectly level, extending from wall to wall; through this let a calm, unruffled, yet muddy streamlet wind its way; let the borders be decked with a few small shrubs, and dwarf trees. Gaze upon the frowning hills, and burning sands, with which you are to suppose yourself half-surrounded; and you will certainly attempt to descend to the lovely scene beneath, and perhaps may resolve to step over the brook, and recline yourself in the shade of a cluster of willows; alas,! if you succeed, how sadly will you be disappointed. The little brook will gladly enlarge itself as you descend, until it becomes a mighty river three hundred yards wide; the bushes will increase in size, and stature, until they become giant cottonwoods; the narrow strip of meadow land between the walls will expand into broad fields of verdure; and you will see, kind reader, in imagination, what many a half-starved trapper has seen in reality, on the Colorado. These walls approach each other so closely in some places, that the bottoms disappear; and the river being compressed to one fourth of its ordinary width, dashes with inconceivable fury, like the Niagara, at the point I have chosen, and which renders its navigation impracticable. Its tributaries are likewise confined by walls, from their junctions some distance; which compels caravans to travel the plains, far from the main river, and depend much upon chance, and rains, for water.[28]

This seemingly is the first published description of the confluence of the Grand and Green rivers and upper Cataract Canyon. It was, however, not widely known, since it appeared in a local literary magazine published in Buffalo, New York. Nevertheless, Ferris's description deserves noting, especially when compared with the descriptions of the Grand and Green rivers and Cataract Canyon by geologist John Strong Newberry in 1859 and explorer John Wesley Powell in 1869 (chapters 3 and 4).

Ferris also drew a map that shows the Green River with most of its tributaries in generally the right places, and the confluence of the Green River and the "Rio Grand" with the "Chanion of the Colorado" beginning just downstream. The map was intended to go with the rejected book but was not found and published until 1940, and hence was unknown to later nineteenth-century explorers. As Robert Utley points out, had the map been published in 1836 or even 1842, when the last of Ferris's manuscripts was published, it would have significantly influenced western cartography.[29]

JOHN CHARLES FRÉMONT

John Charles Frémont (1813–90) was one of those larger-than-life characters of the nineteenth-century American West, made so by his tireless self-promotion and that of his wife, Jessie Benton Frémont, and her father, the powerful U.S. senator from Missouri, Thomas Hart Benton. Frémont made five major expeditions westward between 1842 and 1854. On the second one he came to understand that the hydrographic Great Basin has no outlet to the sea and gave it its name. His published report is said to have been influential in convincing Mormon leader Brigham Young to lead his people into the Great Basin as their place of refuge.[30]

Frémont's last two expeditions, in 1848–49 and 1853–54, were monomaniacal attempts to demonstrate that an all-weather railroad line could be built through the central Rocky Mountains and on to California. To prove his point, he led expeditions into the mountains in the winter. The fourth expedition was stopped in the San Juan Mountains; Frémont retreated to Taos and Santa Fe, going on to California by the southern route, leaving the mountains strewn with the frozen bodies of his men.

In late 1853 he set out again into the Rockies and across the Cochetopa Pass into the Colorado River drainage. In January and early February 1854, he followed the Gunnison River down to Grand Junction, crossed into the Green River drainage, and crossed the river at about the mouth of the San Rafael River. He followed the San Rafael upstream for a short distance but then turned south and crossed into the Frémont River drainage. There he turned upstream, crossed the Awapa Plateau south of Fish Lake, crossed the divide between the Colorado River drainage and the Great Basin, and followed Grass Valley to the Sevier River. He and his men, in wretched and starving condition, finally reached the small Mormon settlement of Parowan on February 8, 1854. One of the men had frozen to death. Frémont wrote, "He died like a man, on horseback, in his saddle, and will be buried like a soldier on the spot where he fell." The topographer Friedrich Egloffstein (chapter 3) and another man left Frémont at that point and made their way to Salt Lake City. Unfazed, Frémont and most of his men went on to California, arriving in early April 1854.[31]

By 1856 Frémont was the newly formed Republican Party's candidate for president of the United States, but he was defeated by James Buchanan. Despite the fact that Frémont spent only a few days passing through the northern edge of the Glen Canyon Country, his name was given to the river he followed, a small community near its headwaters, and the culture associated with the archaeological sites that were first systematically studied along the river in the late 1920s (chapter 13).

EXPLORING THE COLORADO RIVER DRAINAGE BY WATERCRAFT

The adventurers who explored the Colorado River and the Glen Canyon Country from the 1600s to the 1850s did so by horse, mule and burro—and on foot. They were primarily trying to get around, or across, the Colorado drainage wherever they could. Exploring the rivers by watercraft was another matter entirely, given the rapids, the risk of being trapped in deep and very remote canyons, and the kinds of watercraft available. The fur trappers had learned about bull boats from the Plains Indian people who lived along the upper Missouri River. They were easily made—bowl-shaped with a framework of poles covered by bison hides, large enough to carry two or three people. Such boats were useful for going up, down, and across rivers in calm areas, but not suitable for downriver travel in rough water.

In April 1825, the trapper William H. Ashley and his men built two buffalo hide bull boats and set off down the Green River. It's not clear how big these boats were, although historian Dale Morgan thinks they may have been as large as 12 by 30 feet, with a 20-inch draft. In Flaming Gorge the men nearly lost their lives in what came to be called Ashley Falls. This quickly convinced them to portage their boats around major rapids, including Disaster and Triplet Falls and Hell's Half Mile. They later shifted to dugout canoes and made it as far downstream as Minnie Maud Creek before giving up the venture for safer and drier overland travel.[32]

One of the mysteries of water-based exploration of the Colorado River centers on Denis Julien, who inscribed his signature at various spots along the Green River and in Cataract Canyon between 1831 and 1836. During Robert Stanton's survey for a railroad along the Colorado River in the 1890s (chapter 9), he noted an inscription "D. Julien" on a wall in lower Cataract Canyon. The inscription was in a location that led Stanton to think that it had to have been made from a boat during a period of high water. Subsequently, several more Julien inscriptions were discovered along the Green River and its tributaries.

Research by river historian Charles Kelly and others revealed that Denis Julien was born probably in the 1770s and lived in St. Louis from at least 1793. In 1809, Denis and his brother Etienne volunteered for militia duty in St. Louis. Etienne was one of the guides for the Long expedition to the Rocky Mountains in 1820, the second (after Lewis and Clark) of many federally sponsored expeditions sent to explore the West before the Civil War. It was Long's report that established the myth of the "Great American Desert," which he said lay west of the Mississippi. This concept was a central issue through much of the nineteenth century and beyond, and influenced the work and ideas of John Wesley Powell and others.[33] The expedition did name Long's Peak in the Colorado Rockies, which Powell and company claimed they were the first to climb in 1868 (chapter 4).

By the early 1820s, Denis Julien seems to have been a partner of William and James Reed in a trading post on the Uinta River. By 1831, when he began leaving inscriptions, and possibly before, he was exploring and trapping along the Green River and its tributaries. One of the inscriptions includes an image of what seems to be a boat with some sort of sail, and the location of the inscription in Cataract Canyon suggests he was using a boat. The lack of inscriptions below Cataract Canyon has suggested to some historians that Julien drowned, either in Cataract Canyon or somewhere downstream, but his fate is unknown.[34]

There were other trappers and explorers in the Colorado River drainage in the 1820s and 1830s. Some kept journals or diaries, but most, like Ferris's, were not found and published until well into the twentieth century. Everyone agreed the Country was spectacular, but no place for "greenhorns" or "tenderfeet," to use two well-known nineteenth-century terms.

› 3 ‹

MAPPING AND DEFINING THE GLEN CANYON COUNTRY

IN CHAPTER 2 WE SAW HOW EURO-Americans—of Spanish, Mexican, and Anglo heritage—came to know portions of the Glen Canyon Country and adjacent areas from about 1760 to the early 1850s. The few known works they produced were basically chronicles of their journeys, some not published until the twentieth century. A few general maps were produced and found limited circulation. Some showed a river, the Buenaventura, draining westward into the Pacific Ocean. John Frémont searched for it in 1843–44. When he determined it did not exist, he was led to define the Great Basin—the 200,000 square mile region of internal drainage adjacent to the Glen Canyon Country.[1]

Domínguez, Escalante, Frémont, and others preceded those who came into the Glen Canyon Country and onto the Colorado Plateau beginning in the late 1850s. For the next century, topographers, cartographers, geologists, archaeologists, and historians came there to study and map the land, and to write its topographic, physiographic, geologic, and cultural histories. Their stories form the present chapter. But first we need some additional background.

EARLY MAPS OF THE COLORADO RIVER

The area of North America that was named the "Colorado Plateau" in 1858 appeared usually as a blank space, sometimes with a river running through it, on maps produced in Europe as early as 1590. In that year, Abraham Ortelius published an update of his great atlas *Theatrum Orbis Terrarum* (The Picture of the World), a work in progress from 1590 to 1612 as new information became available.[2] One of the maps, *Maris Pacifica*, shows Baja California as a peninsula, the Gulf of California separating it from the mainland, and a "Río Grande" flowing into the Gulf, but no information about the interior or the source of the river.

Matters were confused for much of the 1600s by Henry Briggs's 1625 map, "The North Part of America." It showed California as an island with a

"Río del Norte" flowing from a great interior lake into the channel between "Island California" and the mainland. Briggs's map was often copied, and Island California appeared on some maps as late as 1746. By 1688, other mapmakers at least had a "Río Grande" flowing into the Gulf of Mexico, and another river, sometimes called "Río del Norte," flowing southwestward into the Pacific from the unknown interior.

The 1723–25 map by Bernard de La Harpe had reattached California to the continent and showed a "Río Grande Colorado" flowing into the Sea of California. The great interior "Province of Quivira" is simply blank. An 1802 map of North America by the French cartographer James Pitot shows what appear to be the Green and Grand rivers extending far inland into mountainous country. This map was the most accurate of the country that became the United States, and it figured in the Louisiana Purchase negotiations. But it was Alexander von Humboldt's 1811 great map in his *Political Essay on New Spain* that influenced maps of the American West for years. Humboldt used a copy of Miera's map to show the Colorado Plateau area, although not so named. An 1816 map of the United States used Humboldt's map for the area west of the Rockies. Albert Gallatin's 1836 map of North America accompanying his *Synopsis of Indian Languages* used Humboldt's map as one source and shows the "Río Colorado of the West" in about the right place.[3]

Frémont's 1845 map of his 1842–44 expeditions shows the Grand, Green, and San Juan rivers in about the right places, as does the map drawn in 1848 by his cartographer Charles Preuss.[4] Frémont's maps mark the beginning of on-the-ground mapping of the American West by trained topographers. Frémont was a member of the U.S. Army Corps of Topographical Engineers and was trained at West Point in topographical methods and mapmaking, as were all his fellow officers. Topographical engineers had led the exploration of the American West since Lt. Stephen Long's expedition to the Rocky Mountains in 1819. In addition to Frémont's expeditions in the 1840s, the engineers carried out the railroad surveys of 1853–55 across the continent to determine the "best" route for a transcontinental railroad. These surveys usually had civilian natural historians and artists as members of their teams. We will hear more of them below.[5]

DEFINING THE COLORADO PLATEAU: JOHN STRONG NEWBERRY

The Glen Canyon Country lies within a much larger region called by physiographers the Colorado Plateaus Province. By consensus, there are six subprovinces: the High Plateaus of south-central Utah, the Uinta Basin, Canyon Lands, Navajo Section, Grand Canyon Section, and Datil Section.[6] Even though physiographers use the term "Colorado Plateaus Provinces," the common term for the region is the "Colorado Plateau" unless there is reason to be more specific. There have been other names and definitions, as we will see.

DEFINING THE GLEN CANYON COUNTRY

The geology and physiography of the Glen Canyon Country were defined, over a century and a half, by numerous geologists and topographers who struggled to map and make geologic sense of the encompassing Colorado Plateau. Systematic efforts began in November 1857, when the schooner *Monterey* arrived at the mouth of the Colorado River. The ship off-loaded a disassembled sternwheel, iron-hulled steamboat. It had been built in Philadelphia and then disassembled and shipped to the Isthmus of Panama, hauled overland, and then transshipped to San Francisco, back around Baja California, and up the Sea of Cortés.

A party of U.S. soldiers and civilian mechanics reassembled the craft, the *Explorer,* which had a 45-foot keel. On December 21, the boiler was fired,

3.1. Portrait of John Strong Newberry. From White 1909.

and the boat started up the Colorado River to find the "head of navigation." It was under the command of Lt. Joseph Christmas Ives of the U.S. Army Corps of Topographical Engineers.[7]

Accompanying Ives were Heinrich Balduin Möllhausen, Baron Friedrich W. von Egloffstein, and John Strong Newberry. Möllhausen, born in Prussia in 1825, had married the daughter of the valet of the great explorer and savant Alexander von Humboldt and was one of Humboldt's protégés. On Humboldt's recommendation, he was hired as an illustrator and natural historian with the Pacific Railroad Survey across the Southwest in 1854, led by Lt. Amiel W. Whipple; there he had met Ives. Now he was back in the West at Ives's invitation. In later years his illustrated books chronicling his adventures brought the American Great Plains and Southwest to the attention of Europe and were also popular in the United States.[8]

Egloffstein (1824–85) was of Bavarian origin, the youngest son of Count Wilhelm, Lord of the Manor Egloffstein in Franconia. Egloffstein served in the engineer corps of the Prussian army before marrying and emigrating to the United States. After settling in the large German community in St. Louis, he became a partner in a surveying and topographic firm. On the recommendation of Dr. George Engelmann, the great St. Louis botanist, Egloffstein joined Frémont's ill-fated railroad survey through the central Rocky Mountains in 1853–54. Ill and frost-bitten, he left Frémont's party at Parowan, Utah (chapter 2), and made his way to Salt Lake City. There he recovered, joined the army survey party of Lt. E. G. Beckwith, which was wintering in the city, and traveled with the survey across Nevada and into California. He did some of the illustrations for Beckwith's report. After his work with Ives, he was involved in mapping and studying mining deposits in Mexico, including translating and publishing reports on Mexican mines made by German mineralogists in the 1830s.[9]

John Strong Newberry (1822–92)(fig. 3.1), from an old New England family, was raised in Ohio, where his family had coal mining interests. The fossils in the coal greatly interested young Newberry. He attended Oberlin College and later taught there in the 1840s. While at Oberlin, he was a mentor to a young Ferdinand Vandeveer Hayden. Newberry also studied with James Hall, the great paleontologist/geologist in New York, as did Hayden, at Newberry's urging. He took a medical degree and made additional medical studies in Paris.

But Newberry's real love was natural history. In 1855 he was appointed as a U.S. Army assistant surgeon, geologist, and botanist attached to a topographical engineer survey of the region between San Francisco and the Columbia River. His appointment was a common one for the time. Physicians were often the only people available with training in natural history and hence could serve dual roles on expeditions. After the West Coast

3.2. The steamboat *Explorer* on the lower Colorado River, 1856, by Heinrich Möllhausen. Ives 1860: frontispiece.

survey, Newberry received a similar appointment with the Ives expedition.[10]

Ives's principal assignment was to determine the head of navigation of the Colorado River as a basis for possible future river-borne commerce. More immediately, he was to determine the feasibility of carrying soldiers and military supplies up the river far enough for the U.S. Army to effectively attack southern Mormon settlements should the simmering conflict deepen between the government and the Mormons, the politically ludicrous and confused "Mormon War."[11] No Army supplies or men, however, were shipped up the Colorado beyond Fort Yuma in support of that, or any other, military campaign.

The second part of Ives's assignment was to explore along the south rim of the Grand Canyon, generally following from west to east a route that previous expeditions led by lieutenants Lorenzo Sitgreaves and Amiel Whipple had taken from east to west in 1851 and 1854. Sitgreaves was searching out a wagon road to the Colorado River; Whipple led the railroad survey of the 35th parallel; Ives had been with Whipple as a junior officer.

The *Explorer* (fig. 3.2) struggled up the turgid and shallow river, frequently experiencing close encounters with rocks and sandbars to the great amusement of the Mohave, Chemehuevi, and other Indian people who watched from the riverbanks and sometimes rode on the steamboat. Ives and crew managed to get the vessel to the foot of Black Canyon. There, on March 8, 1858, the *Explorer* had a direct, head-on encounter with a large submerged rock, but miraculously didn't sink. After a 30-mile excursion by skiff farther upstream through Black Canyon to the mouth of Las Vegas Wash, Ives prudently declared the head of navigation to be just downstream from the sunken rock.

When an army pack train, which had trailed along the left bank of the river all the way from Fort Yuma, finally arrived, Ives sent the steamboat back downstream. He then set off with twenty soldiers, the muleteers, three Indian guides, and Egloffstein, Möllhausen, and Newberry to explore the Big Bend of the Colorado River, thence along the south rim of the Grand Canyon, across the Little Colorado River, to the Hopi mesas, and ultimately to Fort Defiance, near the present-day Arizona–New Mexico border.

After several days of difficult travel the party reached the south rim, and Ives wrote perhaps the first published description of the Grand Canyon. The awe with which he and most everyone else who sees the Grand Canyon for the first time is evident:

> a line of lofty bluffs marked the edge of an immense cañon; a wide gap was directly ahead, and through it were beheld, to the extreme limit of vision, vast plateaus towering one above the other, thousands of feet in the air; the long horizontal bands broken at intervals by wide and profound abysses, and extending a hundred miles to the north, till the deep azure blue faded into a light cerulean tint that blended with the dome of the heavens. The famous "Big cañon" was before us; and for a long time we paused in wondering delight, surveying this stupendous formation through which the Colorado and its tributaries break their way.[12]

Ives used the term "Big cañon." Apparently the first published use of the term "Grand Canyon" was on an 1869 map in a report on a private survey in 1867–68 for a railroad along the thirty-fifth and thirty-second parallels. The survey was done under the direction of Gen. William Jackson Palmer (1836–1907), a larger than life character who played major roles in the Civil War and in 1870–71 was the founder of both Colorado Springs and the Denver & Rio Grande Railroad.[13] Over time, "Grand Canyon" won out.

The Ives party descended Diamond Creek to its confluence with the Colorado River. Ives wrote: "Dr. Newberry has had opportunities for observation seldom afforded to the geologist. . . . the sides of the cañons exhibit all the series that compose the tablelands of New Mexico [in 1856 Arizona was not yet a separate territory], presenting, perhaps, the most splendid exposure of stratified rocks that there is in the world."[14]

Newberry had traveled overland from San Diego across the Mojave Desert to Fort Yuma to join Ives. He was on the steamboat to Black Canyon, made the overland traverse to Fort Defiance, and then traveled to Santa Fe and on to Fort Leavenworth, Kansas. His geology report in Ives's general report is a tour de force, a transect across southern California and the Mojave Desert, descriptions of the canyon of the lower Colorado River, the Grand Canyon, the Little Colorado River, "the Navajo Country" (as he called it) between the Little Colorado and Fort Defiance, and all the country he saw between Fort Defiance and Fort Leavenworth.

In two chapters he provided the first succinct description of the geological strata making up the "Structure of the Colorado Plateau," thus giving a name to the region. He also discussed the geological and other forces that shaped,

> the table lands of the upper Colorado. . . . The Colorado [River] rises in a thousand sources, at an elevation of from ten to twelve thousand feet above the sea on the western edge of the Rocky mountains. Descending from their fountainheads its tributaries fall upon a high plateau of sedimentary rock, which forms the western base of these mountains and occupies

> all the interval between them and the great bend of the Colorado. . . .
>
> . . . [T]he great cañons of the Colorado . . . *belong to a vast system of erosion and are wholly due to the action of water*. Probably nowhere in the world has the action of this agent produced results so surprising, both as regards their magnitude and their peculiar character.[15]

Newberry also noted that from about its confluence with the Little Colorado River, the main river's "course trends northeasterly into Utah, where its outline has not been traced."[16]

Newberry's report from the Ives expedition was published in 1861. He provided for the first time a scientific description of the Grand Canyon, postulating that the canyon country was formed entirely by erosional processes acting over untold eons of time. His ideas were soon circulating through the larger scientific community by summaries in scientific journals of the day.[17] Newberry began the description of the many sedimentary strata forming the Colorado Plateau, an effort still ongoing a century and a half later.

To complete this part of our story, Ives had married Cora Semmes, cousin of U.S. naval commander Raphael Semmes and niece of the secretary of war, John B. Floyd, both staunch Southerners. Uncle John had used his influence to secure Ives's appointment to head the Colorado expedition, bypassing several more senior and better qualified officers. When the Civil War began, Ives resigned his commission to join the Confederate Army. He became one of Jefferson Davis's aides de camp, and he and Cora often helped the Davises host dignitaries at the Confederate capitol in Richmond, Virginia. It was a long way in distance and circumstance from the muddy lower Colorado River and the scenic glories of Newberry's Colorado Plateau and the Grand Canyon. He died in New York City in 1868 of meningitis and alcohol abuse.[18]

THE MACOMB-NEWBERRY SURVEY

When he concluded his fieldwork for the Ives survey, Newberry went to Washington to work on his report. At some point he apparently established temporary bachelor's quarters in a "house of ill repute," where he was joined in 1859 by Fielding B. Meek, a paleontologist who worked with Hayden.[19] Newberry was fascinated by the Colorado Plateau and signed on with another topographical engineer party in 1859 led by Capt. John Navarre Macomb (1811–89). Macomb was from a distinguished military family. His father, Gen. Alexander Macomb Jr. (1782–1841), was a hero of the War of 1812. Macomb retired as a colonel in the Corps of Engineers in the 1870s.

The main purpose of the expedition was to explore the general route of the Old Spanish Trail from Santa Fe into Utah and, if possible, reach the confluence of the Grand and Green rivers. The party followed the usual route from Santa Fe to Española before heading up the Chama River valley and into the San Juan River drainage to Pagosa Springs. There they turned westward along the base of the San Juan Mountains and explored around the base of the Mesa Verde. The party then headed diagonally northwestward, briefly stopping to explore an archaeological site that Escalante had noted.[20] They continued on across "the Great Sage Plain," which Newberry named.

The survey party tried to reach the banks of the Grand River by way of a drainage that Newberry called "Labyrinth Cañon," probably Salt Creek, about 4 miles above the Grand and Green river confluence. After they were stymied by a precipitous and impassable jump-up, they retreated to a high mesa where they could see across the confluence and beyond. Below them, across the Colorado, lay the Maze and the Land of Standing Rocks; to the south and east lay the Needles District. Newberry wrote:

3.3. "Lower San Juan, Looking West from near camp 35. J. J. Young from a sketch by Dr. J. S. Newberry." Macomb 1860: plate IX.

> A great basin or sunken plain lay stretched out before us as on a map. Not a particle of vegetation was anywhere discernible; nothing but bare and barren rocks of rich and varied colors shimmering in the sunlight. Scattered over the plain were thousands of . . . fantastically formed buttes . . . pyramids, domes, towers, columns, spires, of every conceivable form and size. Among these by far the most remarkable was the forest of Gothic spires. . . . Nothing I can say will give an adequate idea of the singular and surprising appearance which they presented. . . . Singly, or in groups, they extend like a belt of timber for several miles. Nothing in nature or in art offers a parallel to these singular objects, but some idea of their appearance may by gained by imagining the island of New York thickly set with spires like that of Trinity church, but many of them full twice its height.[21]

Trinity Church, the Gothic Revival masterpiece designed by Richard Upjohn, completed in 1846, was then, as now, situated at the foot of Wall Street in Manhattan. Until the early 1880s, its spire of nearly 284 feet was the tallest structure in the United States. A Manhattan Island full of rock spires nearly twice as high would have boggled the minds of Newberry's readers.

Macomb and Newberry had planned to explore from the confluence of the Grand and Green rivers downstream to the confluence of the Colorado and the San Juan in Glen Canyon, and then turn up the San Juan, but they could clearly see from their lofty observation point that it would

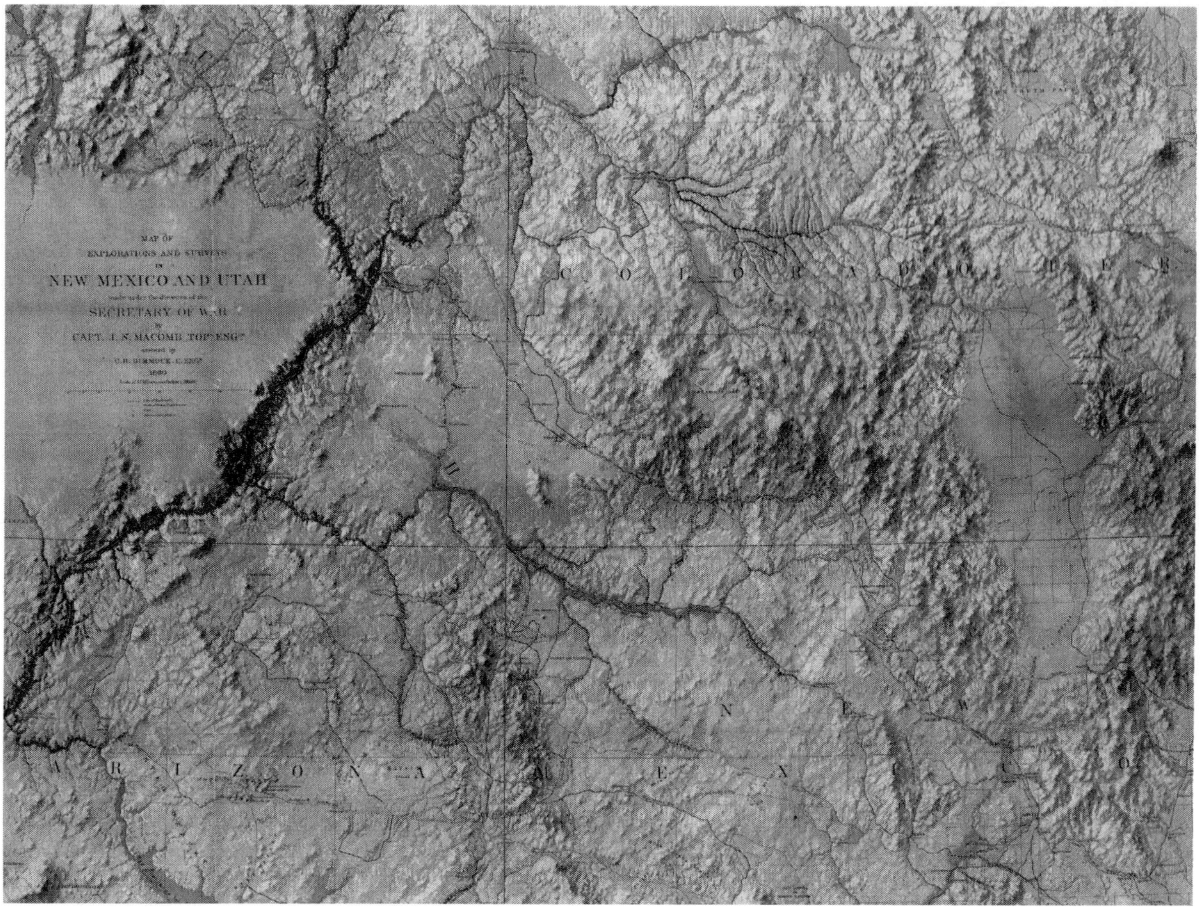

3.4. "Map of Explorations and Surveys of New Mexico and Utah by Capt. L. N. Macomb, Top. Eng." Portion of map accompanying Macomb 1860.

be impossible. Hence, they retreated in a southeasterly direction, passing east of the Abajo Mountains to the San Juan River (fig. 3.3). They followed the San Juan upstream, then turned southeastward back to Santa Fe, passing through Jemez and Santo Domingo pueblos en route.

Newberry's report on his trip to the confluence of the Grand and Green rivers was delayed by the onset of the Civil War and then laid aside. He finally managed to get it into print in 1876, partly in response to John Wesley Powell's reports of his exploration of the Colorado River and descriptions of Colorado Plateau geology, and an article by Grove Karl Gilbert on the "Colorado Plateau Province" (chapter 7).

Newberry served on the U.S. Sanitary Commission during the Civil War and was then appointed Chair of Geology and Paleontology at Columbia University in New York. For a few years he served concurrently as director of the Geological Survey of Ohio. One of his assistants in both jobs was Grove Karl Gilbert (chapter 7). Newberry died in 1892, celebrated as one of the most prominent scientists of the nineteenth century.

IVES'S AND NEWBERRY'S MAPS AND BEYOND

The maps for the Ives and Macomb reports were produced by Egloffstein. By 1856 he had invented a new technique for depicting topographic relief.

The technique was complex, involving plaster scale models of terrain and a half-tone process using daguerreotypy.[22] The resulting maps showed a bird's-eye view of elevational relief with the light coming from the left: the more shadow, the more relief. These "shaded relief" maps were entirely new and "realistically appearing" depictions.

While Newberry's report of the 1859 expedition was long delayed, the army quickly produced a highly detailed map, published in 1860. C. H. Dimmock, a civil engineer accompanying the expedition, compiled topographic and astronomic observations. Those data were turned over to Egloffstein. He incorporated all the map data from the greater Four Corners area accumulated by the topographical engineers since the 1840s and constructed and engraved a shaded relief map that was clearly ahead of its time (fig. 3.4).[23] The scale is 12 inches to the mile, and the map covers an area from about latitude 35.5 to 39.5 north and longitude 104.5 to 111.5 west. Egloffstein's maps for the Ives-Newberry report show a blank just above the confluence of the Colorado and Little Colorado rivers. The 1860 map shows almost all of the Grand and Green river drainages to about 120 miles north of the head of Cataract Canyon. It belies the idea that the Colorado River system canyons between the Uinta Basin and the Grand Canyon were "unknown" (chapter 4).

While Egloffstein's and others' methods of representing topography gave an *idea* of the country shown, the *precise elevation* or *degree of slope* of any place existed only for those points at which actual barometric observations had been made. With the advent of the Pacific Railroad surveys in the 1850s, accurately depicting slopes and grades that trains could run on became imperative. In addition to Egloffstein's method, other methods had included various forms of hachure, but they were insufficient. From the time of the surveys until after the Civil War, hachure lines segued into contour lines of equal intervals. Large-scale geological studies of areas with the enormity of elevational relief and geological complexity of the Rocky Mountains, the Sierra Nevada, and the Colorado Plateau also drove the further development of field topographic mapping and mapmaking.

The Geological Survey of California, begun in 1860 by the great geologist Josiah D. Whitney (for whom Mount Whitney is named), used precisely measured baselines and large-scale triangulation to produce excellent geological maps. Young Clarence King worked on the Whitney survey and carried its methods into his geographical and geological survey of the fortieth parallel. He and Whitney pioneered the use of telegraphic time signals, rather than delicate chronometers, for determining longitude (obviously this only worked where telegraph lines were available). Finally, the Wheeler survey (chapter 6) mapped some 360,000 square miles of the American West, each map a quadrangle of appropriate scale abutting four other quadrangles. Abutting square or quadrangle maps had been used in Europe for some time, as, for example, on the British Ordnance survey maps. We will return to mapmaking later on.

4

JOHN WESLEY POWELL AND THE CANYON COUNTRY, 1867–1869

IN THE SUMMER OF 1859, WHILE MACOMB and Newberry were wending their way to the head of Cataract Canyon, an ambitious twenty-five-year-old rural schoolteacher with a burning interest in natural history set out alone in a skiff down the Illinois River and then up the Des Moines River to study geology and collect mollusks. His name was John Wesley Powell.[1] In previous summers he had made solo boat trips down the Mississippi from near its head to New Orleans, and down the Ohio from Pittsburgh. Longing for a formal education, especially in science, he had managed a couple of years of college when he could afford it. His father, Joseph Powell, was a farmer of necessity, but a circuit-riding preacher of the Wesleyan Methodist persuasion by vocation. He and his wife, Mary, had emigrated from England. Like thousands of other families, the Powells moved westward after the birth of young John Wesley ("Wes") in upstate New York in 1834. There were seven other children. One, Martha Ann, became the mother of Arthur Powell Davis, who would mastermind the Bureau of Reclamation's plans to build dams across the Colorado River (chapter 12). Ellen, six years younger than Wes, would marry Almon Harris Thompson and share her husband's and Powell's adventures in the West and the Glen Canyon Country. Another sister, Eliza, would marry a wagon-maker named Charles Garlick, whom Powell would hire as a member of the U.S. Geological Survey in the 1880s.

At the onset of the Civil War, Powell enlisted in the Union Army as a private, but was soon a Captain of Artillery. At one point he received permission from his commander, Ulysses S. Grant, to take a short leave to go to Detroit and marry his cousin, Emma Dean. She returned to the front with him and remained there for the duration. At the Battle of Shiloh, Powell lost his right arm below the elbow to a Confederate sharpshooter. Nursed back to health by Emma and promoted to major, a title he retained for the rest of his life, Powell returned to the war and was present at the terrible siege of Vicksburg. There he whiled away the lull times by

4.1. Portrait of John Wesley Powell, ca. 1882. Portrait Collection, port 0002. Courtesy of the U.S. Geological Survey Digital Photography Library.

hunting fossils in the trenches that the sappers had dug around the town.

At war's end, Major Powell returned to Illinois, where he became Professor Powell at Illinois State University in Normal. But his eyes were on the West. In 1867 he organized a summer natural history expedition of friends, relatives (including Emma), and students to the Front Range of the Rockies. In Denver, Powell met William N. Byers, owner and editor of the *Rocky Mountain News*. Byers introduced Powell to his brother-in-law, Jack Sumner.[2]

John (Jack) Colton Sumner (1840–1907) was born in Indiana and grew up in Iowa. He enlisted in the Iowa Volunteer Infantry in 1862 and saw much action in the Civil War, often as a sharpshooter and scout. He had come to Colorado in 1866 to serve as a factor for Byers, setting up an outfitting and trading post at Hot Sulphur Springs in Middle Park, where he dealt with Ute Indians and some mountain men. Sumner also had a pack train operation and served as a guide for trips into the Rockies. Powell hired Sumner and his pack train for the student trip. Sumner had come to know the Middle Park country and the areas to the west fairly well, as did some of the mountain men who hung around Sumner's post. Middle Park is part of the headwaters drainage of the Grand River; to the northwest, across a divide, lies the Green River drainage.

Around evening camp fires, Powell and Sumner talked about exploring overland to the upper tributaries of the Grand and Green rivers. That led to discussions of a possible boat trip down the Green River to its confluence with the Grand, thence possibly on down the Colorado through the Grand Canyon. Various stories of Powell's trip stress his heading off into a vague "Unknown" between the southern end of the Uinta Basin and the end of the Grand Canyon. As we saw in chapter 3, the country itself was known and had been mapped in sketchy detail. What wasn't "known" were the canyons themselves and the navigability of the river within them. Sumner would later claim that during the campfire discussions that summer, it was he who convinced Powell to explore the Colorado River below the confluence of the Grand and the Green, which Powell thought "foolhardy and impossible," rather than taking a trip in 1868 through the Dakota Badlands. In fact, Powell had intended the 1867 trip to be into the Badlands, but rumors of Indian difficulties caused him to head instead to the Rocky Mountains.[3] However arrived at, the idea took hold. Slowly, it began to turn into an "expedition," one that would possibly last many months. Sumner would play key roles, not only in planning the expedition, but in helping carry it through.

In the fall of 1867, Powell returned home, where he put together funding from Illinois institutions and his own pocket. He was thus able to launch the Rocky Mountain Scientific Exploring Expedition in the early summer of 1868. One object was to climb Long's Peak, 14,255 feet in elevation, which Powell, Byers, Sumner, Powell's brother Walter, and three others accomplished—apparently the first to make the ascent. They then set out to explore the headwaters of the Grand and Green rivers.

Returning to Sumner's trading post, Powell and Sumner recruited some men who hired out as guides and pack mule wranglers when they could, and hunted, trapped, and prospected at other times. Among them were William Dunn, William Hawkins (in 1868 using the assumed name of "Missouri Rhodes"), Oramel G. Howland, and his half-brother Seneca Howland. A fifth man, Gus Lankin, was recruited but soon disappeared. These men, together with Powell, Emma, Walter, and some others, moved westward to establish winter quarters along the White River at a place now named Powell Bottoms.

A band of "Tabuats" Ute Indians was camped nearby, and Powell began to learn the Ute–Southern Paiute language. He was allowed to observe during curing ceremonies and other rituals, and to collect myths and tales told by the elders to while away the long winter evenings. The Indians named him "Kapurats," meaning "Right Arm Off," a name he was remembered by for decades after among Southern Paiute people in the Glen Canyon Country.[4]

Most of the easterners, except Walter and Emma, left in November via Green River Station, Wyoming Territory—the point the Union Pacific Railroad had reached earlier in the year. Powell and the remaining men explored the country, seeking to learn the lay of the land and whether it would be feasible to run the rivers. Powell heard stories from his men about rapids, waterfalls, and giant whirlpools that would swallow or destroy boats in an instant. There were other tales of the river sinking underground to emerge hundreds of miles away. Powell doubted the stories, especially the waterfalls, since he thought the sediment-filled river was abrasive enough to grind down any abrupt ledges that might create them. He calculated that the Green and Colorado could be run in boats.

In March 1869, Powell and Emma went to Green River Station and boarded an eastbound train. Emma remained in Illinois. Powell stopped in Chicago and ordered some boats built before going on to Washington, D.C., to try to raise money for his trip. He succeeded only in getting authorization to draw army rations at western posts and to borrow some scientific instruments from the Smithsonian Institution. He apparently again used his own funds, and perhaps also funds provided by William Byers.

Powell may not have known that the U.S. Army had on its agenda the exploration of the Colorado River but postponed action when his plans were known. At least one of the parties attached to Clarence King's survey of the fortieth parallel (chapter 6) was in the Green and Yampa rivers area in 1869. Timothy O'Sullivan, King's photographer, took excellent photographs of Flaming Gorge, Lodore Canyon, and Yampa Canyon that year and again in 1872.[5]

While in Washington, Powell also arranged for an army sergeant, George Y. Bradley (1836?–1885), to receive a discharge so he could join the expedition. Bradley had been born in Newberry, Massachusetts, and for some time he worked as a shoemaker, a sailor, and perhaps a cod fisher. He served in the Union Army in the Civil War, achieving the rank of lieutenant, was wounded in 1862, and discharged in 1864. He re-enlisted in January 1867 as a private. He was sent to the High Plains to serve in military units assigned to keep Indians away from the ever-advancing Union Pacific Railroad. By November 1867 he was a first sergeant stationed at Fort Sanders, south of Laramie, Wyoming. Powell somehow met him in late 1868. As noted, Bradley had some sailing and boating experience, and was not enamored of army duty. Throwing in with Powell seemed much more interesting.

In addition to Jack Sumner and Bradley, the other men Powell recruited for his expedition were an odd and interesting lot. Oramel G. and Seneca Howland were half-brothers, both born in Vermont. Seneca Howland (1843–69) was in the Union Army in the Civil War. He was a member of the 16th Vermont regiment, which together with the 13th Vermont stopped Pickett's Charge at the Battle of Gettysburg, turned the tide of the battle, and changed the course of the war.[6] Oramel Howland (1833–69) worked as an editor and printer for Byer's *Rocky Mountain News* throughout the war, was involved in other printing as well as mining ventures, and was well-known in Denver. He spent time exploring the Rockies, hence knew Jack Sumner, and decided to join Powell and Sumner for the expedition. Seneca had joined his older brother in Denver in 1868, and he too decided to go along with Powell.

In 1949 William Culp Darrah wrote, "William Dunn is literally an unknown character. . . . It is to be hoped that some fortuitous find in the future will give to Bill Dunn the flesh and spirit he deserves."[7] Just so. In 2003, some intense archival sleuthing by river historian Don Lago finally gave Dunn "flesh and spirit." William H. Dunn (1845?–69) was born in Ohio. He enlisted in the 15th Ohio Infantry in early 1864 and was involved in several Civil War battles in Georgia and Tennessee. His unit wound up in Texas and remained there for a time after the war ended. He was mustered out of the army in November 1865. His movements thereafter are vague, but at some point he headed to Colorado. He was in the Middle Park area by the summer of 1868. Apparently he was an archetypical image of a mountain man: he dressed in buckskins, had a beard and long hair, and made his living as a hunter, trapper, and mule skinner. Powell obviously judged him to be competent to do more than pull an oar since he placed him in charge of barometrical observations (discussed further below).[8]

Frank Valentine Goodman (1844–1915) was born in England but came to the United States in time to serve in the Union Army during the Civil War. After the war, he returned to England and married, but his wife died of tuberculosis. He was back in the states by about 1867–68. He hired on as a bull whacker for a freight outfit, then worked as a trapper for the Hudson's Bay Company, then trapped on his own up the Snake River and over to the headwaters of the Green River. He sold his furs at Green River City and was apparently hanging around town when he met Powell and signed on for the river trip. Powell hired him as a boatman, but after he lost his clothes and gear in the Disaster Falls debacle (discussed below), he left the expedition at Uinta. He worked briefly at the Uinta Indian agency and then took an Indian wife and became a trapper. He later married an Anglo woman, and he, she, and their children settled in Vernal, Utah, where they scratched out a living as sheep ranchers in the Uinta Basin country until his death.[9]

William Rhodes Hawkins (1848–1919), who sometimes traveled under the names "Billy Rhodes" or "Missouri Rhodes," was born in Gentry County, Missouri. In 1863 he lied about his age and joined the 15th Cavalry of the Missouri State Militia. About a year later he ran afoul of military rules and spent eighteen days under arrest for unspecified charges of "mutiny," but was reinstated. He was later disabled, and still later mustered out on July 1, 1865, owing the Union Army $1.61 for "one waist belt, one gun sling, one shoulder sling and one plate."[10] Rather than pay up, he apparently became "Missouri Rhodes" and headed West. By 1868, he had found his way to the Rockies to prospect and trap. He wore buckskins and long hair, like Dunn. He knew the country around the headwaters of the Grand River. Powell hired him as cook and boatman for $1.50 a day for the duration of the trip. He was never paid.

Powell's younger brother, Walter Henry Powell (1842–1915), was born in Ohio. He managed to get some college education and become a teacher. He enlisted in the Union Army and wound up in brother John Wesley's unit, Battery F, 2nd regiment, Illinois Light Artillery. He was at Shiloh and Vicksburg. He was captured by the Confederates in the battle of Atlanta, but was exchanged as a prisoner of war in March 1865. His prison camp experience traumatized him, and he was moody and sometimes unstable during the expedition. Nevertheless, his brother Wes brought him along on the 1868 trip, and he was a boatman on the 1869 trip. In later years his condition deteriorated; he suffered long bouts of depression and could not hold a job. The Powell family—primarily his sister, Ellen Thompson—cared for him. In his last years he was committed to a military insane asylum in Washington, D.C.[11]

When Powell arrived at Green River station in May 1869, he met Andrew Hall (ca. 1851–82), who was about eighteen. Born in Scotland, Hall had emigrated to the United States with his family in 1858. He had spent five years as a bull whacker, mule driver, Indian scout, and freight wagon guard on the plains and in the mountains. He had some knowledge of boats, hence Powell hired him on the spot.[12]

On May 18, 1869, a Union Pacific flatcar was shunted onto a siding at Green River Station and Powell's four boats were unloaded. The Howlands, Sumner, Hawkins, Walter Powell, and Dunn were already camped there. Before they set out on the river trip, Powell concluded formal written agreements with Jack Sumner, William Dunn, and O. G. Howland specifying duties and recompense "during the proposed exploration of the Green River from Green River City, Wyoming Territory, to the Colorado River, and of the Colorado River from that point to Callville [Nevada]."[13] Sumner was to handle the sextant to track where the party was astronomically. Dunn was to make barometrical observations night and morning and during the day to determine the "altitude of walls of the cañon." That meant periodically climbing out of the canyons to determine the difference in barometric pressure, and thus the height of the walls above river level. O. G. Howland was to "make a topographical drawing of the course of the rivers." The men further agreed to "do a fair proportion of the work necessary in getting supplies and boats safely through the channels of the . . . rivers" and to save "suitable skins of animals" for stuffing. The men were to be given time to prospect for gold and silver, "if not too often," and thirty days for hunting and trapping. They were to receive twenty-five dollars each per month and so much per skin procured for stuffing, ranging from thirty-five cents per squirrel to ten dollars for a "Bear (grown grizzly)." Powell agreed to "furnish boats, supplies, ammunition, etc., sufficient for the use of the expedition."

The agreement was for one year commencing June 1, 1869. Prophetically, however, there was an escape clause: "Should it be necessary to proceed on the journey without delay on account of disaster to boats or loss of rations, then the time specified for hunting may not be required for hunting by either party, nor shall it be deemed a failure of contract to furnish supplies should such supplies be lost in transit."[14] There were apparently no formal agreements with the other men, although Powell seems to have promised each of them various forms of recompense, little or none of which they ever received. On May 24, 1869, Powell and his crew of nine launched themselves down the Green River in the four boats which they had named *Emma Dean* (after Powell's wife), *Maid of the Cañon,* the *No Name,* and *Kitty Clyde's Sister.*

Apparently the Howlands christened the *No Name* after a sloop that Confederate naval officer John Taylor Wood (1830–1904) escaped on to Cuba at the end of the Civil War. Wood was a major war hero to those with Confederate sympathies. The grandson of President Zachary Taylor, he graduated from the Naval Academy in 1853 and saw service in the Mediterranean and elsewhere.

He resigned from the Union Navy in April 1861 and joined the Confederacy soon after. He became naval aide to Confederate president Jefferson Davis—and a scourge of Union shipping. In one raid along the New England coast, he sank thirty-two Northern ships. He was also involved in the abortive attempt at the end of the war to help Davis escape the country. Wood was himself captured, but escaped and pirated the sloop from some Union deserters. According to newspaper reports at the time, when he arrived in Cuba, the customs agent asked the name of the ship and Woods replied "the No Name."[15] Wood later moved to Nova Scotia and became a prominent businessman.

Kitty Clyde's Sister was named for a popular song of the day, "Minnie Clyde, Kitty Clyde's Sister" (1857).

> Oh, long have I sung of sweet Kitty Clyde, who lives at the foot of the hill;
> And though that sweet pretty bird has flown, another is living there still.
> She's blythe and gay as a robin that sings on the tree by the old mill side,
> And if ever I loved a girl in my life, 'tis the charming sweet Minnie Clyde.
> Oh, Minnie Clyde she is my pride, and sure I am no jester;
> For if ever I loved a girl in my life, 'tis Minnie, Kitty Clyde's Sister. . . .

The cover of the sheet music is a print of a pretty young lass, Miss Minnie, looking fetchingly at the robin on the tree branch above her; off in the distance is a mill and mill race. The print is said to be one of the first known published works by a young Winslow Homer (1836–1910).[16]

DOWN THE COLORADO

There are numerous mysteries about the first voyage, some only recently resolved. One surrounds the boats Powell used. In his published reports he wrote that that the boats were "made to my own design." What he apparently meant was that he had some standard boats of the Whitehall design built and then modified to suit his needs. Whitehall boats came into existence in either England or New York City (sources vary) in the 1820s. Probably the quintessential rowboat, the Whitehall was designed to move people and cargo around quickly and efficiently, and the boats were used extensively in harbors and on rivers; indeed, the design continues to be widely used in the twenty-first century.[17] Powell was undoubtedly familiar with such craft.

Powell modified the design to provide covered, watertight cargo spaces in the bow and stern. This, however, left the center section open and easily subject to swamping, as the crew soon found out. Three of the boats were made of oak; a lighter "pilot boat," the *Emma Dean*, was made of pine. One of the questions river historians and expert river runners have pondered is whether or not the boats had steering oars. They probably did not at the start, but some sort of jury-rigged steering oars were perhaps added during the voyage to help cope with running the rapids. The boats on the second trip did have steering oars.[18]

In 1889 Frank Brown, the president of the company proposing to build a water-level railroad down the canyons of the Colorado River to southern California (chapter 9), wrote to Powell asking advice about what sort of boats he should use. Powell replied:

> The boats used by myself and party in the descent of the Colorado River in '71 and '72 were well adapted for the purpose. They were 22 feet long and 4 ft. beam and 22 inches deep; keel bottom, bow sharp, greatest width about 2/5 from bow. The ribs were 3/4 in. square placed 4 inches apart in bow and stern, 8 inches amidship. The planking was 1/2 inch oak and oar locks iron. The boats *not* clinker

> built [that is, not with overlapping side planks, like house clapboards, but fitted smooth]. In bow, stern and amidships were compartments decked over for storing cargo. They were water tight. Rowing oars 12 ft., steering 16 ft. of ash span oars should be taken. Crew of three men—stroke, bow and steersman. Cargo should be enclosed in rubber bags, tools and materials for repairing boats should be taken along. We started from Green River City with 1000 lbs. estimated cargo in each boat.[19]

Unfortunately, Brown did not take Powell's advice, using instead rather flimsy boats, and it cost him his life in the Grand Canyon.

Although Powell and Bradley had some boating experience on the smooth-flowing rivers of the East and Midwest, neither they nor their compatriots were in any way prepared for the rapids and rushing waters they encountered in the canyons of the Green and Colorado on the 1869 trip. Powell, with only one arm, could not row. A major problem was that the person(s) rowing faced the stern, since the power of the stroke is when the oars are pulled toward the oarsman, requiring him to peer over his shoulder to see where the boat was headed. Even with a pilot, this was a problem when running rapids in fast water. It was not solved until the 1890s (chapter 11).

In many places, the men had to either "line" or portage the boats around rapids. Lining involves attaching ropes to the boats and scrambling along the shore while pulling the boats along the edge of the rapids. Sometimes they had to unload the boats first. Portaging, of course, meant unloading the boats and hauling them and the gear around the rapids. It was exhausting and dangerous work, and the men were constantly soaked in the cold river waters. They lost the *No Name* in Lodore Canyon to a particularly nasty rapid they aptly named "Disaster Falls." With the boat went a critical part of their food supply and most of Frank Goodman's clothes—leaving him basically in his red woolen union suit and a pair of shoes. The barometers and a small keg of whiskey were salvaged.

Until Disaster Falls, the rapids had seemed simply thrilling. Now they became dangerous, and the tone of the trip changed. There seemingly was some finger-pointing by the Powell brothers at the Howland brothers, who were in charge of the *No Name*. When the party reached the Uinta (now Duchesne) River, Powell was able to hike to the Uinta Indian Agency and acquire 300 pounds of flour. It was not nearly enough, but may have been all the agency could spare, or all Powell had the funds to buy. Frank Goodman left the expedition at that point, having had quite enough river adventures.[20]

The Uinta Basin had been well known since before fur trapper days. Domínguez and Escalante had crossed there in 1776; a Pacific Railroad Survey party led by Lt. James Gunnison had passed through in 1854;[21] and Powell and his men had partially explored it overland in 1868. So it was known territory, including the river itself. But once Powell and his now eight men in three boats pushed off on July 6, 1869, they were heading into canyons, and down a river, less well known. The river in Gray and Desolation canyons alternated between relatively calm, boring stretches where the upcanyon winds blew so hard they could make no headway, and rapids as difficult as any they had faced so far.

Once they reached the confluence of the Grand and the Green and headed into Cataract Canyon, the journey became continuously difficult. They were experiencing firsthand what Newberry, and probably Ferris, had observed from above (chapters 2–3). For twelve harrowing and exhausting days, they fought through and around some of the biggest rapids on the upper Colorado River. By the time they reached the calm at the upper end of Glen Canyon on July 28, they were tired, bedraggled, irritable, and facing an increasingly serious food shortage. They had fifteen pounds of rancid bacon and a possibly adequate supply of moldy flour, coffee, and dried apples for another month at half rations. A statement by Billy Hawkins, written fifty years after the voyage, suggests that by the time they reached Glen Canyon, there was increasing friction between the Powell brothers and the rest of the men. Powell was seen as arrogant and aloof, partly because he didn't eat with the men but was served off to one side. This may have been a hold-over from Powell's military days—officers don't mingle with the troops. The crew's perceptions likewise may have derived from the time-honored practice of troops bitching about the commander. Some of the friction focused on Bill Dunn, who had purportedly lost Powell's watch in the river; the rest focused on the Howland brothers. Hawkins later asserted that Powell named the Dirty Devil River after Dunn as an insult.[22]

Powell's party reached the mouth of the Paria River on August 4, leaving the serenity of Glen Canyon behind. Marble Canyon and Grand Canyon provided a whole new series of dangerous fast water and rapids, many fiercer and larger than any they had seen before. They struggled on, lining and portaging rapids when they had to, running them when they thought they could. On August 25 they portaged around Lava Falls, one of the more renowned of the Grand Canyon rapids, and that night they opened the last sack of flour. A day later they reached a rapid that seemed impassable. After a day of scouting and fretting, Powell, at Jack Sumner's suggestion, determined to line down the first part of the rapid and then run the remainder.

But the Howland brothers and Bill Dunn had had enough—enough fear and danger, and enough of Powell. They wanted to abandon the expedition, climb out of the canyon, and try to reach the Mormon settlements to the north along the Virgin River. According to Powell, he and O. G. Howland talked at length into the night. Powell then sat up the rest of the night using the sextant to try to determine exactly where they were—and how far it might be to the mouth of the Virgin River and known territory. He concluded they did not have that far to go.

The Howlands and Dunn were not convinced and deeply afraid of the fearsome-looking rapid. They wanted out. On the morning of August 28, they took some of the field notes and two rifles and a shotgun, but refused any rations; they thought they could live off the land. Sumner gave O. G. Howland his watch to give to his sister in Denver, in case Sumner didn't make it. As Sumner described it, Dunn and the Howland brothers

> decided to abandon the outfit and try to reach the settlements on the head of the Virgin River. Each took a gun and all the ammunition he wanted and left us to go it or swamp. The remaining 6 men lifted the two large boats over the rock past some of the rapids, abandoned the small boat as useless property, and pulled out and ran the rest of the damned rapid with a ringing cheer, though at great risk, as the boats shipped nearly half full in a perfect hell of foam.[23]

They had safely run what came to be called Separation Rapid. Later in the day they almost lost both boats in another big rapid, but got through it. It was the last major rapid in Grand Canyon. The other three climbed out to their fate (discussed below).

On August 30, 1869, ninety-nine days after Powell and nine men in four boats had left Green River Station, Powell and five men in two boats reached the mouth of the Virgin River and encountered three men and a boy. According to Powell, they were under orders from Mormon leader Brigham Young to be on the watch for bodies or other remains of his expedition. Several newspapers had carried stories of their demise. Rather than water-bloated corpses, Powell and his men were alive and treated to a fish fry. Sumner recalled that they "settled back on our dignity till the fish was cooked, when we laid our dignified manners aside and assumed the manner of so many hogs."[24] Soon they were able to feast also on bread, butter, cheese, and watermelons sent down from the settlement of St. Thomas by the local Mormon bishop.

Bradley, Sumner, Hall, and Hawkins elected to continue on down the river in the two remaining boats. Although they had been promised money by Powell, apparently they received none. Perhaps he told them he would get it to them later, but he never did. Bradley and Sumner pulled out at Yuma, Arizona; the other two continued on to the Gulf of California. They dispersed in various directions.

By 1882 Hall was driving a Wells Fargo pack train near Globe, Arizona. On August 20 his train, carrying a $5,000 payroll in gold, was ambushed and the gold stolen. Hall managed to trail the robbers, but they spotted him and killed him and another man. A posse caught the robbers two days later. According to a bronze plaque in Globe:

> From a sycamore near this spot L. V. Grime and C. B. Hawley were lynched on Aug. 24, 1852 for the hold up—murder of Andrew Hall, Wells Fargo packer, and Dr. S. T. Vail. The culprits had a fair hearing before JP Allen on Wednesday eve and at 2 AM Thursday on a clear night they were hanged. Saloons were closed and it was an orderly lynching. Sponsors: City of Globe Chamber of Commerce, Downtown Assn. Econ. Dev. Corp. Vigilantes. Donated by Paul Damron Funeral Homes, Miles–Damron Chapel, Globe.[25]

Hawkins settled for a time in Pine Valley, Utah, northwest of St. George, but in later years moved to central Arizona, where he was a prominent rancher and justice of the peace until his death in 1919. George Bradley lived for a number of years in San Diego, working primarily as a fruit grower, and then moved to his family home in West Newbury, Massachusetts, where he died in 1885.[26]

After he reached Yuma, Jack Sumner survived for a time by hunting and trapping, since he had no money. It took him ten months to work his way back to Denver, where his sister and brother-in-law, William Byers, lived. In 1873 Sumner married an Iowa woman, whom he later divorced and then remarried. He lived most of his life in western Colorado. He was involved in mining and irrigation activities in Grand Junction, but was usually in debt and plagued by chronic illness and despondency. Sumner had long nursed a grudge against Powell for abandoning him without money and for not giving him his due as a major player in published accounts of the first expedition, which he certainly was.

On May 24, 1902, thirty-three years to the day from the launching of the first Powell expedition, Jack Sumner stood on the banks of the Green River in Utah, dropped his pants—and castrated himself. When he died five years later, July 4, 1907, the medical examiner noted, "Both testicles have been removed by himself. Operation very successful. Done at a time of supposed temporary insanity."[27]

John Wesley Powell returned to the East via Salt Lake City to find himself something of a national hero. He could have said, as Mark Twain later would, that the reports of his death had been greatly exaggerated. He shrewdly parleyed his moment of fame into an appropriation from Congress to establish the fourth of the so-called "Great Surveys" of the 1870s. Those funds allowed him to make a second river trip in 1871–72 and to begin a program of mapping and studying the geology—and the anthropology—of the Glen Canyon Country and its environs (chapter 5).

POWELL MYTHS AND CONTROVERSIES

Powell's was an epic adventure, made more so by mythmaking that was begun by him and others almost as soon as the first voyage was over. The myths have continued to grow over the fourteen decades since, and Colorado River and Glen Canyon Country historians have struggled for years to sort out fact from myth and legend, and truth from falsehood.

There are two principal areas of disagreement. One is whether Powell and his men were, indeed, the first through the Grand Canyon. The second area has four related issues. First, what really happened between Powell and his men on the first trip that caused Dunn and the Howland brothers to leave the expedition at Separation Rapid, climb out of the canyon, and be killed? Second, who really killed the three men—Indians or other parties? Third, why were the names of Dunn and the Howlands left off the monument to the Powell expedition that stands on the South Rim of the Grand Canyon? Fourth, why did Powell conflate his story of the two river trips of 1869 and 1871–72 into a single narrative with no mention of the men on the second trip? We begin with the "first through the Grand Canyon" issue, which brings us to James White.

The Saga of James White

In the fall of 1867, as Powell was thinking about exploring the Colorado River, sensational news stories were circulating about a man named James White. He was said to have gone through the Grand Canyon "on a rude raft," and had been pulled to shore from the Colorado River near Callville, Nevada, "emaciated and half-demented."[28]

Callville was a small "port" on the Colorado River downstream from the confluence of the Virgin and Colorado rivers, now submerged beneath Lake Mead. The settlement had been established in 1864 at the direction of Brigham Young, and a large stone warehouse was built. A steamboat periodically reached Callville from downstream, but the major traffic, such as it was, were barges that were towed and winched (using large iron rings set in the canyon walls) some 70 miles upstream. Cargos were salt and lime, sent downstream for use in gold smelters.

On September 7, 1867, a group of whites and Indians were loading one such barge when one of the men saw what proved to be a badly battered, badly sunburned, nearly naked man covered with sores and abrasions lashed to some logs drifting down the river. Rescued and nursed back to health, the man said his name was James White. His amazing story was that he had come down the river on the makeshift raft over a period of about two weeks from some point above the Grand Canyon. Given his condition, his rescuers had little doubt that he had been exposed to the elements for a considerable time.

In the next days and weeks, White's story spread by word of mouth, letters, newspaper articles, and telegraph across much of the country. According to an article that appeared in a San Francisco newspaper on September 24, 1867,

> A man by the name of White arrived at Callville on the 7th instant, who had come all the way from Green River on a raft. He was badly bruised, nearly starved and almost entirely naked. Judging from his appearance he has had a rough time, and according to his statements has had many hairbreadth escapes. He gives the following account: He (White) was in the company of two men [Captain Baker and George Strole]. . . . They were prospecting together on a branch of the Colorado that they called the San Juan River. It is between the Little Colorado and the Green Rivers. . . . About the 24th of last month [August 1867] they were attacked by Indians. . . . [Baker was killed; White and Strole got away. The two] succeeded in gathering some rope and some ten pounds of flour and with their guns made for the river. At the river they . . . [made a driftwood raft and headed downstream]. Some three days later . . . Strode [*sic*] was washed overboard and lost. . . . [White continued on for fourteen days. He lost his flour] and he

> was seven days at one time with nothing to eat. Then he luckily struck some Indians, from whom he bought a dog, giving the Indians his revolver. He managed to make out on dog meat until he reached Callville.
>
> He describes the Big Canyon of the Colorado as terrific, a succession of rapids and falls. Some of the falls he thinks are ten feet perpendicular. His raft would plunge over such places, rolling over and over, and he was compelled to lash himself fast to keep from being washed away from it altogether. He says there are rocky cliffs overhanging the river that he believes to be a mile and a half high.[29]

The story was picked up by other newspapers and became a favored topic of saloon gossip across the West, growing wilder and less probable, but "known to be true" with each telling. White was interviewed by a botanist, C. C. Parry, who was connected with the Palmer railroad survey in Colorado and Arizona. In 1868, Parry published an article supporting White's story as true in the *Transactions of the St. Louis Academy of Science.* In 1870, William A. Bell, a physician attached to the same survey, published *New Tracks in North America*, which contained an article by a Philadelphia newspaper man, A. R. Calhoun, who was along with the survey, supporting White's story. The article was taken from Parry's report, but the adventure was even more sensationally elaborated.[30] Thus began the saga of James White and the debate about who was "first through the Grand Canyon"—Powell or White—that continues into the twenty-first century.

It has been said that Powell sought out White before starting on his own voyage but gave little credence to his story. There is no evidence that Powell and White ever met. After Powell's trip, and all the hoopla touting him as the "first" to run the Colorado River, Powell and his supporters denied the claims made by White's advocates. There was no doubt Powell and his men had gone through the Canyons of the Colorado—witnesses had seen them leave Green River City, and others had seen them arrive ninety-nine days later at Callville. White's story was denigrated by those who turned Powell's journey into an epic adventure, par excellence, as indeed it was. The standard anti-White story became that he had somehow only come from the Grand Wash area at the downstream end of Grand Canyon to where he was found. That left Powell's hero status as "first through" intact.

But White's supporters claimed that he had, indeed, come through the canyons—some said all the way from the confluence of the Grand and the Green rivers. Others opined that he at least had come all the way through the Grand Canyon. Very few of the partisans had actually been on the Colorado River below Grand Canyon; few or none had been on the river above it or through it.

In 1917, the U.S. Senate published a sixty-seven-page document, containing most of the published pro-White materials, "An article giving the credit of first traversing the Grand Canyon of the Colorado to James White . . . who it is claimed made the voyage two years previous to the expedition under the direction of Major John Wesley Powell in 1869." In May 1918 a monument was erected on the South Rim of the Grand Canyon that reads, "Erected by the Congress of the United States to Major John Wesley Powell, first explorer of the Grand Canyon."[31]

Such apparent congressional flummery enraged Robert Brewster Stanton (chapter 9). He set out to debunk the White myth once and for all—and did so to his own satisfaction. He published an article in *The Trail*, a publication of a historical group in Denver. Therein he reported that, with a stenographer in tow, he had sought out James White in 1907 at Trinidad, Colorado. White told his story, the stenographer wrote it down, and Stanton told him he was very wrong. Stanton *knew*, based on his own experience, that White *could not* have run the

Colorado River canyons, but had *somehow* traveled overland with his companions from some point on the Grand River to Grand Wash at the foot of Grand Canyon and *then* made the raft trip the rest of the way to Callville. As Stanton reports the interview, it was cordial enough, but he and White agreed to disagree.[32]

Stanton had proper credentials for his inquiry. In 1890–91 he had run the Colorado from the confluence of the Grand and the Green to the Gulf of California, surveying the canyons for a possible water-level railroad from Grand Junction, Colorado, to San Diego. His adventures are chronicled in chapter 9, as are his subsequent unsuccessful attempts to dredge gold from the bottom of Glen Canyon.

In later years Stanton began to compile a major history of the Colorado River. When he died in 1922, it remained unfinished and unpublished. In 1932 two sections of the history were published as *Colorado Controversies*.[33] One section, based on the 1919 article in *The Trail* debunked the White story, at least to Stanton's satisfaction; the other section presented his view of what "really happened" at Separation Rapids during the 1869 Powell trip. We will return to that later.

Stanton's 1919 article in turn enraged William Wallace Bass (1849–1933), one of the legendary characters associated with the Grand Canyon. Bill Bass had come to the area in 1884 seeking to regain his health—and did so. He remained in and around the canyon until he retired in 1923. He became a prospector and miner, a rancher, tour guide, raconteur, champion of the Hualapai Indians, and all-around expert on the Grand Canyon. He established a tourist spot, Bass Camp, on the south rim of the canyon, and widened and stabilized a series of trails within the canyon, creating what came to be known as the South and North Bass trails, going from the south rim to the north rim.

Bass had a camp at river level and, for a time, a cable line to transport hikers across the river to connect the South and North Bass trails. He was a self-trained expert in canyon geology and served as a guide for the first intensive geological surveys of the canyon in the 1890s and later. When he died, his ashes were scattered over the Grand Canyon. A memorial stone in the cemetery there reads, "William Wallace Bass 1849–1933. Pioneer, Guide, Miner, Poet . . . Man of Vision."

In 1920, Bass published *Adventures in the Canyon of the* Colorado,[34] in which he supported White's story and discredited, as Stanton would later do, Powell's version of what "really" happened at Separation Rapid in 1869 (see below). Bass begins by denouncing the "inaccuracies" in Stanton's article on White and then assails "F. S. Dellenbaugh, who has written two books on the Colorado River, viz., 'The Romance of the Colorado River' and 'A Canyon Voyage,' . . . [in which he] openly assails White as a mendacious fabricator of the worst type."[35] Bass goes on:

> F. S. Dellenbaugh, a member of the Powell party of 1872, while on a visit to my camp at Bass Trail, told me his opinion of White's dramatic tale and I later read the same in his "Romance of the Colorado River," wherein he stamps the whole story as a "splendid yarn" (and I may here add, "but well told"). He denounces White's account as an utterly improbable feat to accomplish, but from my first person knowledge of what the river is at the season of year that White's trip was staged, I cannot agree with Dellenbaugh, and never have. From my many years of observation in this section of the Canyon I am thoroughly convinced that during the period of high water, which is from the last of June until late in August, a raft may pass safely through the entire 488 miles of the Canyon without disaster. It would be dangerous in the extreme in low water.[36]

Bass later concluded that "It would not be impossible for me, with my intimate personal knowledge of one portion of the Grand Canyon, extending over a period of nearly forty years, to point out discrepancies and inaccuracies in the published statements of both Stanton and Dellenbaugh, but it is not worth while here to do this. Personally, I have come to believe White's statements."[37]

The principal biographies of John Wesley Powell—published in the second half of the twentieth century by William Culp Darrah, Wallace Stegner, and Donald Worster—all support the Powell-first position.[38] But others continued to think White's story had credibility. Most prominent among them was White's granddaughter, Eileen Adams, who spent thirty years researching his story. In 2001 she had the pleasure of seeing her book about White published by a respectable university press and the validity of her grandfather's saga, as she had painstakingly reconstructed it, widely accepted by Colorado River historians.[39] She died in 2003. That story, as Adams tell it, is as follows.

James White, the youngest of twelve children, was born in 1837 in upstate New York. In 1840 the family settled in Kenosha, Wisconsin. In early 1861 he left home and headed west. He quickly lost most of his modest grubstake in ill-fated prospecting activities in the Rocky Mountains. After a few months, he headed to Virginia City, Nevada, at the height of the Comstock boom. Some found fortunes there; White, like most others, did not. In the fall of 1861 he enlisted in the Fifth California Volunteer Infantry. By May 1862 he was at Fort Yuma on the lower Colorado River. By June 1863 he was stationed at El Paso, Texas.

In September 1864 he and two others were (apparently falsely) accused of stealing 200 pounds of coffee from the army commissary and trading it across the river into Mexico for whiskey. White was court marshaled and sentenced to a year of hard labor and a dishonorable discharge. In April 1865, Army General Order no. 25 pardoned all Union Army prisoners. White was released, given an honorable discharge, and the $100 bonus he'd been promised when he enlisted in Virginia City in 1861. He bought a horse and headed north.

By early 1866 White was driving stagecoaches out of Fort Dodge, Kansas. There, he and another driver, George Strole, met one "Captain" Charles Baker, who may or may not have been an ex-Confederate Army officer, and may or may not have been named Charles Baker. The three men threw in together to go prospecting in the San Juan Mountains of southern Colorado, where Baker had apparently been before the Civil War. Finding little in the area around Silverton, they headed down the Mancos River to the San Juan River to try their hands at placer mining. They followed the San Juan downstream until it entrenched into its deep canyon west of present-day Mexican Hat. Prospects didn't look promising. They decided to head northwest to the Grand River. Perhaps there they could reach the riverbank to prospect. They didn't know how far away the river was, only that it was northwest.

White and his companions swam their horses across the San Juan River and headed up Comb Wash. They climbed out of the wash at Lime Ridge and continued up a westerly fork of Lime Creek onto the Grand Gulch Plateau. Guiding on the Bears Ears, they headed up the Grand Gulch drainage and then swung southwest along the Red House Cliffs, through Clay Hills Pass to Greenwater Spring. Crossing the slickrock barrens of the Red Rock Plateau, they reached not the banks of the Grand River, but the rim of Glen Canyon. Badly in need of water for themselves and their horses, they found a way down one of the stabilized sand dunes that spill over the rim of upper Moqui Canyon, a major left-bank tributary of Glen Canyon upstream from its confluence with the San Juan River.

There they found water and some grazing for their animals and spent the night. The next day they climbed back up the dune with Baker in the lead. At the top they ran into an Indian ambush.

Baker was shot and killed, but White and Strole were able to retreat back down the dune to the canyon bottom. They decided to abandon the horses, which they assumed the Indians were after. They took coats, guns, flour, and lariats and hiked down to the mouth of the canyon. The plan apparently was to somehow find their way down the river. White knew that there were settlements somewhere downstream, but he had no real conception how far they were or what lay in-between.

By moonlight the two men managed to gather some driftwood logs, lash them together into a makeshift raft with the lariats, climb aboard, and push off down the river. Three days later, probably in Marble Canyon, Strole was washed overboard and disappeared. White continued on, lashed to the raft, stopping when he could, but running nearly all the rapids because he could not do otherwise. Finally, he floated out of the Grand Canyon and on down the river to Callville, where by chance the men loading the barge saw and rescued him. Had they not seen him, he would have perhaps floated another 70 miles downstream before there was another settlement, and possibly perished on the way.

Unlike the naysayers, the late Robert C. Euler, a National Park Service archaeologist for the Grand Canyon in the 1970s, thought White's story might be valid. He set out to trace the probable route of the men from where they crossed the San Juan River to where White and Strole climbed aboard the makeshift raft. Euler was able to do some airplane and helicopter surveys over portions of the Red Rock Plateau—the triangular area north of the San Juan and east of Glen Canyon. He determined that Moqui Canyon must have been where the men made their way down stabilized dunes to the canyon bottom. Such "falling dunes," one over 600 vertical feet high, only occur on the Red Rock Plateau in Moqui Canyon (Figures 8.4, 17.11).

The dunes undoubtedly had been used by Indians as trails into and out of the canyon for centuries. John Wetherill led archaeological survey teams down and up the dunes in the 1920s (chapter 13). In the summer of 1960, Calvin Porter, wrangler Keith Rogers, and I led three riding horses and a pack horse down and up one of the dunes. In 1961 a University of Utah excavation team led a string of pack horses down and up another of the dunes several times over the summer to supply their camp in the canyon bottom (chapters 17–18). Thus, according to Euler's searches, the starting point of White's adventure is plausible. Many professional river runners think his trip through Marble and Grand canyons possible, just as William Bass did in 1920, and Robert Euler did in the 1970s. Others disagree, and will continue to do so.[40]

Accepting the veracity of James White's epic adventure in 1867 does nothing, of course, to diminish the accomplishments of John Wesley Powell's epic adventure in 1869, or vice-versa. "Being first" for the sake of being first is only important to those for whom counting coup has some meaning. White's inadvertent adventure and Powell's planned expedition have totally different meanings. White seemingly managed to escape with his life in Glen Canyon, somehow got through Marble and Grand canyons, and lived quietly thereafter until his death at an advanced age. He was a hero by circumstance—a role he apparently rejected. Powell's expedition set in motion many things of great importance to the Glen Canyon Country and the United States generally. He shrewdly used his self-created hero status to advance himself and his goals.

Powell's Men and Myths

In 1875 Powell published his *Exploration of the Colorado River of the West and Its Tributaries,* validating his status as a national hero. He had shrewdly parlayed his 1869 trip into hero status and a congressional appropriation to establish his survey, but the American public and their congressional representatives, then as now, have short-term memories about heroes if not frequently reminded of their valiant deeds.

The previous year Powell had been in danger of losing his congressional appropriation and knew he needed something to propel him back into the limelight. Prompted by his good friend James Garfield, at that time a congressman, Powell's response was to publish a heroic version of the 1869 river trip. But he combined incidents from both the 1869 and the 1871–72 trips, making it seem that everything happened on the first trip. None of the men with him on the second trip were mentioned, to their considerable disgust. That Powell engaged in mythmaking for his own personal gain has rankled many historians ever since. His supporters, including various eminent historians over the decades, have often explained away Powell's historical "errors." Since some of the "errors" have to do with individuals important in the larger story of the Glen Canyon Country, we will look at a few of them.

The Fate of Dunn and the Howland Brothers

The most important "error" has to do with the fate of Dunn and the Howland brothers. In his 1875 report, Powell wrote that in 1870 he and Jacob Hamblin had investigated what happened to the men. They met with some members of the Shivwits band of Southern Paiutes. The story, as Powell later reported it, was that the three had made it out of the Grand Canyon and up onto the Shivwits Plateau. There they encountered some Shivwits people who mistook them for whites who supposedly had killed (and possibly raped) an Indian woman.

Jacob Hamblin purportedly told Powell a more detailed story that he got from one of the Indians. In that version, Dunn and the Howlands were said to have stumbled into their village, "almost starved and exhausted with fatigue [and that] they were supplied with food and put on their way to the settlements. . . . [Soon after] an Indian from the east side of the Colorado had arrived at their village and told them about a number of miners having killed a squaw in a drunken brawl, and no doubt these were the men. . . . In this way he worked them into a great rage. They followed, surrounded the men in ambush, and filled them full of arrows."[41] Having heard this story, Powell seemingly was satisfied; the matter was settled.

The alternate version, developed much later, has several components. One is that the three had managed to get out of the canyon, and having done so, climbed a volcanic peak of the rim of the Grand Canyon to get their bearings. Many years later inscriptions on a rock reading "Dunn, 1869" and "Water" and an arrow were said to have been found atop the mountain. The arrow pointed generally north, toward the Mormon towns on the upper Virgin River. The second component is that the men were found by Mormons and taken to the settlement of Toquerville, Utah. There they were killed in the local ward house (church house) by a Mormon man from Toquerville, and a story was then concocted that they had been killed by Indians.

Why? The story ties back to the Mountain Meadows Massacre of 1857.[42] By 1869, Mormons feared that the federal government had agents, or even bounty hunters, actively seeking the Mormon men thought to be implicated in the massacre. Some of those being sought lived in Toquerville. The story is that Dunn and the Howlands were mistaken for agents or bounty hunters. Their tale of having come down the Colorado River and climbed out of the Grand Canyon was not believed—even though they were on foot, emaciated, and had scarcely any clothing—hardly the physical condition, dress, or mode of transportation one might expect of either federal agents or bounty hunters.

Others report that a few weeks earlier, in 1869, Brigham Young had "ridden circuit" through southern Utah warning of a second impending "war" with the United States, one potentially much worse that the 1858 fiasco. The brethren were to be on the lookout for spies and other suspicious characters possibly in the pay of the federal government. Dunn and the Howlands were, in this scenario, thought to be spies and were captured by Mormons and taken to Toquerville, then the county seat and center of Church authority.[43]

This version of events is based on a letter written in the 1880s that did not surface again until 1983. The writer refers to the killing of three men in the Toquerville ward house, seemingly in 1869, and the 1870 death of Eli Pace, implied to have been the assassin of the three and said to be a son-in-law of John D. Lee.[44] The triple murder was allegedly committed just a few days *before* Powell showed up in St. George asking about Dunn and the Howlands. *After* Powell went on to Salt Lake City, a telegram was sent to Salt Lake saying that word had been received that Indians had killed the men and that "two of the She-bits [Shivwits] were in the Indian camp at Washington [just west of Toquerville] with two of the guns."[45] However, Don Lago, in a careful analysis of news articles from around the time of the supposed incident, demonstrates that the triple murder involved a man who killed his wife and child and was then killed by a sheriff's posse.[46]

Whatever happened, no investigation of Dunn's and the Howlands' deaths was conducted by any locals officials, a most unusual circumstance. In other words, the Mormons pinned the murders on the Indians (as they had the Mountain Meadows Massacre), but nothing was ever done to recover the men's guns or other effects, nor to find and bury their bodies.

Over time, a local legend grew up in support of the Indian theory. One of the Shivwits leaders was a man named Toab, who actively and vehemently opposed the invasion and co-opting of his people's traditional lands by the Mormons. The legend says, "Who was responsible for the murders? No definite proof was ever found, but Toab carried a watch that had belonged to one of the victims."[47] If this were true, one might assume it was Jack Sumner's watch, given to O. G. Howland to take to Sumner's sister in Denver. How Toab came by the watch, if he had it at all, remains a mystery. There is as much veracity to a story that Toab acquired the watch from the reputed Mormon assassin as that he, or other Indians, were themselves the assassins and took the watch off Howland's body.

Many have doubted the authenticity of the Dunn inscription atop Mount Trumbull. No bodies were ever found, nor any of the men's effects, except perhaps the watch. This despite Billy Hawkins's claim fifty years later that "[s]ome years" after the separation in Grand Canyon "I, with a party of some others, buried their bones in the Shewitz Mountains, below Kanab Wash."[48] Hawkins did live in Pine Valley, Utah, north of the Shivwits Plateau, for a while after the river trip and could easily have gone out onto the plateau. Whether or not he actually did so is otherwise unknown.

Jack Sumner had another story. In a 1906 letter that only recently has surfaced, thanks to the indefatigable Don Lago, Sumner wrote to one Lewis W. Keplinger, who was along for part of Powell's 1868 trip into the Rockies. He writes: "the two howlands [*sic*] and Dunn were killed. Powell states by Indians & I Say Killed by the Mormons, Part of the Same old 'Mountain Meadows' massacre gang."[49] Sumner reported that, at Callville, when Powell described the men and the valuable instruments, guns, and Sumner's watch, certain parties who were there suddenly evinced a great deal of interest, and that years later he thought he saw his watch in the possession of one of the interested parties.

Whether or not Powell fully credited the Indians' (or Hamblin's) story, he was aware that he needed to be on good terms with both Indians and Mormons if he was carry out his planned exploration and mapping program scheduled for the following year. So Powell did nothing more, and the Mormon officials did nothing more. For lack of any further action, the matter was closed. The "official" version of what happened became Powell's version, based on what he and Jacob Hamblin heard, or Hamblin said he heard, from the Shivwits. Once Powell published his story in a government report in 1875, that apparently ended the matter. But it did not.

It should be noted that no other incident involving violence by Indians against whites in Utah was *ever* treated in a similar fashion—that is, officially ignored. Even Indian violence against other Indians was dealt with by the law. In the 1890s, when Toab killed Queetuse, a fellow Indian leader, he was tried by a Mormon court and sentenced to the Utah State Penitentiary.[50]

As to why the names of the Howland brothers and Dunn were left off the monument to Powell on the south rim of the Grand Canyon, the consensus seems to be that Frederick Dellenbaugh, who was along on the second 1871–72 river trip and worked for the Powell survey thereafter, is the primary culprit. He was a central figure in the "Powell first" campaign, especially since his book about Powell and the river trips took that position. He apparently was able to convince the government officials who erected the monument that the trio had deserted and therefore did not warrant being named on the monument. And although in Powell's own writings—conflating the two river trips into one—he never mentions the men who were on the second trip, they are listed on the monument. After all, Dellenbaugh was one of them.

5

POWELL AND THE GLEN CANYON COUNTRY

AS POWELL AND HIS MEN PROCEEDED ON their perilous 1869 trip, they were sketch-mapping the canyons, making barometric observations for elevations, and giving names to physiographic features. Their efforts mark the beginning of the systematic study and definition of the Glen Canyon Country. They named physiographic features from the start of the trip—Flaming Gorge, Canyon of Lodore, Disaster Falls, and so on. Once they emerged from Cataract Canyon, after twelve days of battling the rapids therein, they entered the Glen Canyon Country as we have defined it.

Here we pick up their watery trail on July 28, 1869. Powell published a brief description of the voyage in December 1869, shortly after completing the river trip. At the foot of Cataract Canyon, he wrote,

> [a] rocky valley cañon was found here on the left and the river made a bend around a sharp point on the right, which point was set with ten thousand crags and rocks. We called it Mille-Crag Bend, and sweeping around this in a rapid current, our boats shot into Narrow Cañon down which we glided at almost railroad speed, the walls rising vertically from the water 1,300 feet high at its head, and coming down to high-water mark at the foot, seven miles below, where the Dirty Devil, a river of mud, enters from the right. Now we had come again to the red and orange sandstone, and the walls were of beautiful bright rock, low at first, but as we cut down through the strata, rising higher and higher. Now and then, on this and that side, the rocks were vertical from the water's edge; but usually they were cut into mounds and cones and hills of solid sandstone, rising one above the other as they stretched back in a gentle slope for miles. These mounds have been cut out by the showers from the bright orange rock, and glitter in resplendent beauty in the mid-day sun. Hour after hour have we gazed entranced on them, as they faded in perspective and retreated to the rear;

> for the river was gentle, though swift, and we had but to steer our boats, and on we went through this land of beauty and glory.
>
> On the 31st of July we reached the mouth of the San Juan, at the foot of Mound Cañon, and went into camp for a day or two's rest. Then we started again. We had now run once more into dark red and chocolate-colored sandstones, with slate-colored beds below; these usually formed vertical walls, occasionally terraced or broken down, and from the crest of these the orange mounds sloped back, bearing on top of each mound some variegated monument, now vertical, now terraced, now carved by time into grotesque shapes, such as towers, pinnacles, etc. These monuments stood alone or in groups, and spread over the landscape as far as the eye could reach. The little valley of the Paria River terminates this cañon, making it about 100 miles long. We named it Monument Cañon.[1]

This was the first eyewitness description of Glen Canyon ever published. Some additional descriptive materials are contained in the diaries kept by Powell and his men on both river trips. They are of interest in showing how names were derived and sometimes later changed. On July 28, 1869, Powell wrote: "from the bend [Mille-Crag Bend] down to the mouth of Dirty Devil Creek was very direct, very narrow and very quiet. . . . Beautiful view of Mts. through the cleft of Cañon to West." On the same day Jack Sumner wrote: "Camped on the north side at the mouth of a stream 3 rods wide and 2 ft. deep. It is not laid down on any map. The water is about as filthy as the washing from the sewers of some large, dirty city, but stinks more than cologne ever did. It has been named 'Dirty Creek.'"[2]

As an aside, Dirty Devil, the name Powell gave to the river defining the head of Glen Canyon, was a particular favorite because he later would contrast it in lectures with Bright Angel Creek in the Grand Canyon. But, according to Charles Hunt (chapter 7), years later the U.S. Board of Geographic Names was told by a postmistress, probably in Torrey or Hanksville, Utah, that "the nicer people call it Fremont," hence the name Dirty Devil was dropped from U.S. topographic maps in the 1920s. In the 1930s, when Hunt was working in the Henry Mountains region, "I found that most local people still used the name 'Dirty Devil.' I related the earlier protest and was told, 'The nicer people moved away from here a long time ago.' So the Fremont and the Muddy rivers came together to form the Dirty Devil."[3]

On July 31 Powell wrote: "Cool pleasant ride today through this part of Monument Cañon. The large boats racing. Still more cones and rounded points. After dinner soon found the mouth of San Juan [river]." The following day he wrote: "During afternoon I went up into 'Music Temple,' 100 yds. long, 50 yds. wide, cleft of rock above 'sky-light' 25 feet wide. Tinkling cañon Pool. A dozen poplars at entrance. . . . Rock about 500 feet high. Temple 200 ft." On August 2 Sumner wrote: "Half a mile or less from camp there is a curious alcove worn in the sandstone by the rainwater of a gulch. It is large enough to contain 2000 people. Wall 200 ft. high and nearly closed at the top. There are 3 cottonwood trees growing in the clear white sand floor and a little lake of pure water at one side. We christened it 'Music Hall.'"[4]

On August 4 the party reached the end of "Monument Canyon," at the mouth of what Sumner said was a "a small dirty stream coming in from the north called by the Mormons Pahria River." He thought the whole place "desolate enough to suit a lovesick poet."[5] On August 5 they headed into Marble Canyon, leaving Glen Canyon behind. Ahead lay three weeks of toil through the rapids of Marble and Grand canyons, the splitting of the party on August 28, and the final emergence from the Grand Canyon on August 30 as described in the previous chapter.

THE SECOND RIVER TRIP, 1871–72

In 1870 Powell traveled back to Utah to make arrangements for a second river trip and to inquire into the deaths of the Howland brothers and William Dunn. He then traveled to Hopi and on to Fort Defiance with Jacob Hamblin (see below). He then returned to Illinois, ordered some new boats with further modifications, and set out to recruit a new crew.[6] He placed his brother-in-law Almon Harris Thompson in charge of the topographic work. John F. Steward was named geologist. Frederick Samuel Dellenbaugh—seventeen years old and a distant relative of Thompson's—was to be artist and a boatman. Thompson's topographical assistants were Capt. Francis Marion Bishop and Stephen Vandiver Jones, who were friends of Thompson's and knew Powell. Andrew J. Hattan, who signed on as cook and boatman, had met Powell in the army. Powell also hired Frank Richardson as a boatman, but he would leave at Brown's Hole on the Green River early in the trip.

Francis Marion Bishop (1843–1933) was born in upstate New York. His mother, Priscilla Alden Bishop, was a lineal descendant of John and Priscilla Alden of Plymouth Colony fame. He was in the Union Army throughout the Civil War and was discharged with the rank of captain. He then entered Illinois Wesleyan University, where Powell was one of his instructors. In 1870 Powell recruited Bishop to accompany him to southern Utah to arrange for supplies for the river trip. From there they traveled to the Hopi mesas and a meeting with the Navajos at Fort Defiance. He was on the second river trip and remained with Powell until the spring of 1873. He then moved to Salt Lake City, where he lived until age ninety—serving variously as a professor at the University of Deseret (the predecessor of the University of Utah), a businessman, and a justice of the peace.[7]

Stephen Vandiver Jones (1840–1920) was born in Wisconsin and moved to Illinois at age fourteen. He ultimately became a teacher and principal of the Washburn, Illinois, schools, where he met fellow teacher A. H. Thompson and signed on for the second river trip. He remained with the expedition until November 1872, and then returned to Illinois. He later became a lawyer and in 1883 he moved to Dakota Territory, where he became a prominent man of affairs until his death at age eighty. Jones was Thompson's right hand in establishing the Kanab baseline (see below) and in mapping the Pine Valley Mountains, the Virgin Mountains, the Uinkaret Plateau, and the upper Virgin River valley.[8]

John F. Steward (1841–1915) was born in Plano, Illinois. He enlisted in the 127th Illinois Volunteer Infantry in 1862. He met Powell at the siege of Vicksburg while the two were collecting fossil shells in the trenches that the sappers were digging around the city. He later suffered a chest wound and a back injury. Steward was an accomplished amateur geologist and retained an interest in geology throughout his life. His knowledge led Powell to recruit him for the second trip, but his back injury and a rheumatic condition plagued him during the trip, and he resigned. He returned to Illinois to rejoin the March Harvester Company, later merged with the International Harvester Company, and became a high-ranking member of the company's legal department in Chicago. In later years he felt that Powell, in his 1876 report, had not properly credited his contributions in recording the geology of the canyon country.[9]

Powell was aware that the three other federal surveys (chapter 6) had employed professional photographers, so he hired one too—E. O. Beaman of New York. Little is known about Beaman, although he apparently served in the Union Army during the Civil War. He had been a professional photographer for several years and was quite competent at making the wet-process glass plate negatives in use at the time. He made seventy-five or so negatives during the trip, but more importantly, he taught

Jack Hillers the art of the so-called "wet-plate process" of photography. During the 1871 river trip, Hillers volunteered to help Beaman carry the heavy camera and darkroom equipment up and down the cliffs and across the talus slopes so that he might learn about picture making. Wet-plate photography had been perfected in the 1860s and used extensively by Mathew Brady, Timothy O'Sullivan, and others to record both the mundane and the horrors of the Civil War. The process required coating a glass plate with liquid, light-sensitive materials inside a portable darkroom, taking the photograph before the chemicals dried, and developing the negative immediately. The results, properly done, were excellent. After Beaman and Powell had a falling out in January 1872, Beaman went to Salt Lake City, acquired a new photography outfit, and made a trip to the Hopi mesas. He later described the river trip and his journey to Hopi in a series of magazine articles.[10]

Powell planned to have his first cousin Walter Clement Powell (1850–83) become Beaman's assistant and thus learn photography so he could be part of Powell's staff. "Clem" Powell was born perhaps in northern Kentucky. His parents died before he was six years old, and he was raised first by Powell's parents and later by his older brother, Morris. Clem never mastered the intricacies of wet-plate photography, and Powell finally chose Hillers to replace Beaman (see below). Clem returned to Illinois, married, and moved to Omaha, where he developed a wholesale drug and tobacco business. His wife, Mary Breasted, was the sister of the great Orientalist James Henry Breasted.[11]

James Fennemore (1849–1941) was born in London. He found his way to Salt Lake City as a Mormon convert. In 1871 he was working as an assistant to Charles R. Savage, a prominent Salt Lake photographer. Powell came to Savage seeking someone to replace Beaman, met Fennemore, and convinced him to join his expedition in early 1872. Fennemore stayed with Powell from March through August 1872, but left before the trip into the Grand Canyon. He made some good quality photographs and also furthered Hillers's training. He later opened his own studio in Salt Lake City. Fennemore's most famous photograph is that of John D. Lee seated on his coffin just before he was executed on March 23, 1877, for his role in the Mountain Meadows Massacre.[12]

Frederick Samuel Dellenbaugh (1853–1935), was a seventeen-year-old, self-trained artist when he joined the second expedition. Born in Ohio, he was a distant relative of A. H. Thompson. He remained with the expedition until 1873. Thereafter he traveled widely, studied art in Europe, and settled in New York City, where he painted and wrote, and edited several books. He was a founding member of the Explorers Club. It was Dellenbaugh who collected the journals of the Powell expeditions and placed them in the New York Public Library, to the eternal gratitude of river historians. His book *A Canyon Voyage*, published in 1908, was his attempt to tell the story of the second river trip.[13]

Andrew J. Hattan (1841–1919) was born in Ohio. He enlisted in the Union Army in 1861. He met Powell during the war, either at Shiloh or Vicksburg. Powell hired him as cook and boatman for the second trip. After the 1872 trip he returned to the family farm in Ohio. He farmed and worked as a teamster until 1905, when he retired, living thereafter in a disabled veterans home in Illinois until his death.[14]

Finally, there was John K. (originally Johann Karl) Hillers, universally known as Jack Hillers (1843–1925). He was born in Hanover, Germany, and emigrated to New York City with his family in 1852. He apparently had some formal schooling and was working as a clerk when the Civil War began. He may have served briefly in a coastal artillery unit, but he formally enlisted in the regular U.S. Army in June 1861 at Fort Monroe, Virginia. He was assigned to an artillery regiment that apparently spent much of the war in reserve. He did see

5.1. Launch of Powell's second river trip, Green River, Wyoming Territory, May 1871. Photograph by E. O. Beaman. Courtesy of Don D. Fowler.

action at Cold Harbor, Virginia, and his unit was involved in the siege of Petersburg from mid-June 1864 to April 1865, and moved into Richmond during the closing days of the war.

Hillers remained in the army after the war, re-enlisting twice, and was finally discharged in May 1870. He later joined a brother in San Francisco, leaving there about May 10, 1871, for the East. He stopped in Salt Lake City to seek work, and found it with John Wesley Powell, who hired him as a boatman on the spot. Powell apparently liked what he saw. Hillers was about six feet tall, with an affable disposition, a ribald wit, and a taste for ardent spirits appropriate to an ex-army sergeant. Hillers would emerge as one of the great wet-plate specialists of late nineteenth-century photography, alongside William Henry Jackson and Timothy O'Sullivan.[15]

DESCRIBING THE CANYON COUNTRY DURING THE SECOND RIVER TRIP

During the second river trip in 1871 (fig. 5.1), Powell and his men stopped at the confluence of the Grand and the Green, climbed out, and spent hours wandering through, and being fascinated by, the country Newberry and Macomb had gazed down upon in 1859. Stephen Vandiver Jones wrote in his diary: "Major [Powell] and I . . . walked for hours through lovely valleys and alcoves surrounded by steep walls of white rock. At length, after climbing through a steep narrow gorge we came in sight of a splendid view. Towers, columns, pinnacles, turrets, domes in every direction. The Major seemed like one entranced." Powell wrote in his diary for September 16, 1871: "Thompson and I wander among the strange rocks of the Sinav-Tuweap. These rocks are carved out of the upper carboniferous. . . . The columns and beautiful rocks are set about the borders of weird glens at the heads of lateral gulches. The whole country is naked rock. How shall I describe the Sinav-Tuweap?"[16] In Ute–Southern Paiute mythology, with which Powell was familiar (chapter 4), "Sinav," or "Shinauav," is a creator figure. "Tuweap" means "land" or "country." Thus Powell was calling the area "Creator's country" or "a god's country."

On October 2, 1871, Powell and the men cached the *Cañonita* near the mouth of the Dirty Devil River, planning to return overland the following summer to retrieve it (see below). They then continued on into Glen Canyon. Powell wrote: "At certain curves of the river we often obtain a good view of the Unknown Mountains. At noon can see a distant upturned ridge to the west."[17] Powell would later name the "unknown mountains" for Joseph Henry, the secretary of the Smithsonian Institution, and his men would name the "upturned ridge" the Waterpocket Fold. On October 4, 1871, Powell wrote:

> The orange sandstones are composed of two homogeneous beds separated by stratified beds.

> The upper homogeneous has few joints and so weathers into mounds. The lower has many and weathers into monuments. The intervening thinly bedded sandstone formed the bottom of the river for several miles this morning, and grooved ridges of the same would spread across the river causing bad rapids and we had much difficulty. . . . There are many glens along the walls in the thin beds between the two homogeneous [strata]. Glens with springs and oak trees, now and then a cottonwood. There are cañons, shelves and steps up to them. . . . Thompson, Steward and I climb at night into one of these "oak glens" 600 feet above the river.[18]

The following day he wrote:

> The Oak Glens [fig. 5.2] still continue as a characteristic of the cañon. The walls are often quite vertical from the water and beautifully rounded at the curves. . . . Pass the San Juan at 11:00 A.M. Boats go on down to Music Temple while Thompson and I climb up to the west. We obtain a fine view of the mounds and of Mount Seneca Howland.[19]

It is interesting that here Powell was naming Navajo Mountain for one of the Howland brothers. But by 1874, he had decided that Navajo Mountain had precedence, and he used that name thereafter.

After lunching in Music Temple, where some of the men carved their names on a rounded ledge (fig. 5.3), the party continued downstream. A footnote by Frederick S. Dellenbaugh in the 1871 diary of John F. Steward indicates that Powell and most of the crew wanted to climb Navajo Mountain, which they could have done from above Music Temple, although with great difficulty. But Steward was feeling ill and apprehensive about the low state of the food supply, and his "protests prevented."[20] The party continued on downriver. Powell wrote:

5.2. A glen in Glen Canyon, 1872. Photograph by Jack Hillers and James Fennemore. Courtesy of Don D. Fowler.

"Now we are in Monument Canyon and the Monument Buttes are in view. There are many fine stretches of river with beautiful curves and vertical walls and quiet river. The narrow side cañons are very wonderful and very frequent. At night I go up one of these . . . up through the overarching rocks. The overarching rocks are cut at the circumference of the curves, thus the cañon becomes more curved as it cuts down." The next day he wrote: "Long reaches of quiet river. Finely turned curves at vertical walls are still more noticeable today than yesterday. The monuments too are seen on either hand.[21]

Here Powell was referring to Gunsight Butte, Leche-e Rock, Tower Butte, and other prominent "monuments" visible as one proceeds downstream through that section of the canyon. On October 5, Walter Clement Powell wrote:

5.3. The names of Powell's men in Music Temple, 1871–1872: Jack Hillers, Francis Bishop, Frederick Dellenbaugh. Explorers Club flag in picture. Photograph from Julius Stone expedition, 1938. Charles Kelly Collection, 917-85 (10389). Courtesy of the Utah Historical Society.

> We finally started . . . down Monument Cañon. The walls are higher, about 1500 feet on the average and nearly vertical, with very narrow lateral cañons coming in on either side, through which we can see some lonely buttes or monuments (hence the name) rising up from the top of the cañon 500, 600, or 800 feet high, or again we would come to a straight stretch of the river; looking down[stream] could see the vertical undulating cañon walls and then back or beyond rather, see some tall butte looking like some old deserted ruin with peaks and turrets and all of naked rock. . . . 'Tis a grand cañon.[22]

Later that day the river party reached Kane Creek, just upstream from Crossing of the Fathers, to find a supply party waiting for them. Powell left at that point, and the others ran the boats down to Lee's Ferry. They cached them there until the following summer, when they ran through Marble Canyon and into Grand Canyon as far as Kanab Creek.

DESCRIBING THE COUNTRY

Powell's first scientific description of the canyon country was published in 1873 in the *American Journal of Science and Arts*. Therein, he first used the term "great geographical stairway" for the geological formations that step down from the north to the Grand Canyon.[23] He incorporated the article into a larger, more comprehensive report to Secretary Joseph Henry of the Smithsonian Institution in 1874. In the latter, he listed the canyons through which the Green and Colorado run, most of which he and his men had named:

> . . . then Cataract Cañon, a profound chasm below the junction of the Grand and the Green; then Narrow Cañon, which terminates at the mouth of the Dirty Devil River; then Glen Cañon, extending from the mouth of the Dirty Devil River to the mouth of the Paria. . . . Many new mountains have been added to our geographic knowledge. To the north of the Escalante River there is a group of eruptive mountains, the three highest peaks of which attain an altitude of about 12,000 feet above the level of the sea. We have called these Henry Mountains, in honor of the secretary of the Smithsonian Institution. Then we have the Navajo Mountain a little to the south of the mouth of the San Juan River, the greatest single mountain mass known to me within all the territory of the United States; it is nearly 12,000 feet [*sic*] high. . . . [In addition, t]he Dirty Devil River, more than two hundred miles in the length, was discovered and mapped. The Escalante, a river more than one hundred and fifty miles in length, was discovered and mapped.[24]

Here Powell established the names Glen Canyon, Henry Mountains, Navajo Mountain, and Escalante River in print for the first time.

In 1875 Powell published his popular account in which he combined his diaries of the two river trips into one. Under the date August 3, 1869, he wrote:

> The features of this canyon are greatly diversified. Still vertical walls at times. These are usually found to stand above great curves. The river, sweeping around these bends, undermines the cliffs in places. Sometimes the rocks are overhanging; in other curves, curious, narrow glens are found. Through these we climb, by a rough stairway, perhaps several hundred feet, to where a spring bursts out from under an overhanging cliff, and where cottonwoods and willows stand, while, along the curves of the brooklet, oaks grow, and other rich vegetation is seen, in marked contrast to the general appearance of naked rock. We call these Oak Glens.
>
> Other wonderful features are the many side canyons or gorges that we pass. Sometimes we stop to explore these for a short distance. In some places, their walls are much nearer each other above than below, so that they look like caves or chambers in the rocks.
>
> . . . On the walls, and back many miles into the country, numbers of monument-shaped buttes are observed. So we have a curious *ensemble* of wonderful features—carved walls, royal arches, glens, alcove gulches, mounds and monuments. From which of these features shall we select a name? We decide to call it Glen Canyon.
>
> Past these towering monuments, past these mounded billows of orange sandstone, past these oak glens, past these fern-decked alcoves, past these mural curves, we glide hour after hour, stopping now and then, as our attention is arrested by some new wonder. . . .[25]

Thus Powell made it seem that the name "Glen Canyon" was chosen in 1869, rather than in 1874. His 1874 report did not receive wide circulation. His 1875 report did, with its thrilling and romantic tale of Powell, the one-armed hero, and his men conquering the raging Colorado—made more so by combining events from both the 1869 and the 1871–72 river trips and writing as if everything had taken place during the first trip.

But Powell's 1875 report was not meant to be a historical record; it was meant to arouse interest, both among the public and members of Congress. It worked. His congressional appropriation was renewed, and the Powell survey continued until it was subsumed into the U.S. Geological Survey (USGS) in 1879 (chapter 6). Only after Powell died did the story of the second river trip become generally known. In 1908 Frederick S. Dellenbaugh, who, as we saw, was just seventeen when he joined the second river trip in 1871, published *A Canyon Voyage, a Narrative of the Second Powell Expedition Down the Green-Colorado River*. The book was based on Dellenbaugh's own diaries and those of others he had collected, and in his eyes he set the record straight.[26]

As a final note on Powell and the canyons of the Colorado River, during his time working with Ute and Southern Paiute people between 1868 and 1873, Powell recorded many legends and stories about the Colorado Plateau country and how its physiographic features came to be. One is called "The Origin of the Cañons of the Colorado":

> Many years ago when wise and good men lived on the earth, the Great Chief of all the Utes lost his beloved wife. Day and night he grieved and all his people were sad. Then *Tavwoats* [the mythological rabbit deity] . . . appeared to the chief and tried to comfort him, but his sorrow could not be allayed. So at last *Ta-vwoats* promised to take him to a country away to the southwest where he said his dead wife had gone and let him see how happy she was if he would agree to grieve no more on his return. So he promised. Then *Tavwoats* took his magical ball and rolled it before him, and as it rolled it rent the earth and mountains, and crushed the rocks and made a way for them to that beautiful land—a trail through the mountains which intervened between the home of the dead and the hunting grounds of the living. And following the ball, which was a rolling globe of fire, they came at last to the Spirit Land. Then the Great Chief saw his wife and the blessed abode of the Spirits where all was plenty and all way joy and he was glad. Now when they returned *Tavwoats* enjoined upon the chief that he should never travel this trail during life, and that all the people should be warned not to walk therein. Yet still he feared that they would attempt it so he rolled a river into the trail—a mad, raging river into the gorge made by the globe of fire which should overwhelm any who might seek to enter there.[27]

EXPLORING AND MAPPING THE GLEN CANYON COUNTRY

The Powell expedition had much more to do in the Glen Canyon Country than running through the canyons of the Colorado River. Its principal purposes were to map the country and study its geology. From the time the second river party reached Kane Creek in 1871 until the end of 1876, that work fell principally on the shoulders of Powell's brother-in-law, Almon Harris Thompson (fig. 5.4), and the men he commanded. When Powell was in the field, he focused his attention on the Indian people, but most of his time was spent in Washington, D.C., networking and lobbying for yearly appropriations from Congress to keep his survey going.

In 1871, after Thompson and his men had run the boats to Lee's Ferry and cached them for the winter, they headed for Kanab, Utah, and set up a camp near town. They began the tedious work of laying out a 9-mile-long baseline, making astronomical observations, and coordinating time signals by telegraph with an observatory in Salt Lake City to determine the exact latitude and longitude coordinates of a fixed location point in Kanab. The fixed location and the baseline allowed them to establish triangulation points from which topographic maps could be made. In an age of electronic

5.4. Almon Harris Thompson, 1872, in southern Utah. Photograph by Jack Hillers. Courtesy of Don D. Fowler.

transits (total stations) and the Global Positioning System, by which the location of any point on earth can be determined to within a few centimeters, it is instructive to briefly describe how the baseline was established.

The crew made three wooden rods and cast some lead plumb bobs. The three rods were 14 feet long with upright pins in each end and were held by frames, or trestles. The trestles had adjustable legs, which made it easy to allow for elevations or depressions in the land. The rods and trestles were set up in a line and adjusted by sighting along both ends, using the steel pins. Two rods were always kept in place in case of an accidental movement. They were leveled by use of a plummet. Every 100 feet a wooden stake was placed in the ground, and a wire was put in the top of it. The place for the stake and wire was determined by a plummet at the end of the measuring rods. The wires in the stakes created the baseline.[28]

Once the baseline was established, Thompson and his team used it to triangulate outward to the south and west, establishing points from which topographic features could be observed and mapped in. This work occupied them throughout the winter of 1871 and most of 1872.[29] Unfortunately, despite the care they took, the baseline was very inadequate. In 1878 Powell sent Grove Karl Gilbert (chapter 7) to Kanab to examine the it, and he "found the work generally bungled. . . . He had to completely resurvey the topography."[30] It is unclear how many more corrections had to be made. Ultimately, the Powell survey produced four maps published by the USGS in 1886 (chapter 6). They were considered reconnaissance maps, not final topographic presentations.[31]

SEEKING THE DIRTY DEVIL RIVER

In 1870 Powell had contracted with Jacob Hamblin to find an overland route to the mouth of the Dirty Devil River and leave there a cache of supplies for the 1871 river trip. On the first attempt Hamblin's men mistook the San Rafael River for the Dirty Devil, and their Indian guides refused to go farther than about 40 miles downstream. On the second try, Hamblin crossed into the Escalante Basin and, mistaking it for the Dirty Devil drainage, got tangled up in the labyrinth of the Escalante River and its side canyons, and ultimately had to retreat back to Kanab. When Powell's river party reached the mouth of the Dirty Devil in 1871, there were no supplies. They climbed out of the canyon to look at the country to see if they could spot a route. Powell wrote, "Find that we can come around to the north or through the [Henry] mountains and find a way down to the Colorado River at the mouth of Dirty Devil. It would probably be best to come down from the foot of the mountain[s]."[32]

In the early 1870s, the country east of the Sevier River valley and Kanab was little known to white people. Kanab had been established by Jacob Hamblin in 1869; Panguitch had been settled in 1864, but was abandoned from 1866 until 1871 during the period called the Black Hawk War—a desperate, but ultimately unsuccessful, attempt by Utes, some Paiutes, and some Navajos to stop the incursion of Mormons into the territory of central and south-central Utah.

Mormon militia companies were formed during the war, and in August 1866 a cavalry company was formed in St. George, Utah, under the command of Capt. James Andrus. Andrus's adjutant was Franklin B. Wooley, who later wrote a detailed report.[33] They were ordered to examine the country from the Kaibab Plateau to the mouth of the Green River, to deal harshly with any hostile Indians, and conciliate with any others. The troop assembled at Pipe Spring. They headed up Johnson Canyon east of Kanab onto the Skutumpah Terrace and thence to the headwaters of the Paria River, climbing a steep and dangerous slope of bluish clay to come out into lush meadows at the head of the Escalante drainage. They found and enjoyed "Indian potatoes" (*yampa* in Southern Paiute) and named the area Potato Valley. After reconnoitering the upper Escalante drainage and determining they could not cross it, they turned north onto the Aquarius Plateau and ultimately came out on a southeastern point thereof. From there they could see the lay of the land for a hundred miles, including the La Sal and Henry mountains, which they named the Pot-Si-Nip Mountains. From their vantage point, they thought they could see the mouths of the Green River and perhaps the Grand, but they were actually looking into Glen Canyon at about Hall's Creek.

The troop then turned north, down into the Fremont River drainage, headed west along the well-established Indian trail that Frémont had followed, crossed into the Sevier River drainage, and thence south to Parowan and on to St. George. Wooley reported that the only trails they could find were those already known. One of these was the "Old Ute" trail that ran south up the east fork of the Sevier River, over the Great Basin/Colorado drainage divide, into the headwaters of the Paria River, and on to the Ute Crossing in Glen Canyon. The other went around the Kaibab Plateau and on down to the Colorado River at Jacob's Crossing, later renamed Lee's Ferry.

In May 1872, Thompson set out to find a path "around to the north or through the mountains" to the mouth of the Dirty Devil River, where the *Cañonita* had been cached the previous fall. He was accompanied by Frederick Dellenbaugh, Jack Hillers, James Fennemore, Pardon Dodds, who had been with Hamblin in 1871, and others. Thompson and his party started from Kanab with a pack train, following the route of the Andrus Cavalry company. Near the head of the Paria drainage, in what Thompson would call Table Cliff Creek, they found the narrow blue clay hogbacks. Andrus and his men had climbed them in a heavy thunderstorm. So too did Thompson's group, as reported later by Frederick Dellenbaugh:

> [E]arly in the afternoon we reached a series of "hog-backs," up one of which the old Indian trail we were now following took its precarious way. The hog-backs were narrow ridges of half-disintegrated clay-shale, with sides like the roof of a house, the trail following the sharp summit-line. Before we had fairly begun this very slippery, and narrow climb, the thunder boomed and the heavens threw down upon us fierce torrents of rain, soaking everything and chilling us through and through, while making the trail like wet soap. Part way up, one of the worst places, a pack came loose, and slipping back, hung on the rump of the horse.

> There was no room for bucking it off, and there was no trouble so far as the beast of burden was concerned, for he fully realized his own danger. Two of us managed to climb along past the other animals to where he meekly stood waiting on the narrow ridge, with a descent on either side of eight hundred or nine hundred feet, and set things in order once more, when the cavalcade continued the ascent, the total amount of which was some twelve hundred feet.[34]

In his published report of 1875, Thompson laconically reported that:

> Here we climbed a thousand feet up a steep clay ridge, having an average slope of 20° and often not more than five feet in thickness at the top, to the head of a narrow valley called Potato Valley. . . . To the east, low, rounded hills gradually rise higher and higher, till, at an elevation of 1,800 feet above camp, they roll off into a long, narrow plateau, bounded on the west by a well-marked line of cliffs, beginning near the foot of Table Cliff Plateau and continuing southeast 60 miles, to a point on the Colorado River opposite the Navajo Mountain. . . . Its eastern boundary is a line of cliffs, commencing at the foot of Potato Valley and presenting an almost unbroken front to the Colorado River at a point but four miles above the terminus of the western line, thus giving to the plateau a trapezoidal outline, having a length of 55 miles, a breadth at the base of 15, at the apex 4, and standing at an altitude of 9,000 feet [*sic*] above sea level. . . . So far as I have been able to ascertain, we were the first white men to visit the plateau. The Indian name for a small elevation near the north end is Kai-pár-o-wits, so we called the whole plateau by that name.[35]

The term in Southern Paiute translates as "Big mountain's little son," referring to a small peak adjacent to Canaan Peak.[36]

Thompson and his men followed the stream down Potato Valley (now Upper Valley) but soon discovered that their way toward the Henry Mountains was blocked. They climbed a high ridge to get the lay of the land:

> [W]e found we were on the western rim of a basin-like region, 70 miles in length by 50 miles in breadth, and extending from the eastern slope of the Aquarius Plateau on the north to the Colorado River on the south and from the Henry Mountains on the east to our point of observation on the west. A large portion of this area is naked, sandstone rock, traversed in all directions by a perfect labyrinth of narrow gorges, sometimes seeming to cross each other, but finally uniting in a principal one, whose black line could be traced, cutting its way to the Colorado, a few miles above the mouth of the San Juan River. . . . No animal without wings could cross the deep gulches in the sandstone basin at our feet. The stream which we had followed and whose course soon became lost in the multitude of chasms before us was not the one we were in search of but an unknown, unnamed river, draining the eastern slope of the Aquarius Plateau and flowing through a deep, narrow canyon to the Colorado River. Believing our party to be the discoverers, we decided to call the stream in honor of Father Escalante, the old Spanish explorer, Escalante River and the country it drains Escalante Basin.[37]

Thompson's observation cleared up a previous confusion stemming from the fact that on both river trips Powell and his men, eager to find (in 1869) and get to (in 1871) the mouth of the

San Juan River, had passed the slot-canyon mouth of the Escalante on the right bank, perhaps without noticing it. Some later river runners, including me, sometimes had the same problem.

During the 1871 river trip Thompson had expressed disgust in his diary when he learned that Jacob Hamblin had not found a way down what Hamblin thought was the Dirty Devil: "Mr. Hamblin probably made a slight effort to rush the Dirty Devil or some attempt."[38] Having later talked with Hamblin, and with Pardon Dodds, who was with him in 1872, and now gazing on the Escalante Basin, his scorn changed to admiration tinged with fear:

> The perilous character of Mr. Hamblin and party was [now] apparent. For eighty miles they traveled in a cañon, finding in all that distance, but two places where the walls could be scaled. They crossed and re-crossed, waded, and sometimes swam a rapid stream that often filled the gorge from wall to wall. A single shower, on the rock land above, would have changed the stream to a raging torrent, that would have swept them into the Colorado, or imprisoned them in some rock walled alcove, with no possible way of escape.[39]

Thompson could see a possible route to the Henry Mountains up and across the tableland, which the party named the Aquarius Plateau. He also was aware, at least by verbal report, of the Andrus company's ascent onto the plateau. In his diary entry for June 9, 1872, Jack Hillers provided a vivid description of that portion of the trip:

> This mountain travel is fearful—no sooner have you reached the top of some Giant than you will have to climb down again on the other side some thousands of feet. Reaching the bottom or rather the divide you find a canon which cuts you off—now you have to go up to its head. Perhaps you are a lucky Dog and find where the water has undermined the bank and let it slope down at an angle of 60E. Now put on the corsets [that is, cinch up the pack saddles on the horses], but no matter how tight you make them something will give way and away goes your pack. You're lucky if you find everything together again—some is sure to reach the water and then that is the last of it, for the water rushes down with a tremendous force and sweeps it beyond your reach. . . . Followed up quite a stream for about five miles—it ran down at an angle of 30°. It came down leaping, taring [*sic*], rushing, now running down a smooth slope, now taring over big boulders, now leaping down 50 or 100 feet at the bottom of which it finds itself churned into white foam—here it collects itself and is off, never stops until it finds itself in the Pacific Ocean via [the] Colorado River.[40]

After some difficulty, and with some reluctant help from a group of Red Lake Ute people they encountered, Thompson and his men found their way across and down the east slope of the Waterpocket Fold and onto the flanks of the Henry Mountains.

They climbed three of the five peaks and named them Mount Pennell for a friend of Thompson's, Mount Ellen for Thompson's wife, and Mount Hillers for Jack Hillers. Powell and Thompson apparently named Mount Ellsworth, the peak closest to the rim of Glen Canyon, sometime after Thompson's trip and added it to their preliminary maps. When Grove Carl Gilbert climbed the peak in 1875, he knew it as Mount Ellsworth. In all likelihood, they chose the name to honor Col. Elmer Ephraim Ellsworth (1837–61), who was a close personal friend of Abraham Lincoln's and had worked in his 1860 presidential campaign. He went to Washington with Lincoln, and when the secession crisis came, he helped recruit Union soldiers. He organized the 6th (later the 11th) Volunteer New York Infantry Regiment, who were mostly New York City firemen. They called themselves the "Fire Zouaves" because their uniforms were patterned after the uniforms of the French Zouaves, the crack light infantry troop in Algeria made up of Kabyles, a Berber tribe. On May 24, 1861, Virginia seceded from the Union. Ellsworth crossed the Potomac to Alexandria with some troops, intending to secure the railroad station and the telegraph office.

On the way to the latter he saw a Confederate flag flying from the Marshall House Inn. He went inside, tore down the flag, and was killed by the inn owner, James W. Jackson. One of Ellsworth's men then killed Jackson and was later awarded the Congressional Medal of Honor. Lincoln had Ellsworth's body brought to the White House, where it lay in state. He became the first great Union martyr of the Civil War and was regarded as a national hero both during and after the war. Fort Ellsworth in Alexandria was named for him, as were the towns of Ellsworth, Illinois, and Ellsworth, Wisconsin—and, apparently, Mount Ellsworth in the Henry Mountains. Powell started his epic first trip down the Colorado on May 24, 1869, eight years to the day of Ellsworth's death. The coincidence of dates may have helped Powell and Thompson decide to name the mountain for the fallen hero.

Gilbert and Powell named the fifth of the Henry Mountains Mount Holmes for William Henry Holmes, the geologist/artist who was with Clarence Dutton during the latter's Grand Canyon studies (chapter 7). Holmes was with the Hayden survey in the early 1870s and has a peak at the south end of the Gallatin Range in Yellowstone Park named for him as well.[41]

Thompson's party finally found Crescent Wash, which they thought would get them to the Colorado River near where the boat was cached. Hillers wrote, "Being ready we skinned out, and after three hours we reached the head of the gulch which from the top looked dark and gloomy below. After trun[d]ling several pack horses down the cliff, making their hides look like the map of Spain, we finally reached the bottom."[42] The next day, June 22, they reached the river and recovered the *Cañonita.* Thompson and two of the men started back to Kanab with the pack train. Hillers and the others readied the boat for the trip through Glen Canyon to Lee's Ferry (fig. 5.5).

5.5. Refitting *Cañonita* near the mouth of Dirty Devil River, 1872. Photograph by James Fennemore. Courtesy of Don D. Fowler.

When Thompson returned to Kanab, he concluded his report by saying that the party had traveled 280 miles "through a country, for the most part completely unknown. I have not been able to find any evidence that white men ever before visited any considerable portion of the country explored."[43] He was here ignoring the 1866 Andrus company reconnaissance, which he knew about.

5.6. Mouth of Music Temple, Glen Canyon, 1872. Photograph by Jack Hillers and James Fennemore. Courtesy of Don D. Fowler.

But Wooley's report was not published until 1964, and Powell and Thompson were playing up their "we were there first" explorations for the benefit of the public and Congress.

FIRST PHOTOGRAPHS OF THE GLEN CANYON COUNTRY

As noted previously, E. O. Beaman took an excellent series of photographs from the start of the 1871 river trip until he ran out of supplies in Cataract Canyon. The principal reason for caching the *Cañonita* in 1871 and hurrying on to the Crossing of the Fathers was the lack of photographic materials. The plan was to come back overland with a camera and supplies so photographs of Glen Canyon could be made as the boat was taken downstream to Lee's Ferry. James Fennemore arrived in Kanab in time to accompany Thompson to the Henry Mountains.

Powell intended that his cousin, Clem Powell, should learn photography, but Clem was all thumbs. Both Hillers and Clem made photographs during the winter of 1871–72, but Hillers's were clearly superior—which Thompson recognized. That is presumably why Thompson sent Hillers with Fennemore on the *Cañonita* and assigned Clem to the overland party. The trip through Glen Canyon began on June 26. Hillers and Fennemore took numerous photographs, including images of the archaeological sites at White and Red canyons, views near Moqui and Lake canyons, the entrance to Music Temple (fig. 5.6), a "glen" in the canyon (fig. 5.2), and Sentinel Rock at the mouth of Wahweap Creek. They tried to take photographs in Music Temple, but there was not enough light. Hillers did, however, carve his name on the ledge, and Fred Dellenbaugh added his to the others (fig. 5.3).

The party reached the Paria River on July 13, 1872. There they waited a full month for Powell. During that time, Hillers and the others spent much time with John D. Lee and his wife Emma. On July 24, Hillers wrote, "Mr. Lee invited us to spend the day with him, being the anniversary of their [Mormons'] entrance into the Salt Lake Valley. Had a splendid dinner, played cards and sang songs. After supper returned to camp without a change of opinion of Mormonism."[44]

Powell finally appeared on August 13 with various guests, including Mrs. Powell and Ellen Thompson, Powell's sister and A. H. Thompson's wife. Ellen Thompson rode with Hillers and Dellenbaugh through the first rapid at the mouth of the Paria. James Fennemore had been sick throughout the trip to the Henry Mountains and on the river and decided to return to Salt Lake City. Powell listened to Thompson and made Hillers, rather than Clem Powell, the expedition photographer, thus officially launching Hillers on what would be one of the great photographic careers of the later nineteenth century.[45]

On August 17 the party headed into Marble Canyon aboard the *Cañonita* and the *Emma Dean*. The third boat, the *Nellie Powell*, was left behind. Its remnants were exhumed from the Paria sands in 1938 by Russell Frazier and Charles Kelly, and placed on exhibit at the Powell Memorial on the south rim of the Grand Canyon.[46] On September 9, at the mouth of Kanab Creek in the Grand Canyon, Powell decided to end the river trip; the river was running high, and he judged the risks too great to continue. He and Thompson concluded they could map the rest of the Grand Canyon from overland, given the system of triangulation they had established and could extend. As Hillers put it, "Quite a surprise this morning at breakfast. Major told us that our voyage of toil and danger was at an end on the river. Everyone felt like praising God."[47] The party returned to Kanab via Kanab Canyon and proceeded with the mapping work. Powell remained with the party until late fall, primarily working with the local Southern Paiute people (see below), and then left for Washington, D.C. Thompson continued to direct the mapping work from the camp near Kanab. In later seasons he would move west and then north as the mapping project was expanded.

POWELL AND NATIVE PEOPLES IN THE GLEN CANYON COUNTRY

Between 1868–69 and 1880, Powell managed to conduct intermittent studies of the languages and cultures of the Native peoples in the Glen Canyon Country and adjacent areas in Utah and Nevada. He called the people, collectively, the Numa. "This desolate land is the home of a great family of tribes speaking different dialects or languages of the same stock. They call themselves Nu-mes, Nu-intz, Nu-mos, Shi-ni-mos, Nu-nas, etc., all doubtless variations of the same word. We will call them Nu-mas."[48]

Twentieth-century anthropologists and linguists would define a Numic language family, a subdivision of the larger Uto-Aztecan stock. The Numic language family has three major subdivisions: Western, Central, and Southern Numic. Each division has two languages. Western Numic has Mono and Paviotso, spoken in the western and northern Great Basin. Central Numic has Panamint in southeastern California and Shoshone, spoken across the central Great Basin and into the Rocky Mountains. Comanche, spoken on the Southern Plains, is a dialect of Shoshone. Southern Numic has Kawaiisu, spoken by groups in southeastern California, and Ute, comprised of various dialects spoken by the Utes of Utah and Colorado, the Chemehuevi of southern Nevada, and the Southern Paiute of southern Nevada, southern Utah, and northern Arizona.[49]

Powell began his studies during his 1868–69 trip when he wintered along the White River in northwestern Colorado. He worked intermittently with members of a Ute band led by Douglass, who were camped nearby. Legends and myths are told in winter times, and Powell was able to collect several, along with information about doctoring and other topics.

In the fall of 1870, after their meeting with the Uinkarets and Shivwits Paiutes regarding the deaths of his three men, Powell and Hamblin went on to the Hopis via what would soon become the Lee's Ferry crossing of the Colorado near the mouth of the Paria River. While he was not at Hopi for as long as his published article implied, he did gather quite a bit of information.[50]

Most of Powell's work, again intermittent, in 1871–72 was with the Kaibab, Uinkarets, and Shivwits bands of Southern Paiutes. The Kaibabs were on the Kaibab Plateau but also had gathered around the Mormon settlement of Kanab, where Powell had established his field headquarters. The Uinkarets were on the Uinkarets Plateau, and the Shivwits in the vicinity of St. George. During his trips, Powell was often guided by Chuarumpeak, a Kaibab Paiute band leader whom he had first

5.7. Kaibab Paiute leader Chuarumpeak (*second from left*) and family in summer camp outside Kanab, Utah, 1872. Photograph by Jack Hillers, no. 1604. Courtesy of the Bureau of American Ethnology Collection, National Anthropological Archives.

met in 1870 (fig. 5.7). Chuarumpeak accompanied Powell and Hamblin to Lee's Ferry and as far as the Hopi villages, but did not go with them on their journey to meet with the Navajos at Fort Defiance. Chuarumpeak was apparently a very thoughtful and intelligent person, and he appears in various lectures and papers that Powell produced in later years.[51]

In 1873 Powell and an Indian agent, George Ingalls, were directed by the commissioner of Indian Affairs to make a census and extensive sociocultural survey of Indian groups in northern and central Utah, as well as the southern Utah–Arizona Strip area and the Moapa and Las Vegas areas in southern Nevada. They also were directed to make recommendations on the "management" of the various groups. In line with then-current federal policy, Indian people were to be moved onto reservations to get them out of the way of the ever-expanding population of Euro-Americans who wanted their lands, their water, and other resources.[52]

Powell and Ingalls called together conclaves of Indian people when and where they could, aided by Indian agents. Their total head count was 5,522. Of these, there were 528 Paiutes in Utah, 284 in northern Arizona, and 1,031 primarily around Moapa and Las Vegas.[53] They gave synopses of the current conditions of the various tribes and bands, and made detailed recommendations as to which groups were to be sent to existing reservations. Some objected strongly to being moved. For example, representatives of the Southern Paiute people around St. George objected vociferously to being sent to reside with the Utes on the Uintah reservation. The Utes, they said, were "their enemies from time immemorial," who had enslaved and killed the Paiutes (all quite true), and besides were "profoundly skilled in sorcery."[54] In the end, who agreed, or were forced, to go where took years to iron out. The St. George people wound up with a tiny reservation west of Shivwits, near Santa Clara, Utah.

Most of Powell's ethnographic and linguistic work was done with the various Southern Paiute groups in southern Utah, northern Arizona, and southern Nevada, although he never saw "The Kwa-an-ti-kwo-ets, who live on the eastern side of the Colorado River, [and] are nearly isolated from other tribes, and affiliate to a greater or less extent with the Navajos."[55] These were the people encountered by Domínguez and Escalante after they crossed the Colorado River in 1776, and who became known as the San Juan Paiute (chapter 20). From the other groups he gathered materials on myths, legends, chants and songs, vocabularies, kinship terms, and a host of geographic and topographic place-names, some 119 of them. Some—such as Markagunt, Paunsagunt, Kaibab, Toroweap, and Kaiparowits—Powell or his men gave to major landforms. Names of springs (of special importance

5.8. Kaibab Paiute round dance near Kanab, Utah, 1872. John Wesley Powell is standing at left. Photograph by Jack Hillers, no. 1623. Courtesy of the National Anthropological Archives, Bureau of American Ethnology Collection.

to people in the arid environment) and other features were often descriptive, for example Mu-tum-wa-va, "Dripping Spring"—Pipe Spring, southwest of Kanab; Pa'-ga, "Big River," the Colorado River; and Pa'-ga-we-wi-gum, "Cañon (Grand) of the Colorado." At-a-rin-ka has a nice ring to it, perhaps more so than the English "Table Mountain," the part of the Aquarius Plateau escarpment which forms the skyline north of Bryce Canyon.[56]

PHOTOGRAPHING THE NUMA

Jack Hillers took a number of photographs of the Indian people in the vicinity of Kanab in 1872 (fig. 5.8). He was with Powell and Ingalls for much of their 1873 trip, and with Powell in 1874 while he was doing geology studies in the Uinta Basin country. There Hillers took a number of photographs of Ute camps and leaders.[57]

In 1873 Powell invited a reporter for the *New York Times,* Justin E. Colburn, and the famed landscape artist Thomas Moran to visit his operation in Kanab and make trips to the Grand Canyon (fig. 5.9). Moran, Colburn, several of Powell's men, and a Paiute guide, Jim, went first to the Toroweap Valley. They descended to the brink of the inner gorge, where Moran made sketches. They then returned to Kanab to meet Powell, Ingalls, and Hillers, and then made a trip across the Kaibab Plateau to the rim of the Grand Canyon. Moran made

5.9. Thomas Moran (*center*) and Jason Colburn with a young Paiute boy near Kanab, Utah, August 1872. Photograph by Jack Hillers, no. 1592-a. Courtesy of the Bureau of American Ethnology Collection, National Anthropological Archives.

5.10. Posed group of Kaibab Paiutes near Kanab, Utah, August 1872. Beaded clothing is from the Northern Utes; the headdresses were manufactured under direction of Ellen Powell Thompson. Photograph by Jack Hillers, no. 1613-1-2. Courtesy of the Bureau of American Ethnology Collection, National Anthropological Archives.

more sketches, which he turned into his majestic painting *Chasm of the Colorado.* In 1871 Moran had accompanied the Hayden survey party to Yellowstone. His sketches and William Henry Jackson's photographs helped convince Congress to set aside Yellowstone as a national park. Moran then painted his famed *Grand Canyon of the Yellowstone* (1872), which measures 7 × 12 feet. Congress purchased the painting for $10,000 and subsequently purchased the *Chasms of the Colorado* for the same amount. Both hung for years in the U.S. Capitol, were later transferred to the Interior Department building, and are currently (2009) on loan to the National Gallery of Art.[58]

When Moran arrived back in Kanab from the Toroweap trip on August 13, 1873, he wrote to his wife, Mary Nimmo Moran, "Major Powell had arrived and he had all the Indians in camp and all the squaws making Indian toggery for him. He is going to get me an Indian suit made."[59] Hillers was instructed to make a series of photographs of the people to add to those from the previous year. Powell asked Moran to advise Hillers about posing the Indian people, and the photographs are indeed posed (fig. 5.10). Powell's sister, Ellen Thompson, was the one actually in charge of directing the making of the "Indian toggery," including fake headdresses. Powell had also collected clothing items from the Utes in 1868–69. He had some of those shipped out from Washington, D.C. The elaborate beaded clothing in Figure 5.10 is Ute, not Southern Paiute. One photograph shows a woman wearing a buckskin dress with a museum accession number on the bodice.[60] Guided by Moran's aesthetic sense, Hillers posed several buxom Paiute women in Kanab and Las Vegas with their buckskin dresses artfully arranged so that one or both breasts were visible. Then as now, sex sells. In the nineteenth century, photographs of bare-breasted women were acceptable if the women were "savages" and not white. Moran would later do many of the woodcuts for Powell's published articles, basing many of them on Hillers's photographs.[61]

Hillers made two sets of photographs. One was a set of stereographs; the second regular 8 × 10 inch wet-plate images. The stereographs were made into sets for sale; Powell took 40 percent of the profits, A. H. Thompson 30 percent, and Hillers 30 percent. Besides the Indian stereographs, there were many sets of scenery from the 1871–72 river trips and later overland trips. The stereographs were also strategically distributed to congressmen and senators at the time of annual budget hearings. The larger-format photographs became ethnographic documents.

Powell and Hillers were also charged by the Smithsonian Institution to make collections of traditional clothing, tools, implements, and weapons. They did so. For example, the clothing and implements shown in photographs taken in Kanab and Las Vegas in 1873 were purchased off the bodies and out of the hands of their makers.[62]

As an aside, after 1874 Powell was deeply involved in his geology work, exhibits for the Philadelphia Centennial Exposition of 1876, and the political machinations leading to the creation of the U.S. Geological Survey and the Bureau of Ethnology in 1879. However, he was able to do some ethnographic work with Northern Paiute people in 1880 while he was traveling in the West serving on the Public Lands Commission.

Powell used the ethnographic materials he gathered in various lectures and published papers, some as late as 1896.[63] He had planned to write a general report on the Numa peoples and had drafted some sections, but after 1881 he was directing two federal agencies, one of them (the USGS) immersed in a decade of controversy, leaving him little time for the task. All his Numa notes and manuscripts were placed in the Bureau of American Ethnology archives. In 1967–68 Catherine Fowler and I edited and published the report for him, along with all the other ethnographic and linguistic materials he had collected. John Matley and I published an extensive study of the collections of clothing and artifacts that Powell, Thompson, and Hillers had made among the Numa. Both volumes were published by the Smithsonian Institution, an appropriate venue since Powell's beloved Bureau of American Ethnology was administered by the Smithsonian until 1964, when it was merged with the Department of Anthropology of the National Museum of Natural History.[64] Although Powell did not complete his report on the Numa, they are memorialized in a way in the title of his formal portrait that hangs in the foyer of the Cosmos Club in Washington, D.C. It reads, *Kapurats: Major John Wesley Powell.*

› 6 ‹

POWELL, THE U.S. GEOLOGICAL SURVEY, AND THE CANYON COUNTRY

WHEN JOHN WESLEY POWELL HEADED INTO Marble Canyon on August 17, 1872, he saw Glen Canyon for the last time. In the next few years, as he and his men pursued their work and wrote their reports, they not only named Glen Canyon but many other physiographic and topographic features on the Colorado Plateau and in adjacent areas as well. As director of the U.S. Geological Survey between 1881 and 1894, Powell and his staff continued to be actively involved in studying and defining the Colorado Plateau.

When Powell received the initial appropriation from Congress in 1870 to continue his exploration of the Colorado River, he became head of the fourth of the so-called federal "Great Surveys," which had a major impact on the second opening of the West after the Civil War. The full story of the surveys is told in many other places.[1] Here we will simply tell enough of their histories to understand Powell's roles and the actions of his men during the 1870s and 1880s as they relate to the study and mapping of the Glen Canyon Country and the surrounding area.

Prior to the Civil War, all federal western exploration was in the hands of the U.S. Army Corps of Topographical Engineers, but during the war they were merged into the regular Corps of Engineers. After the war new geographical surveys were created, three headed by civilians; only one was under army control. The four surveys had various names, but were best known by the names of their leaders. Clarence King headed the U.S. Geological Exploration of the Fortieth Parallel; Ferdinand Vandeveer Hayden's U.S. Geological and Geographical Survey of the Territories centered its work in the Rockies of Wyoming and Colorado, but in 1875 and 1876 extended westward along the San Juan River and adjacent country. Lt. George M. Wheeler directed the U.S. Geographical and Geological Surveys West of the One Hundredth Meridian, which ranged widely, and sometimes erratically, across the West. Powell's survey was best known as the U.S. Geographical and Geological Survey of the Rocky Mountain Region. The names were very important because they asserted turf rights. Despite his survey's name, Powell concentrated the work of his staff on the high plateaus of southern Utah, the Glen Canyon Country, and the Grand Canyon.

As noted in the previous chapter, Powell published his first scientific paper in 1873 on the Colorado Plateau country, "Some remarks on the Geological Structure of a district of country lying to the north of the Grand Cañon of the Colorado." [2] Therein he described in general terms the sequence of geological strata from the bottom of the Grand Canyon to the top of the Pink Cliffs to the north. In the process he gave names to some of the formations he described. North of the rim of the Grand Canyon, he noted:

> [a] firmly cemented conglomerate containing many fragments of silicified wood, and over its surface are scattered many like fragments, and sometimes huge tree trunks, which are the remnants of rocks at one time overlying the conglomerate but not carried away by erosion. Underlying this cap are variegated sandstones and marls. The whole group is probably of lower Triassic age. The silicified woods so abundant here are called by the Indians who inhabit the Country, Shin-a-rump; or The arrows of Shin-aú-av. (Sinauav is the Hercules of their mythology.)
>
> To the cliffs they give the name Shin-au-rump Mu-Kwan-i-Kunt, and we have adopted as the English name Shinaurump (or Arrow) cliffs. . . . [Further north is] a second line of cliffs, composed of red sandstone and beds of lighter color, which are stained red on the surface. . . . [The Indian name is] Un-Kar Mu-Kwan-i-Kunt, . . . *Vermilion Cliffs.* [Still further north is] another line of cliffs . . . capped by nearly two hundred feet of limestone . . . [atop] a bed of massive light gray sandstone. The Indian name is . . . At-si-gar Mu-Kwan-i-Kunt, or Gray Cliffs [later this formation would be called the White Cliffs]. . . . [Continuing north there] is another line of cliffs composed of limestones and sandstones. . . . The Indian name for this line is Un-tswar-ar Mu-Kwan-i-Kunt, [or] Pink Cliffs. . . . It will be seen . . . that to go from the bottom of the Grand Cañon to the summit of these plateaus, *you must climb by a great geographical stairway, the steps of which have an altitude of many hundreds of feet, and a width of many miles.*[3]

Powell went on to describe the geology of the Country in more detail, including a discussion of the major faults and escarpments, such as a "bold escarpment . . . to which we have given the name, Grand Wash Cliffs, and to the displacement, Grand Wash Fault." He then described another fault extending "from an unknown point south of the Colorado . . . to a point north of Tokerville [*sic*]. . . . The displacement is from 1,300 to 2,800 feet. . . . The broken edges of the rocks on the eastern side of the fault . . . stand in a remarkably steep escarpment, in much of its course a sheer precipice. [The locals have named the cliff] Hurricane Lodge [*sic*], but . . . I have called it Hurricane Cliff . . . the displacement we call Hurricane Fault."

> [Another fault] on the north side of the Grand Cañon . . . is marked by a cañon about thirty miles long, to which we have given the Indian name, To-ró-weap. At the foot of the valley on the brink of the Grand Cañon, the displacement was found to be 820 feet, and it appears to be greater on the south side. We have named this To-ró-weap Fault.[4]

Powell described and named other faults, some of which were later renamed. He then turned to plateaus and described and named the "Sheav-wits" (Shivwits) Plateau; the "Pouns-á-gunt" (Paunsagunt), "Home of the beaver"; and the "Mar-ká-gunt," "Home of the flowering bushes." Finally, "there is an extensive plateau, extending from the Grand Cañon to the foot of the Vermilion Cliffs; the Indian name for this is Kaibáb, meaning Mountain Lying Down, and pleased with its significance we have adopted the name Kaibab Plateau."[5] After extended discussions of monoclines, synclines, and anticlines, and the major volcanic features of the region, Powell ended his article by stating:

> The general history of the geological operations recorded in this desolate waste can be briefly summed [up] in the following statement: The deposition of beds, of many thousands of feet in thickness, in which are enclosed the relics of life which existed when these rocks were formed, and which were buried in their accumulating sands; then the folding and faulting of the whole series, and, *pari passu* with this, the excavation of a wonderful system of gorges, and the carving of a vast network of valleys, leaving behind towering cliffs stretching across the country in every direction, and still, *pari passu*, with the folding, and faulting, and denudation, great floods of lava were poured out from the interior to fill valleys, and form mesas, and tables, and mountain cones. And in the present period we have an *ensemble* of topographical features embossed on the face of the country, wild, grand, and desolate.[6]

In later publications Powell would expand the ideas set forth in the article, but it was an important first step for him. The *American Journal of Science* was the nineteenth-century equivalent of the present-day journals *Science* and, in Britain, *Nature*—the major general science publications by which recognized scientists communicate with their peers. When the editors of the journal accepted Powell's article, they signaled that he was being admitted to the club. For our purposes, his article shows him continuing, as he already had begun, to put names on the geological features of the Colorado Plateau and to lay the groundwork for a geological research agenda that he (and later his staff, particularly Clarence Dutton and Grove Karl Gilbert) would pursue over the next two decades (chapter 7).

By 1876 Powell was ready to set out his own general overview of the geology of the American West in his famous *Report on the Geology of the Eastern Portion of the Uinta Mountains and a Region of Country Adjacent Thereto.*[7] The "adjacent" region of Country encompassed the Rocky Mountains, the entire Colorado Plateau, including the Grand Canyon, and the Great Basin. The major always thought on a grand scale. He began by citing the Newberry quote in chapter 3. He then divided the geology of the western United States into three major provinces: the Park, Plateau, and Basin provinces. By "Park Province" he meant the central and southern Rocky Mountains, with their characteristic high-altitude parks, such as Estes Park, between jutting mountain peaks. "Basin Province" he borrowed from Grove Karl Gilbert's "Basin Range System" (see below), now better known as the Basin and Range Province.[8]

Much of Powell's monograph is taken up with a discussion of the geologic strata of the Colorado Plateau in general. This was derived from his observations in 1868, the two river trips, his trip to the Hopi mesas and Navajo Country in 1870, a brief trip onto the Kaibab Plateau in 1873, two pack trips he made into the Green River Country in 1874 and 1875, and his observations as he traveled between Salt Lake City and southern Utah. There was also a lot of input from John Steward, the geologist on the second river trip.

Having sketched the geology of the West, Powell hoped to be able to continue, with the help of his staff, to fill in the details; that is, to conduct detailed studies of the geology of the Colorado Plateau and make maps—first general topographic maps, and then more detailed maps on which the geology could be shown.

But events intervened. Powell and Hayden both had exhibits at the 1876 Philadelphia Centennial Exhibition, the United States' first major world's fair, celebrating the one-hundredth anniversary of the signing of the Declaration of Independence. Both men were involved in planning government exhibits for the fair. Their staffs spent much of 1875 in the field collecting artifacts and making photographs for the exhibits, and much of 1876 attending to them in Philadelphia. Powell used the fair as a venue to announce a new publication series in anthropology, the Contributions to North American Ethnology, officially signaling his interest in pursuing studies of North American Indian people.[9]

By 1877 political pressure was growing in Congress to consolidate the four surveys. The pressure grew until legislation creating the U.S. Geological Survey (hereinafter, "the Survey" or "USGS") was passed by Congress in 1879. Powell took the opportunity to get language inserted in the legislation that provided funds to "complete" the Contributions to North American Ethnology publications under the auspices of the Smithsonian Institution.

As soon as the legislation was signed, Spencer Baird, secretary of the Smithsonian, appointed Powell "to take charge of the work." Powell immediately had letterhead stationery printed that read "Bureau of Ethnology" and sent three people to the New Mexico and Arizona territories to begin a whole new program of anthropological research. In 1880 legislation provided funds "to continue to complete" the publications. Another bill authorized the printing of the *First Annual Report of the Bureau of Ethnology*, thereby giving the Bureau back-door official recognition. This marked Powell's abandonment of geology, and he would henceforth devote his attentions to ethnology—or anthropology, as it was coming to be called.[10]

But the first director of the Survey, Clarence King, disliked the trench warfare of Washington politics and very much liked *la dolce vita*. He resigned in 1881 to pursue the riches needed to make the good life possible; he found neither. Powell was appointed to replace King by his friend President James Garfield, being allowed to concurrently keep his position as director of the Bureau of Ethnology. The stories of the creation of the Survey and the Bureau, and Powell's assumption of the directorship of both in March 1881, are long and complex, and adroitly told elsewhere by Wallace Stegner and Donald Worster.[11] Here we are concerned with the Survey programs Powell developed from 1881 until 1894 as they related to the Colorado Plateau and the Glen Canyon Country. We turn first to the mapping program.

MAPPING THE CANYON COUNTRY

When Powell set out down the Colorado River in 1869, one of his self-assigned tasks was to map and study the canyons of the Green and Colorado rivers. The area was not "Unknown," as Powell's biographers would have it. Egloffstein's 1860 map (fig. 3.4) had shown the Glen Canyon Country in some detail, but it was an approximation of the courses of the Green and the Colorado. There was Newberry's geology report from the Ives expedition, but his report on the geology of the area around the confluence of the two rivers was not published until 1876. There were, then, lots of "unknowns," but the area was not a total blank. What Powell set out to do was map the topography of the Country in sufficiently accurate detail that detailed studies of the geology of specific topographic features could begin. He did so, and began contributing, along with the other surveys throughout the 1870s, to the ongoing task of producing useful and accurate topographic maps of the West to be used for geology studies, land surveying, road and railroad building and so on.

It was a daunting undertaking. The army topographical engineers were trained—as their name implies—as topographers—mapmakers. Each expedition sent westward, from that of Lt. Stephen Long

6.1. Henry Gannett, 1890s. Portrait Collection, port 0062. Courtesy of the U.S. Geological Survey Digital Photography Library.

in 1819 to Lt. Ives in 1857 and Captain Macomb in 1859, added incrementally to the mapping of the West. Lt. William H. Emory's journal of his 1846 trip from Fort Leavenworth, Kansas, to Santa Fe, and on to California with General Kearney's Army of the West is filled with his descriptions of making astronomical observations to fix the latitude and longitude of the major topographic features along the route. Emory's map was the first to depict parts of the Southwest with any degree of accuracy. He and his staff later continued that work during the Boundary Survey, as they and their Mexican counterparts drew, and redrew, the international boundary between the two countries.[12]

When the Great Surveys were consolidated into the USGS in 1879, producing accurate maps of the United States, especially the West, continued to be top priority. In 1882 Powell reorganized the internal workings of the Survey, placing Henry Gannett (fig. 6.1) in charge of the nationwide mapping program. Gannett (1846–1914), born in Maine and schooled at Harvard University, had become chief topographer for the Hayden survey in 1871. He participated in the first surveys of the Yellowstone region in the 1870s. When the Hayden survey ended in 1879, Gannett went to work for the Tenth Census, demarcating the enumeration districts and working closely with the census chief, Francis A. Walker, in developing cartographic displays of census data; he later worked on the Eleventh and Twelfth censuses. Gannett remained with the USGS throughout his career in various capacities. He was a founder and later president of the National Geographic Society. His pronouncement following the 1890 census that "'the frontier had ceased to exist' prompted the historian Frederick Jackson Turner to formulate his frontier thesis of American development."[13]

Standardizing Mapping

Powell, Gannett, and the Survey staff set out to place geological research and topographic mapping on a standardized basis. As noted in the earlier discussion of the maps made by Egloffstein and others, there was no agreement on how topographic features and elevations were to be represented—indeed, on the procedures for making maps. Army surveys before the Civil War often perforce used what was called the "meander method," measuring distances from a base point that was more or less accurately located, where possible by astronomic observations, and then sketching in observed topography. For surveys on the march, measuring distances usually involved an odometer pulled behind an animal or a wagon. Such devices were first described by Vitruvius, the great Roman engineer and architect, about 23 BCE, and had long been used by armies and topographers.

The U.S. General Land Office used the chain and compass method—a metal chain of known length to measure distance, and a compass to determine angles and directions. The U.S. Coast Survey (later Coast and Geodetic Survey) used an elaborate triangulation system said to be "accurate to a few inches in one hundred miles." But such a system was far too time consuming and costly for the enormous distances of the American West.

Josiah Dwight Whitney, the head of the California Geological Survey in the early 1860s, faced with surveying the multitude of mountains in the Sierra Nevada, set up triangulation points on high mountain peaks and mapped in the intervening country by eye using plane tables and alidades. Young Clarence King, who worked for Whitney from 1863 to 1865, adopted the system for mapping during his surveys along the fortieth parallel, and other federal surveys, including Powell's, followed suit during the 1870s.[14] It worked particularly well in the West, where the clear air and numerous high mountain peaks made sight lines of over 100 miles possible.

In 1878 the International Congress of Geologists began discussions of standardizing map colors, nomenclature, and scales. Powell and his staff were involved in active interchanges with the group for over a decade. In 1882 they presented a standardized color scheme and set of symbols for geological cartography to be used by the USGS. In the sixth annual Survey report for 1884–85, they laid out the principles on which the mapping program would be conducted. These included the scales and sizes of maps to be produced, the type fonts and colors to be used to denote different topographic features, and the conventional symbols and colors to be used to denote cultural features, towns, roads, railroads, rivers, marshes, ditches, and so on .

Contour intervals were to be 10, 20, 50, 100, or 200 feet, varying with the scale of the map and the magnitude of the topographic relief depicted. With some modifications, these conventions have been used by the USGS ever since. For the undeveloped areas of the West, the scale was 1:250,000 (or 4 miles = 1 inch); 1:225,000 for the East, and 1:62,500 for heavily populated areas in the East. Over time the three scales came to be referred to by the number of minutes of latitude and longitude covered on one quadrangle. The 1:250,000 maps were 1 degree in size, that is, 1 degree of latitude by 1 degree of longitude, hence a "60-minute quad"; the 1:225,000 became the "30-minute quad"; and the 1:62,500 became the "15-minute quad." The 1:24,000 scale series, begun early in the twentieth century, became known as "7-1/2-minute quad." Each map, of whatever scale, was given a name, that of a prominent feature shown on the map, and marked with the date of its printing.[15]

Between 1874 and 1886 the Powell survey and the USGS produced ten 60-minute quad sheets covering the Glen Canyon Country and adjacent areas: Mt. Trumbull (1874), Kaibab (1979, 1886), Echo Cliffs (1884), Marsh Pass (1883), and Canyon de Chelly (1883) for Arizona; and Salt Lake (1884), Escalante (1885), Kanab (1879), Henry Mountains (1884), and Abajo Mountains (1884) for Utah.[16]

In the fourth annual report of the USGS, Powell reported that in the 1882–83 congressional appropriation "the Survey was required to make a geologic map of the United States. Authority, therefore, was given to extend the operations of the Survey over the entire country to the extent necessary for the purpose." He noted that the Survey had inherited from the predecessor Great Surveys "a large amount of good topographic material" to build on "[to] prepare a topographic map as a basis for future geologic researches." However, "a large part of [the Wheeler survey] work was on a scale too small, and was done by methods too inaccurate to be utilized for purposes of the Geological Survey."[17] Take that, Lt. Wheeler!

In subsequent annual reports, the Survey published a map of the United States showing "areas surveyed by various organizations prior to July 1st

1881" in relation to work done each succeeding year by the USGS. In the Plateau and Great Basin regions, the previously surveyed areas included the western two-thirds of Colorado, the northwest quadrant of New Mexico, most of Utah, and the Humboldt River drainage in Nevada.[18] The Survey's task, across the nation, was to fill in the gaps. In many areas the gaps were enormous; one such was much of the Colorado Plateau. There the task was made even more arduous by the vast distances and the difficulties of negotiating the terrain.

The Logistics of Mapping: Getting to the Field

Wherever they worked, the first task of the topographers was to establish measured baselines, each anchored on a fixed point, that is a known point of latitude and longitude, established by repeated astronomical observations (together with telegraphic time signals, if possible), as we saw A. H. Thompson and his men doing in chapter 5. The baselines, and their extensions, became the sides of triangles, extended across a region. The aim was to create an interlocking set of triangles, or system of triangulation, from which measurements and sightings could be made to establish where topographic features were in relation to the apexes and lines of the triangles. These could then be mapped in by plane table and alidade.

But before the topographers could measure baselines, establish fixed points, or proceed with triangulation, they had to get to the field—to their assigned work areas. A report by Gilbert Thompson (no relation to A. H. Thompson), one of the Survey topographers, for the 1881 field season, although perhaps an extreme case, illustrates the point. To begin, Thompson could not start work until after July 1. In the nineteenth century, the federal fiscal year was July 1 to June 30. Almost inevitably, the last bill Congress passed each year was the federal budget for the coming fiscal year. That meant no fieldwork could start until Powell, or any other agency head, knew how much money he had to work with. There was always budget horse-trading; funds that had been in submitted budgets throughout the year might evaporate at the last minute. Only with firm figures in hand the first week of July could Powell (or others) proceed to implement plans for the new fiscal year.

Powell ordered Thompson to Fort Wingate, New Mexico, to establish a station for map work on the eastern side of the Colorado Plateau. But first the party had to pass through Kanab, Utah, to pick up equipment and hire some experienced local men who had worked for A. H. Thompson and Clarence Dutton in previous years. Jack Hillers, by this time the Survey's official photographer, was ordered to accompany the party and assist with logistics, and then later do photography.

Hillers arrived by train in Salt Lake City on July 17, 1881, with Thompson to follow. Hillers—with five men, two wagons, eighteen mules, and a horse—left the next day for Kanab, arriving on August 1. Thompson rode the Utah Central Railroad to Marysvale and then went by "special conveyance" (perhaps a hired buckboard) to Kanab, arriving August 7. The next day, Thompson and Hillers—with two assistants, four teamsters, two cooks, a helper, four wagons, and thirty-four horses and mules—left for Lee's Ferry. On August 12, "We crossed the Colorado at the mouth of the Paria, and were nearly broken down over the 'Point.' In the distance of one and a half miles an ascent and descent of 800 feet is encountered. It was fortunate for our animals that we were able to obtain hay of the ferryman."[19] This was the infamous "road" up out of the canyon on the south side of the river.

Six days later the party arrived at the falls of the Little Colorado River but had to continue south for four days before being able to cross because of high water:

> We effected a crossing by making an approach; then, putting the team animals across on the solid ground, we took a strong rope of a length

> greater than the width of the wash, and drew each wagon, half floating, through the quicksands and swift current. Three hours' work put our whole train across . . . and without being obliged to unload the wagons. . . . From this point our travel was without special interest. . . . On August 28 . . . we arrived at Fort Wingate, after a journey of 710 miles, without accident or loss of property, the animals being in much better condition than at starting. The animals from Salt Lake City had traveled 890 miles. The total time was forty days, or thirty seven of actual travel. I wish here to render my thanks to Mr. Hillers and all the other members of the party for their universal good-will and cheerfulness throughout the long journey.[20]

Thus, after nearly six weeks on the road, the members of the party could get to work. Hillers headed for the Hopi villages, Canyon de Chelly, and later the Rio Grande Valley to make what became some of his classic photographs of the Indian pueblos and the grandeur of de Chelly.[21] Along the way he ran into Capt. John Gregory Bourke, the famed ethnologist and aide-de-camp to Gen. George Crook, near Sunset, Arizona. Bourke was making a survey of Indian tribes. Hillers knew Bourke from Washington, D.C. Such a chance meeting called for libations. Hillers went off to forage. According to Bourke, "Hillers reappeared with a mixture of ginger and whiskey. The ginger was all right, but the whiskey, from the Mormon town of Brigham, was as vile as Arizona could produce."[22]

Thompson and his men began to lay out and measure a baseline and establish triangulation points. Thompson had been in the Glen Canyon Country previously with the Wheeler survey. His plan was to connect with previous triangulation points to the west, south, and east established by that survey, and those to the north in Colorado by the Hayden survey. But the area in-between was still largely a cartographic blank: "A large portion of this area has never been mapped. The mighty Navajo Mountain, at the junction of the Colorado and San Juan Rivers, as far as is known, has never been approached or ascended by a white man, and whenever an archaeologic [*sic*] map of the United States is published, this section, with its ruins and inhabited Indian towns, ancient and deep-worn trails, will be one of its most interesting features."[23]

In 1881 Thompson proceeded to work in the general area between Mount Taylor and the Zuni Mountains to the south. The latter offered no high point with a clear line of sight for a triangulation station. Hence, Thompson's men built one, "nearly forty feet in height. To construct this and clear away the heavy pine timbering obstructing the line of sight occupied . . . [a work] party about ten days." By December 11, Thompson surveyors had "occupied" fifteen triangulation stations, with the longest sight line being 80 miles, and in the process made 3,500 theodolite observations for triangulation purposes and 1,380 barometric observations to establish points of elevation. While some of his men were laying out the triangles over a 1,500 square mile area, others were filling in topographic details of 775 square miles by means of plane table mapping. Thompson and his assistant finally left for Washington, D.C., by train on Christmas Eve, 1881.[24]

The difficulties of establishing triangulation points in the canyon country were elegantly discussed by Clarence Dutton in reports of his work and those of his topographers in 1880 on the Kaibab Plateau. The problem for the mappers, said Dutton, was the plateau itself, Powell's "Mountain Lying Down":

> It is a lofty flat mass without a single peak or pronounced elevation anywhere upon its surface. It is densely forest-clad with gigantic pines and spruces. It is loftier by 1,500 to 4,000 feet than the surrounding regions, and to the eye and mind of the topographer, it is merely an obstruction which cannot be crossed by

> his lines of triangulation; and it is extremely difficult to circumvent, for it is nearly 100 miles long and 15 to 40 miles wide. Being devoid of natural objects of sufficient definition to serve as targets for the theodolite, it was necessary to construct artificial ones; and the selection of stations within range of other well-determined stations, and readily distinguished, was not easy; for the nearest ascertained stations were from fifty to eighty miles away and even most strongly individualized points [on the Kaibab] were liable to be confused with others. It was at once concluded that none could be found except upon the brinks of the salients which project out into the broad chasm of the Colorado.[25]

Two such salients Dutton selected, and named, were Point Sublime and Cape Royal: "Here were built large monuments of timber, which were covered with white calico. From both points, the well-determined stations on Mount Emma in the Uinkarets [about 60 miles away] and the San Francisco Mountains [50 miles away], were discernible through the telescope, and satisfactory readings were made upon them from the large theodolite."[26]

Dutton went on to describe the difficulties his topographer, Sumner H. Bodfish, had in shooting the points and in mapping the side canyons draining off the Kaibab into the Grand Canyon: "The very extraordinary topography of the chasm and its accessories [side canyons] called for great skill and ingenuity on the part of the surveyor, but Mr. Bodfish proved equal to all the emergencies, excepting a few which no skill can conquer, and which require wings, rather than skill."[27] Later in the summer Bodfish traveled by pack train to Mount Emma and shot in back sights to confirm his readings from Point Sublime and Cape Royal—a standard topographic practice.

In the 1882 reorganization of the USGS, Powell placed his brother-in-law Almon Harris Thompson in charge of the division located at Fort Wingate, New Mexico (the division has various names in later reports). Gilbert Thompson, who had led the forty-day trek to Fort Wingate the year before, was sent to northern California to develop a major mapping program there. Powell also hired another brother-in-law, Charles Garlick. To add to the nepotic mix, he hired his sister Martha's son, Arthur Powell Davis, who had just graduated from Kansas State Normal School and was ready to see, and map, some part of the West.

It is interesting that Powell sent young Arthur into the canyon country. Perhaps Davis wanted to see the area with which his famous uncle was so closely identified. In later years Davis would become even more closely identified with it in his own right, as director of the U.S. Reclamation Service and key planner of the system of dams on the Colorado River (chapter 12).[28]

Davis started the 1882 season as an assistant topographer but was soon given his own crew. In 1883 he was sent to the "mighty Navajo Mountain" country, but reported unrest among the Navajos forced his recall before any serious topographic work could be done. He did much better in 1884. In his report on the topographic work for 1884–85, Henry Gannett noted that mapping had proceeded in two areas in the Southwest: first, an L-shaped strip along the lower Colorado River and an area as far west as Las Vegas and the Muddy River drainage. Second, in the Glen Canyon Country, the areas mapped were the San Juan Triangle, from the confluence of the San Juan and Colorado rivers northward to the confluence of the Grand and Green and east to about 109° 30", and the area south of the San Juan River from the confluence and west of 111° longitude to the Colorado and Little Colorado south to about latitude 35° 30". Gannett wrote:

> The duty of revising and extending this triangulation was entrusted to Mr. Arthur P. Davis, topographer, with Mr. James A. Maher,

> assistant topographer. . . . [Davis and his crews] occupied twenty nine stations, distributed over the country from the La Sal Mountains on the north and Navajo Mountain on the west to the 35th parallel on the south and the 109th meridian on the east. The area covered within figures [i.e., areas lying beneath triangles] was approximately 29,000 square miles. The greatest length of line observed each way was 137 miles (Mt. Waas [in the La Sal Range] to Navajo Mountain), while the average length of triangle side was 54 miles. The mean error of closure of triangles, after correcting for spherical excess, was 9" 55'. Full connection was established between the Hayden and the Powell surveys.[29]

The report's accompanying diagram shows that from Navajo Mountain, Davis and his crew triangulated with points on Mount Ellen in the Henry Mountains, Mount Waas and Mount Peale in the La Sal Range, Abajo Peak, Ute Peak in southwestern Colorado, Oraibi on Third Mesa in the Hopi country, and San Francisco Peak in northern Arizona.

Davis and his men built a tall triangulation platform atop Navajo Mountain similar to the ones Dutton's men had constructed on Point Sublime and Cape Royal, and that Gilbert Thompson's men had built in the Zuni Mountains. Geologist John O'Brien has suggested that lanterns may have been used on the platforms as targets for siting from and to various points at night, as well as the cloth wrapping that would be visible during the day.[30] Like astronomical observations, each sighting had to be done numerous times to average out errors due to atmospheric disturbances such as heat waves. Anyone who has used an optical transit or theodolite is well aware of the problems caused by heat waves, even at short distances. Sightings over 50-plus miles would create special problems.

As an aside, the triangulation station on Navajo Mountain built by Davis's men in 1884 led to the development of a myth current even into the twenty-first century. The source of the myth was probably John Wetherill (chapter 13), since its promulgators seem to have been associated with him or knew him. For example, Tracy Randall Kelley, who was the field director for the Rainbow Bridge Monument Valley Expedition in 1935 (chapter 13), described Navajo Mountain for prospective recruits: "The top [of Navajo Mountain] is neither a peak nor a ridge, but rather a broad crown, of some hundreds of acres, covered in the center, at its highest, with aspen trees—successors of the pine and fir cut down a century ago [*sic*] by U.S. troops that in Indian warfare needed a clear ground for heliographing."[31]

Later versions of the story were more specific. The heliograph station was built by army troops during the 1864 campaign against the Navajos directed by Kit Carson (chapter 20). Such usage was hardly possible since the heliograph was not invented until 1878 by a British army officer, Sir Henry Christopher Mance (1840–1926), in western Asia. It was, however, widely used by the U.S. Army in the Southwest after 1880.

Excepting a two-year stint with the USGS Irrigation Survey, Davis directed topographic work in the Southwest until 1894, primarily in the eastern section of the Colorado Plateau. The rest of his career is discussed in chapter 12.

In 1894 John Wesley Powell was forced out of the USGS because his views of how western water should be managed were not palatable to developers and western congressmen (chapter 12). He returned to the Bureau of Ethnology (renamed the Bureau of "American Ethnology" to deflect criticism that its anthropology studies were getting too far afield). He began writing rather abstruse papers on philosophy and epistemology, largely ignored at the time and long since forgotten.[32]

He also pulled together his most complete statement on the Colorado River, the Grand Canyon, and adjacent areas: *Canyons of the Colorado,* published in 1895. It is an elaboration of his 1874 report of the 1869 and 1871–72 river trips (still collapsed into one trip), with added descriptions of the surrounding country and Indian people. There are dozens of illustrations taken from Survey and Bureau of Ethnology publications, as well as from magazine articles. Many are engravings based on Jack Hillers's photographs; none are credited. Powell does credit all of his 1869 crew, including Dunn and the Howland brothers, but none of the 1871–72 crew. That would have to wait until Dellenbaugh's *Canyon Voyage* in 1908.[33] Powell's last publication also returned to his beginnings, a truncated history of the exploration of the Grand Canyon and a description of its physical features written for tourists riding the Santa Fe Railway across the Southwest. Therein he describes meeting John D. Lee and his wife at Lee's Ferry and reprints excerpts from his *Canyons of the Colorado.*[34]

More than any other individual, John Wesley Powell put his imprint on the Glen Canyon Country, and the encompassing Plateau Province, by the names he and his men bestowed on topographical features and by the geological studies they initiated. Whatever one's views are of Lake Powell, it was fitting to name it for him—and equally fitting that the name Grand Staircase–Escalante National Monument derives from names first used by Almon Harris Thompson and his brother-in-law John Wesley Powell in the 1870s.

› 7 ‹

LACCOLITHS AND GRAND STAIRCASES

The Work of C. E. Dutton and G. K. Gilbert

IN 1881, IN THE *SECOND ANNUAL REPORT OF the U.S. Geological Survey,* John Wesley Powell and his staff laid out a consensus scheme of geological eras and periods that (with modifications) became the basis for historical geological studies in North America for the next century (table 7.1). Subsequent work and the development of geological dating methods led to various modifications and extensions of Powell's scheme for different parts of North America. Table 7.2 represents a consensus scheme of the geological history of the Glen Canyon Country and adjacent regions as it was developed through numerous studies in the twentieth century up to the 1960s.

The two charts are presented here to remind us that while the Great Surveys and, later, the USGS topographers were triangulating their way across the West, Powell and others had begun systematic studies of the Colorado Plateau's stratigraphy and geological history. In the 1870s Powell set two individuals to work on those studies, Clarence Dutton and Grove Karl Gilbert. Both produced masterpieces of descriptive geology that remain classics in the field.

TABLE 7.1. USGS consensus scheme of North American historical geology, 1880s

ERA	PERIOD
Era of Man	Quaternary
	Pliocene
Cenozoic, or Tertiary	Miocene
	Eocene
	Cretaceous
Mesozoic	Jurassic
	Triassic
	Permian
	Carboniferous
Paleozoic	Devonian
	Silurian
	Cambrian

Source: Powell 1881: xlviii.

TABLE 7.2. Consensus scheme of the geological history of the Plateau Province, 1960s

ERA	PERIOD	EPOCH	DURATION
	Quaternary	Holocene	11K yrs
		Pleistocene	1.6M yrs
	Tertiary	Pliocene	3.7M yrs
		Miocene	18.4M yrs
		Oligocene	12.9M yrs
		Paleocene	8.6M yrs
MESOZOIC	Cretaceous		77.6M yrs
	Jurassic		64.0M yrs
	Triassic		37.0M yrs
PALEOZOIC	Permian		51.0M yrs
EARLIER PALEOZOIC & PROTEROZOIC	Formations seen in Grand Canyon		4.0B yrs

Sources: Hintze 1988: charts 99 and 100; Hunt 1956, 1969; Stokes 1986.

CLARENCE E. DUTTON

Clarence Edward Dutton (1841–1912) was born in Wallingford, Connecticut, the son of a shoemaker and postmaster (fig. 7.1). He entered Yale in 1856 at age fifteen, graduating in 1860 "without distinction," although he rowed crew, won the senior writing prize, and established credentials as a mathematician and raconteur. He later spent two weeks at Yale's theology school until, in his words, he "left before he was thrown out."[1] In 1862 he joined the Union Army and in 1864 received an appointment as second lieutenant in the regular army, serving in the ordnance corps until his retirement. He was promoted to captain in 1873.

Dutton's first postwar assignment was to the Waterliet Arsenal near Troy, New York. There he began studying geology on the side with James Hall and Robert P. Whitfield. Hall (1811–98), a chemist by training, had joined the New York State Geological Survey in 1836 and in 1842 was appointed state paleontologist. Hall's monumental thirteen quarto volume *Paleontology of New York,* published serially between 1847 and 1894, contains nearly a thousand plates, most of them by Whitfield.[2] Stimulated by the two men, Dutton plunged into self-education in geology.

In 1871 Dutton was transferred to Washington, D.C., and soon became part of the network of government scientists centering on the Great Surveys. In 1875 John Wesley Powell, with help from Joseph Henry, secretary of the Smithsonian Institution, got Dutton detailed to his Rocky Mountain survey. Dutton's "geological detail" arrangement lasted for fifteen years. Powell managed to have various other army officers detailed to his research organizations, or ordered to work with them, over the years. The army continued to pay their salaries, and sometimes travel expenses, but they basically became full-time researchers for Powell's organizations; he thought it a capital arrangement.[3]

Dutton moved to the U.S. Geological Survey in 1879 and remained there until 1890. His major interest was volcanoes, and he made significant contributions to vulcanology. In 1890 Dutton and Powell had a falling out, and a new head of

7.1. Clarence E. Dutton, 1882. Portrait Collection, port 0043. Courtesy of the U.S. Geological Survey Digital Photography Library.

army ordnance thought that Dutton's fifteen-year research furlough at full pay was long enough. He was promoted to major and placed in command of the San Antonio Arsenal in Texas, a post he saw as being "in banishment."[4] He retired in 1901 and died in 1912.

Dutton began his western geology career with Grove Karl Gilbert and A. H. Thompson in Utah in 1875. He traveled across the High Plateau country with them and looked out onto the panorama of the Colorado drainage. He was awestruck and spent the next five years studying, mapping, and describing the country. Dutton was a keen observer and a superb wordsmith; his descriptions have defined much of the Plateau country for over a century. He did not make a detailed study of the Glen Canyon Country, as such, but our understanding of it has been shaped by four tours de force: Dutton's major works on the Colorado Plateau. His *Report on the Geology of the High Plateaus of Utah* (1880), *The Physical Geology of the Grand Cañon District* (1882), *Tertiary History of the Grand Canyon District* (1882), and *Mount Taylor and the Zuñi Plateau* (1886) are each rightfully regarded as among the great classics of nineteenth-century geology.[5]

In the introduction to Dutton's *Tertiary History*, John Wesley Powell wrote: "It is the first discussion in monographic form of the results obtained by the study of this remarkable region. The district was for many years the field of research of the present Director. . . . The first exploration of the country was made by himself; its geographic survey was largely made under his own eye; and to its geological structure he has given years of laborious study."[6] But, Powell continued, he "was by circumstances taken" from geology and went on to other things, notably anthropology.

> The change was supposed to be permanent, and he gave up all thought of continuing his work as a geologist. The abandonment of his long-cherished hope and ambition caused less regret from the fact that the subject of study could be transferred to Captain Dutton. . . . Scientific men will regret the change even less than the present Director, for Captain Dutton has pursued wise methods of research and arrived at philosophic conclusions that make his monograph a great contribution to knowledge.[7]

In his works on the Colorado Plateau Province, Dutton painted marvelous word pictures of the geological wonders he saw before him, descriptions quoted time and again over the next century and counting. In 1882, referring to the Colorado Plateau, he wrote: "In no other portion of the world are the natural laws governing the processes of land sculpture exemplified so grandly, nowhere else are their results set forth so clearly."[8] Writing of the Basin and Range Province, he said, "The great belt of cordilleras coming up through Mexico and crossing into United States territory is depicted as being composed of many short, abrupt ranges or ridges, looking upon the map like an army of caterpillars crawling northward."[9]

The cordilleras branch in southern New Mexico, with the east fork ultimately becoming the

Rocky Mountains and the west fork spreading out into the Basin and Range country of the Great Basin and extending northward into Oregon and Idaho. Between the two forks, said Dutton, is "the Plateau country."

> Standing upon any elevated spot where the radius of vision reaches out fifty or a hundred miles, the observer beholds a strange spectacle. The most conspicuous objects are the lofty and brilliantly colored cliffs. They stretch their tortuous courses across the land in all directions, yet not without system; here throwing out a great promontory, there receding in a deep bay, and continuing on and on until they sink below the horizon or swing behind some loftier mass or fade out in the distant haze. . . . In the distance may be seen the spectacle of cliff rising above and beyond cliff, like a colossal stairway leading from the plains below to the domain of the clouds above.[10]

Dutton returned to the images of the "colossal," or "grand," stairway or staircase repeatedly in his publications to describe the country as seen from atop the high plateaus—an image he borrowed from Powell, who first used it in 1873, as noted in chapter 5. Describing the Grand Canyon from that perch, he wrote:

> At the top of the stairs are the broad and lofty platforms of the High Plateaus of Utah; at the bottom is the inner expanse of the Grand Cañon District. The summits of the High Plateaus are beds of Lower Eocene age. Descending southward we cross, step by step, the terminal edges of the entire Mesozoic system and the Permian, and when we reach the inner floor of the Grand Cañon District we find that it consists of the summit beds of the Carboniferous series patched here and there with fading remnants of the Permian.[11]

Dutton's and Powell's staircase image was, of course, the basis for naming the Grand Staircase–Escalante National Monument in 1996.[12]

Dutton, like everyone else who sees the Plateau country for the first time (and indeed ever after), was struck by the colors of the land.

> The character which appeals most strongly to the eye is the coloring. The gentle tints of an eastern landscape, the pale blue of distant mountains, the green of vernal or summer vegetation, the subdued colors of hillside and meadow, are wholly wanting here, and in their place we behold belts of brilliant red, yellow, and white, which are intensified rather than alleviated by alternating belts of gray. Like the architecture [i.e., the landforms], the colors are characteristic of the geological formations, each series having its own group and range of colors. They culminate in intensity in the Permian and Lower Trias [*sic*], where dark brownish reds alternate with bands of chocolate, purple and lavender, so deep, so rich and resplendent that a painter would need to be a bold man to venture to portray them as they are.[13]

Like Newberry before him, Dutton was impressed by that most characteristic feature of the country, the canyons:

> The Plateau country is also the land of cañons, in the strictest meaning of that term . . . those long, narrow, profound trenches in the rocks, with inaccessible walls, to which the early Spaniards gave the name *cajon*, or cañon, are seldom found outside the plateaus. There they are innumerable, and the almost universal form of drainage channels. . . . All these drainage channels lead down to one great trunk channel cleft through the heart of the Plateau Province for eight hundred miles—*chasm of the Colorado*, and the cañons of its principal fork, the Green River.[14]

Dutton, also like Newberry, recognized that the principal formative agent creating the Plateau Province is water:

> Cliff and talus alike are seamed and scored with rain gullies, and if we are fortunate enough to observe the effects of a shower we shall see the waters trickling, spouting or rushing down through every seam and gully, carrying sand, mud, and small fragments with which they are charged to their utmost capacity. The meaning of this is that the cliff is wasting away, and its *locus* through the ages is farther and farther back. This backward movement of the line of frontage by slow wastage is very happily named by Powell the *Recession of Cliffs.*[15]

In an appraisal of Clarence Dutton's works, Wallace Stegner says: "Throughout both *The High Plateaus* and *The Tertiary History*, the best of his books from a literary standpoint, the observer . . . manages to write sound science, and yet to enliven and beautify it with gorgeous nature pictures. His eye is always on the object but he is capable of seeing it for its beauty as well as for its meaning."[16] Just so. But Dutton's elegant wordsmithing was enhanced by the drawings of William Henry Holmes. His panoramic drawings of the Grand Canyon in the text and the atlas of *The Tertiary History* have never been equaled.[17]

In 1871 William Henry Holmes (1846–1933) went to Washington, D.C., to study art. He soon found himself doing scientific illustrations for the Smithsonian Institution. He then signed on with the Hayden survey for the trip to Yellowstone that resulted in the area being designated by Congress as a national park in 1872. The great landscape painter Thomas Moran was on the trip, as well as a young photographer destined to be one of the greats of the nineteenth century, William Henry Jackson. In 1875 Hayden sent Jackson and Holmes into southwestern Colorado, where they discovered and brought to popular attention the "Cliff Dwellers" archaeological sites of the Mesa Verde area (chapter 13). Holmes's great skills at topographic representation made him the obvious choice to illustrate Dutton's study.

7.2. *Smithsonian Butte*, by William Henry Holmes. Dutton 1882: frontispiece.

In 1880 Dutton and Holmes traveled from Kanab, Utah, to Mount Trumbull and spent nearly a month there. Dutton studied the geology; Holmes sketched it. Dutton wrote, "[D]uring our stay at Mt. Trumbull, Mr. Holmes' magical pencil was always busy." He made panoramas from atop Mounts Trumbull, Logan, and Emma of the Toroweap Valley, "and of the superlative spectacle of the Grand Cañon as seen from Vulcan's Throne." They then traveled onto the Kaibab Plateau, where

"Mr. Holmes devoted himself to making sketches of the chasm. Among them is a panorama of the cañon from Point Sublime." They next traveled along the Vermilion Cliffs and into the Virgin River valley, where Holmes made his famed watercolor of Smithsonian Butte (fig. 7.2).[18] Holmes went on to work for the USGS, later for Powell's Bureau of Ethnology, then the U.S. National Museum, and ended his long and distinguished career as the founding director of the National Gallery of Art.[19]

GROVE KARL GILBERT AND THE HENRY MOUNTAINS

When Powell saw the "Unknown Mountains" which he later named for Joseph Henry, the founding secretary of the Smithsonian Institution, they seemed to be anomalies jutting above the sedimentary rocks at their bases (fig. 2.3). Powell was curious about the Henrys and Navajo Mountain but never visited them. Thompson's 1872 observations of the Henrys on the trip to retrieve the *Cañonita* further sparked both his and Powell's interest. In 1874 Powell found the man to study those mountains—a thirty-one-year-old geologist named Grove Karl Gilbert (1843–1918).

7.3. Grove Karl Gilbert, 1910. Portrait Collection, port 0129. Courtesy of the U.S. Geological Survey Digital Photography Library.

Gilbert (fig. 7.3) was born and raised in Rochester, New York. He was a precociously bright young lad, interested in mathematical puzzles and "games of the mind" of all sorts. He graduated from the University of Rochester in 1862 and was hired by Henry A. Ward to work in Ward's "Cosmos Hall." Ward was a faculty member at Rochester who had developed a business, at first on the campus and later as a separate organization, Henry A. Ward's Natural History Establishment. He bought and sold "artifacts of exploration": fossils, minerals, rocks, biological specimens, and Indian artifacts, both originals and replicas. Collectors scoured the world for specimens and sold them to Ward, who resold them—as well as display cases and furniture to keep them in, together with maps, charts, instruments and books—to schools, universities, and the burgeoning number of U.S. museums.

Gilbert worked for Ward for five years. In 1866 Ward sent him to Albany, New York, to help James Hall excavate the skeleton of a mastodon. This ultimately put Gilbert in touch with many leading paleontologists and geologists of the day—including, apparently, Clarence Dutton—and confirmed his interest in geology and geomorphological processes.[20]

In 1869 John Strong Newberry was hired to direct the Ohio Geological Survey. Gilbert applied for a job, but Newberry could only offer him a volunteer position and $50 a month expenses; Gilbert accepted. Newberry directed the survey part of the year and lectured at Columbia University in the winter. Gilbert became an unofficial teaching assistant for Newberry, which greatly broadened his education. Newberry told him about the Colorado Plateau and the geology of the West.[21]

In 1871 Newberry secured Gilbert a position as geologist with Wheeler's army survey. Gilbert, who had never been west of Ohio, "on May 7, 1871, amid snorting mules, blowing alkali, and blaspheming sergeants, . . . arrived at Halleck Station, Nevada" to join the other 149 soldiers and civilians of the Wheeler survey.[22] George Wheeler, like Joseph Ives, had married well, and his wife's relatives had used their influence in Washington to get him an appointment over many senior officers to map much of the West.

Wheeler had graduated from West Point in 1866 and received a commission in the Corps of Engineers. The task of surveying and mapping the West had fallen primarily to civilian surveys after the Civil War. Now the army had only one piece of the action, but Wheeler intended to make the most of it. His agenda was, first, to glorify Wheeler; second, to glorify the army; third, to one-up the other surveys whenever possible; fourth, to prospect for gold and mineral deposits (he had an under-the-table deal with some San Francisco bankers); fifth, to seek out potential military roads within, make maps of, and conduct scientific studies of the area west of the 100th meridian, which the army thought were his sole purposes.

Wheeler's initial orders were to seek feasible north-south roads across the Great Basin. As part of that task, in June 1869 he was ordered to make a "thorough and careful reconnaissance" of eastern Nevada as far south as the head of navigation of the Colorado River. He set out with thirty-six men, eight wagons, forty-eight mules, and thirty-one horses. By October 1 he had reached the confluence of the Virgin and Colorado rivers, where he heard that Professor Powell had arrived the month before.[23]

In 1871, in pursuit of agenda items 1 through 4, Wheeler, to no real purpose, led his survey across Death Valley in midsummer in what nearly was a death march. He then led a rowboat trip up the Colorado River through Black Canyon and as far as Diamond Creek in Grand Canyon. Both Gilbert and Timothy O'Sullivan, the photographer, were along on the trip. It was an arduous and pointless month-long struggle, apparently to one-up Powell, who was coming down the Colorado River that summer, although he stopped at Lee's Ferry. Pulling boats upstream through, and portaging them around, rapids was not conducive to good mapping or geological studies, but it did allow Gilbert to see a portion of the Colorado River and the Grand Canyon he had heard about from Newberry.[24]

As an aside, as part of the one-upping of Powell, but also in pursuit of his stated intent to map the entire West, Wheeler sent a party into southern Utah in 1872. One section of the party moved along the San Juan River. Another section met Thompson and Hillers in Kanab. Maps of the region later published by Wheeler were apparently based on, but not credited to, Thompson's sketch maps and triangulation data. The geologists Gregory and Moore (chapter 8) would later puzzle over the one-upping: "Strangely enough, no mention is made by Wheeler of the work of Thompson or the observations made by Powell's parties of 1869, 1871, or 1872. In fact, Wheeler ignores the work done by all the parties of the Powell survey."[25] Indeed.

In 1872 Gilbert met John Wesley Powell in Salt Lake City while he was waiting for summer fieldwork to start with the Wheeler survey. While waiting, Gilbert made his initial studies of the Pleistocene terraces formed by what he would later call Lake Bonneville. The terraces had first been noted and described by army topographical engineer Howard Stansbury during his survey of the Great Basin in 1849–50.[26]

Powell was impressed by Gilbert and introduced him into the scientific community of Washington, D.C. In 1872 Gilbert ranged widely across southern Utah and the Arizona Strip and again into the Great Basin. In 1873 Wheeler sent him to New Mexico and Arizona. Gilbert spent

1874 in Washington writing a report in which he defined the "Colorado Plateau System" and the "Basin Range System" and discussed them in terms of tectonic and erosional forces. He also published a summary of many of the ideas in his report in an elegant paper, "The Colorado Plateau Province as a Field for Geological Study." It was the first of Gilbert's geological tours de force.[27] We will return to the paper below. The next year he went to work for Powell.

In the 1870s the processes by which volcanoes form were not well understood, and there was much debate on the matter. During his river trips through Glen Canyon, Powell could see that the horizontally bedded sandstones of the country were pushed upward into domelike shapes on the flanks of the Henry Mountains. He further saw what appeared to be "lavas" atop the domes. He sent Gilbert to investigate.

Gilbert arrived at the York Ranch near Nephi, Utah, on June 20, 1875, along with A. H. Thompson, Frederick Dellenbaugh, topographer W. H. Graves, and Jack Hillers. They acquired a pack outfit, including a riding mule Gilbert christened "Lazarus, Duke of York."[28] Given mulish proclivities, it is reasonable to assume that "Lazarus" referred to the creature having to be regularly "raised from the (figurative) dead" to get him to do anything. Possibly the standard old-time Missouri joke about a hefty post or ax handle smartly applied between the eyes was the stimulus.

The party traveled up Salina Canyon, then south past Fish Lake and into the Fremont River drainage, establishing a supply camp in Rabbit Valley. After scouting Boulder Mountain and the Aquarius Plateau, the party reached the headwaters of the Escalante drainage on July 28. They then rode along the flanks of the Kaiparowits Plateau about 25 miles, moved onto the upper bench, and made a trail to the top. On August 3 they rode to the end of the plateau, took some geodetic and topographic bearings, and camped overnight.

The next day they went back down their trail and headed back to Potato Valley, where, as A. H. Thompson reported, they "saw Mormons from Panguitch who talked of making a settlement here and advised them to call the place Escalante."[29] The settlers took Thompson's advice; the village of Escalante was founded later that year (chapter 20). Gilbert then worked along the Waterpocket Fold and into Hall's Creek before reaching the Henrys. He spent about ten days in a reconnaissance of the northernmost peaks. He returned for a detailed, four-month study in the summer and fall of 1876.

Gilbert came to the conclusion that the Henry Mountains are not volcanoes. They do contain many cubic miles of igneous rock, but the rock is *intrusive*, not *extrusive*. Lavas are various forms of igneous matter extruded, or ejected, often violently, from volcanoes. The Henrys, Gilbert thought, were formed by molten igneous rock welling up through sedimentary strata, then bulging out along bedding planes into mushroom-shaped sills. The intrusive bulging pushes up the overlying sedimentary strata into dome-shaped mountains; Gilbert calls them "Bubble Mountains" in his field notebooks.[30] He called these intrusives "laccolites," later changed to "laccoliths." Gilbert's Henry Mountains study is regarded as one of the world classics in geology. It is of some interest that Gilbert's mentor, John Strong Newberry, in his report of the 1859 reconnaissance to the confluence of the Grand and Green rivers, noted that the Abajo Mountains west of Monticello, Utah, were of igneous origin and had pushed up through "the sedimentary strata." Indeed, later studies would define eight laccolithic mountain groups in the Four Corners region: the Henry Mountains, Navajo Mountain, and La Sal Mountains east of Moab, Utah; the Abajos and the Rico, La Plata, and Ute mountains in southwest Colorado; and the Carrizo Mountains in northeastern Arizona.[31]

In the 1930s Charles Butler Hunt (1906–97), of the USGS, restudied the Henry Mountains.

He would later write, "Ours was the last of the big pack-train surveying projects that had begun in the 1850s as surveys for a transcontinental railroad—the end of an era. . . . Our survey has been described as having determined in five years what Gilbert discovered in two months."[32]

Gilbert's Colorado Plateau Province

Gilbert begins his 1876 "Colorado Plateau Province" paper by stating:

> From the western edge of the Plains to the Pacific Ocean the characteristic features are mountains. The strata are bent and broken, and upturned at all angles. The typical structures are structures of displacement. Within this region of great disturbance is a restricted area of comparative calm. Dislocations of strata are not unknown in it; indeed they are of frequent occurrence; but they are less frequent, less profound, and less complex, than in the surrounding region of mountains. Its mountains are few and scattered, and its typical topographic form is the table or plateau. It is called the Colorado Plateau Province.[33]

Gilbert noted that the province covers 170,000 square miles in portions of Utah, Wyoming, Colorado, Arizona, and New Mexico and is drained chiefly by the Colorado River and its tributaries.

> The plateaus which compose it range in altitude from 5,000 to 11,000 feet above the sea, but the lines of drainage are much lower, and the streams run at the bottoms of deep gorges or cañons. The chief mountains and cliffs are of volcanic origin, and they are doubly conspicuous, since they not only constitute some of the loftiest points, but are exceptional to the general character of the topography [i.e., the Henrys and other laccolithic mountains, and various volcanic extrusions along the rim of the Grand Canyon and elsewhere].[34]

The bulk of Gilbert's article advances a brilliant, yet parsimonious, exegesis of the geomorphological processes that give form to the province: "Mountain building by displacement; mountain building by eruption; Stratigraphy, and Erosion."[35] By displacement, Gilbert meant "faults and folds," anticlines, synclines, and monoclines: "In an anticlinal fold, the strata dip in two directions away from the axis. In a synclinal fold the strata dip from two directions toward the axis. . . . [A] third type . . . involves a dip in only one direction. This is a *monoclinal* fold . . . a double flexure connecting strata at one level with the same strata at another level."[36]

Later geologists, particularly Herbert Gregory and his colleagues, would trace out and define the numerous anticlines, synclines, monoclines, and other faults that give the Colorado Plateau Province many of its unique features. For example, there is the Comb Monocline extending from the region of Kayenta, Arizona, along the east side of Monument Valley and across the San Juan River to beyond the Abajo Mountains. In the Kaiparowits region, Gregory, along with Raymond Moore, would define numerous such phenomena; for example, from east to west, the Waterpocket Monocline, the Circle Cliffs Upwarp, the Harris Syncline, the Collett Anticline, and the Escalante Monocline.[37]

Gilbert then goes on to discuss the "great blocks" that have been "unequally uplifted above the ocean which deposited their common sediments, so that each differs from its neighbor in altitude."[38] These are the numerous major and minor plateaus of the Plateau Province, for example the Kaibab, Uinkarets, and Kaiparowits plateaus.

He next turns to the extrusive lava mountains and fields found in the region—for example, in the Toroweap area of the Grand Canyon—followed by a discussion of his laccolithic "bubble domes."

Lastly, Gilbert presents an extended and brilliant discussion of the processes of erosion he calls "The Problem of the Cañons." His mentor John Strong Newberry recognized the critical importance of erosion—water, moved by gravity—in the shaping of the Plateau Province.

To recognize erosion as a major land-shaping force is one thing; to describe in detail how the geophysical processes of erosion *actually work* is another. Gilbert does just that, relating water volumes, duration of flow, and steepness and shape of channels through which water flows to the alluvial materials, from the finest sand grains to huge boulders, that are moved by the water and erode landforms by scouring, a process he calls "corrasion." He sees corrasion as the principal process in formation of canyons in the province. In short, he is saying not just that erosion happens, but *here is how it happens*—here is the *physics* of the erosional processes.[39]

Gilbert would go on to produce other major classic studies in American geology, including that of Lake Bonneville, the Pleistocene lake that at one time covered an area of present-day Utah larger than Lake Superior, and a study of the geology of the moon, presaging by six decades the USGS involvement with lunar and planetary geology. He was especially interested in geophysics and is regarded as a founder of that field. His geophysical interests extended particularly to earthquakes, and he had the scientific good luck, if one might call it that, to be in San Francisco during the 1906 earthquake. Ever the scientist, he coauthored a major report thereon.[40]

> 8 <

GLEN CANYON COUNTRY GEOLOGY IN THE TWENTIETH CENTURY

Herbert Ernest Gregory

AFTER GILBERT AND DUTTON, THE NEXT major geologist to study the Colorado Plateau was Herbert Ernest Gregory (1869–1952) (fig. 8.1). Born in Michigan, he received a bachelor's degree in 1896 and a Ph.D. in 1899 from Yale University. He remained to teach at Yale and in 1904 was named Silliman Professor of Geology. From 1919 to 1936 Gregory was director of the Bernice P. Bishop Museum in Honolulu, but continued to do geology in the Colorado Plateau country. His major studies were published by the U.S. Geological Survey, some in collaboration with Survey geologists or colleagues from various universities.

Gregory first saw the Glen Canyon Country and adjacent areas in 1900 during a field trip led by the geologist-turned-geographer Richard Elwood Dodge (1868–1952) and guided by Richard Wetherill.[1] Between 1909 and 1938 Gregory led many field trips across portions of the Colorado Plateau. In 1910, 1911, and 1913 he explored the Navajo country (as Newberry had originally called it)—the great ovoid area defined on the west by Glen Canyon, Marble Canyon, and the Little Colorado River; on the north by the San Juan River, from its confluence with the Colorado eastward to Farmington, New Mexico; on the east by the Chaco Plateau; and on the south by the Atcheson, Topeka & Santa Fe Railway, which would later be paralleled by a section of U.S. Route 66—an area of nearly 26,000 square miles.

In 1911, guided by John Wetherill, Gregory and two of his students, Joseph E. Pogue and K. C. Heald, climbed Navajo Mountain and visited Rainbow Bridge. Pogue's article in *National Geographic Magazine* in November 1911 was the first published description of the Glen Canyon Country as seen from atop Navajo Mountain.

> Recently, a United States Geological Survey party, consisting of H.E. Gregory, . . . John Wetherill, K.C. Heald, and the writer, stood upon the summit of Navaho [*sic*] Mountain and looked over a country of wildness and grandeur. Fifty miles to the north the graceful

8.1. Herbert E. Gregory, 1901. Portrait Collection, port 3554. Courtesy of the U.S. Geological Survey Digital Photography Library.

> peaks of the Henry Mountains outlined themselves against the horizon; much nearer, the Colorado and San Juan rivers united in the midst of a tilted and disjointed tableland; to the west the Colorado was already beginning to make that wonderful mile deep gash so fitly called the Grand Canyon. . . . Turn in whatever direction one would, the scene was one of overwhelming magnitude. Nearer at hand, surrounding the mountain like an island, surged a billowy sea of red sandstone, carved into fantastic, rounded, and oval masses, colossal in size, between whose cross-bedded and swirling slopes wound deep and tortuous canyons. Hidden away in such a labyrinth, it is not surprising that [Rainbow] bridge remained so long unknown. Yet it is only four miles distant . . . from the mountain's summit, and is visible from this point as a tiny arch, provided one knows exactly where to look.[2]

In 1910, 1915, 1922–23, and 1927–29 Gregory explored the 3,800-square-mile San Juan country—the great triangle defined by the Colorado River on the west, the San Juan River on the south, and the Utah-Colorado border on the east, comprising the Red Rock, Dark Canyon, and Grand Gulch plateaus and the Sage Plain, the latter first defined by Newberry. In 1915, 1918, 1922, 1925, and 1927 he explored what he called the Kaiparowits region, centered on the Kaiparowits Plateau (fig. 2.6), the Escalante River drainage, the Waterpocket Fold, and surrounding areas, comprising about 5,400 square miles. Gregory's and his colleagues' reports on these three areas, published between 1917 and 1938, are classics of reconnaissance geology. Two other major works, on the Zion Park area and the Paunsagunt Plateau, focus on adjacent regions.[3]

Dutton had drawn the big picture. Gregory was taking the next step, as he put it, "to map and interpret the geologic formations in at least sufficient detail to serve as a basis for comparative regional studies in stratigraphy, physiography, and structure."[4] Like Dutton, Gregory had a way with words. In describing the Navajo country, he wrote:

> The region bordering the Colorado canyons between Little Colorado and San Juan rivers and extending southward to the line of the Atchison, Topeka & Santa Fe Railway is difficult of access. Satisfactory maps are lacking, roads are few, and trails are poorly marked, water is scanty and generally poor, and food for animals is scarce. The white population, outside of villages along the railway and the San Juan Valley, . . . numbers 521 and includes Government officials, traders, and missionaries, living at widely separated places. The Indians, who number 32,488, are assigned to six vaguely defined reservations and are none too friendly. . . . [However,] without the kindly assistance of Peter Paquette, superintendent at Fort Defiance, and of the Franciscan Fathers at St. Michaels, who explained my work to the Navajos, the establishment of friendly relations with the Indians might have been difficult.[5]

8.2. "Glen Canyon of the Colorado, three miles east of Crossing of the Fathers, near Meskin Bar; Navajo sandstone in wall." Photograph by Herbert Gregory, 1922. Gregory Collection, ghe 00384. Courtesy of the U.S. Geological Survey Digital Photography Library.

Gregory ranged widely across the country by horseback and pack train, often guided by John Wetherill, or others, including Zeke Johnson (chapter 13). He graphically described the advantage of pack trains in his description of the Hole-in-the-Rock road from Escalante: "The 'road' is of the sort common to southern Utah—a trail along which strongly built wagons may be dragged by 4, 6, or 8 horse teams under the guidance of experienced drivers and where progress is made by 'hardening quicksands,' removing talus blocks, cutting 'dugways,' 'negotiating' sand dunes, and bumping along over knobs and sharp cut depressions of extensive surfaces of bare rock."[6] Pack animals could much more easily negotiate such "roads" as well as the difficult trails across the slickrock and up through notches in cliffs. The routes of travel Gregory followed are amazing. For example, in 1915 he and his party made

> [a] pack train traverse from Lee's Ferry along the north wall of Glen Canyon and thence northeastward across the Kaiparowits Plateau, through a region unmarked by trails [figs. 8.2, 8.3]. From the head of Collett Wash the traverse was continued to Escalante, where supplies and additional horses were obtained, thence down the Escalante River, across the Waterpocket Fold, and through the Henry Mountains to the mouth of Trachyte Creek, where the Colorado was crossed by swimming the horses and ferrying the equipment on a makeshift raft. The work of the season ended with a traverse of White Canyon and the slopes of Abajo Mountain.[7]

Commenting on the vegetation observed along the traverse, he wrote: "The high walls of hundreds of canyons are without plant cover on their faces

8.3. "Kane Spring Valley east of Gunsight Pass." Photograph by Herbert Gregory, 1922. Gregory Collection, ghe 00385. Courtesy of the U.S. Geological Survey Digital Photography Library.

and on their tops. It is possible to follow the rim of Glen Canyon from the Paria to Halls Creek and to continue the journey along the crest of the Waterpocket Fold to the Circle Cliffs without stepping on grass or passing beneath trees."[8]

In 1918 Gregory and his party, with a pack train, started at Green River, Utah, traveling to

> Temple Wash, San Rafael Swell, Pleasant Valley, Tantalus Valley, and along the Waterpocket Fold to the Colorado River at the mouths of Halls and Hanson Creeks. [Then] . . . after crossing the Waterpocket Fold at Muley Twist [Canyon], the next five weeks were devoted to an investigation of the physiography and stratigraphy of the Escalante Valley, the rim of Glen Canyon, and the Kaiparowits Plateau and the examination of the geologic features of the Paria, Wahweap, and Warm Creek Valleys at places not previously visited. . . .[9]

> [In 1925 in the San Juan country] fieldwork . . . included studies of the canyons heading in Elk Ridge, of Upper Red Canyon and of Castle Wash west of the Clay Hills Divide. . . . [T]raverses were extended from Castle Wash to the junction of the San Juan and Colorado Rivers, along Moki Canyon, Cedar Canyon, lower Red Canyon, and Glen Canyon. . . . Routes of travel were chosen with a view of gaining information regarding the large area between Comb Wash and Glen Canyon that had not been visited by scientific parties, thus providing material for a comparison of the structural and stratigraphic features of the Kaiparowits region and upper Glen Canyon with those along the San Juan River.[10]

Gregory's hard-won knowledge of the country is reflected in his description of the area at the confluence of the Colorado and San Juan rivers and nearby canyons on the Red Rock Plateau:

8.4. Gregory pack train descending a falling dune in Moqui Canyon, 1927. Photograph by Herbert Gregory. Gregory Collection, 718. Courtesy of Special Collections, Marriott Library, University of Utah.

> Traverse about the junction of the Colorado and the San Juan is possible only on foot, by scrambling in and out over smooth sandstone walls and following little crooked defiles whose floors break off into terraces toward the river. In a day's walk, covering two miles, twenty five canyons were crossed. It is a region of bare rock towers, alcoves, arches, and deep vertical walled grooves—the roughest country seen in the plateau province. . . . Moki Canyon is a narrow gorge with walls 1,000 feet high, unscalable except where sand dunes or landslides have obliterated the cliffs [fig. 8.4]. . . . Lake Canyon . . . is a trench defined by sandstone walls and joined by short, box-headed gulches.[11]

Gregory undoubtedly knew the overall geology of the regions he studied up close and personal better than anyone else, before or since. His was truly pioneering work—he called it "reconnaissance . . . and exploratory"—identifying strata and tracing and correlating them across the country, knowing (and expecting) that later workers, or he and his colleagues at later times, would amend and correct his observations and hypotheses, as indeed has been the case.

Naming the "Steps" of the Grand Staircase

Beginning with Newberry, geologists defined, redefined, named, and sometimes renamed the geologic strata of the Plateau Province. Geological practice holds that a particular stratum or formation should be named for a specific place where it can be clearly seen. For example, in his 1873 and 1876 publications Powell defined three stratigraphic "groups" prominent in the Canyon Country: the Shinarump Group, the Vermilion Cliff Group, and the White Cliff Group. Gregory named the Navajo sandstone, and grouped the Wingate, Kayenta, and Navajo strata into the Glen Canyon Group, which gives the Glen Canyon Country its particular scenic beauty.[12]

Powell, Dutton, and Gregory sometimes used Indian place-names for geological formations. Two lower groups of formations in the Glen Canyon Country are the Shinarump and Glen Canyon groups. From bottom to top the Shinarump Group contains the Moenkopi, Shinarump, and Chinle formations. Moenkopi, from the Hopi word *Munq pi*, is a place-name for a Hopi village and wash west of the Hopi mesas.[13] The Shinarump Group contains many locales with extensive deposits of petrified wood, including the area within the Petrified Forest National Monument in northern Arizona. According to Powell, "Shinarump means literally 'Shin-au-av's Rock.' Shin-au-av [or mythical wolf] is one of the gods of the [Paiute] Indians of this country and they believe these [petrified] tree trunks to have been his arrows." The linguist Edward Sapir, who studied the Southern Paiute language extensively, has the term Shinarump cïná'-'avi "wolf."[14]

"Chinle" is from the Navajo word *Ch'íní lí* "to flow out horizontally, as stream from a canyon" and refers specifically to the mouth of Canyon de Chelly, where the formation is evident. Indeed the stream emerging from the canyon mouth does spread out across the sand fan there. It was named by Gregory in 1917.[15]

The Shinarump Group is of Triassic age (Table 7.2). It is comprised of the Moenkopi shale, a sandstone and mudstone mixture overlain by the Shinarump conglomerate that contains mixed sandstones and shales, as well as quartz and quartzite pebbles and much fossil wood. Next above is the Chinle Group of shales, marls, soft sandstones, and limestone conglomerates. In Glen Canyon proper, the Chinle is visible at Lee's Ferry, and there is a 320–400 foot section at Hall's Creek where the Waterpocket Fold uplift crosses the river.[16]

The Shinarump and Chinle formations are also exposed in the Little Rincon in Glen Canyon, and I saw numerous large logs of petrified wood on the floor of the rincon when I surveyed there in 1959. Later geologists divided the Triassic formations in Glen Canyon Country into a basal Moenkopi formation and a Chinle formation with three successively younger members: Shinarump, Petrified Forest, and Owl Rock.[17]

In some areas of the Glen Canyon Country, earlier Permian age formations are visible, primarily the Cutler Group, containing shales and sandstones—notably the Cedar Mesa sandstone, which is as much as 800 to 1500 feet thick in some places, and the Halgaito formation, 400–600 feet thick. In the adjacent Monument Valley, the massive and scenic towers and buttes are composed primarily of Permian age De Chelly sandstone, defined by Gregory in 1917, and underlain by Organ Rock shale.[18] Some of the towers and buttes are capped by Moenkopi and Shinarump elements. Some earlier Pennsylvanian age formations are visible in the San Juan River canyon, notably the Honaker Trail formation.[19]

The Glen Canyon Group, defined by Gregory and Moore, is comprised from bottom to top of the Wingate, Kayenta, and Navajo formations.[20] Wingate was named by Clarence Dutton for a formation visible near Fort Wingate, south of Grants, New Mexico. The fort was established in 1862 and named for U.S. Army captain Benjamin Wingate, who was killed in 1862 in the Battle of Valverde, a major military action between Union and Confederate forces in New Mexico during the Civil War.[21]

"Kayenta" is a Southern Paiute term, q'waia -ntuɣwa "to [go] opposite, across." Gilmore and Wetherill say "Kayenta" means "Bottomless Spring three miles from the post"; that is, three miles from the Wetherill trading post near Monument Valley. Possibly the term refers to the spring as being "over there," or "across from" the point at which the viewer is standing. The Navajo name for the spring where the Wetherills built their trading post is Tó Dínéeshzhee', "rivulets or fingers of water," or "where the water runs like fingers out of the hill," which describes a place but is not cognate with "Kayenta."[22] Since the Navajo sandstone is so prominent throughout many areas of Navajo country, Gregory thought it was an appropriate term.

The walls of the main stem of Glen Canyon are comprised primarily of the massive cliff-forming and mound-forming Wingate and Navajo sandstones of Jurassic age. In places the two are separated by the Kayenta formation. The Kayenta is not always present but may be up to 180 feet thick. "In general the [Kayenta] tops a bench of Wingate sandstone and from it the Navajo is stripped back for some distance, thus forming a shelf along which a feasible route extends around the buttresses of Navajo."[23]

Gregory described the Navajo sandstone as follows: "Nearly complete sections are revealed in the walls of Navajo, and San Juan canyons, in Glen Canyon and in the scores of deep, short canyons heading in Navajo Mountain. Like the Wingate sandstone, the Navajo sandstone is everywhere a cliff-maker, but the absence of resistant cover and the friable nature of the rock results in the production of rounded forms, comprising a landscape of remarkable variety and beauty." The Navajo formation may be as much as 600 feet thick.[24]

The Jurassic age San Rafael Group lies above the Glen Canyon Group, made up from bottom to top of the Carmel, Entrada, Summerville, and Morrison formations: "At Fifty Mile Point the whole [San Rafael] group is exposed on a terrace that is capped by Morrison sandstone and underlain by Navajo. . . . On both sides of the Colorado River, the mesas and towers of San Rafael beds, capped by Morrison and Dakota, rise above the wide platforms of Navajo sandstone."[25]

THE SHAPE OF THE COUNTRY

The Glen Canyon Country consists of several thousand feet of sedimentary rocks cracked and crinkled by tectonic forces and featuring the intrusive igneous Henry Mountains and Navajo Mountain. Geologist Donald Baars has succinctly described, for a popular audience, how the major formations in the Glen Canyon Country, as part of the Colorado Plateau, came to be, and we paraphrase his description here.

At the beginning of Triassic times, there was a huge open sea covering what is now western Utah and most of Nevada. The chocolate-brown Moenkopi formation was formed by "clay-rich muds . . . deposited on intertidal mud flats in Early Triassic times, some 240 to 145 million years ago. . . . Mud cracks, small water-formed ripples, raindrop impressions, and worm burrows are ubiquitous on bedding planes throughout the Moenkopi." The sea then "retreated toward the west after the deposition of the Moenkopi, leaving the mud flats high and dry to bake in the hot sun for perhaps 10 million years. By early in the Late Triassic time, streams flowing from the south coursed across Canyonlands country, carving shallow gullies in the Moenkopi flats."[26]

The gullies in the Moenkopi formation "were filled with washed in sands and gravels forming lens-shaped conglomeratic sandstones at the base of the overlying Chinle formation." Masses of leaves, twigs, and tree trunks were also washed into the gullies from the high country. This is Powell's Shinarump conglomerate. Above it, varicolored layers of shales, siltstones, and sandstones ranging in color from grayish green to red to brown to purple were deposited. The layers were formed either as stream or lake bed deposits. They are rich in petrified woods and in uranium; the latter fueled a mining boom in the Four Corners region in the 1950s. The Chinle formation is from 400 to 600 feet thick in many areas of Canyonlands country.[27]

The following geological era is called the Jurassic (210 to 145 million years ago), during which time the rocks of the Glen Canyon Group were laid down. The lower Wingate formation was primarily of windblown origin, the winds coming from the northwest. But no one knows where all the sand came from to form the 300 to 500 foot thick Wingate formation and the 100 to 2,000 plus feet of the younger Navajo formation. It is, as Baars says, "one of the great geological mysteries of our time."[28]

After a time, streams began flowing across the Wingate sands, probably from highlands in western Colorado, laying down the water-deposited Kayenta formation. This was the time of dinosaurs, which left tracks and trails across the mudflats. But climates changed again, and the wind-blown sands of the Navajo formation were laid down in complex, cross-bedded dunes. "It is obvious that the Navajo sandstone is a giant frozen pudding of fossil sand dunes." In places, the Navajo formation is up to 2,000 feet thick, as in the Zion Canyon area. "The Navajo desert . . . was one of the most geographically widespread sand deposits found anywhere in the geologic record"—from western Colorado into Nevada, southward into southern Arizona, and northward into Wyoming.[29]

Resting atop the Navajo formation in the Glen Canyon Country are strata of the San Rafael Group—the Carmel formation, overlain by arch-forming Entrada sandstone, and then the Summerville formation, capped by the Upper Jurassic Morrison formation. Cummings Mesa—as well as many of the towers, mesas, and buttes of the Glen Canyon region (fig. 2.2)—are remnants of the San Rafael Group (for example, Gunsight and Tower buttes). These are Powell's "monuments." The Morrison formation also caps the Grand Bench, which extends westward from the Kaiparowits Plateau above Glen Canyon.

Deposition continued on a large scale in the Cretaceous period (from 146 to about 65 million years ago) on large, shallow sea floors covering much of North America. In the Glen Canyon Country, the strata of the upper portion of the Kaiparowits Plateau, capped by the Straight Cliffs formation, are of Cretaceous age (figs. 2.5, 2.6). The Straight Cliffs formation is very fossiliferous in most places. On the Kaiparowits Plateau the formation contains an estimated 15 billion short tons of coal.[30] During Tertiary times, the area continued to be covered by huge lakes that left sedimentary deposits, ultimately creating the formations seen in Bryce Canyon, Cedar Breaks, and the Pink and White Cliffs at the "top" of the Grand Staircase.

The geological crinkles and cracks—faults, monoclines, anticlines, upwarps, and so on—in the Colorado Plateau result from the forces of plate tectonics. During the years when Newberry, Powell, Dutton, Gilbert, and Gregory were defining the Colorado Plateau and adjacent regions, it was quite clear that there were major uplifting forces at work, but what generated the forces was unclear. The theory of plate tectonics, although proposed in the early part of the twentieth century, was not generally accepted until the late 1960s. How plate tectonics formed (and deformed) the topography of all of western North America, including the Colorado Plateau and the adjacent Great Basin and Rocky Mountains, over billions of years is an extremely complex story.[31]

For our purposes, it is enough to know that at about the beginning of Tertiary times, some 65 million years ago, these forces resulted in some uplifting, cracking, and overthrusting in the Glen Canyon Country that resulted in the San Rafael Swell and Reef, the Circle Cliffs and Waterpocket Fold reef, and Comb Ridge. It was also during Tertiary times, between 65 and 1.6 million years ago (no one is quite sure when within that very long period), that Gilbert's igneous laccoliths began bubbling and oozing upward to form the domes and bulges of the Henry Mountains, Navajo Mountain, the La Sals, and Abajos to the northeast, and the Carrizo Mountains to the east. As the extrusions domed up, the overlying sedimentary strata were attacked by Newberry's and Dutton's forces of erosion, which cut deep canyons in the flanks of the mountains and ultimately exposed some of the igneous extrusives.

FORMATION OF THE COLORADO RIVER SYSTEM

From Triassic through Middle Tertiary times, the Colorado Plateau was at times covered by vast seas or lakes leaving sedimentary deposits, and for a large portion of Jurassic times by enormous dune deposits, as noted above. During Cretaceous and Early to Middle Tertiary times, the lakes, when high enough, flowed out of the region, variously to the northeast or to the west. As the Wasatch Plateau continued to rise during these times, the westward flow would manage to breach and rebreach the plateau, primarily through Salina Canyon. But about 5.4 million years ago, during the later part of Miocene times, the continual uplifting blocked the westward flow, and a channel to the southwest opened. This was the beginning of the Colorado River system.

The erosional forces envisioned by Newberry, Powell, and Dutton were now in play. Cretaceous and, in some places, Tertiary deposits that once covered all of the Glen Canyon Country and the rest of the Colorado Plateau were eroded away, leaving as testimony the remnant Pink and White Cliffs, the Book Cliffs, the eastern front of the Wasatch Plateau, the upper formations of the Kaiparowits Plateau, and the caprock of Factory Butte, near Hanksville. The downcutting continued, exposing Jurassic, Triassic, and, in places, Permian formations, giving form to the core of the Glen Canyon Country, Monument Valley, and adjacent areas.

In the Grand Canyon the erosion proceeded relentlessly downward, deeper and deeper into billions of years old underlying formations.[32] It is this great geological record, from the bottom to the top of the "Grand Staircase," that so fascinated Newberry, Powell, Dutton, and Gilbert in the nineteenth century, and Gregory and dozens of other geologists throughout the twentieth century and into the twenty-first century.

> 9 <

COLORADO CANYON RAILROAD AND GOLD FEVER

Stanton and Spencer

IN 1890 AN AMBITIOUS CIVIL ENGINEER, Robert Brewster Stanton (fig. 9.1), published an article in *Scribner's*, a major popular magazine of the day, titled "Through the Grand Canyon of the Colorado."[1] Stanton recognized the value of publicity. The article was designed to call attention to a scheme he was deeply involved in: construction of a water-grade railroad down the canyon of the Grand River from Grand Junction, Colorado, to the confluence of the Grand and the Green rivers, thence through Cataract, Glen, Marble, and Grand canyons, and on to southern California, ultimately to San Diego. In 1892 he published a lengthy article in the leading American civil engineering journal laying out his scheme for the railroad in some detail.[2]

In 1893 Stanton published another popular and well-illustrated article, "Engineering with a Camera in the Canyons of the Colorado," in *Cosmopolitan Magazine.* Therein he described his canyon surveys and the successful attempt to photograph "all along the line of the survey, as to show almost a complete panorama of the river banks and the walls of the cañons from the head of the Colorado to the Gulf of California, a distance of about twelve hundred miles." In the "most difficult portions, these pictures were made to overlap each other and leave no detail of future construction without its negative to supplement and demonstrate the notes and opinions of the engineers."[3] He declared the effort a great success.

Much of the article is taken up with his version of what happened when his photographer, Franklin L. Nims, fell and shattered his leg and suffered other major injuries in Marble Canyon. Nims was carried unconscious up some 1,700 vertical feet through a narrow canyon by Stanton's men on an improvised stretcher. Stanton then walked 35 miles to Lee's Ferry, got the ferry operator, Warren Johnson, and his wagon, and returned to the canyon head and hauled Nims back to the ferry. Johnson and his wife tended Nims for twelve days while he lay unconscious. When he came to, they were able to arrange for him to be taken by wagon 185 miles to the railroad at Winslow, Arizona. He

9.1. Robert Brewster Stanton at rock art panel, Little Rincon, upper Glen Canyon, 1890s. Photographer unknown. R. B. Stanton Collection, 9-1005. Courtesy of New York Public Library.

ultimately made his way to Denver and recovery after six months. Nims kept a diary of the trip. He ends it by saying, "The company did not pay any of my expenses from the time I fell in Marble Canyon, and cut my salary off January 1st 1890, the day of the accident."[4] Stanton made no mention of this.

The last section of the article describes Stanton (who had to take over the photography) and two of his men making a perilous climb to the top of a high butte within the canyon and spending the night. They awoke to a winter sunrise over the Grand Canyon, and Stanton waxes rhapsodic over the magnificent color changes across the canyon as the sun rose:

Who can measure the force or comprehend the power that has cut these chasms, many miles long, many miles wide, and from a few hundred to six thousand two hundred feet deep?

Cataract and Narrow Cañons are wonderful, Glen Cañon is beautiful, Marble Cañon is mighty. But it is left for the Grand Cañon, where the river has cut its way down through the sandstones, the marbles, and the granites of the Kaibab Mountains, to form these beautiful and awe-inspiring pictures that are seen from the bottom of the black granite gorge, where above us rise great wondrous mountains of bright red sandstones, capped with cathedral

> domes and spires of white, with pinnacles, and turrets, and towers, in such intricate forms and flaming colors that words fail to convey any idea of their beauty and sublimity.[5]

Stanton's effusive prose caught the public's eye by giving a detailed glimpse of the wonders of the canyon country, particularly the Grand Canyon. By the mid-1890s, the Santa Fe Railway was beginning to generate interest in the Grand Canyon as a major tourist destination; Stanton's popular articles added to that interest. But his principal interest lay in the water-grade railroad through the canyons of the Colorado River.

STANTON AND THE RAILROAD

Robert Brewster Stanton (1846–1922) was educated at Miami University in Ohio, where his father, Robert Livingston Stanton, a professor of pastoral theology, was president from 1866 to 1871. Stanton's paternal uncle, Henry Brewster Stanton, was a famed nineteenth-century abolitionist whose wife was the even more famous suffragist and women's rights advocate, the formidable Elizabeth Cady Stanton. Young Stanton had a crippled left arm, but he never let it stand in the way of his ambitions. His first job was with the Atlantic and Pacific Railroad, where he worked from 1872 to 1880, moving up from survey rod man to civil engineer. In 1881 he married Jean Oliver Moore in Denver, and the same year became principal engineer on the Highland Railroad in Colorado, running between Georgetown and Leadville. The high-altitude line was famous primarily because of a 360 degree loop of tracks laid around a series of tight curves, bridges, and trestles that Stanton designed to cope with the steep elevations.[6]

An Arizona prospector, S. S. Harper, in the 1880s had followed an Atlantic and Pacific survey line through the valleys and high passes of the Rockies; he called it the "saw-tooth route."[7] Although he apparently knew very little about the Colorado River, and may even not have known about Powell's river surveys, he proposed a rail line from the western slopes of the Rockies to the California coast along the Colorado River. His idea was taken up by Frank M. Brown, a wealthy Denver realtor, who began actively promoting the idea of a water-grade railroad down the Colorado River from Grand Junction to southern California. Brown incorporated the Denver, Colorado Canyon, and Pacific Railway on March 25, 1889.

There were seemingly attractive economic reasons for building such a railroad. Coal was badly needed in southern California to provide process heat for the booming industries there. Most of the current coal supply came by ship from British Columbia and as far away as Australia. There were large coal deposits in Colorado and eastern Utah; it was thought coal therefrom could be delivered to California at a far lower cost per ton by rail. A railroad following the Colorado River would also "open up" the adjacent country to grazing and mineral exploitation. It all seemed profitable through the rose-colored glasses of speculation.

In March 1889 Brown had funded an initial survey down the Grand River from Grand Junction to its confluence with the Green River. At some point in the late 1880s, Stanton had met Brown and Harper. Now Brown hired Stanton to conduct the main engineering survey of the Colorado River canyons from the confluence to the Gulf of California and to assess resources along the way. While Stanton directed the engineering survey, Brown took personal charge of the logistics. On May 25, 1889, Brown, Stanton, and fourteen other men set out from Green River, Utah, headed for the Gulf of California. Brown had contacted John Wesley Powell seeking information about properly designed and built boats. Unfortunately, he did not pay heed to what Powell told him. Rather, the men rode in five clinker-built, thin-planked cedar boats and a flat-bottomed dory. Despite pleas from Harper and Stanton, Brown refused to take along any life preservers, a particular problem for Stanton, who had only one good arm.[8]

The survey party managed to lose two boats and many of their supplies in Cataract Canyon. Relief supplies were obtained at Dandy Crossing. There, Brown and Stanton met Cass Hite, who regaled them with the mining possibilities in the Glen Canyon Country. There also the crew was split. One group, under W. H. Bush, continued the detailed survey through Glen Canyon. An inscription "DCC + PRR," the names "E. Howard" and "G. A. Sutherland," and the date "7/14/89" were incised at the mouth of Mystery Canyon and may mark the extent of the first survey.[9] Brown and Stanton hurried on, anxious to make a minimal reconnaissance survey through the rest of the canyons.

After waiting for supplies at Lee's Ferry, they started into Marble Canyon on July 9, 1889. The next day, a boat capsized, and Brown was drowned. A few days later there was another upset, and two more men were drowned. As noted, the boats carried no life preservers. The remaining party cached their gear in the cave adjacent to Vasey's Paradise, now called Stanton's Cave, climbed out of Marble Canyon, and made their way to Denver. Stanton, now in charge of logistics, had three boats built of oak with watertight storage compartments and equipped with several safety features. "The best cork life preservers" were acquired, and Stanton required they be worn at all times on the river.[10]

In early December 1889, Stanton and twelve men in the three boats set out from Dandy Crossing. They reached Lee's Ferry just before Christmas 1889, resupplied, and hurried on. One boat was lost in Grand Canyon, but no people, although Franklin Nims fell and had to be rescued (see above). Stanton and seven men in two boats finally arrived at tidewater on the Gulf of Mexico on April 26, 1890. It was an epochal trip, comparable to Powell's first voyage.

Stanton prepared a detailed report touting the viability and eventual economic success of a railroad through the canyons. He projected some 650 miles of roadbed from Grand Junction, Colorado, to Grand Wash, at the foot of Grand Canyon. He estimated that 62.5 percent of the distance would involve "comparatively light work," in earth, loose rock, and talus slopes; 35.5 percent of "heavy" work in solid rock, cliff benches, and sloping granite walls; and 2 percent of "tunneling and half tunneling." Most of the tunneling would be in Glen Canyon, where the crooked course of the river would require "some seventeen to nineteen tunnels from 200 to 6000 feet" in length.[11] The remaining 400 miles of line along the lower Colorado would be relatively easy, Stanton said, from an engineering and road-building standpoint. When John Wesley Powell was asked about Stanton's plan, he said:

> It is an undertaking fraught with difficulties of great magnitude; in fact it is impracticable. No railroad can run along the rocks at the top of the canyon, because the whole region is a labyrinth of stupendous lateral gorges from half a mile to a mile deep. . . . and no engineering known to man can bridge them. In the main canyon the water often rises 40 to 60 feet so that the railroad would have to hang upon the sides of the cliff, which much of the way is perpendicular.[12]

Arthur M. Wellington, an expert on railroad construction, haughtily retorted: "[Powell] did not and could not see it with the eye of an engineer, for he is not one . . . we hold it to be quite impossible for any one not an engineer to form even a valuable impression of a canyon route like this for a railway."[13]

In an earlier article Wellington had said that building a railroad through the Colorado River canyons was indeed possible from an engineering standpoint and urged that it be done.[14] The implication was, given American know-how and technology, anything is possible.

After he had completed his surveys of the canyons, Stanton published a major article in the *Transactions of the American Society of Civil Engineers*, laying out his scheme and asking other leading engineers to discuss the pro and cons of his plan. He also noted that costs could be defrayed by running passenger trains back up through the canyons. But despite Stanton's "engineer's eye" and his detailed engineering, road maintenance, and economic analyses, no venture capitalists came forth with the funds, despite his concerted efforts over the next several years. The economic panic of 1893 and the discovery of oil in southern California undoubtedly contributed to the lack of interest.[15] Whether, indeed, the line could have been built remains mere conjecture. But Stanton wasn't through with the Colorado River, especially in Glen Canyon.

"MOILING" FOR GLEN CANYON COUNTRY GOLD

In his epic poem about the 1898 Yukon gold rush, "The Cremation of Sam McGee," Robert Service wrote, "There are strange things done in the midnight sun by the men who moil for gold."[16] So, too, were strange thing done in the daylight sun by the men who moiled for gold in the Glen Canyon Country from the 1860s through the 1930s.

When his railroad plan failed for lack of backers, Stanton turned to a gold-dredging scheme along the bottom of Glen Canyon. In order to understand what Stanton attempted, and to place his writings about the canyon country in context, it is necessary to develop some background. It begins, as did many stories in nineteenth-century America, with the never-satiated lust for gold.

The Glen Canyon Country was prospected for gold by Anglos perhaps as early as 1861. Gold seekers who entered Navajo Canyon in the 1880s reportedly saw the names "W. E. Mitchell," "F. Smith," something like "Seewer" or "Sethwor," and the date "1861" carved in several places and presumed they were prospectors.[17] Little else is known about these men. John Wesley Powell had contracted with Jacob Hamblin to bring supplies to the river at about the Crossing of the Fathers in 1871. When the Powell party arrived, they found one of Hamblin's men, Pardyn Dodds, accompanied by two prospectors, George Riley and John Bonnemort. Stephen Vandiver Jones, who was with Powell, wrote: "Saw gold washing here for the first time. These men say there is gold all along the river although they have not found it in paying quantities yet."[18] Few would, in the years ahead, although many tried, as we will see.

There had long been stories of Spaniards and Mexicans from New Mexico finding gold or silver south of the San Juan River, somewhere between Shiprock and Navajo Mountain. After the Navajo people returned from the Bosque Redondo captivity in the late 1860s, stories began to circulate that they were mining silver for jewelry making in the same area. No one bothered to notice that all, or nearly all, of the Navajo silver jewelry came from melted down Mexican pesos, or that the Navajos did not possess the technology to smelt ores.

In 1880 a key stimulus for a silver and, possibly, gold rush was created: rumors of a "lost mine." In that year two prospectors, James Merrick and Earnest Mitchell, were killed, perhaps by Navajos, perhaps by Utes, in Monument Valley. Some blamed Hoskininni, the leader of the Navajos who had successfully hidden out in the Navajo Mountain country in the 1860s (chapter 20). Merrick and Mitchell had discovered a "fabulously rich" silver mine, so the story ran, and Hoskininni, or other Navajos, had killed them to prevent knowledge of its whereabouts spreading and bringing other Anglos into the country. It was said that the lost mine might be somewhere in Monument Valley or somewhere around Navajo Mountain. Prospectors began moving into the Glen Canyon Country.[19]

One was Cass Hite (fig. 9.2). Little is known of Hite's early background. It was said he had been with Quantrill's Raiders in the Civil War and had knocked around and been a miner in Colorado and Montana. Hite spent some time searching for the lost Merrick-Mitchell mine, guided—and perhaps misguided—by Hoskininni, who had befriended Hite. Perhaps to keep Hite out of the Navajo Mountain area, Hoskininni told him that there was gold to be found along the Colorado River and perhaps led him there. True or not, in September 1883 Hite arrived at what he would later call Dandy Crossing near the head of Glen Canyon. There Trachyte Creek and North Wash on the right bank and White Canyon on the left bank had long offered Indian people trails from the Fremont River–Henry Mountain area to the northwest to the river and across the river, and to and from the Abajo Mountains and uplands areas to the east. Animals could swim across the river there, and people could either swim or use whatever makeshift watercraft they could devise. Hite established a ranch at the mouth of Trachyte Creek where he lived from 1883 to 1898. He then moved downstream to the mouth of Ticaboo Creek, where he lived until he died in 1912. For years his only close neighbor was Bert Loper (chapter 11), whose place was on the left bank at the mouth of Red Canyon. Both were strong minded and had a prickly friendship that lasted until Hite's death. In 1898 a post office was established in Hite's old cabin to serve the miners who staked claims downstream as far as the confluence of the San Juan River and beyond.

Hite did find small amounts of gold in the gravels along both sides of the river, and he spent most of the next three decades prospecting up and down upper Glen Canyon, knowing that one fine day he would be rich. He died broke. But the word spread, and the never-ending lust for gold drew more prospectors into the country, not only along the river, but up all the side canyons. The discovery of gold along the San Juan River in the early 1890s intensified the rush into the Glen Canyon Country.

9.2. Cass Hite, 1907. Photograph attributed to Byron Cummings. 921 P2 (12522). Courtesy of the Utah State Historical Society.

In Glen and San Juan canyons, extremely fine "flour gold" occurs in alluvial deposits. Most of it was found on the lateral, gravel-covered sandstone terraces or "bars" along the main stems of the canyons. Some were as much as 200 feet above the high-water level of the river. The gravel bars occur in Glen Canyon more frequently above the mouth of the San Juan than below, as well as in the San Juan Canyon itself.[20]

THE SAN JUAN GOLD RUSH, 1892–93

The first major gold rush into the Glen Canyon Country began in 1892 along the San Juan River, a story nicely told by James Aton and Robert McPherson.[21] Most "rushes" in nineteenth-century America were triggered by rumors started by enthusiastic, if often misguided, prospectors. Others were started by individuals or companies who planned to make money not by panning gold but by mining the pockets of eager prospectors and miners. The San Juan rush seems to have been some of both. One story goes that Jonathan P. Williams, an Indian trader who had been in the area for several years, brought some "coal" samples to Winslow, Arizona, from the San Juan area. Charles Cahn, a local businessman, had the samples analyzed, found some gold, and then went to Albuquerque to seek investment capital. He interested officials of the Atlantic and Pacific Railroad (later absorbed by the Santa Fe Railway). They announced a plan to build a railroad to the "coal field." They began sending workers and shipping machinery and lumber to their rail head and freighting it on from there. But an old prospector named French was suspicious, especially since the freighting effort took place at night. French followed the freight wagons to the San Juan and discovered that the equipment included hydraulic machinery for mining gold. Meanwhile, one Karl Snyder, an attorney in the employ of the railroad, somehow managed to become deputy county recorder in the San Juan County, Utah, courthouse and secretly filed claims on the purported gold-bearing sites along the river.[22]

Given the fineness of the aptly named "flour gold," the problem was one of feasible modes of recovery. Some form of sluicing, using hides, was one approach. Water thought to carry gold in solution was run across carpeting or hair-on animal hides. According to William Franklyn Williams, who worked with his father along the San Juan in the 1890s, cattle hides were staked in the river hair side up. The hair collected gold and silt. The hides periodically were taken out, dried and burned. The gold was recovered from the sand and ashes. "By using the hides my father got a full pound of gold (12 ounces) but it cost the company something like ten thousand dollars."[23] The return rate for others was only slightly better, but sometimes enough to keep hopes alive and buy supplies to continue. Cass Hite's hopes burned brightly in Glen Canyon for over three decades. While the Williams's technique sometimes worked in the rivers proper, other means of providing water for sluicing was needed on the gravel bars and in side canyons above river level (see below).

In addition to the "lost" Merrick-Mitchell mine, there was also a story of a "lost" ledge of pure copper. Jim Black, an early prospector in the Navajo Mountain country, related the story. In 1897 Black and two other men, Alf Dickinson and George McCormick, were prospecting along the Colorado River and in Navajo Canyon. In September they decided to return to Flagstaff. Somewhere on the Kaibito Plateau they camped for the night at the base of a ledge. The next morning one of them "noticed the dark color of the flat rocks in the ledge and took a short whack at one piece sticking out. As the [ax] blade hit a small sliver of metal peeled off." Alf Dickinson chopped off some more slivers and carried them back to Flagstaff. He thought they were valueless, "perhaps lead." A couple of years later, someone told Dickinson the slivers were pure copper. An assay proved that to be so. Dickinson did not tell his erstwhile companions about the assay results. Alf took a couple of his best friends, who furnished the money for a grub stake, and went back up there. But the trouble was he couldn't find the ledge where he had camped that night coming away from Navajo Canyon. Alf went back several more times, but to no avail. He finally confided in McCormick. "George swore he could go right back there and so the two of them packed up and went . . . [but] neither could go back to that camp." They told Black, but he did not attempt to return until World War I, when copper prices were high. "Then I couldn't find the place either." Like the Merrick-Mitchell mine, the ledge of "pure copper" remained elusive—to Black, his compatriots, and everyone else.[24]

In Glen Canyon, claims were staked on all the major, and probably most of the minor, bars from the Dirty Devil River to Lee's Ferry. A White Canyon Mining District was organized in the upper end of Glen Canyon in 1885. Prospectors in both

Glen and San Juan canyons sought "color" using a wide variety of placer devices, ranging from simple gold pans at the edges of streams to more elaborate hydraulic schemes using human muscle power, horse power, water power, or steam or gasoline power.[25] The two most elaborate of the latter were those of the Hoskininni Company and the American Placer Corporation, which brings us back to Robert Brewster Stanton.

Glen Canyon as "Nature's Sluice Box"

During the second river trip Stanton chanced to meet Jack Sumner in Glen Canyon. Sumner had been with Powell in 1869 and was now and then prospecting in the canyon. Stanton also met Edward Mesken, who had trapped and prospected in Glen Canyon for several years, and, as noted above, he met Cass Hite, staunch promoter of matters auriferous in Glen Canyon. In his railroad report Stanton had noted the possibility of profitable large-scale placer mining in Glen Canyon. People like Sumner, Mesken, and Hite were sometimes eking out a living from what they could produce with their small-scale placer or panning operations. Stanton thought the only way to make serious money was to scale up and use the high technology of the day; that is, large dredges operated by hydroelectric or some other power source.

In July and August 1891 Stanton formed a company and sent out a prospecting expedition, led by one J. D. Best, from Green River, Utah, to Lee's Ferry, using the second expedition boats and some of the personnel from both previous trips. Various mining claims were staked in Glen Canyon, and the presence of valid existing claims noted.

From 1891 to 1897 Stanton worked on a variety of railroad projects and tried, unsuccessfully, to raise money for Colorado Canyon Railroad, but, more importantly, for a large-scale mining operation in Glen Canyon. In 1897 he traveled to Columbus, Ohio, to meet with some individuals in the coal mining business, including Julius F. Stone, W. R. Mills, and Frank S. Brooks. After extended discussions the three agreed to finance Stanton to explore the possibilities of placer mining in Glen Canyon on a large scale. The Hoskininni Mining Company was formed, with Julius Stone as president, Stanton as vice-president and general manager, Brooks as secretary/treasurer, and Mills as a director. In 1899 the company was reorganized, with John R. Stanton (no relation to Robert Brewster Stanton) as president, J. Wheeler Hardley as secretary, and John Thomson, Julius F. Stone, Mills, and Brooks as directors. R. B. Stanton became vice-president and resident engineer and superintendent.[26]

The financial backing allowed Stanton to get a large drilling machine into the canyon and test the gravels. On the basis of his findings, he developed a prospectus to raise money for large-scale placer mining using dredges. It is interesting to summarize his argument, which was persuasive enough to attract the investment monies needed to undertake the operation—certainly one of the major historical events in Glen Canyon. The Hoskininni Company, Stanton wrote, had 145 placer claims, "in one continuous body, aggregating nearly nineteen thousand acres . . . together with a number of water rights, for mining and power purposes, at several rapids on the river. The property begins at the upper end of Glen Canyon, near Dandy Crossing . . . and extends down the river about 165 miles to Lee's Ferry. . . . The claims are located in one continuous body, and cover the greater part of all the placer gravel on the river for the whole distance."[27] In other words, Stanton had staked out essentially all of Glen Canyon.

Stanton then went on to sketch the geological formation of the Colorado Plateau and the river system. The plateau, "at one time in the geological ages gone by," had been the floor of an inland ocean. As the continent uplifted, the ocean basin was "tipped up on its side and the waters poured out at its southwestern edges, and the whole basin drained." This formed the Colorado River system, and as uplifting continued, the river cut into the bedrock of the old inland sea.[28]

At some point, "either when it was still under water, or about the time the first drainage began," the whole bottom of the vast inland sea was covered by "one general deposit of gold-bearing gravels to a depth of from a few feet to several hundred feet in thickness." The remains of the gravel deposit are found on what are now the high plateaus and benches. These gravels all carry gold, but "not generally in paying quantities." As side canyons were cut, "this gravel, with its gold, has been swept into the main channel and carried down its stream." The gravels and gold did not settle in Cataract Canyon or side canyons, but "precipitated . . . into Glen Canyon, and there it has been to a large extent deposited on account of the comparative level of the canyon. . . . *The gravel has been washing down the river for ages, and thus it is natural to suppose that the canyon has acted as nature's sluice box, and that, especially in the level portion of Glen Canyon, the gravel has been washed over and over and concentrated to a much higher grade*" (emphasis added).[29] Furthermore, Stanton asserted, even more gold-bearing gravel had washed down from deposits in the Wind River Mountains and the western Rockies. To potential investors, Stanton's metaphor of Glen Canyon as "nature's sluice box" was a powerful image—a 165 mile long sluice box filled with auriferous gravels!

Stanton's test borings, so laboriously carried out, demonstrated, he said, the validity of his argument. He found two gravels in the test holes, a lower "ancient" one and an upper "modern" one. The modern gravels were comprised of trachyte, sandstone, and "the usual granite, quartzite and other pebbles," and derived, he thought, from the nearby La Sal and Henry mountains, as well as Navajo Mountain, "these ranges being comparatively modern upheavals." The ancient gravels—comprised of smooth and well-worn granite, quartz, quartzite, slate, and blue limestone—were derived from the "Older Rocky Mountains proper." The ancient gravel fills the ancient river channel and the whole bottom of the gorge. On top is 30–40 feet of the modern gravel, extending from wall to wall, "and through this gravel the present river winds." The "two gravels 'in nature's sluice box,' fill the whole bottom of the '*box*'"—the present-day channel and the low-lying gravel bars.[30]

Then came the clincher: "The locations of the Hoskininni Company cover practically the whole of these low bars and all of the river channel for a distance of 165 miles, together with water rights, reservoirs and dam sites and right of way for pipe and power lines sufficient and available for mining and operating all necessary machines for working the same."[31] The company held 19,000 acres of claims, covering 15,000 acres of placer gravel, 12,000 of which could be dredged. To be conservative, Stanton estimated that there were 10,000 acres of gravel with an average depth of 35 feet—or 544,500,000 cubic yards of gravel. If, conservatively, there was a yield of 25¢ per cubic yard, that meant a gross value of $136,125,000.

The gold, Stanton asserted, was "not *flour* gold, but each little particle is a distinct little 'nugget' and settles in the sluice box with the greatest of ease and certainty when given sufficient water and proper handling. . . . So with the proper supply and adjustment of the water used in washing the screened gravel—a thing most perfectly and easily done by the machinery of a dredging plant—this gold can be successfully saved as if it were a much coarser product."[32]

Unfortunately, Stanton was quite wrong. But in his prospectus, certain that he was right, he envisioned "ten to twenty" dredges up and down Glen Canyon, all driven by hydroelectric power generated where fall of water—at the rapids—made it possible. But that was long-term.

To begin, Stanton proposed a single dredge driven by gasoline engines. Steam power required wood or coal—both in very short supply in Glen

Canyon—and the necessity of hauling a very large boiler 120 miles from the railroad to the canyon. He proposed to run the dredge on the river for six months to test the feasibility of his scheme. He worked throughout 1899 to raise the money to purchase the dredge, ship it to Glen Canyon, construct it, and then run it. His diary reflects the trials and tribulations of money raising. He was swimming with some keen and voracious investment sharks, and he knew it. Nonetheless, he did raise enough money to carry out his plan.

To keep up his claims, Stanton stayed in Glen Canyon from November 29, 1899, to the end of year, posting claims and seeing that assessment work was done. Mining law requires that the equivalent of $100 per year of improvements be done to keep legal possession of each claim. Stanton had 144 claims, hence he had to show improvements worth $14,400. Claims also had to be posted yearly to show that work was done. Otherwise, others could file on them. Stanton did most of the posting personally so he could state in court, if need be, that the posting had been done. This was necessary because others were in the canyon, and there was some claim-jumping. He wrote that he had posted 197 notices, and in so doing, "I walked over rough and rocky ground near, if not over, one hundred miles—and drove over 1200 tacks, to say nothing of the number of times I pounded my thumb in so doing!"[33]

With funding in hand, Stanton put large crews to work at Hite, Wilson Canyon, Hole-in-the-Rock, and Lee's Ferry. Stanton's original plan was to put his first dredge at Lee's Ferry, since there were existing roads to the ferry, such as they were. But in 1900 the south bank of the Colorado River became part of the Navajo reservation, so he shifted his plans upstream. At Hite, George Uden, with twenty-two men and two teams of horses, built a road along the right bank from Hite downstream around Trachyte and some other rapids, thus opening up a wagon road about 6 miles along the river; it was still passable in the late 1950s.

J. W. Wilson and a crew of twenty-five built a road from Hanksville through the Henry Mountains between Mount Hillers and Mount Pennell, through Stanton's Pass, down Hansen Creek, across Cane Springs Desert to Cane Spring, then across Hoskininni Mesa to the head of Wilson [Stanton] Canyon. Between October 20, 1899, and January 10, 1900, Wilson's crew blasted a steep road a half mile long in the right wall of Wilson Canyon, a vertical drop of 150 feet.[34] Stanton had decided to place his first dredge at the mouth of Wilson Canyon. By building the road and the dugway, he solved the problem of bringing the dredge down the river from North Wash, or upriver 2.5 miles and across the Bullfrog Rapids from the Hall's Crossing road.

At Hole-in-the-Rock, Nathaniel Galloway (chapter 11) had twenty-six men, plus a man and a girl for cooks, and a second girl as cook's helper. They carried 8,000 pounds of gear down the trail. Here the effort was to make a usable pack trail up through the "Hole," so they cut a lot of steps. They also built roads and trails upstream and downstream from the base of the Hole-in-the-Rock trail, plus more road work on the left bank of river. Basically this opened up access along the river all the way to the mouth of the San Juan.[35]

In February 1900, after further funding was secured, Stanton ordered a dredge from the Bucyrus (later Bucyrus-Erie) Company of Milwaukee, and gasoline engines from Fairbanks Morse of Chicago. The disassembled dredge, the engines, and all the related machinery, tools, and lumber were shipped by rail to Green River, Utah. There everything was loaded on heavy wagons, pulled by six- to ten-horse spans, and hauled the 100-plus miles to the steep dugway road at Wilson (Stanton) Canyon and then down to the river. The dredge was then assembled about a half mile upstream from the mouth of Wilson Canyon. Thus everything had to be transported upstream by a flat-bottomed scow, a barge, and a power launch. The boats could barely make headway against the current, but finally everything was moved, and the dredge assembled.[36]

The dredge was a flat-bottomed wooden boat 105 feet long and 36 feet wide on which the heavy machinery was installed. The machinery was powered by five gasoline engines, among the very first to be used anywhere for such work. They were all the slow-speed horizontal type. The dredge had forty-six 3 cubic feet buckets fastened to an endless chain that ran on a ladder that could be raised and lowered into the river to dig at different depths. The dredge was anchored to stationary objects on the river banks and moved horizontally by means of winches. The alluvial materials dredged up were automatically dumped into a rotating cylindrical grizzly—a coarse steel screen; while there, the materials were sprayed with high-pressure water to break them up. The gravel, or tailings, dropped onto an endless belt and were carried out over the back of the dredge and dumped back into the river. The fine sand and gravel were sluiced to get rid of the gravel; the sand was then carried over amalgamating tables, and the gold caught in an amalgamation with mercury. The amalgam was then processed in a retort to obtain free gold. This was the theory.

Actual dredging began in late February 1901. The plan was to run twenty-four hours a day, but there were numerous machinery breakdowns. Some days the system ran one or two hours; other days not at all. On March 4 Stanton recorded the "Best day's digging we have had 11 h.40 m. running." Frequent breakdowns led to only working one shift. On April 9, 1901, J. R. Stanton, John Thomson, and F. S. Knox arrived for an inspection visit. The dredge ran well, but when work was stopped and the amalgamation tables "cleaned up" on April 13, a total of $30.15 worth of gold had been recovered. Stanton was mortified. As a diversion, he showed the visitors around the upper canyon.[37]

The dredge was moved to a location suggested by Thomson and restarted. Nothing went right, according to Thomson, who apparently was the only one of the three visitors who knew anything about dredges. On April 22 Stanton recorded "All day on dredge with J.T. . . . J.T. raving and Swearing like an idiot." The party left on April 25. Stanton wrote:

> I cannot understand these men. . . . J.T. began on first arrival & praised the dredge and all work as a whole. [But] *then* he began and from that time up to 6 P.m. last night, picked to pieces every detail of the work to find fault and condemn every detail and every man . . . on the job—swearing and damning every thing and everybody. . . . But in the evening he sang a different tune . . . after swearing and grumbling all day on the dredge he came to the tent and told JRS & Knox "everything was running splendidly & gravel & work much improved"—Curious—Curious—it must be this Mormon air.[38]

Before they left, the party told Stanton that the test should run until he "was satisfied," leaving him in the dark as to what that meant. When he cleaned up again on May 7, the yield was $36.80. The total yield was thus $66.95, not a good return on what was probably an investment of tens of thousands of dollars; no one knows for sure. Stanton's diary ends on May 9 and does not start again until early September, when he met in New York City with Thomson and other directors to discuss putting the Hoskininni Mining Company into receivership. Stanton was appointed to undertake the task. He was in Salt Lake City by September 20. In the end, the biggest losers were Stanton and the Strevell Hardware Company of Salt Lake City. Stanton received about $1,500, against $5,000 he claimed was owed him. When matters were settled, there was $29.86 left to satisfy creditors. Some pieces of the dredge machinery were sold, others high-graded by miners for their own use. The dredge was left in the river; it remained visible at low water until the filling of Lake Powell (fig. 9.3).

9.3. The Stanton dredge, Glen Canyon, 1909. Photograph by Raymond Cogswell, Stone expedition, 1909, NAU. PH.97.34.149. Courtesy of Cline Library, Northern Arizona University.

Despite what Stanton had asserted in his prospectus, the gold in the riverbed and lower bar gravels *was* primarily flour gold. Large-scale dredging or other machinery simply did not work. "The surface tension of the water itself is sufficiently high to float off the powdery gold. Thus, sand, gravel *and* gold were carried right through the . . . dredge."[39] The gold on the high gravel bars was a bit coarser, and a simple sluice box lined with carpeting could catch it. Those who tried to do so with sluice boxes or various other devices sometimes made enough to cover their expenses.

Thus ended Stanton's "moiling" for gold in Glen Canyon. In 1938, at age eighty-three, Julius Stone, who was one of Stanton's investors, revisited Glen Canyon (see chapter 11) with a party that affixed a plaque at Crossing of the Fathers. On the way downriver, according to Roy Webb, "as they floated past the wreck of the Hoskininni dredge, they stopped to explore the ruin and salvage some timbers for that night's campfire. Standing by the fire that night, Stone looked into his coffee cup and reflected that the coffee was the only return he ever got from his investment in the Hoskininni Mining Company. 'This cup of coffee,' he mused, 'cost me $5000.'"[40]

The Colorado Canyon Railroad and the Glen Canyon dredging operation were only two projects in Stanton's long and otherwise successful and profitable career. After 1902 he maintained offices in New York City. He worked as a consulting civil and mining engineer all over the United States, Mexico, Cuba, Nova Scotia, England, Java, and Sumatra. He always maintained an intense interest in the Colorado River and the West, and lectured widely about both, thus bringing his views on the canyon country to many audiences. He compiled some 1,000 pages of materials toward what "would have been a monumental history of the river," including the geology and the archaeology. He died in 1922, with the project unfinished.

SLUICING THE CHINLE AND A PADDLE-WHEEL STEAMBOAT

Hopes for successfully mining Glen Canyon gold did not die with the demise of the Hoskininni Mining Company. Others were convinced that gold could be profitably harvested with the proper equipment and sufficient manpower. In May 1910 one Charles H. Spencer arrived with a group of workmen and much equipment at the fabled Lee's Ferry at the foot of Glen Canyon.[41] Their aim was to mine gold not from the riverbed, but from the Chinle shale formation that occurs at river level in the canyon walls in the area around the ferry.

Charlie Spencer (1879–1968) was born in Walsenburg, Colorado, and grew up in northwestern New Mexico and southwestern Colorado. As a young man he worked in his father's Navajo trading post along the San Juan River and periodically engaged in mining, but more often supported himself as a bull-whacker, hauling freight when and where needed by others engaged in mining and other schemes. He had very little formal schooling, but apparently much native intelligence and a silver tongue able to talk investors into supporting his many mining and other ventures. As a man who worked for him would later say, "His Western manners and the magnitude of his projects and their fabulous possibilities seemed to have an irresistible appeal to the small investor, and when one operation failed or was inconclusive, he always managed to raise more money and try again."[42]

By 1908 Spencer had gotten investors to fund a mining scheme along the San Juan River that involved crushing Wingate sandstone, amalgamating it, and extracting the gold it was thought to contain. It did, but in very minute quantities—certainly not enough to make anything resembling a profit. A second attempt at another location resulted only in more ground-up sandstone and very little gold. But a mining engineer assayed the Chinle shale at the site and determined it contained more gold than the Wingate. Furthermore, the Chinle formation was soft and crumbly—enough so that it could be sluiced with high-pressure hoses. But getting at exposed sections of the Chinle formation where there was enough water for hydraulic mining was not easy. Then Spencer learned that the formation occurred at river level at Lee's Ferry—reachable by the wagon road that used the ferry. Steam heat would be needed to drive the pumps to spray water through high-pressure nozzles. It was said there were coal deposits only a few miles away.

In May 1910, Spencer and his crew arrived at Lee's Ferry and set up shop, using driftwood for the steam boiler while they sought a good coal source. They managed to get the sluicing operation going by the spring of 1911, sending the dissolved Chinle sediments down a long flume to an amalgamator near the river. But the mercury in the amalgamator constantly became clogged, and what gold there was passed on with the tailings instead of being absorbed by the mercury. There seemed to be some "foreign element" causing the clogging. No experts could identify it.[43] Although Spencer and his men did not know what was fouling their process, they persevered.

Meanwhile, a large vein of coal was found about 6 miles upstream in Warm Creek. The mouth of Warm Creek was 28 river miles upstream from Lee's Ferry. A mining operation was established a few miles up Warm Creek from the river (fig. 9.4). Spencer's backers thought the only way to effectively move the coal to Lee's Ferry was by boat. They had a barge built, loaded it with coal, and drifted it down to Lee's Ferry. Spencer's motor launch, the *Violet Marie*, was used to move the

9.4. Remains of Warm Creek coal mine buildings, built 1912. Photograph by A. E. Turner, 1962, P557-430-6900. Courtesy of the U.S. Bureau of Reclamation.

9.5. "Steamboat 'Charles H. Spencer' on the Colorado at Lee's Ferry, [*left to right*] Captain Pete Hanna, unidentified man, 'Rip Van Winkle' Schneider, Smitty Smith, ferryman, Jerry Johnson, Bert Leach, Al Byers, 1912." Photographer unknown. Emery Kolb Collection, NAU. PH.97.34.149. Courtesy of Cline Library, Northern Arizona University.

barge back upstream. Like "The Little Tug That Could," it struggled but did tow the barge to Warm Creek. Clearly, however, it was not efficient, especially in high water. The backers then decided, without Spencer's agreement, to have a paddle-wheel steamboat built in San Francisco, dismantled, and shipped by rail and wagon to the mouth of Warm Creek. It was christened the *Charles H. Spencer* and launched in late February 1912 (fig. 9.5). It probably made two and a half trips—three downstream to Lee's Ferry, two back up. It could even tow a barge.

But by then the whole mining scheme was collapsing: the problem of the fouling of the amalgamator plates by the unknown "foreign element" could not be solved. The value of the mercury was more than the value of the gold recovered. Spencer and his crews soon left, abandoning the mining equipment and the steamboat. The hull and the boiler are still in the river near Lee's Ferry.[44]

Local legend had it that the steamboat had to use all the coal it could carry to get back upstream from Lee's Ferry to Warm Creek and hence was abandoned. Certainly this was the story I heard in the late 1950s. But a careful check of all the records indicated that the boat did make its two and a half round-trips and was abandoned because the overall mining project collapsed.[45]

LOST HOPES OF GOLD ONCE MORE

Individual prospectors continued now and then to seek the elusive gold of Glen Canyon after the demise of Charlie Spencer's sluicing operation and steamboat. There was a final rush, of sorts, in the 1930s by men seeking whatever they might find during the bleak times of the Depression. As noted in the prelude, one of those men was my uncle, Joe Bliss. Neither he nor his compatriots found any gold, and he nearly lost his life hiking up Hall's Creek and across the flanks of the Henry Mountains seeking help for his desperately ill companions. He was found, taken to Torrey, nursed back to health by my grandmother, Nettie Noyes, and ultimately married my Aunt Elva. He spent his life as a farmer and a worker in a meatpacking plant in Utah. He never returned to the Glen Canyon Country.

› 10 ‹

ROMANCING THE GLEN CANYON COUNTRY

THE FORCES OF WATER AND WIND EROSION and gravity have acted for eons on the sedimentary rocks of the Colorado Plateau to produce the many fantastic shapes described with wonder by geologists and others since the time of John Strong Newberry in the 1850s. Prominent among those shapes are natural bridges and arches (figs. 10.1, 10.2, 15.1).

RAINBOW (AND OTHER) BRIDGES

Natural bridges span watercourses; arches are rock openings through which light can be seen. One major area with these features is Arches National Park near Moab, Utah, which has some 2,100 arches of various sizes. Within the Glen Canyon Country there are numerous arches and bridges both north and south of Glen Canyon, several hundred large and small ones in the tributaries of the Escalante River alone, major bridges in White Canyon, and the incomparable Rainbow Bridge.

The three great bridges in White Canyon were known to prospectors and cattlemen by the 1880s. Cass Hite, accompanied by Scotty Ross, Edward Randolph, and Indian Joe, wandered up White Canyon in 1883 and saw all three, naming them "President," "Senator," and "Congressman." In 1895 one Emery Knowles saw the bridges, and in the same year a local cattleman, James Scorup, and two of his cowboys also saw them. In 1903 Scorup and a mining engineer, Horace J. Long, visited the bridges and renamed the two larger ones "Augusta," for Long's wife, and "Caroline," for Scorup's mother; the third they called "the Little Bridge." Long's notes were the basis for a 1904 article in *Century Magazine* by W. W. Dyar that called national attention to the bridges. Dyar's article was in turn quickly summarized in a *National Geographic Magazine* article that contained a drawing showing that Augusta Bridge "would overspan the Capitol at Washington, and clear the top of the dome by 51 feet."[1] In fact, the bridge overspan is 265 feet, and the Capitol is 289 feet high, but the comparison was close enough to give readers a sense of scale—and wonder.

10.1. Sipapu Bridge, Natural Bridges National Monument, 1925. Photograph by W. T. Lee, lwt 03144. Courtesy of the U.S. Geological Survey Digital Photography Library.

In 1905 Scorup guided a party that included a photographer, an artist, and others who were "equipped with scaling ladders and all the necessary paraphernalia" to measure the bridges.[2]

> The measurements taken of the Augusta Bridge were . . . Height, 265 feet; span 320 feet; width in narrowest part, 35 feet; and thickness, 83 feet. The . . . Caroline Bridge [was]: Height 182 feet; span 350 feet; width 60 feet, and thickness 60 feet. . . . The smaller bridge, named . . . the Edwin Bridge, for Col. Edwin F. Holmes, of Salt Lake City, [who had funded the party] measured Height, 111 feet; span, 205 feet; width 30 feet, and thickness, 10 feet, this bridge being the much more graceful and slender of the three.[3]

The artist and photographer made oil paintings and photographs of the bridges, and the former were used as illustrations in a second *National Geographic* article.[4]

The publicity about the natural bridges and the archaeological sites associated with them stimulated Byron Cummings (fig. 13.2) to lead a party to White Canyon in the summer of 1907. The party included two student archaeologists, one being Neil Judd (Cummings's nephew), two engineering students charged with mapping the bridges and ruins, a journalist, and a minister.[5] Cummings and

10.2. Gothic Arch, Soda Gulch, tributary of the Escalante River, 1944. Photograph by Herbert E. Gregory. Gregory Collection, ghe 01244. Courtesy of the U.S. Geological Survey Digital Photography Library.

the students made notes on the bridges and the archaeological sites.

In 1872 Congress had created Yellowstone National Park, using its powers to set aside portions of the public domain for Indian and military reservations and other purposes in the national interest. By the early 1900s Congress was deluged with requests to create national parks—many not of the scale or interest of Yellowstone or Yosemite. In June 1906 President T. R. Roosevelt signed the federal Antiquities Act, the base legislation for all subsequent federal historic preservation legislation. In addition to protecting archaeological sites on public lands, the act gave the president authority to create, by executive order, national monuments—relatively small areas of scenic, historic, archaeological, or scientific interest. This relieved Congress from having to deal with numerous requests to create small-scale national parks. Congress retained the authority, as it still does, to create larger, more significant, national parks.

The Antiquities Act came at a time when the conservation movement that led to creating the national forests and providing other protections for public lands was a major national priority. Some thirty national monuments were created in 1906 and 1907, including Petrified National Forest in Arizona, and numerous archaeological sites, primarily in the Southwest, notably Chaco Canyon.

The General Land Office (GLO) assigned members of its survey staff to study and map places that might be considered, or had been nominated, for national monument status. In 1908 the GLO sent William B. Douglass to map the bridges in White Canyon and evaluate them and the encompassing area for designation as a national

10.3. Rainbow Bridge, looking downstream, 1921. Photograph by S. I. Paige, pai 01475. Courtesy of the U.S. Geological Survey Digital Photography Library.

monument. Douglass's instructions were to record the Indian names for the bridges. According to Neil Judd, the local Utes had no names for the bridges, so Douglass consulted with Walter Hough, an archaeology curator at the National Museum. Hough gave him three Hopi names: Sipapu (Augusta), Kachina (Caroline), and Owachomo (Edwin).[6] Soon after receiving Douglass's report, Roosevelt proclaimed the Natural Bridges National Monument.

The next year Cummings contracted with John Wetherill to lead him to archaeological sites in southern Utah and northern Arizona. Cummings heard from Louisa Wade Wetherill that Indians had described to her a great "rainbow"-like arch somewhere in the Navajo Mountain area. In 1909 Cummings and Douglass jointly "discovered" Rainbow Bridge (fig. 10.3) (see below). Cummings hurried an article into print in the February 1910 issue of *National Geographic*, calling attention to the three bridges in White Canyon as well as Rainbow Bridge, illustrated with Young's spectacular photographs.[7] The *Century Magazine* article, the three *National Geographic* articles, and Young's photographs sparked intense interest across the country—especially in Rainbow Bridge, since it is the largest and the most inaccessible, hence the most mysterious and wondrous.

In 1911 the geologists Herbert Gregory (chapter 8), K. C. Heald, and Joseph Pogue, guided by John Wetherill, climbed Navajo Mountain. They gazed down on Rainbow Bridge, seemingly a "tiny arch" only four air-line miles distant. But to reach the bridge,

> required two days' time and a journey of 35 miles over a very indirect route, a devious and winding course . . . down the bridge canyon over a trail ever difficult and ofttimes dangerous. The way led between lofty and perpendicular cliffs towering to a sheer height of one-fifth of a mile, on whose vertical sides could now and then be descried the crumbling ruins

> of some ancient cliff-dwelling. [On down the canyon the party went, until] a towering arch, rainbow-shaped, of wonderful symmetry, rises nearly sheer from a ledge on the one side, and, spanning the stream, joins the opposite canyon wall on its downward curve. The opening, augmented by a gorge cut by the stream to a depth of 80 feet below the level of the supporting bench, measures a vertical distance of 267 feet; but the total height from stream bottom to the top of the arch is 309 feet, while the abutments at their base stand 278 feet apart. . . . It would easily span, with room to spare, the dome of the Capitol at Washington, or, if hung over the Flatiron Building of New York, its limbs would come within a few feet of the ground, though to the west of Fifth Avenue on the one hand and to the east of Broadway on the other.[8]

The dimensions of the bridge had been determined by William B. Douglass, the government surveyor, in 1909. Pogue's article, illustrated with a number of his full-page photographs of the bridge, added yet again to the sense of wonder the readers of 1911 must have felt, since many were familiar with the general heights of the Capitol (289 feet) and the twenty-two-story Flatiron Building (285 feet), completed in 1902. The statements that the Capitol would fit underneath either Rainbow Bridge or Sipapu (Augusta) Bridge have echoed down through the years in hundreds of articles and tourist brochures. Rainbow Bridge and its canyon (fig. 2.5) were first mapped in detail in 1921 by a U.S. Geological Survey team (chapter 12). In 1923 the *Geographical Review* published their article describing the bridge and discussing how it was formed by forces of erosion during the meandering downcutting of Aztec Creek and Bridge Canyon.[9]

Squabbles Under and Over Rainbow Bridge

Few who came to see Rainbow Bridge were concerned with the details of the formative geological processes that had produced it. It soon was seen in many other frameworks, one of which was who "first discovered" it. As noted above, the Cummings and Douglass party reached the bridge in June 1909. Each man's later claim to be "the first discoverer" of the bridge devolved into an acrimonious catfight over bragging rights conducted by them and their supporters in a small flood of publications and affidavits extending over fifty years. All that is certain is that two overly inflated male egos were involved.[10] The first major public statement about the "discovery" of the bridge, the February 1910 article by Cummings in *National Geographic*, gave equal credit to both parties:

> Few even of the Indians are well acquainted with the [Navajo Mountain] region. It is celebrated as the place where Hoskininni, one of the most revered leaders among the Navajo, successfully evaded Kit Carson in 1866. . . . but not even Hoskininni seems to have penetrated as far as the Nonnezoshi [Rainbow Bridge]. The members of the Utah Archaeological Expedition and of the surveying party of the U.S. General Land Office, *who visited the bridge together* on August 14, 1909, are evidently the first white men to have seen this greatest of nature's stone bridges.[11]

But the "I was first" syndrome soon began to surface. According to an official report by Douglass, dated May 1910:

> The discovery . . . may be said to date from Oct. 7, 1908, when Wm. Boone Douglass . . . reported its existence and location to the Commissioner [of the General Land Office]. . . . The information had come to Mr. Douglass from a Paiute Indian, "Mikes Boy," who later took the name of "Jim," employed as a flagman in the survey of the three great natural bridges of White Canyon. Seeing the white man's

appreciation of this form of wind and water erosion, Jim told of a greater bridge known only to himself and one other Indian, located on the north side of Navajo Mt. in the Paiute Indian reservation. Bending a twig in rainbow-shape, with its ends stuck in the ground, Jim showed what his bridge looked like. An effort was made to reach the bridge in December. Unfortunately, Jim could not be located. On reaching the Navajo trading post at Oljato [the Wetherill post], nothing was known of such a bridge, and the truth of Jim's statement was questioned.[12]

In the 1911 *National Geographic* article, Joseph Pogue backed up Douglass's statement: ""Douglass was acting under instructions from the Department of the Interior, dated October 20, 1908, to investigate a reported natural bridge in southeast Utah, with a view to making it a national monument if found of sufficient interest. An attempt was made in December 1908 to locate the bridge, but was abandoned on account of snow. The search was renewed in August 1909, the party being joined at Oljato by Cummings . . . [and] Wetherill."[13]

Later the squabble became not which man, Douglass or Cummings, *had first heard about* the bridge, but *who had first glimpsed it*, as the combined party rode down the canyon toward it. In 1927, Neil Judd wrote: "I recall vividly the distinct thrill I experienced as I . . . [rode] over the crest of a rounded knoll and saw Professor Cummings, some rods in advance, suddenly draw rein and point down canyon. Then Wetherill reached his side; they stood in silence as others gathered. . . . [I hurried forward and] caught my first glimpse of Rainbow Bridge just as Mr. Douglass joined the silent group on the rim of the inner gorge."[14] Therefore, according to Judd, Uncle Byron made the first sighting. Still later, protagonists argued over *who first rode under* Rainbow Bridge—Cummings or Douglass. Such sophistry need not detain us further. There is good evidence that white men had been to Rainbow Bridge by the 1880s and perhaps earlier (chapter 9).

Cummings's and Pogue's articles inspired even more people to see Rainbow Bridge for themselves. In 1913 one was Zane Grey, who was guided by John Wetherill and Nasja Begay. Grey returned several times over the years and made Rainbow Bridge a powerful symbol in his novels (see below). Later in the same year Wetherill guided Teddy Roosevelt to Rainbow Bridge, accompanied by his young second-cousin Nicholas Roosevelt, soon to become a prominent journalist, diplomat, and author. Teddy Roosevelt wrote, "At last we turned a corner and the huge arch of the Bridge rose in front of us. It is surely one of the wonders of the world. It is a triumphal arch rather than a bridge, and spans the torrent bed in a majesty never shared by any other arch ever reared by the mightiest conquerors among the nations of mankind." Cousin Nicholas thought, "So near is it to being a perfect arch, that it is incredible to conceive that it not made by man." The Roosevelts reported they were the eleventh party who had been there. They were soon followed by numerous others.[15]

Interpreting Rainbow Bridge

Many who made the difficult journey to Rainbow Bridge felt compelled to describe it and put it in some sort of context. In 1935–36 the prolific British essayist, novelist, playwright, broadcaster, and critic J. B. (John Baynton) Priestley (1894–1984) made a journey to America that included a trip to the American Southwest. He and his family drove from Prescott, Arizona, to Red Lake and then on to the Rainbow Lodge on the slopes of Navajo Mountain. They made a pack trip to Rainbow Bridge, led by Bill Wilson, who then ran the lodge. Priestley wrote:

> This must be one of the most wildly spectacular trails in the world. . . . It begins by wandering

in and out of a few canyons, mere little bits of gorges that would be regarded anywhere else as show places, and then suddenly launches you and your mule into the stupendous Cliff Canyon, looking down a clear 2000 feet. Then you go through Red Bud Pass, which had to be blasted out, and could do with plenty more blasting . . . and come into Bridge Canyon. The scenery of this trail cannot be adequately photographed, drawn, painted or described. It is as if the Grand Canyon had been cut up and then thrown about the landscape. . . . [I]magine yourself traveling, at all angles, between colossal sandstone cliffs, golden, orange, rust-brown, vermilion, magenta, sometimes smoothly sliced off for 500 feet or so, sometimes like 1000-foot bastions of burnished copper, sometimes tortured into weird pinnacles. . . . It is the landscape of some mad Arabian Nights story. . . . After breakfast we made our way to the Bridge. . . . The day was perfect. The sky, seen through the vast arch, was an indescribably brilliant turquoise, several shades darker than the shining stone of the bridge itself. . . . Of course, it is not really a bridge . . . but a true arch, almost symmetrical, and though 300 feet high—that is, large enough to span most great public buildings—it has a noble grace and delicacy. The view through it . . . was an enchantment. You felt you only had to walk through that noble arch to find yourself in another and better world, perhaps the Land of Contentment. Everything through there, beyond that magical frame, would be different. . . . As I loitered in that remote magical place . . . I wondered how . . . wise we are . . . when we stare at the noble rock, ask for and receive a geological explanation of its presence . . . and then go away and settle down to a game of cards. We are apt to think that because we can understand how a thing came to be shaped, we know all about it.

But an acoustic study of the workings of strings, reed and brass instruments does not explain the magic of a Beethoven symphony; it only explains the mere machinery of communication between Beethoven's rich passionate mind and ours. How do we know that the Rainbow Bridge . . . is not itself a kind of symphony, no more to be completely explained by geology than Beethoven is by acoustics?[16]

Clyde Kluckhohn (see below), in his book *Beyond the Rainbow*, provided his readers with names given to Rainbow Bridge by Paiute and Navajo peoples, and made a brief reference to legends about it:

> The Paiutes called the Bridge, Barohini—the Rainbow. The Navajos in the Navajo Canyon–Navajo Mountain region call it most often "Tsay-nun-na-ah"—Rock Goes Across the Water. In the Kayenta region, and on the reservation generally, they say "Nonnezoche"—the Arch. Only ceremonially do the Navajo say "Nonnezoche Nadzelid"—Rainbow Arch. Here, according to the Navajo Rain Chant, dwelt the Rain God, and from his home here were stolen his two beautiful wives by the builder of Pueblo Bonito, the Great Gambler of Kintyel, who approached them in the form of a butterfly.[17]

"The Great Gambler" is a Navajo story, and there are various versions of it. One tells of the Great Gambler of Kintyel (a major late Ancestral Puebloan village in northeastern Arizona) who came to Pueblo Bonito in Chaco Canyon when it and the other great houses therein were occupied by their Puebloan builders. According to archaeologists, that was in the 1000–1100s CE (chapter 20). The Gambler was said to be a member of the Butterfly clan. He had a magical substance, a strange gum, that made him a great and very successful gambler. People chewed the gum and became addicted to it and to gambling—they could not stop. Ultimately the Gambler won everything the people had—their moveable property, their villages, and the people themselves, and thus became their ruler. Finally even he became addicted to the gum. No one took care of the cornfields and religious ceremonies. Soon there was drought and starvation. The Great Gambler, blamed for all the disasters, was finally banished and then killed. But the people had to leave Chaco Canyon and settle, it was said, near the present-day pueblo of Zuni.

This version of the story does not tell about the Great Gambler traveling to Rainbow Bridge to steal away the wives of the Rain God. In still other versions, Navajo people come to Chaco Canyon, trick the Great Gambler, and magically transport him far to the south, from which he ultimately returns as the leader of the Nakai—the Mexicans.[18]

In 1927 Neil Judd gave still another version of a Navajo myth about the formation of the bridge:

> [L]ong, long ago one of their hero gods, hunting in the canyon, was suddenly entrapped by a rush of flood waters. In this predicament, with escape cut off, death for the hunter seemed unavoidable. But just then the great Sky Father cast a rainbow before the torrent, the hero god climbed to safety across the arch, the latter turned to stone and has so remained until this very day as proof to all of the omnipotence of our Sky Father and His constant watchfulness over His earth children.[19]

ZANE GREY, RAINBOW BRIDGE, AND WILD HORSE MESA

Several people who came to Rainbow Bridge from about 1913 through the 1930s were inspired to do so by the novels of Zane Grey (1872–1939). Arguably the most famous American writer of the 1920s, Grey set several of his novels in and around the Glen Canyon Country. Born Pearl Zane Gray, he grew up in Zaneville, Ohio, a town named for his great-grandfather, Revolutionary War hero Ebenezer Zane.[20] Grey attended the University of Pennsylvania on an athletic scholarship as a baseball pitcher and studied dentistry. After his 1896 graduation, he established a practice in New York City but slipped away to go fishing at every opportunity. He published his first article in 1902. In 1905 he married Lina Elise (Dolly) Roth, who encouraged him to become a full-time writer and became his editor and business manager. In 1906 they rode the Santa Fe Railway west, stopping for four days in northern Arizona, and rode mules to the bottom of the Grand Canyon. Grey was entranced.

In 1907 Grey attended a lecture in New York given by one Charles Jesse "Buffalo" Jones. Jones claimed to have been a bison hunter on the Great Plains in the 1870s, helping slaughter the animals nearly to extinction. Having done so, he saw the light, so he said, and dedicated his life to saving the species. According to one of Buffalo Bill Cody's biographers:

> I[I]n the 1890s . . . fewer than five hundred [buffalo] remained. At that nadir, a vital genetic resource of buffalo were well-cared for in the Wild West when Cody's good friend, Buffalo Jones, began using animals from [Cody's] herd as breeding stock to begin a serious restoration plan. As a result of Buffalo Jones and Cody's inspired restoration efforts, most of the major buffalo herds that remain in America today were spawned from the healthy animals in Buffalo Bill's Wild West show at the turn of the century.[21]

Jones established a herd on the Arizona Strip north of the Grand Canyon. In 1907 he was touring the East Coast giving lectures to raise money for his animal preserve. He was apparently jeered by many eastern sportsmen, but Grey believed him. Grey offered to travel to Arizona to record and write about Jones's herd to help him raise funds.

Grey traveled with Jones to Flagstaff and then on to Lee's Ferry. In addition to caring for his bison herd, Jones also led hunting parties onto the Kaibab Plateau to rope mountain lions. Grey, Jones, and three others made such a trip. They were then met by Bill Bass, who packed them down and up the Grand Canyon to his camp on the south rim. Grey returned east but came back later in the summer and spent several weeks writing at Lee's Ferry.[22] He returned again to the Kaibab Plateau and the Arizona Strip in 1908 and 1909, when he met Dave Rust (chapter 11).

In 1911 Grey hired Al Doyle to take him across the Navajo reservation. Doyle had worked on the transcontinental railroad and claimed to have been at Promontory Point on May 10, 1869, when the Union Pacific and Central Pacific met. Doyle took Grey across Monument Valley to Kayenta, where he met the Wetherills and heard about Rainbow Bridge. In 1913 Wetherill and Nasja Begay took Grey to Rainbow Bridge, where they spent some days. On the return trip they visited the archaeological ruins of Betatakin and Keet Seel.[23]

In 1914 Grey visited Kayenta and Marsh Pass but did not go into the Navajo Mountain country. In April 1922 John Wetherill again guided Grey and a party of six to Rainbow Bridge. The next year, Jesse L. Lasky, a Paramount Pictures producer, came along for another trip to the bridge. Accompanying the party was Lillian Wilhelm, an artist who was a cousin of Dolly Grey, who sometimes illustrated Grey's books. One of Wetherill's wranglers was Jesse Raymond Smith (1886–1960), a tall, good-looking man who soon caught Wilhelm's eye. They were married in 1924. Smith was apparently the model for Grey's characters Brazos Keene in *Knights of the Range* and *Twin Sombreros*, and Pecos Smith in *West of the Pecos.*

Grey incorporated Rainbow Bridge, Betatakin, Keet Seel, the Glen Canyon Country—indeed the whole canyon country, as well as John and Louisa Wetherill, and Nasja Begay—into his novels, stories, and films. Wetherill became the trader Withers in *The Rainbow Trail* (1915), Weston in *Captives of the Desert* (1952), and Bennet in the serial *The Water Hole* (1927), later published as a novel, *Lost Pueblo*, in 1954. When *Riders of the Purple Sage* appeared in 1912, Grey quickly became the doyen of western novelists, and the book, in time, the most successful western novel ever published in addition to being filmed four times.[24]

In his writing, Grey conveyed a sense of the Glen Canyon Country as a sublime place; sublime in the aesthetic sense as used in the nineteenth century, a place that inspired awe by its grandeur and its almost transcendent beauty. He was equally entranced by the people—Anglos, Indians, and Mormons—and the hard, rough life they led. He was particularly fascinated by the paradoxes (as he saw them) of the Mormons. They intrigued Grey, but he was put off by polygamy, which, despite its 1896 ban by the Church of Latter-day Saints, continued to be covertly practiced in the Arizona Strip country, as indeed it still is in the twenty-first century. He poured all of this into his novels. Jones, and various others Grey met or heard about, appeared in *The Last of the Plainsmen* (1908) and *The Heritage of the Desert* (1910).

Heritage of the Desert set the formula for Grey's western novels, a formula at least a century old when he began writing and continuing in many western novels since. One part is the white man who goes West and learns about life and what it all means from a patriarch/elder, usually by being sent on a quest. Sometimes the white man is a tenderfoot, sometimes a seasoned cowboy, often with a mysterious past, but always young enough to appreciate and worship the virginal white woman he seeks or encounters in his quest. In American literature, the patriarch is oftentimes an Indian elder, as in Cooper's Leatherstocking tales. In *Heritage of the Desert,* the patriarch is a Mormon, James

Emmett, whom Grey had met when he first went into the Country, in the guise of August Naab; in other stories it is John Wetherill under various pseudonyms. Second, there is a love story. Some end tragically if the protagonists are from different social classes or ethnic groups.

In American literature there is a tragic stock character, the pathetic dusky heroine—for example, Helen Hunt Jackson's *Ramona*.[25] She loves the white guy and so sacrifices her virtue, and often her whole self, for him. But it (usually) tragically doesn't work out, and she dies or is abandoned. An example in Grey's work is the eastern white male John Hare and the half-Indian girl Mescal in *Heritage of the Desert*. Another example is the Navajo man Nophaie and the white schoolteacher in *The Vanishing American* (see below). Finally, there is the stark black-and-white struggle of Good versus Evil, raging against the backdrops of the Glen Canyon Country and Monument Valley, both of which Grey described so vividly.

Grey's novels and stories set in the Glen Canyon Country include *The Rainbow Trail* (1915), the sequel to the *Riders of the Purple Sage; Wild Horse Mesa* (1928); *Stranger from the Tonto* (1956); "The Water Hole," later titled *Lost Pueblo* (1927, 1954); and *The Vanishing American* (1922–23, 1925). Grey was particularly awed by Rainbow Bridge, and it became a focal point in various articles and stories, such as *Tales of Lonely Trails* (1922), *The Rainbow Trail,* and *The Vanishing American.*[26]

The Rainbow Trail is the story of a quest by a young, mysterious, failed minister, John Shefford, searching for a young woman, Fay Larkin, in the secret Surprise Valley on the slopes of Navajo Mountain, which Grey had described in *Riders of the Purple Sage*. On the way, at Kayenta, he meets John and Louisa Wetherill in the guise of a trader couple named Withers. Shefford tells Withers that he is only hunting the treasure at the foot of the rainbow, but he is really searching for Fay.[27] He also encounters and befriends Nas Ta Bega, a Navajo educated in Anglo schools, modeled in part on Nasja Begay. Nas Ta Bega leads Shefford into the Navajo Mountain country in search of Fay and the secret valley. They find both. After many adventures and shoot-'em-ups, Shefford, Larkin, Nas Ta Bega, and others arrive at Nonnezsoshe, Rainbow Bridge, "at the foot of the rainbow." Grey describes the way into the bridge as follows:

> [The canyon] became a thousand-foot walled cañon, leaning, broken, threatening, with great yellow sides blocking passage, with huge sections split off from the main wall, with immense dark and gloomy caverns. . . . Its unusual formations of cavern and pillar and half arch led the mind to expect any monstrous stone-shape left by an avalanche or cataclysm. [But the bridge itself enchanted.] Here at last, apparently, was the rainbow of his boyish dreams and of his manhood—a rainbow magnified even beyond those dreams, no longer transparent and ethereal, but solidified, a thing of ages, sweeping up majestically from the red walls, its iris-hued arch against the blue sky. . . .
>
> [That night, the hero, contemplating the bridge, sees it differently:] White stars hung along the dark curved line. The rim of the arch seemed to shine. The moon must be up there somewhere. The far side of the cañon was now a blank, black wall. Over its towering rim showed a pale glow. It brightened. The shades in the cañon lightened, then a white disk of moon peered over the dark line. The bridge turned to silver, and the gloomy, shadowy belt it had cast blanched and vanished.

The next day, as they are leaving,

> Shefford knew that this would be his last look at the rainbow bridge. As he gazed the tip of the great arch lost its cold, dark stone color and began to shine. The sun had just arisen

> high enough over some low break in the wall to reach the bridge. Shefford watched. Slowly, in wondrous transformation, the gold and blue and rose and pink and purple blended their hues, softly, mistily, cloudily, until once again the arch was a rainbow. . . . Ages before life had evolved upon the earth it had spread its grand arch from wall to wall, black and mystic at night, transparent and rosy in the sunrise, at sunset a flaming curve limned against the heavens. When the race of man had passed it would, perhaps, stand there still. It was not for many eyes to see. Only by toil, sweat, endurance, blood, could any man ever look at Nonnezoshe. So it would always be alone, grand, silent, beautiful, unintelligible.[28]

To return to civilization and safety, Shefford and his party must travel to the mouth of Nonnezsoshe Boco, Rainbow Bridge Canyon. When they finally arrive there, they are in the Grand Canyon! By prearrangement, they are met by one of their party coming downriver in a scowlike boat with a steering oar at the back. After a wild ride through the rapids of Grand Canyon, *then* those of Cataract Canyon, and an unnamed smooth-water canyon reminiscent of Glen Canyon(!), Shefford and party emerge at "The Ferry," modeled, of course, on Lee's Ferry. Shefford then marries Fay, and they live happily ever after!

Despite the improbable geography, Grey introduced his readers to Rainbow Bridge, both verbally and in the book's color frontispiece. Grey's hero's fictional quest "to the foot of the rainbow" inspired a young college student, Clyde Kluckhohn (later a famous anthropologist), to make his own horseback quests to Rainbow Bridge and later to the Kaiparowits Plateau, called "Wild Horse Mesa" in Grey's *Beyond the Rainbow* (see below).

Stranger from the Tonto has a gunfighter, Kent Wingfield, from the Tonto Basin in southern Arizona, sent on a quest by a dying prospector and ex-outlaw. He is to save a girl living among a gang of rustlers and outlaws hiding out in a wonderful and secluded ranching oasis on the banks of the Colorado River in Glen Canyon at a place Grey calls "Hole in the Wall," an alternate name for Hole-in-the-Rock.[29] The girl has lived there all seventeen years of her life, innocent of the fact that her father is the "chief" of a band of outlaws. The gunfighter follows a trail that takes him up "Segi" Canyon and past "Kitseel": "Turning a cliff corner Kent came upon a colossal cavern on the left side across the face of which and high up stretched a magnificent cliff dwelling. . . . He did not waste time to halt, but he looked with eyes intent and fascinated, to imprint on his memory that weird bridge of little stone houses crossing the cavern, the vacant eyelike windows, the smoke-stained walls and the vast looming roof of yellow rock."[30]

Wingfield continues on and finds himself on the lower slopes of Navajo Mountain. Grey's description of the Glen Canyon Country as seen from that vantage point is as striking as any ever written:

> He had climbed out onto the Utah uplands. Purple rolling sage, dotted with green cedars and out-croppings of red rock, stretched down for leagues to what appeared a red-streaked haze. Kent could not hold his gaze there because of something looming black and grand to his left. It was a half-round mountain, towering into the blue, banded by sage at its base, by cedars beyond, by green pine to the domelike summit. As striking as was the front of this mountain, the north face dwarfed any other aspect of it. For that side sheered down abruptly, a riven and blasted spectacle of colored crags and cliffs, its lower half vanishing in a red chaos. . . . Kent gaze[d] down these beautiful upland steps to where they fell off into a seared and seamed gulf that reached to infinity. . . . [T]hat gulf was the crust of the

> earth, denuded of soil and green, and endless rock-ribbed region more rough and terrible than the ocean with its hurricanes. . . . [T]his stretch, two hundred miles and more, must be the canyon country of Utah. The lines and cleavages were numberless canyons. The three ragged black irregular demarcations cutting across at all angles with these were the great canyons of which he had heard—the Colorado, the Escalante, the San Juan. Surely this was the grandest scene that man's eyes had ever dwelt upon. The immensity of it limited the faculties of beauty. But an appalling beauty vied with the majesty, the sublimity of the illimitable area of rain-washed, wind-sculptured, sun blasted rock. This was Utah. This was the grand hole in the earth, and down in there somewhere, hidden, all but inaccessible, was the Hole in the Wall.[31]

From his high viewpoint, the hero descends "Noki" Canyon and crosses the San Juan River. Coming out onto the Red Rock Plateau,

> [he] halted to gaze about him in awe. There was no direction in which he could see far over the smooth rock. But all around stood up the grand landmarks that identified this canyon country. Dim black mountains [the Henrys] rose to the north; to the east ran a magnificent red escarpment [Waterpocket Fold], fringed with black, an almost endless barrier which broke off in a purple haze of distance; to the south the red and yellow sloped front of the uplands walled in the canyon area; and to the west loomed the great mountain of the Navahos, with its colossal face of colored crags and cliffs.[32]

Our hero makes his way to the Colorado River and across it to the oasis at the foot of Hole in the Wall, a far larger and more verdant area than existed at the foot of the real Hole-in-the-Rock. He does, indeed, save—and win—the girl.

The sheer eastern escarpment of the Kaiparowits Plateau inspired Grey to write a novel about "the mystery and insurmountable nature of Wild Horse Mesa . . . the last refuge of the great wild stallion, Panquitch, and his band."[33] The plot of *Wild Horse Mesa* centers on an ultimately successful attempt by mustang hunters to capture the great horse, intertwined with various conflicts over women and the usual macho displays of Grey's male characters. In the end, the horse is released and retreats once more to the refuge of the mesa, apparently to live happily ever after with his band of mares.

"The Water Hole" was published in the 1920s as a serial and years later as a novel, *Lost Pueblo* (1954). Set in the 1920s, the story is a totally improbable "Wild West comedy in the desert," as the subtitle of the story says in the magazine version. It takes place at the Kayenta trading post of John Bennet (Wetherill), in the "Segi" Canyon, and the country beyond to the north and west. The plot centers on a young, rich, and spoiled eastern socialite, Janey Endicott, whose father arranges her fake kidnapping by a dashing but honorable and idealistic young archaeologist, Phillip Randolph. The idea is she will come to love this "real man," as opposed to the effete eastern snobs who court her only for her money. Janey learns of the kidnapping in advance but goes along with it. Randolph abducts Janey and heads northwest. The trail they follow is a good description of the one Wetherill usually followed to get to Rainbow Bridge. Randolph's dream is to find a lost and buried ancient ruin called "Beckyshibeta." From the descriptions, Grey seems to have combined features of Betatakin and Keet Seel. Janey actually finds Beckyshibeta, and after various absurd subplot twists, she and the idealistic young archaeologist marry. They will give up the comfortable eastern life and excavate Beckyshibeta, which will make him rich and famous—the rich part being the most improbable plot twist of all!

Aside from all that, Grey's appreciation for the Glen Canyon Country again comes through. Soon after kidnapper and kidnappee arrive at the hiding place, Janey begins to appreciate the Country:

> The place appeared to be simply an enormous cavern with a dome higher than that of the Grand Central Station, which was going some, Janey admitted. It opened on a level bench that extended out over a green canyon, perhaps half a mile wide and twice as long. How refreshing and colorful the different kinds of foliage! It contrasted beautifully with the red and gold of colossal cliffs that sheered up as if to the very sky. . . . The stone walls were higher than any New York sky-scraper. They were full of great caverns and hollows near their base, and above were cracked and stained and covered with moss, with niches and ledges where green growths grew.[34]

Janey explores an area above where Randolph is digging and finds some steps cut in a steep slope. At the top, "[in] the smooth rock she found round polished holes where grain had been ground centuries before. She found the stone pestles lying as if a hand had laid them aside only yesterday. She found the edge of a wall buried in debris. Little red stones, neatly cut and cemented! High up she sighted a cliff dwelling pasted like [a] mud wasp's nest against the shelf of rock."[35]

Zane Grey Films in Glen Canyon Country

Beginning about 1916, 113 movies were produced based on Zane Grey novels. Some, such as *Riders of the Purple Sage* and *The Lone Star Ranger*, were produced four times each; many others two or three times.[36] At first Grey set up his own motion picture company but later sold it to Jesse Lasky, a partner of the founder of Paramount Pictures. In the 1920s Paramount had a special production unit devoted entirely to making Zane Grey movies. Grey insisted that his films be shot on location, and in the 1920s most were. *Heritage of the Desert*—with Bebe Daniels as the half-Indian girl Mescal, and Noah Berry Sr. as the villain (as he was in many of Grey's films)—was shot partly at Lee's Ferry in the fall of 1923. In 1925 *Wild Horse Mesa*—starring Jack Holt, Billie Dove, Douglas Fairbanks Jr., and Noah Berry Sr. (again as the villainous heavy)—was filmed partly at Red Lake and Kaibito, but not on the Kaiparowits Plateau. Film critics regard the 1925 version of *Wild Horse Mesa* as a classic Western, including "beautiful shots of horses running wild through canyons and over rocks." Later versions of the film starred such luminaries as Randolph Scott, Gabby Hayes, and Jim Thorpe in 1932; and Jack Holt's son, Tim, with Nan Leslie, and Jason Robards Sr. in 1947.[37] *The Water Hole* was filmed in 1928 at Kayenta, Monument Valley, and Betatakin, with Jack Holt as Phillip Randolph, the reluctant kidnapper-archaeologist, and the winsome Nancy Carroll as Janey Endicott, the willingly kidnapped socialite. *The Rainbow Trail*, filmed in 1932 partly on location, included George O'Brien as Shefford and Cecilia Parker as Fay Larkin.

The Vanishing American, the most ambitious of the Zane Grey films in the silent era, was shot in 1925 partly at Kayenta and partly at Rainbow Bridge. In the original story, serialized in 1922–23 in the *Ladies' Home Journal*, a young Navajo, Nophaie, falls in love with a white schoolteacher, goes away to the first world war, returns to the reservation, fights a corrupt, land-grabbing Indian agent, and wins and marries the schoolteacher.[38] But in the book version, things are a bit different. Nophaie is raised and educated in schools in the East, leading some critics to suggest that the character was patterned after Jim Thorpe. There he falls in love with Marian Warner, a white coed. Both wind up on the Navajo reservation and are married. Nophaie fights the corruption of the Indian Bureau and evil missionaries, and then goes off to World War I. He returns as a decorated hero, but he has come to recognize the harsh reality of being caught between two cultures.

Seeking to understand his situation, and that of his people, and cope with his bitterness about the whites destroying the Indians, he climbs Navajo Mountain, but finds no answer. Rather, he contracts influenza and almost dies, but recovers enough to make a pilgrimage to Rainbow Bridge from "Withers's" trading post, leaving Marian behind. As he rides toward the bridge, he muses:

> The Indians' deeds are done. His glory and dream are gone. His sun has set. Those of him who survive the disease and drink and poverty forced upon him must inevitably be absorbed by the race that has destroyed him. Red blood into white! It means the white race will gain and the Indian will vanish. . . . [Once at the bridge he holds a vigil beneath its shadow—and finds release from his torment.] Then to Nophaie came the secret of its great spell. Not all beauty and grandeur or mystery or immensity! These were only part of its enchantment. For Nophaie it spelled freedom. Its isolation and loneliness and solitude meant for him the uttermost peace. There dawned upon Nophaie the glory of nature. . . . The world of man, race against race, the world of men and women, of strife and greed, of hate and lust, of injustice and sordidness, the materialism of the Great War and its horrible aftermath, the rush and fever and ferocity of the modern day with its jazz and license and drink. . . . these were not here in the grand shadow of Naza. . . .
>
> For Nophaie . . . [i]n this deserted, haunted hall of the earth, peace, faith, resurging life all came simply to him. The intimation of immortality—the immanence of God! That strife of soul, so long a struggle between the Indian superstitions of his youth and the white teachings forced upon him, ended forever in his realization of the Universal God of the Indian and the white man.[39]

Having found his absolution, Nophaie finds his way back to Marian, only to die in her arms. Thus for Grey, although human life and conflict are transitory, often flawed, and evil, Rainbow Bridge symbolizes, perhaps even embodies, the ultimate, inherent goodness of nature seen as an expression of a universal God. Others came to see the bridge in similar ways.

The 1925 film version of *The Vanishing American* continues the message of history as a succession of stronger races conquering weaker ones. The film has a long prologue, beginning with a quote from Herbert Spencer about the survival of the fittest. Nophaie is a recurring character—the noble but doomed warrior savage. He appears first as a leader of the Navajos as they conquer the Cliff Dwellers. A dying Cliff Dweller predicts that a stronger race will appear and conquer the Navajos and other Native peoples. The Spanish come; Nopaie, now a Pueblo warrior, is killed again, and the Pueblos submit to the Spaniards. Finally, Kit Carson and his men conquer the Navajos, and the symbolic Nophaie dies once more. The Navajos wind up on the reservation. There Nophaie no. 4 confronts a corrupt Indian agent—and falls for the white schoolteacher. She teaches him to read and tells him about Christianity, giving him a small Bible. She convinces him that World War I is a fight for a more just world, and that when it's over, Indians will be treated better. Nophaie and many fellow Indians enlist in the army.

He saves his white rival for the schoolteacher during the war. But when Nophaie and his compatriots return home, things are worse than before. Later, as he tries to stop the fighting between Navajos and corrupt whites, he is killed by a bullet in the chest that goes through the Bible. His death as a Christian martyr brings peace. "The final scene is an extreme long shot of a lengthy procession of Indians vanishing over the horizon as they carry the body of Nophaie away."[40]

Clyde Kluckhohn's Quest for "The Foot of the Rainbow"

Among those inspired by Grey's novels was the young Clyde Kluckhohn (1905–60), who later became a leading scholarly expert on the Navajo Indians from about 1940 until his untimely death.[41] Kluckhohn was born in Le Mars, Iowa, and was adopted and raised by George and Katherine Kluckhohn. He entered Princeton University, but an illness resulting from rheumatic fever as a child forced him to go West to recuperate. He stayed on the ranch of the Evon Vogt family, west of Ramah, New Mexico. There he first encountered the Navajo people who were to fascinate him for the rest of his life. At a community dance in 1923 he heard from a cowboy about the country around Mexican Hat—and also about Rainbow Bridge. He determined to travel by horseback "to the foot of the rainbow," as characters in the Zane Grey stories had done, and continue on from there to the Grand Canyon—his own personal quest.

He set out on a circuitous route from Ramah, going eastward to Acoma and Laguna pueblos and the Rio Grande Valley, then north to Santa Fe and Taos before heading west across the Jemez Mountains. On the way to Santa Fe he encountered one Roy Anderson, a "knight of the road," who was riding from Tulsa, Oklahoma, to the Grand Canyon. Anderson agreed to throw in with Kluckhohn to go see the Rainbow Bridge.

Once across the Jemez Mountains, the men rode to Farmington, New Mexico, looped around to visit Mesa Verde, then headed southwest across the Lukachukai Mountains to Chinle and Canyon de Chelly, and thence to Kayenta and Wetherill's trading post. There they met Louisa Wetherill and various guests. They found that John Wetherill was leading Zane Grey and filmmaker Jesse Lasky to the bridge. The two did not have enough money to hire one of Wetherill's guides, so they set out on their own and ultimately made their way to the bridge.

After returning to Kayenta, the two rode west to Red Lake, then south to Tuba City and Cameron, and on to the Grand Canyon. They were able to sell their horses and gear at the canyon and hitchhiked back to Gallup, New Mexico. During their ride from the Lukachukai Mountains on, Kluckhohn met many Navajo families and became increasingly intrigued by their lifestyle and culture. He began to learn Navajo, ultimately becoming very proficient in the complex subtleties of the language. The trip covered some 2,500 miles and took about five months. Kluckhohn recorded his adventures in *To the Foot of the Rainbow*, published in 1927.

His health restored, Kluckhohn entered the University of Wisconsin, graduating with a degree in classics in 1928. Having been inspired by Zane Grey to go to Rainbow Bridge, Kluckhohn was further inspired to go "beyond the rainbow" to Grey's Wild Horse Mesa—the Kaiparowits Plateau. In 1926, with two fellow students, he set out from Ramah and headed north to Canyon de Chelly. There one of his companions broke a leg, ending the trip for that year. In 1927, with fellow students James Hanks and Lauriston Sharp (later to become a famous anthropologist in his own right), Kluckhohn started out again. This time he reached Navajo Mountain and climbed it. He repeated the erroneous heliograph story. "During 'the Navajo Wars' of the late '60's Navajo Mountain was reached by some troops of U.S. Cavalry who ascended it from the south and profaned the summit by erecting a heliograph station and carving in trees initials which are yet to be seen."[42] As previously noted, it is likely that the source of the heliograph myth was John Wetherill, or those working for him. Aside from this, Kluckhohn's description of the view from atop Navajo Mountain is well worth repeating:

> We reached the top. After a few moments of utter silence Jim said, "Why it makes the Grand Canyon look sick." Grand Canyon is a mile deep and as much as fourteen miles wide, but here we looked down 7000 feet to the Colorado and from fifty to a hundred miles in all directions. . . . To the west a Gothic tangle of tinted and untinted cliffs, clefts and mesas, culminating in the black gash of Grand Canyon. To the southwest the San Francisco Peaks, the highest mountains in Arizona, seem—as in Navajo mythology—to be supporting the blue vault of heaven. To the south all is gray and gold, still and somber. The level plateau has the restfulness of the calm sea, tessellated here and there by the blue shadows of butte obelisks and mesa islands. To the east lies Monument Valley, an archipelago of rock islands. The passion of the landscape to the north absorbs and stills all passion and restlessness of the spirit. It is a fantasy of Titans. In shadowy background one sees the fluted lines of the great plateaux [*sic*] of central Utah. Nearer is the fair dome of Abajo and the square strength of Aquarius Plateau. The whole center of the picture is filled by Wild Horse Mesa, a Colossus amid the Giants, towering above the Colorado, while monstrous buttresses fling out from its flanks like tentacles from an enormous octopus.[43]

Descending from Navajo Mountain, Kluckhohn and his party reached Rainbow Bridge. They then went down Forbidding Canyon to the Colorado River, hoping to cross and gain access to the Kaiparowits from the west, but were thwarted by high water. Kluckhohn determined to try yet again.

By 1928 Ben Wetherill had established a trading post on the north slope of Navajo Mountain. Kluckhohn, Sharp, Hanks, and two others started from there with a Navajo guide named Dogi. Dogi led them across the San Juan, thence across the Red Rock Plateau to the Colorado River. They swam their horses and mules across the river, made their way up through Hole-in-the-Rock, onto and across Fifty-Mile Bench, and onward to the top of the Kaiparowits Plateau, apparently by way of the trail up through the escarpment that emerges at the head of Trail Hollow.

They camped at a nearby spring under the rim and spent about two weeks exploring the southern end of the plateau, and especially under the rim, looking for "cliff dwellings." They found numerous such small sites, now thought to be primarily storage locales, as well as some "pueblo" surface sites in Lake Draw and farther south on the plateau.

The whole point of the journey, as Kluckhohn chronicles it in *Beyond the Rainbow*, was to believe that Zane Grey was right—no white men, at least, had previously gained access to the top of Wild Horse Mesa. But he and his compatriots soon found initials and dates carved on trees (1926, 1927) and spotted a few stray cattle. They finally came to believe that although they were not the first whites on the plateau, theirs was some sort of a moral victory—and perhaps it was. They may have been the first whites to have reached the top of the plateau by crossing the Red Rock Plateau and the Colorado River, and then making their way up through Hole-in-the-Rock, across the lower Escalante Desert, and on to the plateau. But Powell's men were atop the plateau in the 1870s, and geologist Herbert Gregory had been there at least twice, in 1915 and 1918.[44] Cattlemen from Escalante were exploring the Kaiparowits well before the end of the nineteenth century, and from the 1880s on prospectors had scoured the country along both sides of the river.

Having learned that they were not the first whites on the plateau, Kluckhohn at least thought he and his friends were the first to record archeological sites there. Perhaps not until he was hired at Harvard University in 1935 did Kluckhohn learn that Donald Scott, director of the Harvard Peabody Museum, had been on the plateau a few weeks earlier in 1928—recording archaeological sites (chapter 13). Indeed, they were not even the first tourists. In 1922 Dave Rust guided a party across the plateau (chapter 11). In the same summer as Kluckhohn's trip, according to Hoffman Birney, a Mr. and Mrs. Burnham and their nephew, with a guide and pack train provided by Hubert Richardson of Rainbow Lodge, had crossed the Colorado at Lee's Ferry, worked their way northeast across the Kaiparowits to Escalante, trailed down to Hole-in-the-Rock, and thence across the Colorado, the Red Rock Plateau, and the San Juan River. Kluckhohn and his compatriots met Birney and his party on the flanks of Navajo Mountain on their way to Rainbow Bridge.[45]

If nothing else, Kluckhohn was perhaps the first to publish memorable and vivid word pictures of what those of us who have been on the Kaiparowits have seen (figs. 18.2, 18.3). In a chapter called "God's Spies on Horseback," he writes about the views to the east:

> Though prodigal of color in the direct sunlight—an alternating sequence of green and yellow, spotted and dotted with red—the Escalante Desert was usually enveloped in a shimmering haze, a filmy mist like light sea fog, through which points of weathered sandstone glittered like whitecaps. . . . An overlapping line of rose, black, chalk-grey mesas were piled up on the southern skyline like storm clouds. To the southeast . . . [were] the myriad forms of a canyon-cleft valley through which the Escalante Canyon ran like a purple gash. To the north and east of the Escalante Canyon a twisted, gnarled, contorted rock mass of variegated hues rose shelf-like, facing canyon blocks [Waterpocket Fold]. The pink Circle Cliffs rounded off the northern skyline in a curve, while on the east, three majestic black hulks—the Henry Mountains—lay like battleships at anchor.
>
> [Coming through the trees to the rim somewhere on Navajo Point,] . . . the whole sovereign glory of the mountain burst upon us. We had seen Navajo Mountain a hundred times from a hundred angles, but never before had we been vouchsafed at one time the whole 7,000 feet [*sic*] of its height. It was enthroned over mottled maroon and white rock domes, over brilliantly colored Mesa walls, over black vermillion canyons, over the unruffled Colorado, winding like a great brown serpent between purple cliffs. . . .
>
> At first Navajo Mountain completely holds the eye. Then one sees the Henry Mountains and a deep black obelisk, El Capitan, standing sentry near Kayenta and a dark square shape with ruffled edge—Black Mesa. A sharp outline—chalk white like the cliffs of Dover on a clear day—White Mesa seems very near, though it is really just this side of Red Lake. At length the eye comes to rest on the cliffs of Cataract [Grand] canyon, far west in Arizona, and then one becomes conscious of the immensity of the scene. Its grandeur weighs upon one. It is the finest view in the Southwest . . . a master symphony in color. In the theme, red is the dominant and white the sub-dominant. As a whole the symphony keeps to the sonata form, but the view directly between the Mesa and the Mountain is the fugue. It is multi-colored, polyphonic and must be read horizontally, not vertically. The movements of the symphony are distinguished by shifting lights—scurrying cloud racers give the Scherzo.[46]

After recording more archaeological sites and further reveling in the scenery, Kluckhohn and his friends realized it was time to leave—they were running out of food. There was a final crisis. Two of the mules, Segi and Droopy, managed to gain their freedom and join whatever other horses or mules were wild on Wild Horse Mesa in the summer of 1928. Even without the miscreant mules, the party made it back to Ben Wetherill's trading post on the north side of Navajo Mountain and thence back to the world beyond. Kluckhohn tried to make one last trip in 1929, but it failed.[47]

Having finally completed his quests, Kluckhohn went to Europe—first to Vienna, where he was psychoanalyzed and met the Austrian anthropologists centered there. He was a Rhodes Scholar at Oxford in 1931–32. He then returned to the United States, married Florence Rockwood, a sociologist, and was hired as an assistant professor at the University of New Mexico. *Beyond the Rainbow* was published in 1932. In 1935 he was appointed as an instructor in anthropology at Harvard University, receiving his Ph.D. there in 1936. He remained at Harvard until his death in 1960, one of a group of brilliant scientists in the Department of Social Relations. He spent nearly every summer in New Mexico and Arizona studying and working with the Navajo people. His publications on the Navajos continue to be important fifty years after his death. At the time he died, he was one of the best known and highly respected anthropologists in America.[48]

OTHER VIEWS OF RAINBOW BRIDGE

As noted, Kluckhohn and his 1928 party encountered the writer Hoffman Birney and four companions, including John Wetherill's nephew Vent Wade, on the Rainbow Bridge trail. At the bridge, Birney wrote:

> The full moon swept into the sky from behind Navajo Mountain. The bridge was still in darkness although the crests of the lofty walls above it were touched with silver. The light moved downward slowly, down the face of the cliffs and along the canyon. It was as though some master of stage effects was deliberately postponing and delaying the final revelation of his big scene. Then finally the curving crest of the arch was touched by the light, splashed suddenly with silver paint, dripping from the moon. The lumination swept across the arch and down the graceful columns of the buttresses, fluted by vertical cleavages, with a swiftness that was breath-taking in its swift revelation of beauty.[49]

OUTLAWS IN THE GLEN CANYON COUNTRY

Another facet of romancing the Glen Canyon Country has to do with outlaws, legendary and real. The lore focuses on Robbers Roost. The canyon called Robbers Roost enters the Dirty Devil River from the east about 40 miles east-southeast of Hanksville. The sheer canyon walls were thought to make it impregnable. During the 1890s, and for a number of years thereafter, it was a hideout for various outlaws who holed up there, often with herds of rustled cattle. Some of the landmarks are still named for the outlaws who periodically resided there: Bluejohn Canyon and Bluejohn Spring for John Griffith, and Silvertip Spring for James Howells. Griffith, it was said, acquired his nickname because he had one blue eye and one brown eye; "Silvertip" was bestowed on Howells because of the white tip on the end of his beard. The two reputedly were the first outlaws to use Robbers Roost as a hideout, sometime in the early 1890s.[50]

The most famous occasional resident of Robbers Roost was George Leroy Parker, better known as Butch Cassidy. Cassidy supposedly took up periodic residence there after he and his compatriots robbed a mine payroll in Castle Gate, Utah, in 1897.[51] To many people in Utah and Wyoming, Butch Cassidy was a Robin Hood figure. Charles Kelly, in his book about Cassidy and the Robbers Roost gangs, retells a story told in 1938 by one Frank Weber, said to be the oldest resident of Hanksville. According to Weber, Cassidy told him,

> Frank, I'm not as bad as I've been painted. I done a poor feller and his wife a good turn this trip. As I was cutting across the hills I came to a run down looking outfit, but I stopped to see if I could get something to eat. There was an old man and old woman there. They had tried to make a home, but old age hit quicker'n they imagined, and the fact is they were just about to be run off the place by a feller who had a note agin' 'em. I asked 'em who this gent was and they said they looked to see him show up any minute. 'Which way will he come in?' I asks, and the old lady pointed at an old trail. I made the old lady take five hundred dollars, the amount due, and I told her to give it to the feller. I said goodby and left. I hid out along the trail and along comes a feller on a horse. He had on black clothes and I had a hunch this was the collector, so I watched him and he went to the old log cabin and the old lady let him in. Maybe five minutes later he come out. When he came up the trail I stopped him, took the five hundred—and here I am![52]

It is a great story with variants widely current throughout Wayne County and eastern Utah. My own family has two stories about Butch Cassidy. One is that my great-grandfather, Elijah Cutlar Behunin, and Cassidy had known each other for several years, and Cassidy had done "many kind things" for Elijah's family. In 1892, when Elijah, his wife, Tabatha Jane, and the kids were building a stone cabin for their family near Fruita, Butch stopped by. He carved his name in the back wall of the cabin and then had breakfast with the family. During breakfast, "Butch quietly told them that he likely would not see them again. He was leaving the country. . . . [He talked about] the respect he held for them and in parting he sadly told Cutlar that throughout his life he had looked for a woman as good and sweet as Jane! If he ever found a woman, he stated, who could cook bread as Jane could, he would buy her the world and all that was in it!"[53]

The cabin still stands as a roadside exhibit in Capitol Reef National Park. The National Park Service plastered over the carving in the 1990s, convinced it was inauthentic, perhaps having been placed there in the 1960s. Whether or not Cassidy did know Elijah and Tabatha Jane, I'm inclined to agree with James Knipmeyer that the carving is not authentic, but it is still a good story and adds to the lore of the Glen Canyon Country.[54]

The second story is a version of Cassidy and the bank mortgage. Many in my family were convinced (some still are) that a similar thing happened to my grandparents, Fred and Nettie Noyes, in Torrey (Nettie was Elijah and Tabatha Jane's oldest daughter). In the Noyes family version, Cassidy had taken a liking to Grandma Nettie, and once when he stopped for supper with the family, he heard about their plight with a bank mortgage. When he left, they found the mortgage money under his plate. The kicker was that Cassidy had supposedly robbed the bank that held the mortgage, and thus was giving the bank back its own money.

The story was actually told as the gospel truth by a venerable Mormon patriarch at my mother's funeral in the 1990s, but with a moral: even a bad outlaw can be turned to good deeds when he breaks bread with a good Mormon family. But then, in the beginning, George Leroy Parker/Butch Cassidy had come from a good Mormon family from Circleville, Utah. The only problem is, my grandparents did not own property in Torrey until some years after Cassidy fled to South America in 1901. But like the name carved in the wall, it's a good yarn.

Zane Grey wrote his *Robbers' Roost* novel in a variation of his usual format. A mysterious stranger, reputedly with a bad background, appears on the scene to work on a ranch east of the Dirty Devil River.[55] The ranch is owned by an eccentric Englishman who has a beautiful, virginal sister. The woman is kidnapped and taken to Robbers Roost. The mysterious stranger rescues the still-virginal woman from two competing bad guys after a major gun battle ending with a high body count. The two flee Robbers Roost, struggle through some very difficult country, are rescued by a kindly Mormon polygamist, and return to her brother's ranch, where they (maybe) lived happily ever after.

One of the trails leading out of the Robbers Roost country ran generally south to cross the Colorado River at Dandy Crossing, and thence up White Canyon and on into southeastern Utah and southwestern Colorado. Charles Kelly chronicles various trips by Cassidy and others back and forth along the trail. This was part of what he called the "Outlaw Trail"—routes connecting Robbers Roost with Brown's Hole, a large valley along the Green River in the area where Utah, Colorado, and Wyoming converge, and Hole-in-the-Wall in Wyoming. All three were excellent hideouts for rustlers and bank and train robbers for a number of years. The success of the 1969 Paul Newman–Robert Redford film, *Butch Cassidy and the Sundance Kid*; the 1965 Jane Fonda–Lee Marvin spoof, *Cat Ballou*; Robert Redford's 1978 *The Outlaw Trail, A Journey through Time*, a hymn to the trail, the country its branches cross, and the people who lived or passed through it then and now; and later television documentaries and dramas have kept the legends of Robbers Roost and other outlaw hideouts alive, as have various tourist-oriented Internet sites, such as "The Outlaw Trail," sponsored by the State of Utah. Finally, there is Pearl Baker's *Robbers Roost Recollections*. Her parents, Joe and Millie Biddlecome, established a cattle ranch in the Robbers Roost area early in the twentieth century, and it was worked by family members for many decades.[56]

EVERETT RUESS, "A VAGABOND FOR BEAUTY"

One of the enduring romantic stories of Glen Canyon Country is the disappearance of Everett Ruess in 1934. Ruess (1914–34?) was born and grew up in southern California, the son of a social-activist Unitarian minister and an artist mother.[57] After extended camping trips along the California coast and in the Sierra Nevada, in March 1931 he found his way to Monument Valley. He was dazzled by the country—and would continue to be so. He bought a burro for $6, a Dutch oven for $2.50, a tarpaulin for $8, and a supply of food. He wandered across the landscape, enchanted by all he saw. He often simply walked into the hogans of Navajo families—who fed him. He would continue this pattern of wandering back and forth across much of the Glen Canyon Country for portions of the next three years.

In the summer of 1934 Ruess worked for a couple of weeks as a cook for one of the Rainbow Bridge–Monument Valley Expedition archaeology crews in the Tsegi Canyon drainage (chapter 13). In mid-June 1934 he wrote his brother from Kayenta: "There is an archaeological expedition in town now. Some pretty likeable and intelligent young fellows are in it, and I expect to visit their camp when I come back from the mountains."[58]

On July 9, after returning from a solo pack trip to Navajo Mountain and Rainbow Bridge, Ruess encountered the expedition again and determined to join them. Claiborne Lockett was digging a rockshelter high in Degosho Boko (Skeleton Mesa), a site Ruess called "Lasker Marker Cave," later named Woodchuck Cave. It required an hour's climb and another hour back to get in and out of the site. Lockett decided to hire Ruess as cook so the team could camp in the cave for an extended period. Ruess apparently spent his off-duty hours painting or simply gazing out at the landscape. On July 22 Ruess wrote to his parents from the cave:

> At present I am in a cave looking out over the canyons of the Degosho Boko. The cave is in the Navajo sandstone a few feet under the rim. About three hundred [*sic*] feet below and some eighty feet back under, is Twin Caves cliff dwelling, but this cave is far more interesting.

> I have been in this locality about two weeks, working with the expedition. With me in the cave are an archaeologist, his assistant, and a photographer, who also digs. . . .
>
> We have been in the cave four days now. There is a very precarious way down the face of the cliff with footholds in the stone hundreds of years old. The only other way is the horse ladder, six miles up the canyon. We came that way with pack burros, passing the carcass of a horse that slipped. After two days wandering on the mesa top, in the trackless forests, we crossed the bare rock ledges in a heavy cloudburst and came here. . . . I have been doing the packing and the cooking here. Clayborn [*sic*] Lockett, the archaeologist in charge here, is a grizzled young chap of twenty-eight, widely experienced and a magnificent humorist. He is an ethnologist and something of an artist as well. His two helpers are boys of nineteen and twenty from the University at Berkeley. We have great fun up here by ourselves, discovering something new every day, and looking out over everything from our sheltered cave. I'm going down the cliff now to get our mail and a few camp luxuries.[59]

Soon after, Ruess left to continue his wanderings. Around November 1, 1934, he arrived in Escalante, Utah, and camped under the cottonwood trees along the river. He was cordially received and befriended by the people of the village. But in one of his final letters he wrote that he had to move on, fearing that "I would fall in love with a Mormon girl."[60] On November 12, with his two burros, he headed south along the base of the Kaiparowits Plateau. On November 19–20 he camped with two sheepherders near the head of Soda Gulch. The following day he headed out, toward Hole-in-the-Rock, he said, to make sketches. Apparently, no one ever reported seeing him again.

After his parents had received no word from him for three months, they sent inquiries to Escalante. H. Jennings Allen, a Garfield County commissioner, organized a search party. They searched Willow and Soda gulches and found nothing, but in Davis Gulch they reportedly found Ruess's burros penned into an upper part of the canyon by a brush fence. The animals apparently had plenty of grass and water, and were reported to be "fat and healthy."[61]

Searchers found food wrappers, tin cans, and indications of where a bedroll had lain. They also found Ruess's tracks in several places in the canyon, including various high alcoves containing archaeological sites. In one they found "NEMO 1934" carved on a doorway; a second "Nemo" was found elsewhere in the canyon.[62] Ruess's footprints were traced from the Davis Gulch corral to the foot of the Kaiparowits Plateau. What were not found were his bedroll, food, cook kit, paintings and paint kit, journal, and money. The tracks leading to the Kaiparowits suggested he might have used his burros to pack his gear there, returned his burros to the corral, and then climbed on foot up onto the plateau. It was thought perhaps he was then trapped there by heavy snows. A search on the plateau the following spring found nothing.[63] Other fruitless searches were organized later in 1935.

By mid-1935 rumors of what might have happened to Ruess began to circulate. He had crossed the Colorado River and taken up a new life with the Navajo people; he was murdered by cattle rustlers; he had fled to parts unknown. . . . No one knew. The "Nemo" inscriptions generated much speculation. "Nemo" is Latin for "no one"—the name taken by Captain Nemo, builder and captain of the *Nautilus* in Jules Verne's *Twenty Thousand Leagues under the Sea.* Captain Nemo's motto was *Mobilis in Mobile*, "free in a free world"—with no earthly ties. Some have speculated that Ruess was perhaps mimicking Captain Nemo—free in the wondrous world of the Glen Canyon Country, or beyond.[64]

In 1940 some of Ruess's letters, poems, and artwork were printed in a slim volume, *On Desert Trails with Everett Ruess*, generating renewed interest in his fate.[65] Thereafter, his legend grew, fueled by numerous books, articles, films, and in recent years Internet websites.[66]

In 1957 Robert Lister, employed by the University of Utah Glen Canyon Project (chapter 15), and two men from Escalante, Edson Alvey and Lloyd Gates, found some rusted metal eating utensils, kettles and pans, and a box of razor blades from the Owl Drug Company of Los Angeles in Cottonwood Canyon. The canyon is about a dozen miles from Davis Gulch but drains directly into the Colorado River at the foot of the Kaiparowits Plateau rather than into the Escalante River. The items were sent to Ruess's mother, who was uncertain if they belonged to her son.

Then, in May 2009, an article by David Roberts in *National Geographic Adventure* reported that a grave excavated in a narrow rockshelter on Comb Ridge, some 60 air-line miles from Davis Gulch, contained Ruess's remains. The determination had been made based on analyses of the skeletal remains, dentition, and a facial reconstruction by forensic scientists at the University of Colorado, Boulder. Subsequently, DNA samples were compared with those from four of Ruess's nieces and nephews (his closest living relatives). According to the Colorado forensic team, the combined skeletal, dental, facial reconstruction, and DNA evidence "make this an irrefutable case" that the remains were those of Everett Ruess.[67]

The backstory is that in 1934 a young Navajo man, Aneth Nez, purportedly witnessed the murder of a young man by Ute Indians in the streambed below Comb Ridge. They took his "mules" and his possessions. Fearing that Navajo people would be blamed for the death, he placed the body on his horse, moved it to the crevice, and buried it, leaving his saddle, which had been contaminated by the death. He did not tell anyone about the incident for more than sixty years, but finally did so. That set off a chain of events leading to the discovery of the grave.[68] The remaining mysteries are related to the burros purportedly found in Davis Gulch, how Ruess got from there to Comb Ridge, and his apparent demise.

Utah state archaeologist Kevin Jones thought the teeth were not those of a white person: they were ground down somewhat, evidence of a grit-filled diet, typical of Native people who ate corn and other grains ground on stone metates. His conclusion was confirmed by a forensic anthropologist. Jones also managed to help get new DNA tests run by the U.S. Army Forensics Laboratory, which concluded that the DNA analysis done at the ° of Colorado was faulty. When the Colorado lab could not duplicate its results, its denizens had to publicly wipe the eggs off their faces. There is no connection between the DNA from the remains and the Ruess family. So much for the "irrefutable case." The remains found in the Comb Ridge alcove were turned over to the Navajo Nation. The Everett Ruess mystery remains a mystery.[69]

11

PACK TRIPS AND RIVER RUNNING

Exploring the Country for Fun

DURING THE YEARS OF THE GLEN CANYON Project (1957–63), there was a flurry of river trips through Glen Canyon as people rushed to see it before it was inundated by Lake Powell. As river runner and historian Otis "Dock" Marston put it, "The decade of the fifties developed extensive running of the various canyons, including numerous solo runs, taxi service in skiffs and motor craft, an airplane propeller sled and bus-riding on neoprene 'baloneys.' By 1950 there was almost a need for traffic lights; in season campers numbered close to a hundred at the mouth of Aztec Creek."[1]

In 1958 and 1959, when I was on the river with my colleagues, we saw float trips fairly often, but since we spent most days working primarily in the side canyons, we undoubtedly missed many of them. We were acquainted with Frank Wright (see below), who worked with the Utah crew in 1958 and with the Museum of Northern Arizona team for three seasons—especially along the San Juan River. I did encounter the famed "woman of the river," Georgie White Clark, a couple of times. Her very large "baloney boat" rigs were sights to behold, as were the ragtag gaggles of passengers she usually had with her (see below). There were numerous Boy Scout trips led by various groups, of which more later.

What little I learned at the time about the history of boating on the Colorado River came principally in the form of anecdotes from Frank Wright. Only in later years did I begin to appreciate the long history of fast-water river running between John Wesley Powell's 1869–72 trips and the 1950s. In the last twenty-five plus years, river historians, and some expert river runners as well, have enriched that history in numerous archives, articles, and books, many of them listed in the bibliography. This section is based on their collective works and wisdom with deep appreciation.[2] What follows is only a sampling of stories about those who ran the river from 1896 to early 1963, when the gates closed on the diversion tunnels at Glen Canyon Dam.

EARLY RIVER RUNNERS

As already noted, "river running" on the Colorado River and its tributaries has a long history, dating back to at least 1826. Some of the history exists only as legend and lore. Certain individuals are thought to have run greater or lesser sections of the Colorado, Green and San Juan rivers in various sorts of conveyances, but the "evidence" consists of enigmatic inscriptions found on canyon walls, or stories that so-and-so was "said to have" run X section of the rivers in Y craft on Z dates. The word "conveyances" is used advisedly, since the devices people used, or are said to have used, to convey themselves on, or in, Colorado waters over the decades were various—ranging from log rafts to boats made of hides, canvas, wood or metal, to military-surplus neoprene rafts and bridge pontoons (collectively called "baloney boats"), to life preservers, swim fins, and air mattresses. All of these are part of the history of experimentation to discover which boats would best withstand the rapids and frequent pounding on rocks, and which could best be guided through them.

GEORGE FLAVELL AND THE PANTHON

The trips made by Robert Brewster Stanton and his colleagues are discussed in chapter 9. We begin here with those who followed, starting with George F. Flavell, a frontiersman and professional hunter. On August 27, 1896, he and Ramón Montéz, a friend from San Fernando, California, launched a 15-1/2 foot boat at Green River, Wyoming, "with the intention," as Flavell wrote in his journal, "of running down Green River into the Colorado River, and on down through the Grand Canyon to Yuma. . . . As the whistle blew for the noon hour we pushed out on what will, without doubt, be a very interesting if not dangerous trip."[3] Sixty-five days later, they emerged from the Grand Canyon and then continued on to Yuma, Arizona. Flavell kept a detailed journal of the trip, but it did not become available until 1987.

Flavell was born about 1864 in Jefferson, New Jersey, one of six children of Jeremiah and Anna Flavell. He left home at about age fifteen. He apparently learned some sailing and shipwright skills in Philadelphia, then later moved to California, where he supported himself as a commercial hunter and trapper. By about 1890 George and his brother Roland were hunting and trapping beaver, coyotes, and birds from the Colorado River delta to the mouth of Grand Canyon. They spent the cooler months of the year on the California coast. Roland returned east in 1893. The same year George built a 30-foot-long, flat-bottomed, two-masted boat, which he called the *Dart*, and sailed it alone from Yuma to Guaymas, Sonora, and back. He continued to work as a trapper and hunter, mainly along the lower Colorado. At some point Flavell met Ramón Montéz and invited him to come along on a trip down the Colorado River. Montéz apparently knew little about wilderness or river travel, but went along for the ride.

The only description of the *Panthon* is in a letter from John Hislop to Robert Brewster Stanton, written a couple of weeks after he had fed the two men and looked over their boat when they stopped at Green River: "Their boat is a flat bottomed boat with a broad, square stern, two oars worked by one man in the bow who faces to the bow and pushes on the oars. No steering or extra oars. The other man sits on a load in the stern. The oarsman sits on a box when not standing. No airtight compartments. Boat built by themselves and shod with [iron] wagon tires, etc. Have 750 feet of rope."[4]

Flavell's design had three features making it more suitable for running river rapids than were Powell's and Stanton's boats: flat bottomed, shod with strips of iron (recycled wagon tires) as guards against rocks, and the oarsman facing forward, pushing rather than pulling on the oars. As earlier river runners had discovered, running rapids while rowing and looking back over one's shoulder leaves much to be desired in terms of control and safety. Flavell told Hislop that they had only lined four rapids before reaching Green River. They would only line two more for the rest of the trip—a remarkable feat. Flavell didn't mention that they had no life jackets. The two ran all the way through Cataract Canyon in five days. Flavell wrote:

> Cataract Canyon is wonderful, with walls towering thousands of feet high. Oftimes looking upstream, when four or five rapids were in sight, they bore a resemblance to steps, one above the other. I had it in my mind that Cataract was the worst of all the canyons, but rope was only used once. We only broke one oarlock, and got tangled up in only one rapid, and I am compelled to still give the honor to Lodore as being the worst.[5]

On October 5 they emerged from Narrow Canyon and passed the Dirty Devil River at the head of Glen Canyon. They soon encountered Jack Wilson, whom Stanton had met at Dandy Crossing in 1889.

> [Flavell's shout] was answered in a minor key from behind a patch of willows and out popped a man [Wilson], very nimble and robust though his gray hair plainly told that his days were long on the land which the Lord thy God giveth thee. . . . He had expected us to come for some days. We asked him how far it was to Hite, Utah. He told us we were in the city limits then, and within a hundred yards of the post office. . . . We made camp and went over to the village, it being small, only a post office, hotel, and restaurant, all in a room 14×16 feet. The upper half of the cupboard was for letters; the mailbag hung on the bedpost. The house was built of round logs, and over the window a place about a foot long had been hewed so as to make a flat surface and in lead pencil was inscribed, "meals 35cts." We played high five [a card game] with him till it was time for the rooster to crow, and heard some of his history. He had dug for gold until his pick, patience, and soul were worn out, and at last, after 37 years (finding nothing), he had quit in disgust. He was passing his last few days brooding over the campfire, alone, thinking and picturing what he would have done if he had struck it rich.[6]

On October 6 Flavell and Montéz breakfasted with Wilson, sharpened their ax and knives on his grindstone, and headed downstream. Flavell's next journal entry is at Lee's Ferry:

> . . . after seven days winding and twisting through Glen Canyon with its sluggish waters and barren peaks. This has been the most barren spot of our trip. Its walls are almost perpendicular the entire length, 155 miles, with a height of from 500 to 1,500 feet. The top, though level for a mountain, was destitute of vegetation or soil. It seemed as though the elements had took a pride in sweeping and washing it up to have at least one clean spot on the Colorado.[7]

The two spent three days at Lee's Ferry fixing up their boat and preparing for the Grand Canyon. On October 17 they set out, and soon came upon Badger Creek rapid, where they almost capsized. They came next to the infamous Soap Creek rapid, which they portaged, and then headed on down-canyon, running all the remaining rapids in Marble and Grand canyons, a feat not duplicated for three decades.

On October 30 they emerged from Grand Canyon: "We looked back at the high and rugged peaks now left behind. We were safe, a feeling no one could feel while in that terrible place! But now the Great, Grand, Beautiful, Wonderful, Fearful, Desolate Canyon is like yesterday—passed!"[8] Flavell took his time on the rest of the trip, often stopping and visiting people he knew.

Flavell married Lulu Blanch Shaffer in Los Angeles in 1898. He returned to Mexico in 1900 and died in Hermosillo in 1900 or 1901. The Mexican authorities sent his effects to his family in New Jersey, including his journal of the Colorado River trip. It passed down through the family and was donated to the National Park Service at Grand Canyon in 1980.

NATHANIEL GALLOWAY

Although Bert Loper (see below) was perhaps most closely identified with river running and Glen Canyon in the eyes of some, the most notable in the eyes of many river runners was Nathaniel Galloway. As David Lavender puts it: "The more one learns about Nathaniel Galloway, commonly called Than, the more certain it seems that he could have traveled as an equal with Jim Bridger, Jedediah Smith and other fabled mountain men of the 1820s, much of whose country Galloway trapped long after they had left it. He was a crack shot and a superb tracker. He could tinker, repair, improvise, invent. One acquaintance said all he needed for boating was a heavy dew."[9]

Galloway was born in Lehi, Utah, in 1855 but lived in Vernal, Utah, much of his life. He earned a good part of his living trapping beaver along the Green River and its tributaries. He made his first trip from Green River to the foot of Grand Canyon in 1896–97. He had perfected a type of boat well suited to his needs and to the river. The boats "averaged about sixteen feet long, were narrow of beam and shallow, with square sterns and pronounced 'rake'—that is, they were deepest in the mid-section and then rose toward bow and stern."[10] They were light enough to maneuver in rapids, and for one man to haul in and out of the water.

An eminently sensible man, Galloway, like Flavell, saw no reason to row a boat in rapids in the traditional European and Euro-American way: facing the stern and pulling the oars toward you, constantly looking over your shoulder to see where you are going. The advantage of that centuries-old technique comes from the muscle-power of pulling the oars toward the body for good propulsion, which works fine in on lakes and slow-moving rivers. But in rapid-flowing and rapid-filled rivers, the water provides the propulsion, so what was needed was control and the ability to maneuver quickly. Galloway simply turned around to face the bow so he could see where he was going, and used the oars as brakes and rudders, pulling them against the current. To gain speed, if needed, he pushed on them. Galloway seems to have invented this technique, at least on the Colorado River. Flavell had figured out the same technique when he ran the Green and Colorado a couple of months before Galloway, but apparently Galloway had been using it for years. Thus in river history Galloway is regarded as the inventor of the technique.

Galloway liked to work along the Green starting at Henry's Fork and floating on through to Vernal. In 1896 he took his thirteen-year-old son, Parley, along. In Brown's Park they met two prospectors. Sitting around a campfire, Galloway suggested a trapping trip through the Grand Canyon. One of the men, William Richmond, twenty-three and game for adventure, agreed. The other man thought them daft and in the morning left and walked out to the railroad. They dropped off young Parley in Vernal, undoubtedly to his disgust, and then drifted down and picked up another boat that Galloway had cached in Desolation Canyon. At Green River they added wooden decked compartments fore and aft. Later, in Grand Canyon, they used canvas around the open compartments as splash guards.[11]

The two passed through Cataract, Glen, Marble, and Grand canyons with no major accidents and without losing either boat. When they reached the mouth of the Virgin River, below Grand Canyon, they heard that two young men employed at a local mine had been murdered. Coffins had been made from two rowboats, and Galloway and Richmond were prevailed upon to tow the coffins behind their boats to Needles, California. They arrived on February 10, 1897. They sold the boats for $12 each and the furs they had collected for about $600. They also met George Flavell and compared notes on river running.

In the fall of 1897 Galloway ran down the Green and Colorado as far as Lee's Ferry. He then turned back to the placer mines in Glen Canyon. There, in January 1898, along came Robert Brewster Stanton, who employed him as foreman of one of his crews for the great dredge experiment. Galloway continued to run the Green and the Colorado until 1912, when he ended his river sojourns after a trip downriver as far as Lee's Ferry. Before that, however, he made a trip with Julius Stone, from Green River, through the Grand Canyon (see below).[12]

Some braved the river and lost; others came through more or less intact. One Charles Smith made some trapping trips with Galloway in 1910–12. But in 1913, after Galloway had stowed his oars, Smith set out on a trip of his own through Cataract Canyon. Parts of his boat were found near Tickaboo rapids in Glen Canyon; he was not. It was not the only instance in which only the boats of those starting out were found in Glen Canyon. Others were more successful in the canyons of the Green and in Cataract Canyon from 1912 to 1950.[13]

11.1. Bert Loper at his cabin in Red Canyon, 1947. Photograph by Knight B. Kerr, 921 P1 12935. Courtesy of the Utah State Historical Society.

BERT LOPER

The two men most associated with Glen Canyon in historic times were Cass Hite (fig. 9.2) and Bert Loper (fig. 11.1).[14] Loper (1869–1949) was born in Bowling Green, Missouri. In 1867 his father, Jehail Loper, thirty-seven and the father of three young girls from a previous marriage, married America Mettler, age seventeen. By 1869 she had borne him two sons, the youngest being Berta (or perhaps Albert), but generally known as Bert. In 1872 Bert's parents were divorced, and Jehail "walked forever out of the lives of his sons," taking the three girls from his first marriage with him; soon after, America died of tuberculosis.[15] Bert and his brother were raised in a very unhappy atmosphere by strict Baptist relatives. They ran away when Bert was thirteen.

Thereafter, Bert was essentially on his own, earning a scant living as a cow milker and laborer, and managing two years of formal schooling in between. By 1885 he found himself in Durango, Colorado, unhappily working for an uncle digging ditches; later he became a teamster, driving an eight-mule team hauling freight to the mines in the San Juan Mountains, and sometimes milking cows. He turned for a time to coal mining, a job he would return to off and on for many years. In short, he survived.

By 1892 rumors of placer gold along the San Juan River were circulating. Bert apparently met one of the Honaker brothers, "who had some samples of rich placer dirt from the San Juan River."[16]

> Henry and Augustus Honaker were there early, staking and working claims, but also sensed where the real gold was: in the eager gold miners' pockets. They offered stage transportation from the Cortez [Colorado] area to the Mormon town of Bluff, Utah, on the San Juan, with business being equally good in both directions. Thirty miles to the west they pioneered a route into the deepest part of the San Juan canyon to work their own claims and supply other miners.[17]

Bert Loper headed for the San Juan "excitement" and began his fifty-year-plus love affair with the Colorado and San Juan rivers and boating thereon:

> My start in boating was in the fall of 1893 and was a smooth water trip from the Colorado line down the San Juan to Bluff, Utah and from my later experiences was a rather tame affair but it being my first it was sure pack [*sic*] with thrills and I sure enjoyed it very much. . . . [I]n the spring of 1894 I went down the river from Bluff and it was this trip that I had my first rough water and it was then that I got sold on rough water boating.[18]

Loper and some partners tried placer mining on the upper San Juan River in 1893 to little avail. In 1894, as noted, he boated down to the Honaker claims along the San Juan and spent much of the summer up and down the river learning about handling boats in rough water, running rapids, and dealing with sand waves.

In 1894, after much labor and little return from placer mining, Loper found himself in Bluff making bricks. He returned to the Midwest for a time, knocking around from job to job. He enlisted in the army during the Spanish-American War but never left the States. After he was discharged, he moved to Colorado and worked in the mines at Telluride and Cripple Creek, then hobo-ed around the West and Mexico, working mainly as a hard rock miner. By 1907 he was in Goldfield, Nevada, where he linked up with Charles Silver Russell, whom he had met in Telluride.

By early 1907 Russell was in Prescott, Arizona, and was a mining promoter and part owner of the *Arizona Daily Journal Miner*. Being well aware of the prospecting that had gone on along the Colorado River for several years, Russell decided to prospect in the Grand Canyon and at the same time take photographs to sell to newspapers. In Goldfield, Russell linked up with Loper and Edwin R. Monett. The three agreed to make a trip down the Colorado seeking gold and taking photographs. Loper knew about boats from his experience on the San Juan; Russell and Monett did not.

Loper had little money but managed to purchase a camera. Russell and Monett bought a second one. They acquired three 16-foot Whitehall-design steel-hulled boats: the *Arizona*, the *Nevada,* and the *Utah*. On September 19, 1907, they launched the boats from Green River, "heavily laden with food, camping equipment, a perforated gravel screen, gold pans, licks, shovels, retorts, and one hundred pounds of quicksilver, useful for picking up particles of free gold washing through sluice boxes."[19]

They had a very difficult time through Cataract Canyon since only Loper had any white-water experience. They ran the rapids Galloway-fashion—stern first. They capsized a couple of times and got hung up on some rocks, but they got through. Their hopes, however, that Cataract Canyon would yield golden riches were dashed. Stanton had thought Glen Canyon would be nature's sluice box; Loper and his associates thought Cataract Canyon would be. Both were wrong.[20]

The party reached Hite on October 7, 1907. Loper's camera had been damaged during the trip, so he sent it out for repairs. The party resupplied, visited with Cass Hite, and headed into Glen Canyon to prospect. By the end of October they had found little. At the ruins of the Stanton dredge, they agreed to split up. Loper would work his way back upstream to Hite to retrieve his camera, while Russell and Monett worked downstream to Lee's Ferry, where they planned to meet by November 20. It took Loper six days to get back upstream to Hite. Because the camera was late and his boat was damaged, he did a few odd jobs—and he dawdled.

Loper did not start for Lee's Ferry until January 1, 1908, arriving on January 8. Russell and Monett had waited until December 13 and then headed into Marble Canyon, where they lost a boat, possibly in Hance rapid. In the one remaining boat, they made it to Bright Angel Trail, climbed out to the south rim, and were lionized by publicity. They determined to continue. After numerous problems and difficulties, they reached Needles, California, on February 8. They had found no gold. Subsequent newspaper stories made Loper out as a deserter who had had been afraid of the Grand Canyon, an allegation that rankled him for the rest of his life.[21]

Loper, meanwhile, freeloaded on the family who ran Lee's Ferry for two weeks until Bill Emmett asked him to bid on digging a 1,600-foot-long irrigation ditch. Loper concluded he had business back upriver.[22] In icy winter conditions, he rowed and pulled his boat 170 river miles upstream through Glen Canyon, starting on January 26 and reaching the Stanton Dredge on February 18. There he found several men working the gravel bars and was very pleased to get a full meal, as well as a shave and haircut. By February 22 he had reached Tickaboo Canyon and stopped to visit with Cass Hite. He then moved on to the Hite post office, where he spent the winter working for his keep.

Loper prospected the next summer, primarily on Olympia Bar. In the fall of 1908 he was hired to ride the mail from Hanksville to Hite. He also leased Red Canyon Bar from one A. P. Adams. There was a cabin, about a dozen acres cleared for hay fields, and a garden. A system of ditches irrigated the fields and provided water for sluicing gold. Loper finally decided, at age forty, that he had found a home. He continued to work up and down Glen Canyon, staking claims on various bars, living on the food he grew and what little gold he could get from his sluice operation. He boated downstream to visit Cass Hite at Tickaboo, and boated and walked upstream 12 miles to the Hite post office for mail and supplies. When Cass Hite died in early February 1914, Loper helped bury him.

In June 1914 Charles Russell contacted Loper, made amends, and asked Loper to make another river trip with him, with Russell to furnish all expenses. The purpose of the trip was to make a movie, following the lead of the Kolb brothers in 1911 (see below). Loper agreed to go. Russell spent $5,000 on a movie camera and film, and gave Loper a $550 advance. The two met at Green River, and despite Loper's concerns that the boats were too small and shallow, they set out on July 19. They made it as far as Rapid Fourteen in Cataract Canyon without incident, but there Russell capsized in the rapid and lost his boat. The two were forced to hike out with only, it is said, "a package of raisins and a little bag of hard candy."[23] They struggled overland to the Dirty Devil River and on into Hite, and then back to Green River to start over again.

Loper built another boat (but he and Russell later disagreed over who would pay for it). Loper then got a job with the Reclamation Service doing drill testing at the confluence of the Grand and the Green (chapter 12). He left his new boat with a friend and told him not to let Russell have it, but Russell took it anyway. He hired a local, Bill Reeder, as boatman and a man named August Tadje as photographer. Tadje's movie experience apparently was that of gofer for a company making background films around Salt Lake City.[24] When the three arrived at the confluence, Russell and Loper duked it out to an uncertain conclusion, except that Russell kept the boat and went on.

After retrieving the cached boat in Cataract Canyon, Russell promptly sank it at almost the same spot as before. In Loper's boat they reached Hite, but Reeder had had quite enough and left. Russell and Tadje went to Salt Lake City, bought a new boat, hired Tadje's brother-in-law, Goddard Quist, and returned to Hite.

On December 6 they launched the new boat, christened *Titanic II*. They had to chop their boats out of the ice at Lee's Ferry, and Quist quit when they reached Bright Angel. Soon after the *Titanic II* broke loose and floated away. Russell and Tadje hiked up to the south rim and ordered another steel boat. In due time it arrived by train from St. Louis. Russell hired a man named Clements whom Tadje knew. The three hauled the 16-foot steel boat down Bright Angel Trail on a handmade dolly, moving it aside to let the tourist-laden mule trains pass. It took a week. They continued downstream until they jammed the new boat in the rocks of Crystal Rapid. They again climbed out of the canyon; Clement and Tadje in one direction, Russell in another. Somehow they didn't die and were reunited. They managed to get back to Crystal Rapid with gear and winched the boat free, but then promptly jammed it again in the rocks. Pulled free a second time, the boat rolled over, split open, and dumped the cameras and all their gear in the river. In Loper's boat they got to the foot of the Bass Trail. The next morning, defeated, they hiked out, leaving Loper's boat tied up at river's edge. Four years later Russell was declared insane and institutionalized.[25]

Loper continued to work on and off rivers as he could. In April 1916, at age forty-seven, he married Rachel Jameson, age eighteen, a recent emigrant from Scotland, who had settled with her family in Torrey, Utah. In December 1916 the couple rode in a buckboard from Torrey to Hite and made their way to Red Canyon. They stayed there over the winter but left in the spring of 1917, seemingly because Rachel couldn't stand the isolation.

For the next few years Bert worked primarily in the coal mines of Carbon County, Utah, but returned to Glen Canyon when he could to mine for gold, swap yarns with friends at Hite, and enjoy the river. In 1921 he managed to get a job as head boatman with a USGS survey party starting to do the basic topographic and geological mapping along the San Juan and in Glen Canyon that was needed before dam sites and lake levels could be determined. He worked for two years on that project (chapter 12).

Afterward Loper continued to work as a miner and make trips on the Colorado when he could. In 1939, at age seventy, he finally realized his dream of running through Grand Canyon. He made the trip with LaPhene (Don) Harris, who had been with Norm Nevills the previous year (see below). He ran every rapid in Marble and Grand canyons, perhaps exorcizing the stigma of 1907 that he was afraid of the river. He continued to run various river trips with Harris throughout the 1940s, and Boy Scout trips with John Cross and others in 1947–49(see below). At some point in his travels through Glen Canyon, Loper began keeping a log of his trips on Sentinel Rock, at the mouth of Wahweap Creek: "Loper: '07 '08 '11 '12 '21(3)'29 '30 '39 '44 '47 '48."[26]

In July 1949 Loper started another trip through Grand Canyon in celebration of his eightieth birthday. Don Harris and Harry Aleson were the other river runners, and there were a few passengers. Loper had built a new boat, the *Grand Canyon*, for the trip. On July 8, in the middle of the rapid at Mile 24.5, Loper apparently suffered a fatal heart attack. His boat flipped and he fell out, but his passenger escaped. Both Loper and the empty boat were carried downstream. The boat was found lodged on a rock 16 miles downstream, but Loper's body had disappeared. His companions hauled the boat ashore above the flood line and painted on it: "Bert Loper, Grand Old Man of the Colorado, Born: July 31, 1869. Died: July 8, 1949." In April 1975 a hiker found a skeleton near Cardenas Creek between river miles 72 and 73. Forensic anthropologists determined that the bones were probably Loper's remains. Some of them were buried in Sandy, Utah, next to his wife, Rachel, who had died the previous February. The rest were left buried by the river, as Loper would have wanted.

JULIUS STONE

Julius F. Stone (1855–1947) was born on a farm near Devil's Lake, Michigan, the son of immigrant Germans. He had about six years of formal schooling. In 1871, at age fifteen, he became a telegraph operator, but soon began to rise in the business world, especially through investments in coal mining in Ohio, Illinois, West Virginia, and Iowa. In 1903 he turned to manufacturing and banking, including a stint as chairman of the board of the Seagrave Corporation, which manufactured fire engines. Stone moved to Columbus, Ohio, in the early 1880s. There he became an active supporter of Ohio State University, which awarded him an honorary doctorate of science in 1938. He bought Gibralter Island in Lake Erie and gave it to the university for use as an aquatic biological station, and also purchased an 80-ton cyclotron. Stone married in 1900 at age forty-five; he and his wife had five children.

An avid outdoorsman and photographer, Stone had spent a good deal of time in and around the canyon country over the years. He was one of the investors in Stanton's Hoskininni Mining Company. He came to Glen Canyon to see the dredge operation and there met Nathan Galloway, who was working for the company as a boatman, hunter, and sometime construction foreman. Galloway boated Stone up and down Glen Canyon. They subsequently went hunting together in the Henry Mountains and became close friends. Stone also met Cass Hite, John Hite, and others.

Inspired by Powell's Colorado River trips—and perhaps more immediately by Frederick Dellenbaugh's *A Canyon Voyage*, published in 1908—Stone decided to make his own trip. He also decided he would document the geology of the canyons in detail all along the route. In 1909 Stone brought Galloway to Ohio to take charge of the design of the boats they would use. Stone added some of his own ideas, thus resulting in Galloway-Stone boats.[27]

He had four of the boats built. Like Powell's boats in 1869 and 1871, they were delivered by rail at Green River Station, Wyoming. Stone brought two men with him: Charles C. Sharp, an attorney and friend, and Raymond A. Cogswell, Stone's brother-in-law, who also served as photographer. Galloway was hired as lead boatman. He brought along a friend from Myton, Utah, Seymour S. Dubendorff. After some last minute changes and additions to the boats, the party set out on the afternoon of September 12, 1909; they arrived in Needles on November 19 with no loss of boats or men. As an aside, as the party left Green River, a local man gave Stone a quart of rye whiskey in case along the way someone "might need a temporary stimulant badly." According to Stone: "While it is a matter of no importance, still there is a certain gratification in stating that this bottle, unopened, survived the trip through the Canyons, and is still in my possession [in 1931]. Just when the contents will be consecrated to all Colorado River voyagers cannot now be stated, but probably not until some particularly auspicious occasion."[28]

With Galloway and Dubendorff in one boat, and Stone and his friends in the others, the party proceeded. Stone kept a journal of the trip and a log of the nearly 350 photographs he and Cogswell took along the way. In 1932 he published the delightful *Canyon Country: The Romance of a Drop of Water and a Grain of Sand*. The book has a foreword by Henry Fairfield Osborn, the president of the American Museum of Natural History in New York. The book includes "A Borrowed Chapter on Erosion," taken from sections of Clarence Dutton's *Tertiary History of the Grand Cañon District*. As Stone puts it, "Captain Dutton has set forth so clearly the story of deposition and erosion that to attempt to do again the very thing so admirably done by him would be carrying coals to Newcastle. . . . Truth is truth and beauty is beauty wherever one may find them. And so certain pages of Captain Dutton's most memorable writing are herewith reproduced, without further explanation and quite without apology."[29]

On the boats that Stone and Galloway had designed were iron handles for portaging and cloth fenders that could be raised around the cockpits in rapids to fend off waves. Some rapids were run, some lined, others portaged. Galloway often ran the boats through rapids while the gear was carried around. The party made it through Lodore and Split Mountain canyons with no major problems. They stopped at Vernal to rest and resupply, then went on through Gray and Desolation canyons and into Cataract Canyon. They experienced only one major upset in Cataract and arrived at Dandy Crossing and the Hite post office on October 21, 1909. There Sharp received word that required him to return home. One of the boats was given to Fred Gibbons, then living with John Hite at the post office.

In Glen Canyon

After photographing the "prehistoric watch tower" on the bluff below Hite (chapter 16), Stone and the remaining members of the party moved downstream into Glen Canyon, where they encountered Bert Loper. They then stopped at Tickaboo Bar and hiked upcanyon to visit Cass Hite, whom Stone had previously met. Hite was still dreaming of making a fortune from his mining. "Cass tells us he has a deal on whereby he expects to clean up $100,000 for his placer claims, and I hope he does. But the fulfillment of his dreams has already been long delayed. Truly, hope springs eternal."[30]

After photographing portions of the petroglyph panel at Smith Fork (chapter 17), they dropped down to the Stanton dredge, which Stone photographed but did not illustrate in his book. Perhaps the memory of his lost investment was too painful. They passed on through Glen Canyon, noting Hole-in-the-Rock, the mouths of the Escalante and San Juan rivers, and Aztec Creek. Cummings and Douglass had only "discovered" Rainbow Bridge in Aztec Creek two months earlier, so Stone likely did not know about it. Stone was engrossed by the geology of Glen Canyon, describing it in detail and devoting twenty-seven plates in his book to its features.

The party reached Lee's Ferry on October 27 to find that a cache of supplies that Stone had previously arranged and paid for was not there. That left them short of food, but they continued, knowing they could buy more food when they reached Bright Angel Creek. However, they soon were able to shoot a mountain sheep: "All prospect of short rations is now at an end, but alas! Our chance for *adventure* has also gone glimmering. One may only have an adventure if through oversight or lack of information inadequate preparation is made for whatever is to be undertaken. If he then meets with unforeseen difficulty, an adventure may result. [The Arctic explorer] Stefansson, who ought to know, says having an adventure is proof of incompetence."[31] Or, as Professor Jesse Jennings phrased it for his Glen Canyon Project crews (chapter 16), "Only fools have adventures!"

The party continued on, resupplying at Bright Angel. Their one major adventure came when Dubendorff flipped his boat in a rapid and badly cut his head. They emerged from Grand Canyon on November 15, 1909. In 1923 the USGS named the rapid in which Dubendorff had flipped for him, as well as a nearby canyon for Galloway, the creek therein for Stone, and the butte overlooking the area for Cogswell.[32]

In 1938, at age eighty-three, Julius Stone revisited Glen Canyon with a party that affixed a plaque at Crossing of the Fathers. On the way downriver, according to Roy Webb, "as they floated past the wreck of the Hoskininni dredge, they stopped to explore the ruin and salvage some timbers for that night's campfire. As noted earlier, Stone looked into his coffee cup and said, "This cup of coffee cost me $5000."[33]

Julius Stone's *Canyon Country* remains one of the classic works ever written about the Colorado River and its canyons.

THE KOLB BROTHERS

In 1901–2 two brothers, Ellsworth Kolb (1875–1960) and Emery Kolb (1881–1976), arrived at the south rim of the Grand Canyon.[34] The next year they bought a photography business in Williams, Arizona, and moved it to a tent at the head of Bright Angel Trail. The tent was soon replaced by a small wooden studio, which over time expanded into a larger studio, living quarters, an auditorium, and a gift shop. They hiked all over the canyon, taking hundreds of photographs to sell to tourists, including those on the morning mule train. Business was fairly good, although the work was strenuous. Because of a lack of water, they had to run down to Indian Gardens, where there was a spring, to develop the film, and then run back up the trail to print pictures before the mule train returned.[35] But they had found their life's work.

Emery married in 1905, but Ellsworth remained a bachelor. At some point around 1908–9 they began discussing a river trip down the Green and Colorado rivers retracing John Wesley Powell's 1869 voyage. They planned to make both photographs and a motion picture of the trip. They set out systematically, learning all they could about boats, gear, and motion picture cameras. They corresponded with Julius Stone, who had made the trip in 1909 (above). Stone was very helpful, providing detailed information on equipment and the design of his boats.

As to the cameras, "in addition to three film cameras we had 8 × 10 and 5 × 7 plate cameras; a plentiful supply of plates and films; a large dark room; and whatever chemicals we should need for tests. Most important of all, we had bought a motion-picture camera."[36] Obtaining a motion picture camera proved very difficult because of the stranglehold that the Edison Company had on the sale of both cameras and film. Edison held all the key patents and through a trust, the Motion Picture Patents Company, sold cameras only to companies who had agreements with Edison. Since Eastman Kodak was part of the trust, the supply of movie film was controlled as well. But the brothers finally did succeed in acquiring a hand-cranked movie camera and film for it.

Boats for the trip were built in Racine, Wisconsin, and shipped to Green River, Wyoming. After completing their preparations, the two Kolb brothers, with a third man, James Fagen, "an Irish-American aged 22 years, a strong, active and willing chap," set out on September 11, 1911.[37] However strong and willing Fagen may have been, he lasted only until Echo Park, where he left the party. When they reached the confluence of the Grand and the Green, they climbed out, just as John Wesley Powell had, and saw what he had described in 1869 and Newberry a decade earlier:

> To the north . . . were a great number of smooth formations, from one hundred to four hundred, rounded on top in domes, reminding one of Bagdad and tales from the Arabian Nights. . . . But there were other wonders. On

> the south side of the Colorado's gorge, miles away, were great spires, pointing heavenward, singly and in groups, looking like a city of churches. . . . Directly below us was the Colorado River, muddy, swirling, and forbidding. A mile away boomed a rapid, beyond that was another, then the river was lost to view.[38]

Despite numerous difficulties, they managed to get through Cataract Canyon in only four days.

THE KOLBS IN GLEN CANYON

When the brothers arrived at the head of Glen Canyon on November 3, they stopped to visit with John Hite at the Hite ranch and post office. "Hite's home had been a haven for the sole survivor of two expeditions which had met with disaster in Cataract. In each case they were on the verge of starvation. Hite kept a record of all known parties who had attempted the passage through the canyon above. Less than half these parties, excepting Galloway's several successful trips, succeeded in getting through Cataract Canyon without wrecking boats or losing lives."[39]

They noted various placer mining claims downstream from Hite, one of them held by Bert Loper. His claim was "a tunnel in the gravel a hundred feet above the river, and some distance back from the river bank. A track of light rails ran from the river bank to these workings; the gravel and sand was loaded into a car, and hauled or pushed to the bank, then dumped into a chute, which sent it down to the river's edge." Loper's ranch was "a neat little place, with fruit trees and a garden, a horse or two and some poultry."[40] They met Loper downstream, and he rode across the river with them to visit Cass Hite. Continuing on, they noted that

> [s]igns of an ancient Indian race were plentiful in this section. There were several small cliff dwellings, walled up in ledges in the rocks, a hundred feet or so above a low flat which banked the river. At another place [the mouth of Smith Fork] there were hundreds of carvings. . . . Drawings of mountain-sheep were plentiful; there was one representing a human figure with a bow and arrow, and with a sheep standing on the arrow. . . . There were masked figures engaged in a dance, not unlike some of the Hopi dances of today, as they picture them. There were geometrical figures and designs of many varieties.[41]

They described the remains of Stanton's dredge, noting that it "had once represented the outlay of a good deal of money."[42] They wanted to climb Navajo Mountain, hike up to Rainbow Bridge, and hike in to Music Temple, but they did not do so. Further downstream, at the mouth of Warm Creek,

> rounding a turn we saw the strange spectacle of fifteen or twenty men at work on the half-constructed hull of a flat-bottomed steamboat, over sixty feet in length. This boat was on the bank quite a distance above the water, with the perpendicular walls of a crooked side canyon rising above it. It was a strange sight, here in this out-of-the-way corner of the world. Some men with heavy sledges were under the boat, driving large spikes into the planking. . . . [There were] some coal mines, several miles up this little canyon, which bore the name of Warm Creek Canyon. A road led down through the canyon, making it possible to haul the lumber for the boat, clear to the river's edge. The nearest railroad was close to two hundred miles from this place, quite a haul considering the ruggedness of the country. The material for the boat had been shipped from San Francisco. . . . The vessel was to be used to carry coal down the river, to a dredge that had recently been installed at Lee's Ferry.[43]

This was, of course, the *Charles H. Spencer* (fig. 9.5). The Kolbs continued on, arriving at Lee's Ferry in time to have dinner with the dredge workers.

> At the time of our visit, it ["Lee's stronghold"] was occupied by two men; one, a young Englishman, recently arrived from South Africa—a remittance man, in search of novelty—the other a grizzled forty-niner. Much could be written about this interesting group of men and their alluring employment. There were some who had followed this work through all the camps of the West—to Colorado, to California, and to distant Alaska as well, they had journeyed; but it is doubtful if, in all their wanderings, they had seen any camp more strangely located than this, hemmed in by canyon walls.
>
> One feature about the dredge interested us greatly. This was a tube, or sucker, suspended by a derrick about a float and operated by compressed air. This tube was dropped into the sand at the bottom of the river, and would eat its way into it, bringing up rocks the size of one's fist, along with the gravel and the sand. In a few hours, a hole, ten or fifteen feet in depth and ten feet in diameter, would be excavated. Then the tube was raised, the float was moved, and the work started again. The coarse sand and gravel, carried by a stream of water, was returned to the river, after passing over the riffles; the screenings which remained passed over square metal plates—looking like sheets of tin—covered with quicksilver. These plates were cleaned with a rubber window-cleaner, and the entire residue was saved in a heavy metal pot, ready for the chemist.[44]

The Kolbs reached Bright Angel on November 17. After a pause to resupply, they headed out again, now with just one other man, Bert Lauzon, and reached Needles on January 18, 1912. Although they lost a large amount of film, they still were able to produce many stills and a motion picture that was shown almost daily in their studio until Emery died in 1976.[45] Ellsworth had moved to Pennsylvania in the 1920s and later to California, where he died in 1960. Both brothers, but especially Emery, were involved in river running in various ways for many years.

DAVE RUST, PREMIER GUIDE IN THE GLEN CANYON COUNTRY

One theme of this book is that Eliot Porter and the Sierra Club were wrong—calling Glen Canyon "the place no one knew." Many people knew something of it and the surrounding country for millennia. But probably no single individual knew as much of the Glen Canyon Country as Dave Rust (fig. 11.2). He has emerged from historical obscurity only recently through the excellent biography of him by Frederick Swanson.[46] What follows is based on Swanson's work, with appreciation.

David Dexter Rust (1874–1963) was born while John Wesley Powell's men were beginning to map the canyon country, and he died the year Glen Canyon Dam's gates closed and Lake Powell began to fill. His father, George S. Rust, arrived in the Salt Lake Valley in September 1847. He was sent on a Mormon mission in 1854–55 to Kansas, where he met, baptized, and married seventeen-year-old Eliza Brown. By 1857 the family was settled near Payson, Utah, where Dave was born. In 1884 George Rust acquired some property near Cainesville on the Dirty Devil River from Mosiah Behunin, my maternal great-grand-uncle. Dave grew up in the sparse environment getting what schooling he could and learning about the surrounding country while helping herd the family's livestock. He graduated from Richfield High School in 1893 and was hired to teach in Hanksville that fall. He managed two years at the Brigham Young Academy in Provo, working as a cowboy in the summers. In 1896–97 he was principal of the Loa Public School in Wayne County.

11.2. Dave Rust (*left*) and Sarah Fraser in Glen Canyon, 1930. Photograph by George Fraser. Loper Collection, P1136n19. Courtesy of Special Collections, Marriott Library, University of Utah.

George Rust was often away from home, succumbing to the lure of silver and gold, and in 1897 Dave caught the fever and joined his older brothers Will and Orion in the rush to Glen Canyon. Will and Orion had built a 16-foot boat, hauled it down North Wash to the river, and set off downstream to Wildhorse Bar, where they established a camp. Dave took a pack train overland, crossing the Waterpocket Fold at Muley Twist Canyon, thence down the Hole-in-the-Rock Trail, around the base of the Kaiparowits Plateau, and down to the camp. Orion soon went home, but Will and Dave labored on. In early January 1898, Robert Brewster Stanton and his crew came by, staking claims in preparation for Stanton's ill-fated dredge scheme. Rust worked in the canyon until the fall of 1898, sometimes rowing boats for others up- and downstream. In 1899 he tried hard rock mining on the slopes of the Henry Mountains with brother Will and his friend Nathaniel Galloway. He managed a couple more years at the Brigham Young Academy and worked at various jobs in between.

Dave Rust and the Grand Canyon

In 1902 Rust was hired as the principal of the public school in Fredonia, on the Arizona Strip. One of Rust's school friends in Provo was Royal Woolley, son of Edwin D. ("Uncle Dee") Woolley Jr. Dee Woolley was a major figure in Kanab, southern Utah, and the Arizona Strip—a rancher, businessman, civic leader, and president of the Mormon "stake" in Kanab. His uncle was Franklin B. Woolley, chronicler of the Andrus expedition of 1866 to the Aquarius Plateau and its environs (chapter 5).[47] Woolley's number two wife was the daughter of Erasmus Snow, a Mormon apostle and the leader of the southern Utah communities. His number one wife, Emma Bentley, had a daughter, Ruth. Dave Rust was soon courting her, and they were married in the Manti, Utah, temple in May 1903. The couple then went on to California, where Dave was able to complete a year's course work at Stanford University. The following year he taught school in Burley, Idaho, and then returned with Ruth to Fredonia.

Woolley had long had his eye on the north rim of the Grand Canyon. Very aware of the developments on the south rim being undertaken by Ralph Cameron and the Santa Fe Railway, he hoped for a railroad line to the north rim and foresaw automobiles getting there; although the latter happened, the former did not. In 1909 he managed to get a Thomas Flyer and a Locomobile all the way from Salt Lake City to Bright Angel Point on the north rim. More immediately, in 1905 Woolley began planning a trail down Bright Angel Creek, with some sort of cable-way across the river, and a trail up to Indian Gardens below the south rim. Ralph Cameron had a toll trail from the south rim down to Indian Gardens.

Enlisted in the project by his father-in-law, Dave was enveloped in it for the next five years. He worked as construction foreman, cableway/tram operator, and manager of a tent camp he developed at the foot of the Bright Angel Trail. He also began guiding pack trips onto the north rim and beyond. In 1909 he became acquainted with Buffalo Jones and Zane Grey. The latter based one of the characters in *The Heritage of the Desert* on Rust.[48]

Rust worked with a pack trip in 1909 led by Buffalo Jones and Jim Owens, a guide who specialized in roping mountain lions on the Kaibab Plateau. The guests were a group of prominent Bostonians including Charles Sumner Bird, a wealthy manufacturer and supporter of Theodore Roosevelt. Bird's stories of the group's adventures told back in Boston led to Rust being hired in November 1909 by George Russell Agassiz (1862–1951), an astronomer and grandson of the famous naturalist Louis Agassiz, of Harvard, for a pack trip across the Markagunt Plateau.[49] It was the first of many such extended trips Rust would lead over the next several decades. Also in 1909, Julius Stone and Nathan Galloway made their river trip (see above). Rust and Galloway were friends, and Rust was asked to go along, but declined. By the time Galloway and Stone launched their boats, he was working as a guide for the Agassiz pack trip.

Even though Rust never learned how to swim, the river intrigued him. He had been back and forth in Glen Canyon in the 1890s and had boated up- and downstream short distances from Bright Angel with Emery Kolb in 1909. When the Kolbs made their 1911 trip, they invited Rust to join them at Lee's Ferry, but he again declined. (He did, however, ultimately run river trips in Glen Canyon.)

By 1910 Rust was devoting several months a year to guiding small pack trips, primarily for wealthy clients from the East Coast. He took a Massachusetts woman, Helen White Sargent, and two of her women friends on a seven-week trip along the north rim of the Grand Canyon, then to Zion Canyon,[50] then across the Markagunt Plateau to Panguitch Lake and back to Kanab. Other wealthy clients signed on in the following years. But Rust could not devote all of his time to running extended pack trips: he also farmed, ran cattle, worked as a school superintendent, and for a couple of years edited the *Kane County News*, which Uncle Dee had acquired in 1911.

In 1914 George Corning Fraser (1872–1935) and his son George Jr. (1896–1974) hired Rust for a trip to the Zion Canyon and Grand Canyon areas following Clarence's Dutton itinerary when he made his *Tertiary History of the Grand Canyon* studies. The Frasers were from a wealthy New York City family. George Sr. had a degree in geology and was an ardent admirer of Dutton's work. In

1915 Rust and Fraser made a trip to the Fishlake Plateau and Thousand Lake Mountain, climbed Mount Ellen in the Henry Mountains, and then rode across the Aquarius and Markagunt plateaus and on to the top of the Pine Valley Mountains. The following year Rust led Fraser from Kanab to Rainbow Bridge, and then to Monument Valley and on across the San Juan River to Bluff, Utah.

In 1917 Rust led the adventurer Le Roy Jeffers on an extended trip that included Bryce Canyon. Jeffers was an avid mountain climber who made the first recorded ascent of Mount Muir in the Sierra Nevada in 1919 and climbed numerous other peaks in Canada and the United States; he possibly made the first ascent of Mount Moran in the Grand Tetons.[51]

In April 1919 Rust led New York publisher Donald C. Scott across the Navajo reservation and to the top of Navajo Mountain, where they were treated to a magnificent sunset. Scott would later become associate director and then director of the Peabody Museum of Anthropology at Harvard. He would recommend Rust as packer for the Clafflin/Emerson archaeological expedition in the late 1920s (chapter 13).

Later in the summer of 1919, Rust guided two young New Yorkers from wealthy families, Charles Berolzheimer and Arnold Koehler Jr., who had chosen a trip across the Southwest as their high school graduation present. Probably few high schoolers before or since have had such a trip. Rust and his sixteen-year-old son, Jordan, took them from Zion Canyon to Lee's Ferry, thence across the river and on to the Rainbow Plateau, where they encountered Byron Cummings and his students excavating in Red House and Yellow House (chapter 13). They climbed Navajo Mountain, descended to Rainbow Bridge, then traveled northward across Monument Valley and the San Juan River to Bluff. From there they went by car to Mesa Verde, where they were given a tour by Jesse Walter Fewkes of the Smithsonian Institution. In the 1910s and early '20s Fewkes conducted a program of excavation and ruins stabilization at Mesa Verde.

The boys returned for a second trip in 1920. Koehler was by then at Cornell, and Bernheimer at Harvard. Rust and his son Jordan took them to Bryce Canyon, where they hiked to the bottom. They then rode to the south end of the Table Cliff Plateau to Powell Point, then to Escalante, up onto the Aquarius Plateau, north to Fruita, then Capitol Reef, and on to Torrey, Thousand Lake Mountain, and finally to Manti, where the boys caught a train to Salt Lake City and home.

George Fraser was in contact with Raymond C. Moore, a geologist at the University of Kansas who was studying the Kaiparowits Plateau with Herbert Gregory. In 1922 Fraser and his daughter, Jane, contracted with the Rusts for a trip across the Aquarius Plateau and into the Kaiparowits country. They started at Torrey, went up over the Aquarius, across to the south to climb Canaan peak, and then to Tropic. From there they rode down Last Chance Creek and over to Kane Creek, which Rust mistook for the Crossing of the Fathers. They then rode up onto the Kaiparowits, met Moore, and headed down Collett Wash to Escalante. The Frasers went from there by car to Richfield and caught a train home. Fraser was impressed by Jordan Rust and later paid much of his tuition and support at Stanford University.

In 1923 Koehler and Bernheimer returned once again. This time Rust took them east across the Aquarius Plateau and the Waterpocket Fold. They then climbed Mount Ellen, and rode down through the Henry Mountains to the mouth of North Wash to make a boat trip through Glen Canyon. Rust had acquired two 14-foot-long collapsible canvas canoes with steel ribbing and had them delivered to the river. They named the boats the *Powell* and the *Gilbert*. Rust had Powell's report with him to read as they ran downriver. They explored lower Moqui Canyon just a few weeks before Neil Judd and John Wetherill arrived there overland (chapter 13). They stopped at Music Temple and hiked to Rainbow Bridge, then headed on to Lee's Ferry. There they met the USGS survey team led by E. C. La Rue, with Emery Kolb as one of the boatmen (chapter 12). This was the first commercial float trip in Glen Canyon. A local newspaper reported that "D. D. Rust and son Jordan left Monday to accompany a pair of Harvard and Cornell students into the wilds of Southern Utah. They start from Richfield and will journey by pack horses, will boat down the Dirty Devil [*sic*] and Colorado Rivers to Lee's Ferry and back to Kanab."[52]

By 1924 Rust was including his daughter Emma on his trips. She went with him on one across the Paunsaugunt and Aquarius plateaus, and the next year on a trip in Glen Canyon. Stephen Mather, director of the National Park Service, had asked Dr. Frank Oastler of New York City, who was making a Southwest trip with his wife, Maude, to scout out potential national park and monument sites and recommend expansion of existing sites. They had toured the Natural Bridges area with Zeke Johnson, a packer-guide from Blanding and the custodian of Natural Bridges National Monument (chapter 13). He delivered the couple to the mouth of White Canyon. Rust and Emma brought boats down North Wash by wagon, crossed the river, picked up the Oastlers, and proceeded downstream. Jordan met them at Lee's Ferry with a car, and they visited the north rim of Grand Canyon to end the trip. Rust made a second river trip in 1925 with a physician and his wife from Santa Fe, J. P. and Elizabeth Proctor. Elizabeth had been on the 1924 trip across the Paunsaugunt and Aquarius plateaus. The couple were again delivered to Hite by Zeke Johnson, and the Rusts picked them up for the river trip.

Dave and Ruth Rust moved to Provo in 1928, in part so their children could attend Brigham Young University. In 1929 Rust testified in the famous "riverbed case"—federal hearings to determine if the Green, Colorado, and San Juan rivers were navigable. In August 1930 he made a river trip with George Fraser and his daughter Sarah (fig. 11.3). Rust hired Bert Loper to come along as the second boatman. There were numerous other river and overland trips during the 1930s.

Rust continued to lead pack trips and combined pack and river trips all across the Glen Canyon Country until 1941. His work with the Clafflin/Emerson expeditions in the 1920s is discussed in chapter 13. He seldom advertised, relying on word-of-mouth referrals. Most clients were from the East Coast and had Princeton, Harvard, or Johns Hopkins connections. On July 22, 1938, a brief note about one of his trips appeared in the *Kane County Standard*:

> David D. Rust, of Provo, with Dr. L.F. Lowe and Harold Hartshome, of Princeton University, who left Torrey, Wayne County, July 7, on an overland trip to the summit of Hillers mountain before going to Hite and on down the Colorado to Lee's Ferry, arrived at the desired destination safe and sound Sunday, July 17. According to L. Elmer Jackson, who had an interview with the party on his visit to the Ferry last Monday, Mr. Rust was waiting for horses to pilot the party overland into Arizona and then back through the Wayne Wonderland.[53]

Rust's trips were always small, often with just two guests, and six at the maximum. It appears he charged $20 to $25 a day per person for trips that were as much intellectual outings as scenic adventures. Rust came equipped with maps and the reports of Powell, Gregory, Dutton, and their successors. He wanted people to understand the Country, not just "ooh!" and "ah!" as they passed through it. As Rust's biographer puts it, "Taking direction from the nineteenth-century scientist-explorers who had opened the Plateau Province

11.3. George Fraser (*left*), Sarah Fraser, and Bert Loper in Glen Canyon, August 1930. Photograph by Dave Rust, C-187. Courtesy of the Utah State Historical Society,

to modern inquiry, he saw meaning not just in the river corridor, but in the entire Colorado Plateau."[54]

David Rust died January 27, 1963, just a week after the first gate was closed on the diversion tunnels at Glen Canyon Dam and Lake Powell began to form. The Glen Canyon that Rust—and those who came before and after him—knew, was soon to be no more. But the Glen Canyon Country remains. Clearly, no one else had ever ridden over as much of it as Rust, nor knew it as well. And probably no one ever will.

FILMING THE CANYONS

The first to photograph the canyons of the Colorado were E. O. Beaman, Jack Hillers, and Timothy O'Sullivan in the early 1870s. Franklin Nims and Robert Brewster Stanton made and published photographs of Stanton's survey for a railroad down the canyons in the 1890s. While Loper's and Russell's photographic efforts were unsuccessful, Julius Stone's 1909 photographic trip was very successful, although none of the photographs were published until 1932. The Kolb brothers succeeded in making both stills and a motion picture of their journey down the Colorado in 1911–12.

The next major attempts to make movies in the Colorado canyons came in the 1920s, when the USGS was conducting its surveys there. The potential high dam sites in Black and Boulder canyons, as well as in the canyons of the Colorado in general, received a lot of publicity (chapter 12).

Various people decided to cash in on that publicity by attempting to make movies about the river and the surrounding country.[55]

Clyde Eddy and the Pathé-Bray Company

One individual who wanted to make movies in the Colorado canyons was Clyde Eddy (1889–?). Born in Texas, he joined the navy in 1906. He enlisted in the army during World War I, saw combat action, was discharged, and went to work for a pharmaceutical firm in New York. During a trip with his wife to the Grand Canyon, they rode mules down to the river, and Eddy was entranced by it and the canyon country. After reading everything he could about the Colorado, he decided to make a trip and also a film of the journey. He had three Powell-type boats built of mahogany and oak, each weighing 1,000 pounds. Two were 22-footers named the *Powell* and the *Coronado*; the smaller 16-footer was named the *Dellenbaugh*.

Eddy hired Parley Galloway, Nathan's son, as lead boatman and recruited nine college students as crew who paid their own way. He also made a deal with the International Newsreel Company for a cameraman. Accompanying the group were a bear cub Eddy had acquired from the Bronx Zoo, named Cataract, and a dog named Rags.

The team set out from Green River, Utah, on June 27, 1926. They struggled through Cataract Canyon, carved their names on the wall at Mile 202.3, passed through Glen Canyon without any problems, and arrived at Lee's Ferry on July 9. At that point, the cameraman left, taking his equipment with him. Two of the college boys left as well.

Eddy hired a drifter, Oscar Jaeger, whom two of the crew had met on the road while thumbing a ride into Kanab. Jaeger had a hand-held movie camera. They headed into Marble Canyon on July 18, running most of the rapids. Despite losing one of the large boats in Dubendorff rapid, they continued on—eleven men, the bear, and the dog in the two remaining boats. They reached Needles, California, the first week in August. Eddy sold the bear cub for $40; one of the students took the dog home to Wisconsin. Eddy returned to New York without much usable footage for a movie, but having received a fair amount of publicity.

In the fall of 1926 a film combine, the Pathé-Bray Company, was put together specifically to make a film about the Colorado River—perhaps a documentary, perhaps a romantic adventure. If the former, it would be called "Pride of the Colorado;" if a romance, "Bride of the Colorado." Joseph Randolph Bray (1879–1978) was one of the early inventors of animated cartoon films, opening a studio in 1914. By the mid-1920s, his company was producing hundreds of animated shorts and documentaries. The Pathé company was a major European manufacturer of motion picture cameras, film, and projectors. It had invented the newsreel and was a international film distribution company. Bray would produce the film; Pathé would distribute it.

Eugene C. La Rue had just been forced out of the USGS over his opposition to the building of a high dam in Black Canyon (chapter 12). He set himself up as a consultant—an expert on rivers, hydrology, and river running. The Pathé-Bray Company hired him at $150 a day to assemble a group of boats to carry the filmmakers and lead them down the rivers from Green River, Utah. Due to some delays, the flotilla didn't start until November 10, 1926. There were six boats. The crew included La Rue, some boatmen (including two Russian lifeguards from southern California), two cameramen, a director, a publicist, a man who ran a battery-powered radio, a cook, and a dog named Pansy. They struggled through Cataract Canyon and slogged through low water and sand bars in Glen Canyon, making them late in reaching Lee's Ferry.

On November 14, 1926, the Pathé-Bray Company called Clyde Eddy in New York. Their film party was "lost" in Glen Canyon; and they asked if he would come to lead a search for them, and then perhaps take control. On the way into Lee's Ferry, Eddy saw a radio broadcasting rig being set up to send news to a waiting world. The boats arrived, and Eddy met them. They continued, struggling into Bright Angel on December 13. The boatmen hadn't been paid and were about to mutiny, so Eddy hiked out to the South Rim, called the company, got $3,000 from them, rode back to the river, paid off the men—and rode back up the trail and went home. So did Pansy the dog. The party continued on, dropping down to Hermit rapid, where they shot a number of fake rescues and other perilous scenes—running and rerunning the rapids.

At the end, one of the boats was hauled up the Hermit Trail and used in a publicity parade in Hollywood. A huge banquet was held to celebrate the picture's wrap, but it was never released. The two leads, John Boles and Rose Blossom, apparently were never on the river, although they did do some filming on the South Rim. Boles played in various westerns as late as 1936, but then faded. Blossom was a bit player and second lead in a few films, mostly Westerns, between 1925 and 1928, and then faded, as did Clyde Eddy's dream of doing a film on the canyons; as he later said, "The Colorado defeats everybody."[56]

THE UNKNOWN FATE OF THE HYDES

In 1928 a young couple on their honeymoon, Glen and Bessie Hyde, carved "Hyde 11-1-28" on the wall of Narrow Canyon next to the names of the Eddy party from the year before.[57] Entering Glen Canyon, they stopped to visit an unnamed placer miner on an unnamed bar. They passed through Glen Canyon without further comment and arrived at Lee's Ferry on November 8.

The couple had reached that point by most unlikely routes. Glen Hyde's family had settled on a farm near Twin Falls, Idaho, in 1914. Born in 1898, Hyde had attended the University of Oregon and University of Idaho but did not graduate. In 1922–23 he became interested in what were called "sweepboats," scows that had been used on the Salmon and upper Snake rivers since the 1870s. He learned from an old riverman how to make and run them. "Sweepboats were little more than large wooden boxes, crudely built from planks and steered with long, ponderous oar-like sweeps extending from bow and stern."[58] In 1926 Hyde built a 5 × 16-foot sweepboat that he and his sister, Jeanne, successfully ran from Salmon, Idaho, down the Salmon River and then the Snake River as far as Lewiston. They had run several major rapids with very few mishaps, and Glen Hyde was hooked.

Bessie Haley was born in 1905 near Washington, D.C., but grew up primarily in Pittsburgh. She went to Marshall College in West Virginia, much interested in art. In June 1926 she suddenly married a fellow student, one Earl Helmick. Two months later she was in San Francisco, sans Helmick, where she enrolled in the California School of Fine Arts. In 1927 she took an overnight party cruise ship to Los Angeles. On board she met Glen Hyde; both were apparently smitten. They tried to convince Helmick to grant Bessie a divorce, but he refused. Bessie went to Elko, Nevada, for the six-week divorce available at the time. It was granted in February 1928; the next day she traveled to Twin Falls, and married Glen Hyde the day after that.

The Clyde Eddy trip down the Colorado had been much in the news, as was the ill-fated trip by J. R. Bray and Pathé News. Glen and Bessie apparently decided to seek fame—and maybe fortune—by running the Colorado in a sweepboat. She would be the first woman to run the Colorado, and the sweepboat would also be a first. In late October 1928, the couple went to Green River, Utah, built a sweepboat in two days and headed downriver with a goodly food supply but no life preservers. After all, according to Glen, real Idaho sweepmen didn't use them. They managed to get through Cataract Canyon with no major problems and moved quickly through Glen Canyon.

At Lee's Ferry, people tried to dissuade the couple from continuing on—to no avail. After some harrowing experiences in Marble and upper Grand canyons they reached Bright Angel Creek on November 14. They hiked up to the South Rim to resupply and called on Emery Kolb, who, like others, was amazed that they had run all the rapids from Lee's Ferry. They were interviewed by a reporter and mailed letters to their families. Returning to the river, they ran to Hermit rapid, lunched at Hermit Camp, signed the guest book, and departed.

A month later, the scow, with all the Hydes' gear intact and strapped in, was spotted floating in an eddy near the end of the Grand Canyon at river mile 237. Pictures developed from film in a camera on the boat indicated they had been at river mile 165 about November 27. Remains of their camp at Diamond Creek were found, but the Hydes were not. Hyde's father launched an extensive search, aided by the Kolb brothers and others. They were never found.

Their disappearance provided the grist for eighty years of rumors, speculation, and story spinning about their fate. One story was that Georgie White was Bessie (Georgie was christened Bessie), but it wasn't true. The young couple were the most mysterious, star-crossed, and perhaps interesting of those who ran the Colorado River. Their story has been carefully pieced together and artfully told by Brad Dimock, who with his wife, Jeri Ledbetter (both expert Grand Canyon river runners), built a replica sweepboat and re-created the Hydes' trip through Grand Canyon in 1996—but with life jackets and support boats.

BUS HATCH AND HATCH EXPEDITIONS

The most revered Colorado river runner in the minds of many was Bus Hatch (190267).[59] He was a pioneering innovator in building and running boats, and played a major role in the fight to defeat the Echo Park Dam on the Green River in the 1950s. Robert Rafael Hatch, known throughout his life as Bus, was the oldest son of Frank and Annie Swain Hatch of Vernal, Utah. Bus grew up in Vernal, married in 1922, and had children. He was a contractor throughout his life, building and supervising construction of many houses and businesses in the Uintah Basin, Salt Lake City, and elsewhere. He was an active hunter and fisherman, and he was particularly intrigued by the Green River, which flows near Vernal.

In 1929 Parley Galloway, the son of river man Nathan Galloway, was arrested for abandoning his wife and children, and spent several months languishing in the Vernal jail. He had learned boat building from his father and had, as we saw, guided Clyde Eddy through the Grand Canyon in 1927. Bus Hatch and his cousin Frank Swain spent a lot of time visiting Parley, learning about river running. Galloway told them that if they would bail him out, he'd help them build a Galloway boat and guide them down the Green River through Split Mountain Canyon. They raised the bail, and Parley was released, but he immediately blew town. A few years later he was found dead of exposure and starvation near Richfield, Utah.[60]

Based on Parley's sketches, Bus and Frank built a boat, and in August 1931 they and two others attempted a run through Lodore Canyon. They had various accidents, including flipping in Hell's Half Mile. Undeterred, they built new boats, more closely styled on the Galloway model, and had more rapid learning experiences in Split Mountain Canyon. They then linked up with Russell Frazier, a doctor from the Bingham Copper Mine, near Salt Lake City. Plans were made to re-create much of John Wesley Powell's river trips. In July 1933, Hatch, Frazier, and three others in two boats started from Ouray, Utah, with the intention of running Cataract Canyon. They battled their way through the canyon, learning a great deal more about rapids and their ways. At Hite they liberated food from a placer miner's camp, managed to burn down most of the camp, left a polite note of explanation, and headed into Glen Canyon. Using Powell's report, they stopped at various places, including Music Temple, but also Hole-in-the-Rock and Rainbow Bridge. They cached their boats at Lee's Ferry for the year.

In July 1934, with Dr. Frazier, Clyde Eddy, and a newsreel cameraman named Fred Jayne, Hatch and his crew headed into Marble and Grand canyons. Eddy was still trying to make a motion picture of Grand Canyon; he failed yet again. They slugged their way through the canyons, flipped a boat in Lava Falls, and came to Separation Rapid. There they put up a plaque commemorating Dunn and the Howland brothers. Robert Brewster Stanton had expressed disgust in his *Colorado River Controversies* over the omission of their names from the Powell monument on the south rim of the Grand Canyon—a disgust shared by Russell Frazier, who instigated the placing of the plaque.

For the rest of the 1930s and into the 1940s, Bus Hatch and his family became increasingly involved in river running in between work as building contractors. During the early 1950s Hatch emerged as a leader in the fight against the Echo Park Dam. He organized numerous float trips for the Sierra Club and for both Horace Albright, the retired director of the National Park Service, and Conrad Worth, the current director. The campaign was successful—but the trade-off was the Glen Canyon Dam (chapter 21).

After World War II, Hatch, like others, began using surplus inflatable rafts and pontoons for river running. Hatch Expeditions grew into an increasingly larger business as the years went by. They ran the Yampa, the Green, Cataract, San Juan, and Grand canyons, as well as the Middle Fork of the Salmon River in Idaho. Bus Hatch quit river running in 1964 and died in 1967, but Hatch Expeditions continued on, one of the most respected river-running outfits in the West. Bus's son Ted took over the Grand Canyon part of the business, now run in turn by his son Steve. Don, another of Bus's sons, took over the Utah part of the business, running the Green, the Yampa, Cataract Canyon, and the Salmon River. This part of the business was sold but retains the family name.[61]

UPRIVER TO RAINBOW BRIDGE

In the fall of 1930, Frederic A. Stearns, a prominent San Diego attorney, and his friend Pat Flattum decided to make a trip upstream in Glen Canyon from Lee's Ferry to Rainbow Bridge to call attention to Stearns's campaign to get Congress to create a Rainbow Bridge National Park that would encompass Navajo Mountain, part of the Colorado River gorge, and Monument Valley.[62] They also wanted to test out a new steel boat design they had created. Having become acquainted with John Wetherill, they sought his advice.

Stearns and Flattum arrived at Wetherill's home in Kayenta in time for Christmas dinner. They discussed the trip with him, and he agreed to go along. The boat was brought by trailer from Cameron to Marble Canyon Lodge, where it "was loaded with camp duffle and a small supply of dynamite for jams and ice, and one 'Savage' rifle, three cameras, one movie camera, and plenty of gas (as we thought)."[63]

They spent the first four days of January 1931 at Lee's Ferry testing the boat and the motor, a 14 horsepower Indian. The river contained "much ice, cakes from 5 to 40 feet long, about one foot in thickness and which were ground to slush at the rapids above the Marble Canyon Bridge." They found a second "old abandoned [wooden] boat in the river."[64] They tied the two boats together, and the motor seemed capable of pushing both of them upstream. The key question was how much gas to take along: "Tested motor's gas consumption on sharp bend in river to determine how much gas would be needed to reach Rainbow Bridge without over-burdening the boats and motor. Figured 87 miles to bridge canyon and drift of current getting out of ice packs and whirlpools was like figuring how far a frog would jump by the way he sits or looks."[65]

While Stearns stayed behind, Wetherill and Flattum started upstream on January 4, running the steel boat and towing the wooden one. By the end of the first day they had decided to cache the steel boat and use the wooden one. They progressed slowly, dodging ice floes and often lining or pulling the boat through the icy water. On January 5 they made 3 miles; the next day, 8. They continued, dodging ice chunks, packs, and floes, and fell in the water more than once. They stopped for two days at the mouth of Warm Creek to repair the boat and then headed on upstream. On January 11, Flattum wrote, "We have put in a long day's work and only advanced four miles. Our worst enemy is the ice, then the cold! Minus these two traveling would not be so bad, but it seems like I am booked for two to four ice baths a day. Building a fire and wringing out wet cloths and putting them back on, and going back to work in those channels—that should be sport for kings but not for John and I."[66]

On January 13 the boat hit a snag and sunk. All the food except tea and sugar were swept overboard and lost. They managed to raise and bail out the boat. Wetherill wrote, "The ice was coming all the time, but no large pieces hit us. In about thirty minutes we had the boat raised and off the snag. I rowed to shore, Pat swimming behind and pushing. We put in the rest of the evening until 10 P.M. drying our outfits."[67]

After various other icy mishaps, and living on tea and sugar for two days, the two reached the mouth of Forbidding Canyon and hiked to the bridge. Even with all the problems, John Wetherill maintained his appreciation for the country: "We had to line the second rapids this morning about one mile below Bridge Canyon. We made it through in good shape. Had a wonderful trip through a country of much grandeur and beauty. I doubt if it can be surpassed anywhere in the world. The hardships we went through only add value to a wonderful experience."[68]

The owner of Rainbow Lodge, Bill Wilson, kept a food cache at a camp near the bridge. "Had we not found Wilson's deserted camp at Rainbow Bridge with plenty of can goods and sugar and flour as we did, the next day's journey to Rainbow Lodge would have been a long drag—for a hungry man over that steep grade—seventeen miles to the Lodge."[69]

Refreshed by Wetherill's good camp cooking, Flattum hiked to Rainbow Lodge the next day. There he obtained gas and food and brought them back on pack mules. With these new supplies the two continued upriver, reaching the mouth of the San Juan about noon on January 19, then continued on to Hole-in-the-Rock. They camped overnight and managed to kill a deer for fresh meat. They started back downstream and made it to Lee's Ferry in three days, retrieving the fancy steel boat on the way.

It is unclear how much the trip did to advance the cause of a Rainbow Bridge National Park. Stearns published an article about it in the house organ of the Pacific Mutual Life Insurance Company, hardly enough publicity on which to launch a national campaign.[70] The idea remained alive and may have helped influenced Ansel Hall, who, along with John Wetherill, made the Rainbow Bridge-Monument Valley expedition another focal point for pushing for a national park in the area (chapter 21).

THE 1937 AND 1938 RIVER TRIPS

Four trips that were made down the Green and Colorado rivers in 1937-38 generated a great deal of national and international publicity: a trip by Norman Nevills with two women botanists aboard, Elzada Clover and Lois Jotter; a solo trip by Haldane (Buzz) Holmstrom also in 1937; a second Holmstrom trip with a partner, Amos Burg, in 1938; and a kayak trip by two Frenchmen and a French woman in 1938. All four trips are enshrined in the lore of Colorado River running, so it is useful to place the individuals involved in perspective. We begin with Norm Nevills.

Norm Nevills

It is generally agreed that Norman (Norm) Davies Nevills (1908–49) started commercial river running on the San Juan and through Glen Canyon in the 1930s.[71] In good river yarn fashion, he embellished his family history in considerable detail. According to Norm, his grandfather, "Captain" William A. Nevills (1842?–1910–12?), made several fortunes in various gold rushes in California, the Klondike, and Nevada. All this allowed him to live in grandeur in the Palace Hotel in San Francisco until it was destroyed in the 1906 earthquake, whereupon he moved to the St. Francis. In one or both venues he occupied an entire floor, waited on by French servants and doted on by a Spanish mistress.[72]

What can be documented (more or less) from other sources is less spectacular but still flamboyant. William A. Nevills was born in Ontario, Canada, probably in 1842. He moved to California around 1876. He married and had two sons, Emerson and William E. Nevills; either his wife died or the couple divorced.[73] In his later years, the captain's fortunes declined. He and wife Delia did have a suite in the Palace Hotel, and he was badly injured there during the 1906 earthquake. He died in 1910 or 1912, broke.

William (Billy) E. Nevills (1865–1941), Norm's father, apparently was in the Klondike gold rush about 1900 and seemingly designed a boat that could survive the rapids of the Yukon River. At some point he returned to California. There he married Mary (Mae) Davies Nevills. Son Norman was born in Chico on April 9, 1908. In about 1921 Billy headed to southeastern Utah to join in the

11.4. Norm Nevills (*left*) and Bill Wood at Mexican Hat, 1933. "First [*sic*] to shoot Mexican Hat rapids in boat." Photographer unknown, MS-122-750. Courtesy of the Museum of Northern Arizona.

recent oil boom. Mae and Norm remained in California, and Norm attended the University of the Pacific in Stockton from 1925 to 1927.

Billy's wife and son joined him in Mexican Hat about 1928. Billy and Mae built the Mexican Hat Lodge in 1932 to accommodate whatever travel business might come their way. In July 1933 Norm met a vivacious nineteen-year-old, Doris Drown, at a dance in Blanding, Utah. After two (or three) more meetings, they were married in October 1933.

The previous June, Norm (fig. 11.4) had met members of the Rainbow Bridge-Monument Valley expedition (chapter 13) who had come to Mexican Hat to launch their 10- and 15-foot boats built by the Wilson Fold-Flat Company of Los Angeles, for a trip through the canyons of the San Juan and Glen Canyon to Lee's Ferry. The expedition made eleven boat trips, of two to four weeks' duration, between 1933 and 1938, launching either from Mexican Hat or the mouth of Copper Canyon. The expedition leaders judged the fold-boats "to be exceptionally seaworthy and tough."[74] Norm apparently helped the expedition party get the boats launched on their first trip. He began to think about boating the San Juan on his own and set out to build a 16-foot boat.

In December 1933, after caulking the seams with old undershirts and patching knotholes with strips of tin, Norm set out for Copper Canyon, 70 miles downstream, with Doris and their friend Jack Frost. But the boat leaked so badly, they got off at the Honaker Trail and hiked the 20 miles back to Mexican Hat. Norm built a second boat, and in March 1934 he, Doris, and his parents floated to the foot of the Honaker Trail, where they met Frost and his wife. After repairing the old boat, they floated on down to Copper Canyon.[75]

Nevills continued to experiment with boat designs, including what he knew about the boat his father had run on the Yukon. He soon learned, or remembered reading about, the Galloway technique of facing downstream in rapids and pushing or pulling the oars to slow, propel, and maneuver the boat.[76] In 1936, Ernest Hunt, whom Nevills had met with the Rainbow Bridge-Monument Valley group, asked Nevills to guide a party down the San Juan and the Colorado so they could visit Rainbow Bridge. According to family legend, Nevills built a boat for the trip of salvaged boards from an old horse trough and an outhouse, and successfully made the trip.

Nevills, Clover, and Jotter

Nevills's efforts to develop a commercially viable river-running business were greatly aided by a trip in 1938, the principal purpose of which was to "botanize" along the river, and especially in the Grand Canyon. The botanists were Elzada U. Clover, a faculty member from the University of Michigan, and her graduate student assistants Lois Jotter and Eugene Atkinson. Because of the two women, the trip received much national publicity, with headlines proclaiming them "First women through the Grand Canyon!!" The publicity made Nevills well-known and furthered his career as a "professional" river runner, which lasted until his untimely death in a plane crash in 1949.

The prime mover in all this was Elzada Urseba Clover (1897–1980). She was born into a farming family near Auburn, Nebraska. She taught in small schools in Nebraska and then in the Rio Grande Valley of Texas, where her parents had relocated. In 1927 she returned to college at Peru State Teachers College in Nebraska, graduating in 1930. She then enrolled at the University of Michigan, receiving a master's degree in 1932 and a Ph.D. in 1935, both in botany. She was then hired as an assistant curator in the university's Botanical Gardens and Arboretum. Her dissertation was on the vegetation of the lower Rio Grande, particularly cacti, her specialty. There was still much descriptive botany to do throughout the Desert West, and Clover set out to collect and describe as many species as she could. In her last year in graduate school, Clover had roomed with three women; one of them was Lois Jotter.

In August 1937, Clover's summer collecting trips brought her to the Mexican Hat Lodge, where she met the Nevills. She intended to use the lodge as a base for botanizing in the surrounding area and told the Nevills of her dream to botanize through the Grand Canyon. She thought it might be possible to do so with a pack train; Nevills rightly convinced her otherwise, suggesting instead a boating trip. Their discussions deepened, and over the following year arrangements were made for a trip from Green River, Utah, down the Colorado through the Grand Canyon to Lake Mead, by then backing up behind Boulder Dam.

Clover chose two of her graduate students, Atkinson and Jotter, to go along on the trip. Atkinson, born in Michigan, was twenty-five years old, studying zoology, and married with a wife and child. He had done a lot of canoeing, some of it in rough water, and his experience was thought to be helpful. He had accepted a position with a county museum in Michigan beginning September 1; his bosses thought the trip was a good idea and encouraged him to collect zoology specimens in the canyons. His wife gave her okay.

Lois Jotter (1914–?) was born in Weaverville, California. Her father was a forester who worked for the Soil Conservation Service. In 1924 the family moved to Ann Arbor, Michigan, where her father held a faculty appointment at the university; he later moved to Washington, D.C. Lois earned a B.A. in biology in 1935 and master's degree in botany and biology the next year. An avid hiker and camper, in 1937 she had attended an eight-week course for national park naturalists in Yosemite; she also had boat-rowing experience.[77]

Lois Jotter preserved her diary and correspondence from the trip, and the letters back and forth between her and her father discuss the trip in detail. She and he visited Claude Birdseye at the USGS office in Washington (chapter 12). Birdseye gave her a set of his plan and profile maps of the Green and Colorado from his 1923 trip.

Nevills chose two others for the trip. One was LaPhene Harris (who not surprisingly preferred to be called "Don"), a native of Soda Springs, Idaho. He had graduated in 1933 from Utah State Agricultural College (now Utah State University) in Logan and gone to work for the USGS. In August 1937 he was transferred to Mexican Hat and put in charge of measuring the stream flow of the San Juan. He lived in a bunkhouse owned by the Nevills and took his meals at the lodge. Two months earlier, Wilbur (Bill) Gibson, a twenty-four-year-old commercial artist from San Francisco, had registered at the lodge. Both Harris and Gibson enjoyed short rides on the San Juan with Nevills, and both ultimately agreed to go on the longer trip.

The arrangement was that each member of the party would put up $200 toward the cost of building the three boats and supplies needed for the trip. The boats were 16 feet long, 4 feet wide at the stern, 5 feet wide at midship, and had pointed bows and square sterns. The bow and stern had a 6-inch rake from the bottom of the boat. Watertight hatches fore and aft provided storage, and there were splashboards around the cockpit. The frames were covered with Super Harboard marine plywood, which was then covered with 2 × 2-inch oak stripping. The Harbor Lumber Company donated the plywood in return for ownership of one of the boats after the trip (assuming they survived). Don Harris helped Nevills build the boats in return for ownership of another one of them.[78] The boats became known as "Cataract boats" or "sadirons."

When everyone arrived in Mexican Hat, the boats were named the *Wen* (for Billy Nevills's initials), the *Mexican Hat*, and the *Botany*. They launched from Green River, Utah, and the first few days were relatively uneventful. On June 23 the party reached the head of Cataract Canyon. There the *Mexican Hat* got away, but was finally recovered some seven rapids downcanyon. The group had a very difficult time in Cataract Canyon, as others had before and would later. The major problem was that Nevills had never run it before. They ran some rapids and wisely lined and portaged others, such as the Big Drop series, but flipped a boat in Gypsum Canyon rapids. Despite upsets and difficulties, and some anxious nights when they were separated along the river, they emerged intact from Narrow Canyon on July 2 and camped just below the mouth of the Dirty Devil River.

On July 3 they stopped and visited the Chaffins, who fed them a delicious and greatly appreciated home-cooked meal. On July 4 they stopped at California Bar, where they found three Japanese prospectors: "They showed us their placer mining operations. It was amazing to find that these men had somehow urged a Ford through that roadless desert to within a short distance of their present location. Their tents, floored with blue and white linoleum, were spotlessly clean."[79]

Just downstream they tried to get into Moqui Canyon, but were prevented by the well-known quicksand at the mouth, so they moved a few miles downstream to Lake Canyon. "We had piles of fun, . . . found polychrome sherds, a perfect room with a fireplace hole, entrance hole, timbers in ceiling all intact."[80] (This was Wasp House, which I named and excavated in 1960 as part of the Glen Canyon Project [chapter 17]). On July 6 they stopped at Aztec/Forbidding Canyon and hiked to Rainbow Bridge, where they spent the day, plundered the food cache, made lots of biscuits, gobbled them down, and hiked back to the boats in the moonlight. While at the bridge they met three people who had ridden in from Rainbow Lodge. One of them, Mildred Baker, from upstate New York, indicated to Nevills much interest in making a long river trip.

The next day a U.S. Coast Guard plane dropped messages instructing them how to signal if they were okay; they did so. They had been reported late arriving at Lee's Ferry, hence the search.

> After supper we floated down the river by moonlight, now anxious to reach Lee's Ferry. . . . Everyone was stimulated and cheerful after this visitation from the sky, and Don and I played harmonicas as the others sang "When It's Moonlight on the Colorado." I doubt if the song will ever be sung in more appropriate surroundings. The moon was glorious, shining on the water between high walls, the white boats were reflected in ripples, and the oars glistened as they rose and fell to rhythm.[81]

Having been reported "lost," the party found several media people awaiting them when they arrived at Lee's Ferry (fig. 11.5). Buzz Holmstrom (see below) had headed there with his boat to join a possible search, but also, as he admitted, to gain some additional publicity. He became friends with Jotter and Clover during their rest days at Marble Canyon Lodge and corresponded with them for the next several years.[82]

Harris left the party there to return to his job. Atkinson also left, apparently because he'd had more than he bargained for and didn't relish what lay ahead in Marble and Grand canyons. Nevills recruited Lorin Bell, from Tuba City, and Dell Reid, a prospector from Monticello, Utah. Both proved to be good boatmen. They headed into Marble Canyon, running and lining rapids as Nevills judged appropriate. At Bright Angel they picked up Emery Kolb, who went with them to Boulder City. The rapids in Grand Canyon were exciting, but there were no major problems. The party did come across a reminder of earlier days along the river:

> One night toward the end of the trip we camped near a side canyon and Bill Gibson found a cache made by an old prospector. It contained three quarts of navy beans, tea, salt, sugar and condensed milk canned in Iowa in 1901. There were a prospector's gold pan, a pick, 150 feet of rope, Chinese sulphur matches that would still light, knives, forks, spoons, and a roll of blank mining claims dated 1904, some of which were filled out. The following locators were recorded on the claim; W.L. Tucker, J.B. Hall, R.B. Harper, Nellie Aber, J.E. Harper, E.R. Clapp, S.P. Clark, and E.E. Harper. The paper was signed by John S. Wilber, Attorney at Law, and was witnessed by John I. Adams and George S. Cram. The beans went to powder when disturbed.[83]

The trip ended in a blaze of publicity at Boulder City, Nevada, on August 1, 1938. As usual, the media mavens distorted their stories

11.5. Nevills, Clover, Jotter party at Lee's Ferry, 1938: (*left to right*) Clover (*front*), Jotter (*back*), Gene Atkinson (*center*), Don Harris (*back*), Norm Nevills (*center front, looking down*). The other two are possibly Dell Reid and Loren Bell. Photographer unknown, 98.520 P 7. Courtesy of the Utah State Historical Society.

in various ways. Danger, conflict, death, and sex sell newspapers—and, more latterly, sound bytes. After the party reached Lee's Ferry, a *Washington Post* front-page headline read "Six Cheat Death in 300-Mile Rapid Ride."[84] Some griping by crew members got turned into conflict, and when that played out, since there were no actual deaths and no apparent sex, the newshounds were left to marvel, in standard male chauvinist fashion, about how two women could make such a trip. From existing records, Clover and Jotter seem to have done far better throughout the trip than some of their male companions, including, at times, Nevills.[85]

Clover and Bell returned to Mexican Hat to accompany Nevills and a party of tourists down the San Juan and Colorado to Lee's Ferry. This allowed Clover to botanize in the canyons of the San Juan.

> It was a pleasure to be on the water again. The San Juan has cut a canyon more beautiful in many respects than the Colorado. In our little collapsible boat, Lorin and I felt inconsequential traveling at a snail's pace around the great loops of the famous "Goosenecks" near Mexican Hat. Days were peaceful as we floated along enjoying the brilliant blue sky with the

> white clouds piling up on the rim of towering red walls. . . . Pictographs and an occasional Indian ruin gave us a hint of life in the past. Bright-colored lizards sat blinking, unafraid. Wary mountain sheep climbed higher and disappeared.[86]

When the party hiked to Rainbow Bridge, a thunderstorm came up, and soon after, the perceived danger of a flash flood.

> The stream was roaring as we started down [the canyon toward the river]. If the water rose very high there would be danger of drowning where the walls narrowed. We [Clover and Bell] ran two miles, fording the stream several times. It was a surprise to find eventually that we had outrun it. [At the junction of Bridge and Forbidding canyons, they stopped. But,] twenty minutes after our arrival there was a roar, then a dull booming sound which brought back memories of the deadly rapids of the Colorado. The flood waters which had dallied along finally gained momentum and were roaring down the canyon. . . . [Bell tried to get a canteen of water from the creek bed before the flood hit.] He climbed the bank just ahead of a wall of blackish water which marched around a bend, rolling boulders in its path. It was an impressive sight. I slept lightly that night. My bed was near the edge of a narrow, slightly slanting shelf and I had visions of rolling into that surly torrent thirty feet below.[87]

In subsequent years Clover spent a lot of time in the Southwest, pursuing new species of cacti and other desert flora. She hiked in Grand Canyon, rode into Rainbow Bridge, and in 1941 spent part of the summer with the Havasupai people in Havasu Canyon collecting plants. Lois Jotter received a Ph.D. in botany in 1943 from the University of Michigan. She had married biologist Victor M. Cutter Jr. in 1942. He was on the faculty at Yale University before he became head of the Biology Department at the Women's College of North Carolina, later the University of North Carolina, Greensboro. After Victor died in 1962, Lois was appointed to replace him and remained on the faculty until 1984.

The "Two Women Through the Grand Canyon" generated a lot of publicity, which was what Nevills was after. Business, indeed, picked up. Nevills Expeditions, clearly a joint effort of Doris and Norm, did well. In 1940 they planned and successfully ran a trip from Green River, Wyoming, through the Grand Canyon. Accompanying them were Del Reid, Charles Larabee, Mildred Baker (the woman Nevills had met at Rainbow Bridge), John Southworth, and Hugh Cutler, later a river runner and, still later, a famed botanist at the Missouri Botanical Garden. During the Glen Canyon Project, Cutler analyzed all the domesticated plant remains we recovered from various archaeological sites (chapters 15–18).

Barry Goldwater and Anne Rosner joined the party at Green River, Utah. Goldwater(1909–98)—native Arizonan, long-time U.S. senator from Arizona, and presidential candidate in 1964—first visited northern Arizona in 1916 or 1918. He was entranced by the country and the Hopi and Navajo people who lived there. As a young man he began his famous collection of Hopi katsina dolls, which he donated to the Heard Museum in 1969.

Goldwater's fascination with Indian people led him to join the Smoki (pronounced "Smoke eye") in Prescott, Arizona, in 1941. The group was formed in 1921 by a bunch of white males indulging in that peculiar form of bonding behavior noted by Alexis de Tocqueville in the 1830s, a passion for joining lodges and fraternities, and dressing up in strange costumes.[88] Many such groups with Indian themes were founded in the nineteenth century. The famous American anthropologist Lewis Henry Morgan got his start by joining one such group, the Grand Order of the Iroquois, in the 1850s and rose to become the "Grand To-do-de-ho." Like the Boy Scouts, it was all part of white guys' passion for "playing Indian."

The Smokis dressed up as Indians and performed "traditional" dances, usually during Prescott Frontier Days. The group can most charitably be described as a minstrel show in red face. Just as minstrel shows and black-face singers and comedians purported to "honor" African Americans by denigrating them on stage, so too did the Smoki claim to "honor" Indians by their "ritual dances." Apparently it never occurred to the Smoki to ask the Indians what they thought of it all. Others thought very little of it. A *Los Angeles Times* reporter in 1924 called the Smoki ritual "a moronic attempt to be funny . . . a thoroughly offensive, objectionable and indefensible exhibition of bad taste."[89] Barry Goldwater was inducted into the group in 1941 and was a frequent participant for many years. It may have been in bad taste, but it was good Arizona politics. Amazingly, the group did not fade into well-merited oblivion until the 1980s.

Male bonding behavior aside, Goldwater was much interested in the Colorado River and the Glen Canyon Country. During the 1940 trip he kept a diary to which he added historical background material and published in mimeographed form after the trip ended.[90]

Like all river trips, the group had various problems in Cataract Canyon, which Goldwater recounts. On July 20, 1940, they stopped at Hite Crossing and met Arthur Chaffin and his wife. Goldwater noted Chaffin's "stern wheeler . . . which goes up and down the river with supplies for the few placer miners hereabouts." On July 22 they stopped at "Cass Hite's old cabin at the mouth of Red Canyon, . . . across from Ticaboo Creek. . . ." Clearly he misunderstood, mistaking Bert Loper's cabin for Hite's. They stopped at Smith's Fork "to fill canteens and see the petroglyph panel" (fig. 17.4). They soon stopped at the mouth of Moqui Canyon to get out of the sun. On the river it was "Just as hot as hell, 110 degrees, no shade, no clouds."[91]

Downstream they found a mining camp. No one was home. They ate heartily of the miners' food cache—canned shrimp, canned mushrooms and "a good selection of fancy canned goods and sauces of all kinds. . . . What was last night a full cupboard would tonight be a familiar sight to Mother Hubbard. . . . a list was kept of what we used, and we will send a check to cover it." It's hardly likely the miners were pleased when they returned. Goldwater described the cabin and situation:

> This cabin is built right against the red sandstone cliff that forms one back wall. The other three walls are made of rock with the cracks filled in with mud; a dirt floor, roof of iron and canvas. . . . The interior has a stove, two tables, three cupboards, and an oil drum heater in one corner. . . . The mining equipment is all good and in first class condition, showing that a lot of money has been spent here. Their gold log, though, doesn't show much good return.[92]

On July 25 the party camped for two days at the mouth of the Escalante River so that Nevills, Rossner, Baker, Southworth, Larabee, and Cutler could hike upriver to locate what some said was the world's largest natural bridge. They had heard of it from Herbert Gregory, who apparently had heard of it from locals. The hikers reported that they had indeed found the bridge in a side canyon of Forty-Mile Gulch, and although not "the world's largest," it was spectacular nonetheless. Nevills wanted to name the bridge "Nijoni," but the others prevailed and "agreed to send in the name of Gregory," which it officially became.[93] The arch is submerged below Lake Powell.

On July 26 the group visited Hole-in-the-Rock, Hidden Passage, and Music Temple. The next day they camped at the mouth of Forbidding

Canyon and hiked to Rainbow Bridge. Bill Wilson, of Rainbow Lodge, had left a stash of food for the party at his fly camp in Bridge Canyon. Goldwater offered to make Dutch oven biscuits. "We managed to get out the damnedest batch of biscuits anyone ever saw. Their lack of excellence did not stop their being consumed almost immediately, but I have always held that jam well spread can kill a lot of bad bread."[94]

When the party reached Warm Creek and were in Arizona, Goldwater claimed that the air became better, the birds sang sweeter, and so on, and he chiseled an inscription on the rock saying, "ARIZONA WELCOMES YOU."[95]

At Lee's Ferry Goldwater chronicled the story of John D. Lee and the ill-fated *Charles Spencer* steamboat. According to Goldwater, his friend Bill Wilson of Rainbow Lodge was one of five crew members who had worked the coal-laden steamboat downstream from Warm Creek to Lee's Ferry on its maiden voyage.[96] On August 4 the party headed into Marble Canyon for the rest of their voyage, which ended on Lake Mead on August 22, 1940. In 1995, Goldwater "stated without hesitation: 'I enjoyed it as much as anything I ever did.'"[97]

Nevills managed to keep his river-running business going during World War II, principally through numerous San Juan-Glen Canyon trips. One such in 1945 was filmed by Warner Brothers and released in 1946 as one of the studio's Sports Parade shorts (fig. 11.6). The script was by one De Leon Anthony (1901–79), who wrote scripts for dozens of sports films and travelogs from 1928 to 1956. The film, *Facing Your Danger,* won an Academy Award for documentary short subject in 1946. According to those who have seen it, rapids were renamed and shown out of sequence. Dock Marston appears in the film, as does, of course, Nevills himself.[98]

Nevills and Doris expanded their business after the war, running the upper Green River and the Salmon in Idaho in addition to their San Juan-Glen Canyon and Grand Canyon trips. But the San Juan-lower Glen Canyon trips were the company's bread and butter. Nevills made at least forty trips between 1938 and 1949 with parties of various sizes. The trips had standard stops at campsites in both canyons. One was at the mouth of Forbidding Canyon. Nevills and a boatman would climb the cliff on the left side and build a large fire. Nevills, in a booming voice, would then tell the Paiute tale of Tavwoats leading the grieving chief through the river gorge to see his dead wife, and then rolling the great river into the gorge to keep others from following (chapter 5). This was followed by Nevills chanting, "And now, Great God of the River and the Universe, we offer this tribute to you in gratitude for the safe passage you so far have afforded us." Thereupon, he and the boatman would dump the fire over the cliff, like the firefall presented in Yosemite Park for so many years.[99]

Nevills bought an airplane and learned to fly it. On September 19, 1949, he and Doris took off from the dirt strip near their home; the engine failed, and the plane crashed and exploded, killing them both. Later their ashes were scattered over the rivers they loved. Two of their boatmen, J. Frank Wright and Jim Rigg, took over Nevills Expeditions and renamed the company Mexican Hat Expeditions. They began offering trips of eighteen to twenty days through the Grand Canyon, usually in July, using the cataract boats. Another boatman, Don Harris, formed Harris-Brennan River Expeditions. Still another, Kent Frost, formed a tour service for hiking and jeep trips.

In the 1960s the Norm and Doris's daughter, Joan, and her husband, Gaylord Staveley, took over Mexican Hat Expeditions. In 1969 they ran their cataract boats for the last time on a commemorative trip from Green River, Wyoming, to the foot of Grand Canyon, portaging around Flaming Gorge and Glen Canyon reservoirs. The boats were then stored. Mexican Hat Expeditions metamorphosed into Canyoneers, Inc., running pontoon boat trips through the Grand Canyon.

11.6. Film crew with Nevills's boats at Hidden Passage, 1945. Photographer unknown, 917.911 P 7 10450. Courtesy of the Utah State Historical Society.

In 1973 Canyoneers hired a high school kid from upstate New York as a swamper. By 1975 he had made nineteen trips through Grand Canyon and had become a lead boatman. His name is Brad Dimock.[100] He went on to become a major figure in Grand Canyon river running and as a river historian. Dimock linked up with another river runner/historian, Roy Webb, in 1991. Along with river runner/historian Richard Quartaroli, they have done great things for recording the history of the Colorado River. They have been aided and abetted by numerous other river runner/historians—and just plain river historians. Much of this chapter and some of the Powell chapters are derived, with gratitude, from their good works.

The "French Trio"

Perhaps the most unusual pre-World War II river trip was made in 1938 in kayaks by three French citizens: Bernard and Genevieve De Colmont (who were on their honeymoon) and Antoine De Seyne. They planned to go all the way through the canyons to Lake Mead. De Colmont was a photographer for the Paris Museum of Natural History and planned to make a motion picture of their trip, which he did. The idea of an attractive Frenchwoman running the Colorado in a kayak attracted great media attention. They started just below Green River, Wyoming. When they reached Jensen, Utah, they were fêted by the citizenry of Jensen and nearby

Vernal. They continued on through Cataract and Glen canyons but stopped at Lee's Ferry, deterred by cold weather and floating ice. Their motion picture was shown many times in France. Genevieve and Bernard later opened Le Club 55 at St. Tropez on the French Riviera. During the 1950s it became a hangout for French filmmakers, particularly in 1955 during the filming of the Bridget Bardot classic *And God Created Woman*.[101]

Buzz Holmstrom, "The Doing of the Thing"

Buzz Holmstrom is remembered as the only person to run all the rapids along the Green and Colorado rivers.[102] He ran most of them on a solo trip in 1937; the few he portaged or lined in 1937 he ran in 1938. Haldane (Buzz) Holmstrom (1909–46) was born near Coquille, Oregon. He worked in a gas station for several years and was briefly in the Merchant Marine. By 1934 he had become avidly interested in river running—particularly the Rogue River in southwestern Oregon, which by then had a long history of boating on various sections. The Rogue is well named; heading in the Cascade Mountains, it has lots of white water along its upper, middle, and lower stretches before emptying into the Pacific Ocean. Boaters had developed an upturned, flare-sided boat called the Oregon drift boat, some of whose characteristics are similar to Galloway-type boats. It is said to handle better in rough water.

In 1935 Holmstrom built a boat of his own design and ran the Rogue. The trip was not too successful, but hooked him on river running. He was fascinated by the Colorado River and read everything he could get his hands on, including books published by Clyde Eddy and Oscar Jaeger about their trips in the 1920s.[103] He built a new Galloway-style boat but,

> a far better boat. . . . It is shorter and wider, making it far more stable and maneuverable. It had increased upturn at the bow and stern making it ride better and pivot easier over (instead of through) the waves. Although no heavier than a Galloway boat it is easily twice as strong—a feat he accomplished by using thicker planks of native Port Orford cedar. . . . He made the cockpit much smaller than the Galloway boats, allowing for more storage and buoyancy, while reducing the potential for swamping in big water. Lastly its greater width gave far greater leverage on the oars, allowing him to move faster and with greater force.[104]

Holmstrom hauled his boat to Green River, Wyoming, and launched on October 4, 1937. He lined Disaster and Triplet Falls in Lodore Canyon, portaged around Big Drop Three in Cataract Canyon, ran the other rapids, and passed through Glen Canyon. He reached the Navajo Bridge below Lee's Ferry on November 5. He went to Flagstaff to obtain supplies, returned, and resumed his trip on November 7, arriving at Bright Angel on November 12. After hiking to the South Rim and visiting with Emery Kolb, he continued on, running all the rapids in the canyon except Lava Falls, which he portaged. Toward the end of the trip he ruminated in his journal about the Colorado:

> I think this river is not treacherous as has been said—Every rapid speaks plainly just what it is & what it will do to a person & a boat in its current waves boil whirlpools and rocks—if only one will read and listen carefully—It demands respect—& will punish those who do not treat it properly—some places it says—go here safely if you do it just this way—& in others it says—do not go here at all with the type of boat you have—but many people will not believe what it says.[105]

He also pondered what his achievement meant to him—the first person to run the Green and Colorado rivers alone. "I had thought—once past there [Lava Cliff rapid]—my reward will begin—but now—everything seems kind of empty & I find I have already had my reward—*in the doing of the thing.*"[106]

On Thanksgiving Day he finished rowing across the rising Lake Mead and bumped up against Boulder Dam. He sent a telegram to his mother "OK at Boulder Dam, Haldane."[107]

It has been my privilege to run Cataract and Grand canyons with some excellent boatmen. I think they and all their compatriots would agree that "every rapid speaks plainly just what it is" and that what's ultimately important is "the doing of the thing." In this sense, Brad Dimock's summation of Buzz Holmstrom as a "boatman's boatman" is certainly correct.

The trip brought Holmstrom a lot of national publicity. This led Amos Burg to seek him out with a proposal to film Buzz re-creating his river trip. Burg (1901–86) was a native of Portland, Oregon, who had made several solo canoe trips on rivers in the Northwest and western Canada in the 1920s. He became a professional adventurer, running canoe trips on the Columbia, Snake, Yukon, and other Northwest Territory rivers throughout the 1930s and presenting films and slide lectures of his trips nationally.

Holmstrom agreed to the trip. When Julius Stone heard about it, he sent $500 to help defray costs. Holmstrom repainted his boat and named it the *Julius F.* Burg had an inflatable rubber raft custom made by the Goodrich Company. The plan was to start at the headwaters of the Green River in the Wind River Mountains and run all the way to Boulder Dam. Burg's friend, Phil Lundstrom, came along to help with filming. After a couple of days it was evident that the upper Green wouldn't work, so they hauled the boats to Green River, Wyoming, and started from there. Lundstrom left at Vernal, Utah, and the two recruited a local man, Willis Johnson, who stayed with them throughout the trip.

They passed through Cataract Canyon, where Buzz ran Big Drop Three. They ran on through Glen Canyon (see below) and on October 16 headed into Marble Canyon. On November 7 Holmstrom sent another telegram to his mother from Boulder City: "OK again. Haldane."

The film of the trip, *Conquering the Colorado*, was issued as a sports documentary in 1939. Burg went on for many years filming adventure stories around the world, finally settling in Alaska, working for Alaska Department of Fish and Game, making numerous films, and continuing to make river trips until very late in his life.[108]

In early 1939, Holmstrom made an improbable trip with a widow, one Edith Clegg. English born, Clegg lived in Vancouver, B.C. She had long nurtured the dream of re-creating Lewis and Clark's trip across America from west to east. After her husband died, she decided to act on it, despite the trepidations of her children and grandchildren. Holmstrom was recommended to Clegg by Amos Burg. She came to Coquille, met him, and they agreed on the trip. He built two boats that could be run with outboard motors, hired two of his friends as boatmen, plus Willis Johnson, who had been with him and Burg on the 1938 trip.

The trip is artfully chronicled by Vince Welsh, Cort Conley, and Brad Dimock.[109] The route was up the Columbia and Snake rivers, then a portage across the Rockies to the headwaters of the Yellowstone. From that point Holmstrom and Clegg continued alone—down the Yellowstone to the Missouri, on to the Mississippi, up the Ohio and Allegheny to Lake Erie, through the New York State barge canal, and down the Mohawk and the Hudson rivers to New York City. They left Portland, Oregon, on April 23, 1939, and arrived in New York City on September 12.

Holmstrom worked at various jobs in 1940–41, including as driller and boatman for tests for the proposed Echo Park Dam on the Green River and the proposed Bridge Canyon Dam in Grand Canyon. He served in the navy from 1942 to 1945. In April 1946 he was hired as a boatman for a Coast and Geodetic Survey project studying the Grand Ronde River in eastern Oregon. By mid-May he was on the swollen river with nasty rapids, trying to manage an ungainly sweepboat overloaded with gear. On May 18 he borrowed a .22 rifle "to go shoot a chicken," he said. He was found slumped over the gun with a fatal bullet wound in his temple. The coroner ruled it was suicide. He was thirty-seven years old.

Holmstrom in Glen Canyon

Buzz Holmstrom kept a journal of his Colorado River trips, including some descriptions of Glen Canyon. On the way to Green River he stopped in Salt Lake City to talk with Bert Loper, with whom he had been corresponding. He wrote "have been visiting Bert Loper & will stay there tonite—he sure is interesting."[110] At Hite he met a crew planning a road from Hanksville to the river. He gathered some petrified wood on a bench above the river and collected pot sherds in the "Moki Fort." Farther downstream he met one Billy Hay from Torrey, who was working a mining claim on California Bar that he had acquired from Bert Loper. Hay was an

> expert at finding [archaeological] dwellings and writings—went across [river] & up 1/2 mi & took pict of writings at Smith Fk—[Hays] says most relics are off main riv & relics well picked off—found some mummies up Mysterious Canyon (Lake C). . . . up little canyon to R of [Stanton] dredge—Moki granary—wall and small door in front of cave—steps chiseled up there . . . —up here [i.e. in Glen Canyon] Lake Ck is called Mysterious Canon [*sic*]—as there are many dwellings up there . . . several mummies etc have been taken out . . . am sort of disgusted with cliff dwellings as there is nothing much to them.[111]

Holmstrom passed the mouth of Aztec Creek and did not hike up to Rainbow Bridge.

On the 1938 trip with Amos Burg, the party stopped at Hite, then at Smith Creek to see the petroglyphs, and explored a half mile up Moqui Canyon to visit "remnants of cliff dwellings and Indian fort." Burg wrote, "The peculiar characteristic of the red sandstone of Glen Canyon makes it assume many forms under erosion including large caves which the Mokis utilized for homes." The party stopped at Music Temple "to see the names of the Powell Exped. chiseled in rocks." They hiked to Rainbow Bridge. "It surprised us to find that 2800 [*sic*] persons had registered here."[112]

POST-WORLD WAR II RIVER RUNNING

The post-World War II boom in boating through the Colorado River canyons led to the use of all sorts of conveyances. One was a custom-made 18-foot aluminum canoe built by the Grumman Aircraft Company in the early 1950s for Homer Levi Dodge (1887–1983), a prominent physicist at the University of Oklahoma and a canoe aficionado who made trips on rivers all across the United States. Between 1953 and 1963, Dodge made several canoe trips on the Green River and through Glen Canyon, sometimes on his own, sometimes with commercial river runners.[113]

The Boy Scout Brigades

One day in late June 1958, we emerged from one of the Glen Canyon side canyons to see a flotilla of young males drifting by in rubber rafts. They were doing young male things—picking their noses, horsing around, having water fights, some looking terminally bored. One or two were actually looking at the scenery. As they went on around the bend, the noise level faded away. We saw other such groups later that summer and the next, and my compatriots who were on the river in 1961 and 1962 saw still more.

In 1947 the Salt Lake City Council of the Boy Scouts of America had decided that their Explorer

Scouts needed some new outdoor adventures. One council member, John Cross, urged trips through Glen Canyon. There was a major federal surplus center in town where for $10 to $25 one could obtain seven- and ten-man inflatable rafts. Cross bought ten of them. In April 1947 he hired Bert Loper to lead a Boy Scout float trip through the canyon. It was a success. More trips followed in 1947–49 with Loper as leader. Some of the scouts who were with Loper still fondly recall the trips they made with him. Others soon got involved. One was Malcolm Ellingson and another was Albert Quist, both involved with the Boy Scouts. They started Glen Canyon scout trips on their own. Ellingson became known as Moki-Mac, a beloved storyteller around campfires in the canyon.

Some of the scout trips we saw in 1958 and 1959 were probably led by Moki-Mac. Al Quist had three sons—Richard, Clair, and Bob—who literally grew up on the river. The boys started their own commercial river-running business in 1969 and brought in Mac Ellingson as a partner. Thus was born the Moki-Mac river-running company. In 1971, when Wally Schirra and I participated in a re-creation of John Wesley Powell's trip, filmed by CBS News for the Smithsonian Institution (chapter 21), Clair Quist led the float trip from Brown's Hole into the Uintah Basin. In 1981, some family members and I floated Cataract Canyon with Richard and Bob Quist, and the following year, the lower half of the Grand Canyon with a Moki-Mac crew led by Roger Murphy. Perhaps some of the boys we saw in 1958 and 1959 included the Quist brothers; I never did ask them. As of 2010 the Quists were still very much in the river-running business, with trips on the Green River, in Cataract Canyon, Grand Canyon, and elsewhere.[114]

In the early 1950s the official media organ of the Mormon Church, the *Deseret News*, opined editorially that taking Boy Scouts down the river somehow endangered them, or their psyches, or maybe their faith. The Boy Scout Council dropped the program. By sheer coincidence, by that time a new Mormon-led organization had come on the scene, designed to take scouts on river trips and preserve their faith at the same time.

SOCOTWA

One outfit we saw frequently on the river in 1958 and 1959 was SOCOTWA. The organization was named for the Mormon Church South Cottonwood Ward, centered in Murray, Utah—the name probably borrowed from the ward's choir, the SOCOTWA Singers. In 1947–48, two ward members, Dale Labrum and Merlin Shaw, acquired a brand-new surplus ten-man raft complete with paddles and grooved wooden plugs for stopping up bullet holes. They made their first raft trip in Glen Canyon in 1948. They quickly learned of the Boy Scout Council trips and decided to get into the business. Most, but not all, Boy Scout troops in Utah are run by the Mormon Church at the ward or state level. Wallace Stegner, baptized a Presbyterian, grew up in Salt Lake City in the 1930s and managed to become an Eagle Scout in a Mormon troop.

Labrum and Shaw set up a nonprofit corporation, SOCOTWA, "for the purpose of guiding the youth and providing a meaningful relationship with nature."[115] Interest grew rapidly, as did the organization. By 1955–56 the company had more than thirty rafts and associated gear, a fleet of busses and trucks, and were running as many as six trips at a time. The trips were cooperative. One joined the organization for $15 a year and then paid about $50 for a week-long trip. From the outset, women were full participants as guides, boat captains, and trip leaders. All trips adhered to standard Mormon practices: no smoking or drinking, daily prayers, Sunday school, and plenty of opportunities for romance. Presumably that was sufficient for the *Deseret News*.

Trips originated in Salt Lake City. Busses carried participants to Green River, Utah, where they met stake bed trucks loaded with boats and river gear. People threw their personal gear atop the boats and piled on top of that to ride down North Wash to Hite. There the boats were inflated, crews and duties assigned, and they headed out. There were standard stops, including Hole-in-the-Rock (chapter 20). Participants hiked to the top, novices enticed by stories of a mythical Dairy Queen at the top (a sure lure, given the Mormons' love of ice cream). Church services were held in Music Temple, and participants signed a register book kept in a can under an overhang.[116]

There was a ritual hike to Rainbow Bridge and, after returning to the beach at riverside, a "grand fiesta" complete with music and dancing (Mormons love dancing almost as much as ice cream). It's interesting that other river runners complained bitterly about the debris and trash left by SOCOTWA parties on the beach. As noted, there was a lot of sparking. Several couples who met on a trip were later married.

But there was a darker, tragic side. Some trips had inexperienced leaders. In 1958 a SOCOTWA trip came off the river at Kane Creek. The party got all the way to Kanab before they counted noses and came up one Boy Scout short. He had apparently walked over a hill, perhaps to relieve himself, and gotten disoriented. There was a frantic search, but his remains were not found until a year later. In May 1961 one person was killed and a second badly injured during a trip on the Green River. Later that year, leader Walt Scott and four scouts were drowned in a flash flood in Zion Canyon Narrows. In June 1963 a SOCOTWA stake bed truck loaded with people was headed down the Hole-in-the-Rock road when the truck stalled going up out of a steep wash, rolled backward, and overturned. Eight scouts and four adults, including founder Merlin Shaw, were killed, and twenty-six others were injured, some critically.[117]

SOCOTWA's Glen Canyon trips were ended both by tragedy and the filling of Lake Powell. The organization morphed into a group focused on land-based trips and continued into the 1990s.

THE INIMITABLE GEORGIE WHITE

The Salt Lake City Boy Scout Council and SOCOTWA were not the only ones to discover surplus rubber rafts, and soon the rafts were in use not only on the Colorado River system but other rivers across the West, and ultimately across the Western Hemisphere. Some also discovered surplus inflatable bridge pontoons—especially 22- and 27-foot-long models. A 27-footer sandwiched between two 22-footers and steered by an outboard motor at the stern could carry numerous passengers and their gear. Collectively these inflatables were called baloney boats. On the river the big ones looked like floating gypsy caravans, with people perched on the gear and hanging onto the pontoons wherever they could.

Certainly the most flamboyant of the river runners on the Colorado was Georgie White Clark. One of my most vivid memories of Glen Canyon in 1959 was the sight of Georgie and her triple-pontoon raft, covered with a motley array of people, stopped for lunch just below the Little Rincon. Coming down a small side canyon, my partner and I had found one of her passengers, clad only in a swimming suit and hat, squatting in the middle of a luxuriant poison ivy clump, answering nature's call. We walked back to the river with the rather perturbed fellow and recommended that he jump in the river and then ask Georgie if she had any Calomine lotion on board. We talked with her briefly and were struck by her brilliant blue eyes and broad, open smile. I had seen her rig at a distance in 1958 but had not met her then. We had certainly heard stories from other river runners. Like her or hate her, everyone agreed she was an original. If ever anyone deserved the theme song "I did it my way," it was Georgie.

Georgie White (1910–92) was born Bessie De Ross in 1910 in Oklahoma, but as a young girl she took the diminutive of her father's first name, Georgie.[118] She grew up in Denver. In 1928 she married Harold Clark, whom she divorced in 1941. She married James Ray (Whitey) White in early 1942. During World War II she worked in defense plants and trained as a pilot for the Army Air Force Ferry Command. But after completing her 500 hours of flight training, the command was deactivated. Georgie returned to Los Angeles and worked at various jobs.

She had been active in the Sierra Club for several years and did a lot of mountain hiking. At one club meeting she met Harry Aleson (fig. 14.1), who became a major figure in her life for decades. Aleson had served in World War I and had been gassed, which gave him a small disability pension. He worked at various jobs, some around the Colorado River and the Grand Canyon, which became his passions for the rest of his life. By 1945 he was running summer trips on the San Juan and Colorado rivers for Norm Nevills. Later he went on his own (see chapter 14 for additional biography on Aleson).

When Georgie met Harry, he was planning to start from a point within the Grand Canyon, hike up to the North Rim, climb Mount Dellenbaugh, then head across the Arizona Strip to St. George, Utah. Georgie joined in. On August 20, 1944, Harry, Georgie, and a biologist, Gerhard Bakker, set out. They managed to get up out of the canyon with some difficulty. Seven days later, hungry and with badly blistered feet, they were picked up by a government trapper and given a ride to St. George. Undeterred, Georgie and Harry soon were doing other hiking trips in and around the Grand Canyon. Husband Whitey was not pleased by all this, and the couple started divorce proceedings but ultimately reconciled. Georgie claimed her relationship with Aleson was platonic, bound by a love of hiking and the Colorado River.

In late June 1945, Harry and Georgie swam down the Colorado River in Grand Canyon from Diamond Creek to Lake Mead. It was a harrowing trip, but they made it. Soon after Georgie began going along on Aleson's trips through Glen Canyon as a camp helper. In June 1946 the two decided to replicate John White's trip (if it happened) through the Grand Canyon on a raft. They hiked into the canyon from the North Rim to the mouth of Parashant Wash. They had brought along a small inflatable raft which they used to carry supplies and sometimes themselves. They tried to find logs that they could lash together for a raft but did not succeed. They finally emerged from the canyon after about a week and gratefully accepted a ride across Lake Mead in a National Park Service boat.

Their next adventure was to raft through Cataract Canyon on surplus rubber boats. They started in late October 1947, managed to get through, and arrived at Hite on November 5, having run many rapids and lining others. Georgie was now thoroughly hooked on river running. In 1948 the two of them took a raft down the Escalante River, in a place or two having to tip the raft up on its edge to get through narrow spots. Georgie continued to go on rafting trips with Aleson and was receiving a lot of publicity for her exploits.

Georgie and the River Goddesses

The publicity brought Georgie a very strange assignment in 1950, chaperone for five starlets and models for a movie to be made in Glen Canyon.[119] The idea for the film came from one Dave Sutton, a California fashion and pin-up photographer. He wanted to make a "theatrical travelog" in which five young women would have an adventuresome time in Glen Canyon. The film, titled *River Goddesses,* was to be directed by Carl Junghaunatz, who had gone from being an officer in the German Wehrmacht in World War II to a minor film director/producer in Hollywood.

Sutton got in touch with Jim Rigg of Mexican Hat Expeditions, who provided three Cataract boats, one San Juan boat, and two boatmen. Apparently Sutton knew of Georgie White and hired her as chaperone. She also rowed one of the Cataract boats. A friend from the Sierra Club rowed the San Juan boat, used as the platform for filming on the river. According to Georgie,

> All of the girls were under eighteen [*sic*; all were in their early twenties] so they asked me to play chaperone as well as run the boats. When they showed up at Hite they looked like a traveling circus. They had brought six [*sic*; five] gorgeous Hollywood girls, an entire camera crew, and a number of other people to handle the miscellaneous functions. The first thing the director did after they unloaded was to plop down in his chair on the beach and order martinis. I remember watching him drink that martini and thinking, "Boy, this is going to be some trip."[120]

Sutton had chosen five models: Lee Moi Chu, Martha Moody, Becky Barnes, Irene Hettinga, and Irish McCalla. In 1950, Nellie Elizabeth "Irish" McCalla (1928–2002) was a stunning 5'10", twenty-two-year-old blond.[121] Born in Nebraska, she moved to Los Angeles in 1942. By about 1950 she was doing pin-up modeling, including for the famous Alberto Vargas, whose idealized women graced *Esquire Magazine,* the noses of many World War II American airplanes, and, in the 1960s, the pages of *Playboy.* After the filming of *River Goddesses*, McCalla spent a few months as a showgirl at the mob-owned Flamingo Hotel in Las Vegas and played some bits parts in a few 1950s B-movies. She continued modeling and went on to star in the original 1955–56 syndicated television series *Sheena, Queen of the Jungle*, based on the classic 1942–53 comic book character drawn by Will Eisner.[122] In the late 1950s she turned to art, ultimately producing hundreds of paintings and lithographs. She moved to Prescott, Arizona, in 1982 and died in Tucson in 2002 of a brain tumor. Lee Moi Chu had bit parts in three films in the mid-1950s, but little else is known about her or the other women.

Filming for the project began at Hite and continued to Lee's Ferry. There seems to have been numerous T&A shots of the women climbing up the slickrock, purportedly in danger of falling off cliffs or being swept into rapids. According to Georgie, she was asked to deliberately upset her boat several times in the small rapid just below Lee's Ferry. The editing made the rapid look large and the women in danger. There was a flurry of publicity photographs, provided by Sutton, in various magazines in late 1950–early 1951 about the film. According to Georgie, the film was finished and released as *Six Girls Against the Colorado*. No such film is known, and no copy of *River Goddesses* had been found as of 2008.[123]

In a 1990s interview with Richard Westwood, McCalla said she thought the film trip caused Georgie White to think about becoming a commercial river runner in her own right. "I don't know if she ever had the idea before, but I know during the trip, when one of us would fall down something or go off in the wrong direction, she'd rescue us and say, 'I'm going to take people down the river because I can take anybody down, if I can get you dingalings through.'"[124]

Whatever the stimulus, Georgie White did go commercial soon after. She was among those pioneering the use of seven- and ten-man rubber rafts (fig. 11.7). In 1953, in the middle of a Grand Canyon trip, she had the idea of tying three ten-man rafts together broadside to make a triple rig. The idea was that such a rig would go through rapids without upsetting because they would balance each other in big waves. It did work—most of the time. She also started constructing very large rigs consisting of three inflatable bridge pontoons tied together, the center one usually being 27 feet, the side ones 22 feet. Both rigs came to be called "G-rigs" for "Georgie rigs."[125]

11.7. A typical Georgie White rafting party in Grand Canyon, 1950s. White is in the back of the boat at far left. Photographer unknown, NAU 48241. Courtesy of Cline Library, Northern Arizona University.

A major impetus for the large rigs was her "share the expense" concept: passengers paid a fee much smaller than those charged by other commercial outfitters who used wooden or smaller rubber boats and provided often very elaborate meals and services. Larger rigs meant being able to carry more passengers per trip. Passengers also helped with cooking plain rather than elaborate foods and did camp chores. Hence, the cost per person went down. It was a great success. Thousands of people enjoyed her trips and became faithful "Georgie White River Rats."

Georgie White ran trips through Glen Canyon until 1962. She continued to run Grand Canyon and many other rivers until 1991, when she had to stop because of the onset of cancer. She refused treatment and died, as she had lived, on her own terms, in May 1992.

Ken Sleight

Among those running trips for the Boy Scouts in Glen Canyon in the 1950s was Ken Sleight (b. 1929). I did not meet him on the river in 1958 or 1959 that I recall, but I likely saw one or more of his trips. Sleight was and is one of the great heroes of those devoted to the Colorado River and to environmental issues in the West. He was born and grew up in Bear Lake, Idaho. In 1951 he made a float trip through Lodore Canyon with two river runners: Blaine Buzenbark, a nephew of Bert Loper, and Jim Jean, who had boated with Loper on various trips. During the trip they spoke glowingly of

Glen Canyon, and Sleight determined he had to see it. But it took a while. He went in the army, served in Korea, was discharged, went to the University of Utah, and then went to work for the Firestone Rubber Company. But the river kept coming back to him. In 1955 he bought three surplus rubber rafts and started running Desolation and Glen canyons. Soon he was taking Boy Scout trips in Glen Canyon. In 1957 he founded Ken Sleight's Wonderland Expeditions. In 1963 he moved his operation to Escalante, Utah, and began adding overland pack trips to his business as well as running Grand Canyon. In 1966 he left Escalante, primarily because of his opposition to the proposed Trans-Escalante Highway from Bullfrog to Wahweap marinas (fortunately it was never built). In 1969 he moved to Green River, Utah, and opened a bookstore in addition to his river-running business.

In 1967, while Sleight was getting ready for a Grand Canyon run, he met Edward Abbey at Lee's Ferry. They became close friends and remained so until Abbey's death in 1989. In 1985 Sleight and his second wife, Jane Hunter, bought the Pack Creek Ranch in the foothills of the La Sal Mountains, where they ran a dude ranch and pack trip business until his retirement. Sleight is generally regarded as the model for Seldom Seen Smith in Edward Abbey's novels about a group of friends who want to blow up Glen Canyon Dam (see the postlude). He has spoken out on environmental issues since the 1950s and remains an iconic figure among river runners and aficionados of the Colorado River.[126]

› 12 ‹

HARNESSING THE COLORADO RIVER

IN 1963–64, THE GATES CLOSED ON THE Glen Canyon, Navajo, and Flaming Gorge dams, and Lake Powell, Navajo Reservoir, and Flaming Gorge Reservoir began to fill. Twenty-eight years earlier, in 1935–36, the gates had closed on Hoover Dam, and Lake Mead began to fill behind it. In 1938 the Parker Dam on the lower Colorado River came into operation; in 1953 Davis Dam, located between Hoover and Parker dams, became operational; in 1984 McFee Dam on the Dolores River in Colorado came on line. The structures listed are the major components, along with three dozen-plus smaller dams, diversion tunnels, canals, and related facilities constructed by the U.S. Bureau of Reclamation to "harness the Colorado River." Lake Powell is named, of course, for John Wesley Powell; Davis Dam is named for his nephew, Arthur Powell Davis, the second director of the U.S. Reclamation Service and the mastermind behind plans to dam the Colorado as well as the Rio Grande and other western rivers.[1]

Our principal concern in this chapter is to describe the USGS Colorado River expeditions and the reports the staff produced from about 1909 on as they developed plans to "harness the Colorado River." As background context to this part of our story it is useful to begin with John Wesley Powell's famed *Arid Lands Report* of 1878, which contained the outlines of a bold plan for the federal government to develop and manage the water and other natural resources of the American West.[2]

When Powell's *Report* appeared, there were no federal agencies or policies to manage the public domain. The General Land Office (GLO) was created in 1812 to facilitate the surveying, platting, and sale of public lands. It initially administered the Land Act of 1804, and later the follow-on Preemption Act of 1841 and the Homestead Act of 1862. Under these acts, the GLO's job was mainly to facilitate the transfer of the public domain into private land, or into military or Indian reservations. There were no agencies or mechanisms to facilitate scientific data collection and analysis to use in planning for best-use management of the public domain. Powell's 1878 report—but more importantly, his actions once he took the reins of the U.S. Geological Survey (USGS) in 1881—mark the beginnings of such attempts.

The 1879 legislative act that created the USGS, as well as Powell's Bureau of Ethnology as an arm of the Smithsonian Institution, also created a Public Lands Commission. The commission's charge was to inquire into how public lands were being used and gather information about better ways to use and administer them and provide for the interests of small farmers and settlers. Powell was named to the commission. All the other members represented monied interests, particularly big-time western land barons and ranchers. The commission took testimony throughout the West. Its report was a whitewash: it basically said, more of the status quo—let the land barons, the railroads, and the ranchers have their way. Powell acquiesced. None of the ideas he had advanced in his arid lands report are reflected in the commission report.[3] Certainly he knew he was outvoted and that the commission was, in fact, largely a sham. He did get to visit parts of the West he had not previously seen, although he kept his counsel, his ideas would reemerge as events unfolded.

With the creation of the Bureau of Ethnology, Powell seemingly turned away from geology. In the bureau's first annual report, Powell wrote, "[I]t is the purpose of the Bureau of Ethnology to organize anthropologic [*sic*] research in America."[4] Behind the scenes he had supported Clarence King for the directorship of the USGS, but King hated the trench warfare of Washington politics. He wanted the good life, the high life, the life lived by his rich friends in New York and Washington. With no independent means, that was not possible on a salary of $6,000 a year. He resigned in early 1881 to seek the means for the good life; in the end he found neither. Powell's good friend, President James Garfield, immediately appointed Powell to replace King, allowing him to remain as director of the Bureau of Ethnology. Until 1894 Powell ran both agencies out of one office, taking one salary, thereby freeing up funds to support his beloved bureau, which was never able to realize major budget increases.

Powell's *Arid Lands Report* is widely regarded as the historical touchstone for the large-scale development of water resources, principally irrigation agriculture, in the arid West, generally defined as that part of the United States that lies west of the 100th meridian. Irrigation in the West had a long history before Powell's report. Peoples that archaeologists call Ancestral Puebloans, Hohokam, Mogollon, Fremont, and others had developed highly sophisticated irrigation systems many centuries before Europeans and Euro-Americans entered the western Hemisphere, as indeed had the great high civilizations of Mesoamerica to the south and those in western South America. As Yankees, or Anglos, moved into the Mexican province of Nuevo Mexico after 1821, they observed that both the Pueblo and Hispanic peoples used irrigation systems that tapped the Rio Grande and its tributaries. Anglos in various states and territories farther east had used small-scale irrigation systems from at least 1800 on, as individuals or through private water companies. But large-scale irrigation projects, at first privately funded, and later government funded and developed, began only in the decades after the publication of Powell's report.

The complex histories of water in the West, water law, public policies relating thereto, and the plethora of water projects proposed and developed after 1846 when the Mexican provinces of Nuevo Mexico and Alta California became parts of the United States are far beyond the scope of the present work. Those matters are dealt with in magisterial detail by Donald Pisani and Donald Worster.[5] Here we will draw on their works and those of others to tell the stories of the key personalities, expeditions, and research projects that led to the proposed and actual construction of the major dams on the Colorado River system—most particularly, Glen Canyon Dam.

John Wesley Powell was in Utah for varying periods of time in the years 1869–1874. As he traveled back and forth between Salt Lake City and southern Utah and southern Nevada, he was able to observe at close range the irrigation systems the Mormons had put in place after their arrival in 1847. He was particularly impressed with the cooperative administrative structure the Mormons used to allocate water. Water resources were held in common and allocated to individuals through shares. The number of shares an individual held in a particular ditch system determined how much water he was entitled to use during each irrigation year. In most ditch systems water was allocated by time. If an individual owned X shares of water in a ditch, he was allocated Y hours and Z minutes of time to turn the flow of the ditch onto his property. Water ran twenty-four hours a day. I well remember my stepfather getting up at 2 or 3 a.m. to "take the water" for an hour on his half acre in Ogden, Utah.

Powell and his staff studied the Utah irrigation systems and did some preliminary stream gaging—measuring mean annual flows of water in rivers and streams. In his 1878 report, Powell thought that with proper irrigation 2,262 square miles, or 1,447,920 acres, in Utah could be "redeemed" from desert wasteland and turned to the production of crops or forage. As an aside, in 1997, the U.S. Department of Agriculture reported that 1,212,201 acres in Utah were under irrigation.

Powell saw that using large streams for irrigation would require cooperative efforts, similar to the Utah model, although not "under ecclesiastical organization," as the Mormons were doing. Most importantly, he foresaw construction of large-scale storage reservoirs on stream headwaters with canals leading to irrigable lands. To make his cooperative system work, Powell wanted the Homestead Act modified so that, in arid regions, groups could "settle an irrigation district"—rather than individuals "taking up" the usual 160 acres common in the humid East. But first, he thought, western lands had to be surveyed and classified to determine which of them could be irrigated, where reservoirs should be located, and how much water on an average annual basis a particular stream could provide. In a proposed congressional bill, Powell sought to classify "irrigable lands" throughout the West which could then be properly developed in the kinds of cooperative irrigation districts he envisioned: "That all lands in those portions of the United States where irrigation is necessary to agriculture, which can be redeemed by irrigation, and for which there is accessible water for such purpose, not otherwise utilized or lawfully claimed, sufficient for the irrigation of three hundred and twenty acres of land, shall, for the purposes set forth in this act, be classed as irrigable lands."[6]

In 1888, Powell convinced Congress to appropriate an initial $100,000 to create a U.S. Irrigation Survey as a subdivision of the USGS. In the first annual report for the irrigation survey, Powell wrote:

> The area of the arid region is about 1,300,000 square miles—one third of the entire country. I judge that of this area there can be economically reclaimed, by irrigation, within the present generation, at least 150,000 square miles—an empire one-half as large as the entire area now cultivated in the United States. Irrigated, this land would be worth not less than $30 an acre, adding $2,880,000,000 to the wealth of the nation.
>
> In expending the $100,000 appropriated by Congress on October 2, 1888, and a portion of the $250,000 appropriated on March 2, 1889, I have interpreted the law not as authorizing the construction of works of irrigation, but only as directing a comprehensive investigation

> of prevailing conditions: the whereabouts of irrigable land most eligible for redemption and its segregation for homestead settlement; the amount of available water; the location of reservoir sites and canal sites; the seepage; the evaporation; the vested rights and how to maintain them; and, generally, the most economical method of bringing the land and the water together. To this end I have proceeded to expend the money in such a way as to obtain the information required in the shortest time.[7]

Elsewhere, Powell noted that the West contained timber resources in the high country, pasturage in between, and irrigable lands below—and that all three should be protected and properly managed: "My theory is to organize in the United States another unit of government for specific purposes, for agriculture by irrigation, for the protection of the forests which are being destroyed by fire, and for the utilization of pasturage . . . that is to create a great body of commonwealths. In the main these commonwealths would be like counties in the States. . . . Say to the States, If you will allow the people, wherever these interstate districts are found, to organize for the purpose of controlling the water, we will turn all over to them."[8] The government would own the lands, and grant use rights to the timber and pasturage but not full control of either. Powell felt that rationality would prevail so that timber and pasturage would be treated as renewable natural resources; that is, give to the people the right to protect and use the forests and the grass lands.

> Let the general Government organize the arid region, including all the lands to be irrigated by perennial streams, into irrigation districts by hydrographic basins. . . . Then let the people of each such irrigation district organize as a body and control the waters on the declared irrigable lands in any manner which they may devise. . . . Let the Government retain the ownership of reservoir sites, canal sites, and head-work sites; but allow the people of each district to use them, as a body, so as to prevent speculation in such sites, which would ultimately be a tax on agriculture.
>
> Some of these districts would lie in two States. To this arrangement the consent of the states should be obtained, and all the districts should be organized under state laws. The Government should not grant these privileges to the districts until the States themselves ratify the agreement and provide statutes for the organization of the districts and for the regulation of water rights, the protection and use of forests, and the protection and use of pasturage. This is the general plan which I present.[9]

In 1888, Powell put brother-in-law A. H. Thompson in charge of the topographic work and Clarence E. Dutton in charge of the engineering and hydraulic work of the irrigation survey, and studies and mapping began. But when western congressmen and the timber, mining, and ranching interests they represented realized that Powell proposed to withhold any further western settlement until the mapping and classification was finished, and that it might take several years, they raised hell. By 1890 they were hounding Powell and his program. Rather than approving his plans, Congress cut the irrigation survey budget to $165,000—making the survey impossible. Powell battled on until 1892, when the whole USGS budget was cut. Powell was finished. He signaled that he would resign, saw to the appointment of Charles Walcott as his successor, and retired to the Bureau of American Ethnology in 1894.

While Powell's plans and attempts at rational management of water, timber, and pasturage resources were rejected, the concept of "redemption" or "reclamation" (as it came to be called) of arid lands through irrigation continued. By 1890 various private entities had built, or were planning, dams and other water storage devices in the West. An article in *Scribner's Magazine* in 1890 by Walter G. Bates described a number of small- and medium-scale current efforts. Between the 1870s and 1890s, irrigation projects had been developed along the Green River; near Grand Junction, Colorado; and by 1890 at Yuma, Arizona, and on the Salt River. The Salt River projects made extensive use of the Hohokam canals built 500 and more years earlier.[10]

By the time Theodore Roosevelt became president, after the assassination of William McKinley in 1899, western irrigation had become a major political and economic issue. Irrigation congresses were held annually. Pro-irrigation planks were inserted in both the Democratic and Republican platforms in the 1900 election. Increasingly larger visions of a fertile, irrigated West were advanced. In 1902, Frederick H. Newell, whom Powell had appointed as the irrigation survey hydrographer, noted that by 1900 there were about 7,500,000 acres of land under irrigation in the Arid West "this being a little over 1% of the total area of the remaining vacant lands." But if "all the floods were conserved in great reservoirs and all the rivers which could be diverted were turned out from their canyons, . . . there would . . . be water for . . . ten times the area now utilized." He also thought that the population of the West would increase from about 4,000,000 "to at least 40,000,000 people, and possibly far more." He noted that between 1890 and 1900 there had been an increase of irrigated acreage from 4.1 to 7.5 million. But, a limit had been reached.

> Private enterprise has already accomplished what it can in the utilization of the smaller streams, but there still remain great rivers and torrential floods whose control is beyond the possibility of individuals or corporations seeking profitable financial enterprises. The work of reclamation, if done at all, must be through public agencies. . . . President Roosevelt, in his clear-cut decisive fashion, has reached to the very heart of the matter and has recommended that the Government, the great land owner, should construct and maintain the reservoirs as it does other public works. He says that this is properly a national function, and that it is as right for the National Government to make the streams and rivers of the arid region useful, by engineering works for water storage, as it is to make useful the rivers and harbors of the humid region by engineering works of another kind.[11]

John Wesley Powell died on September 23, 1902. His vision for the rational development of the arid West, as he conceived it, was not realized. Millions of acres of land ultimately were "redeemed" or "reclaimed," but not within the political and administrative framework he envisioned. Elements of his vision did come to pass. Much timber and pasturage remain in federal hands, administered by the Bureau of Land Management and the U.S. Forest Service. Irrigation districts do exist within hydrographic basins, but do not have the powers Powell envisioned. The federal government retains control of reservoir sites, dams, and so on. There are interstate water compacts, especially the Colorado River Compact, but they do not also control timber and pasturage.

IRRIGATION, RECLAMATION, HYDROPOWER, AND DAM BUILDING

What Powell did not foresee was hydroelectric power. By 1900 large-scale production of electricity by hydropower and transmission of that electrical power over long distances was feasible. Waterpower as a source of usable energy had long been known. The ancient Romans used horizontal waterwheels placed in rivers to capture energy to drive grist mills and other devices. Vertical waterwheels were developed and perfected during the Middle Ages and provided a major source of energy for the development of the Industrial Revolution in the sixteenth and seventeenth centuries. The principles behind electrical generators were first developed in the 1830s and 1840s independently by Michael Faraday in England and Joseph Henry (later the first secretary of the Smithsonian Institution) in the United States.

The early generators produced direct current (DC) power. The problem is that DC systems are inefficient for long-distance power transmission. Alternating current (AC) is much more efficient for both generation and long-distance transmission of electric power. The first practical AC generator went on line in Germany in 1891. The key person in the United States in the development of AC power was George Westinghouse. In 1893 he won the contract to light the World's Columbian Exposition (the great Chicago World's Fair) using an AC system. Soon after he obtained the rights to develop Niagara Falls using AC generators—what would now be called a major demonstration project. The long-distance transmission of AC power was facilitated by improvements in transformers to step up the voltage coming from AC generators and then step it down at the end of the transmission lines for local uses.

The proponents of DC power generation fought Westinghouse and AC power generation bitterly, but they lost. Thus by about 1905–10, large-scale generation of hydropower and its transmission to distant markets became feasible and increasingly cost effective. That opened the way for realistic discussions of—and planning for—large hydroelectric dams on the Colorado and other rivers around the world. The history of the Bureau of Reclamation is in part one of increasing involvement in generating hydroelectric power for sale and to drive the pumps to move water to irrigation projects and municipalities.

ARTHUR POWELL DAVIS

Arthur Powell Davis (1861–1933) (fig. 12.1) was the son of John Davis and Martha Ann Powell, one of John Wesley Powell's sisters.[12] John Davis had moved his family from Illinois to Junction City, Kansas, where he became a farmer, a nursery owner, and editor of an influential newspaper. In 1891 he ran for Congress on the Populist Party ticket, won, and served two terms in the House of Representatives (1891–94). Young Arthur graduated from Kansas State Normal School (now Emporia State University) and then went to work in 1882 for his uncle Wes as an assistant topographer. He subsequently (1888) earned a B.S. degree from the Corcoran Scientific School of Columbian College (George Washington University). That same year he married Elizabeth Brown, who worked as an astronomical calculator for the *American Ephemeris and Nautical Almanac.*

Davis devoted most of his time between 1882 and 1894 to topographic work, principally in the Southwest. In 1894 he moved to the Division of Hydrography, where he was soon named chief and directed the irrigation survey stream-gaging work nationwide. In 1897 he was assigned to the Isthmian Canal Commission to study hydrographic conditions for the proposed Nicaraguan and Panama canal routes; ultimately (1909) he was a member of the board of engineers reporting on the feasibility and type of canal to be built in Panama.

When the Reclamation Service was established within the USGS in 1902, Davis was named assistant chief engineer; it became an independent agency in 1907 and Davis was named chief engineer in 1908, becoming director in 1914. Between 1903 and 1923 Davis was involved in, or supervised, the construction of more than a hundred dams and projects, including the Newlands Project in western Nevada (the very first Reclamation Service project), major tunnels in Colorado and Utah, the Shoshone (now Buffalo Bill) Dam in Wyoming (completed

12.1. Arthur Powell Davis, 1920s. www.usbr.gov/history/commissbios/davis.html. Courtesy of the U.S. Bureau of Reclamation.

1910), the Roosevelt Dam in Arizona (dedicated 1911), the Arrowrock Dam in Idaho (1915), and the Elephant Butte Dam (1916) in New Mexico.[13] These projects reflected Davis's vision that dams ought to be multipurpose, providing not only irrigation water and flood control, but cheap hydroelectric power and, ultimately, recreational resources.

PLANNING TO DAM THE COLORADO RIVER

"Throughout most of its long history, USGS has rested on a foundation of three disciplines: topographic mapping, geology and geologic mapping, and water-resource assessments."[14] For the arid West, all three are critical for planning the best-use management (however defined) of the public domain. Various Survey divisions at various times were concerned with specific planning functions, including land classification, water storage and distribution, and ultimately power resources and hydro-economics.

Powell had created a Hydrography Division and appointed Frederick Newhall to run it. Its primary task was to collect basic information on stream flow through the establishment of gaging stations. A central task of the irrigation survey was to establish gaging stations on major rivers. The first was on the Rio Grande in 1889. The first one on the Colorado River system was at Green River, Utah, in 1895.[15]

After Powell resigned, his successor, Charles W. Wolcott, faced with the major budget cuts Congress had imposed on the Survey to get rid of Powell, told Newhall his division might be abolished. Newhall then successfully lobbied Congress for funds to expand the division's mission beyond stream gaging to an overall assessment of the nation's water resources. Henry Gannett, director of the Survey's topographic branch, also faced budget problems and asked Newhall if he could assign one of his topographers to hydrography. Newell chose Arthur Powell Davis. Thus it was that Davis moved, administratively, to the division of the USGS directly concerned with water resources.

We have noted that the irrigation congresses, held annually from the 1890s on, were pushing for direct federal involvement in developing water resources, although some delegates disagreed vehemently, holding that development should be done by the private sector. In 1900 pro-federal proponents were led by Congressman Francis Newlands of Nevada. He and his supporters wanted irrigation waters to "reclaim" lands and make them farmable. When Theodore Roosevelt became president in 1901, the reclamation boosters found their champion. Legislation was developed, and Roosevelt signed the Reclamation Act, known also as the Newlands Act, on June 17, 1902.

The act created a "reclamation fund." Monies derived from the sale of public desert lands would be used for surveys and the construction and maintenance of irrigation works in the arid and semiarid lands of the country. Lands classed as such were the (then) fifteen western states and the territories of New Mexico and Arizona. The Department of the Interior had responsibility for administering the act, and the USGS was given lead agency responsibility within Interior. The new Reclamation Service thus became a unit of the hydrography survey. Charles Walcott, as director of the USGS, became the first Reclamation Service director; Frederick Newell became the first chief engineer (remaining also as chief hydrographer). In 1907, when Wolcott resigned from the Survey to become secretary of the Smithsonian Institution, he recommended that the Reclamation Service become an independent unit within the Department of the Interior. Newhall was appointed director, and Arthur Powell Davis became chief engineer.[16]

The Newlands Act created a general framework for the funding of reclamation projects, but each specific project had to be proposed and lobbied through Congress. When a federal bureau begins a campaign to convince Congress to authorize and then fund a project, particularly a complex and expensive project extending over many years, the first step is to develop "the record." The record consists not just of speeches and background materials inserted into the *Congressional Record*, but the proceedings of all congressional hearings on the project, and backup technical and scientific information, and expert testimony and reports. The decision to attempt to "control" the Colorado River system had been reached by the early 1900s. Once that decision had been made, the experts went to work doing the background fieldwork required before dams and related structures could be built. Where might dams be sited in terms of geology and accessibility of construction sites? What kinds of dams were needed, and how many? What might their reservoir storage capacities be? The key players in answering these questions were staff members of the USGS and, later, to a degree, the Reclamation Service.

We begin with the USGS. Among the key documents in "the record" that said, "Yes, dams can, and should, be built to control the Colorado River," were U.S. Geological Survey Water-Supply Papers no. 395 and 556, both written by Eugene C. La Rue and titled, respectively, *Colorado River and Its Utilization* (1916), and *Water Power and Flood Control of Colorado River below Green River, Utah* (1925).[17] The two publications bracket the period of time in U.S. history when discussions of "harnessing" the Colorado moved from "we've got to" to "we will." Three years later, in 1928, Congress passed legislation authorizing the building of a major high dam. It was called the "Boulder Canyon Project," although the actual site was moved a few miles downstream to a geologically more stable location in Black Canyon. La Rue built his case for dam building on data derived from various river trips made through the Colorado River canyons by USGS surveyors, hydrologists, and engineers between about 1914 and 1923.[18]

Eugene Clyde La Rue (1879–1947) was at the center of hydrographic data collection and planning within the USGS from 1909 until 1927. Between 1909 and 1923 he wrote sixty-five reports concerned with water resources data collection and planning.[19] La Rue graduated from the University of California in 1899 and went to work as a stream gager in Idaho and then as a district engineer working under the Carey Act. As an aside, the act provided for grants of irrigable land to the states or assignees provided they were developed for irrigation; it also provided for waterpower sites and certain other public purposes. Like the Homestead Act it provided not more than 160 acres, such lands available only to those who contracted for water rights purposes.

By 1912 La Rue had focused on the Colorado River. He became the chief "field man" to carry out the Survey's investigations of the river (fig. 12.2).

12.2. USGS Grand Canyon survey crew at Lee's Ferry, May 1924: (*left to right*) Leigh Lint, Elwyn Blake, Frank Word, Claude Birdseye, Raymond Moore, Roland Burchard, Eugene La Rue, Lewis Freeman, Emery Kolb. Photographer unknown, NAU 112903. Courtesy of Cline Library, Northern Arizona University.

Between 1914 and 1924, he made ten boating trips on various sections of the Colorado system, including one from Green River, Utah, through Cataract Canyon to Lee's Ferry in 1921, and another from Hall's Crossing to Lee's Ferry in 1922 (see below). He took more than a thousand photographs. The trips allowed him to assess the geology of the canyons in detail and make recommendations as to where various dams might be built.

In his 1916 paper La Rue assembled for the first time a comprehensive overview of existing streamflow data for all the major, and most of the minor, tributaries of the Colorado River system, together with data on geology, irrigable lands, historic precipitation records, current and projected demographics, and other relevant data.

The paper had an introduction by his boss, Nathan C. Grover. Nathan Clinton Grover (1868–1956) was an expert on stream flow and discharge. In 1907 he and John Clayton Hoyt (1874–1946) published *River Discharge,* which became a standard textbook.[20] From 1911 to 1930, Hoyt was in charge of surface-water development, and from 1913 to 1939, Grover was the chief hydraulic engineer, both at the USGS. The two supervised studies of surface waters throughout the United States and were the guiding lights within the Survey for development of the Colorado River.

In the introduction to *River Discharge*, Grover rhetorically asked about the fate of the Colorado River basin:

> What will become of this immense region? Doubtless its forests will be utilized, its mineral wealth will be exploited, its wonderful scenic beauties will be unfolded. Its greatest development must come, however, from its water resources, on which the development of its other resources must largely depend. Without the water afforded by Colorado River and its tributaries this basin would remain forever a barren desert. These rivers make possible not only the construction of large irrigation systems and the growth of towns, cities, and prosperous agricultural communities but also the generation of hydroelectric power for lighting, heating, industrial uses, and the transportation of freight and passengers.[21]

The answer to the water development issue was to build dams—big dams.

In his report La Rue concluded that the Colorado River did not furnish enough water to irrigate all available acreage. He predicted a shortage of 3.8 million acre feet in the Lower Basin. That shortage could be made up by large-scale storage reservoirs, providing somewhere between 18 and 25 million acre feet of storage capacity.[22] This provided a target figure for whatever system of dams would be built. La Rue proposed a dozen dams to create the requisite reservoirs, but many things happened between 1916 and the publication of La Rue's 1925 paper. First of all, detailed surveys of the Colorado River system had to be made. These were conducted between 1920 and 1923. We turn to them next.

THE 1921–1923 SURVEYS: MAPPING THE CANYONS

In order to determine the potential location of dam sites, it was necessary to have accurate topographic maps of canyons and their tributaries. Establishing the elevations of the riverbeds from their origins in the Rocky Mountains to the Gulf of California was step one. Step two was determining the size, extent, and water-surface elevations of reservoir sites at full pool level. The USGS had mapped as much of the relevant country as it could from overland, but much of the Colorado system could only be properly mapped by making rough-water trips down the canyons. Such mapping was difficult and sometimes dangerous, especially given the equipment available in the 1920s. As Boyer and Webb explain:

> In the early 1920s, instrumental surveys—using an alidade and stadia rod—were the only means to obtain accurate map data. These techniques were painstaking and laborious; each topographic point was obtained by observing the stadia rod from an instrument station and making calculations of distance that accounted for vertical angles. The surveying instrument had to be set up on a previously obtained survey point, leveled, and oriented, which took time and care; if the instrument fell out of adjustment or was not carefully used, considerable error would creep into the topographic map. Overall the surveys had to be tied in to existing benchmarks, which was difficult to accomplish in the vertical and labyrinthine river canyons of the Colorado Plateau.[23]

The 1921 trip down the San Juan river provides an example.[24] In addition to a general contour map, the crew was assigned to establish a continuous line at the 3,900-foot elevation, which was the estimated full pool level for a dam that had been proposed to be built in Glen Canyon just upstream from Lee's Ferry. The trip started from near Bluff, Utah, and went down the river to its confluence with the Colorado. It was led by Kelly W. Trimble, an expert USGS topographical engineer, assisted by geologist Hugh D. Miser. Bert Loper was hired as the lead boatman. Robert N. Allen was the recorder, and Henry Elwyn Blake Jr. of Monticello, Utah, and Hugh Hyde of Salt Lake City were the rodmen. There was also a cook, Heber Christensen, of Moab. Wesley Oliver, of Mexican Hat, was the overland packer, bringing supplies to the party down the various trails into the canyon.

The party began its work on July 19, 1921. Because the canyon of the San Juan is relatively narrow in various places, Trimble determined to use two rodmen wherever he could—one on the right bank and one on the left bank. In narrow parts of the canyon or where survey points were adjacent to large rapids, establishing survey points was sometimes dicey and potentially dangerous. The modus operandi was for the rodmen to be delivered to designated points by Bert Loper in one of the boats. Trimble would set up his plane table and take readings from a previously established point. Then, "Robert Allen, the recorder, would write down the information and make the calculations that Trimble would then transfer back onto the plane table as a two-dimensional map with elevation contour lines."[25] At times Blake helped out as a boatman—experience that made him a desirable boatman for subsequent USGS trips in 1922 and 1923 (see below). Most days Loper would deliver the cook and supplies downstream from the previous night's camp and then hike back up along the river for the second boat to help move the rodmen around before delivering them, Trimble, and Miser to the new camp.

The work was meticulous and slow as the crew progressed downstream, with exhilaration and some accidents thrown in from time to time in getting through or around various rapids and coping with the sand waves for which the San Juan is famous. They completed the mapping in good order and arrived at the San Juan-Colorado confluence on October 3 nearly out of food. But the USGS supplier, Tom Wimmer, had left them supplies at a designated point just upstream from the confluence a couple of weeks earlier, so they were okay.

Meanwhile, another USGS party led by William R. Chenowith, a topographical engineer, had been surveying Cataract Canyon. The party also included Frank Stoudt as recorder; two rodmen, Leigh Hunt and Harry Trasker; geologist Sidney Paige; cook John Clogston; and Eugene C. La Rue.[26] The lead boatman was Ellsworth Kolb. Emory Kolb and an assistant came along in the *Edith*, one of the Kolb's boats from 1911. Emory wanted to add to the brothers' stock of Colorado River movies and stills.

The trip was funded by Southern California Edison. The party left from Green River, Utah, in mid-September with four boats. As on the San Juan segment, the survey was carried along the river level and up to the 3,900-foot contour elevation. The party portaged rapids when needed, with Ellsworth Kolb running the empty boats through them. They generally managed to get through in good order until a major rapid at the mouth of Dark Canyon. Kolb tried to take a loaded boat through and got jammed up on rocks about 50 feet from shore. There were mishaps with two of the other boats, and it took until the next day to get the jammed boat loose. Fortunately, Chenowith's maps were not harmed.

They reached the mouth of the Dirty Devil River on October 2. Chenowith had earlier in the season surveyed a section of upper Glen Canyon while waiting for the water level to drop in Cataract Canyon. At Hall's Crossing the party met Tom Wimmer, who had brought in supplies for them and the Trimble party by horse and wagon. The Kolbs, Paige, and La Rue headed on downstream. Chenowith and the remainder of his crew continued to survey to the 3,900-foot level in the Glen Canyon side canyons as far down as the confluence. Given the length and relative flatness of some of the side canyons, such as Bullfrog, Hall's Creek, and Moqui, it took them until early December. Meanwhile, Trimble and his crew carried their survey from the confluence on to Lee's Ferry, finishing about December 15, 1921. For a time the Trimble party linked up with a Coast and Geodetic Survey party who were placing brass-cap benchmarks along and on terraces above the river. One of them was placed 20 feet in front of a cave on a long river terrace adjacent to the mouth of Dangling Rope Canyon. The survey team had painted "3262.2 feet" on the wall of the cave. We found the brass cap and the painted numbers when we excavated Benchmark Cave in 1958 (chapter 14).

The USGS made another river trip in the summer of 1922, from mid-June to mid-August, this time on the Green River through Lodore, Desolation, and Gray canyons. The trip was funded by the Utah Power and Light Company and led by Kelly Trimble again, with Bert Loper, Elwyn Blake, and Leigh Lint as boatman.[27] This completed the surveying of the upper Colorado system, leaving a survey of the Grand Canyon to be carried out the following summer (see below). There was one other river trip that summer, lasting only a few days in Glen Canyon. But it had great significance in terms of where dams would ultimately be built along the Colorado. We will return to that trip after reviewing some additional background events.

WHOSE DAM(S) SHALL BE BUILT WHERE?

For the first decade and a half after its creation, the Reclamation Service was small potatoes among the federal bureaus. Arthur Powell Davis was determined to change that. As we saw, he was involved in various ways in a large number of projects between 1902 and 1914. But during and immediately after World War I, the Service's position became increasingly tenuous. To counter this, Davis turned his full attention to the Colorado River, focusing on water supply and flood control. It was potentially the biggest game in the country, and he took every opportunity to champion the cause of "harnessing the menace of the Colorado."

Colorado waters had been diverted to irrigate the Imperial Valley by a private company, but the river periodically flooded and changed its course, as it had for eons. In 1905–7 major floods caused more such changes, wiping out much of the Imperial Valley farmland and creating the Salton Sea, a story ably told by DeBuys and Meyers in their excellent *Salt Dreams: Land and Water in Low-down California*.[28] Major problems continued over the following decade.

In 1919 a bill was introduced in Congress to authorize construction of a new canal to the Imperial Valley. Arthur Davis's time had come. Simply focusing on a new canal, he said, would leave the area unprotected against the next round of disastrous flooding. He urged a more comprehensive long-term effort—to be led by the Reclamation Service—to develop a system of dams and reservoirs all along the Colorado and its tributaries. The centerpiece would be a major "high dam" to control flooding along the lower Colorado River.

Davis's campaign ultimately resulted in the Kincaid Act, which directed the Department of the Interior to study not only the lower Colorado but other lands adjacent to the river and examine the issues of water control and storage throughout the Colorado River basin.[29] Davis was assigned to develop the report. In 1922 the report was submitted to Congress by Albert Fall and Davis.[30] It was a political tour de force. As Boyce and Webb put it,

> Davis . . . supplied his vision of the Reclamation Service as a three-way broker between the federal government, who had the money; state and local governments, who had the individual tax paying constituents; and the irrigation districts, who needed cheap water to make the desert bloom. His vision fed the ambition of an agency which by the mid-twentieth century would become an enormously powerful bureaucracy that literally changed the landscape of the American West with its network of dams, canals and power lines.[31]

The report called for the construction of a high dam at or near Boulder Canyon to control any future flooding and to generate hydroelectric power. The Newlands Act had called for the sale of public lands to finance reclamation projects. Davis called for projects to be funded by long-term bonds that would be retired by the proceeds from the sale of hydroelectric power and water to the proposed All American Canal that would be built to supply some of the irrigation needs of southern California and southwestern Arizona.

Davis's proposed high dam location at or near Boulder Canyon ran very much counter to the plans Eugene La Rue had been perfecting since 1914 to have a major high dam at the foot of Glen Canyon and a series of other dams both upstream and downstream from it. The stage was set for a head-to-head conflict between these two very strong-willed individuals. The conflict played out against the background of moves toward developing a Colorado River Compact. One act of the conflict took place in Glen Canyon in early September 1922 during the course of a river trip arranged by La Rue.

THE 1922 BIGWIGS GLEN CANYON JUNKET

In addition to La Rue, there was Clarence Stetson, secretary of the Colorado River Commission and assistant to Herbert Hoover, then secretary of commerce; Arthur Powell Davis; Claude Birdseye, chief engineer of the USGS topographic division; Herman Stabler, chief engineer of the USGS Land Classification Board; H. W. Dennis, construction engineer for the Southern California Edison Company; R. E. Caldwell, the Utah state engineer; Franklin Thomas, a professor of civil engineering at the California Institute of Technology; and Robert D. Young, a Mormon leader who was president of the Sevier Stake in Richfield, Utah. One of the key participants was John D. Widtsoe, who kept a journal of the trip.[32]

The party assembled in Richfield and drove in several cars over the mountains into the Fremont River drainage, then on to Fruita and through the Capitol Gorge. At Bowns Ranch on Sandy Creek, they changed to wagons. Two four-horse teams pulled wagons filled with baggage, bedding, and provisions, with the passengers riding atop the gear. They followed the wagon road along the east side of Waterpocket Fold, thence down Hall's Creek. There they were met by six boatmen employed by the USGS, who had brought boats upriver from Lee's Ferry to meet the party. The lead boatman was Tom Wimmer, who had served as packer and supplier to previous USGS trips through Glen Canyon (see above). One of the boatmen was the flamboyant Lewis Freeman, an adventurer and author who wrote about boat trips on major North American rivers and who was collecting materials about the Colorado River water issues. Widtsoe characterized Freeman as "a wild man."[33]

The trip provided an ideal situation for a number of the movers and shakers who were concerned with Colorado River water issues to talk and politic during the day as they floated along the river and at night around the campfire. There was much discussion of how to frame the Colorado River Compact, which would be hammered out in the following months in Santa Fe. But they also took time to enjoy the trip. Widtsoe wrote:

> The scenery is sublime. Great cliffs of majestic proportions and vivid red, and of infinite variety. Immense arches, auditoriums, stadiums, amphitheatres, temples, palaces, nature's writing on the walls. There are hanging gardens, groves and glens, apparently blind alleys that turn everywhere as you come nearer. Occasionally mighty rocks tower out of the river. There is an overpowering quality in the feeling induced by the scenes along the River. One of the most notable days of my life![34]

On September 10 the party camped at the confluence of the Colorado and the San Juan. The following day Widtsoe wrote:

> We pack and are off. High walls on both sides of us; then breaking into lower walls, especially on the east side. The water smooth as a lake. Blue heron on the shores; green patches in crevices of the high walls (about 1200 feet high). Many little side canyons, great arches, caves, ampitheatres, coves, turns, bends, pinnacles, towers, domes; galleries; paths; reflections of wondrous delicacy, broken and softened by the ripples. As the sun rises, the light reflected from the ripples makes the water a golden yellow; where the shadows still lie, the light from the rock walls make the water a lustrous red and gold. It is altogether wonderful. [The party stopped to investigate] . . . an immense ampitheatre, the largest yet seen. . . . It is a narrow, high winding gorge, with a small stream trickling down it. Near the entrance are dense groves of scrub oak, and large patches of poison [ivy]. As we enter, the gorge narrows, a blue rift above is the sky. Where the gorge widens a vast overhanging canopy wholly shuts out the light. A little further on the gorge narrows and water fills the passage way. . . . in this twilight-lighted, moist nook, vegetation is profuse, climbing up the rocky slopes and fastening itself in really impossible places, it seems to us. Man-high is a shelf carrying a most perfect bed, perhaps 10 to 15 feet long, of beautiful maidenhair fern. We name the place *Maidenhair Gorge*.[35]

The name didn't stick; the place came to be known as Hidden Passage. They next stopped to hike up to Rainbow Bridge. Widtsoe copied many of the names in the register book that John Wetherill had placed there and noted a total of 186 visitors, including 36 women.

When the party reached La Rue's number one dam site, 4.6 miles upstream from Lee's Ferry, he unrolled a large map, prepared to show Arthur Davis and the others why this was the optimal place on the Colorado River for a high dam. La Rue, Davis, and some of the engineers repaired to a spot above the river to look at the map and discuss the site. However, as Widtsoe reported:

> We stop at the Ferry Dam Site. Soon after we land the pirates come. They have hoisted a red bandana in front; a white flag, skull and crossbones, at rear boat; all the pirates had handkerchiefs tied around their heads. Three ducks were hung to the front flagstaff. As they passed our camp they sang viciously. "Yoho and a bottle of rum." One of the pirates in the rear boat has a knife between his teeth. As they land below our boat they sing with bloodthirsty voices—Yoho and a bottle of rum. Then a regular piratical college yell.
>
> "We want food!
> Down with the Corporations!
> We're for Public Ownership!
> Give us free maple syrup!
> Fifteen men on a Dead Man's Chest.
> Yoho and a bottle of Rum!
> Drink and the Devil have done for the rest
> Yoho and a bottle of rum!
> [Then,] Down from the hills comes Davis' sonorous voice
> Oh I am a Pirate King
> I am a Pirate King
> It is indeed a glorious thing
> To be a pirate king."[36]

According to Boyer and Webb, the "pirates, replete with biscuit-tin earrings," were led by Franklin Thomas, the Cal Tech professor. They go on to say, "Had the hapless La Rue been able to counter with 'I Am the Very Model Of A Modern Major General,' with 'its many cheerful facts about the square of the hypotenuse,' he might have been able to rescue the moment, but La Rue's repertoire apparently did not include Gilbert and Sullivan's *The Pirates of Penzance*. Indeed, if La Rue had been able to counter with the first two verses of the Major General's song, he may have won the day:

> I am the very model of a modern Major-
> General,
> I've information vegetable, animal, and
> mineral,
> I know the kings of England, and I quote the
> fights historical
> From Marathon to Waterloo, in order
> categorical;
> I'm very well acquainted, too, with matters
> mathematical,
> I understand equations, both the simple and
> quadratical,
> About binomial theorem I'm teeming with a
> lot o' news—
> With many cheerful facts about the square of
> the hypotenuse.
> . . . I'm very good at integral and differential
> calculus;
> I know the scientific names of beings
> animalculous:
> In short, in matters vegetable, animal, and
> mineral,
> I am the very model of a modern Major-
> General.

Unfortunately, La Rue could not rise to the occasion, and the rest of his presentation fell on distracted ears.[37]

When the party reached Lee's Ferry, Widtsoe noted in his journal, "On the road from the Ferry to the Pariah [*sic*], lie iron tubes, pipes, joints, taps, etc. In the River a few rods from the Ferry lies a steamboat, half submerged in the sand with steam boiler, two smokestacks, etc., exposed. Another steam engine plant, partly dismantled, lies further on. Wrecks of human ambition lie scattered all about. It is an interesting commentary on how the world is conquered."[38] The detritus and the steamboat were the remains of Charles Spencer's abortive attempt at hydraulic mining of the Chinle Formation (chapter 9).

Widtsoe, Davis, and others went on overland to view dam sites further downstream, including Davis's Boulder Canyon site. Several of the junketeers then participated in the gathering in November 1922 in Santa Fe, at which the Colorado River Compact was hammered out. Widtsoe is credited with playing a major role in those negotiations.

John A. Widtsoe (1872–1952) was a major figure in Utah higher education and Mormon politics, and an expert on "scientific" dry-farming and irrigation. Born in Norway, the son of Mormon converts, Widtsoe received a B.A. from Harvard in 1894 and a Ph.D. from Gottingen University in 1899. He began his career as a faculty member at Utah State Agricultural College (now Utah State University). He apparently was a master of political in-fighting and behind-the-scenes management of agreements. He engineered the resignation of William Kerr as president of Utah State in 1907 (Widtsoe's mother-in-law was a member of the Board of Regents) and replaced him as president. But Widtsoe knew that the real power lay in Salt Lake City, so in 1916 he left Logan to become the president of the University of Utah. He later became a member of the Council of the Twelve Apostles, the ruling board of the Mormon Church, and remained in that position until his death in 1952.

His reputation as an expert on water matters derived in part from two books that had great influence in the arid West. Widtsoe clearly recognized that John Wesley Powell was right: agriculture in the West is dependent on irrigation. Widtsoe thought, however, that some high desert and upland areas could be "dry farmed" by planting crops in the fall that would take advantage of winter precipitation and the moisture-holding qualities of certain sediments and soils. His *Dry-Farming: A System of Agriculture for Countries Under A Low Rainfall*, published in 1911, had a great impact in Utah and adjacent states.[39] During wet periods of climatic cycles the practice worked often enough to encourage farmers to invest their efforts raising crops on homesteaded lands that had not otherwise not been taken up. When the climate cycled back to drier periods, as it did in the 1930s, the practice did not work, and many marginal farms failed. Widtsoe's reputation as a water expert and his political skills made him a key player in the negotiations over the Colorado River Compact. He and Delphus E. Carpenter, who represented Colorado in western water negotiations, played pivotal roles in creating the compact.[40]

After two months of complex negotiations, the Colorado River Compact was signed in Santa Fe on November 24, 1922.[41] It defined the upper and lower basins, with the dividing point set at Lee's Ferry. It allocated an annual 7.5 million acre feet to each and authorized an additional 1 million acre feet to the lower basin.[42] Some estimates indicated a total availability of perhaps 20 million acre feet, hence the allocation provided for a "reserve" of about 4 million acre feet. No one actually knew what the "real" figures were. Nonetheless, the compact was signed and sent to the seven state legislatures for ratification. The compact did not settle western water wars; it simply moved them to another level. The maxim attributed to Mark Twain, "Whiskey's for drinking, water's for fighting over," remained, as it still is, a stark truism. There were amendments to the compact in 1928; the Arizona legislature did not ratify it until 1944.

For our purposes, the hammering out of the pact and its drawn-out process of ratification is background to our story, which focuses on the planning for dams and reservoirs, particularly in Glen Canyon, however the available water might finally be allocated among the states. In 1923 Claude Birdseye, chief topographer of the USGS, led a survey through the Grand Canyon to complete the surveys of the Colorado River system (fig. 12.2). The story of the survey is masterfully told by Boyer and Webb and will not be chronicled here except to note that Eugene La Rue was on the trip to gather additional data on possible dam sites.[43]

By 1923 numerous other swirls and eddies of the western water wars were boiling up. The Colorado River was only one issue. There are other river systems in the seventeen western states served by the Reclamation Service, notably the Rio Grande, the Columbia and Snake, the upper Missouri, the upper reaches of the Platte, the Arkansas and the Red rivers, and streams and rivers of the Central Valley in California. People living near those waterways were clamoring for federal assistance to control them and make them more productive. There were also ongoing battles over public versus private electric power development. The Reclamation Service had become embroiled in multiple complex political issues centering on water and power development relating to all those river systems, as well as charges of fiscal laxity.

In March 1923 Albert Fall was forced into retirement in the wake of the Teapot Dome scandal. He was succeeded by Hubert Work (1860–1942), a Colorado physician who had became active in Republican Party politics. President Warren Harding appointed him postmaster general in 1922. Now he appointed Work as secretary of the interior. Work promised to reorganize the department in response to widespread criticism, including that directed at the Reclamation Service. In June 1923, Work fired Arthur Davis, replacing him with D. W. Davis (no relation), then abolished the Reclamation Service and created the Bureau of Reclamation, to be administered by D. W. Davis.

Work also appointed a blue-ribbon fact finder's commission to investigate problems within Interior generally and Reclamation in particular. The commissioners included D. W. Davis, John Widtsoe, and Elwood Mead, among others. Mead (1858–1936), a highly respected professor of civil engineering, had been a critic of federal reclamation policies for a decade. The committee report was issued in April 1924 and recommended sweeping changes in reclamation policies that are beyond the scope of our concern but are analyzed in detail by Donald Pisani.[44] Mead became commissioner of the renamed Bureau of Reclamation and served until his death in 1936. During his tenure, Hoover Dam was completed, and Grand Coulee and Owyhee dams were initiated, three of the largest high dams in the country.

Davis was almost immediately hired as chief engineer and general manager of the East Bay Municipal Utility District, which provides water to cities in the East Bay area of California. He continued in that position until his death in 1933. He was reappointed as a consulting engineer to the Bureau of Reclamation in 1933; the appointment was primarily honorific, recognizing his contributions to reclamation in general and, specifically, to the Boulder Canyon project, by then underway. He was too ill to accept the appointment and died soon after. Davis's expertise was recognized far beyond the United States. He was a consultant to both Imperial and Soviet Russia on large-scale irrigation projects, as well as in western China.

MORE LA RUE-DAVIS CONFLICT

Although Davis was out of government, his idea for a high dam in Boulder Canyon was not dead; indeed it was favored by many, and he continued to have strong support, both in Congress and the engineering profession. La Rue valiantly continued to push his plan for a high dam just above Lee's Ferry in Glen Canyon and a series of other dams both upstream and down. By 1924, using all the data he had collected since 1914, including the data collected by the USGS 1921–23 river survey trips, he had developed a complex, but to him, totally rational plan for controlling the entire Colorado River system and conserving (by minimizing evaporation) the maximum amount of water that would back up in the several reservoirs.

In his 1916 scheme La Rue had proposed three dams on the Green River: one in Flaming Gorge, one in Brown's Park, and one downstream from the confluence of the White and Duquesne (Ouray) rivers with the Green. Below that he proposed a dam at the confluence of the Grand and the Green, and one at the head of Marble Canyon, just below the Paria River. These dams were to be between 200 and 244 feet high, the highest being at Marble Gorge. Downstream, La Rue proposed six small stair-step dams in Grand Canyon and a 125-foot-high dam at the "Boulder Canyon Power site."

By 1925 La Rue's thinking was somewhat different. First, there would be a 200-plus-foot-high dam at Bluff, Utah, on the San Juan River specifically to control floods coming out of the 28,500-square-mile drainage basin of the river. Second, Flaming Gorge Reservoir would have a 200-foot-high dam and storage capacity for 3 million acre feet. The dam at the junction of the Green, White, and Ouray rivers would be 170 feet high and have an 8 million acre-feet capacity.[45] But much bigger things were envisioned for Glen and Cataract canyons.

The first was the Dark Canyon Dam, to be sited 3 miles above Dark Canyon in the lower end of Cataract Canyon. The dam would be 532 feet high and 1,060 feet across the top, with a power plant at its base. The reservoir would back up into both the Green and the Grand canyons. On the Green River side the reservoir would come within about 4 miles of Green River City, Utah. "On Colorado River the small settlement of Moab would be submerged, and it would be necessary to relocate the highway bridge at this point. The town of Moab could be moved to a higher and better location on Mill Creek." The reservoir would extend upstream some 15 river miles above Moab.[46]

La Rue's optimal site was his Glen Canyon Dam Site Number One—the site he was trying to discuss with Davis when the "pirate" attack took place during the 1922 river trip. It would be located 4 miles above Lee's Ferry and "would create a storage reservoir with a capacity sufficient to regulate the flow of [the entire] Colorado River." With a storage capacity of 8 million acre feet, "the maximum flood at Yuma . . . may be reduced to 50,000 second-feet or less and the flood menace effectively removed."[47]

La Rue thought his Glen Canyon Site Number One had it all. The "Jurassic sandstone" was judged good for building on and in. Transport would be easy, given the proposed road and bridge across the Colorado canyon below Lee's Ferry (completed in 1929) and because railroads could be built to the dam site from Flagstaff or from a proposed Union Pacific Railroad spur to the north rim of Grand Canyon. The river elevation was 3,127 feet; the crest of the dam would be 3,528 feet.

The site La Rue chose was at the head of an oxbow. He proposed to dig mile-long tunnels through the neck of the oxbow to come out 4 river miles downstream. The tunnels were for spillways and a powerhouse. "However, on account of the distance to market, it is not likely that power will be developed at this site for some time to come."[48]

La Rue considered seven other sites in Glen Canyon, some of which the 1922 river junket had stopped to examine. But in his view they all had problems, primarily the wrong geological footings and/or sidewalls.[49] Foreshadowing issues that would arise when the real Glen Canyon Dam was constructed, La Rue reported that if the reservoir behind his Glen Canyon Site Number One was filled to an elevation of 3,513 feet above sea level, it "would not in any way interfere with the Rainbow Natural Bridge." The backwater would reach only to 1-1/4 mile below the bridge. "In fact, if the Glen Canyon dam were constructed to raise the water to the abutment of the Rainbow Bridge, the storage capacity would have to be about 32 million acre-feet, four times the capacity proposed." Finally, La Rue thought that the reservoir behind his Glen Canyon dam would attract 200,000-plus visitors annually.[50]

Since plans to build dams in the Grand Canyon figured in later disputes relating to the Glen Canyon Dam, it is useful to briefly review what La Rue planned. In his 1916 report, he proposed six 100-foot-high stair-step dams from below Kanab Creek to the Arizona-Nevada border. In 1925 he proposed

> The Mineral Canyon power site [with a 600-foot-high dam] . . . at the bottom of the Grand Canyon, 4,500 feet below the plateau on the south. The end of the railroad at Hotel El Tovar, on the south rim of the canyon is about 30 miles from the dam site. Connection with the dam site could be provided by extending the railroad about 12 miles along the rim and building an inclined railroad into the canyon. At some future time a series of dams may be built in the Grand Canyon, the lower sites being developed first and each making the next accessible by means of the backwater.[51]

The lower sites were at Ruby Canyon, Specter Chasm, and Havasu Creek. In his summary, La Rue again pointed to the dam in Glen Canyon as the key storage site "to regulate the flow of the river in the interest of flood control, irrigation and development of power." The other dams would provide "for the full use of the fall in the river" system.[52]

La Rue then went on to argue against Davis's high dam in Boulder Canyon, suggesting four smaller sites. One site was at Bridge Canyon, 10.5 miles below Diamond Creek in the Grand Canyon. The others were farther downstream.[53] There were other possible options. A high dam could be built at the Bridge Canyon site, more than 800 feet high. He also proposed a gravity system for sending water to southern California. If an 825-foot-high dam were built to an elevation of 1,992 feet above sea level, then a gravity system could be built to send water to southern California by means of a 72 mile tunnel to Topock, Arizona, where the water would be carried across the Colorado River by means of an inverted siphon and thence on to the Los Angeles Basin via an aqueduct.[54]

THE 1924 CONGRESSIONAL HEARINGS

Although La Rue's report was not published until 1925, his plans were known well before that and were actively opposed by Arthur Powell Davis, who continued to champion his Boulder Dam scheme. Although he had been fired by Work, Davis was highly respected by many influential people and members of Congress. La Rue's plan, he said, "would destroy the best reservoir site in the basin [Boulder Canyon] and seriously limit the usefulness of the river." He also challenged the feasibility of La Rue's Glen Canyon site on geological grounds. He was, in fact, correct.[55]

There were congressional hearings in late 1924 at which La Rue testified. His earlier statement that there wasn't enough Colorado River water to successfully irrigate all available lands contradicted the Fall-Davis report and other Reclamation Service reports that there would be water to supply all future irrigation needs. It was not what western boosters, farmers, and politicians wanted to hear. As Langbein points out, La Rue's statement about not enough water is "now [1975] well known to be an unfortunate fact for the Colorado River and the basis for recurrent plans to import water into the basin."[56] His statement is even truer in the early twenty-first century than it was in 1975.

La Rue's position had the support of the recently created Federal Power Commission, but it had little clout. He was pilloried by various senators in the hearings, often the case of a scientist drawing hard-nosed conclusions from his carefully gathered and vetted data versus the rhetoric of politics. Herbert Hoover testified after La Rue. He strongly pushed for Boulder Dam. By 1926 the issue was settled and Boulder Dam was authorized in 1928.

After the hearings La Rue published his report and stridently continued to advocate his position, both publicly and privately. In June 1926 the director of the USGS, George Otis Smith, sent La Rue a telegram officially telling him to shut up. La Rue resigned in July, 1927.[57] He died in 1947.

Construction began on Boulder (Hoover) Dam in the fall of 1930. It was, as it remains, one of the great engineering projects of all time. Arthur Powell Davis lived to see it initiated, but not finished. Parker Dam, constructed between 1934 and 1938, provides water to southern California through the Colorado River Aqueduct, a much simpler system than La Rue's tunnel and inverted siphon. Davis Dam was authorized in 1941 but not constructed until after World War II, being finished in 1953. The major upper basin dams—Glen Canyon, Flaming Gorge, and Navajo—were all built after World War II, realizing some, but not all, of Eugene La Rue's dreams.

The three upper basin dams were not only the dreams of Eugene La Rue, but of Floyd E. Dominy. Dominy was born in Nebraska on Christmas Eve 1909 and died April 20, 2010. Throughout his professional life as a public servant/bureaucrat, he sought to make life better (as he saw it) for people, especially in drought-prone areas of the West. The upper basin dams were authorized when he was assistant commissioner of the Bureau of Reclamation. He was the consummate bureaucrat, and by 1959 he was commissioner of the bureau, having had much to do behind the scenes in getting authorization for the dams through Congress. He was especially proud of Glen Canyon Dam, stating, "Glen Canyon Dam and the creation of the most wonderful lake in the world, Lake Powell, is my crowning jewel."[58] Millions would agree; many others would not (chapter 21).

› 13 ‹

EARLY ARCHAEOLOGY IN THE GLEN CANYON COUNTRY

THE STORY OF ARCHAEOLOGICAL STUDIES in the Glen Canyon Country began in 1874 some distance away, in southwestern Colorado.[1] The photographer William Henry Jackson, employed by the Hayden survey, was sent there to explore and photograph places of interest. Jackson and his guide, John Moss, saw numerous "cliff dwellings," ruins of mesa-top pueblos, and the still-enigmatic "watchtowers" of the Hovenweep area. Jackson's report, *Ancient Ruins in Southwestern Colorado*, provided intriguing descriptions of the archaeology. In 1875 Hayden sent Jackson and the artist/geologist William Henry Holmes back to southwestern Colorado. They recorded more sites, described in a second report.[2]

At the Philadelphia Centennial Exhibition of 1876, Jackson and Hayden's photographs and plaster models of the "Cliff dweller" sites created great interest. The exhibits, widely publicized, established the term *Cliff Dwellers* in both archeological and popular parlance.

In 1880, Benjamin Kite Wetherill his wife and family—Richard, Anna, Benjamin, Alfred (Al), John, Clayton, and Winslow—arrived in the Mancos Valley and established the Alamo Ranch. They ran their cattle in Mancos Canyon and up onto Mesa Verde. They were intrigued by the cliff dwellings and the open pueblos, and began digging in them for artifacts. Sometime in the mid-1880s, Al Wetherill, who was on foot, followed up a side canyon off the Mancos main stem, looked up, and, as he later described it, saw, under an overhanging cliff, a great cavern-like place in which was situated what seemed like a small ruined city. . . . My mind wanted to go up to it but my legs refused to cooperate. At the time I was so tired that I thought later would be the time for closer investigation."[3] A prospector, S. E. Osborn, may have seen the same ruin in 1883–84, according to a story he gave to a Denver newspaper in 1886.[4]

The ruin spotted by Osborn and Al Wetherill, Cliff Palace, was "officially" discovered in December 1888 by Richard Wetherill and his brother-in-law Charlie Mason while hunting cattle on top of Mesa Verde. The same day they also discovered and named Spruce Tree House. The Wetherills and others began digging in the ruins and leading tourist pack trips onto Mesa Verde to visit them.

One such tourist was a young Swedish engineer, Gustaf Nordenskiöld (1868–95), who came in 1891. Gustaf hired the Wetherills to help him excavate several sites and subsequently published a major archaeological report, *The Cliff Dwellers of Mesa Verde*, in 1893.[5] It was the first scientific report on Southwest archaeology and is still in use a century later.

The artifact collections made by the Wetherills and others became a source of income. Two Wetherill collections, one privately purchased, the other bought by the State of Colorado, were exhibited at the 1893 Chicago World's Fair.[6]

In 1890 Charles Lang and a companion headed into Grand Gulch in the San Juan Triangle. Lang photographed several rockshelters and cliff dwellings. His and others' reports of these "untouched" ruins stimulated Charles McLoyd and Charles Graham to go to Grand Gulch in January 1891. They dug for four months throughout the length of the Gulch. Their collection was purchased for $3,000 by C. H. Green of Durango, Colorado, who financed McLoyd for another trip to the Gulch in June 1891.

In the winter of 1891–92, McLoyd and others returned to Grand Gulch and also explored and dug in sites in canyons of the Red Rock Plateau—including Red Canyon, Lake Canyon, "Lost" (probably Moqui) Canyon, and "Deep Canyon."

In the winter of 1892–93, McLoyd, with John Wetherill and others, returned to Grand Gulch and then went on to White, Red, Lake, Lost, and Deep canyons. This was the Wetherills' introduction to Grand Gulch and the Red Rock Plateau.[7]

In 1891 the editor of *The Illustrated American* magazine hired Warren Moorehead of Ohio to lead an expedition along the San Juan River to collect "Cliff Dweller" artifacts for display at the upcoming Chicago World's Fair.[8] The plan was to print articles by members of the expedition chronicling their success "In Search of a Lost Race." Moorehead had some background in Midwest archaeology. The expedition was in the field from April to June 1892. They partially explored the San Juan River and its tributaries from Durango, Colorado, to Grand Gulch. Fourteen articles, some more accurate than others, appeared in the magazine. Ultimately, only forty-six artifacts were displayed in Chicago, and the expedition ended in lawsuits and recriminations.

Also in the summer of 1892, Frederick A. Hyde, a prominent New York physician, and his teenage sons, Talbot and Fred Jr., were taken by the Wetherills on a tour of the Mesa Verde ruins. The boys were studying anthropology at Harvard and were also the heirs to a soap company fortune. When Richard Wetherill renewed his acquaintance with them at the Chicago World's Fair in 1893, they agreed to form and fund a Hyde exploring expedition to Grand Gulch.

In December 1893, Richard, Al, and John Wetherill and others headed for the Grand Gulch region; they stayed four months. They also explored Cottonwood Gulch, Butler Wash, and Red, White, and Step canyons. Richard Wetherill had learned from the meticulous Nordenskiöld the importance of keeping careful excavation notes and observing stratigraphic relationships as he dug sites. In Cottonwood Gulch, he noted an older cultural stratum beneath the Cliff Dweller level. On December 23, 1893, he wrote to Talbot Hyde:

> In the cave we are now working, . . . and curious to tell, a thing that will surprise the archaeologists of the country, is the fact of our finding. . . . [burials] at a depth of five and six feet in a cave in which there are cliff dwellings and we find the bodies under the ruins, three feet below any cliff dweller sign. *They are a different race from anything I have ever seen. They have feather cloth and baskets, no pottery,—six of the bodies had stone spearheads in them.*[9]

Wetherill asked Hyde to pick a name for this new "different race"; Hyde picked "Basket Makers," later shortened to "Basketmakers." Wetherill's "Basket Makers" ultimately were critical keys to the archaeology of the northern Southwest, including the Glen Canyon Country.

In January 1895 Richard and Al Wetherill and Charlie Mason crossed the San Juan River and then trailed across Monument Valley and up Laguna Creek to Marsh Pass. They started up Tsegi Canyon. Not long after, Richard's favorite mule, Neephi, broke his hobbles and wandered away. Richard pursued the miscreant upcanyon, rounded a bend, looked up, and saw the great ruin of Keet Seel. The site soon yielded a rich find of artifacts.[10]

In the summer of 1895 Theophilus Mitchell Prudden (1849–1924) arrived at the Wetherill's ranch. He was a professor of pathology at Columbia University. He was fascinated by the archaeology he saw. For a decade he and Clayton Wetherill systematically sought and recorded sites in the north bank tributary canyons of the San Juan from near its headwaters to Mexican Hat. In 1897 he published the first article to call attention to Richard Wetherill's Basket Maker culture, *Elder Brother of the Cliff Dweller*.[11]

In 1903 Prudden published a sixty-page, illustrated article in the *American Anthropologist*, "The Prehistoric Ruins of the San Juan Watershed," in which he summarized his findings. The accompanying map shows the distribution of hundreds of sites in canyons from Comb Wash eastward beyond the Mancos River. He had surveyed down White Canyon to the Colorado River and reported that Clayton Wetherill had explored sites on the Red Rock Plateau. He explored several miles into Tsegi Canyon but made only a cursory inspection of the canyons that drain into the San Juan off Navajo Mountain.

Prudden's report was a tour de force, giving scholars for the first time a clear picture of the distribution and richness of archaeological sites westward from Mesa Verde to the confluence of the San Juan and Colorado rivers. In 1914 and 1918 he published two more articles about a widespread, often predominant, Ancestral Puebloan settlement pattern on the Colorado Plateau. These were small sites with several surface rooms grouped behind one or more circular pit houses, or kivas. He called them "unit pueblos," a term still current.[12]

In 1906 Prudden published *On the Great American Plateau*, reflecting his exuberant fondness for the country, the archaeology, the Indian people, the traders, and the guides.[13] He retired in 1909 but continued to pursue his interest in the Southwest. About 1914, A. V. Kidder (see below) wrote to Prudden asking advice about working in the area. Prudden gave him not only advice, but a financial contribution for fieldwork, which he continued to provide yearly until he died.[14]

In the spring of 1896 a wealthy Harvard student, George Bowles, appeared at the Wetherill's ranch in the company of his tutor, C. E. Whitmore. Bowles agreed to fund an expedition into Grand Gulch and beyond. In January 1897 Richard led the Whitmore expedition into Grand Gulch and sent others to Tsegi Canyon and on into Moqui Canyon. They found sites that had already been dug in, perhaps by one of the McLoyd parties. Richard dug more in Keet Seel, recovering a large artifact collection that reposes, as yet unstudied, in the American Museum of Natural History.[15]

To add an element of excitement and danger to their expedition, Bowles and Whitmore were purportedly kidnapped by some Navajos. They were held for ransom on Moqui Rock, a pinnacle with about 100 square feet of space on top, while a messenger rode frantically to Bluff City, Utah, for a sack of several hundred silver dollars. The ransom was paid and the haggard captives released—or so the story goes. Documentation of the event, if it happened, is slight; but it's a good yarn.[16]

In 1896, Richard Wetherill, under Hyde expedition auspices, began digging in Pueblo Bonito in Chaco Canyon, New Mexico. The Hyde brothers

13.1. The Wetherill trading post at Kayenta, Arizona, 1930s. Photographer R. Branstead, MS-122-230. Courtesy of the Museum of Northern Arizona.

insisted that the expedition be under the auspices of the American Museum of Natural History.

The great ruins of Chaco Canyon were first described by an army expedition in 1849. Chaco Wash feeds into the San Juan River. Scattered along its upper reaches and on the canyon rims above it are the ruins of a dozen multistory pueblos, each of several hundred rooms. We now know that the Chaco Canyon sites—and related sites to the west, north, and east—were built primarily in the eleventh century and abandoned by the middle of the twelfth century. They were connected by a vast network of "roads." Although studied for over a century, the "Chaco Phenomenon" still puzzles archaeologists.[17] The full story of the Wetherills in Chaco Canyon is beyond our purview, but it is ably told elsewhere by Frank McNitt and Marietta Wetherill, Richard's wife.[18]

For the purposes of our story, however, in 1900 John and Louisa Wade Wetherill (whom we met in chapter 10) opened the Ojo Alamo trading post north of Pueblo Bonito. They later moved to Oljato, just inside the Utah border, and then to Kayenta, Arizona, on the edge of the Glen Canyon Country (fig. 13.1). There they enjoyed long careers as Indian traders and guides, and mentors to dozens of archaeologists and tourists. We'll come back to John and Louisa repeatedly later on.

BYRON CUMMINGS IN THE GLEN CANYON COUNTRY

In early 1906 Edgar Lee Hewett came to Salt Lake City on a lecture tour for the Archaeological Institute of America (AIA). Formed in 1879, the AIA's major focus was on classical Greek and Latin civilizations, but for a time in the 1880s it had supported research in Hispanic America.[19] By 1900 the institute had decided to broaden its membership (and hence its funding base) by re-initiating an

13.2. Byron Cummings at Rainbow Bridge, 1936. Photograph by Tad Nichols. Nichols Collection, NAU 11748. Courtesy of Cline Library, Northern Arizona University.

Americanist program. Hewett was the AIA's newly appointed director of American archaeology, and his job was to stimulate public interest and help form new AIA chapters in western states. In 1907 he became director of the AIA School of American Archaeology based in Santa Fe. In 1909 he founded, and became director of, the Museum of New Mexico, keeping his AIA position as well.[20]

Byron Cummings (fig. 13.2), a professor of classics and administrator at the University of Utah, was in Hewett's Salt Lake City audience. Cummings (1860–1954) was born in upstate New York.[21] In 1893 he answered an ad for instructors at the University of Utah and was hired to teach Latin and Greek. By 1895 he was a full professor, later serving as Dean of Men (1905–15) and also dean of the School of Arts and Sciences (1906–15).

Cummings had included lectures on Old World archaeology in his curriculum. Now, stimulated by Hewett's talk, he turned his attention to the archaeology of Utah. He and Colonel Enos A. Wall formed a Utah chapter of the AIA, and Wall provided some funds for exploration of Utah archaeological sites. Enos A. Wall (1838–1920), a longtime western mining entrepreneur, was co-owner of the Utah Copper Company, which developed the great Bingham copper mine west of Salt Lake City. ("Colonel" seems to have been an honorary title.)[22]

An archaeology program was right down Cummings's alley. He was an avid supporter of athletics (the University of Utah named a playing field for him) and hiking outdoors. Nephew Neil M. Judd wrote that Cummings "was the only Caucasian [as compared, apparently, with Indian people] I ever knew, other than Professor Herbert E. Gregory of Yale, who could out-walk a horse on desert sand."[23]

Cummings's first archaeological foray was a brief trip in 1906 to Nine Mile Canyon in east-central Utah to see the cliff dwellings and the wonderful rock art panels therein.[24] In 1907 he made a trip to White Canyon to see the great natural bridges that had come to national attention in 1903–5. He took along five others, including nephew Neil Judd. The party made some maps of the ruins in the canyon that were later included in the background documentation for the Natural Bridges National Monument nomination.[25]

In 1907 Hewett held the School of American Archaeology's first field school, initially in an area near the Four Corners. He had three undergraduate students from Harvard: Alfred Vincent Kidder, Sylvanus Griswold Morley, and John Gould Fletcher. Hewett took them to a mesa top near McElmo Canyon, waved his arm at the tangled canyons lying between them and Mesa Verde in the distance, and told them to do an archaeological survey "of the area." He then got on his horse and rode away. With a tape measure, a compass, and a cheap camera, they managed to do a respectable job. Kidder and Morley returned in 1908, in the interim having learned a good deal more about how to do archaeology from mentors at Harvard.[26]

Cummings had learned of numerous archaeological sites dotting Alkali Ridge near the town of Blanding, Utah. With some financial support from Colonel Wall and others, he proposed an excavation program there to Hewett, who concurred. When Cummings arrived with Neil Judd and others in tow, he discovered that Hewett had placed A. V. Kidder, with a newly minted Harvard bachelor's degree, in charge. Cummings was rather miffed. Even though he had no archaeological experience, he was, after all, a professor and dean at the University of Utah! He assumed the role of camp cook, as he apparently often did for many years thereafter.[27] Kidder was diplomatic enough to make Cummings co-director, and published a report of the work.[28]

After finishing at Alkali Ridge, Cummings and Judd met John Wetherill at Bluff, Utah, and headed for Oljato. But there was major trouble brewing among the Navajo people, primarily over their children being forcibly sent away to Bureau of Indian Affairs schools. The U.S. Army had been called in. When Wetherill, Cummings, and Judd arrived at Oljato, they found six troops of cavalry, a machine-gun platoon, a wagon train, fifty pack mules, and numerous packers, interpreters, guides, and cooks. Through the good offices of Louisa Wetherill, who spoke fluent Navajo, and with the help of Colonel Hugh L. Scott, an expert army trouble-shooter for Indian disputes, matters were settled, and the army and the Navajos dispersed in separate directions.[29]

Cummings and Judd then went on to explore in Tsegi and adjacent canyons. When they returned to Oljato, they learned from Louisa Wetherill that she had told some Navajos about the White Canyon bridges. The Navajos told her they had heard about a bridge somewhere toward Navajo Mountain "shaped like a rainbow." Cummings determined to come back the next year and search for it.

Cummings, son Malcolm, Neil Judd, and photographer Stuart Young arrived at Oljato in the early summer of 1909. Guided by John Wetherill, they first visited Keet Seel. In early July, John and Louisa Wetherill, with their two young children, and the Cummings party visited a ruin that came to be called Inscription House. The story is that the children found an inscription that Cummings and others interpreted as *Anno Domini 1661,* left, they

13.3. Ida Wetherill and Malcolm Cummings at Keet Seel Ruin, summer 1909. Photograph by Stuart Young, NAU 1468. Courtesy of Cline Library, Northern Arizona University.

thought, by an unknown Spanish explorer. Probably the inscription is *1861*, left by some Mormon missionaries known to have been in the area that year.[30] The party returned to dig in Keet Seel (fig. 13.3) and then headed back to Oljato. On the way they encountered a Navajo woman who told them of a large cliff house in a side canyon. They investigated and found the spectacular ruin they named Betatakin, "Hillside House."

ON TO RAINBOW BRIDGE

Having briefly recorded Betatakin and some other sites, the Cummings party turned to find a way to Rainbow Bridge. As noted in chapter 10, Cummings combined his party with that of the government surveyor William Boone Douglass. The joint Douglass-Cummings party finally reached "the Rainbow Bridge" on August 14, 1909, and fairly quickly fell into a dispute over "who was first" bragging rights.[31]

The backstory to the conflict between Cummings and Douglass began the previous year. It is useful to discuss the conflict briefly because it had to do with interpretation and implementation of the 1906 Antiquities Act. The outcome would, in turn, influence how "salvage archaeology" would begin to be developed in the 1920s and, ultimately, the structure, funding, and implementation of the Glen Canyon Project three decades later (chapter 15).

There was a long struggle, dating back to at least 1889, by archaeologists and their supporters to get federal legislation passed to protect archaeological sites on public lands.[32] Between 1879 and 1906 looting had increased as individuals searched for artifacts to sell to major U.S. and western European natural history museums as well as tourists.

By 1889 American scientific societies were calling attention to the looting problem and issuing pleas for legislation.[33] In 1895 draft legislation began to be submitted to Congress. Key issues were who would be given permission to excavate sites on public lands, and where the excavated materials would be housed. One proposed bill gave control of archaeological sites in the West to a consortium of eastern universities and museums; another gave control of such sites to the Smithsonian Institution. The argument for the latter was that the Smithsonian is, in part, a federal agency and therefore should be in charge of archaeological resources from federal lands. Neither proposal sat well with people in the West.

Finally, in 1906, a bill acceptable to all parties was passed by Congress and signed into law by President Theodore Roosevelt.[34] The regulations to implement the act stated that excavation permits could be issued to any university, museum, or scientific institution in the country—not just to eastern universities or the Smithsonian. But Hewett, Cummings, and others in the West also felt that excavated western collections, no matter who dug them up, should stay in their states of origin—deposited in newly created, or proposed, museums. The eastern institutions, including the Smithsonian, were in hot competition to increase their holdings and strongly disagreed.[35]

William B. Douglass felt there should be full federal control of archaeological sites on federal lands, and artifacts therefrom ought to be in federal repositories. In 1908—9, there was only one such repository: the U.S. National Museum of the Smithsonian Institution.

Natural Bridges and other national monuments needed proper legal surveys and maps. In 1908 Douglass, a federal surveyor, was sent to do the job. He was also instructed to seek out and recommend other national monument sites in the Four Corners states. He set up shop in Bluff, Utah. Keet Seel and other major ruins in the Tesgi Canyon area were either known or rumored. Cummings's foray into the area in 1908 and talk that he would be back in 1909 alarmed Douglass. In March 1909 he managed to get a 160-square-mile area that included Keet Seel, other adjacent ruins, and the yet-to-be discovered Betatakin designated as Navajo National Monument—even though he'd seen only a fraction of the area. Douglass thus thought he would keep Cummings from digging in Tsegi Canyon.[36]

But Cummings was operating under Hewett's antiquities permit. The regulations said permits would be issued to recognized institutions to dig on federal lands—and a national monument was, by definition, federal land. The new Navajo National Monument was within the area designated by Hewett's permit. Douglass argued that the permit had been issued to Hewett, but he wouldn't be there—hence Cummings would be acting illegally. But Hewett could, in his view, delegate authority to Cummings—and he did so.

Following the tense trip to Rainbow Bridge in August 1909, Cummings proceeded with his excavation plans. After the Cummings party returned from the Rainbow Bridge trip, Judd and others returned to Salt Lake City. Cummings stayed in the area and then rode to Beef Basin, northwest of Moab, Utah, to record ruins there.[37] While Cummings was on that trip, Jesse Walter Fewkes of the Smithsonian visited Keet Seel, Betatakin, and Inscription House to initiate surveys and plans for protecting the ruins. In all likelihood, Cummings had learned that Fewkes was coming and chose to be elsewhere. In December, Cummings returned to the Tsegi Canyon area and "cleaned out" Betatakin and several other sites, as he wrote to Hewett.[38]

When Cummings returned to Salt Lake City in December 1909, he hurried three articles into print. Two of them described Rainbow Bridge and the bridges in White Canyon. The third was a brief review of the archaeological sites he had seen and dug in 1908–9.[39]

In 1910 Fewkes recommended that Inscription House be included as part of the national monument (it lay outside Douglass's original area) and the monument boundaries be adjusted. In 1912 the monument was reduced to three separate areas, as it remains: a 40-acre tract around Inscription House and 160-acre tracts around Betatakin and Keet Seel. All intervening areas remain Navajo Nation lands.[40] In 1909 John Wetherill was appointed as custodian of Navajo National Monument at the nominal salary of $1 per year (in fact, it was $1 a month), a position he held for many years.[41]

Between 1911 and 1916, Cummings was back in Tsegi Canyon, or elsewhere on the Rainbow Plateau and Cummings Mesa, digging in at least twenty caves and pueblos. Out of all this he published only a somewhat romanticized paper on kivas in the San Juan drainage.[42] He was apparently reacting in part to an article by Silvanus G. Morley, published in 1908, that called attention to the importance of kivas in the ceremonial lives of historic Pueblo peoples and, by extension, the lives of their predecessors.[43]

Cummings also focused on the ceremonial importance of kivas and the items found therein. He interpreted artifacts based on information elicited from a Navajo chanter or "medicine man." This led him to conclude that Navajo and Hopi priests shared ceremonial materials and knowledge, and therefore "it seems to us to indicate quite a close connection between the Tachinie clan of the Navajo and the Cliff Dwellers of the region."[44]

Questions of the relationship(s) between Navajos and late Ancestral Puebloans ("Cliff Dwellers") would not be resolved to archaeologists' satisfaction for several decades; they are still not resolved in the eyes of the Hopi tribe and the Navajo Nation.

In 1915 Cummings and sixteen faculty members resigned from the University of Utah after a major dispute over academic freedom. Cummings was hired at the University of Arizona, where he built up the Arizona State Museum and a department of archaeology, eventually becoming recognized as "The Dean" of Southwest archaeology.[45]

For many years Cummings's Southwest "excavations" were basically to collect artifacts; he published little. Years later some of his Tsegi Canyon materials were written up as a part of a doctoral dissertation by Keith M. Anderson, who had been on the Glen Canyon Project and later was an archaeologist at Navajo National Monument.[46] Materials from Cummings's digs on Cummings Mesa were incorporated into a doctoral dissertation by Alexander J. Lindsay Jr., the field leader for the Museum of Northern Arizona segment of the Glen Canyon Project.[47]

A. V. KIDDER AND SAMUEL GUERNSEY

News of Cummings's spectacular finds led others to the March Pass–Tsegi Canyon area, among them Alfred Vincent Kidder (1885–1963) and Samuel J. Guernsey from Harvard. Serious attempts to understand and sort out the culture history of the Southwest only began with the introduction of new archaeological methods: stratigraphy and the use of pottery types to provide a relative time scale and establish regional cultural relationships.[48] The "new" methods were introduced after 1910 by several young university-trained archaeologists, especially Nels Nelson and Earl Morris, working for the American Museum; Neil Judd, working for the U.S. National Museum; and Kidder, working for the R. S. Peabody Foundation in Massachusetts and closely linked to the Peabody Museum of Harvard University.

Kidder had attended Hewett's 1907 archaeological field school with fellow Harvard undergraduates Morley and Fletcher. Fletcher became a poet. Morley became an expert on Maya hieroglyphics and a U.S. spy in Central America during World War I.[49] Kidder wrote his doctoral dissertation on southwestern Pueblo ceramics, a key document in the modern archaeology of the Southwest.[50]

In 1914, as Harvard legend has it, Kidder and Samuel Guernsey, a staff member of the Peabody Museum, agreed to launch a systematic field campaign to sort out the chronologies and cultural relationships in the Glen Canyon Country and adjacent areas. One of the problems they wished to pursue was the relationship between Richard Wetherill's Basket Makers and the apparently later in time Cliff Dwellers.[51]

In 1912 Kidder had scouted the southern reaches of the Comb Ridge area and probably met John Wetherill on the advice of T. Mitchell Prudden.[52] In June 1914, "provisioning at Kayenta, the party first took up the exploration of the territory lying between the great Capitan Rock ('Agathla Needle' of the maps) and the 'Monuments,' [Monument Valley] a cluster of enormous eroded pillars of sandstone lying about midway between it and the San Juan River."[53]

One of the Monument Valley sites, Flute Player House, proved to be of particular importance. Just downstream from the site were series of petroglyphs, including a group of "hump-backed creatures apparently blowing on musical instruments, one of which [creature] was phallic."[54] This is an early published depiction of the mythical figure Kokopelli, the "hump-back flute player," who has seeds or other things in his hump (which may also be a burden basket). He seduces and impregnates young girls and is a general symbol of fertility. Rock art images of Kokopelli occur widely across the Southwest, including in Glen Canyon. He and a female counterpart are also kachina figures in Hopi ceremonies.[55] Since the 1960s, Kokopelli, often sans the humpback, has become a familiar image across the land as the name for gas stations, used car lots, rental property companies, car washes, wineries, eateries from bistros to cantinas, hotels, bed and breakfasts, golf courses, housewares, bike trails, and vendors of iPOD parts and accessories, to name only a few (see the Internet).

Flute Player House itself became very important, "for it contained clear evidence of two distinct ancient cultures, one superimposed on the other,"[56] with an intermediate stratum which they speculated might be transitional from "Basket Maker" to "Cliff House." The Kidder and Guernsey report marked a major turning point in southwestern archaeology, demonstrating that the Basket Maker culture was indeed earlier than the Cliff Dweller culture.

DEFINING THE BASKET MAKERS AND THEIR SUCCESSORS

In 1915 Kidder began excavating the great Pecos Ruin, east of Santa Fe.[57] Guernsey continued working in the Tsegi area for the next several years, seeking to better define the sequence of cultures there. He was annually assisted by various Harvard students, including Oliver La Farge (1901–63), who was with Guernsey in 1921, 1923, and 1924 and later became a major novelist (he wrote the Pulitzer Prize–winning *Laughing Boy*) and Indian rights advocate.[58]

The sites that Kidder and Guernsey dug in the Marsh Pass area in 1914–15 suggested to them the "probability" that the Basket Makers were the earliest agricultural inhabitants of the northern Southwest; in 1916 Guernsey's work confirmed this.[59] After World War I he returned to the Tesgi area to "trace the later development" of the Basketmakers and their relationships with the Pueblo peoples.[60] In 1922 he shifted to the lower Chinle Wash, which drains Canyon de Chelly. In 1923, after digging in Poncho House, he headed back to Kayenta for supplies.

> Shortly after arrival, [Guernsey] . . . and two of the men came down with a violent sickness, resembling pneumonia, that in . . . [Guernsey's] case resulted in a prolonged disability. The trouble was doubtless due to a particularly

> pernicious dust during the excavations at Poncho House. The great rubbish heaps at that site, the accumulations of centuries, are composed largely of ashes and pulverized turkey droppings. Every stroke of the pick caused the dust to rise in choking clouds. Only such members of the party as were most exposed suffered from the subsequent long irritation.[61]

Guernsey was forced to leave the field. He and his workers had "desert fever" or "valley fever," formally called coccidioidomycosis, which is caused by a fungus in the soil. Sometimes known as "archaeologists' disease," the infection can be debilitating, even fatal. In 1960 the University of Utah's Glen Canyon Project crew working in Lake Canyon had an "epidemic" of the infection (chapter 17).

In 1924 Kidder published a major synthesis of what was then known and speculated about the archaeology of the Colorado Plateau and adjacent areas, *An Introduction to the Study of Southwestern Archaeology*.[62] He divided the Southwest into several major districts. The "San Juan" district had three subdivisions: Chaco Canyon, Mesa Verde, and Kayenta. He recognized a chronological sequence of "Basket Maker," "Post-Basket Maker," "Pre-Pueblo," and "Pueblo." There was also an ill-defined "Northern Periphery" on the Colorado Plateau of eastern Utah and western Colorado.[63]

In 1927 Kidder hosted an archaeological conference at Pecos Ruin.[64] The resultant "Pecos Classification" is still used, although other systems have been proposed. In 1927 the chronology was "relative"—that is, organized in a sequence known to be stratigraphically correct. The only calendar date that could be assigned was 1540 CE, when the Spanish arrived in the Southwest and "absolute" (that is, Euro-American) calendar time began for the region. After 1929 the development of tree-ring dating allowed pre-1540 calendar dates to be assigned to the sequence. By the end of the 1930s the classification was as shown in Table 13.1.

TABLE 13.1. Pecos Archaeological Classification

STAGE	DATES CE
Pueblo V	1700–present
Pueblo IV	1300–1700
Pueblo III	1100–1300
Pueblo II	~850–1100
Pueblo I	750–~900
Basketmaker III	~450–750
Basketmaker II	1–~500
Basketmaker I	Pre 1 CE

Note: "Basketmaker I" was a hypothetical hunter-gatherer stage preceding the beginning of farming, which appeared to start during Basketmaker II times. "Basketmaker I" is no longer used, replaced by the more general term "Archaic." "Formative" is often used for Basketmaker II through early Pueblo IV times.

By the early 1930s it was apparent that the Pecos Classification applied only to the northern Southwest. Cultures on the Mogollon Plateau in Arizona and the mountains of eastern Arizona and western New Mexico were called Mogollon, and the cultures of the Salt/Gila river basin were called Hohokam. In 1936 Kidder gave the Navajo term "Anasazi" to the cultures of the northern Southwest to distinguish them from Mogollon and Hohokam. Kidder thought the term simply meant "old people,"[65] but, in fact, "Anazazi" means "enemy ancestors." In the eyes of the Hopis and other Pueblo people, "Anasazi" is a pejorative term; they prefer "Ancestral Puebloan" as a substitute. We thus use "Ancestral Puebloan" when not citing or discussing earlier works.

Ancestral Puebloan culture still has Kidder's three subdivisions: the Mesa Verde area is east of the Colorado and north of the San Juan rivers. The Kayenta region is east of the Colorado and south of the San Juan. Along the Virgin River and adjacent areas there is a subdivision called the Virgin Branch or Virgin Kayenta. The Chaco tradition is centered along the Chaco Wash drainage and to the west, with some outliers north of the San Juan. Kidder's "Northern Periphery" was renamed "Fremont" in 1931 (see below).

13.4. Earl Morris (*left*), Charles Bernheimer, and Zeke Johnson during the 1923 expedition to Arizona. Photographer unknown, 294616. Courtesy of the American Museum of Natural History Library.

THE BERNHEIMER EXPEDITIONS

In 1920 Charles L. Bernheimer (1864–1944) (fig. 13.4), a fifty-five-year-old cotton broker and manufacturer from New York City, hired John Wetherill to take him to Rainbow Bridge. Bernheimer, who called himself a "tenderfoot and cliff dweller from Manhattan," was a long way in distance and culture from New York City and his origins. He was born in Germany, came to the United States at age seventeen, and went to work in the family dry goods business. The company expanded and diversified over time, and Charles rose to be president from 1907 to 1928 and chairman of the board thereafter.

Bernheimer began visiting the Southwest in about 1915. In 1919 he made a pack-train trip from Blanding, Utah, to White Canyon to see the great natural bridges, guided by Ezekiel (Zeke) Johnson (1869–1957), who became his close friend and wilderness guardian.

Johnson was a true son of the canyon country. He was the twenty-fourth child of Joel H. Johnson, a Mormon polygamist and early settler in Kane County, Utah, who had 4 wives, 29 children, 112 grandchildren, and 54 great-grandchildren when he died at age eighty-two. Zeke grew up fast. He worked as a farmhand, rode the mail route from St. George to Kanab, punched cows on the Arizona Strip, herded sheep on the Kaibab Plateau, and hauled logs in Flagstaff and freight in Tuba City. In 1898, while herding cattle, he first saw the great natural bridges in White Canyon.

In 1905 he moved to Grayson (later Blanding) and began guiding tourist pack trips to White Canyon. When Natural Bridges National Monument was created in 1908, Johnson became its first custodian, at the usual nominal salary of $1 a year.[66]

When Bernheimer met Johnson, the latter was fifty years old, a great, gentle bear of a man whom the Navajos called Bilagáana Nez, "Tall White Man." His knowledge of the San Juan Triangle and much of the Glen Canyon Country was unparalleled. When Bernheimer contracted with John Wetherill to take him to Rainbow Bridge in 1920, he insisted that Johnson go along. He did so, and was with Bernheimer on all subsequent trips.

Wetherill's people had no trouble accepting Zeke Johnson, but at first thought Bernheimer was a true greenhorn dude. He insisted on wearing pajamas and a wool cap at night, and brought along a large chest of miscellaneous medicines. But he won the men's respect by how he handled himself and his horses. Bernheimer was entranced with Navajo Mountain, Rainbow Bridge, and the surrounding country, so much so that he returned for a second trip in 1921.

Bernheimer kept field notes, later folded into a book about Rainbow Bridge. During the 1920 trip the party stopped in Surprise Valley on the slope of Navajo Mountain.

> Well, I am here in this marvelous little oasis which Zane Grey so cleverly described, and if I may say, accurately [chapter 10]. The approach to it is by a narrow cleft in the rocks, it cannot be reached by any other way. . . . We were one hour on whale back rocks. After they are passed, one reaches the places which Grey describes in the pursuit by Shadd at the end of Rainbow Trail, and just before getting to the small narrow gateway is a fiendish place to come down. How horses can do this I don't know, but our eleven animals did it safely.[67]

In 1920 and 1921 Wetherill followed the same trail to the bridge that he and Nasja Begay had pioneered in 1909 with Cummings and Douglass, which involved a circuit around the north side of Navajo Mountain. In 1920 Wetherill first led Bernheimer to the top of Navajo Mountain, from which he got his first glimpse of Rainbow Bridge: "Away down in the bosom of the earth, nestling in a dark streak of a canyon, we saw what appeared to be a microscopic half of a ring-sausage. Wetherill had no easy task making me see this shape. 'That is your first view of Rainbow Bridge,' he said."[68]

Bernheimer had assumed that the party could descend from the mountaintop straight to the bridge. When he saw the country, he changed his mind. But he thought the trail to the bridge was too long and was convinced that an easier, or at least shorter, one could be developed from the south and west. In 1921 the party made an attempt to get to the bridge from the west, but failed.[69] They had to backtrack and go around Navajo Mountain by the old trail to reach Rainbow Bridge.

In 1922, equipped with dynamite, shovels, sledgehammers, and pry bars, the party blasted a passage, which Bernheimer called "Red Bud Pass," between Cliff Canyon and Red Bud Creek. In his field notes Earl Morris (see below) described the work:

> July 3 & 4 were spent by all hands on the Red Bud trail. . . . The major obstacle was a fissure between great vertical slabs of stone, perhaps 3 ft. wide at the bottom and thirty feet deep. We rolled loose blocks of stone down into it from the cliffs on the W[est] side, then shot down and sledged to pieces the two vertical leaves of stone at the W[est] side of the fissure, until the slit was filled and widened enough for animals to climb down it. July 5. On the morning of this day we . . . rode through Red Bud Pass and down to the Bridge, thus completing the major objective of the trip, that is passing W[est] of Navajo Mountain to the Rainbow.[70]

THE 1921 EXPEDITION

In addition to searching for a new route to the bridge, Bernheimer decided that the 1921 trip should include an archaeological reconnaissance. He was a longtime donor to the American Museum of Natural History in New York and had asked the museum send along an archaeologist. Bernheimer would pay salary and expenses, and any collections would go to the museum. Happy to comply, the museum chose Earl Halstead Morris (fig. 13.4).

In the lore of southwestern archaeology, Earl Morris was the quintessential "field man," or "dirt archaeologist"—one whose real life is "in the field," looking for, finding, testing, and excavating archeological sites. Field men and women know that archaeology is 20 percent fieldwork, the fun part, and 80 percent drudgery—analyzing artifacts, writing reports, filing papers, raising money. They relish the 20 percent and try to avoid the rest.

Earl Morris grew up in Farmington, New Mexico. His teamster father supplemented the family income by digging in local sites, especially Aztec Ruins, for artifacts to sell, and early on he taught

Earl how to dig. After earning bachelor's and master's degrees in anthropology at the University of Colorado, Morris was hired by the American Museum to be excavator and caretaker of Aztec Ruins, which the museum purchased and later turned over to the National Park Service.[71] But his real interest was in the earlier cultures, which he called the "Old People," or "pre-Pueblo"—that is, the Basketmakers. He pursued them across the northern Southwest for much of his professional life.[72]

Thus, when his bosses at the American Museum sent him along with Bernheimer, he reluctantly went, hoping that some "pre-Pueblo" finds would outweigh having to put up with the donor-dude. In fact, Bernheimer became a major supporter of Morris's work. The two apparently hit it off almost immediately. In his field notes for 1921 Bernheimer wrote of Morris, "He is a dandy, fine, clean cut, able and conscientious fellow of a most agreeable personality."[73]

Bernheimer and Morris met Wetherill and his men and animals at Marsh Pass and rode into Betatakin. They moved next to Inscription House, in an upper tributary of Navajo Canyon. They continued down Navajo Canyon but did not go all the way to the Colorado River. They then turned to the task of finding a route from the west to Rainbow Bridge, as described above.

On July 5, 1922, after the party had ridden through Red Bud Pass to Rainbow Bridge, Bernheimer, Wetherill, and Jesse Smith walked downcanyon to the Colorado River. On the way back they detoured up Forbidding Canyon for some miles until

> we came to the largest water pool in the entire country aside from the Colo. River. This forms a barrier in W[est, i.e., Forbidding] Canyon bottom impassable to [pack] animals. On the W[est] side of the canyon just above the pool is a tremendous cave about 350 feet long and 175 [feet] deep. All along the entire wall of this is a deposit of charcoal, etc., of human origin, showing extensive occupation as a camp site, but there are no signs of walls.[74]

The next day Morris returned to the cave and dug in it, finding the burial of a small child covered with pitch-coated basketry trays. He searched for other Basketmaker sites whenever he could during the trip, but found few; most were of later age.

Morris accompanied Bernheimer on five trips into the Glen Canyon Country between 1921 and 1929. In between, Bernheimer funded Morris's search for the Old People in the Carrizo Mountains, Canyon del Muerto, and the Prayer Rock district between the Carrizo and Lukachukai mountains in northeastern Arizona.[75]

THE 1929 TRIP

In 1929 Bernheimer brought together Zeke Johnson, John Wetherill, and Earl Morris for a final horseback trip into the Glen Canyon Country, this time across the Red Rock Plateau. The trip started in Blanding, Utah, and moved southwestward along Grand Gulch, thence westward through Clay Hills Pass into the head of Castle Wash, turning northwestward to the East Fork of Lake Canyon. "On the north brink of East Canyon there is a rectangular fortification some 75 feet in greatest length, with two rooms included in its cliff ward side. The door of one is T-shaped. Among the sherds scattered about Kayenta red is conspicuous."[76] I supervised the excavation of this site in 1960 (chapter 17).

Crossing Lake Canyon, the party turned south, then west and along the left bank of Glen Canyon proper, across the mouth of Slick Rock Canyon, and on to the rim of the Rincon before camping at the head of Cottonwood Canyon. They rode down the canyon to the river and then along the river to the confluence of the San Juan. They followed the Hole-in-the-Rock emigrant trail back to Lake Canyon, then headed into Moqui Canyon, traveling down one of the falling dunes to reach the canyon floor, where Morris spent three days exploring at least three rockshelter sites. (One of those, Bernheimer Alcove, as it was later called, was reexcavated in 1961 by a University of Utah crew [chapter 18]). The party then moved on to Red Canyon, crossed over into White Canyon, and followed it upstream to Bridges National Monument, where they were picked up by an automobile and taken back to Blanding. The trip took twenty-four days. It was Morris's last trip into Glen Canyon Country, but not Bernheimer's. In the 1930s he visited the Rainbow Bridge-Monument Valley Expedition (see below).

NEIL JUDD IN THE GLEN CANYON COUNTRY

Earlier we saw that Neil Judd had accompanied his uncle, Byron Cummings, on trips into the Glen Canyon Country in 1908 and 1909 (fig. 13.2). Neil Merton Judd (1887–1976) was born in Iowa. His mother was Byron Cummings's sister, and in 1901 the Judd family followed Cummings to Salt Lake City. In 1910 Judd attended Hewett's archaeological field school in Frijoles Canyon, New Mexico (now Bandelier National Monument). There he met Frederick Webb Hodge, ethnologist-in-charge of the Bureau of American Ethnology at the Smithsonian Institution. In 1911 Judd graduated from the University of Utah and, with some help from Hewett and Hodge, was hired in the Division of Ethnology in the U.S. National Museum of the Smithsonian Institution. He remained there throughout his career.

In 1915–17 Judd returned to Utah to survey and excavate archaeological sites along the Wasatch Front and near Kanab. He also excavated a number of what would later be called Fremont sites at Paragonah, Utah.[77] In 1917 he directed the stabilization work and some excavation in Betatakin, which uncle Byron had "cleaned out" in 1909.

In 1921 Judd began a seven-year excavation program in Chaco Canyon. The program was funded by the National Geographic Society. Ever on the lookout for another explorer story, *National Geographic Magazine* sent one of its photographers, E. L. Wisherd, and Judd to explore the Red Rock Plateau in the fall of 1923. The two met John Wetherill and his men at Kayenta. They set out to explore "the unknown" (as do all expeditions funded by *National Geographic*): "Bordering on the Rio Colorado in Utah are vast areas which, owing chiefly to their inaccessibility and barrenness, have thus far escaped thorough examination by men of science. Certain portions of these areas, indeed, have never been visited by white men."[78]

This was the usual *National Geographic* hyperbole since Wetherill and others had been in the country since the 1890s. The trip became something of a comedy of errors. Wetherill had contracted with some Navajos to deliver a supply of oats, but they didn't show up. "In this emergency, Wetherill swam the flood [of the San Juan] on a log, walked twenty miles to an oil camp, borrowed a flivver to reach Kayenta and was back at our river camp in two days." They then pastured some of the pack animals at the head of Lake Canyon and rode overland to the river across from Hall's Crossing, "thence along the river edge into Moki Canyon."[79] "Moki Canyon had been represented as about five miles long and enterable, on foot only, at its mouth and extreme head. Mr. Judd not only led his pack train into the narrow gorge, but he advanced with it 18 miles or about two-thirds of the total length, over quicksands and rock ledges that added frequent barriers and not a little danger to the expedition."[80]

Judd and Wetherill climbed out in the North Gulch of Moki, skirted the head of Forgotten Canyon (thus missing Defiance House), and explored Knowles Canyon. They then returned to Moki Canyon and climbed out on the south rim up one of the falling dunes: "Vast accumulations of wind-blown sand had folded down over the south cliff, and one of them, after a long, tedious upward climb, eventually provided our escape."[81] As we noted earlier, there were four such dunes in Moqui Canyon.

At some point Judd and Wetherill visited Bernheimer Alcove (see above), where Wetherill carved his initials and the date in the alcove wall. They then returned to Lake Canyon. For three days the party worked their way across Wilson Mesa through rain and dense fog, finally crossing the San Juan River north of Navajo Mountain, probably via Trail Canyon, and visited Rainbow Bridge, thence on to Kayenta.

Judd carved his name on a ledge at the mouth of Bridge Canyon. He thought that "further, more extended archaeological investigations" were desirable, since "traces of a people older than the cliff-dwellers were observed in several localities."[82]

The trip was a journalistic success. Wisherd took numerous scenic vistas used to illustrate the article that appeared in the *National Geogaphic* in 1924.[83] Judd never returned to the Red Rock Plateau. He did, however, have more to say about it forty-seven years later, when he published a brief article about a bundle of small animal snares, a woven bag, and some beads he had found in an alcove in Moqui Canyon.[84]

Judd finished his work in Chaco Canyon in 1927 and thereafter was deeply occupied with curatorial duties at the National Museum until he retired. In the fall of 1967, Mr. Judd and I met at an anthropology meeting in Washington, D.C. He was then eighty, dressed in a three-piece suit and homburg hat, very much the dapper gentleman/scientist-about-Washington he had been for more than five decades. We discussed places in the Glen Canyon Country—Moqui and Lake canyons and elsewhere—that he had seen between 1908 and 1923, and I had seen between 1958 and 1961. I told him I had seen his name carved on the ledge at the mouth of Bridge Canyon. I had dinner with him a couple of times in the early 1970s when I was in Washington to do research at the Smithsonian.

THE CLAFLIN-EMERSON EXPEDITIONS, 1927–1931

From 1927 through 1931 the Peabody Museum of Archaeology and Ethnology of Harvard University sponsored wide-ranging archaeological surveys in portions of the Glen Canyon Country and adjacent areas. The surveys were named the Claflin-Emerson expeditions for the two men who paid for and also participated in them.

William F. Claflin Jr. was a Harvard graduate and Boston financier. As a boy he was interested in Indian artifacts in his native New England and on Stallings Island, Georgia, where he spent much time with his family. Inspired by Charles Jones's romantic *Antiquities of Southern Indians,* in 1908 he undertook his own dig in a mound site on the island.[85] Claflin spent college summers in the Southwest, visiting the Hopi country and other areas.

Claflin's friend, Raymond Emerson, another Boston financier, was a skilled surveyor. Egged on by A. V. Kidder, Claflin and Emerson agreed to fund a five-year reconnaissance of eastern Utah from the Arizona line to the border of Wyoming. In 1927 the two made a pack trip through portions of southern Utah guided by Dave Rust, who had been recommended by Donald C. Scott, by then associate director of the Harvard Peabody Museum (chapter 11). They visited Boulder, Utah, and saw the Boulder Mound, later named the Coombs site (chapter 15). They also "heard of additional sites on the Kaiparowits Plateau and in the Fremont River drainage."

This led them and their wives to "sponsor an extended reconnaissance program" also funded by the Harvard Peabody Museum. The general plan was to survey the western drainages of the Colorado River in Utah, plus a strip east of the river to

Moab, and the drainage of the Green River north to the Uintah Mountains.[86]

In the spring of 1928, with Rust as guide, Donald and Louise Scott started from Escalante, crossed the Waterpocket Fold, went to the mouth of Hall's Creek, and then made their way upriver to the mouth of Smith Fork to view the major rock art site there (chapter 17). They continued on to Hite, thence up and out of Glen Canyon and across the Henry Mountains to Notom and Fruita, where they recorded some of the famous rock art panels in the Capitol Reef area.[87]

They went on to Torrey to visit with E. P. Pectol and see his artifact collection, including the famous Pectol Shields made of buffalo hide.[88] They then crossed the Aquarius Plateau to visit the Boulder Mound. In Escalante they hired an additional wrangler and made a trip onto the Kaiparowits Plateau. Scott recorded about a dozen sites on the plateau—mostly small rockshelters, a rock art site, and one open site. They then dropped down across the Escalante Desert, briefly visited Davis Gulch, and recorded a site with a large kiva (see chapter 15).[89]

Rust was soon back in Escalante to meet the next member of the expedition—Noel Morss. In 1925 Noel Morss (1904–81), a Harvard student, was inspired by A. V. Kidder to make an archaeological reconnaissance in the region of middle Chinle Wash, north of the confluence of the Canyon de Chelly drainage. He did so and produced a report. In 1927 Morss and two friends explored the area from Tuba City northward onto the Kaibito Plateau, then packed in to Navajo Canyon and across the Rainbow Plateau to Navajo Mountain.[90]

By this time Morss was attending Harvard Law School. He linked up with the Claflin-Emerson expedition in 1928 and 1929 as a way to pursue his fascination with the Southwest and probably as surcease from his legal studies.

In 1928 Morss and a friend, Robert Sanderson, met Rust in Escalante and trailed on to Boulder, where they dug in the Boulder Mound. They moved across the Aquarius Plateau to Temple Creek. In a rockshelter they found artifacts unique to what would eventually be called the Fremont culture: hide moccasins with the hair still on and dew claws on the bottoms for traction, and clay figurines. They went on to Torrey to meet E. P. Pectol and see the buffalo hide shields.

Rust left at that point, while Morss continued with local guides, including excavations in Fish Creek Cove, near Torrey, where he found more moccasins and figurines. In 1929 Morss traveled to Nine Mile Canyon to see the great rock art panels. In 1931 he published a monograph pointing out the differences between the culture he had found in the Fremont drainage and the Ancestral Puebloan cultures to the south. The name Fremont was, in time, given to the culture.[91]

Morss did not actively pursue archaeology as a profession. Rather, he was an attorney and investment counselor.[92] He remained interested in archaeology, especially the enigmatic small clay figurines characteristic of the Fremont culture.[93]

Also in 1929, Dave Rust took another Claflin-Emerson party along the Waterpocket Fold area to the Fremont, Muddy, and Dirty Devil rivers, then into North Wash and on beyond to the San Rafael Desert and the Robbers Roost country. The party was led by Henry Roberts. They also visited Barrier Canyon to see the Great Gallery of "ghost-like" rock art figures.[94]

Other parties sent out by the Claflin-Emerson expedition, and wrangled by Rust, surveyed north of the Glen Canyon Country. In 1931 Donald Scott and John Otis ("Jo") Brew (1906–88) surveyed the Green River area as far north as Vernal, Utah. Brew then began work on the sites along Alkali Ridge outside Blanding, Utah, the sites Byron Cummings and A. V. Kidder had probed in 1908. Brew's doctoral dissertation on Alkali Ridge was published in 1946 and considered a tour de force for its careful consideration of archaeological methods and analysis of Mesa Verde culture.[95]

From 1935 to 1939 Brew supervised the Harvard excavations at Awatovi on Antelope Mesa east of the Hopi mesas, funded in large measure by William Claflin.[96] Brew became the director of the Harvard Peabody Museum in 1948. From 1944 on he was a key behind-the-scenes figure in the development of U.S. "river basin archaeology" and hence indirectly had a major influence on the Glen Canyon Project (chapter 15).

The work of the Claflin-Emerson expeditions stimulated archaeologists from other museums and research centers. Several sent expeditions to various locales on or adjacent to Navajo Mountain, including the University of Pennsylvania, the Arizona State Museum, the Los Angeles County Museum, and the Gila Pueblo Research Center in Globe, Arizona.[97]

JULIAN STEWARD IN GLEN CANYON, 1932

Julian H. Steward (1902–72) was born in Washington, D.C. His parents divorced when he was sixteen, and he was sent to the Deep Creek Boys School (now Deep Creek College) in a desert valley east of Owens Valley, California. The school was also a working ranch. The students studied in the mornings and mowed hay, tended cattle and horses, and mended fences in the afternoons. Steward flourished there. He hiked throughout the area, collecting data on rock art and meeting local Indian people.

In 1921 he studied at the University of California in Berkeley and then went to Cornell. He returned to Berkeley for graduate school and earned a doctorate in anthropology.[98] In 1930 he moved to Salt Lake City to marry an educational psychologist, Dorothy Nyswander, a tenured professor at the University of Utah. Steward was given a position at the university, in effect as a faculty spouse, and a mandate to develop an archaeology program. There had not been an active program since Byron Cummings left the university in 1915.

Steward took his mandate seriously. In 1930–31 he excavated two large caves on Promontory Point on the north shore of the Great Salt Lake, and Black Rock Cave on the south shore, as well as other small caves around the lake. He was guided to the sites by Charles Kelly (see below), who also participated in the excavations. One of Steward's crew members was Kilton Stewart. Kilton arranged for his younger brother, Omer, to be camp cook.[99] We will meet Omer Stewart again (see below).

By the spring of 1932, Steward's marriage was coming apart: he had taken up with Jane Cannon, the willful daughter of the newly appointed editor of the *Deseret News*, owned by the Mormon Church. Jane's grandfather was George Q. Cannon, a major figure in the Mormon Church hierarchy and one of the leaders sent to jail in the 1890s for polygamy. There was an uproar in Salt Lake City over Steward's relationship with Jane, hence he had good reason to stay out of town.[100]

Steward arranged two archaeological reconnaissance trips to southern Utah. The first was a pack trip into the canyons east of Kanab, especially Johnson Canyon and its tributaries. The second was a boat trip through Glen Canyon from North Wash to Lee's Ferry. Those in the river party were Steward, Byron Hughes, Charles Kelly, Hoffman Birney, and John Shoemaker.

Herman Hoffman Birney Jr. (1891–1958) was born in Philadelphia and attended Dickinson College. After army service in World War I, he moved to Tucson and began traveling widely in the West and Southwest. He wrote some thirty books on history and firearms as well as historical novels. From 1943 until his death in 1958 he worked for the federal government, primarily in Texas and Alabama.[101]

Birney's *Roads to Roam*, published in 1930, includes a segment on a mule trip into Rainbow Bridge. His novel, *Forgotten Cañon*, published in 1934, includes a harrowing boat trip by the hero and heroine through Cataract and Glen canyons, escaping bad guys. They finally reach safe haven at Lee's Ferry with a Mormon family. The book is dedicated to Steward and the others who made the Glen Canyon trip in 1932.[102]

Birney's last novel, *The Dice of God* (1952), is about Seventh Cavalry soldiers with General

George Custer at the Battle of the Little Big Horn in 1876. In 1965 it was made into a movie, *The Glory Guys*, and the locale was shifted to southern Arizona.[103] Birney, who was a great stickler for historical accuracy, would have been outraged, but by then he had been dead for seven years.

Charles Kelly (1889–1971) was born in Cedar Springs, Michigan. His father was a hard-shell Baptist preacher who unsuccessfully ran a mission for the poor in Chicago and then founded a religious colony in Tennessee. The father beat Charles and his brothers "once a week for the good of our souls." Charles fled in 1910, briefly attended Valparaiso University, then bummed around the country for several years. After a brief stint in the army in 1918, he settled in Salt Lake City, married, and became a partner in a printing company. He became fascinated by western history, especially tracking historical figures and events across the landscape. His first book was *Salt Desert Trails* (1930), a history of the trails across the Great Basin.[104] He met Steward soon after the latter arrived in Salt Lake City.

Kelly moved to Wayne County, Utah, in 1940. In 1943 he became the custodian of Capitol Reef National Monument; he was made a park ranger in 1950 and promoted to superintendent in 1952. He retired in 1959 and moved back to Salt Lake City, where he died in 1971. He was an iconoclast, notorious for his anti-Mormon rants. Most people regarded him as "difficult," with a "barbed wire personality," but he was said to be very loyal to those who earned his respect and admiration. As Julian Steward's biographer, Virginia Kerns, has written about Kelly, he "did not suffers fools gladly and . . . found them wherever he went."[104] His historical work is highly regarded.[105]

In 1931 Hoffman Birney published a book about Mormon extremists, *Zealots of Zion*. This led Birney and Kelly to collaborate on a book about Porter Rockwell, Brigham Young's hit man, *Holy Murder: The Story of Porter Rockwell*. Kelly later published books on the Mountain Men and on Butch Cassidy and the Wild Bunch, edited John D. Lee's journals for publication, and was one of the editors of the Powell river trip diaries.[106]

Kelly made various trips on the Colorado River over the years. He was along on the 1932 trip partly because of his relationship with Steward. In a letter of June 7, 1932, to A. L. Kroeber, Jesse Nusbaum wrote: "In a letter just received from Julian Steward of the University of Utah, he is planning to leave very shortly for a trip down the Colorado River from Haight's [*sic*; Hite's] Ferry to Lee's Ferry, and then conduct a reconnaissance in the cañons of the Paria. He has five hundred dollars only available for the summer's work, and [has requested] archaeological reconnaissance permits."[107]

Steward wrote, "The party went via Torrey to the Trachyte Ranch at the eastern foot of the Henry Mountains by automobile. From here it was transported the remaining 30 miles down North wash to the river by wagon. Two portable canvas boats proved entirely adequate for river transportation. As the current averaged about 5 miles an hour, only 2 or 3 hours' travel each day covered the necessary distance."[108]

Steward described the "Moqui Fort" (fig. 17.2) at White Canyon, as well as Loper Ruin at Red Canyon. Below Red Canyon the party surveyed primarily along the riverside bars, or more accurately, Hughes did. Steward wrote, "Hughes . . . assumed responsibility for much of the reconnaissance on the [river] trip."[109] The party spent some time around the mouth of Hall's Creek but did not stop upstream at the mouth of Smith Fork Creek, and hence missed the largest rock art panel in the main canyon. They camped at Lake Canyon but seemingly did not hike very far up any side canyons, except to Rainbow Bridge.[110] There was apparently some friction during the trip, but the party reached Lee's Ferry in seeming good order (fig. 13.5), then dispersed.

Steward could see little arable land along the river, and thus no reason for Indians to have been in

13.5. The Steward party at Lee's Ferry, 1932: (*left to right*) Charles Kelly, Hoffman Birney, John Shoemaker, Julian Steward, Byron Hughes. Photographer unknown. Kelly Collection, 917.911 P2 10560. Courtesy of the Utah Historical Society.

the canyon. His summary of Glen Canyon archaeology is brief:

> It appears to have been a kind of a no-man's land which had been very slightly settled by outposts from both Mesa Verde and Kayenta and which had come into contact with the Northern Periphery but had not been strongly influenced by it. Further south, however, near the Arizona border, the sites increasingly resemble those of the Kayenta district and of the Johnson Canyon-Paria River district, to which they are geographically contiguous.[111]

Steward spent the fall of 1932 in Berkeley writing up his two trips, still staying away from Salt Lake City. He was fired by the University of Utah early in 1933. He and Jane then headed to Mexico, where Steward obtained a quicky divorce from Dorothy and married Jane. Dorothy finally consented to a U.S. divorce, and in 1934 Steward and Jane got married again, this time in Tonopah, Nevada, just be sure they were legal. Steward did research on Great Basin Indians in 1934–35 and then joined the staff of the Bureau of American Ethnology at the Smithsonian Institution. His work with Great Basin Indian people in the 1920s and early 1930s resulted in his classic *Basin-Plateau Aboriginal Sociopolitical Groups* (1938), the basis for his later studies in cultural ecology.[112]

THE RAINBOW BRIDGE–MONUMENT VALLEY EXPEDITION

The largest systematic archaeological survey in the Glen Canyon Country prior to the Glen Canyon Project was the Rainbow Bridge-Monument Valley Expedition (RBMVE), conducted between 1933 and 1938. It was a venture unique to American archaeology.[113] The expedition was the brainchild of

13.6. Rainbow Bridge–Monument Valley directors at Wetherill's trading post, Kayenta, Arizona, 1933: (*left to right*) John Armstrong, Alonzo Pond, Bob Kissack (*rear*), Ansel T. Hall, John Wetherill, Ben Wetherill, Tracey Kelly, Lyndon Hargrave. Photograph by R. Branstead, MS-122-236. Courtesy of the Museum of Northern Arizona.

Ansel Franklin Hall (1894–1962). Born in Oakland, California, the son of Charles and Laura Crocker Hall, Hall graduated from the University of California in 1917 in forestry. He joined the fledgling National Park Service (NPS), becoming a naturalist and chief of the field division in 1933. Watson Smith (see below) characterized Hall as follows:

> He [was] an unlikely combination of shrewd promoter and romantic idealist. I never knew in my subsequent acquaintance with him which characteristic dominated the other—perhaps they existed in balanced tension. He had a love of nature and the outdoors, along with the romantic concept of the desirability of indoctrinating . . . [others] with that same emotion. But Hall was also a promoter, . . . and so he conceived a scheme: he would organize an expedition, he would undertake to raise the necessary financial backing, he would induce teachers of the natural sciences to join it for two or three months in the summer, he would induce students of college age to come and pay their [own] way for the privilege of living out in the wilderness somewhere communing with nature and with their fellows in a wholesome environment, thereby tempering their presumably urbanized souls by acquiring practical knowledge of field work in geology, meteorology, botany, anthropology, archaeology, indeed all the natural and social sciences, under qualified professional supervision and he would be in charge of the whole enterprise. What a splendid pedagogic conceit this was![114]

And it worked!

The impetus for the expedition came from efforts by Hall, John Wetherill, and others in the late 1920s and early 1930s to convince Congress to create a national park that would encompass various portions of the Glen Canyon Country and Monument Valley. Hall, in conjunction with Wetherill, made scouting trips into the Monument Valley area in 1930 and 1931. Wetherill and Pat Flattum made an icy trip upriver in Glen Canyon in January 1931 in support of the park idea (chapter 11). The RBMVE was developed partially in support of this effort. Hall credited Wetherill with conceiving the expedition:

> General plans for the fieldwork of the 1933 RBMV Expedition may be said first to have been conceived by the fireside of a desert ranch in the far north of the Navajo country. Mr. John Wetherill, who has followed the frontier in that part of the desert Southwest for more than half a century, pointed out the value—the necessity in fact—of thoroughly exploring the vast region lying north of Black Mesa and south of the San Juan and Colorado rivers. Colorful and spectacular from the scenic standpoint, the complex of canyon, mesa and desert is even more important from the standpoint of the archaeologist, the geologist, and the biologist. . . . Mr. Wetherill pointed out that there was a need for . . . preliminary mapping of an area of some 3,000 square miles and in the determination of outstanding scientific problems which would warrant intensive investigation during future field seasons. In order to accomplish this preliminary reconnaissance the RBMVE of 1933 was organized.[115]

After noting that Lyndon Hargrave developed and directed the 1933 field season (fig. 13.6), Hall continued: "A vast amount of field work still remains to be accomplished in this intensely interesting region. Many canyons and mesas are yet to be explored; areas rich in evidences of early cultures must be studied intensively . . . for several seasons in order that we may approach a solution of the most important archaeological problems." [116]

>•••••••<

WANTED: TEN EXPLORERS

Must be men between the ages of 16 and 45; available from June 3 to August 15 of this summer; interested in exploration, mapping, geology, archaeology, botany, or zoology, but professional training not absolutely necessary; must have had some camping experience—and like it; must be physically fit; must be willing to take part enthusiastically in both scientific projects and camp routine; must be willing to meet share of expenses not to exceed $4.30 per day (includes 3000 miles of travel). Make inquiry regarding sponsors, staff, scientific projects, travel, etc., of Ansel F. Hall, Chief Forester, National Park Service, 333 Hilgard Hall, University of California, Berkeley, Calif.[120]

Hall found several sponsors, among them his close associates Francis P. Farquhar, Duncan McDuffie, and Robert Sibley.[117] McDuffie (1877–1951) was an active conservationist throughout his life, deeply involved in the creation of Yosemite National Park and twice president of the Sierra Club. Robert Sibley (1881–1913), a publisher, banker, and broker, was also an active conservationist. Francis Peloubet Farquhar (1887–1974) was an enthusiastic outdoorsman, conservationist, historian, and bibliophile whose passions were the High Sierra and the Colorado River.[118]

In 1933–34 the expedition was incorporated as the American Exploration Society. Hall put together a strong advisory board including Horace M. Albright, director of the National Park

Service; Wallace Atwood, world traveler and author of two textbooks on North American physical geography;[119] John Collier, commissioner of the Bureau of Indian Affairs; Harold S. Colton, director of the Museum of Northern Arizona; geologist Herbert E. Gregory; A. L. Kroeber, the well-known anthropologist at the University of California, Berkeley; Jesse L. Nusbaum, chief archaeologist for the National Park Service; and Farquhar, Ryerson, and Sibley.

Hall's ad first appeared in the University of California alumni magazine in early spring 1933. But the project soon grew from ten explorers from California to seventy-three from across the country. Staff members' services were contributed by various universities and museums. Without the participants' financial contributions and contributed staff members' time, "it would have been impossible to have maintained such an extensive field program, especially during the lean years of the Depression."[121]

Mindful of the publicity the Dodge Brothers Motor Company had gained by providing vehicles for the famous American Museum of Natural History's Central Asiatic Expedition of the 1920s, led by the flamboyant cowboy-of-science Roy Chapman Andrews, Hall convinced the Ford Motor Company to provide a number of trucks and station wagons (the famed "woodys") for expedition use. Caravans of woodys wended their ways to Kayenta, Arizona, from New York, Chicago, and Berkeley—picking up participants as they went. There were seventy-three participants in 1933; in subsequent years, field parties ranged in size from fifty-four (1936) to twenty-five (1938).[122]

The "Information for Prospective Members of the Scientific Field Staff," issued in 1934, stated: "This is *not* a deluxe expedition. There will be a cook and packer, but each member of the party must expect to bear his share of camp duties, such as gathering fire wood, rounding up pack animals, helping in the commissary department, etc. There will be a few non-technical assignments for those who prefer to serve as 'wranglers' or with preliminary scouting parties."[123]

THE 1937 EXPEDITION FLIER

Field work will include preliminary geographic reconnaissance; base mapping by triangulation; detailed topographic mapping; archaeological survey and excavation; making of measured drawings of cliff dwellings; ethnological work among the Navajo; field research in geology; and collecting and field study in all the major biological sciences. Several projects will continue work of past field seasons; others will be pushed into new territory. It is planned to establish small roving base camps as outposts on Navajo Mountain, in the canyons and in Monument Valley, from which field explorations will radiate. A certain number of men will be chosen to make the 200 mile passage, by boat, through the canyons of the San Juan and the Colorado.[124]

Two women participated in the expedition. One was Grace E. Hoover, a photographer married to Charles Hoover, a professor participant in 1934. The second was Amy H. Andrews, a New York pilot who flew aerial reconnaissance and photo sessions for the expedition in 1937.[125]

Of the some 275 men involved with the expeditions, 10 of them went on to distinguished careers in anthropology or archaeology: Donald Collier (1911–95), Lyndon L. Hargrave (1896–1978), and Omer C. Stewart (1908–91) in 1933 and 1935; Edward T. Hall Jr. (1914–2009) and John B. Rinaldo (1912–80) in 1934; Watson Smith (1897–1993) in 1935, 1936, and 1937; Ralph L. Beals (1901–85) and George W. Brainerd (1909–56) in

13.7. Rainbow Bridge–Monument Valley field crew in 1937: Charles Bernheimer (*standing at right front*); (*front row seated, right to left*) Ansel Hall (next to Bernheimer), Watson Smith, John Wetherill. Richard S. MacNeish is seated on top of the truck cab on left. Others unidentified. Photograph by A. Applegate, MS-122-1971. Courtesy of the Museum of Northern Arizona.

1935, 1937 and 1938; Richard S. MacNeish (1918–2001) in 1937 and 1938; and John W. Bennett (1915–2004) in 1937.

Richard ("Scotty") MacNeish was born in New York City. Small of stature, but great of courage, mind and vision, Scotty was a bantamweight Golden Gloves champion in the same year (1936) he began learning to do archaeology in upstate New York. In 1937 and 1938 he worked for the RBMVE (fig. 13.7). He later wrote that everything he knew about field archaeology he learned from George Brainerd and Watson Smith during his time with the expedition: "Like a hungry puppy I devoured it all."[126] MacNeish had a distinguished, often controversial career (he loved the controversy), highlighted by defining the origins of maize agriculture in Mesoamerica.

Many others went on to distinguished careers in other fields, in public health, medicine, geology, and biology. For example, Theodore H. Eaton Jr., with the expedition in 1933, became a professor of zoology at the University of Kansas. In 1970 he published a well-known book on evolution.[127] Others went into the military. Floyd B. Wood (1908–56) flew aerial reconnaissance missions for the expedition in 1933, joined the U.S. Army Air Corps, and retired in 1954 as a major general. In 1944 Wood and two others flew a Douglas A-20 Havoc into the eye of a hurricane to collect scientific data, the first successful attempt to do so. Walter M. Enger (1914–2003) was with the expedition in 1933. In 1941 he joined the navy and retired in 1972 as a rear admiral in charge of the Naval Civil Engineers, including the Seabees. Suren H.

Babington (1901–75) was the expedition physician for the years 1934–36. In 1950 he published *Navajos, Gods and Tom-toms.*[129]

In a 1935 memo to RBMVE staff, Hall asked individuals to try to recruit artists who could draw artifacts and biological specimens, but also "character sketches of Navajos are desired for ethnological record and publication."[130] The search was successful. Martin Gambee (1905–69) was a watercolorist, printmaker, and illustrator who, as a Works Progress Administration artist, signed on with the expedition in 1936, 1937, and 1938. His experience led him to specialize in southwestern subjects, especially the Navajo people. He later worked as a freelance artist and taught art in Mexico.[131]

Individuals with Utah connections included Angus M. Woodbury (1886–1964), Omer C. Stewart (1908–91), and Walter R. Buss (1905–2000). Stewart, born in Levan, Utah (he never lost his thick "Mormon" accent), was an expedition cook in 1933. He earned a doctorate in anthropology at the University of California and taught for many years at the University of Colorado. He was an expert on Indian peoples of the Great Basin and on the Native American (Peyote) Church. Omer, whom I knew quite well in the 1960s to 1980s, was equally fond of ardent spirits, controversy, and ribald stories, the latter exemplified by his collected essays, entitled "Cannibalism Is an Acquired Taste."[132] Angus Woodbury (1886–1964) was born in southern Utah and for many years was a professor of zoology at the University of Utah. An early proponent of systemic ecology, in 1954 he published a textbook, *Principles of General Ecology.*[133] His career is discussed further in chapter 16. Walter R. Buss was born in Provo, Utah, studied at Brigham Young University, and took a doctorate at Stanford. He was with the expedition in 1933, the year he began teaching at (then) Weber Junior College in Ogden. He taught geography and geology there for forty-one years, a much-beloved professor who introduced many hundreds of students to the geology of Utah, especially its national parks.

Finally, there was Alonzo W. Pond (1894–1986), best described as a wandering anthropologist and desert rat. He was with various archaeological expeditions to Algeria and Mongolia in the 1920s, then knocked around, studying anthropology in Paris and Chicago. He joined the RBMVE for the 1933 season. Having visited Algeria, Mongolia, and the Glen Canyon Country, Pond became a self-styled expert on deserts and wrote desert survival guides for the U.S. Air Force, as well as children's books.[134]

One of the key members of the RBMVE was Watson Smith (1897–1993), a legendary figure in southwestern archaeology. He graduated from Brown University in 1919 and attended Harvard Law School, graduating in 1924 "without distinction," as he put it. He practiced law for a few years, but an inheritance in 1930 left him free to pursue other interests.

Smith met Paul S. Martin, of the Field Museum of Natural History in Chicago, who was excavating the Lowry Ruin near Cortez, Colorado. In 1933 Martin invited Smith to join his party as a shovel hand, and Smith accepted. He moved to the Southwest to begin an active career in southwestern archaeology terminated only by his death at age ninety-six.

Smith spent the 1934–35 academic year at the University of California, Berkeley, studying anthropology.[135] Fellow anthropology students included Isabel Kelly, who made major studies of the Southern Paiute peoples of the Glen Canyon Country and adjacent regions (chapter 18).

In the spring of 1935, Smith "quite fortuitously" met Ansel Hall and was recruited for the RBMVE. According to Smith, "I was soon employed as a staff archaeologist with precious little knowledge, and in June with a group of half a dozen, perhaps ten, automobiles we set out from Berkeley for the western Navajo country."[136] When Smith arrived at Kayenta, he discovered that his two fellow staff archaeologists were George W. Brainerd and Edward T. Hall (no relation to Ansel).

George Brainerd (1909–56) had a doctorate in zoology from Ohio State University. From 1930 to 1934 he worked in Iran on archaeological excavations. He worked for the RBMVE for three summers. A. V. Kidder got him started on ceramic analysis in 1940. This led him to analyze the pottery from the RBMVE—perhaps the most excruciatingly detailed analysis of a single southwestern pottery collection ever made. He was hired as assistant professor of anthropology at UCLA after World War II. Apparently a workaholic, he died of a heart attack at age forty-seven.

Ralph L. Beals (1901–85) grew up in a Populist and Fabian socialist family in Kansas, received a doctorate in anthropology in 1926, and founded the anthropology department at UCLA. He joined the RBMVE in 1935, principally to learn some archaeology to help him develop the anthropology department into a four-field department.[137]

Edward T. (Ned) Hall (1914–2009) grew up in Montana, Missouri, Europe, Santa Fe, and up and down the Rio Grande, where he spent a good deal of time with the various Pueblo tribes. He met the sons of the charismatic John Collier (1884–1968), the commissioner of the Bureau of Indian Affairs in the Roosevelt administration.[138] Collier instituted WPA-like programs on Indian reservations to build roads and other things, and in 1933 he hired Hall to work on the Navajo reservation.[139] His experiences with Navajo and Hopi people, and the careful tutoring in cross-cultural understanding he had received from the Indian trader Lorenzo Hubbell, are artfully chronicled in Hall's *West of the Thirties: Discoveries Among the Navajo and Hopi,* and his autobiography, *An Anthropology of Everyday Life*. Most important were Hall's lessons from a renegade Protestant missionary, "Shine" Smith, and some of his Navajo and Hopi coworkers, about the differences in, and meanings of, nonverbal communication between Navajos, Hopis, whites, and Hispanics. It was the start of Hall's lifelong quest to understand and explicate the crucial but little understood, culturally defined nonverbal systems of communication all humans use. In his famed works, beginning with *The Silent Language* (1959), which had sold nearly 1.75 million copies by 2001, then *The Hidden Dimension* (1966), *Beyond Culture* (1976), and *The Dance of Life: The Other Dimensions of Time* (1983), Hall taught the world to be aware of "body language," as it is now called, as well as differences in the uses of personal space and attitudes toward and the uses of time.[140]

Hall joined the RBMVE in 1934 and the following two seasons worked for the Peabody Museum of Harvard University excavations at the Awatovi site in northeastern Arizona.[141] He received his Ph.D. in anthropology from Columbia University just in time to enter the U.S. Army in World War II. Promoted to captain, he commanded a regiment of African American soldiers in Europe and the Philippines. After the war he became increasingly involved in his studies of body language and proxemics. In the 1950s he and others worked for the U.S. State Department, developing programs to sensitize foreign service and foreign aid personnel about the nuances of body language, personal space, handling of time, and so on—in short, to help make them not-quite-so-ugly Americans.

FIELD DIRECTORS

The field director for 1933 and 1934 was Lyndon L. Hargrave (1896–1978), an archaeologist and ornithologist on loan to the expedition from the Museum of Northern Arizona (fig. 13.6).[142] Hargrave has a special place in the lore of southwestern science. Born in Franklin, Georgia, he was fascinated by both archaeology and ornithology from a young age. He served in World War I and then worked as a hydrographer for the expansion of the Roosevelt Dam project in Arizona in 1920–21. There were many archaeological sites in the project area, and Hargrave began studying them, encouraged by Byron Cummings. He also became a student at the University of Arizona. When the

13.8. Rainbow Bridge–Monument Valley river crew camping at San Juan–Colorado River confluence, 1935. Photograph by C. Bond, MS-122-1701. Courtesy of the Museum of Northern Arizona.

Coolidge Dam on the Gila River was constructed in 1924–1928, Hargrave did some salvage archaeology on the sites to be drowned by the reservoir. Hargrave was employed by A. E. Douglass on the dendrochronology project and participated in the key excavations in 1929 that "closed the gap" between an earlier "floating" chronology and the Euro-American calendar (see above). The same year he was hired by the Museum of Northern Arizona in Flagstaff as assistant director. For the next decade he made numerous contributions to both southwestern archaeology and ornithology.[143]

It was Hargrave who gave central direction to the RBMVE and turned its major focus toward archaeology, with other studies being ancillary. Hall had planned touchy-feely projects similar to those he had previously developed for Boy Scout outings and tourist nature walks in the national parks. Hargrave, backed by Colton and Kroeber, envisioned a systematic program of archaeological survey and limited excavation, with biological studies being made in their own right, but also contributing to archaeological interpretation.

Hargrave's approach centrally influenced the organization and procedures of the later Glen Canyon Project used by both the Museum of Northern Arizona and the University of Utah. His systemic thinking in the later 1920s/early 1930s ultimately had major impacts on the work of Walter W. Taylor (see below) and Julian H. Steward. The central point was that archaeological sites should be seen in their ecological contexts as well as their place in space, time, and cultural relationships.[144]

A basic problem for the RBMVE teams was the lack of usable topographic maps. The USGS teams of the 1880s had accomplished basic triangulation of the region but produced only scattered topographic maps. The central focal point of the RBMVE was the Tsegie Canyon drainage: a major task of the expedition throughout its existence

13.9. Rainbow Bridge–Monument Valley river crew in Glen Canyon below Kane Creek, 1936. Photograph by C. Bond, MS-122-1737. Courtesy of the Museum of Northern Arizona.

was the production of an accurate topographic map of it. As the map was developed, plotting sites accurately became possible, and data to realize Hargrave's hope for a "human ecology of [the] region" also became possible. The map was itself a major achievement. None of the previous expeditions had been particularly concerned with maps, since there weren't any. Rather, they had relied on those in John Wetherill's head.

THE RIVER TRIPS

"In the six summers that the Expedition was in the field no less than eleven passages were made by boat through the canyons of the San Juan and Glen Canyon of the Colorado." The trips (figs. 13.8, 13.9) lasted from two to four weeks and ran from Mexican Hat or the mouth of Copper Canyon to Lee's Ferry. "The trips were made in ten- and fifteen-foot boats built by the Wilson Fold-Flat Company of Los Angeles. These craft proved to be exceptionally seaworthy and tough."[145]

The 1935 river trip was led by Bayne Beauchamp, "well-known Arctic explorer and organizer of expeditions on rivers of the far north."[146] Beauchamp made adventure films, including one called *Mother Yukon* (1938). He corresponded with the river runner Norm Nevills between 1935 and 1939.[147]

Among the staff archaeologists was Henry Claiborne (Clay) Lockett (1911–84), later a prominent figure in Arizona archaeology, publishing, and Indian arts and crafts marketing. He joined the RBMVE in 1934 and supervised the excavation of Woodchuck Cave and other sites.[148] While he was working at Woodchuck Cave, Everett Ruess wandered in and served as cook for a couple of weeks (chapter 10). Lockett later worked for the Bureau of Indian Affairs, and then opened a Southwest Indian arts and crafts shop in Tucson that he operated until 1963, after which he operated the gift shop in the Museum of Northern Arizona until his death in an car accident in 1984. He was also closely associated with Northland Press of Flagstaff.

In the end, the only major report produced by the Rainbow Bridge–Monument Valley Expedition was a monograph on the archaeology by George Brainerd, Ralph Beals, and Watson Smith.[149] It was, and remains, a useful addition to the scientific literature on the archaeology of the Glen Canyon Country. When the project ended, Ansel Hall went on to run the concessions at Mesa Verde National Park. He also developed a summer "Explorers' Camp" for boys, ages fourteen to seventeen, running six or twelve weeks, based in Mancos, studying Mesa Verde and various abandoned mining towns in the La Plata Mountains. The camp began during World War II and ran until 1949.[150]

THE CARNEGIE MUSEUM EXPEDITIONS

In 1944 an anonymous donor gave the Carnegie Museum of Pittsburgh some funds to support an archaeological survey in southeast Utah. Three surveys were made for an undetermined numbers of days in the summers of 1945, 1946, and 1947. Apparently some excavations were done in Butler Wash, as well as in the northern tributaries of White Canyon and in Fable Valley and other tributaries of Gypsum Canyon. No report was produced, and the artifacts remain on deposit at the Carnegie Museum. The collection was studied in 1961 as a supplement to the Glen Canyon Project. Nearly all of the material was Mesa Verde and dated to late Pueblo II–early Pueblo III times.[151]

THE "PUEBLO ECOLOGY" PROJECT

Among the lesser-known archaeological projects in Glen Canyon Country, and in many ways the oddest, was the so-called Pueblo Ecology Project of 1951–52. It was the brainchild of archaeologist Walter W. Taylor (1913–97), who is best described as one-of-a-kind.[152]

Taylor took an A.B. in geology at Yale in 1935. In the summers of 1935–37 he excavated some sites in the Kayenta area for the Museum of Northern Arizona (MNA) under the direction of Lyndon Hargrave. Taylor began graduate work in anthropology at the University of New Mexico (UNM) in the fall of 1935.[153] He was a student foreman for the UNM field school in Chaco Canyon in 1938 and 1939. The 1939 guest field director was Frank Setzler, then curator of anthropology in the U.S. National Museum of the Smithsonian Institution. Taylor was eager to try out archaeological excavation methods and analyses based on the holistic ecological approaches of Hargrave and Donald Brand, a UNM faculty member. Setzler had worked in the Big Bend country of Texas and suggested that Taylor could profitably excavate in various cave sites across the Rio Grande in Mexico.

In 1938 Taylor enrolled in the doctoral program at Harvard University. He developed a proposal for a research program focused on some Coahuila cave sites and did fieldwork there in 1940 and 1941 using monies funneled through the Smithsonian.[154]

Clyde Kluckhohn, Taylor's mentor and dissertation advisor, was something of an iconoclast in matters archaeological, although he was principally an ethnographer, and was highly critical of the culture history approach being used by the Carnegie Institution of Washington's Maya studies program, which had been underway since 1914.[155] Taylor's dissertation was, in effect, an extension of this critique.

In early 1942 Taylor enlisted in the U.S. Marine Corps. He was assigned to the Office of Strategic Services. Since Yale University has a very long history of sending its graduates into federal service, clandestine and otherwise, the assignment is not surprising. In August 1944 Taylor parachuted behind German lines as part of the invasion of southern France. He was wounded and captured, spending three months in hospitals and more months in 1944–45 in prison camps, where he spent part of his time teaching an introductory anthropology course to his fellow prisoners.[156]

After the war Taylor settled in Santa Fe and completed his Coahuila fieldwork in 1947. His revised dissertation was published by the American Anthropological Association, which gave it great cachet.[157] The published version, *A Study of Archaeology*, was a closely reasoned critique of the culture history approach of Americanist archaeology that had been predominant since the 1920s. Taylor asserted that archaeology should be done as Lyndon Hargrave had proposed in the 1930s, using a "conjunctive" approach—that is, a human ecological, or cultural ecological, approach. He also mildly criticized some major figures of the time, particularly A. V. Kidder. Some saw the book as archaeological heresy—how dare this young upstart, even if he does have a Harvard Ph.D., criticize the great Kidder and our sacredly scientific culture history approach to archaeology?!! Over time Taylor's critics became increasingly vociferous and mean-spirited, especially since he failed to produce any sort of "conjunctive" report of his self-ballyhooed work in Coahuila; and, in fact, never did.[158]

In 1949 Taylor turned his attention back to the Glen Canyon Country, specifically the Kayenta region. He decided that the region would be a good place to develop a new project to demonstrate his "conjunctive" approach.[159] More specifically, he wanted to address a specific "culture-environmental relationship . . . whether the alleged Great Drought of 1276 to 1299 A.D. affected the Anasazi culture of northeastern Arizona, and if so, in what way." In 1949 the existence and impact of the Great Drought were still debatable issues.[160]

Taylor decided that to meet his goals, he would need to locate "cliff house" sites of the right age, from about 1240–50 to 1300 C.E.—sites filled with dry, undisturbed deposits containing not only artifacts but ecofacts—floral and faunal remains; that is, "such places as Kiet Seel and Betatakin [once] *were*" before they were excavated. He would use all available biological, environmental, and archaeological data and pertinent ethnographic data to demonstrate his approach and resolve the Great Drought problem. He headed to the field and spent two whole days in October 1949 in Tsegi and Dogoszhi canyons. He looked at six sites, all previously recorded; none were deemed suitable.[161]

In August 1950 Taylor attended the Pecos Conference in Flagstaff, where he met then-graduate student William Y. (Bill) Adams (see chapter 19 for more on Adams). Adams had spent the summer of 1950 conducting an ethnographic survey among Navajo people in the Navajo Mountain–Tsegi Canyon area. Taylor was delighted; here was an ideal field person who knew the Kayenta country and who spoke some Navajo besides! If there were undiscovered cliff houses, "like Keet Siel and Betatakin [once] were," Adams would be the one to find them.

In early 1951 Taylor offered Adams a summer job to survey "the canyons around Navajo Mountain . . . and from the San Juan and Colorado Rivers on the north to the Tuba City-Kayenta road on the south."[162] According to Adams:

> [Taylor] offered me $500 for the summer's work—which seemed to me at the time a princely sum, since I was just exhausting the last of my G.I. bill benefits. But as it turned out, out of that sum I had to pay all the costs of the actual survey (i.e. running my truck and hiring Navajo guides, horses and a mule), and in the long run I did so much damage to my pickup that the survey cost me more than I made. . . . Although Taylor . . . talked about "coming over every two or three weeks to look over my work," in fact I had personal contact with him only twice, at the beginning and at the end of the project. I won't go on to talk about the survey . . . [except to say that] Taylor wasn't at all involved in any of it. . . . All the

> sites I recorded were either shown to me by others (mainly Navajos) or I was told about them. I had the same advantage that John Wetherill always had: if you want to find ruins, just ask the Navajos.[163]

Adams covered the major canyons and adjacent mesas around Navajo Mountain and made a reconnaissance into Monument Valley and Chinle Wash to the east.[164] At summer's end he reported to Taylor that there were two possible sites in the Chinle Wash drainage and took him on a three-day trip to evaluate them.

> We camped for the night below Poncho House (which in those days was very hard to reach), and my most vivid memory was that he had brought along a small barrel full of New England oysters and clams packed in ice. He told me he received a fresh shipment every three weeks, and that he never went camping without them. I suppose my Stoic soul was offended by that blatant display of Epicurianism, though I did enjoy eating the shellfish. Taylor concluded . . . that both [sites] were too remote and difficult of access to be practically feasible for excavation. I had been thinking . . . about showing him a couple of the sites in Navajo Canyon . . . but they were more remote still. . . . Thus ended my direct association with the Pueblo Ecology Survey.[165]

In 1952 Taylor shifted his gaze to the Monument Valley area and spent five days with a USGS mapping team that had recorded about a hundred site locales. He visited forty-one sites and made surface collections from seventeen of them.[166] In November 1952 the geologists submitted their own archaeological report to the Bureau of American Ethnology at the Smithsonian, listing ninety-six sites, including those visited by Taylor.[167] Taylor found no sites suitable for his purposes.

In 1958 Taylor published a brief report on his "pueblo ecology" project, basically a taxonomic description of the pottery types. No "conjunctive" data or interpretations were presented. In the end, his vaunted approach, both in Coahuila and the Glen Canyon Country, appeared to come to naught. But not entirely.

The real contribution of Taylor's abortive study was Bill Adams's 125-page report, which, despite Taylor's promises, was never published.[168] Adams had spent some time as a young man on the Navajo reservation and had traveled widely across it (chapter 19). During his 1950 socioeconomic survey project around Navajo Mountain he had examined numerous archaeological sites.[169]

Adams took the job with Taylor because, as he said, he needed the money. He was in the field from June 20 through September 18, accompanied some of the time by Robert Tallsalt, a Navajo friend who knew the country intimately. He kept a detailed field diary and an equally detailed set of site records.[170] His manuscript report is titled "Archaeology and Culture History of the Navajo Country, Report on Reconnaissance for the Pueblo Ecology Study, 1951." He later added a subtitle, "*or* Kidder Up to Date: A Reintroduction to the Study of Southwestern Archaeology." The report is, quite simply, an excellent work, well ahead of its time. Adams presents the site data he collected in detail and discusses the pottery types he observed. He then discusses Kayenta culture history, linking demographic and ecological perspectives—doing what Lyndon Hargrave had proposed in 1931–32, and Taylor had set out to do, but did not.

According to Adams, Kayentans, from Basketmaker II to Pueblo III times, were small-scale farmers, exploiting whatever arable land was available in any given year and living most of the time on small farmsteads. They came together, seasonally perhaps, for social and ritual purposes and to exchange genes and information. Only in Pueblo III times was it possible, briefly, to assemble in larger villages, many probably for defensive purposes. This picture has been fleshed out by sixty years of subsequent research, as we shall see. In my view, Adams's report is, indeed, a study of Kayentan *pueblo ecology*, accomplishing in part what Taylor failed to do. It is most interesting that while Taylor had Adams's full report, he did not use it.

The second half of Adams's report, the "Kidder up to date" portion, is equally prescient. Adams rightfully castigates the anal-retentive obsession with pottery types that had dominated southwestern archaeology from before the 1927 Pecos Conference until the mid-1950s and beyond. Finally he presents an extensive and reasoned discussion of the culture histories and interrelationships of the regional variants of the Anasazi (Ancestral Puebloan)—Kayenta, Mesa Verde, Chaco, and Little Colorado—most of it confirmed by research over the subsequent fifty-plus years since Adams wrote.[171] We will meet Bill Adams again in chapter 19.

› 14 ‹

THE ENAMORED EXPLORERS

MANY PEOPLE MADE FLOAT TRIPS THROUGH Glen Canyon in the 1950s, especially after word got around that the Bureau of Reclamation was planning to build a major dam there. Of all those who came to the canyon in those years, two trios of individuals stand out. One called themselves "Canyon Surveys"; the other, "We Three." The individuals members of each trio were, and remain, improbable and wonderful characters in the history of the Glen Canyon Country. All were deeply enamored of Glen Canyon and highly offended by the plans for—and later, the reality of—Glen Canyon Dam. Both trios often started their trips at Hite, where they visited with Arthur ("Arth") Chaffin (chapter 20) before starting out.

THE CANYON SURVEYS TRIO

The first trio consisted of Richard W. (Dick) Sprang, comic book artist extraordinaire; his wife, Dudy Thomas; and the eccentric river runner Harry Aleson, whom we met briefly in chapter 11.

Harry Aleson (fig. 14.1) was closely linked to Glen Canyon in the 1940s and 1950s, making trips as early as 1942.[1] We have already noted his relationship with Georgie White Clark. Harry Le Roy Aleson (1899–1972) was born in Waterville, Iowa. He quit high school to work as a chemist's helper in an iron mine. In 1918 he enlisted in the army and was assigned to the aviation section of the Signal Corps and sent to France. On a reconnaissance mission his plane crashed, and he was gassed. He later received a total disability pension. After the war he managed to finish high school and a couple of years of college.

Harry knocked around at various jobs. He married Thursa Arnold in 1928, but they were separated in 1940, in part because Harry had discovered the Colorado River, fell in love with it, and spent all his time near it and on it. Around 1940 he set up a tent camp in Quartermaster Canyon, near the end of Grand Canyon, and called it "My Home, Arizona." From this base he began exploring the Grand Canyon and its tributaries. By the early 1940s he was making trips as a river guide, sometimes

14.1. Harry Aleson fixing a boat motor in Glen Canyon. Photographer unknown, C 187. Courtesy of the Utah Historical Society.

working for Norm Nevills before going out on his own. In April 1945 he made the first motorboat trip upstream in Glen Canyon from Lee's Ferry to Hite in five days. That same year he and Georgie White Clark made their 61-mile life-preserver trip in Grand Canyon, and in 1946 they completed their 81-mile trip (chapter 11).

By 1945 Aleson was working winters as a night clerk in a hotel in Richfield, Utah, for room and board, using the long nights to organize his river-running business, primarily San Juan–Glen Canyon trips. In 1947 he joined other river runners in acquiring navy surplus rubber rafts. Given the room on the rafts, he was able to offer extended trips (fig. 14.2) with stops for hikes up side canyons to visit particularly scenic places, and along the rivers to visit mining and archaeological sites. By 1952 he had made over forty trips in Glen Canyon.

Richard W. (Dick) Sprang (1915–2000) was born in Fremont, Ohio. From an early age he worked at odd jobs as a professional illustrator. After college he worked for the Scripps-Howard newspaper chain as an artist, doing magazine jobs on the side. He moved to New York and found work illustrating pulp magazines such as *Popular Detective*, *Popular Western*, and others. In the late 1930s he began working as a comic book illustrator and became a ghost artist for the Batman and, later, Superman series at DC Comics. Being told that he could live and work "anywhere there's a mailbox," he moved to Sedona, Arizona, in 1946, later lived in the Wayne County area in Utah, and finally moved to Prescott, Arizona, in 1972, where he remained until his death. He met and married Dudy Thomas, who had long lived in the canyon country and was a close friend of the Wetherill family.

Sprang bought a surplus ten-man rubber raft, outfitted it with a rowing frame, and in the fall of 1951 set out down Glen Canyon with Dudy and a friend from Sedona, Elmer Purtymun.[2] On October 10 they encountered Harry Aleson camped at the mouth of the Escalante River. The four camped together and immediately hit it off. In early 1952 Sprang proposed to Aleson that they develop a complex system of carefully recording what they saw on their river trips. The idea was to produce detailed sets of environmental, archaeological, geological, and other data on Glen Canyon and its environs that could be used, added to, and corrected by future researchers. They called their project Canyon Surveys.

They planned to live along the river or other areas for four to six weeks at a time in the fall after the tourist season. They also brought along Dick's dog and Dudy's cat. As Sprang explained to Eleanor Inskip,

> Two additional members of our party may surprise you: Pard, my splendidly level-headed shepherd dog . . . and Mickey, Dudy's

14.2. Harry Aleson river party in Glen Canyon, 1940s. Aleson is cooking at the campfire. Photographer unknown, 551.47 P2. Courtesy of the Utah Historical Society.

> supremely tough, gray and white, short-haired tomcat, who was built like a buffalo, had the heart of a lion, and walked the canyons, wading water, with a tiger's stride, utterly fearless, militant, shrewd, never a problem, always keeping up, and thoroughly at home, loving to doze in Anasazi ruins. We called him our Moki cat [figs. 14.3, 14.4, 14.5].[3]

Following the 1914 and 1921 surveys of the Colorado and San Juan rivers, the USGS had issued a detailed topographic map of the course of the rivers and adjacent areas of both riverbanks. Aleson and Sprang had a set of these maps. Sprang also acquired a set of U.S. Soil Conservation Service aerial photo stereographic pairs of the main canyons and areas beyond those shown on the USGS river map. The coverage was sufficient to show the full lengths of many of the tributary canyons.

During his winter months at the Richfield hotel, Aleson laid out a detailed exploration plan focusing on Glen Canyon from Hite to the confluence with the San Juan. The party arrived at Hite on October 10, 1952, and started downriver—stopping to survey and hike out the places Aleson had picked. Aleson kept a detailed daily journal of the trip.[4] On October 19 they camped on the left bank of the river in the "north edge of oak grove nearest entrance to canyon opposite Smith Fork. Since '45 I've called this 'No Name' Canyon. On their [Sprang and Thomas's] 1951 trip suggested calling this 'Forgotten' Canyon. It is a good name. Let us hope it may become known as Forgotten Canyon."[5]

On the USGS river map the canyon was shown to be short and unnamed. The stereographic pairs revealed a much longer and complex canyon. On October 20 the party hiked up the canyon about a mile to what Aleson called "the Narrows." There the canyon bottom narrowed to 1–2 feet and was filled with chest deep and, in the final pool, over-the-head-deep, very cold water. In 1951 the Narrows had looked impassable, but Sprang thought there was a way around them up over the slickrock. Aleson wrote: "He brought tools from Sedona for cutting 'Moki steps.' . . . We are busy until about 4:30 cutting the steps . . . with a stone facing tool and a heavy hammer. For over half the day we worked on slick rock slope averaging sixty degrees." They were then able to set a transverse line to hold onto while crossing the steps and set anchors for ropes to get back down to the canyon floor.

The next day Sprang and Thomas carried their gear (with the cat in a fishing creel) across the slope; Aleson swam the dog through the Narrows, and they proceed upcanyon. "We continue up the main canyon . . . now thru narrows, then brush, over rocky bottom until after 3:00 PM Dick stops, looking up into a high cave, saying, 'Look at that.' There are 3 large, white paintings, figures holding raised shields. . . . I spot a Cliff Dwelling . . . to the left of the paintings" (figs. 17.10, 17.11, 17.12). Aleson and

14.3. Dudy Thomas, Dick Sprang, and their cat Mickey, Glen Canyon, 1953. Sprang Collection, NAU 53545. Courtesy of Cline Library, Northern Arizona University.

Sprang climbed to the rockshelter and described in detail the structures they found there. "Dick remarks that it appears that this is a virgin find. No sign of any visitors here since final abandonment."[6]

The party spent the rest of the day exploring to the head of the canyon, noting that both its upper forks boxed up a couple of miles upstream from the site. They camped in the canyon that night and explored and recorded the site in more detail the next day—the three people, the dog, and the cat. They decided to call it "Three Warriors Ruin." In 1959, when the University of Utah Glen Canyon Project rerecorded and then excavated the site, we called it "Defiance House" (chapter 17).

14.4. Mickey the cat at Anasazi Ruin, Glen Canyon, 1953. Sprang Collection, NAU 54657. Courtesy of Cline Library, Northern Arizona University.

14.5. Dudy Thomas, Pard, and Mickey hiking on slickrock, Glen Canyon, 1953. Sprang Collection, NAU 54824. Courtesy of Cline Library, Northern Arizona University.

They then turned back downcanyon, discovering as they went several additional sites that the Utah crew would record and excavate in 1959 (fig. 17.10). After their trip the trio submitted the name "Forgotten Canyon" to the USGS. It was accepted and was on the quad sheet I used when I surveyed the canyon in 1959 (chapter 17).

The three plus two continued on downriver, resupplied by two airdrops that Aleson had arranged. Sprang and Aleson explored Moki and Lake canyons by hiking from Lake Canyon across the slickrock back to Moki Canyon and then down one of its major falling sand dunes.[7] Aleson thought it was the dune Judd and Wetherill used in 1923 to get in and out of the canyon. Moving on downstream they explored gravel terraces and side canyons all the way to the confluence of the Colorado and the San Juan. Aleson stopped at the mouth of the Escalante River, where he kept a "private register" in a bottle under a ledge. He copied out all the entries, noting that the October-November 1952 trip was the forty-ninth time he had been there in ten years.[8] By the time they reached Music Temple, it was November 19 and getting quite cold. They made a few more brief stops and arrived at Lee's Ferry on November 22. The next day they headed home in a snowstorm.

In 1953 the three turned their attention to the San Juan River, including a trip from Mexican Hat to Lee's Ferry and explorations of Grand Gulch. They made their last Glen Canyon trip together in 1955. Pard the dog and Mickey the cat went along on all the trips, hiking across the slickrock and helping explore the ruins. In 1957 Dudy Thomas died during an operation to remove a brain tumor.

After Dudy died, Dick Sprang remarried, and he and wife Elizabeth made a five-week float trip through Glen Canyon in the fall of 1959. Years later Elizabeth Sprang published an eloquent memorial of the trip. In her October 13 entry at Smith Fork Bar she wrote, "Today we saw a great panel of petroglyphs that had been vandalized. For the purpose of taking impressions, blue latex paint had been sloshed and dribbled down over the figures, permanently spoiling their looks."[9] Mea culpa, Elizabeth. 'Twas I who sloshed and dribbled the blue rubber latex (not paint) to make the impressions the previous July (chapter 17).

Despite the trio's good intentions of producing reams of data to be used, updated, and augmented by future researchers, it all came to naught. They did record much, but it remained unpublished and primarily in Sprang's hands until his death in 2000. As Gary Topping points out, those of us surveying the ecology, archaeology, and history of Glen Canyon in the late 1950s had no knowledge of the data, or even of the Canyon Survey itself.[10] But the Sprang-Thomas-Aleson records did ultimately find their way into archives, and collectively they give us a detailed glimpse of five intrepid explorers (counting Pard and Mickey) exploring and learning about the wonders of the Glen Canyon Country.

WE THREE

The members of the second improbable trio were Frank Wright, Katie Lee, and Tad Nichols (fig. 14.6). John Franklin Wright (1903–2002) was born in Fruitland, Colorado, one of seven children.[11] The family moved to Grayson (later Blanding), Utah, in 1915. Except for a few years in the early 1930s living near Salt Lake City, where he met and married his wife, Dora, Frank lived in Blanding all of his life. A man of many talents, Frank farmed, taught music, was an accomplished photographer and ham radio operator, and for forty years was the official local weather observer. He was also a barber, an auto mechanic, and welder. He learned to fly a plane in 1947. But he is remembered best as a master boatman on the San Juan and Colorado rivers.

In 1948 Frank made a river trip with Norm Nevills from Bluff to Mexican Hat—his first river experience. A week later Nevills recruited him as a boatman for a commercial trip from Mexican

14.6. "We Three" in Glen Canyon, 1953: Tad Nichols (*left*), Frank Wright, and Katie Lee. Photographer unknown. Courtesy of Katie Lee and Roy Webb.

Hat to Lee's Ferry. When Nevills was killed in a plane crash in 1949, Wright and Jim and Bob Rigg bought the company and renamed it Mexican Hat Expeditions. In 1951 the Rigg brothers ran one of their boats from Lee's Ferry through the Grand Canyon to Separation Rapid in thirty-eight hours. In 1953 they led a boat trip from Green River, Utah, on down through the Grand Canyon. In 1952 they acquired two Chris Craft motorboats and ran the Grand Canyon in them. Tad Nichols (see below) went along to make a film of the trip. In 1957, at the start of the Glen Canyon Project, the

Museum of Northern Arizona hired Frank Wright for three years as boatman (fig. 19.3), and sometimes cook and shovel-hand for their archaeological surveys along the San Juan River and the left bank of Glen Canyon below the confluence of the San Juan and the Colorado (chapter 19).

After the completion of Glen Canyon Dam, Wright, in partnership with others, established a marina and ferry service at Hall's Crossing. At various times Wright carried VIPs on trips on the still-filling Lake Powell, including senators Frank Moss and Robert Kennedy, Stewart Udall, and others, usually to Rainbow Bridge.

But the glory years for Frank Wright and others were from 1949 to 1963. Frank ran various Glen Canyon trips and at least one Grand Canyon trip per year. From 1954 to 1963 he made a series of trips with Katie Lee and Tad Nichols, primarily in Glen Canyon after the regular tourist season. They called themselves "We Three." It was a friendship that lasted until Nichols's and Wright's deaths, and is memorialized in many of Katie Lee's writings and songs.[12]

Kathryn (Katie) Lee was born in Tucson, Arizona, in 1919 and grew up there. Her father was a architect and builder, and her mother taught music, including to Katie, and later dealt in real estate. Katie began singing and playing the guitar at sixteen. She and some compatriots would sometimes go to the cathouses in Nogales, Mexico, to learn the folk songs sung there. She graduated from the University of Arizona, married in 1942, and was divorced in 1945. In 1948 she started a professional career as a film actress and sometimes character actress on radio shows and early television in Hollywood, including "The Great Gildersleeve," the "Gordon MacRae Railroad Hour," the "Halls of Ivy" with Ronald and Benita Coleman, and others. She worked with Burl Ives, Josh White, Dorothy Dandridge, Pete Seeger and Ronnie Gilbert of the Weavers, Cisco Houston, Woody Guthrie, and many others, and toured widely across the country on concert and coffee house circuits for ten or eleven years.

In March 1953 Katie saw her long-time Tucson friend Tad Nichols's film of the Rigg brothers' first Chris Craft run through the Grand Canyon the previous year. The film was shown by Jim Rigg. In June 1953 Rigg invited her to come along on the second Chris Craft run through the Grand Canyon for the cost of her food if she would bring her guitar and sing for the passengers. It was the beginning of her love affair with the canyon country that continues more than fifty years on and counting.

Immediately after the Chris Craft trip, Rigg and his partners ran an oar-powered trip from Green River, Utah, on through the Grand Canyon. Katie was invited to the farewell dinner for the trip in Boulder City, Nevada. There she met Frank Wright. In the fall of 1953, when Wright came to the Los Angeles area to show river movies and hustle customers, Katie helped him meet people.

In June 1954 Frank invited Katie to come along on a commercial trip down the San Juan from Mexican Hat to Lee's Ferry. Again, she paid her way by playing and singing, and helping out with chores. Her friend Tad Nichols was on the trip. In July and August 1954 she made two trips with Wright and Jim Rigg through Glen Canyon from Hite to Lee's Ferry. She was totally entranced by Glen Canyon, a romance that continues to the present day.

But the commercial trips were too hurried; there was no time to stop and explore all the intriguing side canyons and alcoves during a seven- or eight-day trip. When Katie asked Wright or Rigg what was up some of the side canyons they were passing, they often didn't know. She began thinking about a different kind of trip—slow and leisurely, with time to explore all those side canyons, to climb out and see the country. Ultimately, with Frank Wright and Tad Nichols, she was able to make such trips.

Edward Tatnall (Tad) Nichols (1911–2002) was born in Springfield, Ohio; his family later moved to Cambridge, Massachusetts. He suffered from asthma, so his family sent him to a boy's ranch school in Arizona. It was life-changing. As Nichols said, "I date my life as starting when I came to Arizona."[13] He graduated from the University of Arizona with degrees in geology and anthropology. In 1934 he made a trip to the Monument Valley area with a fellow student and met John Wetherill, who told them about the trip he had made upriver in Glen Canyon in the winter of 1931.

The next year, 1935, Nichols was a student at Byron Cummings's archaeological field school on Cummings Mesa. Afterward Cummings took the students to Rainbow Bridge (fig. 13.2), as well as to Keet Seel, Betatakin, and Monument Valley, and finally to a dinner at the Wetherills' home in Kayenta.

Nichols studied photography at a school in Tucson and later with both Brett Weston and Ansel Adams. This led over time to numerous photography assignments with scientific expeditions to many parts of the world. He began making training films for the Army Air Corps during World War II. After the war he made documentaries for the U.S. Indian Service on reservations in the Southwest. Still later he made documentary films for Walt Disney and the Sierra Club, among others.

In 1950 Nichols had been hired to help make a television film of a trip through San Juan and Glen canyons. The trip was organized by Mexican Hat Expeditions—the Rigg boys and Frank Wright. It was the beginning of long friendships with all three. Nichols ran the Grand Canyon with Wright and the Riggs brothers in 1951 and 1952, and filmed the latter trip. Other Grand Canyon trips would follow over the years until 1968. But Nichols, like Lee, was fascinated by Glen Canyon. As he later said:

> That first trip with Frank Wright down San Juan River and into Glen Canyon, I was so intrigued with Glen Canyon and the beauty of it, that for the next at least seven or eight years, I borrowed, begged, or stole a boat of some kind, and almost every summer went down through Glen Canyon, each year exploring a different side canyon. Each one was different and each one was extraordinary. I had just never really thought such a place in the world existed.[14]

Nichols made thirty some trips through Glen Canyon between 1950 and 1963. Several of them were with Frank Wright and Katie Lee. The first "We Three" trip was in September 1955.

The trips started either at Hite or at the Mexican Hat bridge across the San Juan River. Most of them focused on three or four side canyons per trip, which the three would explore thoroughly. They named several of the canyons and submitted the names to the USGS. Some of them appeared on the quad sheets produced in 1956–57 for use during the construction of the dam—for example, Cathedral, Dangling Rope, and Dungeon. Some didn't. "Iceberg" seems a better name than "Wilson" Canyon, given the sometimes icy pool of water that was a short way upcanyon from the river.[15]

Nichols also made Glen Canyon trips with other photographers. He had first met Eliot Porter in 1935. He would later take Porter and his family through Glen Canyon on his boat, as Porter, like Nichols, photographed "the place no one knew."[16] Nichols took many wondrous photographs of Glen Canyon, admired by all who saw them. Many of them were finally brought together in the hauntingly beautiful *Glen Canyon: Images of a Lost World*, published in 1999.[17]

For Katie Lee, all of Glen Canyon and its river were hauntingly beautiful:

> I stand by the river on the cool, wet sand, watching the colors fade and breathing the river-scented air. Stars begin to arrange and concentrate their battalions in the eastern sky, sending out a few to reconnoiter before the troops advance. Beaver slap at their work, and

birds make sleepy peeps and rustling sounds of settling in for the night. Bats careen through pinkish twilight, silent of wing, dipping water that turns from salmon to silver-grey, in streaks and swirls, in circles and ruffles, an ever-changing pattern, alive and moving, breathing, throbbing, stroking . . . encored with silt.

> Wind changes from up-canyon to down. Nocturnal sounds slip in to replace those of day, as the new moon, a golden eyelash in a sea of turquoise, drifts on the horizon and disappears. Sand banks fall to the shameless advances of the water. In the shallows where the river runs over smooth-as-velvet rocks, I hear his seductive night conversation.[18]

On one trip the trio camped by the petroglyphs at the mouth of Smith Fork (fig. 17.7).

> On a darkly varnished wall near the mouth of Smith Fork is an Anasazi story board. It pictures squiggles, dots and spirals, suns and snakes, animals and bugs; human and super-human figures armed with bows and arrows, others with arrows through them; much game, many hunters; hands, a lot of feet and bird prints; heavy-hung shaman figures with goofy headdresses, Kokopelli from the mythical (?) world, with his hump and his flute—and things that archaeologists, anthropologists and other educated guessers will never figure out.[19]

The Navajo Sandstone—comprised of those thousands-of-feet-thick petrified sand dunes eroded into so many fantastic shapes and forms—fascinated Katie as it did many others. During a trip in October 1959, she wrote:

> The most perfect time of the year. The side canyon pulled me through every kind of sandstone magic—pools to swim, ledges to crawl, open spaces with sandy bottoms and redbud trees, fluted narrows, banks drenched in maidenhair fern, monkey flowers and penstamon—to where there really could be no more surprises. I leaned against a water-cut rift no wider than my living room to take the scene in through every pore, and to bless the gods that let me find this Eden. . . .
>
> I climbed a sluiceway to top out at many small cataracts where water played soft musical notes beneath an overhang. Everything was in faerie light, refracted down through the curvaceous sandstone walls rising two hundred feet on either side. To my right, bordering the stream, the stone resembled the open fan of a pleated skirt. About that lay a ridge of chipped ice, then long sweeps of Navajo tapestry, topped with a lacy border of honeycomb depressions dribbling colors from maroon to pink-gold down fifty feet of wall. Some of the depressions were large enough to crawl into; others no bigger than your head. Homes, of course, for owls and canyon wrens and those spunky little lizards who constantly hug these walls to make sure they don't go away. My God! The place was out of this world. Alice never knew what a wonderland was.[20]

For Katie Lee and many others, all of Glen Canyon was a wonderland. No one has sung its praises better or more lyrically than she. And no one has mourned its drowning more deeply nor sorrowfully, done in by the "Bureau of Wreck-the-nation," as she calls it. *Salud*, Katie Lee!

› 15 ‹

THE GLEN CANYON PROJECT

Beginnings

IN JUNE 1957 THE NATIONAL PARK SERVICE issued contracts to the University of Utah and the Museum of Northern Arizona to initiate what was formally known as the Upper Colorado River Basin Archaeological Salvage Project—hereinafter the Glen Canyon Project (GCP). The final contracts were issued in 1963. Summary reports were published, one by Jesse D. Jennings in 1966 and one by Alexander J. Lindsay Jr. and his associates in 1968. [1] The GCP was the largest single archaeological salvage project undertaken in the United States up to that time. It resulted in 200-plus scholarly publications and became a model for later projects, not only in the United States but in Latin America, as American archaeology morphed from salvage archaeology into cultural resources management. It is useful to briefly place the project in historical context.

BACKGROUND

When Euro-Americans began spilling over the Appalachian Mountains in the very early 1800s, they encountered thousands of "mounds"—archaeological sites built by then unknown peoples at unknown times, who came to be called Mound Builders. Many of the sites were enormous, covering dozens of acres. The mounds excited great interest among the general public and the antiquarians of the day. Since many of them were on prime farmland, they began to be leveled, yielding hundreds of thousands of intricately made artifacts. Antiquarians and other interested scholars called for some form of protection for some of the sites, and a few were protected one way or another.

The Smithsonian Institution was created in 1846 as a quasi-governmental, quasi-private organization (as it remains). Its first major publication in 1848 was a massive volume, *Ancient Monuments of the Mississippi Valley*, containing dozens of maps and descriptions of mound sites in the Ohio and Mississippi river valleys, most of them later subsumed under the cultural labels "Hopewell" and "Mississippian."[2] The authors, E. G. Squier and E. S. Davis, had personally mapped many of the sites and described artifacts from them before they were leveled for farms and town sites. In effect, the mapping was a form of "salvage archaeology"—the maps and the artifact descriptions representing public information about the sites. Some of the artifacts found their way into the collections of public institutions, such as the American Antiquarian Society in Worcester, Massachusetts, or the numerous natural history societies and state historical societies that sprang up as public lands became territories and then states during the nineteenth century.

Also in 1846, the United States invaded Mexico and took possession of the provinces of Nuevo Mexico and Alta California. Those entities then became the territories of New Mexico and California (Arizona was split off from New Mexico in 1863). Several major surveys by the Army Topographical Engineers were carried out in the 1840s–50s. Their assignments were to survey and map the territories, plot out potential railroad and wagon routes to the West, and study and describe the natural resources, as well as the Indian tribes and archaeological sites, therein. By the 1850s the already famous site of Casa Grande and the various great houses in Chaco Canyon, as well as many other archaeological sites, had been described in reports published by the Army Topographical Engineers. These "ruins" excited much interest across the country, and calls were made to preserve them for future study and the benefit of the public.[3]

The next major step was the creation of Yellowstone National Park in 1872. The previous year the Hayden survey (chapter 5) had gone into the Yellowstone area, studied it, and made photographs and other illustrations. The materials were shown to Congress, and there was a rather quick legislative move to "set aside," or "reserve," the area as a national park, as a place of scientific and scenic interest for the benefit of the public.[4] Since the Yellowstone area was part of the public domain, Congress could "reserve" it using the same powers it had to set aside Indian reservations and military reservations. Yellowstone thus became the first national park in the United States—and in the world.

In 1879 John Wesley Powell managed to get his Bureau of Ethnology funded by Congress and placed administratively under the wing of the Smithsonian Institution (chapter 5). He immediately launched a major, long-term collecting and research program in the Southwest, including recording and excavating archaeological sites. In 1889, responding to a petition from numerous prominent Boston Brahmins, Congress set aside Casa Grande in the Gila River drainage of Arizona Territory. By that time anthropology (including archaeology) had become a small but viable scientific discipline within the growing Science Establishment during the last quarter of the nineteenth century.

As the frontier continued to expand ever westward, archaeological sites were increasingly subject to looting. The nineteenth century has been called the "Age of Museums." There were art museums, generally given to celebrating the rise of European and Euro-American civilization. There were also natural history museums, generally given to celebrating European and Euro-American domination over the natural world, including subjugated peoples and their pasts, many styled as aboriginals or "savages." Nineteenth-century anthropology was concerned with subjugated peoples and their pasts, hence anthropology (earlier in the century, ethnology) was usually a part of natural history museums.[5]

The major U.S. and European natural history museums, including the U.S. National Museum of the Smithsonian Institution, were in keen competition to assemble as large and "complete" collections of ethnographic and archaeological materials as they could. The competition created a market for archaeological and ethnographic artifacts. From 1879 through the end of the century, railroad cars full of archaeological and ethnographic objects were shipped from Arizona and New Mexico to the Smithsonian, the American Museum of Natural History, and other museums in the United States and abroad. The rise of tourism after 1880, promoted by the railroads, further contributed to the market. Locals in western states, particularly the Southwest, responded to that market by digging up sites and selling the artifacts to middlemen who sold them to the museums and tourist agencies.[6]

By the 1880s it was understood that indiscriminate digging, or looting, produced no scientific data about the sites, their internal relationships, and the relationships of the artifacts. Standards for note taking and recording of excavations and the provenance of artifacts from within the sites began to be developed. The successive stratigraphic layers of a site and the provenance of artifacts within those layers had to be carefully recorded so that the full culture history of a site could be understood—as well as its relationship with other sites.

By 1899 organizations such as the American Association for the Advancement of Science, the Archaeological Institute of America, and the professional staffs of major museums in Boston, New York, Philadelphia, and Washington, D.C., began lobbying Congress for federal antiquities legislation that would protect sites on public lands. They also wanted a permitting system that allowed only individuals from qualified universities, museums, and other scientific organizations to excavate sites on public lands. It took seven years to hammer out legislation acceptable to all parties, but in 1906 Congress passed the federal Antiquities Act, which is the base legislation for all subsequent federal antiquities and historic preservation legislation.

The act did three things. One, it prohibited excavation of archaeological sites on federal lands without a permit from the government. Two, it gave the president authority to set aside, by executive order, relatively small portions of public land called "national monuments" to protect the cultural, historical, or scientific phenomena thereon. Congress reserved to itself, as it still does, the authority to create larger national parks. For our purposes the importance of the act is that it attempted to protect sites on public lands and implicitly established federal responsibility for cultural resources that might be impacted by federally funded, sponsored, or licensed projects. Three, it established a uniform set of rules and procedures for granting permits and monitoring the results of archaeology done under the permits.[7]

THE ORIGINS OF SALVAGE ARCHAEOLOGY

It is generally agreed that what came to be called "reservoir salvage archaeology" began in Egypt in 1907. Between 1889 and 1902 the British had constructed a dam across the River Nile at Aswan. But it proved inadequate, and in 1907 its height was raised, threatening to flood a number of sites that were excavated by the famed Egyptologist George Reisner. The dam was raised again in 1929, prompting more salvage work, and in the 1960s the Aswan High Dam, 4 kilometers upstream from the original dam, was built. That led to a massive archaeological salvage program involving several American scholars, including William Y. Adams (chapter 19), and the removal of the great temple of Abu Simbel to a position above Lake Nasser.[8]

In 1918 the federal government began work on the Wilson Dam at Muscle Shoals, Alabama. The new reservoir would, and did, drown many archaeological sites. In 1922, at the request of the Tennessee Valley Historical Society, the Bureau of American Ethnology of the Smithsonian Institution sent archaeologist Gerard Fowke to conduct "salvage" excavations in sites before they were inundated by the rising lake. He sampled just two.[9]

Fowke's excavations, small though they were, seemingly mark the beginning of federal involvement in reservoir salvage archaeology in the United States. Later in the 1920s, Neil Judd of the Smithsonian Institution and Clark Wissler of the American

Museum of Natural History, began organizing state-level conferences through the National Research Council (NRC) to deal with issues of the depletion of the archaeological record; the conferences also called national attention to the destruction through looting of archaeological sites across the country.[10] The 1906 Antiquities Act forbade excavation of sites on federal lands without a permit, but there were no real enforcement mechanisms in place. In the East and Midwest, where there was very little federal land, sites could be looted—or protected—at the will of the landowners—and there was far more looting than protecting.

The basic premise of the NRC-sponsored conferences was that archaeological sites, historic towns, and other sites, buildings, or objects constitute valuable, nonrenewable parts of the nation's shared cultural and scientific heritage, whether they be on public or private lands. Archaeological sites were seen as containers of scientific data; the sites must be excavated by trained archaeologists and the information and artifacts found therein preserved for the public good. If the sites were looted or, in the case of reservoirs, drowned before they were properly studied, the information would be lost. Salvaging the information from the sites made the data available to the scientific world and ultimately to the public through museum exhibits, textbooks, and popular articles.[11] Few at that time questioned whether or not reservoir or other public works projects should proceed—after all, they represented Progress. Rarely in the first half of the twentieth century did anyone question the reality and importance of Progress, even if they couldn't define it.

As we saw in chapter 12, by the early 1900s the Reclamation Service/Bureau of Reclamation had grandiose plans for damming the rivers of the West for irrigation, flood control, hydroelectric power, and recreation. Soon after, similar plans were being formulated for the entire Mississippi Valley drainage, including the Missouri, Ohio, and Tennessee river basins. Irrigation wasn't an issue there, but erosion and flood control, hydroelectric power, navigation, and recreation were. As these projects were realized, the idea of salvage archaeology continued to develop. With the advent of the Depression, salvage archaeology, especially in the Southeast, became big business under the auspices of the Civil Works Administration (CWA) (1933–35), the Works Progress Administration (WPA) (1935–41), and the giant reclamation program begun in 1933 by the Tennessee Valley Authority (TVA).[12]

Many of the major figures in American archaeology of the 1940s–70s cut their professional teeth on CWA/WPA/TVA archaeology projects. One was Jesse D. Jennings, a graduate student at the University of Chicago who in 1933 supervised 100 CWA workers in the excavation of Peachtree Mound in North Carolina.[13] In the West, the construction of Boulder (Hoover) Dam triggered an archaeological salvage program along the Virgin River in southern Nevada conducted by Mark R. Harrington of the Southwest Museum in Los Angeles. Those sites were later flooded by an arm of Lake Mead. Some salvage archaeology was done before World War II in advance of dam building on the Columbia River, but most such work came during the 1950s and early 1960s.[14]

Although by the mid-1930s the idea of "salvage archaeology" was slowly gaining acceptance, or at least being tolerated, by federal agencies, making it work was a matter of catch-as-catch-can lobbying and persuasion on a project-by-project basis. There was a sense of responsibility that archaeological and other historic places ought to be preserved, or at least salvaged, but there was no clear legal mandate to do so.

Congress and the executive agencies had been feeling their way for several decades in the areas of conservation and protection of both natural and cultural resources (the term "cultural resources" was not coined until 1972). In 1916, partly to resolve management problems of the increasing numbers of national parks and monuments, Congress created the National Park Service.[15] In 1935, to further clarify and consolidate management issues relating to parks, monuments, national battlefields, as well as problems relating to historic preservation in the broad sense, Congress passed the Historic Sites Act. Most important for our story was the assignment of the National Park Service as the "lead agency" in all federal matters having to do with historic preservation, including salvage archaeology and related issues and projects. Although there was no clear mandate defining how "reservoir salvage archaeology" would be funded, at least it was clear that available funding for such projects would be channeled through the Park Service, which would implement the projects through contracts with universities, museums, and other agencies.

After World War II, various federal agencies took many plans off shelves where they had resided for the duration—plans for as many as 108 reservoirs, large and small; plans for what became the interstate highway system; plans for major urban renewal of American cities; plans for flood control and improvement of navigation on major rivers. Energy companies began planning large long-distance electric transmission lines and oil and gas pipelines. Some American archaeologists foresaw the impacts all these plans would have on cultural resources. In 1944–45 they created a Committee for the Recovery of Archaeological Remains (CRAR—a small, informal, but influential group of archaeologists who began lobbying Congress and federal agencies for salvage archaeology funding. The group also provided a forum for advice on matters archaeological for the National Park Service.[16]

Of most immediate concern to the Park Service were the reservoirs and the flood control and navigation projects within the Columbia, Colorado, and Missouri-Mississippi river basins that were on the drawing boards of the Bureau of Reclamation and the U.S. Army Corps of Engineers. By law, the Corps is responsible for development projects of all sorts relating to any river within the country deemed to be "navigable." ("Navigable" is very broadly construed to include such streams as the Walker River in Nevada and eastern California, which is now and then navigable by canoe or raft, at best, and usually only during spring runoff, in years when there is such.)

In response to Corps of Engineers and Bureau of Reclamation plans, the Park Service created a "River Basin Surveys" program. In each basin the Park Service contracted with various universities and museums to undertake salvage archaeology projects in advance of dam building, channel straightening, lock construction, and so on. In the Missouri River basin, the principal contractor was the Bureau of American Ethnology (BAE) of the Smithsonian Institution.[17] In 1946 the assistant director of the BAE was Frank H. H. Roberts Jr., an archaeologist who had joined the bureau in 1927, just as he was finishing his doctorate. He became director of the River Basin Survey program in Washington, D.C.

Roberts's chief administrative contact in the Omaha, Nebraska, office of the National Park Service was Jesse D. Jennings. Jennings had taken his doctorate at the University of Chicago and joined the Park Service in 1937. He served as a naval officer in World War II and, as he would humorously say, had "fought and bled" at desk jobs in Bermuda and Iceland for the duration of the war. When he was discharged from the navy, he rejoined the Park Service and was assigned to Omaha. His principal job was liaison between the Park Service, the River Basin Survey program, and in time, various local universities and museums that became part of the overall "salvage" effort. There he became intimately familiar with how reservoir salvage projects were funded and operated, and he was able to help create administrative and fieldwork changes that made them work better.[18]

In early 1948 the Park Service asked Jennings to move to Washington, D.C., as an archaeologist within the Office of History, managed by the extremely able Ronald Lee. Jennings resisted; Lee persisted. There was an offer of a associate professorship at the University of Utah. Jennings and his wife, Jane, weighed all the options. "No matter how we viewed the question of staying with the service or going to the university, all advantages clearly lay with staying put." But was life long enough to live it in the pressure cooker of Washington politics, making policy and pushing paper, instead of doing archaeology? "Waiving common sense, fiscal wisdom and advice, we calmly decided to leave a comfortable future in the warm but restricting bureaucratic womb and try something new."[19] Jennings accepted the offer to go to the University of Utah and build up an anthropology department. The history of archaeology in the American West for the next four decades, and the ultimate lives and careers of many grade school and middle school students (as of 1948), and others not yet born, would have been very different had Jennings chosen to remain in the "warm . . . bureaucratic womb" of the National Park Service.

ANTHROPOLOGY AT THE UNIVERSITY OF UTAH

In September 1948 Jennings arrived at the University of Utah to take up his position as associate professor. His mandate, as he saw it, was to build an anthropology department, a statewide archaeology program, and ultimately, a natural history museum. When he arrived, there were two other anthropologists on the faculty, Elmer Smith and Charles Dibble. Smith had a master's degree from Utah and had been around since the mid-1930s. During World War II he had worked with the Japanese American internment camps in Utah and had become morally outraged by the treatment the people had suffered. He was equally outraged by any form of discrimination against ethnic minorities. He delighted in controversy, not for its own sake, but as a way to press issues of social justice and fair treatment for all citizens. His classes were wondrous, full of wit, good knowledge, and vitriol. In 1961 he was cashiered out of the university by a vindictive vice-president.

Dibble had been an undergraduate at Utah and then taken a doctorate at the National University of Mexico—he was fascinated by the high civilizations of Mesoamerica. With Arthur J. O. Anderson, he undertook the definitive translation of the great Florentine Codex: a compilation over fifty years of traditional Aztec ethnography and ethnohistory by Fray Bernardino de Sahagún in the latter half of the sixteenth century. The translation project took thirty-five years.[20] Dibble's classes, especially his course in Mesoamerican archaeology, were delights. Charlie was an elflike figure with a shy/wry smile and a twinkle in his eye, especially when attractive coeds were in view. He had learned all his archaeology in Spanish and would sometimes lapse into Spanish in the classroom for up to ten minutes, finally catching himself and sheepishly apologizing, saying he "had been dreaming in Aztec again."

By 1954 Jennings had managed to get anthropology separated from sociology and was given three new positions. One went to James Gunnerson, who was hired as the state archaeologist with some teaching duties. A second was Gordon Gibson, an Africanist who left in 1959 to become curator of African anthropology in the Natural History Museum of the Smithsonian Institution. I had courses with Gordon at Utah and later knew him quite well at the Smithsonian. The third was Robert Anderson, an ardent disciple of Leslie White, of the University of Michigan, proponent of "the Science of Culture." Anderson was a true missionary, indoctrinating his students in the deterministic straitjacket of "culturology" as the only "valid" approach in anthropology. I didn't shake off some of that until I was in the doctoral program at the University of Pittsburgh.

In addition to getting a statewide archaeological survey underway, Jennings started an archaeological field school. He focused on some cave sites on the western edge of the Great Salt Lake salt flats hard on the Utah/Nevada border. One site, Danger Cave, proved to contain some 13 feet of dry, stratified cultural deposits. In 1949 Willard Libby invented the process of radiocarbon dating. Jennings was able to submit samples from Danger Cave to Libby that demonstrated a ten-millennium time span of occupation of the site. At the same time Luther Cressman of the University of Oregon submitted sandals and other materials he had excavated in the 1930s from Fort Rock Cave in Oregon; they proved to be equally old. Similarly, Emil Haury of the University of Arizona submitted samples from Ventana Cave in Arizona. They too demonstrated a roughly 10,000-year time span of human occupation. In 1940 Julian Steward, whose work was reviewed in chapter 13, had opined that Great Basin cultures were no more than about 2,000 years old. Now, by the mid-1950s, the radiocarbon data demonstrated the presence of humans in the Great Basin for five times as long.

Jennings pulled all the data together from Oregon, Arizona, and his own work, and in his masterful study, *Danger Cave*, proposed the concept of the Desert Culture. The Desert Culture denoted a hunter-gatherer lifeway closely adapted to the arid conditions of the Desert West that had persisted for ten millennia. He would later rename the concept the Desert Archaic, and finally the Western Archaic.[21] The publication of *Danger Cave* in 1957 established Jennings as a major player in American archaeology. Serendipitously, that same year he took on the task of organizing and directing the Glen Canyon Project.

ORGANIZING THE GLEN CANYON PROJECT

When Jennings turned down the National Park Service archaeology position in Washington, Ronald Lee asked whom he would recommend in his place. Jennings recommended John M. Corbett (?–1975). Corbett had taken his doctorate at Columbia University and done archaeology in both North and South America before signing on with the Park Service. As Jennings said of him, he had great confidence, "an almost patrician presence (he stood about six foot five inches), a quick mind . . . diverse field experience . . . [and] could find his way through the Washington jungle best of any."[22] Jesse Nusbaum (1887–1975), another tall, lanky guy, after stints with the Museum of New Mexico and the Museum of the American Indian, had joined the National Park Service in 1921 as superintendent of Mesa Verde National Park. In 1927 he was appointed as Park Service's lead archaeologist, and later as departmental consulting archeologist (DCA) for the Department of the Interior. In 1946 he moved to the Santa Fe Park Service office and retired in 1957.

Corbett quickly found his way around the Washington jungle. In 1957 he took over Nusbaum's title of DCA and established a Division of Archeology, one part of which was an Inter-Agency Archeological Salvage Program (IASP).

The Park Service administered reservoir salvage activities in the West out of the Santa Fe regional office. The key people there were Charles R. Steen Jr. (but universally known as Charlie) (1908–97) and Erik Kellerman Reed (1914–90). Steen and Reed, with Corbett in the background, played central roles in the development, funding, and administration of the Glen Canyon Project. They were quite a trio. Corbett was tall, lanky, lean, with a hawk nose, a garrulous manner, an endless font of ribald stories, and an intense liking for gin martinis. Steen was a somewhat rotund 5'6"–7", with a twinkling eye, a ready smile, and an unending font of gentle humor. Reed seemed to be both the field man and the scholar. He was also a thespian in the local theater in Santa Fe and widely famed as a raconteur.

With a bachelor's degree in anthropology from the University of Denver in hand, Charlie Steen had started at Wupatki National Monument in 1934 as an archaeology assistant and was appointed as an archaeologist in 1936. He served in the army in Southeast Asia in World War II. From 1951 to 1966 he was regional archaeologist for the Park Service's Southwestern Region, in Santa Fe. Reed had received a bachelor's degree in anthropology from George Washington University in 1932, a master's from Harvard in 1933, and a Harvard doctorate in 1945 after his World War II military service. He had supervised various salvage archaeology jobs in 1934–37 and then was assigned to the Park Service office in Santa Fe, where he remained until he retired.[23]

All three men were wise in the ways of intragovernment politics and pushing the envelope to get things done. While I did not know them well during the Glen Canyon Project, I did in later years in both Washington, D.C., and Santa Fe, and appreciated them greatly. They were among the unsung heroes in the development of American archaeology between 1950 and 1974—the latter date marking the transition from "salvage archaeology" to "cultural resources management."[24] They exemplified the best in federal service: they were "public servants," not "bureaucrats."

POLITICKING THE PROJECT INTO EXISTENCE

In April 1956, Congress authorized the Upper Colorado River Basin Project to include the construction of Glen Canyon, Navajo, and Flaming Gorge dams and some ancillary facilities. Construction of the Glen Canyon and Navajo dams was to start almost immediately. The story of the Bureau of Reclamation and the construction companies gearing up to build the dams, and their subsequent construction, is artfully told in Russell Martin's *Story That Stands Like a Dam* and will not be rehearsed here.[25] At the same time, the National Park Service and the Committee for the Recovery of Archaeological Remains began gearing up to lobby for salvage funds on the Washington level. Jesse D. Jennings and C. Gregory Crampton at the University of Utah, Edward B. Danson at the Museum of Northern Arizona, and Fred Wendorf at the Museum of New Mexico began developing research plans and contacting their congressional representatives to seek contracts for the salvage work. Utah, Arizona, and New Mexico all had powerful senators in Congress, and all had supported the authorizing legislation for the dams. Now the archaeologists in their states needed their help to gets funds authorized for the archaeology.

Initially it was unclear which institutions would handle which projects, assuming they were funded. In the end the Museum of New Mexico handled the Navajo Reservoir Project, Utah handled Flaming Gorge, and Utah and the Museum of Northern Arizona (MNA) jointly undertook the Glen Canyon Project. MNA was responsible for the San Juan River canyon and its tributaries, and the left bank of the Colorado River downstream from the confluence of the Colorado and the San Juan. Utah was responsible for both sides of the Colorado River above the confluence and the right bank below it.

On June 29, 1956, John Corbett wrote to Jennings telling him about the upper Colorado project authorization and suggesting that at least the Glen Canyon and Flaming Gorge projects would be of interest to him; Jennings agreed. On July 31 Corbett flew to Salt Lake City for "a little informal conference 'a deux.'"[26] The next day Jennings wrote a long memo to Sterling McMurrin, then dean of the College of Arts and Science. In it he basically laid out a plan of how the Glen Canyon Project should—and in fact did—develop. There would be "a staff of field and laboratory archaeologists, which would be completely apart from the regular academic staff [having] . . . a specific laboratory for analysis, classification, and all other phases of archaeological study." There would be a phased program of site survey, some initial testing, and "a full scale excavation of sites . . . deemed valuable enough for such intensive study on the basis of the evaluation arrived at through the testing program." Jennings would supervise the overall project.[27] And so it ultimately came to be.

There had been hope that some supplemental funding would be available for fiscal year 1956–57 (then July 1–June 30). By August 10 it was clear that was not going to happen.[28] Lobbying and negotiations continued for the next several months. CRAR swung into action behind the scenes, supporting efforts to fund the upper Colorado projects as it had supported those in the Missouri and Columbia river basins. On February 14, 1957, Jennings met with Charlie Steen and developed a tentative contract for the Glen Canyon Project of $127,000 and agreed to the Utah/MNA division of areas to be covered, as noted above.[29]

But it was rough going. In early March, $205,650 for upper Colorado River basin salvage projects was eliminated by congressional committees. But lobbyists, like Yogi Berra, know that it ain't over 'til it's over. All parties redoubled their efforts. By late May 1957 there was hope of some reduced funding, but by June 1 the word was there would be no contract, no project, and hence no student jobs—at least that year. At that point several students, including me, left the university to find summer work elsewhere. On June 6, 1957, the Park Service came through with $17,000 of contingency funds.[30] With some backup university funds, the monies allowed Jennings to get Robert Lister into the field to begin surveying in the Escalante River drainage. Some other contingency funds allowed MNA to put a crew into the field. The Glen Canyon Project was underway.

During the summer and fall of 1957, lobbying intensified and was carried through in subsequent years. The Bureau of Reclamation did little to help; they wanted all the money they could get for the dams and related infrastructure installations. But the funding got a little easier, and amounts improved. For the final four years of the project, Utah had $80,000–$90,000 per year, and MNA $35,000–$50,000. For 1961 and 1962 Jennings received "sizeable outside grants" from the National Science Foundation and the Wenner-Gren Foundation for Anthropological Research, primarily to support work on the Kaiparowits Plateau and in the Virgin River drainage to the west (chapter 18).[31]

Although none of the institutions ever got all the funding they requested, there was sufficient money to see the projects to completion. Jennings was able to fund not only the archaeology program, but Crampton's history project and the University of Utah Biology Department's ecology studies. None of the regular Utah faculty involved, including Jennings, received extra salaries. The project paid for logistics, food, equipment, lab personnel, and analysis and publication data. Student field workers received hourly wages (based on an eight-hour day, about two-thirds of a normal field workday). The Park Service paid Utah 29 percent overhead on salaries and wages.[32] Contracts in smaller amounts funded the work in Flaming Gorge.

The funding for the Glen Canyon and Navajo dams salvage projects, as well as others in the early 1960s, continued to be secured through catch-as-catch-can lobbying. Matters began to change drastically with passage of the National Historic Preservation Act in 1966 and the Reservoir Salvage Act in 1969. The latter specified that up to 1 percent of the total cost of a federal project could be spent on salvage archaeology. The Reservoir Salvage Act was lobbied through Congress by the members of CRAR, led by Charles R. McGimsey of the University of Arkansas and Carl Chapman of the University of Missouri. It was a masterful, although exhausting, effort on their parts and the dozens of individuals and agencies that supported them.[33]

The National Environmental Policy Act, which included language concerning the conservation of cultural resources, was passed in 1969. In 1971 President Richard Nixon signed Executive Order 11593 directing all federal agencies to become actively involved in the inventory, assessment, and management of cultural resources in their respective purviews. The three pieces of legislation and the executive order laid the groundwork for salvage archaeology to metamorphose into cultural resources management. It did so in March 1974 at a conference of federal and academic archaeologists in Denver, Colorado.[34] I was there, and it marked the beginning of a thirty-five-year personal involvement in cultural resources management, historic preservation, and the "archaeo-politics" of making them work. But that's another story for another time.

THE 1957 SEASON

Once the initial contract for the project was signed, Jennings moved quickly. He had asked Robert Lister of the University of Colorado, an eminent southwestern archaeologist, to get the fieldwork underway. Lister and a crew were in the field by June 22, continuing until September 5, 1957. On July 22 Jim Gunnerson took charge of a small excavation crew testing sites in the Escalante drainage which Lister had recorded. Lister's assignment was to do a reconnaissance survey along the right bank of Glen Canyon from Wahweap Creek to and including the Escalante River—that is, Wahweap Creek, Warm Creek–Cottonwood Wash, Gunsight Canyon, Navajo (Padre) Canyon, Kane Wash, Last Chance Creek, and Rock Creek. He, and some of the land-based survey teams in 1958, were aided somewhat by the crude roads (and some airstrips) bulldozed all across the Four Corners area during the great "uranium frenzy" of the early 1950s.[35]

The logistical challenges faced by Lister are succinctly summed up in his weekly reports. His team covered the drainages from Wahweap Creek to Navajo (Padre) Canyon by jeeps equipped with winches—tools that were often used. They then moved into the Escalante drainage, covering Harris Wash and some of the other upper tributaries by jeep; then its lower side canyons by horseback. With the horses, they entered the Escalante drainage at Clear Creek and came out at Coyote Gulch to Willow Tank. They surveyed the major right bank tributaries: Indian Creek, Clear Creek, Davis Gulch, Soda Gulch–Fifty Mile Gulch, Willow Gulch, Coyote Gulch, and Twenty Five Mile Gulch, as well as Stevens, Cow, and Fence canyons on the left bank.[36] The crew admired the several natural bridges in the Escalante drainage: Gregory Arch in Soda Gulch; Moqui Window and Nemo Arch in Davis Gulch; Jug Handle Arch, Coyote Bridge, and Lobo Arch in Coyote Gulch (fig. 15.1); and Stevens Arch, near the mouth of Steven Canyon. In Twenty Five Mile Gulch, the party saw what would later be named the Gates Roost site (see below).[37] Some excerpts from Lister's weekly reports indicate the difficulties and problems of the assignment.

> Last Monday we jeeped to the trailer on the rim of the lower Escalante [river], a distance of about 68 miles from town [Escalante]. The last 7.1 miles is over the world's worst 'road'—and requires about one and one half hours to negotiate. Three horses and a wrangler joined us at the trailer and packed our gear into the canyon. We made two camps on the river, one opposite Clear Creek and the other about a quarter mile above the gaging station. Working with pack animals is the only possible way to do this job. However the animals are used only to move our camp—all surveying must be done on foot. We have averaged about 10 miles a day. Most of the walking is done with wet feet. In fact we are wet to the knees almost constantly. This has caused some of the boys to have blistered feet, plus the fact that having water and sand in our

15.1. Lobo Arch, Coyote Gulch, Escalante River drainage, 1957. Photograph by Robert H. Lister. Archaeology Center Collection, 41KA00-75. Courtesy of Special Collections, Marriott Library, University of Utah.

shoes makes walking very uncomfortable. But all members of the party are in good shape and a weekend of rest will find us ready to go next Monday. . . . We have found the town to supply our needs quite well, as well as being a friendly place.[38]

Ten days later Lister reported: "Five camps were made during the nine days we were on the [Escalante] river, one at Soda Gulch, a second at Willow Creek, third at Peters Creek, four at the mouth of Coyote Gulch, and last in Coyote Gulch. . . . One day the river rose to such a stage

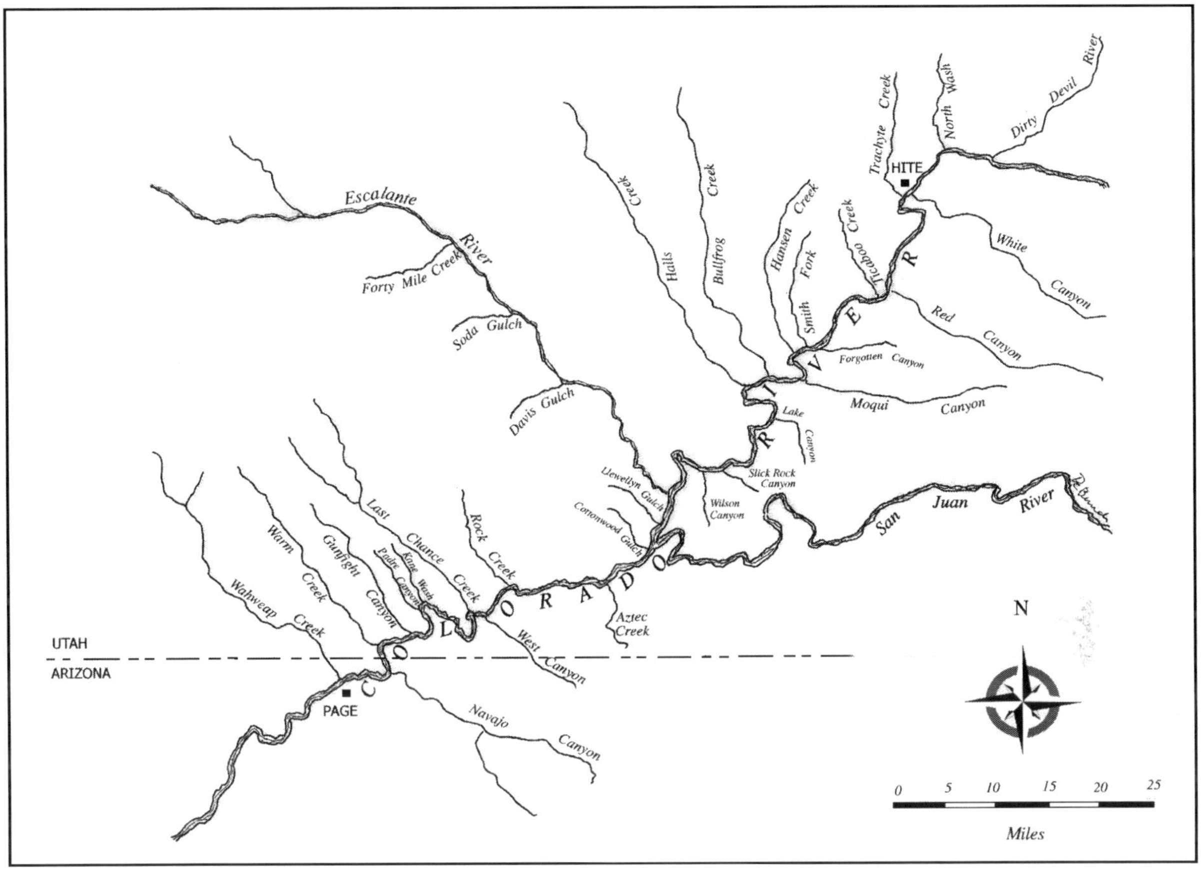

MAP 3. Glen Canyon and major tributary canyons surveyed during Glen Canyon Project. Map by Patricia DeBunch.

that operations were slowed, but using horses to 'ferry' us across the waters we kept going."[39] On July 28, 1957, he wrote,

> Loyd Gates has proven to be a very satisfactory wrangler. He helps in a great many ways, including baking excellent bread in the bread [Dutch] oven. . . . We camped at Soda Spring, and worked Llewellyn Gulch [in one day]. [Then two days in Cottonwood Gulch] . . . We packed our bedrolls and some grub into the canyon and stayed there overnight. Friday and Saturday we worked Davis Gulch from Moqui Window to Nemo Arch, again spending a night away from our base camp. . . . Of interest in Cottonwood [Gulch] was the finding of someone's camping gear which appeared to have been purposely hidden. Included were tin and aluminum pots, pans, plates and cups, a canteen and a knife, several empty tin cans, several jars and a tube of medicine, and a package of razor blades. Could this have been the last camp of Everett Ruess? We have turned the material and story over to the county sheriff.[40]

The mystery of Ruess's disappearance is discussed in chapter 10. The finds did not, apparently, help solve the mystery at the time.

At the end of July, Lister, his crew, Edson Alvey, Loyd Gates, and Jesse Jennings and his sons, Herbert and David, made a pack trip onto the Kaiparowits Plateau: "We jeeped approximately 40 miles south of [Escalante] to Willow Tank, turned west off the desert road and drove up onto the

Kaiparowits bench at the foot of the Middle Trail. There our gear was transferred to pack animals and we walked to the top of the plateau, making camp at Mud Hole Springs, approximately 2 miles west of the point where the trail tops out. . . ."[41]

Lister's next report presented a summary of surveys of Wahweap, Cottonwood, Gunsight, Navajo, the Big Bend of Colorado just above Wahweap mouth, and Warm Creek. There were very few sites, mainly chipping stations, places where hunters had made or resharpened hunting tools.

Lister had one more task to complete his summer assignment. With wrangler Lindsey Wilson, he and one of his crew made a five-day horseback trip up the Middle Trail to the top of the Kaiparowits,

> [then] southwest across the plateau passing the area known as the Lake, and down into Rock Creek. The three forks of Rock Creek, the terrace above the Colorado River between Rock and Last Chance creeks, and the lower end of Last Chance were surveyed by horseback. . . . [then rode back up over the plateau and down Middle Trail] I estimate we rode 130 miles during the five-day trip. Only casualty during the trip was the loss of one canteen which fell from a saddle while a horse was being led over a steep section of the trail and rolled several hundred feet into steep canyon below.[42]

Finally, in describing the climate of the country, Lister caught its essence: Daily temperature "ranges of 50°F. are not unusual. . . . Fortunately, the high temperatures and great daily range are accompanied by dry air. In the sun the heat of summer is intense; but in the shade of a rock or a tree coolness prevails. The line between scorching heat and fairly cool temperature is drawn at the edge of the shadow."[43]

Normally there is a hiatus of many months, sometimes years, between the completion of archaeological fieldwork and publication of a final report, for some reason especially in the Southwest. Professor Jennings knew this syndrome well and would have none of it; neither would Professor Lister. It was written into the contract between the National Park Service and the University of Utah that a report, acceptable to the Park Service, would be in agency hands before the next field season. Robert Lister's report of his work from June to September 1957 was not only accepted but published in March 1958, thus setting a standard that all subsequent crew chiefs and authors had to meet—and most did. The prompt publication also told the federal agencies and Congress that the University of Utah was serious about the work and would meet all contract-stipulated schedules before the completion of Glen Canyon Dam in 1963.

Lister's report, like those to follow, was basically descriptive: Here is the country, here are the sites within it, here are the time-marker and culture-marker artifacts found thereon. It was clear that the sites in the Escalante drainage were a mixed bag—some Kayenta Ancestral Puebloan and some Fremont artifacts were found, not only in the surface surveys but in the excavations conducted in 1957 and again in 1961 (see below).

In December 1957 Jennings wrote a brief note to *Teocentli*, an archaeological newsletter sent out biannually beginning in 1922, in which American archaeologists report what was currently going on in their field and laboratory work. (The newsletter, now an annual, has persisted into the twenty-first century.)

> Major activity, which consisted mostly of chasing paper and seeing people, was the initiation of a contract with the National Park Service for the study of archaeological, historical and ecological values in a part of the Glen Canyon reservoir area. In the 1957 season, Robert Lister participated as did Jim Gunnerson and I. The first season . . . has ended. We have some interesting and we think important information

> and will begin on laboratory analysis of this material about the first of November. . . . I have had pleasant visits with Charlie Steen, John Corbett, [Jean Carl] Pinky Harrington, Ned Danson . . . in conjunction with this Glen Canyon project. I am still looking for men with sufficient experience to run small excavation units entirely on their own resources. The Glen Canyon Country is so remote, so difficult and in some ways so dangerous, that the party leaders need about as much experience in survival training as in archaeology.[44]

C. Gregory Crampton's Historical Surveys in Glen Canyon

The Glen Canyon Project was unique among salvage archaeology projects because of the attention paid to historic archaeological sites and objects. It was perhaps serendipitous that C. Gregory Crampton was a faculty member at the University of Utah, along with Jesse Jennings.

Charles Gregory Crampton (1911–95) was born in Kankakee, Illinois, to parents who were both osteopathic physicians.[45] The family had a deep interest in plants and agriculture, which led them to move in 1922 to a small farming community, Delhi (pronounced "Del High" for the Delta Highline Canal), in the Central Valley of California. But the farm was not very good, and during the Depression the family opened a small roadside stand along Highway 99 to sell produce and Indian and Mexican handicrafts. The handicrafts business began to do so well that soon there was a Crampton Trading Post. Young Greg traveled all across the West with his father buying handicrafts and artifacts to sell at the stand.

Crampton attended Modesto Junior College from 1929 to 1931, then worked at odd jobs for two years. In 1933 he entered the University of California, Berkeley. Deeply interested in western history, he studied with the great historian Herbert Eugene Bolton (1870–1953), who was head of the history department and director of the Bancroft Library. Bolton is a legendary figure in the field of American history. He and his students invented Borderlands Studies—the shifting boundaries in North America between the Spanish (and later Mexican) Empire, and the French, British, and finally the Yanqui (American) territories. During his time at Berkeley, Bolton supervised 350 master's students and 104 doctoral students, including Crampton.[45]

Bolton was a firm believer in "ground truthing" the history he winnowed out of documents. He traced the life and work of the great seventeenth-century Jesuit explorer and missionary Father Eusebio Kino from his native Austria to Mexico and into the American Southwest, and Coronado's routes (1540–42) from Mexico to the Rio Grande, to Kansas, and return. Similarly, he retraced the 1776 route of Domínguez and Escalante from Santa Fe, through Utah, across Glen Canyon, and back to Zuni (chapter 2). Bolton trained his students to do as he did—literally follow the tracks of those you study and pay close attention to the landscapes and any and all material traces of their having been there—wherever "there" was. Most of his students gained further appreciation for landscapes and material culture through courses from the geographer Carl Sauer and the anthropologist A. L. Kroeber, who were Bolton's colleagues at Berkeley.

In 1941 Crampton drove Bolton from the south rim of the Grand Canyon up through Kayenta and Monument Valley to Mexican Hat, Utah. Bolton had contracted with river runner Norman Nevills for a float trip from Mexican Hat down the San Juan River and lower Glen Canyon so Bolton could see where Domínguez and Escalante had crossed the Colorado. Crampton did not go on the river trip, but he was entranced by the canyon country and remained so for the rest of his life.

After receiving his doctorate in 1941, Crampton traveled and studied in Latin America for a year under a Rockefeller Foundation fellowship.

15.2. Frank Wright (*left*) and C. Gregory Crampton in Glen Canyon, 1959. Photograph by Christy Turner, P.GCP.39.24. Courtesy of the Museum of Northern Arizona.

In 1942 he went to work for the FBI, working on surveillance projects relating to Latin America. In 1944 he transferred to the Army Quartermaster Corps in Oakland, California. In 1945 he was hired as an assistant professor at the University of Utah. Promoted to full professor in 1955, he remained at the university until he retired in 1978.

As a student of North American history in the 1930s, Crampton was aware of the historic archaeology excavations (1936–41) then ongoing at the site of Jamestown in Virginia and the search for Walter Raleigh's "Lost Colony" on Roanoke Island, North Carolina, led by Jean Carl Harrington (1902–98). Historic archaeology—that is, the archaeology of places, landscapes, and artifacts from the European period in North America, after 1492—had its beginnings with the restoration of Colonial Williamsburg in Virginia, starting in the 1920s, but especially with Harrington's work at Jamestown and Roanoke.[46]

In 1949 Crampton was able to go on a float trip through Glen Canyon aboard a World War II rubber raft—a baloney boat. He loved the scenery but was also fascinated by the material remains of the gold rushes in the canyon—the waterwheel at Olympia Bar, the caterpillar tractor on Gretchen Bar, the remains of the Stanton dredge, and all the rest of it. He managed a second trip in 1950 and began to record the historic sites and artifacts in the canyon—that is, to do historic archaeology. Between 1950 and 1955 Crampton was able to make several overland trips into the Glen Canyon Country and the area around it. Like many before and after him, he fell in love with it.

When the Glen Canyon Project got underway, Jennings was able to persuade the Park Service to include some funds to support Crampton's archival and field studies. He produced a series of highly valuable monographs on the history and historic archaeology of both Glen Canyon and San Juan Canyon, and summarized much of it in his masterful *Ghosts of Glen Canyon.* He also produced major works on Robert Brewster Stanton (chapter 9).[48]

The senior scholar in the University of Utah history department in the 1950s was Leland H. Creer (1895–1968), who also had been trained at the University of California by Herbert E. Bolton. In 1935 he was president of what was then Weber Junior College in Ogden, then moved in 1937 to the history department at the University of Utah, where he remained until his death. He was a major twentieth-century figure in Utah historical research and writing, especially his *The Founding of an Empire*. For the Glen Canyon Project, Creer produced two quicky and minimally useful monographs, one on Jacob Hamblin and the second a survey of Mormon towns in the region of the Colorado.[48]

THE ECOLOGY SURVEYS

Jennings managed to get an ecological survey of Glen Canyon included in the project budget, and in later contracts for Flaming Gorge, Navajo Reservoir, and the Curecanti Reservoir on the Gunnison River. The titular leader for these projects was Angus M. Woodbury (1886–1964), a renowned biologist and ecologist who had joined the University of Utah biology department in 1931. Woodbury was born in southern Utah, the son of Mormon pioneers who had come to Utah in 1847. From 1908 to 1920 he worked for the U.S. Forest Service. He then started college, earning a bachelor's degree at Brigham Young University in 1927 and a doctorate from the University of California in 1931. During the summers of 1925–27 he worked in Zion National Park, pioneering interpretative ecological programs and writing a history of southern Utah. Woodbury was a early leader in the ecological approach in biology, ultimately publishing a textbook widely used in college courses.[50]

While Woodbury was the senior scholar for the reservoir studies, the field supervisor was Stephen Durrant, assisted by Seville Flowers. Stephen David Durrant (1902–75) was born in Salt Lake City. He attended LDS High School and Weber Academy, graduating in 1921.[51] He served as a Mormon missionary in French-speaking Switzerland in 1922–25, then traveled for a few months in Europe, Turkey, Egypt, Palestine, and Syria. He received a B.A. in 1929 and an M.A. in 1931 from the University of Utah. He was an assistant professor at Utah from 1932 to 1941. In 1938–39 he was a doctoral student at the University of California, Berkeley, with E. Raymond Hall (1902–86), universally regarded as the dean of North American mammalian taxonomy and biogeography. Durrant helped Hall collect mammals in Nevada in 1939 and vowed that he, Durrant, would produce a work comparable to Hall's *Mammals of Nevada* (1946), which, according to biologists, set the standard for state faunal surveys. Durrant had planned to complete his doctorate at Berkeley, but Hall moved to Kansas in 1944. Hence, Durrant finally got his doctorate at Kansas in 1950, after spending a semester there in the spring of 1945. His *Mammals of Utah* was published in 1952, and it is, indeed, comparable in scope to his mentor's work on Nevada.[52]

Durrant was universally regarded by his colleagues as an excellent scholar, but more importantly by many as a great raconteur, and by generations of awed students as a superb teacher. Many recall his class on "Man" in the old biology building at the University of Utah. The classroom had exposed water pipes hanging below the ceiling. Durrant demonstrated primate behavior by brachiating around the room on the pipes, which in later years, given his girth, was an amazing sight to behold. Durrant was famous for his field trips at the conclusion of his course on mammalogy. Different areas of Utah were visited each term. Students and other faculty often went along, with spouses if they had such. Sometimes as many as thirty-five or more people were in the party. A large truck was rented, and a cook employed. There were campfire song fests and yarn spinning, most often by Durrant.

Another member of the survey team was Seville Flowers (1900–1968), a professor of botany with a specialty in bryophytes (mosses and related plants). He was the opposite of Durrant in personality but obviously an excellent scientist. Legend at Utah had it that he kept his precious type specimens in plastic bags in wastebaskets in his office. This filing system was well known to—and carefully avoided by—the janitors in the biology building. But one night a substitute janitor efficiently emptied the wastebaskets. The next day, a frantic tracking of the university garbage to where it had been dumped in the Salt Lake municipal landfill recovered the precious specimens. Flowers died in 1968, leaving his magnum opus on western mosses unpublished. It was, however, seen through to publication in 1973 and is still regarded as a classic, notable for its beautiful and accurate illustrations drawn by Flowers himself.[53]

When he became field director of the Glen Canyon ecological survey, Durrant simply took his end-of-the-semester traveling road show onto the river and extended the time to most of the summer. Two large baloney boats carried a crew of eighteen. The party moved downstream from Red Canyon, stopping at side canyons to survey and collect plants and critters. In July 1958 we encountered Durrant and his team just below Music Temple and spent some time visiting their camp. I still recall hearing Durrant sing the "Amphioxis" song on a beach in Glen Canyon. The song is known to generations of biologists in several variants, but the chorus of the version I learned from Durrant (sung to the World War I tune "It's a Long Way to Tipperary") is as follows:

> It's a long way from Amphioxis; it's a long way to us
> It's long way from Amphioxis to the meanest human cuss
> So goodbye to fins and gill slits, hello nails and hair
> It's a long, long way from Amphioxis,
> But by Gawd we're there.[54]

Recent versions are more politically correct, the last line being, "But we all came from there." Durrant would not have approved. Woodbury, Durrant, and Flowers published five monographs on the ecology of Glen Canyon in the University of Utah Anthropological Papers. The first appeared in 1958, as did Lister's archaeology survey report and Creer's two papers on aspects of Glen Canyon history. Collectively, they provided firm evidence of the Glen Canyon Project's commitment to scholarship and timely publication.[55]

› 16 ‹

IMPLEMENTING THE GLEN CANYON PROJECT

BY EARLY 1958 IT WAS CLEAR THAT SUFFICIENT funds would be available to implement the Glen Canyon Project as Jennings had envisioned it. In April he made a river trip (fig. 16.1) with key federal personnel to look at Glen Canyon proper and figure out what sort of boats the inexperienced crews could use. Accompanying Jennings were Frank Wright, river runner extraordinaire (chapters 11 and 14) and his son Otis; Lloyd Pierson, chief ranger at Natural Bridges National Monument; Benny Bullard and Urban Rogers, National Park Service recreation planners from Santa Fe; Stan Rasmussen, Bureau of Reclamation photographer; geologist Maurice (Spade) Cooley, nicknamed after a popular country western singer of the day; and Norris Bradbury, director of the Los Alamos National Laboratory and an active member of the New Mexico Archaeological Society.

According to Pierson,

> Bradbury's contribution to the scientific side of the trip was to figure out how much bourbon whiskey to allocate each of the drinking members each happy hour based on what had been brought and the number of days to be spent on the trip. This was a problem worthy of a trained atomic physicist, which Dr. Bradbury was, as the size of the bottles and the amount of contents was highly variable. He apparently did a good job as I heard no complaints from those involved and the booze lasted the entire trip.[1]

As to the boats, Jennings decided that something similar to Frank Wright's "San Juan boats" would work. San Juan boats had blunt sterns, both bow and stern curved upward, and watertight compartments, both to keep things dry and to provide buoyancy if they flipped in the rapids. Fortunately for novice river runner/archaeologists, Glen Canyon offered few rapids likely to flip a boat, although sand waves could be a problem. Jennings consulted with a boat purveyor in Salt Lake City and acquired two square-prowed, flat-bottomed,

16.1. Jesse D. Jennings in Glen Canyon, April 1958. Photograph by and courtesy of Lloyd Pierson.

but curved upward at the bow, aluminum boats with enclosed seats for buoyancy.

The boats were part of a line of watercraft called Arkansas Travelers, built by the Southwest Manufacturing Company of Little Rock. The "Arkansas Traveler" name derived from the folk legend/fiddle tune/song/stage performance story that apparently began in 1840 and ultimately came to mean many things within and far beyond the state of Arkansas.[2] From the front the boats looked like the scows that the characters in *Pogo* polled across the pages of the famed cartoon strips drawn by Walt Kelly in the 1950s and 1960s. Both boats had splash guards installed on the prows (fig. 16.2). The "Little Boat" had one outboard engine at the rear. The "Big Boat" had dual outboards and a steering wheel and throttle at the front. They did yeoman service for four seasons, or parts of seasons, that crews were on the river.

THE 1958 FIELD SEASON

As Jennings continued to plan the university's part of the Glen Canyon Project, he made a basic decision that wherever possible the fieldwork would be done by students, either those at Utah or recruited from elsewhere. None of us who were hired had much, if any, survival training, but we did "cope" (see below). That meant, of course, that the field seasons were tied to the academic year. The Museum of Northern Arizona, employing full-time staff, was able to keep its crews in the field for much longer periods each year.

For 1958, Jennings planned to have five teams in the field. After completing excavations at the Coombs site at Boulder, Utah (see below), Robert Lister led a survey party east of the Waterpocket Fold. A second, "roving" team, led by James Nichols, scouted the headwaters of the right-bank drainages above the pool level, the Escalante

16.2. Keith Anderson (*left*) and Don Fowler with the University of Utah boats in Glen Canyon, 1958. Photograph by William Lipe. Archaeology Center Collection, 42KA00-199. Courtesy of Special Collections, Marriott Library, University of Utah.

Desert, Grand Bench, the Circle Cliffs area, and the flanks of the Henry Mountains. Thomas Matthews led a party into the San Juan Triangle; James Gunnerson led a team onto the Kaiparowits Plateau. The Lister, Nichols, and Matthews teams were equipped with jeeps with power winches; two of them could be mounted with dual wheels front and rear. The fifth party, a combined survey and testing team, was in Glen Canyon proper, working from the confluence of the San Juan and Colorado rivers downstream to Lee's Ferry.[3]

THE LISTER PARTY

In the first part of the 1958 season, Robert Lister supervised an archaeological field school at the Coombs site in Boulder, Utah, as he also did in 1959. The site, on land owned by Ephraim Coombs, was well known. In 1927 William Claflin and Raymond Emerson had been taken there by Dave Rust to see what was then called the Boulder Mound (chapters 11, 13). In 1928 Noel Morss recorded the site and made a small test excavation as part of his survey of the region's Fremont sites. He noted that the sherds he collected from the surface were all related to the Kayenta Anasazi culture south of the Colorado River, and that the ceramics and visible architectural features were different from the Fremont sites to the north along the Fremont River.[4] The site was larger than anything recorded the previous year by Glen Canyon Project personnel. That, coupled with ceramics perhaps indicating some sort of Kayenta "outpost" north of the Colorado River, made it of much interest.

Since the site lay well outside the areas covered by the Park Service salvage contract with Utah, other means were needed to support the excavations. Jennings was acquainted with William Purdy, a history teacher at St. Marks School for Boys in Salt Lake City who had a special interest in archaeology. Purdy recruited seven of his students for a two-week field school at the site led by Jennings and Jim Gunnerson and assisted by Bill Lipe (see below). Robert and Florence Lister, assisted by graduate student Richard Ambler, arrived in mid-June with twelve students from the University of Colorado field school for an additional month of excavations. One of the 1958 students, Mary Mulroy, from Barnard College, later became a graduate student at Utah and joined the laboratory staff of the Glen Canyon Project. Lister directed a second Colorado field school at the site in 1959 and uncovered additional structures. The ceramics continued to indicate a primary occupation related to the Kayenta Anasazi in the late 1100s (chapter 20).

By early 1959, Jennings and Lister had begun discussing the idea of the Coombs site becoming a state park. Jennings brought the key people together to further this idea, as he wrote to Lister in May:

> Dear Bob: Yesterday we moved a little further toward our goal. I brought, after three abortive attempts, Director of State Parks, Chet Olsen and Eph Coombs together in Boulder. They dickered and talked for several hours. As a result, Eph Coombs . . . will donate the Coombs site to the State. Olsen, on the other hand if Coombs goes through with his donation, is committed to the purchase of the adjacent acreage sufficient to make up the first State archaeological monument. . . . The progress Olsen and Coombs made in their talks yesterday is, I presume, confidential. Certainly any great discussion of it before the deed of gift is made over to the state might jeopardize the whole thing. No matter how much Olsen and Coombs discuss it, it seems to me that you and I ought to be fairly vague about the whole thing.[5]

The site and adjacent lands were ultimately acquired by Utah State Parks. Park archaeologists conducted additional excavations between 1970 and 1991. The Listers, and later the State Parks division, excavated ninety-seven rooms, perhaps half of those contained in the site. Tree-ring dates indicate a primary occupation between 1129 and 1169 CE; the site may have been burned and abandoned by about 1175 CE. State Parks stabilized sections of aboveground masonry structures and pit houses, and constructed a visitors center, including a six-room replica of the aboveground rooms. The complex is now called the Anasazi State Park Museum.[6] The place of the Coombs site in the Ancestral Puebloan history of the Glen Canyon Country is discussed in chapter 20.

Lister closed the 1958 field school at the Coombs site on July 10, and by July 18 he was in Escalante with a survey team to continue working on the right-bank tributaries. His team included J. Richard Ambler, a Colorado University graduate student; William Buckles, Wilfred Husted, and Richard Ross, Colorado undergraduates; and Norman Ritchie, a Utah undergraduate loaned to Lister from Jim Gunnerson's Kaiparowits crew. The assignment was to survey the portions of the canyons that would be inundated by the lake east of the Waterpocket Fold—Hall's Creek, Bullfrog Creek, Hansen Creek, Smith Fork, Ticaboo Creek, Trachyte Creek, North Wash, and the Dirty Devil River. Lister's weekly reports are filled with instructions of roads to follow and where water resources could be found. The archaeology was minimal, in some cases nonexistent, in the lower reaches of the canyons as they deeply entrenched toward the river. In lower Ticaboo no sites were noted except the remains of Cass Hite's homestead.

Lister did note that the 54-mile corridor of Hall's Creek headed at a low divide between the drainage of the Fremont River—and offered a major route to and from the Fremont area and the Colorado River. He thought that intermittent water sources along Hall's Creek and the numerous tanks—the "water pockets" which prompted Powell's men to give the Waterpocket Fold its name—would aid those traveling along the corridor.[7]

THE NICHOLS PARTY

The roving party led by James Nichols, a graduate student at UCLA, was to make reconnaissance surveys in the heads of right-bank drainages west of the Kaiparowits Plateau, especially Wahweap and Last Chance, then along the Rees Canyon–Collett Wash road that crossed the upper end of the Kaiparowits Plateau, and to look at areas on Grand Bench and in the Escalante Desert, as well as areas in the Circle Cliffs, the Henry Basin, and the upper North Wash and Dirty Devil River. The survey was designed to be a sampling exercise, sometimes called a "gumshoe survey"; that is, go into assigned areas, pick likely site locales, and investigate them. It was hoped that this approach would turn up sites related to Southern Paiute and Ute peoples, known to have been in those areas when the first Euro-Americans arrived in the 1770s. It did not. That led to a different approach, carried out in 1961–62 by Catherine Sweeney (see chapter 18).

Nichols worked out of Escalante, Utah and had just one crew member with him. For the first part of the season it was John Price, a Utah student; later it was Richard Ross, a student of Lister's who worked on the Coombs site the first part of the season. Nichols followed out jeep roads, sometimes trails rather than roads, and managed to record 174 sites, most of them lithic scatters or campsites.[8] His weekly reports reflect the wide-ranging nature of his assignment, the sites he recorded—and problems with his jeep. It had been equipped with dual wheels, front and back, since Jennings thought they would give maximum traction in sandy situations. However, Nichols reported that

> [w]ith eight wheels on the jeep and a full seven day load [of supplies], the jeep was not only difficult to handle but a large power loss was noted. Dual front tires threw so much dust that passengers and equipment were literally covered with 1/8" coat of dust. To remedy power loss and the dust problem, I am having the front duals removed and am reducing equipment load by utilizing "C" rations and cutting the water supply by one half. . . .
>
> [Later, Nichols reported] the jeep in general is feeling the strain of the rough roads . . . and is suffering from a bad case of loose nuts and bolts.[9]

THE SAN JUAN TRIANGLE SURVEY

A second extensive roving survey was conducted from April through early October 1958 in the area known as the San Juan Triangle—the apex of the triangle being the confluence of the San Juan and Colorado rivers, the southern boundary being the San Juan River itself, the northeast-southwest boundary the Colorado River from the confluence to Hite, and the eastern boundary Comb Ridge (map 1). The survey was led by Thomas (Tommy) Mathews, a well-known archaeologist who had worked in the Southwest for several years.

From April 15 to June 1, 1958, Mathews and Downey Raibourne, who had been with Jim Gunnerson in 1957, worked out of Natural Bridges National Monument. Bates Wilson, then superintendent of the monument, and a dedicated public servant rather than a bureaucrat, provided them with a "shack" in which to store equipment and the use of the campgrounds as needed. The two did some surveying but primarily scouted all across the area—some 1,700 square miles—locating roads and springs for possible campsites, and talking with locals about the country and the archaeology therein. They also participated in a pack horse trip through the upper section of Grand Gulch. One member of the party was Chet Olsen, of Utah State Parks, who was investigating possible areas for "archaeological monuments" (see above).

In mid-June, Mathews returned to the field with three University of Utah students, one of whom, Dirk van der Elst, went on to earn a doctorate in anthropology and taught for many years at Fresno State University in California. Another student, from the University of Chicago, Sterling Robbins, was 6′4″ and looked much like Clint Walker of the famed "Cheyenne Bodie" television series of the 1950s. Sterling also played a mean western guitar, which, as I recall, the original Clint did not. Later in the season Mathews added some local men to the crew to increase areal coverage. Most of the survey was in the canyons and adjacent uplands of the two major physiographic features of the Triangle, the Red Rock Plateau and the Grand Gulch Plateau. Since the lake would back up into the San Juan River canyon, the lower reaches of side canyons that drain into the San Juan from the north were thoroughly surveyed from Grand Gulch on downstream.

The second foci were the upper reaches of canyons draining across the Red Rock Plateau into the Colorado River. The lower reaches were surveyed from the river up to the pool level of the lake (see below). The portions of canyons that would be submerged by the lake were intensively surveyed. For example, Mathews and Raibourne hiked the lower 18 miles of Grand Gulch in four days—two days in, two days out. Upland areas were sampled at 5-mile intervals, working from roads crossing those areas.

For a few days in mid-September the Mathews party linked up with the river crew to gain access to the lower reaches of Knowles and Cedar canyons (see below). Overall, Mathews recorded nearly 200 sites, ranging from small lithic scatters to architectural sites in rockshelters and alcoves. They ranged in age from Basketmaker III to Pueblo III and were principally affiliated with the Mesa Verde culture to the east.[10]

THE KAIPAROWITS SURVEY

Earlier we saw that the young Clyde Kluckhohn had surveyed a southern portion of the Kaiparowits Plateau in 1928, as had Donald Scott from Harvard's Peabody Museum. Jennings had made a very brief reconnaissance in 1957. It was clear that there were many archaeological sites on the plateau. Jim Gunnerson's 1958 assignment was to survey the top of the plateau from the Upper Trail southward to the end of the plateau. He had a crew of four students: Peter Cousins, Herbert Alexander, Norman Ritchie (fig. 16.3), and C. Melvin Aikens. Loyd Gates, who had been with Gunnerson in the fall of 1957, provided the pack animals and hired Millard Davis as wrangler. The pack animals were generally okay, with one exception, as Gunnerson reported from Escalante: "One of the horses is so old that we are afraid to use him and will take up a replacement. I don't think he could make it to the top again." Later Gunnerson wrote, "A small mule was substituted for the old horse. He has worked fairly well but has tended to buck with packs and will not stay near camp or with the other animals at night."[11] The crew named this creature "Rat" for his size and appearance.

Gunnerson and crew made a systematic survey of well over 12 square miles of the plateau top—no mean feat given the dissected terrain. They recorded some 253 sites, concentrated primarily on knolls and in rockshelters along the east rim. But "material is to be found all over the plateau. There is probably not a spot that is more than fifty feet from a sherd, chip, or projectile point."[12] Two rockshelter sites and three open masonry sites had Rainbow Bridge–Monument Valley Expedition site numbers painted on them. The expedition had sent a party on to the southern end of the Plateau in 1937.[13]

16.3. Herbert Alexander, "Manure," and Norman Ritchie on the Kaiparowits Plateau, 1958. Photograph by C. Melvin Aikens. Archaeology Center Collection, 42KA00-236. Courtesy of Special Collections, Marriott Library, University of Utah.

Gunnerson and his team made a 1 inch to 1,000 foot plane table map of the portions of the plateau they surveyed—a major accomplishment, given the terrain and the area they covered (fig. 16.4).[14] The archaeology of the plateau is discussed further in chapter 18.

After the 1958 season Jim Gunnerson returned to his regular duties as Utah state archaeologist, but then resigned the following year to return to Harvard and finish his dissertation.[15] He taught at Northern Illinois University for several years as a professor of anthropology and later moved to Lincoln, Nebraska, where he was director of the University of Nebraska State Museum from 1974 to 1980, when he retired. He continued as an active scholar until his death at age eighty-six in January 2009. C. Melvin Aikens went on to earn a doctorate in anthropology from the University of Chicago and had along and distinguished career as an archaeologist and museum administrator at the University of Oregon. He is an expert in the archaeology of the American West and of Japan.

16.4. C. Melvin Aikens mapping on the Kaiparowits Plateau, 1958. Photograph by Peter Cousins. Courtesy of C. Melvin Aikens.

Norman Ritchie went on to a career in the National Park Service before retiring to private business.

THE RIVER TEAM

Previous surveys by Julian Steward in the early 1930s (chapter 13) and reports of sites recorded in the early 1950s for the Museum of Arizona (chapter 19) made it clear that there were archaeological sites in the main stem of Glen Canyon and the lower reaches of its tributary canyons. Those surveys were sporadic and cursory. The contract between the Park Service and Utah called for a systematic survey of all tributary canyons at least to the projected lake level. Utah was responsible for both banks of the river above the San Juan–Colorado confluence and the right bank downstream therefrom. During his May scouting trip Jennings had determined that it was possible to move both upstream and downstream in motorboats, and that students, who would be very novice river runners, could (hopefully) run the boats and get the archaeology done as well.

The river crew was placed in charge of Bill Lipe, then a graduate student at the University of Oklahoma, who already had some experience in southwestern archaeology. The rest of the crew were Joe Jorgensen, Lynn Robbins, Keith Anderson, Peter Bodenheimer, Wayne Coon, and me. Peter was a physics major at Harvard; Coon was an anthropology graduate student at the University of Colorado; the rest of us were anthropology students at Utah (fig. 16.5).

On June 10 the crew and Jennings arrived after dark at Kane Creek Landing just upstream from the famed Crossing of the Fathers. We tossed our sleeping bags out on the slickrock and turned in. Early the next morning we arose to find Jennings assembling breakfast. We unloaded the boats from the truck and put them in the water. About that time Dick Grimm, from Wahweap Lodge, appeared from his camp downstream with a large motorboat. We packed all our food, gasoline, camping gear, excavation equipment, and personal gear into the three boats. When we were ready, Jennings called us together and said that we were going to go *upstream* about 20 river miles to the confluence of the San Juan and the Colorado. We were to follow Grimm's boat closely, keep our eyes open, and learn something about running the rapids and avoiding sandbars as we proceeded upstream. This was apparently Lesson One of our survival training.

As we headed to the boats, Jennings turned to me and said, "Get into the small boat and follow us." All my lifelong avoidance of the outdoors, and of water deeper than a bathtub, suddenly came to a crisis point. "But," said I, "I've never run a motor boat before—and I don't know how to swim!" Amidst some unprintable but colorful phrases, Jennings said, "Put your [bleeping] life jacket on, and watch." I did so, and he showed me how to start the motor and steer with it. My compatriots looked on slightly bemused; they were to ride in the other boats, and they could all swim. But since we were all total novices in river running, there was not too much jocularity at my expense, at least within my hearing.

As we started upstream, my gaze turned to the spectacular canyon walls, buttes, and mesas. Fairly soon I was gaping at the river, the water birds, and

16.5. University of Utah river crew, 1958: (*left to right*) William D. Lipe, Don D. Fowler, Joseph G. Jorgensen, Peter Bodenheimer, David Dibble, Lynn Robbins. Photograph by Keith M. Anderson. Archaeology Center Collection, 42SA00-26. Courtesy of Special Collections, Marriott Library, University of Utah.

the cliffs and not following the other boats closely enough—and had the first of many encounters with sandbars. Seemingly some few years, but in fact only a few hours, later we arrived at a large slickrock shelf on right bank of the river just upstream from Hidden Passage.

Across and downstream was Music Temple; across and upstream was the confluence of the San Juan River. Hidden Passage was just downstream below our camp. The end of the Kaiparowits Plateau loomed almost 4,000 feet above us. We unloaded the gear, bade good-bye to Dick Grimm, who hightailed it back downstream, and set up camp on the slickrock. Jennings appointed Peter Bodenheimer as cook and proceeded to give him basic (very basic) lessons in the arts of camp cuisine. We finished our meal and blew up our air mattresses as we began what would be an unending, summer-long, and losing battle with voracious mosquitos and no-see-ums.

The next morning we climbed into a high alcove above the camp to test an archaeological site therein—our first excavation in Glen Canyon proper. Coon professed some ability to take pictures and was appointed photographer. Jennings had decided that all photography was to be done in both black-and-white and color. He further decided that all excavation shots would be done with a 4 × 5–inch (negative size) Graflex "Press" Camera—the kind used by news photographers from the 1920s to the 1960s. They were heavy and cumbersome, but made great photographs. Color was shot with 35 mm cameras, and the survey teams (thankfully) used 35 mm cameras for both black-and-white and color. Cameras with built-in light meters were not generally available in 1958, so we all carried light meters. Much of the correspondence between the field parties and the lab in Salt Lake City every year had to do with camera and light meter problems: sand, sometimes water, and rough treatment are not conducive to the proper operation of such delicate equipment.

Jennings spent the day doing what he did best—teaching novices how to do dirt archaeology. After dinner he reiterated what he had told us in Salt Lake City—that Bill Lipe was the crew chief, in charge of excavations, logistics, data collection, and crew health and safety. My job was to assist with the excavations as needed, but primarily to survey for new archaeological sites on the gravel bars along the main stem and up the side canyons. I was to concentrate on the right bank since the Museum of Northern Arizona was to deal with all sites along the San Juan and on the left bank below the confluence of the San Juan. I did, however, hike one to several miles up a number of the left bank side canyons. Some of them, such as Dungeon Canyon, were among the most scenically spectacular in Glen Canyon, as was, of course, Bridge Canyon, containing the unforgettable Rainbow Bridge.

On the third day a party of river runners stopped to say hello and see what we were doing. Jennings hitched a ride with them downriver to Kane Creek. His parting instructions were, "Do all the archaeology between here and Lee's Ferry between now and September 15th; come into Kanab every two weeks to ship your specimens and data to the lab; I'll see you in Salt Lake in September." He boarded the boat, made a roll-your-own, and headed downstream with the river runners. He didn't say it at that point, but he had deeply impressed on us Maxim Number One for surviving in difficult country: "Only fools have adventures." Only much later did we learn from Mrs. Jennings that he returned to Salt Lake and bit his fingernails to the elbows until we telephoned from Kanab two weeks later to say we were there and all still alive. We had suffered only one slight case of dehydration and one case of poison ivy (which was luxuriantly rampant in some glens and canyon bottoms).

The first weeks were probably the most intense learning experience of any of our lives. We learned to get along with each other; we learned that mosquitos are insatiable and can penetrate any and all unguents, balms, sprays, or creams designed to thwart their sanguinary tastes. We fought unending and unsuccessful battles with no-see-um gnats. We became closely acquainted with the tribes of small kangaroo rats who came out at night to scamper over our sleeping bags and check us out. We began the long learning process of digging and recording to try to understand what the ancient folk were doing in Glen Canyon in centuries past.

But most immediately, we began to learn to run the river and to enjoy the wonder of the place. Powell and his men had found the relatively calm waters of Glen Canyon a welcome respite after the watery turmoil of Lodore and Cataract canyons and remembered them fondly as they tossed in the roiling rapids of Marble and Grand canyons. Later river runners were equally pleased by the placidity of the stream. With few exceptions, they all went only downstream, whereas we had to go both up- and downstream daily to do our work—downstream to Kane Creek, and back up to our camps. I, with one other person, was up and down the river every day.

The rapids were the least of our problems; there weren't very many, and they weren't very big, although negotiating them upstream took some doing, especially at low water. The major problems were the ever-moving sandbars, occasional sand waves (although they are more common on the San Juan, we did experience them a few times), and the upcanyon winds, which could whip up amazing whitecaps in short order. We would carefully note where the sandbars were in relation to shore landmarks as we headed either down- or upstream in the morning. By afternoon the bars were either gone or had cunningly moved clear across the river from where they were in the morning and were awaiting us as we came 'round the bend.

Outboard motors are equipped with shear pins—cotter keys which, in theory, break before the propeller does when it hits an obstacle. And most of the time they did. We became highly proficient at standing in water ankle to midcalf deep on a sandbar in the middle of the Colorado River, one holding the boat, the other changing the shear pin. We used them by the dozen. My vague recollection is that we also destroyed about a dozen propellers during the season—and we shattered at least one drive shaft.

Serendipitously, on our first trip to Kanab, and of dire necessity thereafter, we reached the Salt Lake–Kanab Freight Company office before 5 p.m. on a Friday, when its truck left for Salt Lake City. At least one, and sometimes two, of our wounded outboard motors had to be packed up and shipped. They were delivered at 9 a.m. the next morning to Salt Lake Marine Supply, repaired, and shipped back at 5 p.m. the same day, with a new supply of shear pins and propellers. We received them on Sunday morning, loaded them, gasoline, and food onto the trucks, and headed to Kane Creek and back upriver to camp.

Kanab was a busy oasis in the summer of 1958. Page, Arizona, was just being built, and the Glen Canyon bridge wasn't finished, so the Bureau of Reclamation and construction company headquarters for the dam were there. There was a motel, Aikens Lodge (still there in 2008), with a swimming pool containing clear (not red) water, and a nearby laundromat. The Trail's End Cafe, presided over by its congenial proprietor, Merle "Peaches" Beard, provided cuisine of seemingly unsurpassed excellence. Peaches, according to his own legend, was a drifter from Texas who had wandered into town during the Depression, met a nice Mormon girl, married her and settled down (at the end of his personal trail) to become a purveyor of good food. But before he reached his Nirvana in Kanab, he had been a cook at the fabled Marble Canyon Lodge near Lee's Ferry in the 1930s. Above the café door there was a neon sign replica of James Earl Fraser's famous "End of the Trail" statue (the Indian warrior and his horse, with drooped heads) first exhibited at the 1915 San Francisco World's Fair.

Peaches liked a taste or two of various distillations of wheat and corn, and he introduced us to the Buckskin Bar, strategically located about 50 yards across the Arizona state line a few miles from Kanab in that odd section of Arizona called The Strip—the area north of the Grand Canyon. Unlike Utah and its then-arcane liquor laws, requiring ownership of a permit that allowed one to purchase bottles of hootch that one then carried into bars and poured into purchased "setups," civilized Arizona allowed bars to simply sell individual drinks made to order.

There was a dance band (of sorts) at the Buckskin on Saturday nights, and we danced with and tried to romance the local lovelies—but to little avail.

Back in the canyon we soon turned to the excavation of Talus Ruin, a string of masonry rooms at the top of a talus slope behind which rose a south-facing cliff several hundred feet high. While we were there, the ecology survey crew came by; their thermometers registered the air temperature at noon at 123°F, and the ground temperature at about 140°F, or so they said.

Later we moved downriver to a long terrace with a deep narrow alcove at the base of the cliff.

There was a U.S. Coast and Geodetic Survey brass cap benchmark set 20 feet in front of the cave, and the elevation of "3262.2" feet was painted on the cave wall (chapter 12). The cave was at the base of the cliff and looked out onto a large, approximately 60-acre terrace covered with prickly pear and shrubs. The site became Benchmark Cave. I supervised some testing of the site, which proved to be deep and filled with organic remains, and contained various artifacts, including a small buckskin bag filled with cotton seeds. Some distance up nearby Dangling Rope Canyon was a wonderful spring, a great respite from the Halazone tablets we often used to settle and more or less purify the river water for drinking and cooking. Besides Benchmark Cave and Talus Ruin, we excavated or sampled several other sites.

In mid-August we traveled to the Pecos Conference, a summer gathering of southwestern anthropologists first instituted by A. V. Kidder in 1927 (chapter 13). We traveled from Kanab southward across the Navajo Bridge at the head of Marble Canyon and on to the Hopi mesas, stopping to gawk at Oraibi on Third Mesa, a Hopi village already long established when the occupants ran out Father Garcés in 1776 (chapter 2). We continued on to Gallup, New Mexico, to the Gallup Ceremonial, held annually as the town's answer to Santa Fe's Indian Market. There we met David and Barbara Breternitz and their two-year-old son, Corey. Dave was already a seasoned archaeologist who had worked briefly for the Museum of Northern Arizona's portion of the Glen Canyon Project (chapter 19) and would later run major projects at Mesa Verde and in the Dolores River area. (As an aside, in 2008, at the annual meeting of the Society for American Archaeology, Dr. Corey Breternitz became a member of the society's board of directors.)

The Pecos Conference was, and is, a "field conference." The tradition is that people come to an agreed-upon conference site, camp out, present field reports of what they've done during the summer, and indulge in serious partying. In 1958, however, the conference had been invited to the University of New Mexico campus in Albuquerque. Participants were quartered in a brand new, several-story dormitory—single men down one hallway, couples down a second, and women down a third on the fifth floor. There were two bath and shower rooms on the floor, but gender occupancy thereof was not clearly defined, leading to some occasional surprises.

The partying was, indeed, serious. The senior archaeologists of the day had all grown up during the Depression era. Many, indeed most, had been in World War II military service. Jesse Jennings had been a commander in the U.S. Navy. W. W. Taylor, a well-known and controversial figure, had been in the Marine Corps, attached to the OSS, and had been captured behind German lines. Robert Euler had been a major in the Marine Corps and was wounded at Iwo Jima. There were dozens more. All were hard drinkers; most everyone smoked either cigarettes or pipes. My first glimpse of Julian Hayden, then and later a legendary figure in southwestern archaeology, was of him and Erik Reed, the National Park Service archaeologist, walking down the dormitory hall to their room carrying a full case of Johnny Walker Black Label scotch to be consumed and shared as needed.

The first evening the entire conference was invited to a party at the house of a UNM student's parents. There were cases and tubs of beer, and two 10-gallon thermos jugs filled with Tom Collins that were refilled as they got low. We students gazed in awe at the famous names among whom we circulated—Clyde Kluckhohn and his wife, Florence; Fred Eggan, Richard and Nathalie Woodbury, Frank Hibben, Joe Ben and Pat Wheat, Raymond and Molly Thompson, Emil Haury, Bob and Florence Lister (who of course we already knew), Gordon Vivian, and others. Most of them and many more would become my friends and colleagues in years to come.

Somewhat later in the evening, the Albuquerque police broke up a song fest in the middle of Central Avenue at the entrance to the UNM campus. We had circled the Utah red jeeps and sat in the middle of the street to sing folks songs, accompanied by Sterling Robbins on guitar. Oddly, Jennings never said much about the song fest. He may, in fact, have been secretly pleased.

The next night a group including me, the Listers, and several others found ourselves on the rooftop deck of the UNM dormitory in possession of several bottles of bourbon and vodka. Tom Kane, then director of the Heard Museum in Phoenix, who tooled about in an elegant Jaguar cabriolet sedan, lay down on the deck parapet, opened his shirt, poured some vodka on his chest, and lit it aflame. We all cheered. At the end of the conference the UNM regents decreed that due to the condition of their dormitory, the Pecos Conference would never again be held on the UNM campus—and it never has been.

Somewhat subdued, we found our way back to Kanab, resupplied, and set out for the river to continue our work. For me, apart from the hangovers, the conference was a defining moment. Southwestern archaeologists are an egalitarian lot. Senior scholars, then as now, make a point of getting to know students and what they're doing. This is partly because by the time they get to be senior scholars, they're mainly doing paperwork and raising money, and the students are doing all the fun fieldwork. Many such eminences went out of their way to introduce themselves to me and others of our crew. Jennings and the Listers saw to it that we met still others. We did have a modicum of cachet—we were part of the Glen Canyon Project, and Lipe, our crew, and I were actually running up and down the Colorado River in pursuit of archaeology. Jennings, ever on the lookout to one-up his colleagues, had made sure that all the field crews (and some of the lab crew) were there—as we tooled into town in our bright red jeeps, each with a large white U painted on it.

Back on the river, by late August we had worked our way to Kane Creek. We loaded the trucks and started toward the head of Glen Canyon. Several hundred miles later, after a roundabout trip via Blanding, Utah, we were again alongside the river at the mouth of Red Canyon, camped next to Bert Loper's cabin (fig. 16.6). We began work on the archaeological site that John Wesley Powell had recorded in 1869, and did additional work there in 1959, naming it Loper Ruin. On September 10, Tom Mathews and his Triangle Survey crew arrived in our camp. We ferried them downstream to Olympia Bar so they could survey the lower portions of Knowles and Cedar canyons, thus completing their survey of that section of the Triangle. Three days later we retrieved them. By that time the river was quite low, and we had to cross Ticaboo rapids—a long, gravelly stretch. Mathews later wrote in his report, "After pulling the boats up through Ticaboo #1, I know now I don't want to be a pirate."[16]

After a crew photo opportunity on the last day (fig. 16.5), we packed up and headed for Salt Lake City, fall quarter classes, and lab work. We were now seasoned river-running novices—only river runners with years of experience ever became "veterans." We had more or less met Dr. Jennings's hopes; first, that we had survived in good health; second, that we could move both upstream and down in our boats to carry out the survey and testing program; third, that we could do so under the normal twelve- to sixteen-hour days that camping out, hiking, and working required; and fourth, we could do it for three months at a time.

Jennings had told me I was to remain in charge of the equipment—cleaning and stowing it for the next year. Now he told me that I was to write up the results of my survey. The other crews, and the field school, had been equally successful during the summer. The lab crew had become a highly organized and skilled unit. Our mandate to get artifact analyses and reports done and ready to go to press was taken very seriously. No putting off reports for

16.6. Bert Loper's cabin at the mouth of Red Canyon, 1958. Photograph by William Lipe. Archaeology Center Collection, 42Sa00-24. Courtesy of Special Collections, Marriott Library, University of Utah.

the future, as Neil Judd did with his Chaco Canyon reports; he finished his fieldwork in 1927, but the final reports didn't appear until 1954 and 1964.

Jennings would have none of that. Another of his maxims was "unpublished data don't exist," largely true in pre–copy machine days. As noted in the previous chapter, he had it written into the annual contract with the National Park Service that reports from the previous year's fieldwork had to be ready to go to press before the crews left for the next field season.

To facilitate this, he set up a production line laboratory at the university in Salt Lake City. Each time, at two- to three-week intervals, that the various field crews came into their supply point towns—variously, Kanab, Escalante, Blanding, or St. George—they shipped to Salt Lake all artifacts and their provenance sheets, field notes, exposed film, original maps, and detailed weekly reports. These were received in Building 405 at the university by a staff of artifact processors and catalogers. Artifacts were cleaned, labeled with provenance data, and temporarily stored in drawers in open racks. Black-and-white film was processed, and positives printed in-house. Color slides were sent out for processing.

At the end of each field season, when the crews arrived back at the university, all materials except what they'd brought with them from their last two- to three-week stint were already processed and catalogued and ready to be analyzed. Under Jennings's system, ideally the persons who had supervised the actual fieldwork also analyzed the materials and wrote the reports. But his system of note taking, artifact cataloguing, and data processing was so thorough that (in theory) any trained person could write a scientifically acceptable report. As the analysis began, so too did drafting of maps and drawings of artifacts, and selection of photographs for illustrations. As manuscripts were produced by the field folk, or their surrogates, they were edited. Edited manuscripts were then typed on "multilith" gelatin masters and sent to the University of Utah Press, across the street and down the block, for printing and binding. Both multilith masters and IBM Executive typewriters, cutting-edge word-processing technologies of the day, appeared just in time to be used by the Glen Canyon Project. Most, but not all, manuscripts were "in press" by the time the crews headed for the field the following summer.

"The Lab" was supervised for the first couple of years by Dee Ann Suhm (her later married and professional name is Dee Ann Story). Dee Ann had done extensive archaeological fieldwork in Texas and had just acquired a Ph.D. in anthropology at UCLA. Now she suddenly had a desk job. The editors, both highly proficient, were Carol J. Stout (Condie) and Norma Mikkelsen. Most of the people working in the lab were women.

Jennings and the MNA staff were very much products of their time: fieldwork, especially in "dangerous" places like the Glen Canyon Country, was for men. Women, being good at "housekeeping"-type chores such as washing and labeling artifacts, staffed the labs. On the Utah side of the project, Dee Ann and others of her staff were only allowed to go to the field for a couple of weeks after the regular field season was over. They were sent only to places to which jeeps and carryalls could be driven—not on the river or into areas requiring pack horse/mule-assisted logistics. And a couple of more or less trustworthy males were sent along to make sure the women "would be OK." The only woman who was sent to do fieldwork on her own on the Utah side of the Glen Canyon Project was Catherine Sweeney, but that's another story (chapter 18).

The production line system worked with few hitches or glitches. Artifacts and field notes got analyzed, and reports got written and sent to press. *The Glen Canyon Archaeological Survey*, in three volumes, totaling 803 pages, appeared in May 1959.[17] My part was 95 pages. I was a published author and had yet to graduate! Certainly, from then on, my fate was sealed. Meanwhile, most all of us—lab and field staff—were going to school, usually full-time. As in most other university research programs, we simply worked as required—usually sixty to seventy hours per week—with classes and research intermixed. The jobs got done, and classes got taken and hopefully passed. Partying took place whenever possible. We loved it.

In December 1958 the Park Service hosted a "summit meeting" in Santa Fe that involved key staff people from Utah, the Museum of Northern Arizona, and the Park Service. Jennings, Gunnerson, Lister, Lipe, Mathews, Nichols, and Suhm represented Utah. William Y. Adams, David Breternitz, Maurice Cooley, Alexander J. Lindsay Jr., and Christy G. Turner II represented MNA. Erik Reed and Charlie Steen represented the Park Service. The MNA contingent is further introduced in chapter 19. Alfred E. Dittert Jr. represented the Navajo Reservoir Salvage Project on the upper San Juan River, which was getting underway at the same time.

The meeting resulted in final agreement as to which entities would be responsible for which areas within the project area, as well as some common procedures and goals. It was also agreed that both Utah and MNA would do limited test excavations in selected areas above the pool level of the lake where sites might suffer from secondary impacts from the projected increase in visitors once the lake filled. It was also clear that to fully understand the archaeology in the lower canyons, sites in the uplands needed to be sampled. This allowed MNA in later years to excavate sites on the flanks of Navajo Mountain and on various mesas atop the Rainbow Plateau.[18]

But it was also understood that areas such as the Kaiparowits Plateau would probably not suffer secondary impacts. Hence work there needed to be, as it was, funded from other sources. As noted previously, the Utah program was tied to the university academic year, but the MNA program was not. Hence, field seasons and various operating procedures differed as well. What did occur in an ongoing fashion was exchange of data as results of each field season were written up. The Glen Canyon Project was now fully underway.

› 17 ‹

THE 1959 AND 1960 SEASONS

IN EARLY JUNE 1959, I AND HUNDREDS OF others marched through graduation ceremonies in the University of Utah football stadium, where I became the proud possessor of a document that I could trade in at the registrar's office for another one proclaiming me a Bachelor of Arts in anthropology. Three days later we would leave for Glen Canyon. The day before we left, Jennings called me into his office and told me I had been awarded a three-year National Defense Education Act (NDEA) graduate fellowship in American studies. The NDEA act had been created in response to the suddenly accelerated space and arms race between the United States and the Soviet Union, and a perceived need to increase the production of university professors. The act created an initial 1,000 fellowships distributed to universities nationally; three had come to the University of Utah, and one of those was awarded to me. Given my overall grade point average of two-point something, some behind-the-scenes legerdemain seemingly had gone on. The administrator of the fellowships at Utah was William Mulder, an eminent professor of English. He and Jennings often shot pool in the faculty club in the Student Union. I sometimes wondered if Jennings had won the fellowship in a game of Eight Ball. I later learned that I would continue as a staff archaeologist for the Glen Canyon Project, but that the fellowship would provide my support during the school year. I had Sputnik to thank—that puzzling, beeping satellite that we had learned about when we came into Escalante in October 1957.

THE 1959 SEASON

We arrived at Red Canyon late at night on June 14. The next day we set up camp and proceeded with the continued excavation of Loper Ruin and some small sites nearby. The following day David Dibble, the project photographer, and Dee Ann Suhm, the lab supervisor, flew in to the airstrip at White Canyon, and Jennings and his son David arrived by jeep. Dee Ann was with the excavation party for two

17.1. Loper Ruin excavation, June 1959: (*left to right*) David Dibble, unidentified, Tom Roth, Floyd Sharrock. Photograph by William D. Lipe. Archaeology Center Collection, 42SA364-114. Courtesy of Special Collections, Marriott Library, University of Utah.

weeks and supervised digging at three small sites in lower Red Canyon. Since she had far more field experience than any of us except Jennings, it was his way of giving her a little field time before the lab at the university would swing into full operation. Dibble's job was to do still photography and shoot a 16 mm film of the excavation of Loper Ruin, which John Wesley Powell and his men had first recorded in 1869. Situated on a knoll just above Bert Loper's cabin, the site was also well known to river runners. It proved to be a two-story affair with a kiva in the middle of its L-shaped format (Fig. 17.1).

My job, as in the previous year, was to survey the gravel bars and side canyons for sites. We made a quick trip to see "Fort Moqui," sometimes called "the Watch Tower," on a bluff above Hite (see chapter 20), a two-story masonry structure (Fig. 17.2). Powell had noted the site during his trips, and Beaman had photographed it from below in 1871. All later river runners usually stopped to see it and collect souvenir sherds. It was already in the Utah State Survey site files, and there was little left to excavate. I then started surveying downstream in the Little Rincon—an old river meander with much petrified wood on the surface. Bill Lipe later looked around there and found a site I'd missed, Creeping Dune, of which more anon (chapter 20).

After a few days I took one of the crew, Dick Ross, who had been with Lister and Nichols the previous year, and set out downstream with the "little boat" and a military surplus seven-man rubber raft filled with jerry cans of gasoline, gear, and supplies (Fig. 17.3). The arrangement worked tolerably well. At the end of the first week I wrote, "The raft

17.2. "Fort Moki," or "the Watch Tower," upper Glen Canyon: Harry Aleson (*left*) and Ralph Badger, ca. 1946. Photograph by Charles Kelly, C87-P58 2145. Courtesy of the Utah State Historical Society.

requires twice a day pumping, but it is still afloat. The two boats tied together make a very good rig except we had to move the raft farther forward to prevent backwash from slopping into the boat when negotiating rapids or rough water."[1] We carried a Coleman stove for heating up canned foods, but sometimes ate directly from the cans (Fig. 17.4).

My assignment was to survey all the gravel bars and benches along the main stem of the canyon, and all the side canyons on both sides of the river up to the ultimate pool level of the lake—that is, the 3,310 foot contour interval—except those side canyons surveyed by Lister and Mathews in 1958. We were to be out about three weeks at a time and would leave notes at the mouths of canyons recommending sites to test. Bill Lipe, following along downstream with the dig crew, would review the sites and decide which ones should be tested.

At the end of each period we moored the raft at some convenient point, loaded our artifacts, film, and records in the boat, and headed upstream—first to the dig camp, then to the trucks at Red Canyon and on to Blanding. After showers at the Cliff Palace Motel (where the owner-lady at the desk listened in to all our telephone calls to Salt Lake), some Jim Beam (which we had to drive to Monticello to acquire at the state liquor store and illegally transport back in a state vehicle), and several always unique gastronomical experiences at the Elk Ridge Cafe, we resupplied at the Redd Mercantile, drove back to Red Canyon, loaded the boat to the gunnels with supplies and gas, and headed downriver to the dig camp. There I picked up a different crew member, motored downstream to the raft, pumped it up (we never did find the slow leak), and headed out again.

By the end of the second session we were a long way downriver. That and the dropping river level made the upstream run particularly interesting, especially through the rapids. One of my reports notes the demise of five shear pins and one propeller in a stretch between Lake and Moqui canyons. We usually hauled, rather than ran, the boat upstream through rapids. At the beginning of the third month, we joined forces with the dig crew at Wilson Canyon and floated on down to Kane Creek, where the trucks had been ferried around by the lab crew to await us.

My three compatriots—Dick Ross, later a professor at Oregon State; Bob Kiste, later a professor at the University of Hawaii; and Wilfred Husted, later an archaeologist with the National Park Service—were good company. During the three-week stints we often saw only each other for days on end. We hiked long miles, wondering at the beauty of the side canyons, recorded sites, and cursed the mosquitos, gnats, and our World War II surplus C-rations toward the end of the period when we ran out of more palatable canned food. A couple of times we outran flash floods that came rumbling down the side canyons, rolling boulders, logs, and an occasional dead cow on their crests. The problem was that the floods sounded like the military jets overhead in the variable echo chambers of the canyons, and we never knew which one we were hearing. We slept in the open, or under tarps if it rained, on the sandbars. A tent (in those long-ago pre–nylon pop-up tent days) weighed too much and was too much trouble since we were always on the move.

Each duo had various experiences. We had two Coleman lanterns and would lie on our sleeping bags to read in the evening. One night I looked up to see a large skunk reading over Bob Kiste's shoulder. The kibitzing continued for some time, until Kiste noticed that I was very quietly staring just above and to the left of his head. When the skunk and Kiste finally made eye contact, they fortunately leapt in opposite directions, and the skunk decided not to leave an olfactory memento of his visit.

Some days later we were morosely contemplating the remains of our food supply—C-rations and two cans of sardines. We were to head upstream the next day. As we sighed and cursed our fate, around the bend came a raft with four tourists who had a large chest filled with goodies, including steaks on dry ice and two bottles of Old Crow. They were kind enough to share in return for our tall tales about our experiences in the canyon. Both parties left somewhat later than they should have the next day.

17.3. Don Fowler at the mouth of Moqui Canyon, 1959. Photograph by Richard Ross. Archaeology Center Collection, 42SA00-120. Courtesy of Special Collections, Marriott Library, University of Utah.

Perhaps because of a certain fogginess of perception, coupled with the noise of the motor, as we headed into the rapid at Hall's Crossing we missed seeing the guy high up on the rim of the canyon who was shouting, waving his arms, and throwing rocks to get our attention. A month later, when we pulled our truck with the boats on top in front of the Glen Canyon City Bar, we learned from the owner-bartender that he had been up on the cliff. He saw the boats and greeted us with "Why the hell didn't you SOBs rescue me last month?"—then broke into a laugh.

17.4. Don Fowler lunching in Wilson Canyon, August 1959. Photograph by Wilfred Husted. Courtesy of Don D. Fowler; gift of Wilfred Husted.

It seemed he had left the Salt Lake airport in his Cessna late of an evening and, suffering from his own certain fogginess of perception, forgot to file a flight plan. He was headed to Page, Arizona. Dawn found him far to the east of the Kaiparowits Plateau with an empty gas tank. He managed to land on one of the numerous airstrips left over from the uranium boom of the early fifties and made his way to the rim of Glen Canyon at the mouth of Hall's Creek. He had no food nor water. We went by and didn't see him, despite his frantic gesticulations and shouts. He managed to walk back up the rim, get down into the canyon, find a spring, slake his thirst, and then hike to the river. He knew where he was, so he launched a driftwood log for transport and floated down the river hoping to be found by river runners or someone else. He was finally rescued by some Bureau of Reclamation surveyors headed upriver to Rainbow Bridge.

The 1959 season gave me my greatest appreciation of Glen Canyon itself. The play of light on the cliffs and the reflections of the cliffs in the water (Figs. 17.5, 17.6) were wondrous. Every gravel bar and every side canyon presented unique scenery. Early morning thunderstorms produced rivulets of water running down the cliffs or spouting out into the river from the cliff tops. We photographed the remains of the various attempts to extract gold from the bars but didn't record them in detail because Gregory Crampton was doing so (chapter 15). We met various river runners and their tourist charges; the adults were usually enchanted with the place; the Boy Scouts were usually badly sunburned and terminally bored, as only acned teenagers can be. We avoided the luxurious poison ivy; some tourists did not, as related in chapter 11.

The highlights of the summer were forays into left-bank side canyons, particularly Moqui, Forgotten, Wilson, Lake, and the Rincon, as well as Smith Fork on the right bank. The story of Smith Fork and Forgotten Canyon is best told by portions of my weekly reports: "Smith Fork Bar, June 27, 1959. . . . The latexing of petroglyphs at Smith Fork was completed this morning. To insure durability of the molds we applied six coats of latex. A total of 22 molds were made covering 90% of the glyphs. The panel was also chalked in and photographed [Figs. 17.7, 17.8] so that a composite picture can be made. . . . Tourist traffic has been brisk. We had lunch with Georgie White (legs still look good) [Jennings was a well-known "leg man," hence the now male-chauvinist observation]. . . . Other parties have been somewhat of a nuisance while we were working on the glyphs."[2]

17.5. Cliffs and water opposite Music Temple Bar, August 1959. Photograph by W. J. Owen. Courtesy of Don D. Fowler; gift of W. J. Owen.

Among the "other parties" was a man from Brooklyn with a ten-year-old daughter and twelve-year-old son in a canoe. The man had decided his

17.6. Cliffs along the river below Meskin Bar, lower Glen Canyon, September 1958. Photograph by Christy Turner, S.GCP.482. Courtesy of the Museum of Northern Arizona.

kids should see Glen Canyon, so he borrowed a canoe and headed west. They stopped by our camp to ask directions to Moqui Canyon, since the only map they had was a small cutout from *Sunset Magazine*. We told them that Moqui Canyon was just a few miles downstream on the left; they made their uncertain way back onto the river and headed out. We assumed they survived, since we never found a capsized canoe caught in the driftwood anywhere downstream, nor heard anything of their demise.

Forgotten Canyon was directly across the river from Smith Fork Bar. "Both Forgotten and Smith Fork have deposited fans of boulders and cobbles into the river. The river has been able neither to clear the accumulation away nor to cut a single deep channel through it; instead the water spreads out into a shallow flow over the boulder mass and down a minor rapid at the lower end. . . . when the water is low, the river can be forded easily just above the rapids."[3] Smith Fork heads in the flanks of the Henry Mountains; Forgotten Canyon provided access onto the Red Rock Plateau east of the river. The two provided a pathway in either direction across the Colorado River.

> Forgotten Canyon, July 5, 1959. . . . Forgotten Canyon was surveyed only 2 1/2 miles upstream. There we were stopped by deep pot holes full of water. . . . We plan to continue up the canyon tomorrow. This is feasible, since with Lipe now camped here we have the gear to build a way around the barrier.[4]

Lipe and the excavation crew had arrived and started excavation of a site just inside Forgotten Canyon. While I was working downstream for a

17.7. Section of rock art panel, Smith Fork Bar, 1959. Photograph by Don D. Fowler. Archaeology Center Collection, 42Ga367-1. Courtesy of Special Collections, Marriott Library, University of Utah.

17.8. Richard Ross (*right*) and Don Fowler chalking petroglyphs at Smith Fork Bar rock art panel, July 1959. Photograph by W. J. Owen. Courtesy of Don D. Fowler; gift of W. J. Owen.

couple of days, Lipe and Floyd Sharrock had gotten around the pot holes, hiked into the upper canyon, and saw what we came to call "Defiance House." When I returned, Dick Ross and I used Lipe's "gear"—star drills, lag shields, and eye bolts—to set horizontal sliding ropes and, further upstream, vertical ropes.

> July 11, 1959. . . . Access into Forgotten Canyon was gained by setting a series of four ropes at points that allow passing by the pot holes in the two narrow parts of the canyon [bottom]. We found that apparently the Indians used the same path, as there are two sets of steps cut up and [horizontally] along the [slickrock] benches above the pot holes.[5]

The two ropes along the steps (Fig. 17.9) were set for the excavation crew to hang on to while traversing the benches laden with excavation equipment; the other two vertical ropes for getting up onto and back down from the slickrock benches in the upper canyon.

> A total of eight sites were recorded in the first five miles of the main canyon. Two of these, 42SA597 [Fig. 17.10] and 42SA598, have several structures, including kivas. 42SA598 in particular is a spectacular site, consisting of 5 contiguous semi-circular rooms, 3 storage structures, 2 square rooms with intact roofs, a long retaining wall or defensive wall and a kiva with an intact roof. The ladder into the kiva is still in place. Also, there are three 4 foot high pictographs of men with shields [Figs. 17.11, 17.12], and, on the surface, several large collapsed jars. The pottery [has] . . . the mosquito net B/W [black-on-white] designs of . . . late PIII times. . . . All the sites recorded thus far in the canyon are undisturbed, a somewhat unique phenomenon.[6]

The threatening postures of the pictograph figures led Bill Lipe and his excavation crew to name the site "Defiance House." Since the site is above the pool-level of Lake Powell, the National Park Service later stabilized it (Fig. 21.5), and it has been visited by thousands of boaters. One of the figures, minus a certain appendage, became the logo of the University of Utah Press (see the spine of this book).

Initially we thought we were the first to see Defiance House since its builders had gathered up their children and some of their possessions and walked away about 1300 CE. But the excavation crew found two men's names and the date 1954 scratched on the wall at the rear of the site (the notes unfortunately don't give the names). Much later we learned that the "Canyon Surveys trio" (chapter 14) had been there in 1952, accompanied by Pard the dog and Mickey the cat.

I have since learned from other veteran river runners that they, too, had found a way around the deep pools and gotten into the upper canyon before 1959. They, too, were properly awed by Defiance House and its setting and respectful of its integrity. But the deep pools seemingly did discourage most of the more casual river runners and tourists, thereby preserving the sites largely intact. Then too, the upper forks of the canyon boxed up, thus preventing cattle from straying in from the mesa top, and hence cowboys from coming into the canyon after them. The earlier archaeological forays led by John Wetherill also skirted around Forgotten Canyon. The complex of archaeological sites on both sides of the river at Smith Fork and Forgotten Canyon are discussed in chapter 20.

While Lipe and his crew excavated Defiance House and several other sites, I moved on downstream to survey Moqui, Lake, Slickrock, and Wilson canyons, and the Rincon, as well as the terraces on both sides of the river. In 1958 Robert Lister had surveyed, overland, Smith, Hall's, and Bullfrog

17.9. Keith Anderson (*foreground*) and Thomas Roth on horizontal steps cut into the wall of Forgotten Canyon, 1959. Photograph by Floyd Sharrock. Archaeology Center Collection, 42Sa00-324. Courtesy of Special Collections, Marriott Library, University of Utah.

creeks. In Moqui Canyon we surveyed up the main stem as far as North Fork, and a couple of miles up the latter to about lake pool level. In Lake Canyon, certainly one of the more beautiful, we surveyed upstream to pool level. Both canyons are much longer, and it was clear we would have to come into their upper reaches overland, which we did in 1960 and 1961. Slickrock Canyon boxed up about 5 miles above the river, as did Wilson Canyon. All four canyons contained important sites that were excavated in 1960–62. In 1959 excavation efforts focused on lower Moqui Canyon and Wilson Canyon.[7]

17.10. Crumbling Kiva site, Forgotten Canyon, July 1959. Photograph by William D. Lipe. Archaeology Center Collection, 42Sa597-4. Courtesy of Special Collections, Marriott Library, University of Utah.

Following the work in Moqui and Wilson canyons, we dropped downstream to Music Temple. By early August the river was low, and we camped on the sandbar at the base of the terrace in front of Music Temple, across and just downstream from Hidden Passage. One of my tasks was to make latex molds of the Powell expedition names carved in the sloping walls of Music Temple. My notes also contain a copied-out passage from Powell's diary about Music Temple. I did not know it at the time, but it marked the beginning of my long involvement with Major Powell and his men, particularly Jack Hillers, that would continue off and on for the next several decades.[8]

Since I had surveyed most of the right-bank side canyons in 1958, I spent some time further exploring some of the left-bank canyons below the San Juan–Colorado confluence and below Kane Wash, the take-out place on the river. After our last supply run upstream to the trucks at Red Canyon and on into Blanding, a crew from the lab in Salt Lake City had moved the trucks around to the Kane Creek landing.

After we reached that point, two of the crew and I drove the trucks around to Lee's Ferry. Lipe and the rest of the crew floated on down to the dam site, where, by arrangement with the Bureau of Reclamation and the engineers working on the dam, they were able to float on through during a shift change of construction workers on the bridge. No one wanted to risk a rivet or tool dropping 800 feet onto someone's head. With the exception of bureau and construction-related boats, the University of Utah crew was perhaps the last, or nearly the last, group to float on down to Lee's Ferry.

With the season over, we returned to the university. I wrote up my survey materials for the upper Glen Canyon, but my major concerns were my graduate classes in American studies, since that was what my fellowship was all about. My earlier courses in philosophy and political science (chapter 1) had sharpened my interest in intellectual history. Now I had courses in European and American history, as well as European and American literature, and political and social history. The courses I remember most were, first, those with Don Walker, a superb English professor who reintroduced me to my childhood (indeed, lifetime) favorite author, Mark Twain. When I was nine years old, my mother had given me a set of *Tom Sawyer* and *Huckleberry Finn* with illustrations by Norman Rockwell. I had read each of them a dozen times or more. Now Don Walker guided me to all the rest of the Twain oeuvre and that of his contemporaries. My second favorite was William Mulder, the administrator of the NDEA fellowships, who gave me a larger appreciation of American intellectual history.

In previous years when I returned from the field, I had shared an apartment with various fellow students, most of them guys I'd gone to high school with. Now, however, I rented an apartment in a two-story, deteriorating, Queen Anne–style,

17.11. Pictographs at Defiance House site, Forgotten Canyon, 1959. Photograph by William D. Lipe. Archaeology Center Collection, 42Sa598-51. Courtesy of Special Collections, Marriott Library, University of Utah.

Charles Addams–looking house situated immediately south of where Fourth South Street curves around to become Fifth South. The site has long since been occupied by a high-rise apartment building.

The house, divided into four apartments, had a concrete plaque on the north wall reading "Lafayette Villa." It was owned by a nice, elderly Greek immigrant lady who never set foot on the premises, probably for good reason. It had been first rented by graduate students several years before, and as each one moved on, they passed their apartment on to a friend. In the fall of 1959, one of the apartments passed to me. My fellow graduate students, who were in medicine, pharmacy, and psychology, and I threw frequent parties. The Villa parties were loud, alcohol-fueled, and attended by many, some of them even invited. One attendee was a modern dance major from southern California named Janet Ary. We courted, married in the early winter of 1960, and soon found we were to be parents. She went home to California in the summer of 1960 while I went to the field.

1960 Season

In 1960 the major effort of the Glen Canyon Project focused on Lake Canyon. Access was from Blanding, Utah, over slickrock and sand dune "roads" for the last portion of the trip. The plan was to evaluate and excavate some previously recorded sites. A second task was to survey the upper reaches of Lake Canyon. A third was to evaluate sites in the upper reaches of Moqui Canyon, which had been visited earlier by the Wetherill and Bernheimer parties (chapter 13) but had not been reached by

17.12. Don Fowler (*lower right*) recording house structure, Defiance House, 1959. Photograph by Richard Ross. Courtesy of Don D. Fowler; gift of Richard Ross.

the 1958 Triangle Survey, nor by me in 1959, coming upstream from the river.

We had a large crew of a dozen. Bill Lipe was crew chief, Floyd Sharrock, David Dibble, and I were assistant crew chiefs, and there were a number of others from several universities. Among them was Richard Gould, then a Harvard undergraduate, later to do ethnoarchaeology in Australia and work for the American Museum of Natural History before settling in to a distinguished career at Brown University. Another was a Haverford College undergraduate named Alexander Sharp, whose

17.13. Camp Number 1, Lake Canyon, 1960: (*background, left to right*) unidentified, Calvin Porter, "The Cook," Alan Howard, unidentified; (*foreground, with head turned*) Alexander Sharp, Frank Weir (*with hat*), others unidentified. Photograph by Floyd Sharrock. Archaeology Center Collection, 42SA00-293. Courtesy of Special Collections, Marriott Library, University of Utah.

father, Lauriston Sharp, had been with Clyde Kluckhohn on the Wild Horse Mesa/Kaiparowits Plateau trip in 1928 (chapter 10).

The first week in June, Bill Lipe and I went to the area to scout out access and a place for an initial camp in the upper reaches of the canyon. The last part of the route, after leaving the Fry Canyon road, was across slickrock and sand dunes but was passable. On the advice of Clarence Rogers of Blanding, who would provide pack and saddle horses for us, we found a campsite under a large alcove that (fortunately) was shaded by about 1:30 in the afternoon. There was a small waterfall in a side canyon about half a mile upstream that provided culinary and drinking water as well as a shower.

On June 14–15 we arrived with the full crew, our wrangler, Keith Rogers (Clarence's son), and four horses. Keith, large of frame, full of smarts, and generous of spirit, had played football as a tackle and guard at Brigham Young University. His wife's excellent cooking had added to his bulk after he graduated and became a teacher. He saw the field season as a chance to diet, so he "ate" only Metrocal, a popular diet drink of the day, and drank only water for the month he was with us. As he visibly lost bulk, his horse looked increasingly relieved. On August 1, Keith returned home to prepare for the school year and was replaced by Brigham Stevens, then in his fifties. Brig was a wise, gentle, soft-spoken man who knew much about horses, the Glen Canyon Country, and the world at large. He also worked with the Moqui Canyon crew in 1961.

As it turned out, the archaeology in Lake Canyon proved very interesting, and the field season itself quixotic in several senses. First the quixotic. One of the students in Professor Jennings's spring 1960 Anthropology 1 class was a man (who shall remain nameless, but shall be called "The Cook") in his forties. He claimed to be a mathematics major who had given up life as a cowboy in the San Juan Triangle to get an education. He also claimed to be a veteran of World War II. He wore a sweat-stained Stetson and a mustache, and affected a macho demeanor. Jennings, who had his own macho streak, was completely horn-swoggled. Jennings hired the man as cook, since he evinced familiarity with the nuances of Dutch ovens and related camp cuisine. With considerable enthusiasm, Jennings informed us that here was a "real man" who would show us young, callow lads "how it was done" in the wild. Since we had been "doing it" rather well for two or three years previously, we found his enthusiasm both amusing and off-putting.

After various vehicle breakdowns, we arrived on the rim of upper Lake Canyon. We cleared the floor of our alcove home (Fig. 17.13) of a large stand of poison ivy, which The Cook proposed to burn before a couple of us intervened (inhaling the smoke from burning poison ivy is not a good thing). The crew quickly found the waterfall. Given the heat, it was wondrous. We could shower in it and lug our drinking and culinary water to camp in 5-gallon jerry cans. We set about excavating three nearby sites, including one aptly named Horsefly Hollow (Fig. 17.14). The horseflies there and throughout the canyon were numerous and omnivorous—they had a taste for *Homo sapien* as well as equine flesh.

It soon turned out that The Cook's idea of camp cuisine was very much of the "greasy sack" genre shunned by our wrangler of yore, Loyd Gates. "Real man" food, as produced by The Cook, was inedible for the most part. Grumbling soon began, fueled by further complications. It was extremely hot, so much so that after a day of working in the sun, the crew could only retreat to the camp alcove and loll flaccidly about, sweating and whining. Some now and then succumbed to heat prostration.

Very soon other health problems began to appear: some began to complain of flu-like symptoms and chest pains. Ultimately, it turned out that some crew members had contracted coccidioidomycosis—desert fever, or valley fever—the same fungus that Samuel Guernsey and his crew had encountered in Chinle Wash in the 1920s (chapter 13). It almost became an epidemic, in the sense that of our population of thirteen, 25 percent were either in the hospital in Monticello (where an alert medical resident recognized it for what it was and confirmed his diagnosis in consultation with a professor of medicine at the university), recuperating in Blanding, or in the field but not working. We were all tested, and only I and two others tested negative. In my case, I had probably been exposed the year before; I recalled having what I thought was a bad cold for a few days while I was on the river.

Meanwhile, things continued to go awry in camp, centering on The Cook. One day as we came over a slickrock knoll from where we were working, we heard shots and the whine of bullets. It turned out The Cook was practicing "quick draw" with his .357 Magnum pistol (which he was not supposed to have; Jennings had a strict rule about no guns in the field) by shooting at a large cottonwood tree—immediately behind which were the trucks and 40 gallons of gasoline. He was, at least, a fairly good shot. The denouement came soon after. We had decided that to beat the heat we would get up at 3:30 in the morning, have breakfast, and then work until 1 p.m., after which we would shade up in the alcove (even though it functioned not unlike a reflector oven). The first morning of the new regime, The Cook served leftover fried carrots and little else except the vile camp coffee that "real men" savored. It didn't set well.

The Cook had an unending fund of self-promoting stories. During the invasion of France,

17.14. Jesse Jennings (*in cap*) instructing Richard Gould in the finer points of archaeological recording at the Horsefly Hollow site, June 1960. Photograph by William D. Lipe. Archaeology Center Collection, 42Sa544-5. Courtesy of Special Collections, Marriott Library, University of Utah.

he said, he had parachuted behind German lines, suffered a badly sprained back when he landed, but accomplished his mission and raped a few nuns for good measure. The variation was he was thrown from his horse way out in the San Juan Triangle, suffered a sprained (sometimes it was broken) back, but managed to crawl to Blanding, raping a few Navajo women along the way. There were other tales of similar veracity. It was quickly noticed that The Cook never took a bath. He never wore a shirt either, the better to show off his dirt-streaked physique. He did, however, go to the waterfall and watch while the other men showered. He carried a very large bowie knife with a 10- to 12-inch blade on his belt at all times.

The Cook's credibility ended one afternoon as he and some of the crew were walking back from the waterfall and he was regaling them with more tall tales of his bravado. There was a rustle in the bushes alongside the trail. The Cook whipped out his bowie knife and assumed a crouched fighting position. A small ground squirrel emerged from the bushes and looked rather defiantly up at him. The crew dissolved into uncontrolled fits of laughter. The Cook's macho facade shattered and ran down his dirt-streaked chest. The next day he asked to leave. Lipe quickly agreed, and Sharrock drove him to Blanding and bought him a bus ticket for Salt Lake City.

Some time later, court records show that The Cook was an accomplice in a murder in which a woman killed her lesbian girlfriend's boyfriend. The Cook turned state's evidence and got off, but court records showed that he had been in the Utah State prison for aggravated assault during the years he purportedly was working as a cowboy in the San Juan Triangle.

One of the young men from Blanding, Lyle Palmer, became cook, and the cuisine improved 100 percent; those who had been sick recovered (except two who had to go home), and the field season went on to be a success. Professor Jennings said very little thereafter about "real men." Perhaps the fact that a dozen callow high school, undergraduate, and graduate students all hung in there and did yeoman service under very difficult circumstances demonstrated to him that wearing sweat-stained Stetsons, carrying big knives and guns, not bathing, chewing snuff, and being an unconfessed convicted felon didn't necessarily define male gender-hood.

The day after The Cook made his exit, we moved the camp about 6 miles downcanyon to a nice shady grove of cottonwood trees where there was water in the creek. We treated the water with Halozone, which precipitated out the mud and, in theory, killed disease-causing microbes. We were lucky, because there were beaver ponds just below our camp, and beaver are known carriers of *Giardia lambia*, as are cows, and there were cows in the canyon. In fact, as we worked downstream from the camp, we routinely waded through the beaver ponds twice daily, much to the annoyance of the inhabitants. Perhaps we were only fated to suffer one epidemic that year.

My job, as previously, was to survey for sites. I had been several miles up Lake and Moqui canyons in 1959, surveying from the river. Now I rode out the upper arms of Lake Canyon and found more sites, some of which we tested. We photographed the remnants of deposits around the site of Lake Pahgahrit. The "lake" had formed behind a falling dune, and when first described in 1880 by the Mormon Hole-in-the-Rock party, who paused there during their epic trek (chapter 20), it was J-shaped and about a half mile long by a quarter of a mile wide at the widest, and 50 feet deep at the sand dam. In November 1915 there were three days of intense rains, filling the lake to overflowing, cutting the sand dam, and releasing its water to roar downstream and flush out much of the sediment in the canyon as it rushed to the Colorado River. The breach was witnessed by J. A. Scorup, the veteran cattleman who controlled much of the Red Rock Plateau.

I spent a few days in Moqui Canyon with wrangler Keith Rogers and one of the crew. We gained access into the upper part down a 600-vertical-foot-high falling dune spilling at the angle of repose over the canyon wall (Fig. 17.15). We led the horses zigzag down, and later back up, the dune. It and two other falling dunes had long been used as ways in and out of the canyon, as difficult as they were (Fig. 8.4). As noted earlier, James White and his companions perhaps climbed down, up, and then down again one of the dunes in 1867 as they fled the Indians. The Wetherills leading Neil Judd and the Bernheimer parties into Moqui Canyon in the 1920s also used the dunes.

In Moqui Canyon we recorded a dozen sites—several of them rummaged in by the Wetherill, Judd, or Bernheimer parties, others not previously recorded.[9] We spotted a portion of a masonry wall and what appeared to be a hearth jutting out of the alluvial cut-bank about 40 feet above the streambed. This site was later excavated and proved important for interpreting the culture history of Moqui Canyon—and Glen Canyon in general (chapter 20). The surveys of upper Lake and Moqui canyons did not take long, and I spent the rest of the summer digging various sites in Lake Canyon. We usually had four sites being tested or excavated

17.15. Falling Dune (Dune 2) in Moqui Canyon, 1961. Photograph by David Dibble. Archaeology Center Collection, 42SA00-387. Courtesy of Special Collections, Marriott Library, University of Utah.

at the same time.[10] One of them we named "Wasp House" (Fig. 17.16) for the pestiferous yellowjackets who had taken up residence there. It was a mile or so upcanyon from the river and had been seen and photographed by most river runners who had passed through Glen Canyon. It still had a smoke-blackened roof of made beams, cross-laid willows, and earth, a fireplace, and anchors for an upright loom set in the floor.

By August 20 we felt we had an adequate sample of Lake Canyon sites, so we packed up, moved back upstream to the trucks, and headed back to the Little Rincon to finish work on the reservoir site I had missed—and Lipe had found—in 1959, the Creeping Dune site (chapter 20). We camped, once again, next to Bert Loper's cabin at the mouth of Red Canyon and were able to drive along the river nearly to the site. On September 1 we headed back to Salt Lake City. On September 9 Floyd Sharrock and a small crew returned to finish up the site.[11]

We went back to school, and back to analyzing artifacts and writing reports. But first I went to southern California to bring Janet back to Salt Lake

17.16. Wasp House, lower Lake Canyon, 1960. Photograph by Don D. Fowler. Archaeology Center Collection, 42Sa373-01. Courtesy of Special Collections, Marriott Library, University of Utah.

City. We sent up housekeeping and awaited the birth of Mark Charles Fowler in January 1961. Once he arrived, we attempted to be parents, but the marriage did not work. We were divorced in May 1961 before I left for the field. Later, when Mark was twelve, he came to live with me and my wife, Kay. He graduated from high school, went on to college in computers, became a successful information technology maven, married, and has a wonderful wife and son of his own.

› 18 ‹

THE 1961 AND 1962 SEASONS

TWO GLEN CANYON PROJECT CREWS WERE sent out in 1961. One went into upper Moqui Canyon. The other, under my charge, went first into Harris Wash, an upper tributary of the Escalante River, and then onto the Kaiparowits Plateau. Neither Harris Wash, and certainly not the top of the Kaiparowits Plateau, would be flooded by Lake Powell, but to understand the culture history of Glen Canyon proper, we needed to connect it with that of adjacent areas. I've previously noted the work at the Coombs site near Boulder, Utah. Now the idea was to do some work in the area between Boulder and Glen Canyon. Since this area was well outside Glen Canyon proper and the areas of secondary impacts from boaters on Lake Powell, and thus could not be funded by the National Park Service, Jennings had secured grants from the National Science Foundation and the Wenner-Gren Foundation for Anthropological Research to cover the costs of our work. The Moqui Canyon work was covered by funds from the National Park Service.

By 1961 word was out that there were jobs doing archaeology in an interesting place, the Glen Canyon Country, hence we had crew members from all across the land: C. Melvin Aikens, previously introduced; T. J. Barrette, University of Minnesota; Richard Gould and Thomas Lynch, University of Chicago; Alan D. Koloseike, UCLA; Jon Morris, Northwestern University; Leslie Pennington, University of Texas; Oliver (Buddy) Thomas, Louisiana State University; and Wylie Wilson, University of Wisconsin. Calvin Porter, from Escalante, had been on the 1960 crew in Lake Canyon. Richard Gould was previously introduced. Tom Lynch took his doctorate at Chicago, had a distinguished career at Cornell University, and did major work on early archaeological sites in South America. The others went on to careers in a variety of fields.

The sites in Harris Wash included several large, dry alcoves containing many cultivated plant remains, including whole ears of maize, gourds, and a mixture of Anasazi and Fremont cultural

18.1. "Fowler's Folly," Harris Wash, June 1961. Photograph by Thomas Oliver. Courtesy of Don D. Fowler; gift of Thomas Oliver.

items.[1] The excavations were routine; the time marked principally by an occurrence later known as "Fowler's Folly" (fig. 18.1), when I got the truck stuck in a flash flood. The incident was memorialized by a camp folk song, "Twas a sad day when the green jeep went down."

The Kaiparowits Plateau is one of the major landmarks in the Glen Canyon Country. It is sometimes known as the "Straight Cliffs" for the east face. Locals in Escalante called it "The Fifty," or "Fifty Mile Mountain," since it is about that distance from Escalante to the end of the plateau at Navajo Point. A dirt road roughly paralleled the cliffs along the floor of the Escalante Desert, leading to Hole-in-the-Rock.

Access to the top of the Kaiparowits on the east side was by one of three trails. The trail farthest north was known as the Upper Trail, or the "Golden Stairs," since the ranchers had blasted some steps near the trailhead through a portion of the Morrison Sandstone, which has a yellowish hue. Given that one seemed to be climbing to the top of the world, the stairs were aptly a kind of metaphorical reminder of the stairway to heaven. We gained access by driving up onto Fifty Mile Bench as far as we could go, and then hiking about 1,800 vertical feet up the Middle Trail. Gear and supplies were hauled up by four faithful, but always willful, mules owned by Loyd Gates and wrangled by Cecil Griffin, from Escalante. I had met three of the mules in 1957 in Twenty Five Mile Gulch.

Cecil was extremely competent and full of good cheer. The critters did the usual mulish things. They could, and regularly did, wander 2 to 4 miles a night, despite hobbles; when hobbled two together, they would hop in tandem. When ridden,

>••••••<

MULES

The *Oxford English Dictionary* defines a mule as: "An animal born of a mating between a male ass and a mare or loosely between a female ass and a stallion (hinny); used esp. as a draught animal and for bearing loads and proverbially regarded as the epitome of obstinacy." Just so!

Many of those who explored portions of the Glen Canyon country prior to the building of the dam, including me, had close encounters of the unpleasant kind with these mischievous miscreants. Hoffman Birney, writing of the mules he and his party used on their 1928 trip into Rainbow Bridge, said:

> One thing I know: a mute could never handle a pack-mule. There is something about a mule—the innate mulishness of the brute, as it were—that absolutely demands language. Horses are horses, but mules are distinctly individualists. I am convinced that they have a sense of humor and equally certain that their wit is motivated entirely by Poe's Imp of the Perverse. They will deliberately take a deep breath and hold it while they're being cinched—plenty of horses know that trick, too—and exhale that breath with diabolic pleasure in finding their girths comfortably slack. They will wait until one is standing tip-toe to reach a lashing and then lazily side-step just sufficient distance to throw the packer off his balance. They will delight . . . in lying down fully packed and having to be unpacked before they can rise, in scraping your bedroll against every tree and rocky wall they encounter, and in perpetually maintaining an air of bland, long-eared innocence that makes the well known expression of the cat that has just eaten the canary look like the furtive guilt of Judas Iscariot! There's only one thing they really understand—language. The more sulphurous it is the better a mule likes it and the better he works. If you can't curse, learn before starting out with a mule train; if you have scruples against profanity hire somebody who hasn't and plug your ears.[2]

they excelled at scraping their riders off by heading beneath the nearest pinyon branch that cleared their ears, but not the torsos of their passengers. No amount of verbal abuse or kicking or lashing of their flanks kept them from this near-daily ritual. We named archaeological sites after them: Ava site, Bridgette site, and Sophia Cave. However, the powers-that-were vetoed "Manure Manor" for a fourth site, and it become the much more prosaic Three Forks Pueblo.

The four long-eared Imps we had in the summer of 1961 fully lived up to Birney's description. On the other hand, they can carry far more than a pack horse over the same distance in the same period of time, and we could not have functioned without them.

The top of the Kaiparowits Plateau was a place of wonder. There were periodic springs and seeps. One, Mud Hole Spring, where we located our camp, was in a grove of quaking aspen, or "quakies," those amazing single-organism plants, called "collective clones," pretending to be groves of individual trees.[3] There were scattered groves of pinyon and juniper on the knolls, two relic stands of ponderosa pine, and large flats covered with rabbitbrush and sagebrush, some individual plants over 6 feet tall.

We concentrated our efforts on the southernmost 18 to 20 miles of the plateau. Here a series of canyons head at—or almost at—the Straight Cliffs side of the plateau and drain generally southwestward to the Colorado. These include the tributaries of Dry Rock Creek that cut down through the wondrous amphitheater formed by the crescentic cliff line called Harvey's Fear; others to the northwest feed into other branches of Rock Creek or into Last Chance Creek. There are various flats and hollows at the heads of the canyons, and some flats on the larger ridges between canyons. We marveled at all we saw, especially the spectacular views from the rims (figs. 18.2, 18.3), which Clyde Kluckhohn had so elegantly described in *Beyond the Rainbow* (chapter 10).

Given the logistics, once on the plateau we tried to go to Escalante only every three weeks. We only had one radio that worked spasmodically. Hence, our first clues to events in the greater world that summer had to do with an increase in the number of the giant push-propeller B-36s being refueled high overhead. When the radio did finally work, we got some inkling of the Berlin Crisis of that summer, but only got full details later.

Since all our food had to be hauled up in the panniers on the mules, we were limited to compact canned goods. But fresh meat was ardently desired. The situation was resolved by an emergency declaration. Numerous fat buck deer were abroad on the plateau. They looked dangerous to us, scheming to attack our camp at any moment and lay waste to our hard-won scientific data. Clearly periodic counter-insurgency strikes were required. If one of the threatening deer was dispatched, then eaten, we reasoned, it would be a warning to the others. The wrangler had a Winchester .30-30. The fresh meat was excellent, as was the jerky, soaked in brine made from a cake of cow salt and smoked over scrub-oak coals. Both beat SPAM (also known as "donkey dick"), canned tuna, and Dinty Moore stew hands down.

The town of Escalante, as previously noted, was then at the end of the paved road from U.S. Highway 89. But for a field crew, it had all the necessities: a gas station, a pay telephone, a motel complete with showers and a laundry room, a garden of gastronomic wonders (as in "I wonder what this is?") called Ruby's Café, a movie house (open Saturday nights and Tuesday evenings after Mutual, pronounced "Mew-chull"), a grocery store (in which there was a Utah state liquor store), and a hardware store. "Mutual" is a peculiar Mormon institution, short for "Young Men's Mutual Improvement Association" and "Young Women's Mutual Improvement Association." They meet jointly and are devoted to socialization activities such as dances, theater, Boy Scouts, and good works for teens, but mostly to allow supervised courting as teenage hormones begin to roil.

Several of the businesses in Escalante were owned or controlled by Claren Griffin, bishop of the local ward. Claren was a friendly, shrewd, able individual who was of great help to us. We, in turn, were of some considerable help to his bank balance over the course of the summer. I had only been in Escalante briefly in the fall of 1957. Now, in 1961, I was back with a crew of nine male college seniors and graduate students. After our second trip into town, it dawned on us that there were no nubile girls visible—most peculiar for a Mormon town, or any small community. The mystery was solved during an unscheduled visit I made to town about midsummer. Our normal town trips were scheduled so we would have room reservations in Claren's motel. I had unexpectedly come to town in search of some badly needed hardware.

At the hardware store an elderly man kindly inquired as to how we were doing "out there on the Fifty." I said that all was well, save the broken hardware. He then asked, "Where are all you boys from?" I replied that my troops were from Texas, New York, Chicago, Berkeley, and other exotic places, and that I was from Ogden but had been

18.2. View to the south off the Kaiparowits Plateau from Harvey's Fear, with Millard Davis (*seated left*) and Peter Cousins. Photograph by C. Melvin Aikens, 1958. Archaeology Center Collection, 41KA00-446. Courtesy of Special Collections, Marriott Library, University of Utah.

born in Torrey, across the Boulder Mountain to the north. There was a sudden silence among the several women in the store. Then came the key question: "Torrey? Who was your granddaddy?" "Fred Noyes," said I. "Why," said the man, "I used to herd sheep with Fred Noyes out in the Henrys in '06 and '07." The women's internal Mormon genealogical computers were suddenly awhirl. "If he's Fred Noyes's grandson, that means he's related to X, and Y, and Z, . . . here in Escalante."

The next week when I came to town with the crew, Claren came to the motel and invited us to a

18.3. View to the west off the Kaiparowits Plateau from Harvey's Fear, with Millard Davis (*left*) and C. Melvin Aikens, 1958. Photograph by Peter Cousins. Archaeology Center Collection, 42KA00-452. Courtesy of Special Collections, Marriott Library, University of Utah.

barbeque at his house. There, suddenly, was a bevy of teenage girls, as self-aware of their dresses and still-being-honed coquettishness before all us college boys as we were of our own testosterone-fueled, gangly behavior before these pulchritudinous lovelies. However, it was clearly flirt and talk, but not touch. The lesson, we later decided, was the power of Mormon kinship connections. If I was somehow, even distantly, related to half the town, then I was probably okay. Bishop and Mrs. Griffin, at least, were willing to take a chance that my compatriots were likely okay as well and might behave ourselves,

18.4. Excavation crew in Moqui Canyon, 1961: (*back row, left to right*) Vance Fowler, Kent Day, Edward Keane, Ernst Shurer, William Lipe, Floyd Sharrock, David Jennings; (*front row, left to right*) David Read, Brigham Stevens, John Conway, Lyle Palmer, Alan Howard. Photograph by David Dibble. Archaeology Center Collection, 41SA00-373. Courtesy of Special Collections, Marriott Library, University of Utah.

at least in a chaperoned context. We did, but there was no subsequent socializing, although the girls remained visible when we came to town. Nonetheless, the niceties had been observed, and we certainly appreciated the food, since it was much better than that usually served up at Ruby's Café.

Jim Gunnerson and his team had surveyed much of the southeastern end of the plateau in 1958 and recorded numerous sites. Now the plan was to excavate a sample of those and make further surveys to better determine the cultural affiliations of sites on the plateau. We worked from our camp at Mud Hole Spring since it seemingly was the only certain source of water that year. Some of the sites, such as one at the head of the Upper Trail, required stub camps, with water and supplies being brought in every two or three days by Cecil and the faithful mules. The system worked tolerably well. We walked and rode across many areas from Basin Canyon to the end of the plateau, finding more sites and marveling the while at the vast world we could see far beyond the rim.

It seemed that the flats at and between the heads of the many canyons had served as numerous farmsteads for Ancestral Puebloans. We found various small house remains out in the flats that we decided were "field houses," places to be near and watch the crops, as well as harvest them. On the knolls and ridges were dozens of small pueblos, or perhaps pueblitos—two-, three-, and four-room masonry structures. Many had fire hearths in prepared clay floors. None seemed to be more than one story. All had melted into piles of masonry rubble. In our view, people had come onto the plateau mainly to farm in the summer, retreating to lower and warmer climes in the winter.[4] More of that in chapter 20.

MOQUI CANYON ONCE MORE

While my crew and I were reveling in the grand scenery visible off Zane Grey's Wild Horse Mesa, my compatriots—led by Floyd Sharrock and Dave Dibble, with Bill Lipe and ten others, as well as Brigham Stevens, the wrangler from Blanding—were back in Moqui Canyon across the river (fig. 18.4). The sites I had recorded in 1959 and 1960, together with what was known from other information back to the 1920s, made it clear that Moqui Canyon was an important place. Access to the upper canyon was by driving to Greenwater Springs on the road through the Clay Hills Pass, leaving a vehicle there, then driving over the slickrock to the rim of the canyon. The crew then hiked and led the pack horses down one of the vertical falling dunes previously described (Dune 1, probably the one shown in figure 8.4).

Once the crew reached the canyon floor, there was some confusion. The problem was, in 1960 Keith Rogers and I had gone down and up a higher and steeper dune (Dune 2) farther downcanyon (fig. 17.11) than the one to which Brig Stevens led the 1961 crew—and the one used by Herbert Gregory in 1927 (fig. 8.4). I had located a potential campsite a short distance from Dune 2. When Sharrock and company arrived at the base of Dune 1, no such campsite was to be found. After some frantic searching (and undoubtedly cursing Fowler's ineptitude), the crew found Dune 2, then the campsite I had located. They wisely retreated to a much better campsite closer to Dune 1 that had nearby springs. There they established camp on a rock ledge well above the creekbed (fig. 18.5)—placement that proved wise when a couple of flash floods roared down the canyon later in the summer.

A SHATTERED LEG AND MYSTERY RUSTLERS

Two notable, but very different incidents occurred during the Moqui Canyon sojourn. The canyon has a long side canyon called "the North Fork" (sometimes "Secret Canyon"). I had gotten a couple of miles into it in 1959. In 1960 I had concentrated on the main canyon, but the rest of North Fork needed to be surveyed. Now, in 1961, Sharrock sent Ed Keane and Johnny Conway (a high school student from Blanding) on horseback to survey the rest of North Fork, and they had proceeded accordingly for two days.

The June 28, 1961, entry in Sharrock's weekly reports states,

> Keane and Conway returned to camp at 3 p.m. with [Keane suffering from a] fractured tibia, cuts and abrasions. . . . Sharrock, Day, [Vance] Fowler, and Stevens took Keane to parked vehicles. Fowler, Sharrock and Day continued with Keane, stopping at Green Water Springs to exchange jeep for Dodge pickup. . . . Sharrock called ambulance from Natural Bridges, continued 15 miles toward Blanding before meeting County ambulance. Arrived with Keane at San Juan hospital in Monticello at approximately 11 p.m., put him in care of Dr. C.D. Goon.[5]

The good doctor looked at the X-rays and said he could not properly set the leg. The next

18.5. Field camp in Moqui Canyon, 1961. Photograph by David Dibble. Archaeology Center Collection, 42SA00-497. Courtesy of Special Collections, Marriott Library, University of Utah.

morning, Keane was flown to the University Hospital in Salt Lake City, where he was operated on. Despite early fears that he would be permanently crippled, he recovered and within a year was back skiing and racing sports cars.

The backstory is that Keane and Conway had located a high alcove site about 3 miles upstream from the confluence of the North Fork and the main stem of Moqui Canyon. There were some "Moqui steps"—hand- and toeholds cut into the Navajo Sandstone—leading up to the site. Keane was about 20 feet up the steps when he slipped and fell, shattering his left leg. Keane was 6' tall; Conway about 5'4", but a tough ranch kid who also played football. He made a splint for Keane's leg from some cottonwood branches and a rope, got him on his horse, and started for camp. At the confluence of the two canyons, the horse fell on Keane, further injuring his leg. Conway somehow got Keane back on the horse, and they trailed upstream to the camp. There Keane was given a shot of painkiller. Sharrock and the others got him back onto the horse and led the horse up the sand dune to the trucks and on to Blanding, as related above.

The second incident had to do with an apparent cattle rustling, as described by my brother, Vance Fowler. He was then eighteen. Professor Jennings had agreed to hire him, perhaps on the theory he couldn't do any worse than his older brother. Vance recalls the rustling incident as follows:

> On an otherwise uneventful Sunday, our one day off, we were relaxing after a hearty breakfast of Spam and hot cakes when a few head of Hereford cattle came round the bend from down-canyon. They belonged to the Scorup Land and Cattle Company, who had the grazing rights to much of San Juan County. Playing toreador, I chased them back down the canyon, but they reappeared a few minutes later. I started after them again, when an Indian girl carrying a lever-action rifle and leading a burro packing, probably, a slaughtered cow lashed under a tarp, came round the bend. She was accompanied by a large Indian of indeterminate sex on horseback. They spotted a dozen startled young men and a grizzled old cowboy staring at them. I have no idea who the two Indians thought we were. But the girl never breaking stride or looking at us, cocked her .30-30. Brig Stevens reached inside his tent, brought out, and cocked his .30-30. You could have heard a pin drop as they passed by on up the canyon. Not a word was spoken.
>
> The following day, Dave Dibble and I rode horseback downstream to the mouth of the canyon. We could see the cattle, horse and girl's tracks in the wet sand at the mouth of the canyon. Another crew working up canyon that day followed their tracks clear to the top of the canyon. They disappeared as mysteriously as they had come.[6]

BASKETMAKERS, PUEBLOANS, AND BURIED SITES

Moqui Canyon drains about 250 square miles of Mancos Mesa. From its headwaters at about 6,200 feet, it had a gradient of about 70 feet per mile for 30 miles. When the alluvial fill was in place, there was about 500 acres of arable land. Given what we had seen on previous surveys, we thought there might be significant sites related to farming on the alluvium that we assumed was there when the Indian people were there. Also, we knew that artifact collectors had been in Moqui Canyon in 1891–93 and 1897, and that John Wetherill had led Neil Judd there in 1923, and Bernheimer and Morris in 1929.

At least three of those parties had dug in sites with earlier Basketmaker materials in them. We had been singularly unsuccessful in finding clear evidence of Basketmaker occupations elsewhere. Hence, it was thought that relocating the Wetherill/Bernheimer sites might yield some remains of Basketmaker age that could be scientifically excavated rather than ripped out of the ground. Some of said sites were relocated and excavated by Sharrock's crew. It also turned out that the small wall section I had spotted protruding from the alluvial cut-bank became a key to understanding the downcutting and filling of alluvium in Moqui, and by inference, other lateral canyons (chapter 20).

The work of both the Kaiparowits and Moqui Canyon crews was deemed successful. The crews dispersed to homes or schools, and Sharrock, Dibble, and I turned to the job of analyzing the artifacts and writing up our reports.[7]

ETHNOGRAPHIC INTERLUDE

But before I did that, I spent six weeks in Lander, Wyoming, and on the adjacent Wind River Indian Reservation in my one, not very successful attempt to be an ethnographer. Since I had the NDEA fellowship in American studies, the thinking was that perhaps I should do a dissertation, or at least a master's thesis, on some topic that combined anthropology and American history. This ultimately led to a plan to study the ethnohistory of the Eastern Shoshone people—then living on reservations in northern Utah and on the Wind River reservation in Wyoming. Toward that end I had done much reading and archival work on the histories of said Indian people. I also applied for and received a Wenner-Gren Foundation predoctoral fellowship that provided funds for me to spend six or seven weeks in Wyoming and, later, at the Bancroft Library at the University of California, Berkeley.

I was given a three- or four-day crash course in how to do ethnography by Warren d'Azevedo, a marvelous ethnographer and great human being who would later figure very prominently in my professional and personal life. Warren had arrived at Utah in early 1961. He was, and is, an expert in both Great Basin Indian people and the peoples of West Africa. I had taken his seminar in Great Basin Indians in the spring term of 1961, where I met an undergraduate student named Catherine Sweeney.

In late September 1961, I drove my 1956 Chevrolet to Lander and found a reasonable motel where I could camp out for the duration. There was no place to stay on the reservation. The day I arrived it was 26 degrees and snowing. It got colder and stayed that way. Every day that I drove to the reservation, ice would accumulate under the car, and I'd often have to have it towed the next morning to the gas station to get it thawed out before it would start. My attempts to talk with the Indian people were not very successful. One elder and her daughter took me in for a while, I think because they felt sorry for me driving around in the cold. It never got above freezing, or so I remember, the entire time I was there. I did do some useful archival work in the Lander County Library—at least it was warm there. But it was clear that ethnography was not for me.

I returned to Salt Lake City, warmed up, and then drove to Berkeley, California, where I spent a glorious ten days working in the Bancroft Library at the University of California. There I met the eminent western historian Dale Morgan, who spent much time with me and gave me great guidance about how to do archival research. Through the good offices of Warren d'Azevedo, I met Robert Murphy, a well-known anthropologist, and Sydney Lamb, then just starting out as an anthropological linguist, both then on the faculty at Berkeley. They were extremely helpful and generous with their time. Ultimately, I did write a doctoral dissertation on Eastern Shoshone ethnohistory, at the University of Pittsburgh.[8] At the end of December I returned to Utah and went back to writing up my Glen Canyon Project work.

THE 1962 SEASON

Two Utah crews were in the field in 1962. One, led by Floyd Sharrock, was on the river for the first part of the season and then in the Greenwater Spring area in the San Juan Triangle. The second crew, led by me, was sent to the Virgin River valley for work centered on St. George and Zion Canyon.

THE RIVER CREW

The plans for the season were to accomplish three tasks. One was to finish up some details and mapping of the Creeping Dune site in the Little Rincon. The second was to use the boats and rafts to move downstream, work some additional sites at the mouth of Moqui Canyon, and evaluate and possibly dig some sites in Slickrock Canyon, downstream from Lake Canyon. These were sites I had recorded in 1959. Following that, the crew would move to Benchmark Cave, which Lipe and I had tested in 1958 and which we suspected was deeper and more complex than we'd determined in the time we had. A related task was to take pollen samples in cut-banks along the river and in the alluvial remnants in the side canyons, particularly Moqui and Lake canyons, to aid in reconstructing the ecological environments at the time prehistoric Indian people were there.

Sharrock and crew left their trucks at the mouth of Red Canyon—our old camp spot next to Bert Loper's cabin. Later in the season two of my crew and I drove from St. George to Red Canyon via Blanding, moved Sharrock's trucks to Kane Creek, then returned to St. George. It was a long three days and 1,300 miles, most of it, fortunately, over paved, or at least passable, roads.

Sharrock's weekly reports for the river trip record that the sites at the mouth of Moqui Canyon that we thought might be deep were not. Slickrock Canyon, the next canyon downstream, was a different matter. I had recorded sites on high ledges in alcoves. They turned out to contain numerous storage structures and small kivas (frontispiece). The importance of the canyon was not so much the structures, but that the alluvial fill in the canyon had not washed out as it had in the longer canyons such as Moqui, Lake, and most all the others (chapter 20). After Slickrock Canyon, the party moved downstream to Benchmark Cave.

In 1958 I had dug a long trench from outside the dripline to the back wall of the cave to a depth of about 7 feet. The deposits were dry, and we recovered yucca-fiber sandals, a hide pouch full of cotton seeds, another filled with paint, a sickle made on a mountain sheep horn, and a corrugated pot filled with coarse salt covered by an inverted bowl. There were remnants of cotton, yucca, agave, and prickly pear plants, some corncobs, remains of domesticated squash, and bones of mountain sheep and beaver. The pottery indicated people of the Kayenta tradition had used the site in the mid-1100s.[9]

However, as we mulled over the site, more questions came up—hence the return in 1962. Sharrock and his crew reopened and greatly expanded and deepened the main trench. What we in 1958 had taken to be the sterile "bottom" of the site was simply a layer of windblown dune sand, below which lay other culture-bearing levels. The "fire pits" we found in 1958 turned out to be roasting pits for prickly pear pads. The cave was excavated to bedrock, some 14 feet below the surface, far below our 1958 "sterile" layer. It was still assumed, based on the pottery, that the primary occupation had been intermittent during the mid-1100s. The people may or may not have grown the corn and beans, and possibly some cotton, on the broad terrace in front of the site.

But the story doesn't end there. In the 1990s, Phil Geib, during a restudy of the Glen Canyon area, had three of the sandals from the cave radiocarbon dated, and they proved to be between 5,800 and 3,200 years in age.[10] In other words, people had visited the cave long, long before the Kayentans of the 1100s CE stopped by to dine on roasted prickly pear pads, corn, squash, mountain sheep, and beaver. More on all this in chapter 20.

The moral of the story is the ongoing value of carefully collected and carefully curated collections and related documentation. Geib was able to go to the University of Utah Natural History Museum, check the accession records, find the sandals, and have samples of them taken and submitted for radiocarbon dating. Those data, and many others carefully collected and analyzed by Geib, permitted a revamping and retelling of the history of the people who sojourned in Glen Canyon, far earlier than we suspected in 1958 or 1962.

The crew was camped on the sandbar in front of Benchmark Cave for some time. My brother, Vance, was the cook, a step up from his shovel bum status of the previous year. The U.S. Coast and Geodetic Survey was doing some mapping and placing elevation markers, apparently where the full pool level of Lake Powell would be, in various areas of the canyon that summer. They had hired a helicopter firm to move them around, bring in supplies, and so on. One day the helicopter set down near the crew camp, and the pilot—an African American Korean War vet—came over for a cup of coffee. For the next couple of weeks he would stop by when he could. One day a National Geographic film crew arrived by boat to shoot some footage of the excavation. At the same time, Hugh Cutler, of the Missouri Botanical Garden, and his party arrived. Cutler was a former river runner, but also an expert on domesticated plant remains. He identified all the specimens we excavated during the project. Brother Vance fed all these luminaries, including the helicopter pilot.

At some point it was quietly mentioned that the crew was running out of toilet paper but not scheduled to go to town for about ten days. The next day the helicopter came by, hovered long enough to drop off a twelve-pack of TP, and flew away. They never saw him again.

When they finished at Benchmark Cave, Sharrock and his crew floated on down to Kane Creek Landing, where my crew and I had moved his trucks, and headed for the Castle Wash area in the San Juan Triangle. There they continued the work they had started at the end of the 1961 season. What they found there is incorporated into chapter 20.

THE VIRGIN RIVER AREA

In the work done on the Kaiparowits Plateau in 1958 and 1961, various materials, mainly pottery, relating to what was then called the "Virgin Branch of the Anasazi culture" had been collected. In the 1930s, Harold Colton and his compatriots at the Museum of Northern Arizona had defined various "branches" of various cultural traditions primarily on pottery types (see below). The Virgin Branch (for the Virgin River in Utah and Nevada) was assumed to basically be Kayenta West. The sites salvaged in the early 1930s along the lower Virgin River (later to be inundated by Lake Mead) by Mark Harrington of the Southwest Museum were also deemed to be Virgin Branch. To link the Kaiparowits materials to the Virgin Branch sites proper, Jennings obtained a grant from the National Science Foundation to support a season of fieldwork. Mel Aikens and I led a crew of five. T. J. Barrette came back for another season; others were Robert Jacka, Wichita State University; Walter Schumsky, Fairmont College; Alan Kosse, University of Chicago; and David Jennings, Salt Lake City. We were based out of St. George, the largest (then and certainly now) of the cluster of Mormon settlements in "Utah's Dixie." We initially camped along the Santa Clara River, a tributary of the Virgin River.

The crew's only complaints were the summer heat (the St. George area is about the same elevation as Las Vegas) and the no-see-ums, the ever pestiferous gnats. We ate well, since we could nip into St. George, about 5 miles away, for fresh produce and meat as needed, as well as feasting on hamburgers and malts at the Sugar Loaf Cafe. After our Kaiparowits cuisine of the previous year, Aikens and I thought we were in culinary heaven. There was also a bar where we could drink cold beer and play pool with the Arizona Highway Department engineers then starting to build I-15 down through the Virgin River canyon below St. George.

We began excavating a village site overlooking the Santa Clara River. We called it Three Mile Ruin. It was a semicircular unit pueblo with a courtyard inside the circle. We excavated twelve rooms, and there were probably eight or ten others in another section of the semicircle. It contained Virgin Branch ceramics dating from about 900 to 1200 CE.

There was a local chapter of the Utah State Archaeological Society in St. George, avocational archaeologists who volunteered to help us, and some did. Mel Aikens and I attended a meeting of the chapter. Both of us, coming from Mormon backgrounds, were not surprised that the opening prayer included the hope that divine guidance would be forthcoming to help chapter members find lots of artifacts. Said guidance was apparently for those who signed on to help us, and those who might dig elsewhere, whether it was legal to do so or not.

After Three Mile Ruin we sampled a small site on a bluff overlooking the goose necks of the Virgin River south of St. George and a second, very badly vandalized site east of St. George. Both were Virgin Branch in affiliation.

We next moved to a camp in Parunuweap Canyon at the mouth of Zion Canyon. The east fork of the Virgin River runs through the canyon and joins the north fork of the Virgin, which drains Zion Canyon proper. On the advice of the Zion Park naturalists, we worked on two village sites above the river. One of them, it turned out, had been excavated in the 1930s—a second "Fowler's Folly," in effect. No harm was done, just a waste of a few man days and a red face for the crew chief. The second site proved to contain thirteen masonry storage cists, probably built to hold foodstuffs grown on the floodplain below the knoll. We also sampled some caves and related dune areas at about 5,000 feet elevation, west of the boundary of Zion National Park, but found little.

Lastly, the crew moved to Johnson Canyon, near Kanab, Utah. In 1871 John Wesley Powell's men had established their survey camp in the mouth of the same canyon. Johnson Canyon contains spectacular scenery. Looking upcanyon one can see some of the "stair-step" cliffs of Powell's and Dutton's Grand Staircase. The canyon also then contained a western town movie set used in one of the many shoot-'em-ups filmed in the Kanab area in the 1940s and 1950s.

One of the archaeological sites, later named Bonanza Dune, proved to be a major find. It contained a series of house floors and a kiva at different levels totaling some 20-plus feet of deposit. We didn't finish the site, but Mel Aikens went back in 1963 to work on it some more.[11]

ETHNOARCHAEOLOGY IN THE GLEN CANYON COUNTRY

One of the culture history problems that Professor Jennings wanted to pursue during the Glen Canyon Project was determining the locations of traditional camping and resource areas used by Southern Paiute people in historic times (after 1760–76) and before. Domínguez and Escalante had encountered Southern Paiute people from about present-day Cedar City, Utah, southward into the Virgin River drainage and west of Navajo Mountain after they crossed the Colorado River in Glen Canyon. The Mormons encountered them also around Kanab, on the Kaibab and Shivwits plateaus, and in the Escalante and Fremont river drainages, as well as along the lower Virgin River and in the Las Vegas Basin.

In the 1930s anthropologists had done several distribution studies of Paiute and Ute tribes, drawing lines on maps delineating "traditional" band and tribal territories. The maps were part of a larger "culture element distribution" study administered by A. L. Kroeber, the senior anthropologist at the University of California, Berkeley, in the 1930s. The basic assumption of the so-called "culture history school" had its roots in nineteenth-century German anthropology.[12] The principal assumption was that cultures are made up of conglomerations of "traits" or "elements."

A culture trait was whatever the analyst wanted it to be—designs on baskets or pots; shapes or manufacturing techniques of baskets or pots; styles of moccasins; styles of bows; shapes of projectile points; masonry techniques in architecture; a particular myth or legend; and so on. A specific "culture" was the sum total of the elements that made it up. One task of anthropology—and particularly archaeology—was to trace the distributions of traits, or the conglomerations of traits making up specific cultures, through space and time. But traits—for example, pottery design styles—could obviously be borrowed from one group of people to another. Thus, in the Glen Canyon Country, the same pottery design styles were found on vessels from the Kayenta and Mesa Verde subareas of the Ancestral Puebloan culture. While the designs were the same, the temper and paste of the pottery were not; hence, different "pottery types" that visually looked alike could be distinguished by the cognoscenti.

But what about the historic ethnic groups—the tribes or bands that were encountered on the land when Euro-Americans arrived? In the Great Basin there were various Paiute, Ute, Shoshone, Goshute, and other groups who spoke variants of Numic languages—the groups that had interested John Wesley Powell (chapter 5). But what were their cultural-historical connections? Aside from language, how did they relate to each other? Kroeber and his compatriots thought that detailed distribution studies of a standard list of "culture elements" would resolve the question.

Accordingly, Kroeber sent his graduate students to find out: to California, to parts of the Northwest Coast, and to the Great Basin. Julian Steward conducted such studies for Kroeber across the central and western Great Basin after he was fired from the University of Utah in 1933. Those studies ultimately resulted in his major work on Great Basin peoples, published in 1938.[13] Another graduate student, Isabel T. Kelly, was sent to the southern reaches of the Great Basin and the adjacent Glen Canyon Country to delineate and study the various Southern Paiute groups found there. Her work later would be critical to the Glen Canyon Project and to subsequent studies of, and with, Southern Paiute people.

Isabel T. Kelly (1906–82) was born and grew up in Santa Cruz, California.[14] An excellent scholar and athlete, she intended to major in physical education at the University of California, Berkeley. But due to an administrative mix-up she was denied admission into the P.E. program and registered for an anthropology course instead. She received her bachelor's degree in anthropology in 1926 and was admitted to graduate school at Berkeley the same year under the benign, if demanding, tutelage of A. L. Kroeber, Robert Lowie, and Edward Gifford in anthropology, and Carl Sauer in geography. Kelly wanted to be an archaeologist, and she attended an archaeological field school in 1929 sponsored by the Laboratory of Anthropology in Santa Fe and directed by A.V . Kidder. But her mentor, Kroeber, thought that women should either work in museums or be ethnographers. On her own, Kelly studied a Northern Paiute community in Surprise Valley, California, and a Coast Miwok group in northern California. Her doctoral dissertation was a library study, "Fundamentals of Great Basin Culture," a culture element and culture history treatise.

Kelly received her doctorate in 1932 in the midst of the Depression, a time when there were very few jobs for anthropologists, male or female. However, she received a two-year fellowship from the National Research Council to study Great Basin tribal geographic and subsistence bases. She chose to work with the Southern Paiute peoples, whose traditional territories spanned, as we have seen, the southern Great Basin and much of the Glen Canyon Country. In addition to the fellowship, Kelly received a total of $650 to purchase collections of traditional material culture for Berkeley, the Harvard Peabody Museum, the Laboratory of Anthropology, and the American Museum in New York. She ultimately collected 325 well-documented items.

Kelly got on well with her Native consultants. In September 1932, she wrote to Kidder, "The past week I have been camped in the wilds at Indian Peak, sixty miles from here [Cedar City, Utah], on exceedingly chummy terms with 7 Paiute, 9 horses, and countless canines resident there. This does not include the amiable bobcat which wandered into my tent one moonlit night."[15] She ultimately collected a large body of excellent information on traditional Southern Paiute cultures from the San Juan Paiute, north of Navajo Mountain, to the lower Virgin and Las Vegas valleys, as well as the related Chemehuevi people in the Mojave Desert and along the west bank of the lower Colorado River. By the mid-1934, Kelly wound up her work with the Southern Paiute and Chemehuevi. She published a couple of excellent articles but took the bulk of her materials with her to Mexico.[16]

Isabel Kelly lived in Mexico for the rest of her life, doing what she had always wanted to do—be an archaeologist. She made major contributions to Mexican archaeology, especially western Mexico, but also worked as an applied anthropologist, not only in Mexico, but around the world. In 1960 Jesse Jennings contacted Kelly and asked if she would write up her materials on the Southern Paiute groups most closely connected to the Glen Canyon Country. She did so, and her monograph appeared in the Glen Canyon series in 1964.[17]

While Kelly's monograph provided a general framework for Southern Paiute culture history, Jennings wanted more ethnohistoric and on-the-ground surveys. He took two steps. One, he hired Robert C. Euler, a well-known anthropologist with expertise in western North American archaeology and ethnography. Two, he hired a promising undergraduate anthropology major, Catherine (Kay) Sweeney.

Robert (Bob) C. Euler (1924–2002) was born in New York City but grew up in Manitou Springs, Colorado.[18] When Euler was in high school, James Henry Breasted, the great Middle Eastern archaeologist from the University of Chicago, came to lecture at the local high school. He told Breasted of his interest in American Indian cultures and asked career advice. Breasted recommended the University of New Mexico (UNM).

Euler took his advice, but after a year and a half left to join the Marine Corps in October 1942. After boot camp and officer training he was commissioned a second lieutenant. In February 1945 he found himself leading his platoon onto the beach at Iwo Jima. On the nineteenth day of the horrific battle he was wounded, and spent months recovering in military hospitals before he was discharged. He returned to school at Arizona State College (now Northern Arizona University) and earned bachelor's and master's degrees in economics. He was then hired as a ranger at Wupatki National Monument, where he undertook a study of the economics of the Navajo people who lived nearby. In the fall of 1948 he returned to UNM and completed his doctoral course work, ultimately writing his dissertation on the culture history of the Hualapai people who live on the south rim of the Grand Canyon.

In 1952 he was hired as an ethnologist at the Museum of Northern Arizona and then curator of the Department of Anthropology. He did ethnography, archaeology, and ethnohistory. When the Indian claims cases began in the 1950s, he did ethnographic and ethnohistoric research for the Hualapai, Chemehuevi, and Southern Paiute tribes.[19] In 1956 he was hired by Arizona State College to establish an undergraduate major in anthropology there, which he did, also continuing ethnohistoric work on the claims cases. It was Euler's expertise in Southern Paiute ethnohistory that led Jennings to hire him part-time to help develop a program to study Southern Paiute ethnohistory and archaeology in the Glen Canyon Country.

Catherine (Kay) Sweeney (b. 1940) was born in Missoula, Montana. Her paternal grandfather had emigrated from Ireland to Montana, where he married and worked as a stage driver and various other occupations. Her mother's grandparents were of French Canadian descent and had come from Montreal to Butte, Montana, in the 1890s. Kay's parents, Vincent and Elizabeth Coburn Sweeney, were married in 1937, and Kay was born three years later. Vince then worked for the U.S. Forest Service. At the start of World War II he went to work as a civilian employee of the U.S. military in supply, a career he pursued until his retirement. When World War II began, the government established major army and navy supply depots in northern Utah; Hill Field, later Hill Air Force Base, had been established in 1940. The locations were chosen because they were beyond the range of Japanese bombers, and connected to major east-west rail lines that went through Ogden and Salt Lake City. The Sweeneys moved to Ogden, where Vince worked as a logistics administrator in the army supply depot for many years, later transferring to Hill Air Force Base. Kay grew up in Ogden, where she attended Catholic primary and high schools and was active in the Girl Scouts.

In 1956 and 1957 Kay traveled to Santa Fe, New Mexico, to participate in a Girl Scout–sponsored "Dutton's Dirty Diggers" program. From 1947 through 1957, Bertha Dutton, a curator at the Museum of New Mexico, ran a two-week summer field program for senior Girl Scouts fifteen to seventeen years old. The programs, called Mobile Camps, included visits to ongoing archaeological digs, Pueblo dances, and national parks and monuments (Chaco Canyon, Mesa Verde, and others). In 1954 a second program was added during which the girls participated in the excavation of Pueblo Largo—a late Pueblo site in the Galisteo Basin south of Santa Fe. Kay participated in two Mobile Camp programs, and they provided her introduction to anthropology and archaeology.

As an aside, over the decade of its existence, more than 280 Girl Scouts participated in the program. Dutton inspired many to go on to university, business, and medical careers. Several went on to careers in anthropology. Three of them ultimately worked for the Glen Canyon Project: Nettie Kessler Adams and Mary Anne Stein at the Museum of Northern Arizona (chapter 19) and Catherine Sweeney at Utah.

Although anthropology intrigued her, Kay really wanted to be a large animal veterinarian. She had owned horses from age twelve and worked for a veterinarian in the summers. But she was told that women did not do large animal veterinary medicine. So she opted for anthropology. After two years at Weber Junior College, she arrived at the University of Utah anthropology department in 1960. Jesse Jennings and other faculty members soon recognized her smarts. In the summer of 1961 she was hired as the anthropology department secretary when the regular secretary left suddenly. In the fall of 1961 she was put to work on background ethnohistory studies and a bibliography on the Southern Paiute as a student–staff member of the Glen Canyon Project. Her work was guided by Bob Euler.

In March 1962 Kay traveled to Flagstaff to meet with Euler and look at collections and records at the Museum of Northern Arizona. On the way there she began what would become a lifelong relationship with the family of Carl and Minnie Jake, prominent Southern Paiute elders who lived in Cedar City. Their son, daughter-in-law, and three other elders were also present at their first meeting. From Carl, Kay learned that Tom Mix and Jimmy

Timmican, of Richfield, had lived on the west side of the Henry Mountains and would be likely to help her. Carl and his people knew the country all around Cedar City, had traveled as far northwest as Panguitch Lake, but son Mike, especially, had hunted on the Kaiparowits Plateau and in the high country to the west of the plateau. He would know all the springs in the region and their names, as well as other prominent topographic features.[20]

After her trip to Flagstaff, Kay went to Hurricane, Utah, to meet with Vilate Hardy. Vilate was a remarkable woman—warm, generous, with a wry sense of humor—a homemaker, gardener, and amateur archaeologist with a marvelous southern Utah Mormon accent. She was well acquainted with many Indian people who respected her. Vilate put Kay in contact with Southern Paiute people in Santa Clara, Utah, at the Shivwits reservation and in Moccasin, Arizona, at the Kaibab reservation. At Kaibab, Kay met people whose grandparents had known John Wesley Powell in the 1870s. Memories of "Kapurats"—right arm off—had been passed down through the generations.

One elder at Santa Clara, Tony Tillohash, proved to be of special interest. As a young man he had been sent to the Carlisle Indian School in Pennsylvania. The school had been established in 1879 by Richard Pratt as a boarding school for Indian children. The idea was to bring them there from all over the country and forcibly (if need be) enculturate them into white culture, whether or not they, or their families, wanted that to happen.

Tony had been sent there in 1908. The famous anthropologist/linguist Edward Sapir found him and used him as a consultant to compile a massive Southern Paiute volume of texts and dictionary.[21] Tony was taught to be a harness maker, a totally useless skill by the time he returned west. Tony was not able to give Kay too much help with identifying traditional Paiute places in the Glen Canyon Country, but he was later to be of enormous help to her and me in annotating all the Southern Paiute place-names John Wesley Powell had collected in the 1870s.[22]

On a second visit with Carl and Minnie Jake, Kay met Lavan Martineau, an Anglo man married to a Southern Paiute woman. He affirmed the names of Paiute elders living in Richfield who were born in or knew the Escalante drainage country and the Henry Mountains. Martineau would later publish a book on rock art and another on Southern Paiute culture and language.[23]

Kay continued to compile bibliography and background materials in consultation with Bob Euler. She had been assigned a cubicle on the second floor of the GCP lab. My office was there as well. We began going for coffee, and then out to dinner. As June approached, we both prepared to go to the field—I with my crew to St. George, Kay to start field trips with Paiute elders.

While we were digging near St. George, Kay came to visit a couple of times. On the first trip she wrote to Jennings, "Don's crew seems to be surviving in the heat and the site is most interesting! I was very fascinated as I have not seen archaeology in action except on two occasions."[24] She and I also went with my crew to Summit, Utah, near Cedar City, to visit the UCLA archaeological field school, then excavating a large Virgin Branch site, the Evans Mound.[25] Mary Mulroy, who had worked for Utah on the Glen Canyon Project, was one of the field supervisors. The visit was an occasion for a lengthy party, which I remember principally because I heard Beethoven's *Ode to Joy* played for the first time on a five-string banjo (a Pete Seeger standard, I later learned).

SEEKING SOUTHERN PAIUTE SITES

The day after the party Kay arrived in Richfield, Utah, to keep an appointment she had made with a Paiute elder, Tom Mix, who had agreed to go with her into the Escalante country.[26] Tom had been given the nickname because he had worked as an extra in various Westerns shot in and around Kanab in the 1940s and 1950s. When she couldn't find him, she consulted with the local police chief, who had him in the hoosegow on a drunk charge. The local Mormon bishop assured Kay that Tom now and then was a guest there, but was a good guy. And so he proved to be.

Kay and Tom set out for Escalante. Along the way he gave her place-names and told her that he was born in Bryce Canyon. In Escalante the ever-helpful Loyd Gates had arranged for a local senior man, Joe Pollock, to go with her and Tom out into the country to look for sites. They began along the Hole-in-the-Rock road, and Tom was able to point out places he and his family had camped, including an often used winter camp at Panther Seep. The next day they investigated the Pine Creek area northwest of Escalante. There Tom was able to identify sites where wikiups had been built, including one where his wife and child had died of smallpox, as well as a dance circle and a pine nut gathering camp. The following day they visited a place west of Escalante that Tom's father had homesteaded about 1905. They also visited an ochre-gathering site where Tom's father and others had gathered the paint materials and traded it north to Ute people and south to Navajos. They recorded more place-names and information about trails leading cross-country.

Tom Mix had lived in Escalante in his younger days and was well known by local residents. As Kay wrote to Professor Jennings, "He enjoys talking about the old times, and is most happy here at Escalante. Most all of the town's people know him and hold him in high esteem. He goes through town after our work is finished and visits with everyone. People stop him on the street and chat at length."[27]

A local man, Edson Alvey, took Kay to visit sites he knew about, where they observed burials in rock crevices containing a mixture of Indian and white artifacts and tools. Alvey also led her to various Paiute residential sites with grinding slabs, manos, and the distinctive Southern Paiute brownware sherds.

While Kay was in Escalante, Bob Euler came to visit and check on her progress and visited some sites. He was working as time permitted with Southern Paiute people at Moccasin, Arizona.

Kay had also met the second Paiute elder, Jimmy Timmican, in Richfield. He claimed to have grown up in the Henry Mountains area. Accordingly, a second field trip was arranged. As it turned out, his knowledge of the Henry Mountain area was second-hand, but he did know about sites around Torrey near Fish Creek. He also led Kay and Joe Pollock to a complex pronghorn corral and associated hunting blinds on Parker Mountain, and to his birthplace south of Loa.

The Great Basin Anthropological Conference was held in Carson City on September 7–8, 1962. Kay (with Euler as junior author of one paper) presented her first two papers at a professional meeting. Mel Aikens gave a report on what he and I had done in southwestern Utah in the summer of 1962, and Kent Day, another Utah graduate student, reported on the final work in the Glen Canyon area and the salvage work Utah was then conducting in the Flaming Gorge area.[28] It was all part of Jennings's pushing to develop his students into professionals.

The week before the conference I had returned with my crew to Salt Lake City, my six-year periodic sojourn in the Glen Canyon Country at an end. I spent a couple of days with my new fiancée, Kay Sweeney (we had agreed to wed during one of her visits to St. George), and hopped on a plane to Pittsburgh. There I entered the University of Pittsburgh's doctoral program in anthropology. The following June I returned to Salt Lake and married Kay in the living room of David and Esther Pendergast (see below), with our relatives, friends, and Warren and Kathleen d'Azevdo, as well as Jesse and Jane Jennings, looking on. We then loaded a small U-haul trailer, attached it to our 1956 Chevy sedan, and headed to Pittsburgh. Kay had also been admitted to Pitt's doctoral program. We finished our doctorates and ultimately both became professors at the University of Nevada, Reno.

But we were not through with the Glen Canyon Country and those associated with it. During a year at the Smithsonian Institution (1967–68), we edited and later published John Wesley Powell's manuscripts on the Numic peoples (with place-name annotations by Tony Tillohash), as well as Powell's and Hillers's diaries of the 1871–72 river trip and Powell's collection of Numic material culture. In 1969 we helped celebrate the centennial of Powell's first river trip.[29]

In 1970–72, the Smithsonian Institution, in collaboration with CBS News, briefly sponsored a series of intellectual adventure documentaries starring Wally Schirra, famed as one of the original seven astronauts. Schirra had joined CBS a couple of years earlier as a commentator. The powers that be decided that a documentary re-creating John Wesley Powell's first river trip would be good. Having recently been at the Smithsonian working on Powell's archives, and just appointed as a research associate in anthropology, I became the Smithsonian's "Powell expert."

The plot line was Wally—with his wife, Jo, and daughter Susie—accompanying me on a trip down the Green and Colorado rivers. We began shooting in Green River, Wyoming, and ended at Separation Rapid in the Grand Canyon. The float trip through Lodore Canyon and Split Mountain was managed by Clair Quist of Moki Mac. The producer, who was along on the trip, was Isaac Kleinerman (1917–2004), a legendary producer and film editor at NBC and later CBS News, whose credits included the *Victory at Sea* and *Twentieth Century* and *Twenty-first Century* series. It was a great experience and led to my being a talking head on other documentaries relating to Powell over the next three decades, particularly an *American Experience* film in 1999.[30]

Kay became a nationally recognized expert on Numic languages and cultures, as well as American Indian art and ethnobiology, studies she still pursues fifty years later and counting, along with other interests.[31] Ultimately, she was appointed as a trustee of the National Museum of the American Indian of the Smithsonian Institution, serving her third term as of 2010.

WHAT DID IT ALL MEAN?

In later years, as I have given illustrated lectures about Glen Canyon thither and yon across the country, I've been asked two major questions. One, what did I learn from my six years of working on the Glen Canyon Project? Two, did I (or "we" who collectively worked on the project, especially on the river) mourn the loss of Glen Canyon? The answers to question one are, first, only fools have adventures. The maxim in variant wordings has been attributed to several different explorers for at least a century. The core of its meaning is, if you have adventures—placing yourself and/or others in harm's way—you haven't properly and adequately prepared for the task at hand and/or have taken unnecessary risks. It's a maxim I drilled into my students and staff from 1966 to 2004 when I ran field research programs of my own. Second, archaeology requires teamwork, both in the field and in the laboratory. You can't do it alone. Third, if it's not published, it doesn't exist. Fourth, large-scale archaeology projects cost lots of money. If you don't develop the skills to raise monies from federal grants and contracts, foundations, and (rarely) well-off donors, you're in the wrong business.

The second question, the loss of Glen Canyon, is addressed in chapter 21.

CODA: FOLK SONGS FOR ARCHAEOLOGISTS

Archaeologists who camp out in the wilds traditionally entertained themselves, at least in pre–microelectronic music box days. Usually someone could play a guitar, banjo, or ukulele (often very loudly to cover a lack of talent). Every crew developed a repertoire of favorites. Often a known song, folk or popular, would be given new words reflecting the experiences of the field crews, the verses full of inside jokes. Thus, the immortal ditty, popular in Harris Wash in 1961 for two or three days, "'Twas a sad day when the green jeep went down," composed and sung off-key by Tom Lynch, was based on the folk song *There Was a Ship Titanic:* " . . . it was sad when the great ship went down," and so on.

The Utah anthropology department was fortunate to have a resident songwriter, David Pendergast, who had joined the faculty in 1960. He was something of a prodigy, had done archaeological work in western Mexico, and had written and defended a doctoral dissertation at UCLA in a very short time, then turning it into published articles. He and his wife, Esther, were only a couple of years older than those of us working on the Glen Canyon Project. We naturally partied together often, drinking beer and Jim Beam, watching Ernie Kovacs and Edie Adams specials and Bugs Bunny cartoons on TV, and sharing a feigned disdain for authority in the person of Professor Jennings. While Dave did not go into the field with us, he listened to our stories and turned them into songs. There were several, the most notable being:

> "THE DIGGER: OR, THE ARCHAEOLOGIST'S LAMENT," BY DAVID M. PENDERGAST, MAY 1961, SUNG TO TUNE OF "THE FROZEN LOGGER." Printed by permission of the author.
>
> As I walked out one evening
> To an old Southwest café
> My thoughts were of my field crew
> They were many miles away.
>
> My order of peanut butter
> With a slab of bread did come
> But alas, there was no knife, so
> I had to spread it with my thumb.
>
> As I sat there a-spreading,
> A haggard broad walked by
> And glanced down at my sandwich
> With a bleary, bloodshot eye.
>
> She sat down right beside me;
> I could not get away
> It was clear that there was something
> She was trying hard to say.
>
> She turned her fair lips to me,
> And I smelled that Jim Beam reek;
> And then those fair lips parted,
> And she started in to speak:
>
> I see that you are a digger,
> A kind of a common bum.
> For nobody but a digger
> Spreads peanut butter with his thumb.
>
> My lover was a digger,
> And one of the very best.
> He could dig from dawn 'til sunset,
> And never stop to rest.
>
> He lived on stale C-rations
> And lumps of sour dough
> But when asked, "Do you call this living?"
> He'd smile and say, "Hell no."
>
> His favorite sport was drinking
> White lightning on the rocks
> You could find him every evening
> Straining sterno through his socks.

He signed on the Glen Canyon
One sad and fateful day.
He could not know by signing
he had thrown his life away.

He dug down in the Canyon
And up on the Plateau.
And he did it not for money,
But for science, as you know.

He explored the Colorado,
Using twenty props a day.
If it had not been for puddles,
He could have walked it all the way.

He mushed on down the river
And climbed each talus slope.
And emblazoned on his forehead
Was the magic slogan, "Cope!"

He dug at Crumbling Kiva
And Horsefly Hollow too,
And the year was almost over
When he met his Waterloo.

He started out one morning
And climbed the cliffs so high
To dig another PIII structure,
Though he vaguely wondered why.

At last he reached the ledge, and
He started in to work.
In the true GC tradition,
He was shoveling like a Turk.

At noon the dig was finished;
He began his homeward trip.
And 'twas just as he was leaving
That he made his fatal slip.

He forgot that he was standing
On a mighty narrow ledge.
He stepped back to take a last look
And then tumbled off the edge.

His final words resounded
As he hurtled down the cliffs:
"Dig it all by natural levels,
And don't chalk those petroglyphs!"

And so I lost my lover,
And to this café I came;
And here I wait 'til someone
Spreads peanut butter with his thumb.

There are several inside jokes in the song, but two need noting. Jennings had the habit of delegating incoming letters or memos requiring some sort of action to staff members whenever he could. He would send a memo with "DF Cope. JDJ" scrawled across the top. I, or whoever the addressee was, did so. "Don't chalk those petroglyphs" referred to a letter from J. O. Brew, known from his rotund form as the "D-shaped Director" of the Peabody Museum of Anthropology at Harvard University. "Jo" (as he was known to all) had requested some slides of rock art in Glen Canyon. Jennings had sent him copies of slides I had taken at the mouth of Smith Fork Canyon. We had chalked in the figures so they would show up better and photographed them before we slathered them over with six coats of rubber latex. Brew's response was, "We at Harvard never chalk our petroglyphs." At the time we all thought it an instance of Harvard snobbery. But in later years, after I got to know Brew a bit, I decided it was a joke of his own on Harvard stuffiness. At the same time, he was right. Ideally, rock art should never be enhanced before it is photographed. But at Smith Creek we had no time to wait for cloudy days (there was a lot of glare on the rock surfaces), and the figures were to be covered with six coats of rubber latex, then peeled off, despite Elizabeth Sprang's displeasure (chapter 14), and would soon go under several hundred feet of water.

> 19 <

THE MUSEUM OF NORTHERN ARIZONA AND THE GLEN CANYON PROJECT

IN 1912 HAROLD S. COLTON AND MARY-Russell Ferrel were married. Both were from prominent eastern Pennsylvania families. Colton was a zoology professor at the University of Pennsylvania. They spent their honeymoon on an extensive camping trip through New Mexico and Arizona. They fell in love with the Southwest, particularly the Colorado Plateau and the area around Flagstaff, Arizona. In 1916 they rode in a mule-drawn wagon from Flagstaff to the Hopi mesas to witness a Snake Dance at Oraibi. There they met archaeologist Byron Cummings (chapter 10, 13). The same summer, they found their first archaeological site while picnicking east of Flagstaff. They were hooked, and began a systematic survey of sites in the Flagstaff area each summer. By 1928 they had recorded and published data on 1,250 sites.

As early as 1922 the Coltons were discussing the possibilities of a regional museum with the citizens of Flagstaff. In 1927 they incorporated the Northern Arizona Society of Science and Art. The previous year they had purchased 100 acres of pine forest along Fort Valley Road, just west of Flagstaff. There, in time, the Coltons and their associates built the Museum of Northern Arizona (MNA), with Harold Colton as director. In 1929 Lyndon Hargrave was hired as assistant director; in 1930 Katherine Bartlett was hired as curator of anthropology, and John C. McGregor as curator of archaeology.

Mary-Russell Colton became curator of art (she was an accomplished artist) and began the museum's program of collecting, studying, and encouraging the development of Navajo and Hopi arts and crafts that continues into the twenty-first century. From the outset MNA was, as it remains, a natural history and art museum devoted to the geology, biology/ecology, archaeology, ethnography, and arts of the Colorado Plateau.[1]

In the 1930s Colton, Hargrave, and McGregor expanded the museum's archaeology program to include the Tsegi Canyon/Marsh Pass and Navajo Mountain sections of the Glen Canyon Country. Hargrave was also the brains behind the archaeology program of the Rainbow Bridge–Monument Valley Expedition in the 1930s, of which MNA was a cooperating partner (chapter 13).

Harold Colton began moving toward retirement in the early 1950s. He convinced Edward (Ned) Bridge Danson Jr. to become a museum trustee in 1951 and assistant director in 1956, turning the directorship over to him in 1958. Ned Danson (1916–2000) was born in the Midwest. He found his way to Arizona and took a bachelor's degree in anthropology at the University of Arizona in 1940.[2] After naval service in World War II, he earned his doctorate at Harvard in 1952. His dissertation was on the archaeology of the upper Gila River area in eastern Arizona. He was on the faculty at the University of Arizona until he became the MNA assistant director in 1956. Ned was very much aware of the development of salvage archaeology programs after World War II—including highway and pipeline archaeology. He moved to position MNA to be involved in salvage programs while still a museum trustee. When the Glen Canyon Project began, MNA was prepared to play a central role.

THE MUSEUM OF NORTHERN ARIZONA AND THE GLEN CANYON PROJECT

The Museum of Northern Arizona's involvement with Glen Canyon began in 1952. Gene Foster had begun recording archaeological sites during river trips in Glen Canyon in 1952 and depositing her data with MNA. Gene Field Foster was born January 17, 1917 in Tomahawk, Wisconsin. She was named for her maternal grandfather, Eugene Field (1850–95), the famed Chicago newspaper columnist whose satirical daily column, "Sharps and Flats," delighted and sometimes enraged his readers with its mixture of satire and poetry, especially when skewering politicians. He also wrote children's poetry and is best remembered for "The Gingham Dog and the Calico Cat," "Little Boy Blue," "Wynken, Blynken and Nod," and others that became part of American culture.[3]

Foster moved to Flagstaff in the late 1940s. During a river trip she become enamored of Glen Canyon and purchased two ten-man rubber rafts and two Johnson outboard motors to run her own trips. As noted, she had begun recording archaeological sites and depositing her records with the MNA.

In the spring of 1957, when it appeared that contracts would be forthcoming for the Glen Canyon Project, Foster was hired to make additional surveys in lower Glen Canyon. In April 1957 she put together a volunteer crew that included Katherine Bartlett, by then MNA librarian, and three others. Foster made three trips between April and October 1957. David Brugge, an MNA research associate who would go on to a long and productive career as an archaeologist, Indian trader, and expert on the Navajo people, accompanied her on the second trip. The site data Foster collected were later incorporated into a survey and excavation report on lower Glen Canyon.[4]

One of the first tasks facing the contractors who were hired to build the dam was to build a company town. The nearest towns of any size were Flagstaff, 120 miles to the south, and Kanab, Utah, 80 miles to the northwest. U.S. Highway 89, connecting Kanab and Flagstaff, crossed the Colorado River at Lee's Ferry at the foot of Glen Canyon. A new 25-mile road had to be built from Bitter Springs, 14 miles south of Lee's Ferry, up through the Echo Cliffs, onto the Kaibito Plateau, and on to the Page town site. Road surveyors encountered an archaeological site in a rockshelter and asked MNA to undertake an emergency salvage project. David Breternitz was then a museum staff archaeologist, and he quickly took on the project. The site was difficult of access and was named Heltagito Rockshelter. The museum had already initiated a survey of Navajo Canyon prior to the Glen Canyon Project. The canyon is a major tributary entering

Glen Canyon a few miles upstream from the dam site. Breternitz and an MNA volunteer, William Miller, completed the survey in the fall of 1957 and the spring of 1958.[5]

Danson also hired William Y. (Bill) Adams, introduced briefly in chapter 13. Bill Adams has a unique history in twentieth-century American anthropology.[6] He was seven when his father, a UCLA history professor, died. Adams's mother, Lucy Adams, was a strong and brilliant woman. She went to work for the Bureau of Indian Affairs (BIA), taking Bill and his brother, Ernie, with her to Window Rock, Arizona, then the newly established administrative center for the Navajo, Hopi, and Southern Ute reservations. Bill lived there from 1937 to 1941. During World War II he led a somewhat nomadic life as many children did while their parents were involved in the war effort. His mother had various government jobs, both in the United States and Europe; Bill lived with relatives in California much of the time. He entered Stanford University in 1943 at age sixteen. At the end of his second year he enlisted in the navy. After he was discharged, he had two undergraduate years at the University of California, Berkeley, and then started graduate school there. In the summer of 1950 he received a grant to do a socioeconomic survey on the Navajo reservation. It was his report of this work at the 1951 Pecos Conference that led Walter Taylor to hire him for the Pueblo ecology study (chapter 13). After he finished his stint with Taylor, Adams wound up helping run a sheep drive from the Shonto Trading Post to the Santa Fe railroad. This led to a job as trader at the post, which lasted intermittently for several years.

In 1954 Adams enrolled at the University of Arizona instead of returning to Berkeley. He signed up for a class taught by Edward Spicer, a renowned ethnologist/ethnohistorian.[7] Sitting in the front row was "this lovely young undergraduate from Tulsa" named Nettie Kessler. Adams sat down next to her. He decided, "This is the one," and three weeks later asked her to marry him; she accepted.[8] They agreed to always work together as a team, and have done so very productively for fifty-five years and counting.

Nettie Kessler Adams, like Bill, was, and is, a remarkable person. As a Girl Scout she had been one of Bertha Dutton's "Dirty Diggers," participating in both the tours and the digs for two summers (chapter 18). She went with Adams back to the Shonto Trading Post, living in a hogan while he continued as a trader and ultimately wrote his doctoral dissertation on the role of traders in Navajo society.[9]

THE ADAMS AT THE MUSEUM OF NORTHERN ARIZONA

Once Ned Danson had a contract in hand for the MNA portion of the Glen Canyon Project, he hired Bill, as Adams says, "not so much because of any archaeological expertise but because I knew the area and the people."[10] His initial assignment was to survey the lower San Juan River; Nettie went along (fig. 19.1). The decision to start on the lower 71 miles of the San Juan Canyon was a logical one. Access to the lower canyon from overland is possible in very few places. In the fall of 1957 Bill and Nettie made overland trips by jeep to the canyon from the north side and recorded what sites they could. During the winter of 1957–58 Adams compiled information about previous Glen Canyon area surveys.[11] In March 1958, Bill and Nettie and Navajo wrangler Floyd Laughter made a pack trip from Navajo Mountain to the mouth of Paiute Creek where they recorded the Paiute Farms sites (chapter 20).[12]

In May and June 1958, Bill and Nettie Adams, with Frank Wright, made a river trip down the San Juan Canyon from Mexican Hat to the confluence, and later a motorboat trip on the Colorado from the confluence to river mile 13 to complete their survey.

19.1. Bill and Nettie Adams on the San Juan River, 1959. Photographer unknown, PO25C Box 2, ID 3, Grp. 7. Courtesy of Special Collections, Marriott Library, University of Utah.

It was clear to Danson as the Glen Canyon Project expanded that several additional surveys and test excavations would be needed and additional help would be required. Accordingly, he hired Lex Lindsay and Christy Turner.

Christy G. Turner II had begun as an archaeologist and photographer with MNA in 1956. He later went on to a major career as a physical anthropologist at Arizona State University. Alexander (Lex) J. Lindsay Jr. (fig. 19.2) was born in 1929, grew up in Denver, and graduated from the University of Denver. After military service as an army officer in Korea, he entered the graduate program at the University of Arizona. He came to MNA in late 1957 and the following year was placed in charge of the museum's field operations for the Glen Canyon Project. He was a staff member of the museum for many years, managing various salvage archaeology programs. After Glen Canyon he continued to work in the Kayenta region, producing a landmark dissertation on the Kayenta Anasazi.[13] Lex ultimately moved to Tucson, where he remains actively involved with research programs at the Arizona State Museum.

Following the Adams's San Juan survey, Bill Adams, Lex Lindsay, Christy Turner, and Frank Wright surveyed lower Glen Canyon and its tributary canyons. They investigated small pueblo sites at the mouth of Forbidding Canyon. The sites were visited by nearly every river trip that stopped to hike upcanyon to Rainbow Bridge and had been damaged over the years. They also investigated other small sites with evidence of temporary occupancy in Catfish and West canyons, as well as sites on the large river terraces. The latter were primarily lithic workshops.

Over the millennia the river had deposited gravels on the terraces (some of them the same gravels from which miners had tried to sluice gold). The gravel nodules were a major source of tool stone for people who had frequented the terraces—stone from which knives, scrapers, drills, projectile points, and other needed implements could be fashioned (chapter 20).[14]

Bill Adams left the MNA Glen Canyon Project at the end of 1959, partly because there was internal disagreement about Nettie being in the field, and partly, as he later wrote, "I left because I was offered the opportunity to plan archaeological salvage work along the River Nile, where the Aswan Dam was to be built—an opportunity so preposterously improbable that I could not refuse it." He and Nettie would be engaged in Nile Valley and Sudan research for many years thereafter, in 1959–66 and 1969–1984 becoming "so heavily involved . . . that . . . [we] have never [as of 1993] been able to disengage." He also played a major role in developing the anthropology department at the University of Kentucky, and ultimately retired from there as a distinguished professor.[15]

In 1959 a river-based crew led by Lindsay and assisted by Frank Wright excavated sites along both the San Juan and Colorado rivers. When Bill and

19.2. Alexander (Lex) J. Lindsay Jr. at a site in the Navajo Mountain area, 1961. Photographer Paul V. Long, P.GCP.65.10. Courtesy of the Museum of Northern Arizona.

Nettie Adams made their San Juan survey, they noted evidence of stone-lined farm plots and irrigation ditches near the mouths of Castle, Paiute, and Beaver creeks. The largest of these, at Beaver Creek, had earlier been recorded by the Rainbow Bridge–Monument Valley Expedition river trip survey in 1935. Lindsay and his crew excavated the Beaver Creek site, finding a sophisticated complex of ditches, rock-bordered garden plots, small houses, and a kiva (chapter 20).[16]

Later in the season, Lindsay and his crew moved into Glen Canyon proper and tested or excavated a series of sites between about river miles 71 and 38. One of the sites was on the left-bank terrace at Crossing of the Fathers. Pottery found in a small alcove indicated that people had been at the crossing by at least 1050 CE and in the fourteenth and fifteenth centuries.[17]

In 1960 Lindsay and his crew were again in Glen Canyon late in the season. His crew members (fig. 19.3) included Frank Wright; Calvin R. Cummings, who would go on to a fruitful career as an archaeological administrator in the National Park Service; and Michael E. Mosely, who became a distinguished archaeological expert on Andean civilizations.[18]

MNA RESEARCH IN THE UPLANDS

MNA assumed responsibility not only for the left banks (downstream orientation) of the San Juan and Colorado river canyons destined to be flooded by the dam, but also for a large section of the Rainbow Plateau and adjacent areas, in the midst of which Navajo Mountain (fig. 2.4) rises in its majesty. As Lex Lindsay wrote, “Navajo Mountain, a laccolith, has been lifted and formed by the forces of nature to such signal and magnificent proportions that it the most individually awesome in the Glen Canyon Basin. Whether seen nearby or from afar there is no mistaking its symmetric, nearly circular

19.3. Museum of Northern Arizona excavation crew in West Canyon, 1959: (*left to right*) Daniel Perin, Michael Mosely, Calvin Cummings, Alexander Lindsay Jr., Frank Wright. Photograph by Tad Nichols. Nichols Collection, NAU 22912. Courtesy of Cline Library, Northern Arizona University.

uplifted form—a solitary dome, rising above the Rainbow Plateau as a symbolic and majestic guardian of the Lower Glen and San Juan region."[19]

Some of the lower-elevation upland areas would be covered by the lake. Others, such as Cummings Mesa and Paiute Mesa (map 3), would not. But they would be accessible by boats once the lake filled, hence subject to vandalism. There was also a good scientific reason why the uplands needed to be investigated: given what was known from previous surveys and what had been learned by both the MNA and Utah teams by the end of the 1959 season, it was clear that the larger Ancestral Puebloan occupational sites were in the upland areas.[20] It seemed apparent that people moved down into the lower side canyons and along the river to farm, hunt, and collect tool stone during the summer months, but then most returned to the uplands (chapter 20).[21] Thus, for both scientific reasons and the potential problems of vandalism, the National Park Service agreed that it was appropriate to fund the MNA uplands work.

The agreement allowed the museum staff to schedule field seasons of up to six months, starting in 1958–59. In the early spring, when the rivers were high with winter runoff, teams could survey and begin excavation projects in upland areas. Later, May through October, teams could work from the river. The work both from the river and in the uplands was done with the permission and cooperation of the Navajo Nation.

For surveys and excavations in the uplands—the Rainbow Plateau and Navajo Mountain areas—the MNA teams faced the same logistics problems as the various earlier parties led into the area by John Wetherill. This was especially true in the so-called Bald Rock Crescent area and Nasja Mesa, lying between Navajo Mountain and the confluence (map 3).[22] Nasja Mesa is bounded on the east by Nasja Canyon, the upper end of which, on the flanks of Navajo Mountain, is Surprise Valley, which so delighted Zane Grey, Charles Bernheimer, and others who managed to find their way there (chapters 10, 13). The major canyons in the Crescent area include Mystery, Forbidding/Bridge canyons, and those draining the northern side of Cummings Mesa—Cathedral, False Entrance, Catfish, and Dungeon. It is extremely difficult country (figs. 19.4, 19.5). Lex Lindsay wrote of it, "Travel through this sub-area is slow by foot, tedious by horse, and impossible by automobile."[23] West of Cummings Mesa, the major canyons surveyed were West, Face, Labyrinth, Antelope, and Navajo.

19.4. Museum of Northern Arizona pack train on a slickrock area on Navajo Mountain along the trail to Cummings Mesa, April 1961. Photograph by Alexander J. Lindsay Jr., S.GCP.343. Courtesy of the Museum of Northern Arizona.

During the 1959 river survey, when the MNA team arrived at Mystery Canyon they could not get much beyond the mouth because of a high, steep jump-up. There was a series of pecked hand- and toeholds going up and around the jump-up, but it was too dangerous to attempt. After several attempts overland by pack train, a team led by Christy Turner, using the Rainbow Bridge Trail, were able to get into some sections of the canyon and its tributaries and record a few Pueblo II–III sites. The party included Noel Morss, who had surveyed in Navajo Canyon and on the Kaibito and

19.5. Museum of Northern Arizona pack train on the Oak Canyon trail, October 1960. Photograph by Christy Turner, S.GCP 611. Courtesy of the Museum of Northern Arizona.

Rainbow plateaus in 1927 (chapter 13), and Otis (Dock) Marston, river runner and indefatigable collector of Colorado river-runner history and lore.[24]

In April 1960 Lex Lindsay and J. Richard (Dick) Ambler (who was introduced in chapter 16), along with a small team, began a survey on Cummings Mesa. "Cummings Mesa, a dissected remnant of the Jurassic sediments which once covered all the Glen Canyon region, is one of the prominent topographic features in Lower Glen Canyon. . . . Like a three-fingered hand, the extremities of the mesa extend toward the Colorado River and rise above the river gorge in a series of vertical cliffs and ledges." The mesa is bounded on the west by Navajo Canyon. Other tributaries of the river, notably West, Dungeon, Catfish, Cathedral, and False Entrance canyons, "have carved a fantastic network of deep canyons and barren rock slopes on both sides of Cummings Mesa as well as the steep-sided inner gorge of Lower Glen Canyon."[25]

Elevations atop the mesa range from nearly 6,500 feet at the southern end to about 4,800 feet near the river. Logistics for the survey and excavation parties onto the mesa were difficult, reachable only by foot or on horseback. Two Navajo wranglers, Floyd Laughter and Eugene Holgate, were employed, "periodically negotiating the precipitous trails with supplies and equipment."[26]

> The starting and returning point for the two mesa top survey and excavation expeditions was Rainbow Lodge. The mesa was reached over several stock trails built and used by the

> Navajo Indian inhabitants of the area. . . . These hazardous stock trails lead west from Rainbow Lodge over a dune and sand-capped rock platform which terminates at the rim of Forbidding Canyon. Descent into the canyon is at the northern boundary of the "Kettle," so named by John Wetherill for its vast network of rugged canyons which coalesce in Forbidding Canyon to form the collecting basin for Aztec Creek. Proceeding westward the trails join into one, then ascend a series of talus slopes and precipitous ledges to reach the summit of the mesa's eastern escarpment.[27]

The MNA team began excavations on Cummings Mesa in April 1961. The team included Lindsay, Ambler, and Paul Long, a graduate student at the University of Arizona. Personal gear and basic food supplies were carried to the mesa top by pack mule. It was easier, however, to get excavation equipment and additional food supplies there by parachute. On April 20, 1961, Paul Long wrote in his journal,

> Food and equipment arrived today by an air drop. The supplies had been transported to Page to be dropped for us when we arrived in camp. It was a stirring sight to see shovels, picks, and dig boxes floating across the sky. We immediately scattered out to retrieve the supplies. Finally, the boxes of food came gyrating down. Most of the food was freeze dried packets. However, it was great to have something other than sandwiches for breakfast, lunch and dinner.[28]

MNA was fortunate to have a cadre of volunteers, many of them well trained in archaeological surveys and excavations. Several of them participated in the Cummings Mesa work, particularly William C. Miller, Charles Kearns, and Robert Sears, astronomers and photographers associated with the Mount Palomar and Mount Wilson observatories in California. A crew of Navajo workmen, who lived in the Navajo Mountain area, were recruited for the excavations in 1960, 1961, and 1962. Only a few of them worked all three seasons, but all of them were excellent workers who quickly learned the finer points of archaeological excavation and contributed greatly to the success of the MNA project.

The archaeological sites on Cummings Mesa and the upper reaches of its tributary canyons that were situated in open areas proved to be generally small—one- to three-room pueblos. One site, Surprise Pueblo, had a unit pueblo room block with pit houses along the back wall, as well as a large courtyard enclosed by a low rock wall. There was a small kiva inside the courtyard. Various small storage structures were found in several small overhangs below the rims of the tributary canyons.

Most of the open sites were occupied in the twelfth century and the beginning of the thirteenth—the same Pueblo II–early Pueblo II period as in the lower canyon areas. The large open site, however, had evidence of periodic Pueblo occupation into historic times. Most sites near any source of water were also occupied in historic times by Navajo people, principally as camps for grazing their animals.[29] There was also some indications of Basketmaker II occupation in some of the tributary canyons, but not on the mesa top.

Following their work on Cummings Mesa, the MNA teams moved on to other upland areas north and east of Navajo Mountain. The teams—led by Lex Lindsay, Dick Ambler, Paul Long, and Philip Hobler—made extensive surveys in several areas. They also carried out excavations at several sites that, collectively, provided a deep time depth for the occupation of the upland areas.

One area was Segazlin Mesa, sometimes called Lost Mesa, a small, steep-sided mesa near the base of Navajo Mountain. The crew established a base camp at the foot of the mesa with wall tents, an open ramada for cooking, and an artifact processing facility. The logistics were relatively easy with the Navajo Mountain Trading Post about a mile away. Several Ancestral Puebloan sites were excavated or sampled on the mesa.

Much more important in terms of understanding the overall culture history of the Glen Canyon Country were two cave sites in adjacent areas: Dust Devil and Sand Dune caves, both excavated in 1961 by Dick Ambler. Sand Dune Cave is located on the northeast side of Navajo Mountain on a tributary of Paiute Creek. It is 8 meters wide at the mouth and 24 meters from front to back, and had undisturbed archaeological deposits. Dust Devil Cave is located on the northeast side of Navajo Mountain in the upper reaches of Desha Creek. Both sites contained long records of Archaic occupations for several millennia before Ancestral Puebloan people were in the upland areas.[30] The sites are discussed in more detail in chapter 20.

ESTABLISHING FIELD LABS

Until early fall of 1961, basic artifact processing (washing, labeling, and cataloguing) for the Glen Canyon Project had been done at the MNA in Flagstaff, usually after the end of the field seasons. However, Lindsay thought that it would be more efficient to have the processing done at the field camps, at least for excavation projects where a team would be in one place during the course of work in a particular area. Elizabeth Galligan had been directing the laboratory processing in Flagstaff but had left to take another position. She recommended a fellow "Dutton's Dirty Digger," Mary Anne Stein, for the job.

Mary Anne Stein had been on both of Dutton's field programs and had met Elizabeth Gilligan on one of them. Dutton wrote a strong letter of recommendation to Edward Danson on Stein's behalf, and she was hired to direct the Glen Canyon Project laboratory. With a newly earned bachelor's degree in anthropology from the University of Oklahoma in hand, Stein arrived at MNA in early September 1961. She was almost immediately sent to the field with Lindsay, Long, and Ambler to the Segazlin Mesa camp to finish up excavation work there. Stein was an accomplished horsewoman and had camping experience with Dutton and elsewhere, but no experience in the fine art of four-wheeling in sand and across slickrock. She credits Lex Lindsay for being an able tutor in that regard.[31]

In 1962 one major focus for the MNA team was Paiute Mesa. Preliminary surveys, in addition to information from various reconnaissance trips in the 1920s and 1930s, indicated the presence of large pueblo sites on the mesa top. The logistics were fairly daunting. There was a road, sometimes more tracklike than roadlike, some of it along a precipitous rim of Paiute Canyon, that took at least four hours in low four-wheel drive from the nearest telephone and supply point at the Inscription House trading post. Lindsay, Ambler, and Hobler were the crew chiefs, and there were four undergraduate students. As in previous years, the Navajo workers from the Navajo Mountain area proved to be excellent excavators.

Lindsay again decided that a field laboratory would be the most efficient. Stein was already on board as laboratory supervisor. Two other women, Ada Hatch and Dorothy Diehl, were hired. Edward Danson was not pleased, but Lex Lindsay and, one suspects, Jane Lindsay, prevailed.[32]

A camp was established at the base of the mesa, and a large ramada style kitchen/field lab was built by local Navajo men. Water had to be hauled in a 300-gallon tank trailer from a spring-fed sheep tank a few miles away, and every effort was taken to conserve water. Stein reports that the women washed their hair and then used the water to wash pot sherds.

Traditional Navajo family camps, called "outfits," are centered on a senior woman, her daughters, and their husbands and children (chapter 20). The

Bitsinnies' family outfit was about a quarter mile from the excavation camp. One of the daughters, Fannie, was hired to work in the lab, and other family members sometimes helped. Later in the summer the crew were invited to attend the wedding of Fannie Bitsinnies to one of the Navajo workmen, Willie King.

The major focus of the 1962 season was Pottery Pueblo, a large site on Paiute Mesa, although other sites were excavated as well. The three women were periodically taken to sites under excavation to catalogue large ground stone items—metates, mauls, and so on—that were left in the field after being studied and photographed. However, the women were not asked to do any of the excavations. A helicopter was used to survey parts of Paiute Mesa and adjacent areas—and sometimes to make a trip to a trading post for ice cream for the crew. As Loyd Gates (chapter 1) said, "Don't greasy sack it when you don't have to."

One of the more amusing aspects of the 1962 season was the recurrent appearance of Mormon missionaries on their never-ending quest to convert the local Navajos. They drove International Scout vehicles. Stein reports that whenever the Scouts appeared, the Navajo workmen on the digs disappeared.

The field lab was a great success, and even though the women did not get to do any digging, they regarded the summer experience as extremely valuable. Ada Hatch became a teacher, Dorothy Diehl a nutritionist, and Mary Anne Stein went on to co-author two MNA Glen Canyon Project reports, earn a Ph.D. in anthropology, and later a law degree.[33]

The National Park Service was supposed to provide funding for an additional field season (1963) for MNA fieldwork and to write up the Paiute Mesa excavations. Even though the University of Utah, for Flaming Gorge, and the Navajo Reservoir Project were funded, MNA was not. Supported by other funds, Mary Anne Stein directed a survey on Paiute Mesa in the summer of 1963 and wrote a master's thesis on the results. She had an International Scout as a field vehicle and witnessed several Navajos running away to hide when they saw it coming, thinking she was a Mormon missionary.

Stein later wrote up the Pottery Pueblo material for her doctoral dissertation at Southern Methodist University.[34] In 1964–65 she was in charge of the field laboratory of the Snaketown re-excavation project, directed by Emil Haury of the University of Arizona.[35] Phillip Hobler wrote up Neskahi Village on Paiute Mesa for a master's thesis and later had a long career as a professor of anthropology at Simon Fraser University. Ambler finished a doctorate at the University of Arizona and taught at Northern Arizona University in Flagstaff for several years before suffering a debilitating automobile accident in 1985. The results of the 1959–62 surveys and excavations around the base of Navajo Mountain appeared in 1968, co-authored by Lindsay, Ambler, Stein, and Hobler.[36] The report was, as it remains decades later, a major contribution toward our understanding of the Kayenta and earlier cultures. It is discussed further in chapter 20.

› 20 ‹

LIVES AND TIMES OF SOJOURNERS IN THE GLEN CANYON COUNTRY

FORMAL FIELDWORK ON THE GLEN CANYON Project ended in 1963. Between 1957 and 1968, the project researchers published more than 200 monographs and technical papers on the Glen Canyon area.[1] It was an astonishing output, validating Professor Jennings's dictum that "unpublished data don't exist."

Equally important was the practice strictly observed by both Utah and the Museum of Northern Arizona that "the data" themselves, the artifacts and their associated provenance materials—notes, maps, photographs, and so on—were permanently preserved and accessible for future use. And they are, in the Museum of Northern Arizona Research Center and the Utah Natural History Museum, where they have been consulted by many scholars over the years.

The work of project archaeologists and historians belied the assertion that Glen Canyon was "the place no one knew." By 1968 it was clear that various groups of people had sojourned in the Glen Canyon Country at various times for at least 9,000 years, perhaps more. Here we briefly sketch what was thought to be known about people in the Country as of 1968–69, when the last major study was published, with notes about later work that has updated and clarified those findings.

We saw in chapter 13 that by 1929, archaeologists had created a chronological framework for the culture history of the Southwest: the Pecos Classification. At first the chronology was *relative*; that is, older than/younger than, but with no calendar dates attached. The development of tree-ring dating in 1929 and thereafter made possible a very fine grained *absolute* chronology tied directly to the Gregorian calendar. Artifacts found in direct association with tree-ring datable wood could be dated by association.

By the mid-1930s it was evident that the Pecos Classification did not fit all of the Pueblo cultures in the American Southwest. Artifact and architectural styles differed enough that subregions were defined—Anasazi, Mogollon, and Hohokam being the major ones. The Hohokam centered along the

Salt and Gila rivers in Arizona and southward into northern Mexico. The Mogollon centered on the Mogollon Plateau and adjacent mountains in eastern Arizona and western New Mexico. The term "Anasazi" was advanced in 1936 by A. V. Kidder to define the Pueblo cultures in the San Juan Basin and adjacent areas—including most of the Glen Canyon Country.[2]

Differences in artifact types and architecture warranted dividing Anasazi into three subdivisions: Chaco, Mesa Verde, and Kayenta. Kayenta had a western subdivision, the "Virgin Branch," centered on the Virgin River in southern Nevada.

Styles and construction materials of tools, textiles, clothing, and other manufactured items change over time in all known cultures. In twenty-first-century world culture, styles of clothing, cars, cell phones, and thousands of other contemporary artifacts change yearly, sometimes more often. In southwestern Pueblo cultures before 1540 CE, the pace of change was far slower, but was ongoing as manufacturing techniques and fashions in designs changed.

Pottery "types"—design styles, vessel forms, and manufacturing techniques—were particularly sensitive to change and could be correlated with the tree-ring data to produce time-sensitive index artifacts. Thus, in 1959, when I stated in my weekly report that the pottery we found at Defiance House in Forgotten Canyon (chapter 17) had "mosquito net black-on-white designs of . . . late PIII times," informed readers knew that the pottery was of Kayenta Anasazi origin and dated between 1250 and 1300 CE. Therefore the site had been occupied at least during that time period.

Pottery was (and is) the key index artifact in southwestern Pueblo archaeology generally. Between 1910 and the late 1950s, archaeologists sorted literally hundreds of thousands of busted pieces of crockery (sherds) and hundreds of whole vessels into increasingly narrower "types" thought to be culturally and temporally significant. John McGregor wrote in 1941: "Ceramics have . . . [been] subjected to almost every conceivable treatment, with the result that types have been established and subdivided until the intricacies of classification approach those of the animal kingdom."[3]

This effort, as A. V. Kidder jokingly said in the 1950s, was caused by a "ceramic bacillus spawning a taxonomic orgy that has spread, like the Black Death in the Middle Ages, and has resulted in so hopeless a situation that only recently have attempts been made to haul our archaeological heads out of the still rising floods of nomenclature that threaten to engulf us."[4]

A major contributor to the "taxonomic orgy" was Harold Colton, who once wrote, "If differences are not pointed out they will be overlooked and so will never be recognized. . . . *for analysis, we must split to the limit or something important might be missed.*"[5] Both ceramic and lithic analysts have ever since classified themselves as "lumpers" or "splitters."

To some, pots took on virtual lives of their own, leading Jesse Jennings to wonder at "all those southwestern pots, galloping across the dunes on their little legs, meetin', matin', and miscegenatin'" to produce new types.[6] While most archaeologists didn't consciously anthropomorphize pots, they generally thought that specific pottery types more or less equaled specific populations or ethnic groups. If there were mixtures of types from different cultural subdivisions on a site, say Mesa Verde and Kayenta, most analysts (including me) wrote vaguely about "influences"—which could imply anything from trade, to migration, to intermarriage.

By 1966 the chronology for the Anasazi region was as shown in Table 20.1.

The archaeological work of the Glen Canyon Project was summarized by Jesse Jennings in 1966, by Alexander Lindsay and his colleagues in 1968, and by doctoral dissertations by William Lipe, Alexander Lindsay, and Mary Anne Stein.[7] What follows is a synthesis of those works and relevant

TABLE 20.1. General Ancestral Puebloan chronology

Stage	Dates
Pueblo V	1700–present
Pueblo IV	1300–1700 CE
Pueblo III	1100–1300 CE
Pueblo II	~850–1100 CE
Pueblo I	750–~900 CE
Basketmaker III	~450–750 CE
Basketmaker II	1–~500 CE
Pre-Puebloan Archaic	8000+ to 0 BCE

others about the histories of peoples who sojourned in the Glen Canyon Country over ten millennia and possibly more.

PALEO-ARCHAIC PEOPLES

Current archaeological evidence has people in North America by at least 14,000 years ago.[8] The people who spread across the land from the northwest and north were hunter-gatherers. By 10,000 years ago, people living in the Great Basin and the Greater Southwest had developed simple yet sophisticated cultures well adapted to desert environments and the exploitation of available animal and plant resources. Jesse Jennings named them the Desert Cultures and, later, Western Archaic. More recently, the earliest of these variants have been called Paleoarchaic.[9]

These cultures were carried by small, highly mobile groups moving through an annual round across environments they knew intimately. The first such people came to the Glen Canyon Country about 9,000 years ago. They made and used easily portable tools—baskets, nets, mats, sandals, hide clothing, a variety of stone, bone, and wood tools such as knives, scrapers, and drills—and atlatls, or spear-throwers, and spears tipped with carefully chipped projectile points.

During the Glen Canyon Project, five sites with Archaic components were excavated. Two of them were on the north slope of Navajo Mountain: Sand Dune Cave and Dust Devil Cave. Some sandals therefrom were dated to between 8,000 and 7,000 years ago. On the basis of the dates, Dick Ambler defined what he called "the Desha Complex." Ambler returned to Dust Devil Cave in 1970. Dates from that study ranged from about 9,000 to 7,000 years ago.[10]

Three sites in lower Glen Canyon proved to contain Archaic components, although we did not clearly recognize them as such at the time. The three were within a mile of each other on the right bank of the river: Lizard Alcove, the Hermitage, and Benchmark Cave. Access from the uplands was by way of Dangling Rope Canyon. In the early 1990s, Phil Geib had sandals from the three sites radiocarbon dated, and they turned out to be 5,800 to 3,200 years old.[11]

One of the attractions of Glen Canyon proper for Archaic and later groups was the gravel-covered terraces. The gravels were a major source of tool stone for knives, projectile points, scrapers, and other implements. How often various Archaic groups visited the Glen Canyon Country is not clear. They were in the Escalante area by about 9,000 years ago and likely throughout the country as well at various times.[12]

BASKETMAKERS IN THE GLEN CANYON COUNTRY

As corn (maize) and, later, squash came into the Southwest from Mexico, some Archaic groups began to learn to plant and grow them.[13] Both have to be planted, watered, protected from predators, and harvested. This requires some settling down by at least some members of a social group for part of the year. Archaic peoples had long been aware of the relationships between plants and water, and had likely practiced some forms of management to help the plants they harvested produce more seeds or fruits. But corn and squashes provided more food per plant than many nondomesticates and hence were worth the time investment. Both can be dried and stored for winter use.

In the Ancestral Puebloan Southwest, some Archaic groups began to experiment with domesticates by about 300 BCE. The culture of those groups is called Basketmaker II. Sometime after 300 BCE, Basketmaker II farmers were occupying Grand Gulch and adjacent canyons draining into the San Juan River from the north.[13] It is a relatively easy route from Grand Gulch westward toward Glen Canyon. Perhaps a few of these early farmers—who had excellent baskets and textiles, and used the atlatl—headed west through the Clay Hills Pass. They likely explored several canyons, but found Moqui Canyon to be most suitable for their purposes.

Moqui Canyon had about 500 acres of arable land, and numerous large alcoves and rockshelters very much like the ones in Grand Gulch. The people moved into some of them, in particular those later called Bernheimer Alcove and Rehab Center. Both faced east, hence there was solar gain for warmth during cold times. The Rehab Center alcove was sheltered from high winds blowing upcanyon and had a small spring of excellent water inside the alcove proper. The people planted their crops, hunted small and large game, and collected numerous wild plant foods, including pinyon nuts from the slopes of Mancos Mesa to the north. From Glen Canyon and Grand Gulch excavations we get other glimpses of their lives. Some textiles were made of human hair; apparently the women cut their hair for this purpose. Life was sometimes violent: some Grand Gulch sites contained burials with spear points in them.

It is unclear how long the Basketmaker folk stayed in Moqui Canyon; possibly no more than a few years, or, if they came intermittently, a few decades. There was very little evidence of Basketmaker II occupations in other Glen Canyon side canyons. In the uplands there were occupations on the flanks of Navajo Mountain and on Paiute Mesa at various times. But sometime around 500 CE, the people moved away from Glen Canyon proper and the Navajo Mountain uplands. Occupation continued, however, on the eastern edge of Glen Canyon Country, in the Tsegi Canyon–Marsh Pass area, along the upper San Juan River, and the on mesas north of the river.

In time, new cultural elements came in: beans, pottery, and the bow and arrow, marking the transition to the Basketmaker III stage about 500 CE. Beans were a major dietary addition in two ways. First, they are nitrogen fixers for soil; when planted between rows of corn, they replace the nitrogen that corn extracts. Second, beans are a major source of vegetable protein. They also contain lysine, which helps make the protein in corn more digestible, thus enriching people's diets.

The bow and arrow were introduced between 200 to 500 CE, earlier in the north than the south. The spear and spear-thrower (atlatl), used for so many millennia, were slowly replaced by the new technology. Pit houses began to be built, and farming intensified. But with the exception of a possible outpost in Navajo Canyon, few people ventured into the core of the Glen Canyon Country during this time.

About 700 CE a new architectural style, multiroom surface structures—Prudden's (chapter 13) "unit pueblos"—began to appear. Often the unit rooms faced onto some sort of plaza, and there was a kiva, or ceremonial structure, in or adjacent to the plaza. Most sites were small—five to twenty rooms. There seems to have been a general increase in population over time, and some pueblos grew relatively large. Even so, few people ventured into the core of the Glen Canyon Country until about 900–950 CE. After 900 BCE, favorable climatic conditions and increasing populations to the east and north pushed people back into the upland areas around Navajo Mountain and nearly all the side canyons of Glen Canyon proper. Pueblos of thirty to forty rooms were built in the uplands. It was during this

20.1. Reservoir structure at Creeping Dune site, Little Rincon, upper Glen Canyon, September 1960. Photograph by Floyd Sharrock. Archaeology Center Collection, 42Sa701-100. Courtesy of Special Collections, Marriott Library, University of Utah.

time that the intensive occupation of the Kaiparowits Plateau took place; numerous small pueblos were built on the knolls, and the adjacent flats were farmed by rainwater agriculture.

In some areas perennial streams or springs made it possible to develop small-scale irrigation farming. At the Creeping Dune site (fig. 20.1) in the Little Rincon of upper Glen Canyon, there was a double-walled reservoir built around a small spring that emerged from the joint plane between the Chinle and Wingate formations. The reservoir was about 11 × 28 feet and 6 feet deep. A sandstone slab with a hole drilled in the middle served as a metering gate that let water out into a ditch that apparently served feeder ditches leading to a relatively flat area of about an acre. The ditches had largely eroded away, but the presence of lines of notched stone slabs suggested gates for directing water flow. Pottery types indicated the reservoir was in use in the early 1100s, during early Pueblo III times.[14] Nothing similar to the Creeping Dune reservoir was recorded elsewhere in the region.

There was also an extensive farming community at the mouth of Cha Canyon, which feeds into the lower San Juan River. There, several slab-lined ditches from 30 to 100 feet in length were found

20.2. Stone-lined ditch at Beaver Creek agricultural community, San Juan Canyon, 1959. Alexander J. Lindsay Jr. in photograph. Photograph by Christy Turner, P.NA7175.3. Courtesy of the Museum of Northern Arizona.

(fig. 20.2). Notched stone slabs were set across the ditches at intervals to control water flow. Grid lines of upright stone slabs defined numerous fields. Some fields were terraced. The Kayenta occupation was between about 1100 and 1250 CE. Similar farming communities were recorded at the mouths of Castle and Paiute creeks.[15]

The period from 850 to 1100 CE, Pueblo II, was a time of expansion and cultural elaboration all across the Ancestral Puebloan region. During this time the great houses were built in Chaco Canyon, composed of hundreds of rooms up to five stories high. Chaco Canyon seems to have been the center of a vast network of roads and great houses extending north beyond Mesa Verde and west as far as Bluff, Utah.[16]

It was a time of plentiful rainfall, allowing more food production and a consequent population increase. The major occupation of the Glen Canyon Country occurred during this time. People lived in the great rockshelters in some canyons and built small unit pueblos, such as Loper Ruin, in open areas. Larger pueblos were built in the uplands, some with dozens of rooms and several kivas, such as Pottery Pueblo on Paiute Mesa.

But after about 1150 to 1175 the climate began to change, and areas less favorable for farming were slowly abandoned. By 1250, arroyo cutting had begun to deplete farmland throughout the Ancestral Puebloan country.

This process was clearly seen in Glen Canyon tributaries by project personnel. Geologists Maurice Cooley and John Lance documented cycles of alluvial aggradation (filling) and degradation (downcutting) in the tributary canyons.[17] By 900 CE a period of aggradation had filled tributary canyons with as much as 100 feet of sediment, providing many acres of good farmland. By 1150 a period of degradation had begun again, flushing out some or all of the canyon sediments. Later, after the Ancestral Puebloans had moved away, the tributaries filled up again, only to erode away after 1850 or so, perhaps in part as a result of overgrazing by cattle and sheep. At the time the Gates Roost site in Twenty Five Mile Canyon (chapter 16) was occupied by Puebloan peoples, the alluvium was just below the alcove floor. When we arrived there in 1957 to excavate the site, the stream flowed on bedrock, 40 feet below the alcove (fig. 1.1). Lake Pahgarit, at the head of Lake Canyon, breached its sand dam in 1915 and flushed out as much as 80 feet of alluvium.[18] By the time we arrived in 1960 to study the sites in Lake Canyon, the stream flowed on bedrock except for areas where beaver ponds existed.

As conditions deteriorated after 1200, there was increased competition for land and food. Hunter-gatherers, perhaps Numic-speaking peoples coming from the north and west, may have begun to invade, seeking the foodstuffs of the local farmers. As conflict escalated, people in both the Kayenta and Mesa Verde areas began to move onto defensible mesa tops and into rockshelters difficult of access.[20] A few Kayentans moved across the Colorado River and up the Escalante drainage to take up residence at the Coombs site at Boulder for a time in the 1200s.[19]

By 1225–50 Kayenta people had left most of the Glen Canyon Country. One or two places in Glen Canyon reflected the time of stress and conflict: the "Fortress" in Lake Canyon (chapter 17) and especially Defiance House. The latter, high in its rockshelter atop a steep talus slope, would have been easily defended. The great pictographs (fig. 17.7) of warriors brandishing clubs and shields is perhaps the most graphic symbol anywhere in the Kayenta country of a time of trouble and conflict. The enigmatic "Fort Moqui," or "Watch Tower," on the bluff above Hite (fig. 17.2) in upper Glen Canyon may also have been built during this time for defensive purposes. By about 1275 or soon after, even Defiance House was abandoned. By 1300 the Glen Canyon Country, lowlands and uplands, lay empty once again.

By 1300 at the latest, the Fremont people north of Glen Canyon seem to have disappeared as well. After seventy years of research it is still not clear what happened to them. Some may have migrated eastward beyond the Rocky Mountains to become one of the historic Plains tribes, possibly some of the Apachean groups. Some may have migrated southward with the Kayentan peoples. Some may have gone back to being hunter-gatherers and emerged into historic times as some of the Numic groups. All three hypotheses have their proponents. There are valid reasons why, and why not, each hypothesis may be right.[21] To use a standard archaeological maxim, "More work needs to be done."

NUMIC AND NAVAJO PEOPLES IN THE GLEN CANYON COUNTRY

What we do know is that by the 1770s, when Domínguez and Escalante made their epic trip across Glen Canyon (chapter 2), the people historically called Ute and Southern Paiute were in place. Ute and Southern Paiute are dialects of the same language, called Southern Numic. Utes historically lived in the Uintah Basin and the Plateau and Rocky Mountain country to the east and south, including the Henry Mountains. Southern Paiute people were spread across the southeastern Great Basin, along the Utah high plateaus, the Virgin River drainage, the upper Escalante Basin, and across the Colorado River around the base of Navajo Mountain.[22]

Occasionally, Havasupai people who lived, and still live, in a side canyon on the south rim of the Grand Canyon came into the Glen Canyon area to hunt and possibly to trade. Broken Hopi pottery found here and there across the Glen Canyon region attests to the occasional presence of Hopi hunters after perhaps 1450.

THE COMING OF THE NAVAJOS

Archaeologists think that the Navajos arrived in the Southwest about 1450 to 1500 CE. They and their linguistic cousins, the Apaches, migrated over several generations from northwestern Canada. By the mid-1600s, people the Spanish called "Apaches de Nabajo—Apaches of the Fields," were centered in the Gobernador region west of the Pajarito Plateau in present-day New Mexico. The Navajos took over sheep, goats, horses, and cattle from the Spanish and learned to farm and weave from the Pueblo people.

As their population increased, Navajos pushed westward and southward, impinging on the traditional lands of the Hopi and Zuni tribes. By the early 1800s, Navajos were moving toward the Rainbow Plateau–Navajo Mountain area from the south and east. There they met small bands of Southern Paiutes. Over time there was some intermingling and intermarriage. Some Paiutes took up herding of sheep and goats, and lived much the same as their Navajo neighbors, but kept their own language.

From at least the mid-1600s, and certainly throughout the 1700s, the Navajos, Utes, and Paiutes were involved in various ways in the Spanish slave trade. Slaves were used in villages and on Spanish haciendas in New Mexico and, after the 1770s, in California.

Both Utes and Navajos raided Paiute bands for slaves, especially women and children. The Spanish (and after 1821 the Mexicans) raided all three. The Utes and Navajos, having horses and sometimes guns, could and did fight back. The Paiutes in the Glen Canyon Country and along the Virgin River had neither horses nor guns and could only try to hide wherever they could.

The intensity of the conflicts between the Spanish/Mexicans and the Utes, Navajos, and Apaches increased between 1800 and 1860. Slave taking and related hit-and-run guerilla warfare were almost constant. There were no innocent parties. Finally, in 1863, the U.S. government attempted to round up the Navajos and some Apache people, and move them to a 40-square-mile reservation in the Bosque Redondo area in the Pecos River valley in New Mexico. The campaign was led by Kit Carson. Between 8,000 and 9,000 Navajos and about 400 Apaches were forcibly moved there. There was great suffering, and many died during "the Long Walk." Some few, led by Hoskininni, managed to escape into the Navajo Mountain country.

The entire endeavor was a disaster, and in 1868 a treaty between the Navajo people and the federal government allowed them to return to their homeland, a 3.5-million-acre reservation that included most of the Glen Canyon Country east of the Colorado and south of the San Juan river. Over time the reservation was expanded to the present-day 17 million acres (26,000 square miles) in Arizona, Utah, and New Mexico.[23]

Various Navajo family groups moved into the areas around Navajo Mountain, Rainbow Plateau, Shonto Plateau, and Paiute Mesa after 1868 to join Hoskininni's group and others who had escaped the Long Walk. There, as elsewhere, the people farmed where they could and herded sheep and goats for sustenance. Navajo Mountain itself, as well as the Colorado and San Juan rivers, became incorporated into localized Navajo origin myths (see below).

NAVAJO SOCIETY AND IDEOLOGY

There is an old joke among anthropologists, and probably among the Navajo people, that a traditional Navajo "outfit," or extended family group, consists of a senior woman, her unmarried children, her daughters and their husbands and children—and an anthropologist. Certainly the Navajos have been studied by more anthropologists than any other Native group in the United State from the 1880s on.[24]

Navajo family, kinship, inheritance patterns, and religion have fascinated Anglos since the late 1840s. Many early Anglo observers, steeped in their taken-for-granted patterns of male-dominant family structure and inheritance, were astounded by Navajo matrilineal kinship and inheritance patterns, and the idea that Navajo women and men regarded each other as equals. They were either mystified by, or came to greatly appreciate, the complexities and philosophical subtleties of Navajo religion, for example the magisterial studies by Washington Matthews in the 1880–90s. Between 1900 and 1940 several anthropologists studied either Navajo kinship and family, or religion, or both.[25]

Family organization, kinship, and tribal governance studies were all the rage among American anthropologists in the 1950s and early 1960s. Studies made before 1963–64 among the Navajo people in the Glen Canyon Country and immediately adjacent areas include the late Jerrold Levy's study of basic Navajo family social organization. He defined a "camp" as a basic unit—essentially the same as an "outfit," as I have defined it.[26]

In 1960–62, anthropologists Mary Shepardson and Blodwen Hammond made extensive studies of family, kinship, gender status, and governance of the Navajo Mountain Community, building in part on a 1938 study by Malcolm Carr Collier, not published until 1966.[27] They were working at the same time and in the same area as the Museum of Northern Arizona Glen Canyon Project team. Their study is of interest because it draws a picture of traditional Navajo life in the early 1960s.

Extended family outfits lived in small clusters of hogans, herded sheep and goats, farmed where they could on small plots, and participated in a full and rich ceremonial cycle, partly centered on Navajo Mountain. The trading posts at Shonto and elsewhere were focal points for economic activities. There were no paved roads; travel was by wagon or pickup truck.

But change was looming. With the completion of Glen Canyon Dam, by 1970 Lake Powell had encroached well within the Glen and San Juan side canyons that were part the Navajo Mountain country. A radio tower had been built at the very top of Navajo Mountain, a major sacred place. Worse still, the waters of Lake Powell were flooding up to and under Rainbow Bridge. The bridge has been a central focus for Navajo sacred legend and cosmology for at least a century, possibly longer.

The Bureau of Reclamation had at first promised the Sierra Club, other conservationists, and the Navajo Nation that the waters of the lake would not encroach on the bridge—obvious flummery for anyone who could read a contour map. The Bureau then argued that the encroaching waters would do nothing to erode or undermine the bridge—an argument impossible to validate, except as the smoke screen it obviously was.

In 1971, Navajo people from the northwestern areas of the reservation took an extraordinary step. The waters of Lake Powell had intruded below Rainbow Bridge. The people sought assistance from the Navajo Nation legal services, "claiming that important religious interests were being infringed upon by the flooding." Ultimately, the Nation engaged Karl Luckert, a well-known expert on Native American and comparative world religions to investigate "whether religious significance can indeed be documented for Rainbow Bridge." Many Navajos have been loath to entrust their sacred traditions "to tape recorders and paper." But given the seriousness of the situation, it was decided that "The gods will not object when we, their people, try to protect their own sacred places and bodies."[28]

A panel of knowledgeable and prominent elders, many of them Singers—experts in one or more of the Navajo ceremonial chantways—from the general Navajo Mountain area were assembled. They were Robert Long-Salt, Floyd Laughter, Buck Navajo, Ernest Nelson, Buster Hastiin Nez, Paul Goodman, and La Mar Bedonie. Floyd Laughter had worked for the Museum of Northern Arizona as a wrangler in the late 1950s–early 1960s (chapter 19). Each person made an extensive presentation about his personal knowledge of how Navajo Mountain, many specific landmarks and places thereon, and especially Rainbow Bridge, figure in traditional Navajo religious ideology.[29]

The result is an extraordinary picture of Navajo cosmology as centered on the Navajo Mountain area. It is clear that Rainbow Bridge was known and revered as a sacred place of pilgrimage long before any Anglos came on the scene. In chapter 10 we outlined some stories about the bridge said by Anglos to be based on "Indian legends." Here the stories are laid out in far more detail than any known before.

Navajo cosmology does not have a written liturgical canon, unlike Anglo religions. Rather there is general knowledge of the major events and actions in the myths that are parts of the cosmology and of individual chantways. Thus, the specific origin of Rainbow Bridge and its purposes differ slightly in the telling of the various elders.

In his summary of what the elders said, Luckert writes that a pilgrimage downcanyon toward the bridge will lead one past four Holy People who chose to become permanently fixed to the canyon wall as Stone People. "Their bodies merged nearly halfway into the canyon wall. And so they stand forever looking up the canyon, ready to spot any human intruder who dares to enter their sanctuary. As soon as one of them is heard, his walking noises and voice are passed down the canyon, repeated and amplified by one Holy-person after another. White people call this 'Echo Canyon'; traditional Navajos know better."[30]

Farther downcanyon there is a Stone Person sentinel, stationed at a corner so he can see both up- and downcanyon. "He is a remarkable person. Long ago, in anticipation of the day on which a Navajo would come through here, he put on the mask of a Navajo *yé'ii*-impersonator. A little further down the canyon another group of Holy People stationed itself. The attentive visitor will notice that these are menfolk and women, as well as children." Still further down, the echoes "follow only about a syllable behind the original words." They come from "Talking Rock, looking your way. Below his tall hat his face is complete—his protruding nose, his squinting eyes, and his mouth contorted as he imitates your words exactly, however strange or foreign these may sound. . . . If you look a little closer you will discover another face looking at you. Talking Rock girl lies reclined and has her head right below the chin of Talking Rock Boy."[31]

Farther on is a sacred spring. "In due time, Navajo explorers discovered that this is a sacred Spring-person who cooperates with a similar divine personage at the top of Navajo Mountain, also with a Rainbow farther downstream." From a ledge above the spring one can see "the most remarkable of all the Rock people who have stationed themselves in this canyon—a petrified Rainbow person." Ultimately, Navajos determined that this Rainbow person is, in fact,

> two Rainbows, a male and a female one, arching together in perfect marital union. Now this certainly explains how all sorts of Rain people, such as young Rainbows and Clouds, originate from this place and float from here into Navajo-land to bless its plants, its animals, and its people with moisture and with life. . . . This place is the very home of Rainbow.[32]

If one looks back from the downstream side of the Rainbow, one can see the top of Navajo Mountain, which "visibly links its own sacred Pool up there with the Rainbow down here, also with the spring whose ravine is visible beneath the arch in the near background."[33]

Karl Luckert published *Navajo Mountain and Rainbow Bridge Religion* in 1977. The Navajo Nation hoped federal agencies would heed the message that Rainbow Bridge and its canyon are sacred places that should be protected. The response of the National Park Service and the Bureau of Reclamation was to build boat docks just downcanyon from Rainbow Bridge, making it even easier for increasing hordes of tourists to get there. But, the agencies reminded people, they should be "respectful" and not walk under the bridge because it is offensive to Navajo people to do so. Few have ever paid any heed.

MERICATS AND MORMONIS IN THE GLEN CANYON COUNTRY

Yankee, or Anglo, trappers and traders came into the Colorado River drainage soon after 1800, but were seldom seen in the Glen Canyon Country until after the U.S. invasion of Mexico in 1846. By the 1850s new peoples appeared in the Country in increasing numbers. The Paiutes quickly learned to distinguish between Anglos, or "Mericats," and "Mormonis," or Mormons, just as earlier they had distinguished between themselves, "The Numa," and Mexicans, "Ukwatsi-ngwi," meaning "weavers."[34]

We have chronicled the sojourns of various Mericats and Ukwatsi-ngwi in previous chapters. The histories of Mormon settlements in the Glen Canyon Country are documented by an enormous and easily accessible literature and will not be rehearsed in any detail here.[35] There is one settlement, however, Escalante, and one major event—the Hole-in-the-Rock trek—that need discussion because stories about both were written by two individuals who came into the Country to research and write those stories, Lowry Nelson and David E. Miller, and a third individual, Jerry C. Roundy, who has written an excellent historical story of his hometown.

Lowry Nelson (1893–1974) was a rural sociologist who wrote a classic study of Escalante and other Mormon villages. Nelson was born in Ferron, Utah.[36] He first studied Escalante in 1923 for his master's degree at the University of Wisconsin. Later he studied Ephraim, American Fork, and three Mormon communities in Alberta, Canada. He ultimately took a doctorate in sociology at the University of Wisconsin and joined the faculty of the University of Minnesota, where he became a leader in the development of rural sociology. In 1952 he brought together his various studies of Mormon communities and added some new data. His book, *The Mormon Village,* is a classic in the field.

We recall that in 1875 A. H. Thompson and his party were in the upper Escalante River valley (chapter 5), where they encountered "four Mormons from Panguitch who are talking about making a settlement here. Advised them to call the place Escalante."[37] They heeded Thompson's advice and so named the town, although locals have always

20.3. Aerial view of Escalante, Utah, 1937. Rainbow Bridge–Monument Valley Expedition Flight 3. Photograph by E. Beckwith, MS-122-2266. Courtesy of the Museum of Northern Arizona.

favored "Escalant," with the accent strongly on the last syllable. Even if "Escalante" is used, it's the Mormon English pronunciation, Ess-cuh-lant-ee, not the Spanish, Ace-cah-lahn-tay, or something like that.

The scouts laid out the arable land in roughly 160-acre tracts, later subdivided into 22.5-acre farms to be taken up by other settlers to follow. The next spring, when the first settlers arrived, the town site was laid out and divided into eighteen 5-acre blocks (fig. 20.3). This was a departure from the standard Mormon plat of 8- or 10-acre blocks. Otherwise, the town site conformed to the plan that Joseph Smith and others had developed in the 1830s, the so-called "Plat of the City of Zion," an idealized town plan with broad streets oriented to the cardinal directions.[38]

Each of the 5-acre blocks was divided into four lots of 1.25 acres, one lot per family. Each lot had a house and a yard, with much of the lot being taken up with orchards and vegetable gardens. The actual farmlands lay outside the town, the standard Mormon practice. Water for gardens, orchards, and the farms came from two irrigation ditches tapping Escalante and Pine creeks, flowing from the high mountains west and north of the town.[39]

As a rural sociologist, Nelson was particularly interested in the interrelationships between land distribution and tenure, social structure, and ideology. He describes how those factors played out in Escalante and other Mormon villages. Nelson's book should be read in tandem with Jerry Roundy's history of his hometown, "Advised Them to Call the Place Escalante," published in 2000.[40] He places Escalante in regional context from the time of its founding until the creation of the Escalante–Grand Staircase National Monument.[40] For me the book brings back the warmth and interest of the people and the character of the town as I knew them in 1957 and 1961.

THE HOLE-IN-THE-ROCK EPIC

Finally, we cannot leave the Glen Canyon Country without taking note of perhaps the most amazing sojourn therein, the Hole-in-the-Rock trek by some 200 intrepid individuals in 1879–80. During the first week in April 1880 more than 200 "weary, worn out, galled" men, women, and children in wagons pulled by equally weary, worn out, and galled teams of horses, oxen, and sometimes mules and cows, reached the San Juan River just east of Cottonwood Wash.[41] They were Mormons "called" from Panguitch, Paragonah, and adjacent settlements by the Church of Jesus Christ of Latter-day Saints to settle the "San Juan Mission." Most had been on the trek for six months over the course of an often severe winter.

Their route of travel was totally improbable. They had gone from their homes across the mountains to Escalante, thence 50-plus miles south along the base of the Kaiparowits Plateau to a cleft in the cliff above Glen Canyon called Hole-in-the-Rock. They had blasted and hacked a roadway some 2,000 vertical feet down through the cleft to the Colorado River, ferried eighty-three wagons, swam hundreds of livestock across the river, struggled up a steep dugway, and traveled across the Red Rock Plateau and on to their final destination. They built roads and dugways as they went, including a final, back-breaking one up and around the end of Comb Ridge where it is cut by the San Juan River. They were supposed to go on another 18 miles or so to the mouth of Montezuma Canyon but stopped instead and founded Bluff City.

David E. Miller (1909–78) was a history professor at the University of Utah from 1947 to 1977, and a colleague and close associate of C. Gregory Crampton. Miller was born in Syracuse on the shores of the Great Salt Lake. His great-grandfather, Henry Miller, ran sheep on Fremont Island and for a time the island was called "Miller's Island." David Miller took his B.A. and M.A. at Brigham Young University, and a Ph.D. at the University of Southern California in 1947, the year he joined the history faculty at Utah. He was an excellent researcher and popular professor. He began researching the Hole-in-the-Rock trek about 1950. His book, aptly titled *Hole-in-the-Rock, An Epic in the Colonization of the Great American West,* was first published in 1959.[42] The story is indeed epochal in the true sense of the word, a chronicle of the most improbable group of people to sojourn in the Glen Canyon Country.

We saw earlier that the Mormons had begun expanding eastward beyond the Wasatch Front in the early 1870s. The church leaders wanted to secure what is now eastern and southeastern Utah against cattlemen coming in from the Great Plains, and miners from Colorado. They were also interested in establishing missions among the Indians, following their policy of feeding Indian people instead of fighting them, and their belief that once all the Indians had become Mormons, they would metamorphose and become "white and delightsome."

The Mormon system of colonization was to issue "calls" to specific families to leave established lives and homes, and pick up and go where they were sent. In chapter 1 I noted that various of my ancestors had been "called to the Muddy Mission," others "called to Dixie," and later to settle along the Fremont River.

In April 1879 some thirty people were called to undertake a scouting mission to seek a route from the Panguitch and Paragonah area to the San Juan River. They traveled south, crossed the Colorado River at Lee's Ferry, went on to Moenkopi, then turned northeast through Marsh Pass, traveling across Monument Valley and on to the San Juan just above Montezuma Wash. They arrived there at the end of May. Members of the party scouted along the river and to the north for potential town sites and farm and grazing lands during June and July. In mid-August most of the party headed north

20.4. Dance Hall Rock, near Forty-Mile Spring, Escalante Desert. Photograph by Charles Kelly, C-311. 10051. Courtesy of the Utah State Historical Society.

along Recapture Creek, past the site of future Monticello and on to the Old Spanish Trail. They followed the trail to Moab and westward to Sevier Valley, arriving about mid-September, having made a circuit of about 1,000 miles.[43]

The explorers reported that the route to the San Juan by way of Lee's Ferry was too difficult. Once across the Colorado they were on Navajo lands. The Navajos were hostile, especially to large parties driving teams of draft animals and droves of cattle across their minimal grazing lands with few water sources. The most practical route to the San Juan was to return back along the Old Spanish Trail, following the route the explorers had just opened. Wagons could easily have been taken that way again.[44] But *that way* was 450 miles to get to a point 200 miles almost due east. It was thought that there must be a shortcut; eyes turned eastward toward Escalante, just recently established. "Perhaps a new road [to the San Juan] could be cut by way of this remote outpost."[45] The decision was made to go via Escalante. Like many committee decisions, it was the wrong one.

By 1879 a few cattlemen were running herds down the Escalante Desert in the shadow of the Kaiparowits Plateau. One of them, Charles Hall, scouted a possible route to the rim of Glen Canyon. He is credited with finding Hole-in-the-Rock. The top of Hole-in-the-Rock was 2,000 vertical feet above the river. Looking across the river from that vantage point, Cottonwood Creek seemed to provide a good wagon road—and it did for the first 4 to 5 miles. Hall reported that "It would be something of a problem to get wagons down to the river, but once down and across, it would be a simple matter to move on to the San Juan about sixty miles away."[46]

Two others, Andrew P. Schow and Reuben Collett, made a more thorough reconnaissance in the summer of 1879. They built a wagon box boat and carried it on a two-wheeled cart to the rim of the canyon. They got the boat to the river (not down through Hole-in-the-Rock), crossed it, did some scouting on the other side, and decided that a road could be made through the country to the site of the planned San Juan settlement. The two made their report to the church leaders at Parowan. The Lee's Ferry route exploring party returned soon after with their negative report—the route was "impossible." The decision makers deemed the Old Spanish Trail route "too long." Therefore, the settlers should take the "shortcut" via Escalante and Hole-in-the-Rock. Those called to make the journey were told they should be en route for about six weeks; they were actually on the road for six months.

The people had been preparing for the trek during the summer of 1879. The vanguard set out in the middle of October. Parties traveled in small groups to Escalante and beyond, on down the desert to Forty-mile Spring. Beyond that the route became increasingly difficult because of deep canyons heading close to the Kaiparowits. By December 5 more than 200 people, 1,000-plus head of loose cattle, and hundreds of horses were assembled at the spring. Some people had brought violins and other instruments. The people kept their spirits up by dancing in the alcove of Dance Hall Rock (fig. 20.4). Another scouting party had been sent ahead. They managed to get across the river and look over the country once again for possible routes. They returned with conflicting reports: some said go; some said no go. On December 4, 1879, the decision was made to go.

The "Hole-in-the-Rock" was a narrow cleft in the edge of the cliff face—barely wide enough for a man to squeeze through. At great effort the cleft was blasted out wide enough to drive a wagon through (fig. 20.5). The "road," blasted and filled in down the notch, descended at about a 45 degree angle. Below that, about a third of the way down, a "road" was built out on poles set in holes drilled into the cliff face to get around a 50-foot sheer drop. Below that the road was hacked out at a steep angle to the river terrace.

Once the roadway was completed, the wagons' rear wheels were rough-locked with chains so that the chains were at the bottom to help act as brakes by digging into the ground. "The wagons were all driven down that narrow defile with horses or oxen hitched to the front, a driver in the wagon, and as many men hanging on behind as could find footing."[47] On January 26, 1880, forty wagons were driven down, and twenty-six of them ferried across the river.

Charles Hall had cut timber in the mountains above Escalante, milled and precut it into materials for a ferry boat, and hauled them to the top of the cleft. The materials were hand carried to the river. Using an improvised kiln to extract pitch from pine trees, Hall produced caulking for the craft. Assembled, it was about 16 × 18 feet, big enough to accommodate two wagons and teams at a time. Ultimately, eighty-three wagons were ferried across the river, and the livestock were swum across.

On the east side, a dugway (fig. 20.6) was built up and around the sheer canyon wall, some 250 vertical feet. A relatively easy road from there led up Cottonwood Canyon for a few miles. From there on, however, all the way to the San Juan, the route alternated between stretches of relatively level ground, dugways that had to be hacked out of solid rock walls and ledges, and gulches that had to be filled in.

There was a brief period of surcease when the party reached Lake Pahgahrit near the head of Lake Canyon. The "lake" had formed behind a huge falling dune. In 1880 it was about a half-mile long,

20.5. Top of Hole-in-the-Rock, 1959. Charlie Steen (?) is on the right; the figure on the left is unknown. Photographer unknown. Archaeology Center Collection, 42Ka00-200. Courtesy of Special Collections, Marriott Library, University of Utah.

a quarter of a mile wide, and 50 feet deep near the dam. There the party rested, washed clothes, and recouped for a few days. They then continued on—sometimes over relatively flat country, but often hacking the roadway up many more solid rock walls and ledges, and filling in gulches, some small, many large, all the way to Comb Wash. There, where the wash runs into the San Juan and the river cuts through Comb Ridge, they hacked and cut their final roadway up, around, and down the end of the

20.6. Dugway up the cliff face across the river from Hole-in-the-Rock. Photograph by David Miller, B-311. Courtesy of the Utah State Historical Society.

ridge, then traveled on a few miles to Cottonwood Creek. They were supposed to go another 18 miles to Montezuma—the small outpost where some members of the 1879 exploring party awaited them. They did not; they stopped. It was early April 1880. They had been traveling for six months on the "quicky shortcut" via Escalante to get 200 air line miles east of where they began. The epic trek was finally over.

The people laid out lots in standard Mormon village fashion and started building houses and digging an irrigation ditch for crops soon to be planted. Bluff City came into existence in the next few months.

The Hole-in-the-Rock road continued to be used as a wagon route for a couple of years but was soon superceded by Hall's Crossing, on the far side of the Waterpocket Fold. The Hole-in-the-Rock itself was modified by others in the 1880s and '90s, most notably by a crew in the employ of Robert Brewster Stanton in support of his ill-fated dredging operation up the river (chapter 9).

There is little doubt that the sojourn of the members of the "San Juan Mission" was the most dramatic, indeed, epochal in historic times in the Glen Canyon Country. The full story is artfully told in David Miller's book, which should be read by all those interested in one of the great stories of human perseverance and ultimate triumph in the nineteenth-century West.

THE PLACES AT THE ENDS OF GLEN CANYON

Finally, we need to note three places that figured in the history of the Glen Canyon Country and Glen Canyon proper: Hite and White Canyon at the upper end of the canyon, and Lee's Ferry at the lower end.

Lee's Ferry figures prominently in the history of the Glen Canyon Country and areas beyond and has been well described in detail by P. T. Reilly, Evelyn Measeles, and Bud Rusho and Gregory Crampton.[48] Only portions of that history will be sketched here. Lee's Ferry is at the confluence of the Paria and Colorado rivers. It marks the official boundary between the upper and lower basins of the Colorado River, hence has enormous importance in the division of river waters under the Colorado River Compact (chapter 12). It also is at Mile Zero, the official beginning of Glen Canyon: river miles within the canyon start from there and are counted upstream. River miles through Marble and Grand canyons start from there and are counted downstream.

In 1776, Domínguez and Escalante did not find a way to cross the Colorado there, but other Euro-Americans perhaps did later in the century, and it was seemingly known to Indian people for an undetermined amount of time. By the early 1850s the Mormons were planning to expand southward into what would become northern Arizona (Arizona was officially part of New Mexico Territory until 1863) and to proselytize the Hopis. Jacob Hamblin, Ira Hatch, and others were sent to scout potential routes across the Colorado River. Two routes swung far to the southwest to skirt the Grand Canyon. One such went from St. George down the Virgin River drainage to cross the Colorado at Stone's Ferry, or Bonelli's Ferry, as it was often known. A second went from St. George generally down Grand Wash to cross at the mouth of the wash or a few miles upstream at Pearce's Ferry.

Jacob Hamblin and his compatriots first learned of the Ute Ford/Crossing of the Fathers in November 1858 and used it on several occasions. But it was impossible to take wheeled vehicles across the river there. Hamblin and his compatriots continued looking for a place that wagons could cross or be ferried across. He was aware of the confluence of the Paria and Colorado, and the possibility of a crossing there, but did not accomplish it until the spring of 1864. Hamblin and his people built a rough driftwood raft and were able to cross in both directions in March and April 1864 using the raft and swimming their animals. The crossing offered a shorter and more direct route to the Hopi mesas and on to the upper Little Colorado River area that the Mormons wished to colonize.

Hamblin guided John Wesley Powell and his two men, Francis M. Bishop and Walter Graves, from Kanab to the Hopi country by way of the Paria crossing in the fall of 1870. He had a rough scow built, which Graves christened the *Cañon Maid*, to ferry the party across the river.[49]

By 1870, John D. Lee was becoming the scapegoat/fall guy for the Mountain Meadows Massacre.[50] On the advice of Brigham Young, he traveled to the mouth of the Paria in November 1871 with three of his wives and some of his children to hide out and establish a ferry. His first passengers were a group of Navajos who appeared on the left bank on January 19, 1872, and wanted to be ferried across the river. Lee refurbished the boat that Hamblin and others had built and ferried them across, being paid, apparently, in blankets.

Lee and his family hosted many travelers wanting to cross the river, and from July 13 to August 13, 1872, Jack Hillers, James Fennemore, and Frederick Dellenbaugh after they brought the *Cañonita* down from the Dirty Devil in preparation for Powell's 1872 trip into the Grand Canyon (chapter 5).

Lumber and other materials were hauled in, and by January 11, 1873, an 8 1/2 × 26–foot ferry boat and auxiliary skiffs were built. Lee operated the ferry for about six months, earning substantial sums from the Mormons on their way to Arizona and sometimes from miners. The ferry boat was lost in a storm in June 1873. Another ferry was built and was in operation by October 1873.

In November 1874, Lee was arrested in Panguitch, where he had gone to visit one of his

20.7. Lee's Ferry, ca. 1925. Photographer unknown, 386.1 P2. 992. Courtesy of the Utah State Historical Society.

families. He was tried twice, convicted the second time, and sentenced to die. He chose to be shot rather than hanged. He was taken to Mountain Meadows, where on March 23, 1877, James Fennemore took a photograph of him "calmly sitting on his coffin, his eyes bound. . . . [He] raised his hands and placed them over his head so the firing squad could get a clear shot."[51]

After Lee's arrest, the Mormon Church appointed Warren Johnson to assist Lee's wife, Emma, in running the ferry, and when she left, he continued running it for more than twenty years. Johnson, like Lee, hosted many travelers. In December 1889 he and his wife hosted Robert Brewster Stanton and his party. Soon after, Johnson brought Stanton's photographer, Franklin Nims, in his wagon from the rim of Marble Canyon to his house after Nims fell and fractured his leg, and perhaps his skull. Johnson and his wife nursed Nims for twelve days before he could be taken to Winslow (chapter 9). When Johnson left, others operated the ferry service (fig. 20.7) until the completion of the Navajo Bridge across the Colorado canyon just downstream from the ferry site in 1929.

Until 1958, river runners making the Glen Canyon run pulled their boats from the river at Lee's Ferry. Before 1958, some Grand Canyon river parties started at Lee's Ferry, beginning with John Wesley Powell's 1872 trip. Since 1958, Grand Canyon river parties by the hundreds have started from there.

HITE AND WHITE CANYON

The mouth of the Dirty Devil River, 169.4 official miles upstream from Lee's Ferry, marks the upper

20.8. Hite Ferry, September 18, 1946. Photographer unknown, 386.1 P7. 1000. Courtesy of the Utah State Historical Society.

end of Glen Canyon. Downstream from 167.5 to 161.3 river miles is (or once was) the Dandy Crossing area, named, as we saw in chapter 9, by Cass Hite in 1883. Travelers coming down Trachyte Creek or North Wash could cross the river to White Canyon, or vice-versa. There, in 1883, at Mile 162, Cass Hite built a cabin, planted a garden, and settled in to get rich from the gold that his Navajo friend Hoskininni told him was there. There wasn't much, so in 1898 he moved about 14 miles downstream to the mouth of Ticaboo Canyon and set up shop anew. He remained there—still seeking the main chance, still moiling for gold—until he died and was buried there in 1914.

When Hite abandoned his upstream cabin and land, the cabin was taken over for the post office, and Hite became an official place to service the various miners downstream. Hite's brother, and later others, ran the post office and sometimes a store to supply those who, like Hite, moiled for the gold they sought in the river gravels and on the terraces of Glen Canyon. There was just enough to keep some men going for a number of years, including Bert Loper, who settled in his snug hermitage at the mouth of Red Canyon in 1908 and remained for four decades. Various people served as postmaster, and sometimes storekeeper, at Hite over the years and were visited by river parties that passed through (chapters 9, 11).

By the 1920s all but a few diehards had abandoned the search for gold in Glen Canyon. But in the 1930s, with the second rush to the canyon sparked by the Depression, people came again to Hite and its environs. One was Arthur Chaffin (1896–1979). Born in Cedar City, Utah, Chaffin, known as "Arth," first came to Glen Canyon at age twelve to help his older brothers with their mining claims at Hansen Creek. The enterprising Chaffin started up a trading post nearby and seems to have successfully traded with the Navajos for a time. He then went elsewhere for twenty years, returning to Glen Canyon in the 1930s to buy up the Cass Hite properties along the river. He and his wife planted orchards and gardens, and often shared their largesse with river runners who stopped by. In 1932 he borrowed a bulldozer and cut a road, known for its scary curves, down North Wash.

In 1945 the State of Utah built a road down White Canyon from Blanding. The way for trans-Colorado tourism seemed open. Chaffin cobbled together a ferry, powered by a Model T Ford (later replaced by a Model A) which pulled the ferry along a cable strung across the river (fig. 20.8). It operated until 1964, when the rising waters of Lake Powell submerged it.

Finally, there was the small, ephemeral company town of White Canyon, opposite Hite—a mining boomtown in the true sense of the word. From 1949 to 1954 it was occupied not by men moiling for gold, but by men working in a mill owned by the Vanadium Corporation of America to produce uranium. The uranium boom began in 1949 and engulfed the Four Corners area until about 1956.[52] Some individuals, such as Charlie Steen of Moab, got very rich. Others got moderately rich, including Joe Cooper and Fletcher Bronson of Monticello, who bought the Happy Jack Mine for $1,000.

The mine, located at Copper Point on the Red Rock Plateau about 20 miles to the northwest of Fry Canyon, yielded copper ore, but the ore contained uranium, which prior to 1949 was a waste product and impeded the profitable extraction of the copper. The previous owners had given up and were apparently happy to sell what looked like a losing proposition. Soon after the sale came the uranium boom, and the Bronson and Cooper Mining Company wound up selling over 26,000 tons of uranium ore to the Vanadium Corporation. The mill was built at White Canyon because the Colorado River provided the water needed to process the ore. Raw ore was trucked in from the mine and put through a first-stage process. The resultant uranium sodium diuranate, "yellowcake," was trucked out in 350-pound metal casks to Durango, Colorado, where it was further processed and sent on to federal government facilities for incorporation into atomic bombs.

Tom McCourt, who spent time in White Canyon with his grandparents, who ran the company boarding house, described the mill as a

> remarkably unimposing . . . collection of buildings, smoke stacks, holding tanks, acid baths, leaching tables, conveyor belts, and catwalks. It was unpainted and unadorned and looked rusty and crude. . . . The place looked more like a train wreck than an important nuclear facility. The mill rumbled and growled and belched as it chewed and digested the rich and spicy uranium ore. Mineral waste stacked up in the dooryard like a manure pile near a stable, and smokestacks vented vile, acid-soaked gasses out into the unsuspecting sunshine.[53]

There were a dozen cabins of rough-cut boards, tarpaper, and asphalt, each occupied by two men. There was also a bathhouse and a cookhouse, or boardinghouse, to feed the resident workers and staff. All these were on the south side of White Canyon Wash. Scattered haphazardly on the north side of the wash were a schoolhouse, a post office, a store and gas station, and various rough cabins and camp trailers. The workers with families and a few others lived on the north side. The two sides of town were joined by a heavy wooden planked bridge. The store and gas station owner was also the postmaster, rented trailers or cabins to those who needed them, and sold clean water to residents and provided them with electricity from his diesel generator, which was shut down at 10 p.m. nightly. There was no indoor plumbing. A small airstrip was laid out along the river below the north side of town. All food and other supplies came in either from Blanding and Monticello to the east, or Hanksville and Price to the northwest. Arth Chaffin's ferry provided the link across the river.

Tom McCourt's grandmother, Bertha Winn, ran the boardinghouse, cooking and serving seventy to seventy-five, or more, meals a day, seven days a week. Tom and his brother, as young boys, got to visit their grandmother periodically. They explored, chased lizards, and visited nearby "Fort Moqui" (fig. 17.2) to look for arrowheads. In their young eyes White Canyon was a wondrous place, and it remained so in Tom's eyes over the next four decades and counting, as is evident in his account of "the little town at the bottom of Lake Powell."

The uranium boom ended in about 1956, leaving the scars of hundreds of mines and test pits, bulldozed roads, and rough airstrips across the lands of the Glen Canyon Country and beyond. When Tom McCourt went back to White Canyon for the last time in 1959, the town was gone—bulldozed into piles of rubble and burned. The mill had been dismantled and taken elsewhere. All that remained was the decaying schoolhouse and the radioactive purple-gray tailings pile at the mill site. The Atomic Energy Commission determined that 43 percent of the uranium in the processed ore remained in the tailings pile. It also determined that no hazard would be posed when the tailings pile was submerged by the lake, since any residual radioactivity would be diluted within the lake, and the pile would be sealed by layers of sediment.[53]

By 1965 Lake Powell had covered Dandy Crossing and the remains of other ephemeral places—places first established by men who sojourned there searching for the gold that would give them *la dolce vita*; and last by men producing the material that made it possible to blow up the world.

Since 1965 millions of people have come to the Glen Canyon Country, nearly all seeking the frantic surcease of water-based recreation. Some few still come seeking that which "We Three" and others of like mind found before 1963: a unique place of wonder. Each knew, or will know, the place in her or his own way.

› 21 ‹

POSTLUDE

The Glen Canyon Country of the Imagination

THE CLOSING OF THE GATES ON THE diversion tunnels of the Glen Canyon Dam in late 1962 and early 1963 marked the turning point for the Glen Canyon Country from wilderness to playground. Work continued on the dam the until 1966 (figs. 21.1, 21.2), by which time Lake Powell had risen and flooded most of the side canyons.

But even before the dam was finished, and just as the waters were beginning to rise, Hollywood came to call. From early 1962 until early 1963, the people of Page, Arizona, and Kanab, Utah, were in a frenzy. Areas in the Wahweap and Kane Creek drainages had become the settings for a cinematic extravaganza, *The Greatest Story Ever Told*, directed by George Stevens and starring a plethora of big names. They included Max von Sydow as Jesus, Charlton Heston as John the Baptist, Dorothy McGuire as the Virgin Mary, Claude Rains as King Herod, Telly Savalas as Pontius Pilate, and John Wayne as a Roman centurion. Some casting was true to type: Pat Boone as an angel, and Donald Pleasance as the Devil. There were re-creations of Jerusalem, Bethlehem, Nazareth, and other biblical places, and a row of crucified dummies on the road to Kane Creek (figs. 21.3, 21.4). Some 3,000 people in Page, Kanab, and elsewhere worked directly or indirectly on the film through much of 1962 and early 1963. It was one of the greatest Hollywood widescreen spectaculars of the 1960s—and cost $20 million, an enormous sum at the time.

Meanwhile, work went forward on the dam. Russell Martin has wonderfully and sardonically described the simultaneous filming and dam building during that time.

> It was almost Christmas before the scenes by the riverside had been shot, just a month before the diversion tunnel would be closed and this River Jordan would begin to resemble the Sea of Galilee. . . . [There were weather delays of the filming] on the bench land above the creeks, above the quickly invading slackwater, until well after Lem Wylie [the chief construction foreman at the dam site] had locked the

21.1. "The Last Bucket of Concrete," Glen Canyon Dam, September 13, 1963: (*left to right*) L. F. Wylie, project construction engineer, and Jim Irwin, project manager for Merritt-Chapman and Scott, the project's prime contractors. Photograph by Mel Davis, P557-420-8794. Courtesy of the U.S. Bureau of Reclamation.

> west tunnel gates and the water indeed had begun to rise—the last images of that part of primeval Glen Canyon ironically captured in a film about the Bible. By the time the set crews burned Bethlehem in April—Stevens and the cameramen getting their final outdoor footage—the gates in both diversion tunnels had been screwed down and a motionless lake nearly reached Jerusalem.[1]

The saga of the filming was later memorialized by Bruce Berger and Natalie Gignoux, who were on a float trip through Glen Canyon with Katie Lee in October 1962. They arrived at the Kane Creek take-out in the middle of one of the movie camps to find the sandstone benches covered with plastic olive trees. There they learned that George Stevens had gone to see the real River Jordan in Israel, but discovered "It's just a pathetic little creek that no one would believe, so we came here. The Colorado looks like the Jordan is *supposed* to look." They also learned that Stevens wanted the scene where John the Baptist baptizes Jesus to be there, and asked the ranger how deep the water was, "then Stevens stepped in and disappeared. The ranger had to pull him out downstream. So they're building a

21.2. Glen Canyon Dam and Lake Powell, August 12, 1984. Photograph by W. L. Rusho, C557-400-2849NA. Courtesy of the U.S. Bureau of Reclamation.

21.3. Crucified dummies on the road to Kane Creek, a set for George Stevens's film *The Greatest Story Ever Told*, 1963. Photograph by A. E. Turner, P557-420-7790. Courtesy of the U.S. Bureau of Reclamation.

platform underwater so that John and Jesus will only be in up to their waists."[2]

As Berger and Gignoux thought about this strange encounter, they decided it ought to be appropriately memorialized:

GREATEST STORY EVER TOLD
Oh, little town of Bethlehem
How swift we see thee rise
Beneath the true and cobalt blue
of Southern Utah skies.
While in the dark streets riseth
Walls of 'papier mache'
T'was here that Charlton Heston
Was born on Christmas day.

The mighty Colorado
That carved the Canyon Grand
Here vaunts a scenic beauty
That man not God hath planned
And where the great George Stevens
Slipped in above his knees
Kane Creek is planted all about
With plastic olive trees.

How silently, how silently
A lake will climb thy wall
And who will dream that Bethlehem
To water's flood did fall,
Or that 'neath the Wahweap basin
Where plastic olives grow

21.4. Set for George Stevens's film *The Greatest Story Ever Told*, 1963. Photograph by W. L. Rusho, P557-420-7790. Courtesy of the U.S. Bureau of Reclamation.

> 'The Greatest Story Ever Told'
> Was filmed in Todd-A-O.[3]

Actually, Max von Sydow played Christ, "born on Christmas Day"; Charlton Heston played John the Baptist; and the film was shot in Ultra Panavision—but the irony is appropriate.

Despite the slackwater of nascent Lake Powell being at hand, the filmmakers thought it not appropriate as a proxy for the Dead Sea, so segments set there were shot at Pyramid Lake in western Nevada with members of the Pyramid Lake Paiute Tribe as extras. Pyramid Lake, although only slightly saline, does indeed bear a visual resemblance to the Dead Sea. Seen forty-five years later, the film is still spectacular, especially scenes shot atop various mesas with Grand Bench, the Kaiparowits Plateau, Cummings Mesa, and the Colorado River (as the surrogate River Jordan) providing terrific scenic backdrops.

GLEN CANYON MORPHS INTO LAKE POWELL

As the dam became operational, the construction town of Page, Arizona, became a residential community for the Bureau of Reclamation employees operating the dam and, later, the National Park Service employees administering the 1.2 million-acre Glen Canyon National Recreation Area that was created in 1972. New motels, eateries, gas stations,

21.5. Defiance House, Forgotten Canyon, as restored by the National Park Service, September 1970. Photograph by Harry Gilleland, P557-400-1444. Courtesy of the U.S. Bureau of Reclamation.

and other tourist amenities soon sprang up there, as well as at the Wahweap, Bullfrog, and Hall's Crossing marinas. A floating pit stop for boats was set up at Dangling Rope Marina.

Millions came annually to boat, water-ski, jet-ski, fish, litter, loll about on houseboats, and explore. Defiance House in Forgotten Canyon (fig. 21.5)—perhaps seen for the first time in 600-plus years in 1952 by Mickey the cat, Pard the dog, and their compatriots Sprang, Thomas, and Aleson (chapter 14)—was restored and stabilized by the National Park Service. People could boat right to it, and very soon some miscreants began to vandalize the restoration, upholding the true American tourist tradition of defacing public places. The Bureau of Reclamation's vision of Lake Powell as a place of recreation for the masses was now a reality—for better or for worse.

In 1996 most of the rest of the Glen Canyon Country, as we have defined it, became part of the federally controlled southern Utah tourist wonderland when President Bill Clinton issued an executive order under the 1906 Antiquities Act creating the 1.9 million-acre Grand Staircase–Escalante National Monument.[4] The term first applied to the geology of the Country by John Wesley Powell in 1873 now became official.

The new national monument, coupled with Canyonlands National Park, Rainbow Bridge

National Monument, the Glen Canyon National Recreational Area, Vermilion Cliffs National Monument, Capitol Reef National Park, and the Navajo Nation Monument Valley Park, in effect fulfilled the dreams of John Wetherill, Ansel Hall, the National Park Service, and many others dating to the 1930s and before, that the Glen Canyon Country and adjacent areas become a giant national park.[5]

MOURNING GLEN CANYON

In chapter 12 we traced the history of the planning by the Reclamation Service/Bureau of Reclamation, aided and abetted by the U.S. Geological Survey and western electrical power companies, to "harness" the Colorado River. The Colorado River Compact of 1922 allocated the river waters to the Upper Basin and Lower Basin states in roughly equal amounts and left it to the states in each region to portion out their shares. Given that, the next issue was where the dams would be built for "optimal" flood control and storage purposes in both basins. Boulder/Hoover Dam was completed in the 1930s.

After World War II, the Bureau of Reclamation turned its attention to construction of dams in the Upper Basin and in the Grand Canyon in the Lower Basin. Potential dam sites were reviewed and decisions announced as to locations of construction sites. The Bureau and its allies paid little attention to the ideology behind national parks and monuments—that they are inviolate places, permanently set aside for the scientific, scenic, and educational uses of the public. They also ignored the idea of "wilderness" held by many, and discounted the willingness of people to exercise their rights through the political process to express their own ideas about what should happen on and to the public lands.

When the Bureau announced a plan to build a dam in Echo Park that would drown much of Dinosaur National Monument, citizens began to say, "Wait a minute." We have noted how river runner Bus Hatch (chapter 11) became a leader in developing opposition to the dam, and how the Sierra Club and many others, individuals and groups, became involved. The fight against the Echo Park dam is well chronicled elsewhere, as are the fights to keep dams out of Grand Canyon National Park.[6]

What is equally well chronicled is that the trade-off for not building a dam that would flood Dinosaur National Monument was the Glen Canyon Dam—Eliot Porter's "The Place No One Knew." As we've seen, the place *was known*, by many, for millennia. What Porter meant was the place wasn't known well enough to David Brower, his compatriots in the Sierra Club, other conservationist and environmental communities, and individuals who might have rallied in its defense.[7] From their perspectives this wondrous place was lost out of ignorance—"Gee, we didn't know, or we would have/might have. . . ." But no one did, except for last-ditch efforts that did not avert, in Brower's words, "America's most regretted environmental mistake."[8]

In fact, Brower and his compatriots *did* know: they had cut a deal with the Bureau of Reclamation that five dams would be built in the Upper Basin if their waters did not encroach on Dinosaur National Monument or other national parklands. Russell Martin has wondered if Porter's *The Place No One Knew* was somehow the Sierra Club's expiation of a "sense of guilt about its loss by fibbing about its anonymity."[9]

Be that as it may, some did know, and the haunting beauty of Glen Canyon emblazoned in their memories spurred them to outrage and action early on. One such was the indomitable Katie Lee (chapter 14), whose fight against the Glen Canyon Dam began as soon as she heard about the "Bureau of Wreck-the-nation's" plans for it, and continues unabashed and unabated into the twenty-first century in her writing, songs, poetry, and public speaking.[10]

Others were equally outraged, none more so than the late Edward Abbey. His writings reflect the developing coherence of his rage over Glen Canyon Dam, Lake Powell, and the ongoing destruction of wilderness in the West, beginning in *Desert Solitaire*. Therein he indulged in "idle, foolish, futile daydreams," as he called them, about planting explosives inside the dam, set to go off at its grand opening ceremony. Such dreams of eco-anarchy (or eco-terrorism) became more coherent and elaborate in *The Monkey Wrench Gang* and *Hayduke Lives*![11] These and Abbey's other writings were, and are, seminal to the development of the environmental literature focused on the Glen Canyon Country and the larger canyon country which encompasses it.

The idea of blowing up the dam and in so doing creating the biggest, most awesome rapid on the Colorado River gripped the imaginations of many river runners, and the imaginary breached dam became known as "Dominy Falls." All this was expressed in a poem by Vaughan Short called "Floyd's Void." It was written, Vaughn tells us, in response to Bureau of Reclamation propaganda about the wonders of Lake Powell, and Floyd Dominy's assertion that only the effete rich made float trips in Glen Canyon and wanted to keep it for themselves. Dominy was commissioner of the Bureau of Reclamation (1959–69) during the building of the Glen Canyon, Flaming Gorge, and Navajo Reservoir dams, and he was an ardent and abrasive promoter of Lake Powell and its recreation potential for the masses. As we noted in chapter 12, Dominy regarded the Glen Canyon Dam and Lake Powell as his "crowning jewel." Others thought otherwise.

"FLOYD'S VOID," BY VAUGHAN SHORT

There's a breed of men who sit at their desks
And they like their water tame,
They like to damn the rivers up,
Then give the lakes a name
They do
Then give the lakes a name.
So give three cheers for the Bureau boys
And a special rah for Floyd
He built his dam and he built it well
And then he said "In spite of hell,
I'm going to fill that void
I am
I'm going to fill that void."
Now with this void, created by Floyd,
Was a special thing or two,
Reserved for the sight of the filthy rich
And a very greedy few
They were
A very greedy few.
So give three cheers for the Bureau boys
And a special rah for Floyd.
For Floyd did say, "I'll change this plan,
I'll open it up for the common man
I will
I'll open it up for the common man."
"What value the trees? What value the grasses,
Compared to the rights of the down-trodden
masses?"
Floyd said, "I'll make it so easy
I'll make it so simple,
They can all speed their boats over Music
Temple
How about that?
Speed right over the top of Music Temple!"
So give three cheers for the Bureau boys
And a special rah for Floyd
For now we know beneath the blue
Is a revered spot once seen by few
How sad
Before Floyd's void seen only by a few.
To see the Rainbow—aloof—remote—
You had to hike or you had to float.
Denied it was to that jolly old chap
By his houseboat rail in his yachting cap

Oh my!
Poor old chap in his yachting cap.
So give three cheers for the Bureau boys
And a special rah for Floyd
He buried them all deep under his lake
But he did it for the people's sake
He did
He did it for the people's sake.
For the power hungry man with the dollar sign
eyes,
Who lights up the neon in the evening skies
For the poor down-trodden in his speeding
boat,
For the jolly old chap in his yachting cap
Who had no water to float
Poor guy
He had no water to float.
So give three cheers for the Bureau boys
And a special rah for Floyd
Though he buried the Moqui and he shortened
the wall,
He did it for the good of all
He did
He did it for the good of all!
But there's a breed of men both hardy and free
Who lie at night on the lonely bars
And there beneath the glittering stars
They dream of TNT
They do
They dream of TNT
So give three cheers for the Bureau boys
And a special rah for Floyd
He built his dam and though he built it well,
These dreamers swear in spite of hell
They're going to void Floyd's void
They are
They're going to void Floyd's void.
They dream of a mighty boom and a quake.
They dream of a swirl in a vanishing lake
They dream of a river wild and free
Freed from its shackles by TNT
Sweet bliss
Freed from its shackles by TNT.
Now! Let's have three cheers for the boys on
the bars
Who dream their dreams 'neath the glittering
stars.
Who dream of a wild and a wonderful treat—
*A houseboat running Dominy Falls at a million
second feet*
Ah yes
*A houseboat running Dominy Falls at a million
second feet*![12]

Others dreamed less violent dreams than those of Abbey and Short, hoping that some combination of public opinion and enlightened government action (if that is not an oxymoron) would lead to the Glen Canyon Dam being decommissioned or its floodgates left permanently open so that ultimately Lake Powell would drain away, leaving Glen Canyon in time to be cleansed of its accumulated silt and returned to its pristine glory by the forces of Nature. No group has worked more ardently toward that goal than the Glen Canyon Institute. As we move into the second decade of the twenty-first century, the hopes of the Institute members and others may happen by default, rather than government action, as the level of Lake Powell continues to diminish.[13]

Finally, a personal note. Over the years after I joined the professorial ranks, I gave numerous lectures at universities, and for the Smithsonian Institution around the country, about John Wesley Powell and about the archaeology of Glen Canyon and the Glen Canyon Country. Many wanted to know how I and my compatriots on the Glen Canyon Project felt, at the time, about what would happen to the canyon, post-dam. Did we feel a sense of impending loss? Having seen Glen Canyon and the surrounding country up close and personal over many months, did we think the dam should not have been built? I was fully aware at the time that Glen Canyon was a wondrous place and we were fortunate to get paid to work there and revel in the scenery. But the dam was under construction and was supposedly a good thing for the country. I accepted that at the time, and went on my way.

I did not go back into the Country until 1971 (except to fly over at 37,000 feet on various airliners), when I participated in the film documentary with Wally Schirra re-creating Powell's trip. The trip through Lodore, Whirlpool, and Split Mountain canyons and on into the Uinta Basin was my first real whitewater experience. Clair Quist of Moki Mac was lead boatman. It was terrific. CBS News had arranged for four chartered Cessnas to move us around. We flew from Vernal to Moab and went by jet boat to the confluence, shot some scenes there, then flew to Page. It was my first low-level aerial view of the Glen Canyon Country and Lake Powell. I thought the lake was beautiful in its setting. We shot a scene at Lee's Ferry and then flew on to Las Vegas, thence traveled up Lake Mead in jet boats for a final scene at Separation Rapid.

In 1980 Kay and I were asked to be among the experts who went along on the annual National Park Service first trip of the season through Cataract Canyon. In 1982 we ran Cataract again with Richard and Bob Quist of Moki Mac. Both times we came out onto Lake Powell before take-out, and I began to feel a sense of loss for Glen Canyon. It finally came to full flower in 1999 when I went on a houseboat trip with Ken Verdoia and his KUED television crew from Wahweap Marina to Hole-in-the-Rock and back.

As we proceeded upcanyon, the upper cliffs of the canyon and Powell's "monuments" were visible close up, and I knew what lay 400–500 feet below—where in 1958 and 1959 I had continued my transition, begun the year before, from wannabe urban lounge lizard to nascent archaeologist. When we returned to Salt Lake City, I attended one of the early meetings that led to the Glen Canyon Institute—and I met Katie Lee. She autographed *All My Rivers Are Gone* for me. I read it on the plane going back to Reno. I had already started to write this book. But Katie and Katie's book made me think in a very different way about Glen Canyon and the Country encompassing it. Maybe it would be a good thing if the lake was drained.

Whatever else we learned from the Glen Canyon Project—as archaeologists and paleoclimate people elsewhere in the Southwest knew then and know now—is that the Country is subject to long-term major droughts. If currently predicted climate changes continue, the lake may drain naturally.

From Powell's time on, many have sojourned in the Country and the Canyon, some to study, map and describe what they saw; others seeking elusive riches they wanted to believe were there; still others simply and most profoundly to commune with the wonders therein. None of those sojourners came away unaffected by the place, including me.

NOTES

PREFACE

1. See the bibliography for a full list of sources by authors consulted for the book.

CHAPTER 1

1. Woodbury 1944: 155–57.
2. Mulder 1959: 61.
3. Fleming 1967.
4. Murphy 1996: 80, 117.
5. Murphy 1996: 117; Jay Lynn Torrey (1852–1920) scrapbook, Finding Aid, Special Collections, Rolla Library, University of Missouri, Rolla, http://web.mst.edu/whoncinfo.
6. Murphy 1996: 330.
7. Gunnerson 1969.
8. Gunnerson 1959.
9. Fowler and Fowler 1971; Fowler 1989; Fowler, Euler, and Fowler 1969; Hillers 1972.
10. Fowler 1969; Porter 1969.

CHAPTER 2

1. Porter 1963.
2. Hunt 1988: 4.
3. Winship 1896: 329–400; see also Bolton 1949.
4. Winship 1896: 350–402.
5. Jacobs 1992: 200–223.
6. Jacobs 1992: map 2.
7. Jacobs 1992: n. 28.
8. Jacobs 1992; Cutter 1977; see also Hill 1930.
9. Garcés 1965: 65–75.
10. Garcés 1965: v–ix.
11. Domínguez 1956.
12. Chavez and Warner 1976. The Domínguez-Escalante journals were first fully published by the great Spanish Borderlands historian Herbert Bolton (1950). The later Chavez-Warner edition (1976) corrects some problems in the Bolton edition and adds useful data, hence is used herein.
13. Chavez and Warner 1976: 90.
14. Chavez and Warner 1976: 94.
15. Chavez and Warner 1976: 94.
16. Chavez and Warner 1976: 95.
17. Chavez and Warner 1976: 95.
18. Chavez and Warner 1976: 94, n. 367.
19. Chavez and Warner 1976: 100.
20. Chavez and Warner 1976: 101.
21. Bolton 1950: Miera map.
22. Humboldt 1811: map; Pike 1925: map; Biddle 1962, vol. 1: map; see also Goetzmann 1966: 69.
23. Chavez and Warner 1976: 101–3.
24. Crampton 1960a: 274.
25. Pattie 1962; Goetzmann 1966: 71–75; Kroeber 1964
26. Weber 1971: 134–36.
27. Ferris 1940: xlii.
28. Ferris 1940: 40, 319–20. Since Ferris was from Buffalo, New York, his use of Niagara Falls for comparative purposes seems natural.
29. Utley 2004: 147–48.
30. Frémont 1845, 1856.
31. Spense 1984: 439–60, 470.
32. Ashley 1954–55: 167; Morgan 1964: 106–7, 115–16.

33. Goetzmann 1979: 40–45.
34. Kelly 1933; Knipmeyer 2002.

CHAPTER 3

1. Fremont 1845, 1856.
2. This section draws on Bagrow 1985 and Harvey 1980.
3. Humboldt 1822: map; Gallatin 1836: map.
4. Fremont 1845, 1846; Preuss 1848.
5. There is a rich historical literature on the U.S. Army Corps of Topographical Engineers; see especially Goetzmann 1959, 1966; and Wallace 1955.
6. Fenneman 1928: map 1; Hunt 1967.
7. Ives 1861; Pace 2004; MacKinnon 2008: 417–33; Wallace 1955: 174–293; Goetzmann 1966: 306–7.
8. Huseman 1995.
9. Egloffstein 1864.
10. Newberry 1857, 1861, 1876; White 1909; Kenys 1893; Goetzmann 1966: 491.
11. Furniss 1960; MacKinnon 2008.
12. Ives 1861: 99.
13. Palmer 1869: map.
14. Ives 1861: 100–101.
15. Newberry 1861: 41, 45, emphasis added.
16. Newberry 1861: 41, map 2.
17. Hyatt 1868.
18. Fowler 2000: 47–49.
19. Goetzmann 1966: 492.
20. The site, north of Cortez, Colorado, is now known as the Escalante Ruin and is part of the Anasazi Heritage Center, administered by the Bureau of Land Management.
21. Newberry 1876: 97.
22. Egloffstein 1857; see also Krygier 1997: 32–50. Egloffstein is also credited with the invention of the first commercial half-tone printing process in America (Falk 1999, vol. 3: 3418; Hanson 1993).
23. Egloffstein 1860; McKinney 2000.

CHAPTER 4

1. Biographical materials on Powell are copious. See especially Aton 2010; Darrah 1954; Fowler and Fowler 1969; Stegner 1962; and Worster 2001. See also Thomas 2004. Diaries relating to Powell's 1869 river trip were first published in *Utah Historical Quarterly*, edited by William C. Darrah (1947); see also Marston 1969 and Rusho 1969a. Recently, Michael Ghiglieri (2003) has compiled, retranscribed, and re-edited the diaries (correcting numerous errors), together with much very useful background and contextual information on the events of 1867–69 leading up to the first river trip, as well as on the trip itself and its aftermath. Since 1971 there have been various television documentaries of the 1869 river trip; see especially Kleinerman 1971; Greystone Productions 1994; and Davis 1999.
2. This section draws heavily on Ghiglieri 2003: 1–76; and Lago 2008.
3. Sumner, quoted in Ghiglieri 2003: 42; Powell 1867: 3.
4. Fowler and Fowler 1971: 12. The formal portrait of Powell in the Cosmos Club in Washington, D.C. (the club was founded in Powell's living room in 1878) is titled *Kapurats: Major John Wesley Powell.*
5. Rabbitt 1979: 2; illustrations pp. 170–72. Originals in Hague and Emmons 1877; Jurovics et al. 2010; plates 68–83.
6. Ghiglieri 2003: 23–26.
7. Darrah 1947: 94.
8. Materials on Dunn are from Don Lago (personal communication, 10/29/08); see also Ghiglieri 2003: 16.
9. Ghiglieri 2003: 16–17.
10. Materials on Hawkins/Rhodes provided by Don Lago (personal communication, 10/29/08); see also Ghiglieri 2003: 20.
11. Ghiglieri 2003: 279; Darrah 1947: 89.
12. Ghiglieri 2003: 17–19.
13. Ghiglieri 2003: 48–50.
14. Ghiglieri 2003: 49.
15. Ghiglieri 2003: 61.
16. The song was written and published by L. V. H. Crosby in 1857, often sung by him on the concert stage, and was apparently popular for several years, at least as late as 1869. Original sheet music in the L. S. Levy Collection, Johns Hopkins University Library, Baltimore, http://levysheetmusic.mse.jhu.edu.
17. Brad Dimock, personal communication, 4/6/06; Dimock 2010; Ghiglieri 2003: 51–55; see also http://www.whitehallrow.com/legacy.
18. Ghiglieri 2003: 53–56.
19. J. W. Powell to F. Brown, USGS correspondence, National Archives. Courtesy of Dove Menkes, personal communication, 10/12/07. Apparently the

12-foot oars were too long and were shortened before the trip began.

20. For more on Goodman, see http://www.powellmuseum.org/Goodman.html.
21. Goetzmann 1979: 283–85.
22. Hawkins, cited in Bass 1920: 23.
23. Sumner 1947: 122.
24. Sumner 1947: 123.
25. Dolnick 2001: photograph between pp. 180–81; Ghiglieri (2003: 274–78) chronicles the robbery and ambush in more detail.
26. Bass 1920: 13–14; Darrah 1947:30.
27. Cited by Lago 2003a: 3.
28. Stanton 1932: 3.
29. Cited by Stanton 1932: 3–5.
30. Parry 1868; Bell 1870; *American Naturalist* 1870.
31. Cited in Stanton 1932: 5–6.
32. Stanton 1919.
33. Stanton 1932. The publication of *Colorado Controversies* was underwritten by Julius F. Stone, who had been an investor in Stanton's failed gold dredge scheme in Glen Canyon, but who continued to have very high regard for Stanton as a person. Stone had made his own river trip from Green River City in Wyoming to the Gulf of Mexico in 1909 (Stone 1932; see chapter 11). He commissioned James M. Chalfant to edit Stanton's pieces on White and Powell. In the preface thereto, Chalfant wrote regarding the 1917 Senate resolution, "Surely . . . this must be accounted one of the drollest of all gestures of a Congress notoriously given to sporadic asininity" (Chalfant 1932: xxvi).
34. Bass 1920.
35. Dellenbaugh 1904, 1908.
36. Bass 1920: 31.
37. Bass 1920: 36.
38. Darrah 1954; Stegner 1962; Worster 2001. See Dimock 2002 for a summary and critique of other publications by "Powell firsters" and "White firsters."
39. Adams 2001.
40. For the most recent iterations of the debate see Dimock 2008a, 2008b; and Myers 2008.
41. Powell 1875a: 129.
42. Bagley 2002; Bigler and Bagley 2008; Novak 2009; Novak and Rodseth 2006.
43. Ghiglieri 2003: 271.
44. Larsen 1993.
45. Cited in Krakauer 2003: 244.
46. Lago 2003b.
47. Brooks et al. 1961: 302.
48. Bass 1920: 29.
49. Lago 2003a, quoted by Ghiglieri 2003: 293.
50. Brooks et al. 1961: 302.

CHAPTER 5

1. Powell 1869: 23–24.
2. Powell 1947: 127; Sumner 1947: 116.
3. Stegner 1962: 98; Hunt 1988: 6.
4. Powell 1947: 127–28; Sumner 1947: 117.
5. Sumner 1947: 118.
6. Several of the men kept journals of the trip. Most were published between 1939 and 1949; see Darrah 1947; Darrah, Chamberlin, and Kelly 1948–49; and Thompson 1939. See also Rusho 1969c for the maps drawn by Francis M. Bishop during the river trip. Powell's diary of the second trip and Hillers's diary did not surface until 1967–68, when I found them in the National Anthropological Archives of the Smithsonian Institution; see Powell 1968; Hillers 1972; and Fowler 1989.
7. Chamberlin 1947.
8. Gregory 1948–49: 11–18.
9. Darrah 1948–49a: 175–79.
10. Beaman 1874; Darrah 1948–49b: 491–503.
11. Kelly 1948–49: 253–55.
12. Darrah 1948–49b: 492–95.
13. Darrah 1948–49b: 497–99; Dellenbaugh 1908.
14. Darrah 1948–49b: 503.
15. Fowler 1989: 15–23.
16. Jones 1948–49: 84; Powell 1968: 30.
17. Powell 1968: 30.
18. Powell 1968: 30.
19. Powell 1968: 30.
20. Steward 1948–49: 245, n. 45.
21. Powell 1968: 30.
22. W. C. Powell 1948–49: 340–41.
23. Powell 1873: 456–65.
24. Powell 1874: 6–7, 10.
25. Powell 1875a: 96–97. Powell incorporated portions of three articles (Powell 1875b–d) in this report. He later (Powell 1895, 1964, 1987) included the *Explorations . . .* in a larger expanded work, *Canyons of the Colorado*.
26. Dellenbaugh 1908. In 1878 *Scientific American* magazine issued a supplement that included an article titled "The Cañons of the Colorado, Compiled from

sources of the Professor J.W. Powell Expedition." The article includes quotations from Powell's 1875 report and a series of woodcut illustrations based on Beaman's and Hillers's photographs taken between 1871 and 1873.

27. Fowler and Fowler 1971: 76–77.
28. Olson 1969: 263; see also Johnson n.d.: passim.
29. Thompson 1939: passim.
30. Pyne 1994: 62, 71.
31. Gregory and Moore 1931: 9.
32. Powell 1968: 30.
33. Crampton 1964c.
34. Dellenbaugh 1908: 198.
35. Thompson 1875: 137.
36. Fowler and Fowler 1971: 141.
37. Thompson 1875: 137.
38. Thompson 1939: 42.
39. Thompson 1875: 137–38.
40. Hillers 1972: 118.
41. Gus Scott, personal communication, 1/2/03; also, William Cox, Smithsonian Institution Archivist, personal communication, 11/23/02, to Barbara Ekker, forwarded to Don Fowler 12/31/02; see also Hunt 1988; and Wikipedia, http://en.wikipedia.org/wiki/Elmer_Ephraim_Ellsworth.
42. Hillers 1972: 124.
43. Thompson 1875: 140.
44. Hillers 1972: 130.
45. Fowler 1989.
46. Reilly 1999: 406–7.
47. Hillers 1972: 142.
48. Fowler and Fowler 1971: 5.
49. Miller 1986.
50. Powell 1875d.
51. Powell 1896b.
52. The 1873 Powell-Ingalls report is reprinted in full in Fowler and Fowler 1971: 97–118.
53. Fowler and Fowler 1971: 107–18.
54. Fowler and Fowler 1971: 106.
55. Fowler and Fowler 1971: 107.
56. Fowler and Fowler 1971: 133–43.
57. Fowler 1989: plates 31–32.
58. Thomas Moran, http://www.nga.gov/feature/moran/west8.shtm.
59. Thomas Moran, http://www.nga.gov/feature/moran/letterwife.shtm.
60. Fowler and Fowler 1971: fig. 29.
61. Fowler 1989: plate 27.
62. Fowler and Matley 1978.
63. Powell 1896b.
64. Fowler and Fowler 1971; Fowler and Matley 1978.

CHAPTER 6

1. Goetzmann 1966: 355–601; Bartlett 1962; Wilkins 1958.
2. Powell 1873.
3. Powell 1873: 458–59, emphasis added.
4. Powell 1873: 459–60.
5. Powell 1873: 462. Powell's Southern Paiute ethnographic field notes contain some variations of the names he used in his article, as well as over 100 additional place-names, some of which he, or his men, applied to landscape features in later publications; e.g., Uinkarets Plateau, Kwagunt Creek, Tapeats Creek, Kaiparowits Plateau. See Fowler and Fowler 1971: 133–43; and Powell 1874, 1875a, 1876.
6. Powell 1873: 465.
7. Powell 1876.
8. Powell 1876: 3, 6. Later Powell (1896a: map 98–99) used "Basin Ranges," "Colorado Plateaus," "Park Mountains," and "Stony Mountains." His Colorado Plateaus area extends north to the extreme end of the Green River drainage in Wyoming. For more recent nomenclature see Hunt 1967.
9. Fowler 2000: 220–32.
10. Fowler 2000: 88–89.
11. Stegner 1954: 202–350; Worster 2001: 297–436.
12. Emory 1848; Fowler 2000: 38–78.
13. Meyer 2000: 2. For the details of the USGS reorganization see Cloud 1980; and Rabbitt 1979, vol. 2: 57–126.
14. Rabbitt 1979, vol. 2: 145.
15. Powell 1881: xlix–liv, plates I–VIII; Powell 1886: iv–xxi; Cloud 1980: 160. Standardizing map colors, nomenclature, and representations of elevation and relief were subjects of much debate in the 1880s and 1890s, most of it through the International Congress of Geologists (Frazer 1888; Powell 1882b, 1886, 1888). When the USGS began shifting to the metric system in the 1960s, contour intervals changed, and appropriate number scales were added to the edges of the maps to accommodate the Universal Transverse Mercator grids used by the Global Positioning System (GPS).
16. Moffatt 1985: viii.
17. Powell 1884: xiii–xv. See also Moffat 1985: 2.0–2.2, 46.0–46.2. The Wheeler survey produced some

small-scale maps of portions of the Glen Canyon Country; see Schmeckebier 1904: 60, 62.

18. Gannett 1885b.
19. G. Thompson 1883: 34.
20. G. Thompson 1883: 35–36.
21. Fowler 1989: 96.
22. Bourke 1884: 354. On Bourke's ethnological survey see Fowler 2000: 134–35.
23. Thompson 1883: 37.
24. Thompson 1883: 38, 40.
25. Dutton 1882a: 6.
26. Dutton 1882a: 7.
27. Dutton 1882a: 7.
28. Bissell and Weymouth 1935: 1582.
29. Gannett 1885a: 13.
30. John O'Brien, personal communication, 6/13/02.
31. Kelley 1935: 1.
32. For a list of Powell's philosophical and anthropological publications after 1894 see Thomas 2004: 107–26.
33. Powell 1895; Dellenbaugh 1908.
34. Powell 1902.

CHAPTER 7

1. Pyne 2000: 1; see also Stegner 2006.
2. Hall 1847–94.
3. Fowler 2000: 117–39.
4. Pyne 2000: 1.
5. Dutton 1880, 1882a, 1882b, 1882c, 1886.
6. Powell 1882a: xii–xiii.
7. Powell 1882a: xiii–xiv.
8. Dutton 1882b: 49.
9. Dutton 1882b: 116.
10. Dutton 1882b: 51.
11. Dutton 1882b: 69.
12. Hill 1997.
13. Dutton 1882b: 52–53.
14. Dutton 1882b: 53.
15. Dutton 1882b: 58.
16. Stegner 2006: 14.
17. Dutton 1882c: frontispiece.
18. Dutton 1882a: 9–10. Holmes's sketches are in Dutton 1882b (plates x, xix, xxiii, xxxi) and throughout Dutton 1882c.
19. Fowler 2000: 82–84.
20. Pyne 1994: 12–19. On Henry Ward's establishment see Kohlstedt 1980.
21. Pyne 1994: 20–24.
22. Pyne 1994: 37.
23. Rabbitt 1979, vol. 2: 182–83.
24. Dawdy 1993; Pyne 1994: 41–47.
25. Gregory and Moore 1931: 8–9.
26. Pyne 1994: 48; Stansbury 1988.
27. Gilbert 1875, 1876.
28. Hunt 1988: 2.
29. F. Dellenbaugh to H. Gregory, personal communication, n.d., cited in Gregory and Moore 1931: 9; see Thompson 1939; Roundy 2000.
30. Hunt 1988: 8.
31. Gilbert 1877; Newberry 1876: 100; Witkind 1975. In his famous review of Gilbert's monograph, the Harvard scholar James Dwight Dana gave his seal of approval to Gilbert's thesis: "The facts brought out appear to sustain Mr. Gilbert's conclusions that the mountains were made such, out of horizontal strata by the ascending trachyte" (Dana 1880: 22). But Dana gently chided Gilbert for his improper use of Greek suffixes in naming "laccolites": "Since the termination *ite* is distinctive in science of names of *kinds* of minerals and rocks, the modified form of the term laccolith (analogous to monolith) would be better and is used below as essentially Mr. Gilbert's" (Dana 1880: 18). Despite this gentle scholarly upbraiding, Gilbert continued to use "laccolite" for twenty years (Hunt 1980: 27).
32. Hunt 1988: 11.
33. Gilbert 1876: 16.
34. Gilbert 1876: 17–18.
35. Gilbert 1876: 21–22.
36. Gilbert 1876: 21.
37. Gregory and Moore 1931: 119–20 and plate 16.
38. Gilbert 1876: 24.
39. Gilbert 1876: 89–101.
40. Gilbert 1890, 1893, 1914; Gilbert and Brigham 1902; Gilbert et al. 1907. See also Davis 1918; Hunt 1980; and Yochelson 1980.

CHAPTER 8

1. Davis 1900.
2. Pogue 1911: 1048.
3. Gregory 1917, 1938, 1950, 1951; Gregory and Moore 1931.
4. Gregory 1938: 1.
5. Gregory 1917: 8, 10. The mission at St. Michaels, along the road from Gallup, New Mexico, to

Ganado, Arizona, was established in the 1890s. It remains very active in the twenty-first century.

6. Gregory and Moore 1931: 12.
7. Gregory and Moore 1931: 1.
8. Gregory and Moore 1931: 12.
9. Gregory and Moore 1931: 1.
10. Gregory 1938: 1–2.
11. Gregory 1938: 14.
12. Powell 1876: 53, 69; Gregory 1917: 57–59, 157; Gregory 1938: 52–53; Gregory and Moore 1931: 52–53; Baker, Dane, and Reeside 1936: 5, 17.
13. Hopi Dictionary Project 1998: 261.
14. Powell 1876: 69; Sapir 1931: 660.
15. Gregory 1917: 42; Young and Morgan 1980: 290.
16. Gregory 1917: 42.
17. Hintze 1988: chart 100.
18. Gregory 1917: 16.
19. Hintze 1988: fig. 165 and charts 100 and 101.
20. Gregory and Moore 1931: 61–69.
21. Dutton 1886: 136–137; Nusbaum et al. 1940: 322–23.
22. Sapir 1931: 646; Gillmor and Wetherill 1953: 189; Young and Morgan 1980: 706.
23. Baker, Dane, and Reeside 1936: 5, 17; Gregory 1938: 52–53; Gregory and Moore 1931: 64.
24. Gregory 1917: 57.
25. Gregory and Moore 1931: 69.
26. Baars 2000: 54–55.
27. Baars 2000: 55.
28. Baars 2000: 58.
29. Baars 1972: 171–72, 2000: 59.
30. Hintze 1988: 60.
31. Hintze 1988: 94–103.
32. This section is a pastiche based on Baars 1972, 1993, 1995, 2000; Baker 1946; Baker, Dane, and McKight 1936; Hintze 1988; Hunt 1956, 1969; and Stokes 1986.

CHAPTER 9

1. Stanton 1890.
2. Stanton 1892.
3. Stanton 1893.
4. Stanton 1893: 294–97; Nims 1967: 76. Stanton later incorporated his version of Nims's accident and rescue into a section of his work on the Colorado River (Stanton 1965: 114–29).
5. Stanton 1893: 300–302.
6. http://www.georgetownlooprr.com.
7. Stanton 1965: 23–27.
8. Stanton 1965: 33–36.
9. Crampton 1988: 75; on Hite's relationship with Hoskininni see Kelly 1953.
10. Stanton 1965: 95.
11. Stanton 1892; see also Stanton 1965: 223–27.
12. John Wesley Powell (1889), quoted in *New York Tribune*; cited in Stanton 1965: 13.
13. Wellington 1889a: 278–79; cited in Stanton 1965: 13.
14. Wellington 1889b: 813–14.
15. Stanton 1892. I am indebted to Al Holland and Richard Quarteroli for noting the influence of the 1893 economic panic and the discovery of oil in southern California as contributing to the lack of interest in Stanton's scheme.
16. Service 1968: 33.
17. Black 1930.
18. Jones 1948–49: 99.
19. The following section draws particularly on Crampton and Smith 1961; Smith 1960, 1962; and Smith and Crampton 1987. See also Topping 1997: 119–43 for a more extended summary of the gold rushes in the Glen Canyon Country.
20. Crampton and Smith 1961: 74.
21. The section on mining along the San Juan draws particularly on McPherson and Kitchen 1999; and Aton and McPherson 2000: 113–28.
22. McPherson and Kitchen 1999: 69.
23. Williams 1929: 8.
24. Black 1930: 12–13.
25. Crampton and Smith 1961: xiii, 88, 107.
26. Crampton and Smith 1961: 71–72.
27. Quoted by Crampton and Smith 1961: 72.
28. Crampton and Smith 1961: 71–72.
29. Crampton and Smith 1961: 72–73, emphasis added.
30. Crampton and Smith 1961: 75.
31. Crampton and Smith 1961: 78–79.
32. Crampton and Smith 1961: 112.
33. Crampton and Smith 1961: 95, n. 5.
34. Crampton and Smith 1961: 99, 113–14.
35. Crampton and Smith 1961: 121–40.
36. Crampton and Smith 1961: 135, 139.
37. Crampton and Smith 1961: 142–43.
38. Crampton and Smith 1961: 80, n. 5.
39. Cited in Webb 1994: 101.
40. Cited in Smith and Crampton 1987: xii. In 1932 a portion of Stanton's magnum opus, *Colorado River Controversies*, was edited and published by the historian E. L. Chalfant (Stanton 1932) and is discussed

in chapter 4. Part of his compilation of materials was an annotated historical map (Stanton 1908). There is a copy in the Library of Congress. The first eleven chapters of volume 2 of Stanton's opus, which he called "The River and the Canyon," were edited and published by the historian Dwight Smith as *Down the Colorado* (Stanton 1965). His four volumes of detailed field diaries and his engineering notebooks of the two river trips were edited and published in 1987 (Smith and Crampton 1987). The bulk of Stanton's 1890–1922 manuscripts and other materials relating to his experiences in the canyon country are in the New York Public Library (Stanton 1851–1960).

41. This section is based on Rusho and Crampton 1992: 66–80; Carrell, Bradford, and Rusho 1987; and Reilly 1999: 215–39.
42. Carrell, Bradford, and Rusho 1987: 8. I am also indebted to W. L. Rusho (personal communication, 4/7/10) for some additional details about the boats Spencer used.
43. The "element" was rhenium, a soft metal only identified many years later. It is a superconductor of electricity, and in very recent years has been combined with boron to produce a "superhard" material, rhenium diboride, hard enough to scratch diamonds (Dumé 2007).
44. Carrell, Bradford, and Rusho 1987; Rusho and Crampton 1992: 71–79.
45. Rusho and Crampton 1992: 76.

CHAPTER 10

1. Dyar 1904; *National Geographic Magazine* 1904: 367–68. For additional background on natural bridges and arches in the Glen Canyon Country and adjacent areas, see Moore 1955; Munthe 2002; and McVickar 2001.
2. Holmes 1907.
3. Holmes 1907: 203.
4. See also McPherson 1999: 345–46 for additional background on the discovery and reporting of the bridges.
5. Judd 1968: 4–14.
6. Judd 1968: 17–18.
7. Cummings 1910a, 1910b.
8. Pogue 1911: 1048, 1053.
9. Miser, Trimble, and Paige 1923.
10. See Stephen Jett 1992 for the definitive review of the squabble.
11. Cummings 1910a: 165, emphasis added.
12. Douglass 1910.
13. Pogue 1911: 1053.
14. Judd 1927: 13.
15. T. R. Roosevelt, cited in Babbitt 1990: 46 (originally 1913); Nicholas Roosevelt cited in Babbitt 1990: 58 (originally 1913); see also Babbitt 1987. John Wetherill placed a small book register at the bridge for visitors to sign. The register is now in the archives of the Glen Canyon National Recreation Area office in Page, Arizona. In 1922, when John Widtsoe and the USGS party visited the bridge (chapter 12), Widtsoe copied many register entries in his journal and counted a total of 187 visitors, including 36 women (Widtsoe 1955: 217–18). These included Zane Grey's trips in 1913 and April 1922; the Roosevelt party in 1913; parties led by Byron Cummings in 1919 and 1920; and Bernheimer's trips in 1920, 1921, and 1922 (chapters 10, 13).
16. Priestley 1990: 106 (originally published 1938); see also Atkins 1981.
17. Kluckhohn 1932: 117.
18. Another version of "The Great Gambler" story was published by Louisa Wade Wetherill and Byron Cummings (1922).
19. Judd 1927: 14.
20. There are several biographical and interpretive sources on Zane Grey. The major ones are Gruber 1970; Jackson 1973; Kant 1984; May 1997; and Ronald 1975.
21. Bridger 2002: 9.
22. Reilly 1999: 205–6.
23. Kant 1984: 21–25.
24. Gruber 1970: 252.
25. Jackson 1884.
26. Grey also described Rainbow Bridge in various magazine articles over the years (Gruber 1970: 263); see, for example, "Down into the Desert" (Grey 1924).
27. Grey 1915: 45, 48–49.
28. Grey 1915: 333, 335, 338. Grey, following the lead of Byron Cummings and Joseph Pogue, in 1910 and 1911 *National Geographic Magazine* articles on the Utah natural bridges called Rainbow Bridge "Nonnezoshe." Cummings (1910a: 162–67) spelled it "Nonnezoshi"; Pogue (1911: 1049) spelled it "Nonnezoshe."

29. Grey's "Hole in the Wall" is not to be confused with the outlaw hideout in Wyoming.
30. Grey 1957: 75.
31. Grey 1957: 76–77.
32. Grey 1957: 90.
33. Grey 1928: 1.
34. Grey 1954: 90–91.
35. Grey 1954: 113.
36. Gruber 1970: 253; Kant 1984: 139, 141–42, 144–45.
37. See Zane Grey films, http://imdb.com. Jack Holt (1888–1951), by the by, was the epitome of the square-jawed, pencil-mustachioed hero. He became the model for cartoonist Chester Gould's Dick Tracy.
38. Grey 1922–23, 1925.
39. Grey 1925: 294, 301–2. The recycled description of the bridge comes from Grey's "Down into the Desert" (1924: 44).
40. Hilger 1986: 7–8; see also Stedman 1982: 176–78.
41. Biographical information on Kluckhohn is drawn from Parsons and Vogt 1962.
42. Kluckhohn 1932: 107.
43. Kluckhohn 1932: 110–11.
44. Geib, Collette, and Spurr 2001: 399–440.
45. Birney 1930: 283–84.
46. Kluckhohn 1932: 232–35.
47. James Hanks, who was with Kluckhohn on his final trips, made movies and still photographs of the trip onto the Kaiparowits Plateau. These are now in Special Collections, Cline Library, Northern Arizona University, Flagstaff.
48. See, for example, Kluckhohn 1962; and Leighton and Kluckhohn 1947.
49. Birney 1930: 290.
50. Kelly 1938: 152–53.
51. Kelly 1938: 127–34.
52. Kelly 1938: 149–50.
53. Tippets 1961: 112.
54. Knipmeyer 2002: 124; Tippets 1961: 112.
55. Grey 1930.
56. Baker 1991; Hill and Goldman 1969; Silverstein and Newman 1965; Redford 1978. See also Utah Tourism, *The Outlaw Trail*, http://www.utah.com/oldwest/robbersroost.html.
57. This section is based principally on W. L. (Bud) Rusho's (excellent study *The Mystery of Everett Ruess* (2010) and David Roberts's "Finding Everett Ruess" (2009).
58. Cited by Rusho 2010: 179.
59. Cited by Rusho 2010: 190–91.
60. Rusho 2010: 203.
61. Rusho 2010: 213.
62. Rusho 2010: 210.
63. Rusho 2010: 214–20.
64. Rusho 2010: 239.
65. Ruess 1940.
66. Rusho 2010; see also Roberts 1999; Orr 2000; and numerous Internet sites in English, French, and German devoted to Ruess's life, art, and possible fate.
67. Roberts 2009; Maugh 2009.
68. Roberts 2009: 76–77.
69. Rusho 2010: 258–59.

CHAPTER 11

1. Marston 1960: 308.
2. Major sources on Colorado River runners include Baker n.d.; Clark and Newcomb 1977; Cook 1987; De Ross 1958; Dimock 2001, 2003; Dimock, ed., 2003; Flavell 1987; Kolb 1914; Kolb and Kolb 2003; Lavender 1985; Nelson 1991; Reilly 1987; Suran 2003; Swanson 2007; Webb 1989, 1994, 2004, 2005; Webb and Dimock 2000; Welsh, Conley, and Dimock 1998; Westwood 1992, 1997. Major archives on Colorado River runners include the Marston Collection at the Huntington Library, and the several collections in the Cline Library, Northern Arizona University, Flagstaff; and the Marriott Library, University of Utah, Salt Lake City.
3. This section is based on Flavell 1987.
4. Hislop to Stanton, October 4, 1896, quoted in Flavell 1987: 11.
5. Flavell 1987: 44.
6. Flavell 1987: 44–45.
7. Flavell 1987: 45–46.
8. Flavell 1987: 73.
9. Lavender 1985: 36.
10. Lavender 1985: 36.
11. Lavender 1985: 37.
12. Marston 1960: 293.
13. Marston 1960: 293–98.
14. This section based on Dimock 2007.
15. Dimock 2007: 18.
16. Bert Loper, cited by Dimock 2007: 37.
17. Dimock 2007: 37–38.
18. Loper, cited by Dimock 2007: 39.
19. Lavender 1985: 45.

20. Dimock 2007: 99–108.
21. Dimock 2007: 128–32.
22. Reilly 1999: 208.
23. Baker n.d.: 80.
24. Lavender 1985: 51.
25. Lavender 1985: 53–54; Webb 1994: 67–68.
26. Crampton 1960b: 86.
27. Webb 1994: 91.
28. Stone 1932: 46.
29. Stone 1932: 4.
30. Stone 1932: 79–80.
31. Stone 1932: 85.
32. Webb 1994: 93.
33. Webb 1994: 101.
34. This section is based on Kolb 1952 (first edition 1914) and the Kolbs' diaries and correspondence edited by William Suran (2003); see also Webb 1994: 68–69.
35. Webb 1994: 68.
36. Kolb 1952: 4.
37. Kolb 1952: 10.
38. Kolb 1952: 123.
39. Kolb 1952: 153.
40. Kolb 1952: 156.
41. Kolb 1952: 159–60.
42. Kolb 1952: 161.
43. Kolb 1952: 171–72.
44. Kolb 1952: 179–80.
45. Webb 1994: 70.
46. Swanson 2007.
47. Swanson 2007: 166.
48. Swanson 2007: 66–68.
49. In the 1950s, Agassiz had a radio telescope named for him at Harvard University's observatory station in Texas.
50. A portion of Zion Canyon had been designated in 1909 as Mukuntuweap National Monument—John Wesley Powell's name for the canyon.
51. Jeffers 1923.
52. *Kane County News*, June 29, 1923; courtesy of Dove Menkes 12/20/01. Rust's boats apparently still exist in a National Park Service warehouse at Grand Canyon (W. L. Rusho, personal communication, 4/2/2010).
53. *Kane County Standard*, July 22, 1938.
54. Swanson 2007: 202.
55. This section draws principally on Lavender 1985 and Webb 1994: 57–75.
56. According to IMDB (www.imdb.com) there was an animated short film issued in 1928 titled *Conquering the Colorado*, but there is little further information about it. Eddy is quoted by Lavender 1985: 76.
57. This section is based on Brad Dimock's (2001) excellent book on the Hydes; see also Dimock 2003.
58. Dimock 2001: 29.
59. This section is based principally on Webb 1989.
60. Webb 1989: 24, 157, n. 1.
61. See www.hatchriverexpeditions.com; www.donhatchrivertrips.com.
62. This section is based on Wetherill, Flattum, and Stearns 1961.
63. Wetherill, Flattum, and Stearns 1961: 34.
64. Wetherill, Flattum, and Stearns 1961: 35.
65. Wetherill, Flattum, and Stearns 1961: 35.
66. Wetherill, Flattum, and Stearns 1961: 40.
67. Wetherill, Flattum, and Stearns 1961: 42.
68. Wetherill, Flattum, and Stearns 1961: 43.
69. Wetherill, Flattum, and Stearns 1961: 43.
70. Stearns 1931.
71. The major sources on Nevills are Roy Webb's (1989) edition of Nevills's river diaries, as well as Nelson 1991; Cook 1987; and Reilly 1987.
72. Cook 1987: 7; Nelson 1991: 1.
73. Ferrari 1987–88: 2.
74. Beals, Brainerd, and Smith 1945: 7.
75. Webb 1989: 4–5.
76. Nelson 1991: 4; Cook 1987: 7–10; Webb 1989: 5; Jotter 1997.
77. Cook 1987: 12.
78. Nelson 1991: 7–8.
79. Clover 1939: 7.
80. Jotter 1938: 12.
81. Clover 1939: 8.
82. Welsh, Conley, and Dimock 1998: passim.
83. Clover 1939: 12.
84. Cook 1987: 66.
85. Cook 1987: 116–19; Webb 1989: 16–60.
86. Clover 1939: 9–10.
87. Clover 1939: 11.
88. de Tocqueville 1945.
89. Cited by Iverson 1997: 164.
90. Goldwater 1940.
91. Goldwater 1940: 25–26, 28.
92. Goldwater 1940: 30.
93. Goldwater 1940: 33.
94. Goldwater 1940: 34.
95. Goldwater 1940: 44.
96. Goldwater 1940: 50.
97. Iverson 1997: 39.

98. www.imdb.com; Roy Webb, Clioriver digest 120.
99. Webb 1993: 36, 46–47.
100. Dimock 2005.
101. Webb 1994: 81, 104–5.
102. This section is based on Dimock 2003; and Welsh, Conley, and Dimock 1998.
103. Eddy 1929; Jaeger 1932.
104. Dimock 2003: xv.
105. Dimock 2003: 115.
106. Dimock 2003: 115, emphasis added.
107. Dimock 2003: 117.
108. The film was later reissued by 20th Century Fox Sport Show with narration by Mel Allen (www.imdb.com); see also Capital Communications Broadcasting 1992 and Oregon Historical Society n.d.
109. Welsh, Conley, and Dimock 1998: 171–220.
110. Dimock 2003: 33.
111. Dimock 2003: 74–75.
112. Dimock 2003: 194–95, 197.
113. Center for the History of Physics 2009.
114. Moki Mac, http://www.moki mac.com.
115. Webb 2004: 2.
116. The Music Temple registers are now in Special Collections, Marriott Library, University of Utah, Salt Lake City.
117. Webb 2004: 9.
118. This section is based principally on Westwood 1997; see also De Ross 1958 and Clark and Newcomb 1977.
119. This section is based on Westwood 1997: 35–38, and an Internet website devoted to Irish McCalla (Wickham 2005–9).
120. Clark and Newcomb 1977: 73.
121. Georgie remembered her as "Iris McCollough a tall, dark, buxom girl" (Clark and Newcomb 1977: 73).
122. Brooks and Marsh 1999: 911.
123. Clark and Newcomb 1977: 72–73; Wickham 2005–9.
124. Westwood 1997: 38.
125. Westwood 1997: 58.
126. Stiles 1999; Verdoia 1999b.

CHAPTER 12

1. Davis 1917.
2. Powell 1878.
3. Worster 2001: 373–79.
4. Powell 1881: xi.
5. Pisani 1992, 2002; Worster 1985, 2001.
6. Powell 1879: 1.
7. Powell 1890a: vii.
8. Powell 1890b: 355.
9. Powell 1890b: 357.
10. Bates 1890; Gressley 1988.
11. Newell 1902: 8, 88.
12. Langenheim 2000.
13. Davis 1917.
14. Boyer and Webb 2007: 33. This section is based on Langbein 1975 and Boyer and Webb's (2007: 1–98) excellent historical summary of the development of the USGS and the Reclamation Service in the years between 1894 and 1928 in relation to the Colorado River.
15. Boyer and Webb 2007: 34.
16. Boyer and Webb 2007: 38.
17. La Rue 1916, 1925.
18. Here we drew particularly on the excellent works by Robert Webb and his colleagues on Cataract and Grand canyons: Boyer and Webb 2007; Webb, Belnap, and Weisheit 2004; and Langbein 1975.
19. Langbein 1975: 2–3.
20. Hoyt and Grover 1908.
21. Grover 1916: 10.
22. La Rue 1916: 198.
23. Boyer and Webb 2007: 51.
24. The 1921 trip is chronicled in detail in Westwood 1992: 1–61.
25. Westwood 1992: 12.
26. Webb, Belnap, and Weisheit 2004: 30.
27. Boyer and Webb 2007: 53.
28. DeBuys and Meyers 1999.
29. Boyer and Webb 2007: 41.
30. Fall and Davis 1922.
31. Boyer and Webb 2007: 43.
32. Widtsoe 1955.
33. Boyer and Webb 2007: 590; Widtsoe 1955: 200.
34. Widtsoe 1955: 205.
35. Widtsoe 1955: 221.
36. Widtsoe 1955: 222.
37. Gilbert and Sullivan 2010; Boyer and Webb 2007: 54–55; see also Freeman 1924: 209–210.
38. Widtsoe 1955: 223.
39. Widtsoe 1911.
40. Tyler 2003.
41. Tyler 2003: 123–241; Worster 1985: 209–11.

42. Colorado River Compact 1922: articles III a–b.
43. Boyer and Webb 2007: 46–47.
44. Pisani 2002: 136–53.
45. La Rue 1925: 18–20.
46. La Rue 1925: 48 and plate xviii.
47. La Rue 1925: 19, 23.
48. La Rue 1925: 23.
49. La Rue 1925: 26–27.
50. La Rue 1925: 25–28.
51. La Rue 1925: 59, 61–62.
52. La Rue 1925: 59.
53. La Rue 1925: 70–75.
54. La Rue 1925: 76–77.
55. Langbein 1975: 5.
56. Langbein 1975: 6.
57. Langbein 1975: 8–9; Boyer and Webb 2007: 263–75.
58. Floyd Dominy, cited by Couch 2010: 25.

CHAPTER 13

1. This section draws on Adams 1960; Blackburn and Williamson 1997; Fowler 2000: 81–84, 187–202, 256–60, 289–93; and McNitt 1966.
2. Jackson 1876; Holmes 1876.
3. Wetherill 1977: 110.
4. Blackburn and Williamson 1997: 21.
5. Nordenskiöld 1893.
6. Fowler 2000: 210. Some Wetherill collections were exhibited at industrial expositions in Minneapolis in 1891–92. For a complete history of the collections see Osborne 2004: 3.
7. Blackburn and Williamson 1997; Osborne 2004: 5.
8. James Knipmeyer (2006) has done an excellent job of chronicling the expedition and reprinting all the articles.
9. R. Wetherill to T. Hyde, cited by McNitt 1966: 65, emphasis added.
10. McNitt 1966: 80–84.
11. Prudden 1897.
12. Prudden 1903; see also Prudden 1918.
13. Prudden 1906, 1914, 1918; Cordell 1997: 280–85.
14. L. Prudden 1927: 179.
15. Anderson 1969: 7. Keet Seel is also spelled "Kiet Siel" in archaeological and southwestern travel literature. Herein we follow the spelling used by the National Park Service—Keet Seel—unless it is in a quote.
16. McNitt 1966: 162; M. Wetherill 1992: 79–83.
17. For succinct summaries of Chacoan archaeology see Noble 2004; Lekson 2006; and Cameron 2009.
18. McNitt 1966; M. Wetherill 1992.
19. Fowler 2000: 172–80.
20. Fowler 2000: 261–74.
21. This section is based on Judd 1954 and Bostwick 2006.
22. Salmon 2009. Wall's mansion on South Temple Street in Salt Lake City was occupied by the L.D.S. Business College until 2006.
23. Judd 1968: 3.
24. See Schaafsma 1994.
25. Judd 1968: 3–18.
26. Fowler 2000: 261–69.
27. Judd 1968: 22.
28. Kidder 1910.
29. Judd 1968: 27. Col. (later Gen.) Hugh Lenox Scott served in the U.S. Army from 1876 to 1919. One of his first assignments was to mark the army graves at the Little Big Horn battlefield. He became an expert in Indian sign language and cultures, and served in numerous posts, including superintendent of West Point (twice), a soldier in the Spanish-American War, and finally as chief of staff of the U.S. military from 1914 to 1917. See Scott 1928.
30. Jett 1992: 48, n. 24.
31. Jett 1992.
32. Fowler 2005: 21–22.
33. Thompson 2000.
34. Thompson 2000; Lee 1970.
35. Fowler 2000: 247–74.
36. Rothman 1991: 19.
37. Cummings 1910c: 29–30; Rudy 1955: 3.
38. B. Cummings to E. L. Hewett, 11/5/09, cited in Fowler 2000: 259.
39. Cummings 1910a, 1910b, 1910c.
40. Rothman 1991: 28–29.
41. Rothman 1991: 24–26.
42. Bostwick 2006: 61–67; Turner 1962a; Cummings 1915.
43. Morley 1908: 609.
44. Cummings 1915: 282.
45. Bostwick 2006.
46. Anderson 1969.
47. Lindsay 1969; see also Lindsay et al. 1969 and chapter 19.
48. Nordenskiöld 1893.
49. Kidder 1915; Fowler 2000: 265–66, 284–88; Harris and Sadler 2003.

50. Kidder 1914; Givens 1992.
51. Prudden 1897; Pepper 1902.
52. Kidder and Guernsey 1919: 47.
53. Kidder and Guernsey 1919: 14–15.
54. Kidder and Guernsey 1919: 41, 195, fig. 96.
55. Hawley 1937; Parsons 1938; Titiev 1939; Malotki 2000.
56. Kidder and Guernsey 1919: 41.
57. Kidder 1916.
58. La Farge 1929, 1937, 1945; Pearce 1972.
59. Guernsey 1931: iv; Guernsey and Kidder 1921.
60. Guernsey 1931: 9.
61. Guernsey 1931: 55.
62. Kidder 1924.
63. Kidder 1924: 167–251 and fig. 12.
64. Kidder 1927.
65. Kidder 1936; Cordell 1997: 158–79; McNitt 1966.
66. Leake and Topping 1987:149–50; Topping 1997: 260.
67. Bernheimer 1920–21: 6.
68. Bernheimer 1924: 9.
69. Morris 1922a: 512.
70. Morris 1922b: 6.
71. Morris 1919; Fowler 2000: 290–91.
72. Morris 1939.
73. Bernheimer 1920–21: 3.
74. Bernheimer 1920–21: 7.
75. Morris 1939.
76. Morris 1929: 3–4.
77. Judd 1926.
78. Judd 1924b: 77.
79. Judd 1968: 95–96.
80. Judd 1924a: 78.
81. Judd 1968: 99.
82. Judd 1924a: 81–82.
83. Judd 1924b.
84. Judd 1970.
85. Jones 1873; Smith 1992: 152.
86. Gunnerson 1969: 23 and figs. 2A-2B; Swanson 2007: 221–24.
87. Swanson 2007: 208.
88. Kreutzer 2005: 21–22.
89. Swanson 2007: 227–28.
90. Morss 1927, 1931a.
91. Morss 1931b; Gunnerson 1969: 33; Kreutzer 2005: 22–23.
92. Brew 1982: 344.
93. Morss 1954.
94. Swanson 2007: 230–33; Gunnerson 1969, n. 53.
95. Brew 1946.
96. Davis 2008: 19.
97. Hayden 1930; Mason 1945.
98. Steward 1931.
99. Janetski 1999: table 2.1; Kerns 2003: 127; Steward 1936, 1937.
100. Kerns 2003: 139–43.
101. Thrapp 1990, vol. 1: 116.
102. Birney 1930, 1934.
103. Birney 1952; Peckinpah and Laven 1965.
104. Kelly 1930; Kerns 2010: 77.
105. Thrapp 1990, 2: 767.
106. Birney 1931; Kelly and Birney 1934; Kelly 1938; Kelly and Howe 1937; Lee 1938; Darrah, Chamberlin, and Kelly 1948–49.
107. J. Nusbaum to A. L. Kroeber, 6/7/32. A. L. Kroeber Papers, Bancroft Library, University of California, Berkeley.
108. Steward 1941: 325.
109. Steward 1941: 282.
110. The "huge cave" is probably a site tested by the University of Utah in 1958; Steward's Site 13 is probably Talus Ruin (chapter 16).
111. Steward 1941: 354.
112. Steward 1938, 1977; Kern 2003.
113. This section is based on Beals, Brainerd, and Smith 1945; Christenson 1983, 1987; Smith 1963, 1992: 123–38; and the Ansel Hall Papers in the Bancroft Library, University of California, Berkeley; see also Elliot 1995: 189–212.
114. Smith 1963: 228–29.
115. Hall 1934a: 5.
116. Hall 1934a: 7.
117. Beals, Brainerd, and Smith 1945: iii. Unless otherwise noted, the thumbnail biographical sketches in this section derive primarily from the several volumes of *Who Was Who in America* (Marquis Who's Who 1954–98), *Who's Who in Engineering* (American Association of Engineering Sciences 1922–64), and the twelfth edition of *American Men and Women of Science* 1971–86 (Bowker Publishing, New York).
118. Farquhar's interest in the Sierra led him to edit and republish William H. Brewer's *Up and Down California in 1860–1864,* and Clarence King's classic *Mountaineering in the Sierra Nevada* (Farquhar 1930, 1935). His Sierra scholarship culminated in his magisterial *History of the Sierra Nevada* (Farquhar 1965). Mount Francis Farquhar in Kings Canyon

National Park is named for him, and the Sierra Club gives an annual mountaineering award in his name (Clinch 1975). His interests in the Colorado River led to a major bibliography, *The Books of the Colorado River and Grand Canyon* (Farquhar 1953). That led him to rediscover Lt. George Horatio Derby's *Phoenixiana* satires (Farquhar 1937).

119. Atwood 1940, 1945.
120. Hall 1934a: 49.
121. Beals, Brainerd, and Smith 1945: iii.
122. Individuals associated with all six expeditions are listed in Beals, Brainerd, and Smith 1945: iii–v.
123. Hall 1934a: 2.
124. Christenson 1983: fig. 2.
125. Christenson 1983: 11.
126. MacNeish 1974: 209–10.
127. Eaton 1935, 1970.
128. Smith 1992: 132.
129. Babington 1950.
130. Hall 1935a, 1935b.
131. Martin Gambee. http://69.15.66.178/gambee.htm.
132. Stewart 1987,1998.
133. Woodbury 1944, 1954.
134. Pond 1928, 1965. The results of the Mongolia archaeology project were not published until fifty-five years later (Fairservis 1993).
135. Smith 1992: 126.
136. Smith 1992: 127.
137. Beals 1982: 2–11.
138. Collier 1963.
139. Hall 1994: 3–4.
140. Hall 1959, 1966, 1976, 1983, 1992, 1994.
141. Davis 2008: 63, 65.
142. Christenson 1983: 14; see also Christenson 1987.
143. The foregoing is based on Taylor and Euler 1980 and Nash 1999.
144. Hargrave 1931, 1935: 20. In theory the expedition focused on all the natural sciences, but only mimeographed reports on zoology and herpetology were produced (Clark 1935, Cole 1935, Eaton 1935).
145. Beals, Brainerd, and Smith 1945: 7; Rinaldo 1935.
146. Hall 1935a: 3.
147. Nevills Papers, Box 5, Fd 12, 1935–39; thanks to Roy Webb, personal communication, 7/11/02.
148. Lockett 1933, 1934; Lockett and Hargrave 1953. Lockett's mother, Hattie Greene Lockett, received her master's degree in 1932, also from Arizona. Her published thesis, *The Unwritten Literature of the Hopi*, became a local best-selling book (Lockett 1933).
149. Beals, Brainerd, and Smith 1945.
150. Hall 1944, 1947.
151. Sharrock and Keane 1962.
152. Taylor 1958. This section is drawn from Fowler 2010.
153. Fowler 2003: 325.
154. Taylor 2003: 4–5, 1988.
155. Kluckhohn 1940.
156. W. W. Taylor 1945; Euler 1997; Dark 2010; Fowler 2010.
157. Taylor 1948.
158. Only portions of such a report were published six years after his death (Taylor 2003).
159. Taylor 1958: 1, n. 1.
160. Taylor 1958: 1; Nash 1999.
161. Taylor 1958: 3.
162. Taylor 1958: 3.
163. Adams 2003.
164. Adams 1951; Taylor and Adams 1953: 1–71.
165. Adams 2003.
166. Taylor and Adams 1953: 97–118.
167. Witkind, Thaden, and Lough 1952.
168. Adams 1953.
169. That project, subsequent ethnographic work, and stints as an Indian trader at the Shonto trading post ultimately led to his landmark dissertation on Navajo Indian traders, later published by the Bureau of American Ethnology (Adams 1963; see also Adams 1993: 309).
170. Adams 1951; Taylor and Adams 1951–53: 1–71.
171. Cordell 1997; Cordell and Fowler 2005.

CHAPTER 14

1. Information on Aleson based on Topping 1984, 1997: 244–45, 319–27; and Wisheit 1993.
2. This section draws on Topping 1997: 321–27.
3. Dick Sprang to Eleanor Inskip, 1995, cited in Inskip 1999: 15.
4. Aleson 1952: 1–4.
5. Aleson 1952: 22.
6. Aleson 1952: 24–26.
7. Aleson 1952: 28.
8. Aleson 1952: 45–46.
9. Sprang 1992: 12.
10. Topping 1997: 327. Sprang's papers and records are now in the Utah Historical Society archives, Salt Lake City; many of his photographs, as well as

Aleson's 1952 journal, are in the Colorado Plateau digital archives, Cline Library, Northern Arizona University, Flagstaff.
11. This section based on City of Blanding 2005.
12. This section draws on Katie Lee's delightful autobiographical books and DVD (1998, 2004, 2007), and on personal communications by email and telephone with me from August 2009 to January 2010.
13. Nichols 2000: 1.
14. Nichols 2000: 2.
15. Lee 1998: map.
16. Nichols 2000: 35; Porter 1963.
17. Nichols 1999.
18. Lee 1998: 105.
19. Lee 1998: 115.
20. Lee 2004: 157.

CHAPTER 15

1. Jennings 1966; Lindsay et al. 1969.
2. Squier and Davis 1848.
3. Fowler 2000: 38–49.
4. Fowler 2000: 82–83.
5. Fowler 2000: 203–32.
6. Fowler 2005.
7. Thompson 2000.
8. Brew 1968.
9. Haag 1985: 2.
10. Fowler 1986a.
11. Jennings 1963; Fowler 1982, 1986a.
12. Ultimately, the Tennessee Valley Authority developed fifty dams and reservoirs, eighteen coal-fired power plants, and (later on) three nuclear-fueled power plants. http//www.tva.gov/sites.
13. Jennings and Setzler 1941; see also Haag 1985; Fagette 1996; Lyon 1996.
14. Harrington, Hayden, and Schellbach 1930; Osborne 1957.
15. Dilsaver 1994; Everhart 1972; Rettie 1995.
16. Wendorf and Thompson 2002.
17. Jennings 1963.
18. Jennings 1994: 131–56.
19. Jennings 1994: 138.
20. Sahagún 1950–82.
21. Jennings 1957; Cressman 1942; Haury 1950; Steward 1940. See also Fowler 1986b: 17–21; and Fowler and Fowler 2008.
22. Jennings 1994: 159.
23. Steen 1981; Lambert 1983.
24. Fowler 1986a. "Salvage archaeology" came to encompass more than reservoirs, especially pipeline archaeology, invented in 1950 by Jesse Nusbaum, Fred Wendorf, and others, and highway salvage archaeology, invented by Fred Wendorf and the New Mexico Highway Department in 1953 (Wendorf 2008: 59, 66–71).
25. Martin 1989.
26. J. M. Corbett to J. D. Jennings, 6/29/1956, GCPA.
27. J. D. Jennings to S. McMurrin, 8/1/1956, GCPA.
28. J. M. Corbett to J. D. Jennings, 8/10/1956, GCPA.
29. J. D. Jennings to S. McMurrin, 2/15/1957, GCPA.
30. Telegram from C. Steen to J. D. Jennings, 6/6/1957; J. D. Jennings to S. McMurrin, 6/7/1957.
31. J. D. Jennings to Frank Moss, various letters 1958–62, Moss Papers, Special Collections, Marriott Library, University of Utah, Salt Lake City.
32. Memorandum of Understanding, National Park Service and University of Utah, 6/24/1957, and subsequent renewals, 1958–62, GCPA.
33. McGimsey 1985.
34. Lipe and Lindsay 1974.
35. Ringholz 2002.
36. Lister 1958: 9–19.
37. Lister 1958: 26 and fig. 12.
38. R. Lister weekly report, 7/6/1957, GCPA.
39. R. Lister weekly report, 7/16/1957, GCPA.
40. R. Lister weekly report, 7/28/1957, GCPA.
41. R. Lister weekly report, 8/3/1957, GCPA.
42. R. Lister weekly report, 9/5/1957, GCPA.
43. Lister 1958: 5.
44. Jennings 1957: 13; Teocentli 61, p. 13.
45. Peterson 1995.
46. Fowler 2000: 185.
47. Harrington 1952.
48. Crampton 1959, 1960a, 1960b, 1962, 1964a, 1964b, 1964c, 2009; Crampton and Smith, eds., 1961.
49. Creer 1947, 1958a, 1958b.
50. Woodbury 1954.
51. Behle 1977.
52. Hall 1946; Durrant 1952.
53. Flowers 1973.
54. See Newcomer 2008 for the five verses that accompany the "Amphioxus" chorus.
55. Woodbury 1965; Woodbury et al. 1958, 1959; Woodbury, Durrant, and Flowers 1959.

CHAPTER 16

1. Pierson 1998.
2. Hudgins 1971; Lankford 1982.
3. Fowler et al. 1959.
4. Morss 1931a, 1931b.
5. J. D. Jennings to R. Lister, 5/27/1959, GCP archives.
6. Lister, Ambler, and Lister 1959–61; see also Utah State Parks, http://stateparks.utah.gov/parks/anasazi.
7. Lister 1959a, 1959b.
8. Suhm 1959.
9. Nichols 6/23/58, 8/12/58.
10. Weller 1959.
11. Gunnerson 7/31/58, 8/13/58.
12. Gunnerson 7/16/58.
13. Beals, Brainerd, and Smith 1945: 6.
14. Gunnerson 1959: fig. 46.
15. Gunnerson 1969.
16. Mathews 9/14/58.
17. Fowler et al. 1959; Lipe 1960.
18. Adams, Lindsay, and Turner 1961: iii–iv.

CHAPTER 17

1. Fowler 6/27/59.
2. Fowler 6/27/59.
3. Lipe 1960: 70.
4. Fowler 7/5/59.
5. Fowler 7/11/59.
6. Fowler 7/11/59.
7. Lipe et al. 1960.
8. Fowler 1989; Fowler and Fowler 1971; Fowler and Matley 1978; Hillers 1972.
9. Fowler 1960.
10. Sharrock et al. 1963.
11. Sharrock et al. 1961.

CHAPTER 18

1. Fowler 1963.
2. Birney 1930: 276–77.
3. Lanner 1984: 134–37.
4. Fowler and Aikens 1963.
5. Sharrock 6/28/61.
6. Vance Fowler, personal communication, 7/4/2004.
7. Sharrock et al. 1963.
8. Fowler 1965.
9. Lipe 1960: 91–99.
10. Geib 1996: table 5.
11. Aikens 1965.
12. Fowler 2000: 275–78.
13. Steward 1938.
14. This section is based on Fowler and Kemper 2008.
15. Cited by Fowler and Kemper 2008: 151.
16. Kelly 1934, 1939.
17. Kelly 1964.
18. The following is based on House 2002.
19. In the early 1950s, Congress passed legislation allowing Indian tribes to sue the federal government for losses of "traditional" tribal lands. Anthropologists were hired both by the Justice Department and attorneys representing tribes or tribal coalitions to determine boundaries of "traditional" lands. Courts decided boundaries and adjudicated disputed areas, and awarded monetary damages to the tribes. This was thought to quiet (in the legal sense) all claims that Indian tribes had to lands outside reservations.
20. Sweeney, weekly report, 4/15/1962, GCPA; Sweeney 1961.
21. Sapir 1930–31.
22. D. Fowler and C. Fowler 1971; C. Fowler and D. Fowler 1986.
23. Martineau 1973, 1992.
24. C. Sweeney to J. D. Jennings, 7/8/1962, GCPA.
25. Alexander and Ruby 1963.
26. The following section is based on Sweeney's weekly reports, 6/8–15/62, 6/16–22/62, 7/16–22/62, GCPA.
27. C. Sweeney to J. D. Jennings, 7/22/1962.
28. Only the Sweeney and Euler 1963 paper was published.
29. Fowler and Fowler 1971, 1981; Fowler and Matley 1978; Fowler 1989; Hillers 1972.
30. Davis 1999; Greystone Productions 1994; Kleinerman 1971; Verdoia 1999a.
31. C. Fowler 2004, 2005, 2006, 2008, 2010; C. Fowler and D. Fowler 1981.

CHAPTER 19

1. The foregoing is based on Fowler 2000: 371–72.
2. Thompson 2001; Edward (Ted) Bridge Danson III became a well-known actor on *Cheers* and other television shows.

3. Field 1900, 1922.
4. Adams, Lindsay, and Turner 1961.
5. Breternitz 1957; Miller and Breternitz 1958a, 1958b.
6. This section is based on Adams 2010: 5–74.
7. Spicer 1962.
8. Adams 2010: 105.
9. Adams 1963.
10. Adams 2010: 116.
11. Adams and Adams 1959; Adams 1960.
12. Adams 2010: 119.
13. Lindsay 1969.
14. Adams, Lindsay, and Turner 1961.
15. Adams 1993: 309, 2010: 131–258; see also Adams 1984.
16. Adams and Adams 1961: 16–17; Rinaldo 1935: 2; Lindsay 1961.
17. Long 1966: 4–10.
18. Moseley 1975, 1993.
19. Lindsay et al. 1969: 8.
20. Turner 1962a.
21. Turner and Cooley 1960.
22. Turner and Miller 1961; Turner 1962b.
23. Lindsay et al. 1969: 10.
24. Turner 1960.
25. Ambler, Lindsay, and Stein 1964: 2.
26. Ambler, Lindsay, and Stein 1964: iv.
27. Ambler, Lindsay, and Stein 1964: iv, 4.
28. Long n.d.: 1; courtesy of Mary Anne Stein.
29. Ambler, Lindsay, and Stein 1964: 88–89.
30. Lindsay et al. 1969: 30–120.
31. Stein 2009.
32. This section draws on Stein 2009 and Carnine 2009: 7.
33. Stein 2009; Carnine 2009.
34. Stein 1966, 1984.
35. Haury 1976.
36. Lindsay et al. 1969.

CHAPTER 20

1. See the bibliography in Jennings 1966.
2. Kidder 1936.
3. McGregor 1941: 30.
4. A. V. Kidder, cited in Fowler 2000: 285.
5. Colton 1939: 12, emphasis added.
6. J. D. Jennings, oral seminar presentation, April 2, 1962, and various instances thereafter.
7. Jennings 1966; Geib 1996; Lindsay et al. 1968; Lipe 1967; Lindsay 1969; Stein 1984.
8. Beck and Jones 2010; Meltzer 2009; Goebel, Waters, and O'Rourke 2008; Jenkins 2007.
9. Jennings 1989; Fowler and Fowler 2008: 35–54.
10. Ambler 1996: 43.
11. Lipe 1960; Geib 1996: 18 and table 5.
12. Janetski et al. 2005.
13. This section draws on Blackburn and Williamson 1997 and various Glen Canyon Project reports.
14. Sharrock, Dibble, and Anderson 1961.
15. Lindsay 1961.
16. Cameron 2009; Lekson 2008.
17. Cooley 1962; Lance 1963.
18. Lipe et al. 1975.
19. Lister, Ambler, and Lister 1959–61.
20. Haas and Creamer 1993.
21. Geib, Collette, and Spurr 2001; Janetski 2008; Madsen 1989; Madsen and Simms 1998.
22. Bunte and Franklin 1987; Franklin and Bunte 1983; Kelly 1934; Knack 2001.
23. McPherson 1988, 1992, 2001; Roessel 1973; Thompson 1976.
24. See especially Ortiz 1983: 489–683 for overviews and bibliography.
25. See Fowler 2000: 39–49, 321–42 for a history of Navajo studies from 1846 to 1940.
26. Levy 1962.
27. Shepardson 1995; Shepardson and Hammond 1970; Collier 1966.
28. Luckert 1977: vii.
29. Luckert 1977: 39–154.
30. Luckert 1977: 12.
31. Luckert 1977: 16–17.
32. Luckert 1977: 17–24.
33. Luckert 1977: 23.
34. Catherine Fowler, personal communication, January 2, 2010.
35. See, for example, Brooks 1972, 1980; Brooks et al. 1961; Fleming 1967; McPherson 1999; Larson and Peterson 1989; Campbell 1989; the county histories and *Utah Historical Quarterly* articles in Utah Historical Society 2000; Historical Views 2001; and McCourt 2003.
36. Biographical information on Nelson is taken from Utah State University 2010.
37. Cited in Roundy 2000: 2.
38. Nelson 1952: 34–40.

39. Nelson 1952: 89.
40. Nelson 1954, 1969; Roundy 2000.
41. Redd 1950: 23–24, cited in Miller 1966: 140.
42. Miller 1959, 1966. Biographical information on Miller from Utah Historical Society 1980. Miller's book should be read by all, especially for the numerous diaries, journals and letters of the participants included in the book.
43. Miller 1966: 17–33.
44. Miller 1966: 34.
45. Miller 1966: 35.
46. Charles Redd 1950: 7, cited in Miller 1966: 37.
47. Miller 1966: 111.
48. Measeles 1981; Reilly 1999; Rusho and Crampton 1992.
49. Reilly 1999: 7–16.
50. Brooks 1972: 303–34; Bagley 2002.
51. Measeles 1981: 28.
52. Ringholz 2002.
53. McCourt 2003: 222–23.

CHAPTER 21

1. Martin 1989: 207–8.
2. Berger 1994: 33–34.
3. Reprinted with the permission of Bruce Berger.
4. Bureau of Land Management 2000; Chesher 2000; Hill 1997; Keiter, George, and Walker 1998.
5. National Park Service 1950.
6. Carrier and Richardson 1992; and Farmer 1999 and references therein.
7. McPhee 1971.
8. Cited in Lee 2007: 1.
9. Martin 1989: 6, 11.
10. Lee 1954, 1998a–c, 2004, 2007.
11. Abbey 1968: 188, 1975, 1982, 1990; Ronald [1982] 1988; Cahalan 2001.
12. Short 1978: 40–43.
13. Powell 2008.

BIBLIOGRAPHY

Abbey, Edward
1968 *Desert Solitaire: A Season in the Wilderness.* Simon and Schuster, New York.
1975 *The Monkey Wrench Gang.* Harper and Row, New York.
1982 *Down the River.* E. P. Dutton, New York.
1990 *Hayduke Lives!* Little, Brown and Co., Boston.

Adams, Eilean
2001 *Hell or Highwater: James White's Disputed Passage through Grand Canyon 1867.* Utah State University Press, Logan.

Adams, William Y.
1951 Diary, Pueblo Ecology Survey. W. W. Taylor Papers, Box 20, National Anthropological Archives, Smithsonian Institution, Washington, D.C.
1953 Archaeology and Culture History of the Navajo Country, Report on Reconnaissance for the Pueblo Ecology Study, 1951. *Or* Kidder up to Date: A Re-introduction to the Study of Southwestern Archaeology. Unpublished ms., W. W. Taylor Papers, Museum of Northern Arizona, Flagstaff.
1960 *Ninety Years of Glen Canyon Archaeology, 1869–1959.* Museum of Northern Arizona Bulletin 33, Glen Canyon Series no. 2. Flagstaff.
1963 *Shonto: A Study of the Role of the Trader in a Modern Navaho Community.* Bureau of American Ethnology Bulletin no. 188. Washington, D.C. (Originally issued 1958 as a Ph.D. dissertation in anthropology, University of Arizona.)
1984 *Nubia: Corridor to Africa.* Princeton University Press, Princeton, NJ.
1993 Growing Up in Colonial Navajoland. In *Papers from the Third, Fourth, and Sixth Navajo Studies Conferences,* edited by June-el Piper, pp. 305–10. Navajo Nation Historic Preservation Department, Window Rock, AZ.
2010 *The Road from Frijoles Canyon: Anthropological Adventures on Four Continents.* University of New Mexico Press, Albuquerque.

Adams, William Y., and Nettie K. Adams
1959 *Inventory of Prehistoric Sites on the Lower San Juan River, Utah.* Museum of Northern Arizona Bulletin 31, Glen Canyon Series no. 1. Flagstaff.

Adams, William Y., Alexander J. Lindsay, Jr., and Christy G. Turner II
1961 *Survey and Excavations in Lower Glen Canyon, 1952–1958.* Museum of Northern Arizona Bulletin 36, Glen Canyon Series no. 3. Flagstaff.

Aikens, C. Melvin
1965 *Excavations in Southwest Utah.* University of Utah Anthropological Papers 76, Glen Canyon Series 27. Salt Lake City.

Aleson, Harry L.
1952 Harry Aleson's Glen Canyon Journal. October–November, 1952. Colorado Plateau Digital Archives, Cline Library, Northern Arizona University, Flagstaff.

Alexander, Wayne, and Jay W. Ruby
1963 [The] 1962 Excavations at Summit, Utah: A Progress Report. *Nevada State Museum Anthropological Papers* 9: 17–32.

Ambler, J. Richard
1996 Dust Devil Cave and Archaic Complexes of the Glen Canyon Area. In *Glen Canyon Revisited,*

by Phil R. Geib, pp. 40–52. University of Utah Anthropological Papers no. 119. Salt Lake City.

Ambler, J. Richard, Alexander J. Lindsay, Jr., and Mary Anne Stein

1964 *Survey and Excavations on Cummings Mesa, Arizona and Utah, 1960–1961*. Museum of Northern Arizona Bulletin no. 39, Glen Canyon Series no. 5. Flagstaff.

American Association of Engineering Societies

1977–2001 *Who's Who in Engineering*. American Association of Engineering Societies, New York.

American Men and Women of Science

1971–86 *American Men and Women of Science*, 12th–14th eds. Bowker Pubs., New York.

American Naturalist 1870 Voyage through the Grand Canon [*sic*] of Colorado. *American Naturalist* 2(12): 655–56.

Amsden, Charles

1949 *Prehistoric Southwesterners from Basketmakers to Pueblo.* Southwest Museum, Los Angeles.

Anderson, Keith M.

1963 Ceramic Clues to Pueblo-Puebloid Relationships. *American Antiquity* 28(3): 303–7.

1969 Tsegi Phase Technology. Doctoral dissertation in anthropology, University of Washington, Seattle.

Ashley, William H.

1954–55 The Diary of William H. Ashley, March 25–June 27, 1825: A Record of Exploration West Across the Continental Divide, Down the Green River and into the Great Basin, Parts I–III, edited by Dale L. Morgan. *Bulletin of the Missouri Historical Society* 11: 9–40, 158–186, 279–301. St. Louis.

Aton, James M.

2010 *John Wesley Powell.* University of Utah Press, Salt Lake City. (Originally published 1994, Boise State University.)

Aton, James M., and Robert S. McPherson

2000 *River Flowing from the Sunrise: An Environmental History of the Lower San Juan.* Utah State University Press, Logan.

Atkins, John A.

1981 *J. B. Priestley: The Last of the Sages.* J. Calder, London.

Atwood, Wallace W.

1940 *The Physiographic Provinces of North America.* Ginn and Co., Boston.

1945 *The Rocky Mountains.* Vanguard Press, New York.

Baars, Donald L.

1972 *Red Rock Country: The Geological History of the Colorado Plateau*. Doubleday/Natural History Press, Garden City, NY.

1993 *Canyonlands Country*. University of Utah Press, Salt Lake City.

1995 *Navajo Country: A Geology and Natural History of the Four Corners Region*. University of New Mexico Press, Albuquerque.

2000 *The Colorado Plateau: A Geologic History*. University of New Mexico Press, Albuquerque. (Originally published 1983.)

Babbitt, James E. (editor)

1987 Across the Painted Desert: Nicholas Roosevelt in Northern Arizona, 1913. *Journal of Arizona History* 28(3): 11–23.

Babbitt, James E. (compiler)

1990 Rainbow Trails. *Early-Day Adventures in Rainbow Bridge Country*. Glen Canyon Natural History Association, Page, AZ.

Babington, Suren H.

1950 *Navajos, Gods, and Tom-toms.* Greenberg Pubs., New York.

Bagley, Will

2002 *Blood of the Prophets: Brigham Young and the Massacre at Mountain Meadows.* University of Oklahoma Press, Norman.

Bagrow, Leo

1985 *History of Cartography.* Transaction Pubs., New Brunswick, NJ.

Baker, A. A.

1946 *Geology of the Green River Desert–Cataract Canyon Region of Emery, Wayne, and Garfield Counties, Utah*. U.S. Gov't. Printing Office, Washington, D.C.

Baker, A. A., C. H. Dane, and E. T. McKnight

1936 *Geology of the Monument Valley–Navajo Mountain Region*. U.S. Geological Survey Bulletin 865. Washington, D.C.

Baker, A. A., C. H. Dane, and J. B. Reeside, Jr.

1936 *Correlation of Jurassic Formations of Portions of Utah, Arizona, New Mexico, and Colorado*. U.S. Geological Survey Professional Paper 183. Washington, D.C.

Baker, Pearl

1991 *Robbers Roost Recollections.* Utah State University Press, Logan.

n.d. *Trail on the Water*. Pruett Publishing Co., Boulder, CO.

Bartlett, Katherine
1957 Field Notes, Glen Canyon Expedition, April–May, October–November, 1957. Manuscript on file, Museum of Northern Arizona Library, Flagstaff.

Bartlett, Richard A.
1962 *Great Surveys of the American West*. University of Oklahoma Press, Norman.

Bass, William W.
1920 *Adventures in the Canyons of the Colorado: By Two of its Earliest Explorers, James White and W. W. Hawkins.* Published by the author, Grand Canyon, AZ.

Bates, Walter G. 1890 Water-storage in the West. *Scribner's Magazine* 7(1): 3–17.

Beals, Ralph L.
1982 Fifty Years in Anthropology. *Annual Review of Anthropology* 11: 1–23.

Beals, Ralph L., George W. Brainerd, and Watson Smith
1945 *Archaeological Studies in Northeast Arizona: A Report on the Work of the Rainbow Bridge–Monument Valley Expedition*. University of California Press Publications in American Archaeology and Ethnology 44(1), 236 pp.

Beaman, E. O.
1874 The Cañon of the Colorado and the Moqui Pueblos. *Appleton's Journal* 11: 481–84, 513–16, 545–48, 590–93, 623–26, 641–44, 686–89.

Beck, Charlotte, and George T. Jones
2010 Clovis and Western Stemmed: Population Migration and the Meeting of Two Technologies in the Intermountain West. *American Antiquity* 75(1): 81–116.

Behle, William H.
1977 In Memoriam: Stephen David Durrant (1909–1975). *Journal of Mammalogy* 58(1): 111–16.

Bell, William A. 1870 *New Tracks in North America: A Journal of Travel and Adventure Whilst Engaged in the Survey for a Southern Railroad to the Pacific Ocean during 1867–8.* 2 vols. Chapman and Hall, London.

Berger, Bruce
1994 *There Was a River: Essays on the Southwest.* University of Arizona Press, Tucson.

Bergera, Gary J.
1999 "The Murderous Pain of Living": Thoughts on the Death of Everett Ruess. *Utah Historical Quarterly* 67(1): 48–67.

Bernheimer, Charles L.
1920–21 Field Notes, Bernheimer Expeditions, 1920–21. Library Archives, American Museum of Natural History, New York.
1923 Encircling Navajo Mountain with a Pack-Train. *National Geographic Magazine* 43: 197–224.
1924 *Rainbow Bridge: Circling Navajo Mountain and Exploration in the "Bad Lands" of Southern Utah and Northern Arizona*. Doubleday Page, New York.

Biddle, Nicholas (editor)
1962 *The Journals of the Expedition Under the Command of Capts. Lewis and Clark. . . .* 2 vols. Heritage Press, New York. (Originally published 1814.)

Bigler, David L., and Will Bagley (editors)
2002 *Innocent Blood: Essential Narratives of the Mountain Meadows Massacre, 1857.* Arthur H. Clark Co., Norman, OK.

Birney, Hoffman
1930 *Roads to Roam*. Penn Pub. Co., Philadelphia.
1931 *Zealots of Zion*. Penn Pub. Co., Philadelphia.
1934 *Forgotten Cañon*. Penn Pub. Co., Philadelphia.
1952 *The Dice of God.* Henry Holt, New York.

Bissell, Charles, and P. E. Weymouth
1935 Arthur Powell Davis, Past President, Am. Soc. C.E. *Transactions of the American Society of Civil Engineers* 100: 1582–91.

Black, James W.
1930 Statement of James W. Black, 07/10/1930. Rainbow Bridge Collection, Manuscript 239, folder 13. Special Collections, Cline Library, Northern Arizona University, Flagstaff.

Blackburn, Fred M., and Ray A. Williamson
1997 *Cowboys and Cave Dwellers: Basketmaker Archaeology in Utah's Grand Gulch.* School of American Research Press, Santa Fe.

Blanding, City of
2005 John Franklin (Frank) and Dora Wright Family. *Blanding Centennial Family Histories: 1905–2005*, pp. 1603–12. Shumway Family Publishing, Yorba Linda, CA.

Bolton, Herbert E.
1919 *Kino's Historical Memoir of Pimería Alta; a Contemporary Account of the Beginnings of California, Sonora and Arizona.* Arthur H. Clark Co., Cleveland.
1949 *Coronado on the Turquoise Trail: Knight of Pueblos and Plains.* University of New Mexico Press, Albuquerque.
1950 *Pageant in the Wilderness: The Story of the Escalante Expedition to the Interior Basin, 1776.* Utah Historical Quarterly 18. Salt Lake City.

Bostwick, Todd W.
2006 *Byron Cummings: Dean of Southwestern Archaeology*. University of Arizona Press, Tucson.

Bourke, John G. 1884 *The Snake Dance of the Moquis of Arizona*. C. Scribner's Sons, New York.

Boyer, Diane E., and Robert H. Webb
2007 *Damming the Grand Canyon: The 1923 USGS Colorado River Expedition*. Utah State University Press, Logan.

Breternitz, David A.
1957 Heltagito Rockshelter (NA6380). *Plateau* 30(1): 1–16.

Brew, John O.
1946 *Archaeology of Alkali Ridge, Southeastern Utah*. Papers of the Peabody Museum of Archaeology and Ethnology, vol. 21. Harvard University, Cambridge.
1961 Emergency Salvage Archaeology: Salvage in Advance of Technological Progress. *American Philosophical Society Proceedings* 105(1): 1–10.
1982 Noel Morss, 1904–1981. *American Antiquity* 47(2): 344–45.

Bridger, Bobby
2002 *Buffalo Bill and Sitting Bull: Inventing the Wild West*. University of Texas Press, Austin.

Brooks, Juanita
1972 *John Doyle Lee: Zealot-Pioneer Builder-Scapegoat*. Arthur H. Clark Co., Glendale, CA.
1980 *Jacob Hamblin: Mormon Apostle to the Indians*. Westwater Press, Salt Lake City. (A historical novel that recounts incidents in Hamblin's life.)

Brooks, Juanita, et al.
1961 Utah's Dixie. . . . The Cotton Mission. *Utah Historical Quarterly* 29(3): 289–302. Salt Lake City.

Brooks, Tim, and Earle Marsh
1999 *Complete Directory to Prime Time Network and Cable Television Shows, 1946–Present*. Ballantine Books, New York.

Brugge, David M.
1957 Journal of Glen Canyon Archaeological Survey, 24 May–20 June, 1957. Manuscript on file, Museum of Northern Arizona Library, Flagstaff.
1964 Vizcarra's Navajo Campaign of 1823. *Arizona and the West* 6(3): 223–44.

Bulgar, Harold A.
1961 First Man Through the Grand Canyon. *Missouri Historical Society Bulletin* 18: 321–31.

Bunte, Pamela A., and Robert J. Franklin
1987 *From the Sands to the Mountain: Change and Persistence in a Southern Paiute Community*. University of Nebraska Press, Lincoln.

Bureau of Land Management
2000 *Grand Staircase–Escalante National Monument: Approved Management Plan, Record of Decision*. Bureau of Land Management, Grand Staircase–Escalante National Monument, Cedar City, UT.

Cahalan, James M.
2001 *Edward Abbey: A Life*. University of Arizona Press, Tucson.

Campbell, Eugene E.
1989 Early Colonization Patterns. In *Utah's History*, edited by T. G. Alexander, E. E. Campbell, D. E. Miller, and R. D. Pohl, pp. 133–52. Utah State University Press, Logan.

Cameron, Catherine M.
2009 *Chaco and After in the Northern San Juan: Excavations at the Bluff Great House*. University of Arizona Press, Tucson.

Capital Communications Broadcasting
1992 *The Journey of Amos Burg*. VHS New Dimensions Media, Chicago, o.p.

Carnine, Dorothy Diehl
2009 Memories of Paiute Mesa . . . 7713 and Other Upper Digs. Manuscript in author's possession.

Carrell, Toni, James E. Bradford, and W. L. Rusho
1987 *Glen Canyon National Recreation Area Submerged Cultural Site Report: Charles H. Spencer's Mining Operation and Paddle Wheel Steamboat*. National Park Service Southwest Cultural Resources Center Professional Paper 13. Santa Fe.

Carrier, Jim, and Jim Richardson
1992 *The Colorado: A River at Risk*. Westcliff Pubs., Englewood, CO.

Center for the History of Physics
2009 *Finding Aid to the Homer Levi Dodge Papers, 1852–1994*, www.aip.org/history/ead/.

Chalfant, James M.
1932 Preface to R. B. Stanton's *Colorado Controversies*. Dodd, Mead and Co., New York, pp. xv–xxxii.

Chamberlin, Ralph V.
1947 Francis Marion Bishop (1843–1933). *Utah Historical Quarterly* 15: 155–58.

Chavez, Fray Angelico, and Ted J. Warner (editors)
1976 *The Domínguez-Escalante Journal*. Brigham Young University Press, Provo, UT.

Chesher, G. K.
2000 *Heart of the Wild: Grand Staircase–Escalante National Monument*. Bryce Canyon Natural History Assn., Bryce Canyon, UT.

Christenson, Andrew L.
1983 The Archaeological Investigations of the Rainbow Bridge–Monument Valley Expedition, 1933–1938. In *Honoring the Dead: Anasazi Ceramics from Rainbow Bridge Monument Valley Expedition,* by Helen Crotty, pp. 9–22. University of California, Los Angeles Museum of Cultural History Monograph Series 22.
1987 The Last of the Great Expeditions: The Rainbow Bridge/Monument Valley Expedition, 1933–38. *Plateau* 58(4): 3–32. Flagstaff.

Clark, C. C.
1935 Report on the Zoology of Navajo Mountain. Mimeograph. Copy in Ansel Hall Papers, Bancroft Library, University of California, Berkeley.

Clark, Georgie White, and Duane Newcomb
1977 *Georgie Clark: Thirty Years of River Running.* Chronicle Books, San Francisco.

Cloud, Preston
1980 The Improbable Bureaucracy: The United States Geological Survey, 1879–1979. *American Philosophical Society Proceedings* 124(3): 155–67.

Clover, Elzada U.
1939 Danger Can Be Fun. *Michigan Alumnus Quarterly Review* 44(14): 1–11.

Cole, La Mont C.
1935 Report on the Herpetology of the Navajo Country. Mimeograph. Copy in Ansel Hall Papers, Bancroft Library, University of California, Berkeley.

Collier, Malcolm Carr
1966 *Local Organization among the Navaho*. Human Relations Area Files, New Haven.

Cook, William
1987 *The Wen, the Botany, and the Mexican Hat: The Adventures of the First Women through Grand Canyon, on the Nevills Expedition*. Calisto Books, Orangevale, CA.

Colton, Harold S.
1939 *Prehistoric Culture Units and Their Relationships in Northern Arizona*. Museum of Northern Arizona Bulletin 17. Flagstaff.
1962 Steamboating in Glen Canyon of the Colorado River. *Plateau* 35(2): 57–59.

Colorado River Compact
1922 http://colorado.edu/colorado_river/docs/Colorado River Compact.pdf.

Cooley, Maurice E.
1958 Physiography of the Glen Canyon–San Juan Area, Parts I–III. *Plateau* 31(2–4): 21–33, 49–56, 73–79.
1962 Late Pleistocene and Recent Erosion and Alluviation in Parts of the Colorado River System, Arizona and Utah. *USGS Professional Paper* no. 450-B, pp. B48–B50. U.S. Gov't. Printing Office, Washington, D.C.

Cordell, Linda
1997 *Archaeology of the Southwest.* 2nd ed. Academic Press, San Diego.

Cordell, Linda A., and Don D. Fowler (editors)
2005 *Southwestern Archaeology in the Twentieth Century.* University of Utah Press, Salt Lake City.

Coues, Elliot
1900 *On the Trail of a Spanish Pioneer.* F. P. Harper, New York.

Crampton, C. Gregory
1959 *Outline History of the Glen Canyon Region, 1776–1922.* University of Utah Anthropological Papers 42, Glen Canyon Series 9. Salt Lake City.
1960a Historic Glen Canyon. *Utah Historical Quarterly* 28(3): 274–90.
1960b *Historical Sites in Glen Canyon, Mouth of San Juan River to Lee's Ferry*. University of Utah Anthropological Papers 46, Glen Canyon Series 12. Salt Lake City.
1962 *Historical Sites in Glen Canyon, Mouth of Hansen Creek to Mouth of San Juan River*. University of Utah Anthropological Papers 61, Glen Canyon Series 17. Salt Lake City.
1964a *Historical Sites in Cataract and Narrow Canyons and in Glen Canyon to California Bar*. University of Utah Anthropological Papers 72, Glen Canyon Series 24. Salt Lake City.
1964b *The San Juan Canyon Historical Sites*. University of Utah Anthropological Papers 70, Glen Canyon Series 22. Salt Lake City.

Crampton, C. Gregory (editor)
1964c Military Reconnaissance in Southern Utah, 1866. *Utah Historical Quarterly* 32: 145–62.
1965 *Standing Up Country: The Canyon Lands of Utah and Arizona*. Alfred L. Knopf, New York, and University of Utah Press, Salt Lake City.

1968 *Historical and Prehistoric Cultural Resources of the Upper Colorado River Region.* University of Utah Press, Salt Lake City.
1988 *Ghosts of Glen Canyon: History Beneath Lake Powell.* Publishers Place, St. George, UT. (Revised edition 2009, University of Utah Press, Salt Lake City.)

Crampton, C. Gregory, and Dwight L. Smith (editors)
1961 *The Hoskininni Papers, Mining in Glen Canyon, 1897–1902.* University of Utah Anthropological Papers 54, Glen Canyon Series 15. Salt Lake City.

Creer, Leland H.
1947 *The Founding of an Empire: The Exploration and Colonization of Utah, 1776–1856.* Bookcraft, Salt Lake City.
1958a *The Activities of Jacob Hamblin in the Region of the Colorado.* University of Utah Anthropological Papers 33, Glen Canyon Series 4. Salt Lake City.
1958b *Mormon Towns in the Region of the Colorado.* University of Utah Anthropological Papers 32, Glen Canyon Series 3. Salt Lake City.

Cressman, Luther S.
1942 *Archaeological Researches in the Northern Great Basin.* Carnegie Institution of Washington Publication no. 538. Washington, D.C.

Cross, Whitman 1894 The Laccolitic Mountain Groups of Colorado, Utah and Arizona. *U.S. Geological Survey Annual Report* 14, pt. 2, pp. 165–241.

Cummings, Byron
1910a The Great Natural Bridges of Utah. *National Geographic Magazine* 21(2): 157–67.
1910b The Great Natural Bridges of Utah. *University of Utah Bulletin* 3: 4–16.
1910c *The Ancient Inhabitants of the San Juan Valley.* Bulletin of the University of Utah, 2nd Archaeological number, vol. 3(3), pt. 2.
1915 Kivas of the San Juan Drainage. *American Anthropologist* 17(2): 272–82.

Cutter, Donald C.
1977 Prelude to a Pageant in the Wilderness. *Western Historical Quarterly* 8: 5–14.

Couch, Julianne
2010 Floyd Dominy, the Colossus of Dams, Dies at 100. *High Country News* 42(8): 25.

Dana, J. D. 1880 G. K. Gilbert's Report on the Geology of the Henry Mountains. *American Journal of Science*, 3rd series 19(109): 17–25.

Danson, Edward B.
1958 The Glen Canyon Project. *Plateau* 30(3): 75–78.

Dark, Philip J. C.
2010 Walter Taylor: POW, Professor and Colleague. In *Prophet, Pariah and Pioneer: Walter W. Taylor and Dissension in American Archaeology,* edited by A. L. Maca, J. E. Reyman, and W. J. Folan, pp. 103–17. University Press of Colorado, Boulder.

Darrah, William C.
1948–49a John F. Steward, 1841–1915. *Utah Historical Quarterly* 16–17: 175–79.
1948–49b Beaman, Fennemore, Hillers, Dellenbaugh, Johnson, and Hattan *Utah Historical Quarterly* 16–17: 491–503.
1954 *Powell of the Colorado.* Princeton University Press, Princeton, NJ.

Darrah, William C. (editor)
1947 Biographical Sketches and Original Documents of the First Powell Expedition. *Utah Historical Quarterly* 15: 9–148.

Darrah, William C., Ralph V. Chamberlin, and Charles Kelly (editors)
1948–49 Biographical Sketches and Original Documents of the Second Powell Expedition of 1871–72. *Utah Historical Quarterly* 16–17: 1–540.

Davis, Arthur P.
1917 *Irrigation Works Constructed by the United States Government.* U.S. Gov't. Printing Office, Washington, D.C.
1925 Dams on the Colorado River. *American Society of Civil Engineers Transactions, 1925*: 389–90.

Davis, Hester A.
2008 *Remembering Awatovi: The Story of an Archaeological Expedition in Northern Arizona, 1935–1939.* Peabody Museum Monographs, no. 10. Harvard University, Cambridge.

Davis, Mark J. (writer and producer)
1999 *Lost in the Grand Canyon.* Film documentary. The American Experience, WGBH, Boston.

Davis, William M.
1900 An Excursion to the Grand Canyon of the Colorado. *Harvard College Museum of Comparative Zoology Bulletin* 38 (Geological Series 5): 107–98.
1918 Grove Karl Gilbert. *American Journal of Science* series 4, vol. 46: 669–81.

Dawdy, Doris O.
1993 *George Montague Wheeler: The Man and the Myth.* Swallow Press/Ohio State University Press, Athens.

DeBuys, William, and Joan Meyers
1999 *Salt Dreams: Land and Water in Low-Down California.* University of New Mexico Press, Albuquerque.

Dellenbaugh, Frederick S.
1904 *The Romance of the Colorado River.* G. P. Putnam's Sons, New York.
1908 *A Canyon Voyage: The Narrative of the Second Powell Expedition down the Green-Colorado River from Wyoming, and the Explorations on Land, in the Years 1871 and 1872.* G. P. Putnam's Sons, New York.
1969 F. S. Dellenbaugh of the Colorado: Some Letters Pertaining to the Powell Voyages and the History of the Colorado River (edited by C. G. Crampton). *Utah Historical Quarterly* 37(2): 214–44. Salt Lake City.

De Ross, Rose Marie
1958 *Adventures of Georgie White: TV's "Woman of the Rivers."* Desert Magazine Press, Palm Desert, CA.

Dilsaver, Lary M. (editor)
1994 *America's National Park System: The Critical Documents.* Rowan and Littlefield, Lanham, MD.

Dimock, Brad
2001 *Sunk without a Sound: The Tragic Colorado River Honeymoon of Glen and Bessie Hyde.* Fretwater Press, Flagstaff, AZ.
2002 White Lies, Major Distortions, and Several New Stabs at the Truth: 8 Recent Publications on James White and Major John Wesley Powell. *Boatman's Quarterly Review* 5(1): 1–4.
2003 A Letter from Bessie Hyde. *Boatman's Quarterly Review* 16(3): 1–4.
2005 Foreword to *High, Wide and Handsome: The River Journals of Norman D. Nevills,* edited by Roy Webb, pp. vii–xii. Utah State University Press, Logan.
2007 *The Very Hard Way: Bert Loper and the Colorado River.* Fretwater Press, Flagstaff, AZ.
2008a The James White Debate. In *Reflections of Grand Canyon Historians: Ideas, Arguments and First Person Accounts,* edited by Todd R. Berger, pp. 123–124. Grand Canyon Association, Grand Canyon, AZ.
2008b The Case for James White's Raft Trip through Grand Canyon: The Story of White's Story. In *Reflections of Grand Canyon Historians: Ideas, Arguments and First Person Accounts,* edited by Todd R. Berger, pp. 131–36. Grand Canyon Association, Grand Canyon, AZ.
2010 If Boats Could Talk. *Sojourns/Collections* 5(1): 38–43.

Dimock, Brad (editor)
2003 *Every Rapid Speaks Plainly: The Salmon, Green and Colorado River Journals of Buzz Holstrom.* Fretwater Press, Flagstaff, AZ.

Dolnick, Edward
2001 *Down the Great Unknown: John Wesley Powell's 1869 Journey of Discovery and Tragedy Through the Grand Canyon.* Harper Collins, New York.

Domínguez, Francisco A.
1956 *The Missions of New Mexico, 1776.* Edited by E. B. Adams and A. Chavez. University of New Mexico Press, Albuquerque.

Douglass, William B.
1910 The Discovery of Rainbow Natural Bridge. *General Land Office Records* 182: 133–64. (Reprinted 1955 in *Our Public Lands* 5(2): 8–9, 14.)

Dumé, Bell
2007 Another Superconductor Shows Up. http//:www.advancedphysics.org/forum.

Durrant, Stephen D.
1952 *The Mammals of Utah: Taxonomy and Distribution.* University of Kansas Press Museum of Natural History Publications, vol. 6. Lawrence.

Dutton, C.E.
1880 *Report on the Geology of the High Plateaus of Utah, with Atlas.* U.S. Geographical and Geological Survey of the Rocky Mountain Region. U.S. Gov't. Printing Office, Washington, D.C.
1882a Report of Capt. C. E. Dutton. *Second Annual Report of the U.S. Geological Survey for 1880–81,* pp. 5–10.
1882b The Physical Geology of the Grand Cañon District. *Second Annual Report of the U.S. Geological Survey for 1880–81,* pp. 49–166.
1882c *Tertiary History of the Grand Cañon District.* U.S. Geological Survey Monograph no. 2. Washington, D.C.
1886 Mount Taylor and the Zuñi Plateau. *Sixth Annual Report of the U.S. Geological Survey for 1884–85,* pp. 113–98.

Dyar, William W.
1904 The Colossal Bridges of Utah. *Century Magazine* 68: 505–11.

Eaton, Theodore H., Jr.
1935 *Report on Amphibians and Reptiles of the Navajo Country.* Rainbow Bridge–Monument Valley Expedition Bulletin no. 2.
1970 *Evolution.* Norton Pub. Co., New York.

Eddy, Clyde
1929 *Down the World's Most Dangerous River.* Frederick A. Stokes Co., New York.

Egloffstein, F. W.
1857 *New Style of Topographic Drawing.* N.p., New York.

1860 Map of Explorations and Surveys in New Mexico and Utah Made Under the Direction of the Secretary of War by Capt. J.N. Macomb, Topographical Engineers. Department of War, Washington, D.C.

Egloffstein, F. W. (editor)
1864 *Contributions to the Geology and the Physical Geography of Mexico, Including a Geological and Topographic Map with Profiles and Some Mining Districts.* D. Appleton Co., New York.

Emory, William H.
1848 *Notes of a Military Reconnaissance from Fort Leavenworth, in Missouri to San Diego in California. . . .* 30 Congress, 1st Session, Senate Executive Document no. 1, pp. 1–126.

Euler, Robert C.
1964 Southern Paiute Archaeology. *American Antiquity* 29(3): 379–81.
1997 Walter Willard Taylor, 1913–1997. *SAA Bulletin* 15(4): 1–2.

Everhart, William C.
1972 *The National Park System.* Praeger, New York.

Fagette, Paul
1996 *Digging for Dollars: American Archaeology and the New Deal.* University of New Mexico Press, Albuquerque.

Fall, Albert, and Arthur P. Davis
1922 *Problems of Imperial Valley and Vicinity.* 67th Congress, 2nd Session, Senate Executive Document 142.

Falk, Peter H.
1999 *Who Was Who in American Art, 1564–1975.* 3 vols. Sound View Press, Madison, CT.

Farmer, Jared
1999 *Glen Canyon Dammed: Inventing Lake Powell and the Canyon Country.* University of Arizona Press, Tucson.

Farquhar, Francis P.
1953 *The Books of the Colorado River and Grand Canyon, A Selective Bibliography.* Ward Ritchie Press, Los Angeles.
1965 *History of the Sierra Nevada.* University of California Press, Berkeley.

Farquhar, Francis P. (editor)
1930 William H. Brewer's *Up and Down California in 1860–1864.* Yale University Press, New Haven.
1935 Clarence King's *Mountaineering in the Sierra Nevada.* W. W. Norton, New York.

Fairservis, Walter A., Jr.
1993 *Archaeology of the Southern Gobi of Mongolia.* Carolina Academic Press, Durham.

Fenneman, Nevin M.
1928 Physiographic Divisions of the United States. *Annals of the Association of American Geographers* 18(4): 261–353, map.

Ferrari, Carlo de
1987–88 Captain Nevills Builds a Hotel in Sonora, 1896. *The Sierra Escape* (Winter–Spring 87/88) 2(1): 1–3.

Ferris, Warren A.
1940 *Life in the Rocky Mountains: A Diary of Wanderings on the Sources of the Rivers Missouri, Columbia, and Colorado from February, 1830 to November, 1835.* Edited by Paul C. Phillips. Old West Publishing Co., Denver.

Field, Eugene
1900 *Sharps and Flats.* 2 vols. Collated by S. Thompson. Charles Scribner's Sons, New York.
1922 *The Poems of Eugene Field, Complete Edition.* Charles Scribner's Sons, New York.

Flavell, George F.
1987 *The Log of the Panthon: An Account of an 1896 River Voyage from Green River, Wyoming to Yuma, Arizona through the Grand Canyon.* Edited by N. B. Carmony and D. E. Brown. Pruett Publishing, Boulder, CO.

Fleming, L. A.
1967 The Settlements on the Muddy 1865 to 1871: "A God Forsaken Place." *Utah Historical Quarterly* 35(2): 147–72.

Flowers, Seville
1973 *Mosses; Utah and the West.* Edited by Arthur Holmgren. Brigham Young University Press, Provo.

Foster, Gene
1959 Glen Canyon Archaeology. Manuscript on file, Museum of Northern Arizona Library, Flagstaff.

Fowler, Catherine
2004 "Timbisha Shoshone" and "Ecological-Cosmological Knowledge and Land Management among Hunter-Gatherers." In *The Cambridge Encyclopedia of Hunters and Gatherers*, edited by R. B. Lee and R. Daly. Cambridge University Press, Cambridge.
2005 Uto-Aztecan Languages. *Encyclopedia of Languages and Linguistics* 4: 62–72. Elsevier, London.
2006 Great Basin Plants. In *Handbook of North American Indians,* vol. 3: *Environment,* edited by Dennis Stanford, Bruce D. Smith, Douglas Ubelacker, and Emoke Szathmary, pp. 331–50. Smithsonian Institution, Washington, D.C.

2008 The Great Basin and The People. In *American Indian Places*, edited by Frances Kennedy, pp. 218–24. Houghton Mifflin Co., New York.

2010 *Northern Paiute Dictionary*. With Sven Liljeblad, Harold Abel, and Glenda Powell. University of Utah Press, Salt Lake City.

Fowler, Catherine S., and Don D. Fowler

1981 The Southern Paiute: A.D. 1400–1776. In *The Protohistoric Period in the North American Southwest*, edited by D. R. Wilcox and B. Masse, pp. 129–62. Arizona State University Anthropological Research Papers 24. Tempe.

1986 Edward Sapir, Tony Tillohash and Southern Paiute Studies. In *New Perspectives in Language, Culture and Personality*, edited by W. Cowan, M. K. Foster, and K. Koerner, pp. 41–65. John Benjamin Pub. Co., Philadelphia.

Fowler, Catherine S., and Don D. Fowler (editors)

2008 *The Great Basin: People and Place in Ancient Times.* School of Advanced Research Press, Santa Fe.

Fowler, Catherine S., and Robert Van Kemper

2008 Isabel T. Kelly: A Life in the Field. In *Their Own Frontier: Women Intellectuals Re-Visioning the American West*, edited by Shirley Leckie and Nancy J. Parezo, pp. 137–19. University of Nebraska Press, Lincoln.

Fowler, Don D.

1959–62 Weekly Field Reports, Glen Canyon Project. University of Utah Archives. Accession 499, Boxes 25, 28. Salt Lake City.

1960 [The] 1960 Reconnaissance of Upper Moqui Canyon. Manuscript on file, Archaeology Center, University of Utah.

1963 *[The] 1961 Excavations, Harris Wash, Utah*. University of Utah Anthropological Papers 64, Glen Canyon Series 19. Salt Lake City.

1965 Cultural Ecology and Culture History of the Eastern Shoshoni Indians. Unpublished Ph.D. dissertation, University of Pittsburgh.

1969 Foreword and Notes. In *Down the Colorado: John Wesley Powell: Diary of the First Trip Through the Grand Canyon*, pp. 9–23. E. P. Dutton, New York.

1982 Cultural Resources Management. *Advances in Archaeological Method and Theory* 5: 1–50. Academic Press, New York.

1986a Conserving American Archaeological Resources. In *American Archaeology Past and Future*, edited by D. J. Meltzer, D. D. Fowler, and J. A. Sabloff, pp. 135–62. Smithsonian Institution Press, Washington, D.C.

1986b History of Research. *Handbook of North American Indians,* vol. 11, *Great Basin,* pp. 15–30. Smithsonian Institution, Washington, D.C.

1989 *The Western Photographs of John K. Hillers: Myself in the Water*. Smithsonian Institution Press, Washington, D.C.

2000 *A Laboratory for Anthropology: Science and Romanticism in the American Southwest, 1846–1930*. University of New Mexico Press, Albuquerque. (Reprinted 2010, University of Utah Press, Salt Lake City.)

2003 E. L. Hewett, J. F. Zimmerman, and the Beginnings of Anthropology at the University of New Mexico, 1927–1946. *Journal of Anthropological Research* 59(3): 305–27. Albuquerque.

2005 The Formative Years: Southwest Archaeology, 1890–1910. In *Southwest Archaeology in the Twentieth Century*, edited by Linda S. Cordell and Don D. Fowler, pp. 16–26. University of Utah Press, Salt Lake City.

2010 Walter W. Taylor in the Southwest. In *Prophet, Pariah and Pioneer: Walter W. Taylor and Dissension in American Archaeology,* edited by A. L. Maca, J. E. Reyman, and W. L. Folan, pp. 299–313. University Press of Colorado, Boulder.

Fowler, Don D., and C. Melvin Aikens

1963 *[The] 1961 Excavations, Kaiparowits Plateau, Utah*. University of Utah Anthropological Papers 66, Glen Canyon Series 20. Salt Lake City.

Fowler, Don D., Robert C. Euler, and Catherine S. Fowler

1969 *John Wesley Powell and the Anthropology of the Canyon Country*. U.S. Geological Survey Professional Paper 670.

Fowler, Don D., and Catherine S. Fowler

1969 John Wesley Powell, Anthropologist. *Utah Historical Quarterly* 37: 152–72.

Fowler, Don D., and Catherine S. Fowler (editors)

1971 *Anthropology of the Numa: John Wesley Powell's Manuscripts on the Numic Peoples of Western North America, 1868–1880*. Smithsonian Contributions to Anthropology 14. Washington, D.C.

Fowler, Don D., and John F. Matley

1978 *Material Culture of the Numa: The John Wesley Powell Collection, 1867–1880*. Smithsonian Contributions to Anthropology 26. Washington, D.C.

Fowler, Don D., et al.

1959 *The Glen Canyon Archaeological Survey, Pts. I–III*. University of Utah Anthropological Papers 39, Glen Canyon Series 6. Salt Lake City.

Franklin, Robert J., and Pamela A. Bunte
1983 *The Paiute*. Chelsea House Pubs., New York.

Frazer, Persifor
1888 A Short History of the Origin and Acts of the International Congress of Geologists, and of the American Committee Delegates to It. *American Geologist* 1(1): 3–11.

Freeman, Lewis R.
1924 *Down the Grand Canyon*. Dodd, Mead, New York.

Fremont, John C.
1845 Map of an Exploratory Expedition to the Rocky Mountains in the Year 1842 and to Oregon and North California in the Years 1843–44. U.S. Senate, Washington, D.C.
1856 *The Life of Colonel John Charles Fremont*. Miller, Orton and Mulligan, New York.

Furniss, Norman F.
1960 *The Mormon Conflict, 1850–1859*. Yale University Press, New Haven.

Gallatin, Albert H.
1836 A Synopsis of the Indian Tribes of North America. *Archaeological Americana: Transactions of the American Antiquarian Society* 2: 1–44. New York.

Gannett, Henry
1885a Report of Mr. Henry Gannett. *Sixth Annual Report of the U.S. Geological Survey, 1884–85*, pp. 3–17.
1885b Map of the United States Exhibiting the Progress Made in the Geological Survey During the Fiscal Year 1884–5. *Sixth Annual Report of the U.S. Geological Survey,1884–85*, end pocket.
1889 Report of Mr. Henry Gannett. *Eighth Annual Report of the U.S. Geological Survey, 1886–87*, pp. 97–120.

Garcés, Francisco
1965 *A Record of Travels in Arizona and California, 1775–1776*. Translated and edited by John Galvin. John Howell Books, San Francisco.

Geary, Edward A.
1992 *The Proper Edge of the Sky: The High Plateau Country*. University of Utah Press, Salt Lake City.

Geib, Phil R.
1996 *Glen Canyon Revisited*. University of Utah Anthropological Papers 119. Salt Lake City.
2000 Sandal Types and Archaic Prehistory on the Colorado Plateau. *American Antiquity* 65: 509–24.

Geib, Phil R., Jim H. Collette, and Kimberly Spurr
2001 *Kaibabitsinüngwü: An Archaeological Survey of the Kaiparowits Plateau*. Utah Bureau of Land Management Cultural Resources Series 25. Grand Staircase–Escalante National Monument Special Publication no. 1. Salt Lake City.

Ghiglieri, Michael P.
2003 *First Through the Grand Canyon: The Secret Letters and Journals of the 1869 Crew Who Explored the Green and Colorado Rivers*. Puma Press, Flagstaff.

Gilbert, Grove K.
1875 Report on the Geology of Portions of Nevada, Utah, California and Arizona Examined in the Years 1871 and 1872. *Report upon Geographical and Geological Explorations and Surveys West of the One Hundredth Meridian*, vol. III, pt. I, pp. 17–187. U.S. Gov't. Printing Office, Washington, D.C.
1876 The Colorado Plateau as a Field for Geological Study. *American Journal of Science and Arts*, 3rd Series 12: 1–24, 85–103.
1877 *Report on the Geology of the Henry Mountains*. U.S. Geographical and Geological Survey of the Rocky Mountain Region, Washington, D.C.
1890 *Lake Bonneville*. U.S. Geological Survey Monograph no. 1. Washington, D.C.
1893 The Moon's Face: A Study of the Origin of Its Features. *Philosophical Society of Washington* 12: 241–92.
1914 *The Transportation of Débris by Running Water*. U.S. Geological Survey Professional Paper 80. Washington, D.C.

Gilbert, Grove K., and Albert P. Brigham
1902 *Introduction to Physical Geography*. D. Appleton and Co., New York.

Gilbert, Grove K., Archibald R. Marvine, Edwin E. Howell, and J. J. Stevenson
1876 Geology. *U.S. Army Engineers Exploration and Surveys West of the 100th Meridian*, vol. 3. Washington, D.C.

Gilbert, Grove K., et al.
1907 *The San Francisco Earthquake and Fire of 1906 and Their Effects on Structures and Structural Materials*. U.S. Gov't. Printing Office, Washington, D.C.

Gilbert, W. S., and Arthur Sullivan
2010 *The Pirates of Penzance or the Slave of Duty*, http://GaS/pirates/pirates_lib.pdf.

Gillmor, Frances, and Louisa Wade Wetherill
1953 *Traders to the Navajos: The Story of the Wetherills of Kayenta*. University of New Mexico Press, Albuquerque.

Goebel, Ted, Michael R. Waters, and Dennis H. O'Rourke
2008 The Late Pleistocene Dispersal of Modern Humans in the Americas. *Science* 319: 1497–1502.
Goetzmann, William H.
1959 *Army Exploration in the American West, 1803–1863.* Yale University Press, New Haven. (Reprinted 1979, University of Nebraska Press, Lincoln.)
1966 *Exploration and Empire: The Explorer and the Scientist in the Winning of the American West.* Alfred A. Knopf, New York.
Goldwater, Barry
1940 *A Journey Down the Green and Colorado River, 1940*. H. Walker Pub. Co., Phoenix. (Reprinted 1970 as *Delightful Journey Down the Green and Colorado Rivers,* Arizona Historical Foundation, Tempe.)
Gregory, Herbert E.
1917 *Geology of the Navajo Country: A Reconnaissance of Parts of Arizona, New Mexico, and Utah.* U.S. Geological Survey Professional Paper 93. Washington, D.C.
1938 *The San Juan Country: A Geographic and Geologic Reconnaissance of Southeastern Utah.* U.S. Geological Survey Professional Paper 188. Washington, D.C.
1945 Scientific Exploration in Southern Utah. *American Journal of Science* 243(10): 527–49.
1948–49 Stephen Vandiver Jones (1840–1920). *Utah Historical Quarterly* 16–17: 11–18.
1950 *Geology and Geography of the Zion Park Region Utah and Arizona.* U.S. Geological Survey Professional Paper 220. Washington, D.C.
1951 *Geology of the Paunsaugunt Region, Utah.* U.S. Geological Survey, Washington, D.C.
Gregory, Herbert E., and Raymond C. Moore
1931 *The Kaiparowits Region, A Geographic and Geologic Reconnaissance of Parts of Utah and Arizona.* U.S. Geological Survey Professional Paper 164. Washington, D.C.
Gressley, Gene M.
1988 Arthur Powell Davis, Reclamation and the West. *Agricultural History* 42(3): 241–57.
Grey, Zane
1908 *The Last of the Plainsmen*, Outing Pub. Co., Chicago.
1910 *Heritage of the Desert*. Harper and Bros., New York.
1912 *Riders of the Purple Sage*. Harper and Bros., New York.
1915 *The Rainbow Trail: A Romance.* Harper and Bros., New York.
1922–23 The Vanishing American. *Ladies Home Journal* (Nov.–Dec. 1922; Jan.–April 1923).
1923 *Wanderer of the Wasteland.* Harper and Bros., New York.
1924 Down into the Desert. *Ladies Home Journal* (Jan. 1924): 8–9, 42–46.
1925 *The Vanishing American*. Harper and Bros., New York.
1927 The Water Hole. *Collier's National Weekly Magazine,* vol. 80 (October–December).
1928 *Wild Horse Mesa.* Harper and Bros., New York.
1930 *Robber's Roost.* Harper and Bros., New York.
1952 *Captives of the Desert*. Harper and Bros., New York.
1954 *Lost Pueblo*. Harper and Bros., New York.
1957 *Stranger from the Tonto*. Harper and Bros., New York.
Greystone Productions
1994 *John Wesley Powell.* 60 minute documentary. The Real West Series, Arts and Entertainment Television, Los Angeles.
Grover, Nathan C.
1916 Introduction to *The Colorado River and Its Utilization*, by Eugene La Rue USGS Water Supply Paper 395, U.S. Gov't. Printing Office, Washington, D.C., pp. 1–12.
Grover, Nathan C., and Arthur W. Harrington
1943 *Stream Flow: Measurements and Their Uses.* John Wiley and Sons, New York.
Gruber, Frank
1970 *Zane Grey, a Biography*. World Pub. Co., Cleveland.
Gunnerson, James H.
1957–58 Field Reports and Correspondence, Glen Canyon Project. University of Utah Archives. Accession 499, Box 25. Salt Lake City.
1959 *[The] 1957 Excavations, Glen Canyon Area.* University of Utah Anthropological Papers 43, Glen Canyon Series 10. Salt Lake City.
1969 *The Fremont Culture. A Study in Cultural Dynamics on the Northern Anasazi Frontier Including the Report of the Claflin-Emerson Expedition of the Peabody Museum.* Papers of the Peabody Museum of Archaeology and Ethnology, vol. 59, no. 2. Harvard University, Cambridge.

Guernsey, Samuel J.
1931 *Explorations in Northeastern Arizona: Report on the Archaeological Field Work of 1920–1923.* Papers of the Peabody Museum of Archaeology and Ethnology, vol. 12, no. 1. Harvard University, Cambridge.

Guernsey, Samuel J., and A. V. Kidder
1921 *Basket-Maker Caves of Northeastern Arizona.* Papers of the Peabody Museum of Archaeology and Ethnology, vol. 8, no. 2. Harvard University, Cambridge.

Haag, William G.
1985 Federal Aid to Archaeology in the Southeast, 1933–1942. *American Antiquity* 50(2): 272–80.

Haas, Jonathan, and Winifred Creamer
1993 *Stress and Warfare Among the Kayenta Anasazi of the Thirteenth Century AD.* Fieldiana: Anthropology, n.s. 21. Field Museum of Natural History, Chicago.

Hafen, Leroy R. (editor)
1947 Armijo's Journal. *Huntington Library Quarterly* 11: 87–101.

Hague, Arnold, and S. F. Emmons
1877 *Descriptive Geology.* U.S. Geological Exploration of the Fortieth Parallel Reports, vol. 2. Washington, D.C.

Hall, Ansel F.
1933 Wanted: Ten Explorers. *University of California Alumni Monthly Magazine* (March): 49–50.
1934a Information for Prospective Members of the Scientific Field Staff. *Rainbow Bridge–Monument Valley Expedition Bulletin no. 1.*
1934b *General Report: Rainbow Bridge–Monument Valley Expedition of 1933.* University of California Press, Berkeley.
1935a Expedition Newsletter to Members of Qualifications Committee and Advisory Board. Mimeograph. Copy in A. F. Hall Papers, Bancroft Library, University of California, Berkeley.
1935b Expedition Administrative Circular. Mimeograph. Copy in A. F. Hall Papers, Bancroft Library, University of California, Berkeley.
1944 Preparing for Explorers' Camp. Printed flier. Copy in A. F. Hall Papers, Bancroft Library, University of California, Berkeley.
1947 Announcing the Mesa Verde Explorers' Camp for Boys, June 19 to September 9, 1947. Printed flier. Copy in A. F. Hall Papers, Bancroft Library, University of California, Berkeley.

Hall, Edward T.
1959 *The Silent Language.* Doubleday, New York.
1966 *The Hidden Dimension.* Doubleday, New York.
1976 *Beyond Culture.* Doubleday, New York.
1983 *The Dance of Life: The Other Dimensions of Time.* Doubleday, New York.
1992 *An Anthropology of Everyday Life: An Autobiography.* Doubleday, New York.
1994 *West of the Thirties: Discoveries Among the Navajo and Hopi.* Doubleday, New York.

Hall, Eugene Raymond
1946 *Mammals of Nevada.* University of California Press, Berkeley. (Reprinted 1995, University of Nevada Press, Reno.)

Hall, James 1847–94 *Contributions to the Paleontology of New York.* 13 vols. Various printers and publishers, Albany, NY.

Hanson, David A.
1993 Baron Frederick W. von Egloffstein: Inventor of the First Commercial Halftone Process in America. *Printing History: The Journal of the American Printing History Association* 15(1): 30–41.

Hargrave, Lyndon L.
1931 The Influence of Economic Geography Upon the Rise and Fall of the Pueblo Culture in Arizona. *Museum of Northern Arizona, Museum Notes* 4(6): 1–4.
1934a A Recently Discovered Basket Maker Burial Cave in the Tsegi. *Museum of Northern Arizona, Museum Notes* 7(4): 13.
1934b Archaeological Investigations in the Tsegi Canyons of Northeastern Arizona in 1934. *Museum of Northern Arizona, Museum Notes* 7(7): 25–28.
1935 *Report on Archaeological Reconnaissance in the Rainbow Plateau Area of Northern Arizona and Southern Utah: Based upon Fieldwork by the Rainbow Bridge–Monument Valley Expedition of 1933.* University of California Press, Berkeley.

Harrington, Jean C.
1952 Historic Site Archaeology in the United States. In *Archaeology of the Eastern United States,* edited by J. B. Griffin, pp. 335–44. University of Chicago Press, Chicago.

Harrington, Mark R., Irwin Hayden, and Louis Schellbach III
1930 *Archaeological Explorations in Southern Nevada: Report of the First Sessions Expedition, 1929.* Southwest Museum Papers 4. Los Angeles.

Harris, Charles H., III, and Louis R. Sadler
2003 *The Archaeologist Was a Spy: Sylvanus Griswold Morley and the Office of Naval Intelligence.* University of New Mexico Press, Albuquerque.

Harshburger, J., C. A. Repenning, and J. H. Irwin
1957 *Stratigraphy of the Uppermost Triassic and Jurassic Rocks of the Navajo Country.* U.S. Geological Survey Professional Paper 291. Washington, D.C.

Harvey, P. D. A.
1980 *History of Topographical Maps: Symbols, Pictures and Surveys.* Thames and Hudson, New York and London.

Haskell, Horace S.
1958 Flowering Plants in Glen Canyon; Late Summer Aspect. *Plateau* 31(1): 1–3.

Haury, Emil W.
1950 *The Stratigraphy and Archaeology of Ventana Cave, Arizona.* University of Arizona Press, Tucson.
1976 *The Hohokam: Desert Farmers and Craftsmen, Excavations at Snaketown, 1964–1965.* University of Arizona Press, Tucson.

Hawley, Florence
1937 Kokopelli, of the Prehistoric Southwestern Pantheon. *American Anthropologist* 39(4): 644–46.

Hay, Fred J.
2000 Clyde Kay Maben Kluckhohn. *American National Biography Online,* www.anb.opac.80: art 14.

Hayden, Irwin
1930 Preliminary Report on Two Caves in Southwestern Utah, Explored in July and August, 1930 by the Van Bergen–Los Angeles Field Party. Manuscript on file, Los Angeles County Museum Archives, Los Angeles.

Heald, Weldon F.
1955 Who Discovered Rainbow Bridge? *Sierra Club Bulletin* 4(8): 24–28.

Hilger, Michael
1986 *The American Indian in Film.* Scarecrow Press, Metuchen, NJ.

Hill, Joseph J.
1930 Spanish and Mexican Exploration and Trade Northwest from New Mexico into the Great Basin, 1765–1853. *Utah Historical Quarterly* 3(1): 1–10.

Hill, Linda M. (editor)
1997 *Learning from the Land: Grand Staircase–Escalante National Monument Science Symposium Proceedings, 1997.* U.S. Bureau of Land Management, Utah Office, Salt Lake City.

Hill, George Roy (director), and William Goldman (writer).
1969 *Butch Cassidy and the Sundance Kid.* 20th Century–Fox Studios.

Hillers, John K.
1972 *"Photographed All the Best Scenery": Jack Hillers's Diary of the Powell Expedition, 1871–1875.* Edited by D. D. Fowler. University of Utah Press, Salt Lake City.

Hintze, Lehi F.
1988 *Geologic History of Utah.* Brigham Young University Geological Studies, Special Publication 7. Provo.

Historical Views
2001 *The Utah History Suite.* 3rd ed. CD. Historical Views, Provo.

Holmes, Edwin F.
1907 The Great Natural Bridges of Utah. *National Geographic Magazine* 18(3): 199–204.

Holmes, William H.
1876 A Note on Ancient Remains of Southwestern Colorado. *Bulletin of the U.S. Geological and Geographical Survey of the Territories* 2, no. 1: 3–24.

Hopi Dictionary Project
1998 *Hopi Dictionary, Hopìikwa Lavàytutuveni: A Hopi–English Dictionary of the Third Mesa Dialect.* University of Arizona Press, Tucson.

House, Dorothy
2002 Robert C. Euler: Scholar. In *Culture and Environment in the American Southwest: Essays in Honor of Robert C. Euler,* edited by David Phillips, Jr., and John A. Ware, pp. 203–17. SWCA Environmental Consultants, Phoenix.

Howell, Edwin E.
1875 Geology of a Portion of Utah, Nevada, Arizona and New Mexico, Explored and Surveyed in 1872 and 1873. In *Report Upon Geographical and Geological Explorations and Surveys West of the 100th Meridian,* vol. 3: *Geology,* pp. 231–301. U.S. Gov't. Printing Office, Washington, D.C.

Hoyt, John C., and Nathan C. Grover
1908 *River Discharge; Prepared for the Use of Engineers and Students.* John Wiley and Sons, New York.

Hudgins, Mary D.
1971 Arkansas Traveler—a Multi-Parented Wayfarer. *Arkansas Historical Quarterly* 30: 145–60.

Humboldt, Alexander von
1811 *Political Essay on the Kingdom of New Spain, with Physical Sections and Maps.* Riley, New York. (Reprinted 1970, Longman, Hurst, Ree, London.)

Hunt, Charles B.
1953 *Geology and Geography of the Henry Mountains Region, Utah.* U.S. Geological Survey Professional Paper 228. Washington, D.C.
1956 *Cenozoic Geology of the Colorado Plateau.* U.S. Geological Survey Professional Paper 279. Washington, D.C.
1967 *Physiography of the United States.* W. H. Freeman Co., San Francisco.
1969 *Geologic History of the Colorado River.* U.S. Geological Survey Professional Paper 669C. Washington, D.C.
1980 G. K. Gilbert on Laccoliths and Intrusive Structures. In *The Scientific Ideas of G. K. Gilbert,* edited by E. L. Yochelson, pp. 25–34. Geological Society of America, Boulder, CO.

Hunt, Charles B. (editor)
1988 *Geology of the Henry Mountains, Utah, as Recorded in the Notebooks of G. K. Gilbert, 1875–76.* Geological Society of America Memoir 167. Boulder, CO.

Huseman, Ben W.
1995 *Wild River, Timeless Canyons: Balduin Möllhausen's Watercolors of the Colorado.* Amon Carter Museum, Forth Worth.

Hyatt, A.
1868 The Chasms of the Colorado. *American Naturalist* 2(7): 359–65.

Inskip, Eleanor (editor)
1995 *The Colorado River through Glen Canyon before Lake Powell: Historic Photo Journal 1872 to 1964.* Inskip Ink, Moab, UT.

Iverson, Peter
1997 *Barry Goldwater: Native Arizonan.* University of Oklahoma Press, Norman.

Ives, Joseph C.
1861 *Report Upon the Colorado River of the West Explored in 1857 and 1858.* U.S. Gov't. Printing Office, Washington, D.C. (See also McKinney 2002.)

Jackson, Carlton
1973 *Zane Grey.* Twayne Pubs., Boston.

Jackson, Helen H.
1884 *Ramona: A Story.* Roberts Brothers, Boston.

Jackson, William Henry
1876 A Notice of Ancient Ruins in Arizona and Utah Lying About the San Juan. *Bulletin of the U.S. Geological and Geographical Survey of the Territories* 2, no. 2: 25–45.

Jacobs, G. Clell
1992 The Phantom Pathfinder: Juan Maria Antonio de Rivera and His Expedition. *Utah Historical Quarterly* 60: 200–223.

Jaeger, Oscar R.
1932 *Great Grand Canyon Adventure: A Narrative of Rapid-shooting on the Colorado River.* O. R. Jaeger, Dubuque, IA.

James, Edwin
1822 *Account of an Expedition from Pittsburgh to the Rocky Mountains, Performed in the Years 1819 and '20 . . . by Major Stephen H. Long.* Carey and Lea, Philadelphia.

Janetski, Joel C.
1999 Julian Steward and Utah Archaeology. In *Julian Steward and the Great Basin: The Making of an Anthropologist,* edited by R. O. Clemmer, L. D. Meyers and M. E. Rudden, pp. 19–34. University of Utah Press, Salt Lake City.

Janetski, Joel C., et al.
2005 *Life on the Edge: Archaeology in Capitol Reef National Park.* Museum of Peoples and Cultures, Brigham Young University Occasional Paper no. 11. Provo, UT.

Jaques Cattell Press (editors)
1971–86 *American Men and Women of Science.* 12th–14th ed. Bowker Pubs., New York.

Jeffers, Le Roy
1923 *The Call of the Mountains: Rambles among the Mountains and Canyons of the United States and Canada.* Dodd, Mead Co., New York.

Jenkins, Dennis
2007 Distribution and Dating of Cultural and Paleontological Remains at the Paisley Five Mile Point Caves in the Northern Great Basin. In *Paleoindian or Paleoarchaic? Great Basin Human Ecology at the Pleistocene/Holocene Transition,* edited by Kelly E. Graf and Dave N Schmitt, pp. 57–81. University of Utah Press, Salt Lake City.

Jennings, Jesse D.
1957 Annual letter. *Teocentli* 61: 13.
1959 Annual letter. *Teocentli* 63: 17.
1963 Administration of Contract Emergency Archaeology Programs. *American Antiquity* 28(3): 282–85.
1966 *Glen Canyon: A Summary.* University of Utah Anthropological Papers 81. Salt Lake City.

1985 River Basin Surveys: Origins, Operations and Results, 1945–1969. *American Antiquity* 50(2): 281–96.

1989 *Prehistory of North America*. 3rd ed. Mayfield Publishing Co., Mountain View, CA.

1994 *Accidental Archaeologist: Memoirs of Jesse D. Jennings*. University of Utah Press, Salt Lake City.

Jennings, Jesse D., and Frank Setzler

1941 *Peachtree Mound and Village Site, Cherokee County, North Carolina*. Bureau of American Ethnology Bulletin no. 131. Washington, D.C.

Jett, Stephen C.

1973 Testimony of the Sacredness of Rainbow Natural Bridge to Puebloans, Navajos and Paiutes. *Plateau* 45(3): 133–42.

1992 The Great "Race" to "Discover" Rainbow Natural Bridge. *Kiva* 58(1): 3–66.

Johnson, William D., Jr.

N.d. *William Derby Johnson, Jr. and the Powell Expedition of 1871–1872*. Compiled by Dale M. Clawson. N.p.

Jones, Charles C., Jr. 1873 *Antiquities of Southern Indians, Particularly of the Georgian Tribes*. Appleton, New York.

Jones, Stephen V.

1948–49 Journal of Stephen Vandiver Jones (edited by Hebert E. Gregory). *Utah Historical Quarterly* 16–17: 19–174.

Jotter, Lois

1938 Trip Log, Lois Jotter Colorado River Trip, 1938. MS 69, folder 3. Special Collections, Cline Library, Northern Arizona University, Flagstaff.

1997 Interview with Lois Jotter. *Boatman's Quarterly Review* 10(4), http://www.gcrg.org/bqr/10-4/jotter.htm.

Judd, Neil M.

1924a Explorations in San Juan County, Utah. *Smithsonian Miscellaneous Collections* 76(10): 77–82.

1924b Beyond the Clay Hills. *National Geographic Magazine* 45(3): 275–302.

1926 *Archeological Observations North of the Rio Colorado*. Bureau of American Ethnology Bulletin 82. Washington, D.C.

1927 Rainbow Bridge. *The National Parks Bulletin* no. 54: 6–13.

1954 Byron Cummings—1860–1954. *American Antiquity* 20(2): 154–57.

1968 *Men Met Along the Trail: Adventures in Archaeology*. University of Oklahoma Press, Norman. (Reprinted 2009, University of Utah Press, Salt Lake City.)

1970 Basketmaker Artifacts from Moki Canyon, Utah. *Plateau* 43(1): 16–20.

Jurovics, Toby, Carol M. Johnson, Glenn Willumson, and William F. Stapp

2010 *Framing the West: The Survey Photographs of Timothy H. O'Sullivan*. Yale University Press, New Haven.

Kant, Candace C.

1984 *Zane Grey's Arizona*. Northland Press, Flagstaff.

Keiter, Robert B., Sarah B. George, and Joro Walker (editors)

1998 *Visions of the Grand Staircase–Escalante: Examining Utah's Newest National Monument*. Utah Museum of Natural History and Wallace Stegner Center, Salt Lake City.

Kelley, Tracy R.

1935 The Northern Navajo Country. Mimeograph fact sheet in A. F. Hall Papers, Bancroft Library, University of California, Berkeley.

Kelly, Charles

1930 *Salt Desert Trails: A History of the Hastings Cutoff and Other Early Trails which Crossed the Great Salt Lake Desert*. Western Epics, Salt Lake City.

1933 The Mysterious "D. Julien." *Utah Historical Quarterly* 4(3): 79–81.

1938 *Outlaw Trail; a History of Butch Cassidy and His Wild Bunch . . .* Self-published, Salt Lake City.

1948–49 Walter Clement Powell (1850–1883). *Utah Historical Quarterly* 16–17: 253–55.

1953 Chief Hoskininni. *Utah Historical Quarterly* 21(3): 219–26.

Kelly, Charles, and Hoffman Birney

1934 *Holy Murder; the Story of Porter Rockwell*. Minton, Balch, New York.

Kelly, Isabel T.

1934 Southern Paiute Bands. *American Anthropologist* 36(4): 548–60.

1939 Southern Paiute Shamanism. *University of California Anthropological Records* 2(4): 151–67.

1964 *Southern Paiute Ethnology*. University of Utah Anthropological Papers 69, Glen Canyon Series 21. Salt Lake City.

Kelly, Isabel T., and Catherine S. Fowler

1986 Southern Paiute. *Handbook of North American Indians*, vol. 11, *Great Basin*, pp. 368–397. Smithsonian Institution, Washington, D.C.

Kenys, J. F. 1893 Memoir of J. S. Newberry. *Geological Society of America Bulletin* 4: 393–406.

Kerns, Virginia
1999 Learning the Land. In *Julian Steward and the Great Basin: The Making of an Anthropologist*, edited by R. O. Clemmer, L. D. Meyers, and M. E. Rudden, pp. 19–34. University of Utah Press, Salt Lake City.
2003 *Scenes from the High Desert: Julian Steward's Life and Theory*. University of Illinois Press, Urbana.
2010 *Journeys West: Jane and Julian Steward and Their Guides*. University of Nebraska Press, Lincoln.

Kidder, A. V.
1910 Explorations in Southeastern Utah in 1908. *American Journal of Archaeology*, 2d series 14: 37–59.
1924 *Introduction to the Study of Southwestern Archaeology*. Yale University Press, New Haven.
1927 Southwestern Archaeological Conference. *Science* 66(1716): 489–91.
1936 Speculations on New World Prehistory. In *Essays in Anthropology: Presented to A. L. Kroeber in Celebration of His Sixtieth Birthday, June 11, 1936*, edited by R. H. Lowie. University of California Press, Berkeley, pp. 143–52.

Kidder, A. V., and S. J. Guernsey
1919 *Archaeological Explorations in Northeastern Arizona*. Bureau of American Ethnology Bulletin 65. Washington, D.C.

Kino, Eusebio F.
1919 *Kino's Historical Memoir of Pimería Alta . . .* 2 vols. Arthur H. Clark, Cleveland.

Kleinerman, Issac (producer)
1971 *99 Days to Survival*. 60 minute documentary. CBS News for Smithsonian Television, New York.

Kluckhohn, Clyde
1927 *To the Foot of the Rainbow*. Century Company, New York.
1932 *Beyond the Rainbow*. Christopher Publishing House, Boston.
1940 The Conceptual Structure in Middle American Studies. In *The Maya and Their Neighbors*, edited by C. L. Hay et al., pp. 44–51. D. Appleton Century, New York.
1962 *The Navaho*. Rev. ed. Natural History Library, Garden City, NY.

Knack, Martha C.
2001 *Boundaries Between: The Southern Paiutes, 1775–1995*. University of Nebraska Press, Lincoln.

Knipmeyer, James A.
2002 *Butch Cassidy Was Here: Historic Inscriptions of the Colorado Plateau*. University of Utah Press, Salt Lake City.
2006 *In Search of a Lost Race: The Illustrated American Exploring Expedition of 1892*. Xlibris Corp., n.p.

Kolb, Ellsworth L.
1952 *Through the Grand Canyon from Wyoming to Mexico*. Macmillan Co., New York. (Originally published 1914.)

Kolb, Ellsworth L., and Emery C. Kolb
2003 *The Brave Ones: The Journals and Letters of the 1911–12 Expedition down the Green and Colorado Rivers*. Transcribed and edited by W. C. Suran. Fretwater Press, Flagstaff, AZ.

Kohlstedt, Sally G.
1980 Henry A. Ward: The Merchant Naturalist and American Museum Developer. *Journal of the Society for the Bibliography of Natural History* 9: 647–71.

Krakauer, Jon
2003 *Under the Banner of Heaven: A Story of Violent Faith*. Doubleday, New York.

Kreutzer, Lee
2005 Archaeological, Historical, and Ethnographic Research at Capitol Reef National Park. In *Life on the Edge: Archaeology in Capitol Reef National Park*, by Joel C. Janetski et al., pp. 19–36. Museum of Peoples and Cultures, Brigham Young University Occasional Paper no. 11. Provo.

Kroeber, Clifton B. (editor)
1964 The Route of James O. Pattie on the Colorado in 1826: A Reappraisal by A. L. Kroeber. *Arizona and the West* 6: 119–36.

Krygier, J. B.
1997 Envisioning the American West: Maps, the Representational Barrage of 19th Century Expedition Reports, and the Production of Scientific Knowledge. *Cartography and Information Systems* 24(1): 27–50.

La Farge, Oliver
1929 *Laughing Boy*. Houghton Mifflin, Boston.
1937 *The Enemy Gods*. Houghton Mifflin, Boston.
1945 *Raw Material*. Houghton Mifflin, Boston.

Lago, Don
2003a The Madness of Jack Sumner. *Boatman's Quarterly Review* 16(2): 1–8.
2003b The Toquerville Myth. *Boatman's Quarterly Review* 16(3): 9–16.

2008 New Evidence on the Origins and Disintegration of the Powell Expedition. In *Reflections of Grand Canyon Historians: Ideas, Arguments and First Person Accounts*, edited by Todd R. Berger, pp. 119–22. Grand Canyon Association, Grand Canyon, AZ.

Lambert, Marjorie F.
1983 Charles R. Steen, Jr. In *Collected Papers in Honor of Charlie R. Steen, Jr.*, edited by Nancy L. Fox. Papers of the Archaeological Society of New Mexico 8: 1–9.

Lamparski, Richard
1985 *Whatever Became of . . . ?* Crown Pubs., New York.

Lance, John F.
1963 Alluvial Stratigraphy in Lake and Moqui Canyons. Appendix IV of *Excavations in the Glen Canyon Area*, by Floyd W. Sharrock, Kent C. Day, and David S. Dibble. University of Utah Anthropological Papers 63, Glen Canyon Series 18, pp. 347–76.

Langbein, Walter B.
1975 WRD Historical Note I. L'Affaire La Rue. *Water Resources Division Bulletin* (April–June): 1–12.

Langenheim, Ralph L.
2000 Arthur Powell Davis. *American National Biography Online*, http://www.anb.org/articles/13/13-00399.html.

Lankford, George
1982 The Arkansas Traveler: The Making of an Icon. *Mid-America Folklore* 10: 16–23.

Lanner, Ronald M.
1984 *Trees of the Great Basin: A Natural History.* University of Nevada Press, Reno.

Larsen, Wesley P.
1993 The "Letter": Or Were the Powell Men Really Killed by Indians? *Canyon Legacy* 17: 12–19.

Larson, Gustave, and Charles S. Peterson
1989 Opening the Colorado Plateau. In *Utah's History*, edited by T. G. Alexander, E. E. Campbell, D. E. Miller, and R. D. Pohl, pp. 371–86. Utah State University Press, Logan.

La Rue, Eugene C.
1916 *Colorado River and Its Utilization.* U.S. Geological Survey Water Supply Paper 395. Washington, D.C.
1925 *Water Power and Flood Control of the Colorado River Below Green River, Utah.* U.S. Geological Survey Water Supply Paper 556. Washington, D.C.

Lavender, David
1982 *Colorado River Country.* E. P. Dutton, New York.
1985 *River Runners of the Grand Canyon.* Grand Canyon Natural History Assn. and University of Arizona Press, Tucson.

Leake, Harvey, and Gary Topping
1987 The Bernheimer Expedition in Forbidding Canyon, Utah. *Utah Historical Quarterly* 55(2): 137–66.

Lee, John D.
1938 *Journals of John D. Lee, 1846–47 and 1859.* Western Printing Co., Salt Lake City.

Lee, Katie
1954 Folk Songs of the Colorado. *Arizona Highways* (May 1954): 2–4.
1998a *All My Rivers Are Gone: A Journey of Discovery through Glen Canyon.* Johnson Books, Boulder, CO. (Reprinted 2006 as *Glen Canyon Betrayed: A Sensuous Elegy,* Fretwater Press, Flagstaff, AZ.)
1998b *Colorado River Songs.* Music CD. Katiedid Books and Music, Jerome, AZ.
1998c *Glen Canyon River Journeys.* Katiedid Books and Music, Jerome, AZ.
2004 *Sandstone Seduction: Rivers and Lovers, Canyons and Friends.* Johnson Books, Boulder, CO.
2007 *Love Song to Glen Canyon: Images, Words and Songs.* DVD. Katiedid Books and Music, Jerome, AZ.

Lee, Ronald
1970 *The Antiquities Act of 1906.* National Park Service, Washington, D.C.

Leiby, Austin N.
1985 Borderland Pathfinder; The Diaries of Juan Maria Antonio de Rivera. Doctoral dissertation, Northern Arizona University, Flagstaff.

Leighton, Dorothea C., and Clyde Kluckhohn
1947 *Children of the People: The Navaho Individual and His Development.* Harvard University Press, Cambridge.

Lekson, Stephen H.
2006 *The Archaeology of Chaco Canyon: An Eleventh Century Pueblo Regional Center.* SAR Press, Santa Fe.
2008 *A History of the Ancient Southwest.* School for Advanced Research, Santa Fe.

Levy, Jerrold E.
1962 Community Organization of the Western Navajo. *American Anthropologist* 64(4): 781–801.

Lindsay, Alexander J., Jr.

1961 The Beaver Creek Agricultural Community on the San Juan River, Utah. *American Antiquity* 27(2): 174–87.

1969 The Tsegi Phase of the Kayenta Cultural Tradition in Northeastern Arizona. Doctoral dissertation in anthropology, University of Arizona.

Lindsay, Alexander J., Jr. and J. Richard Ambler

1963 Recent Contributions and Research Problems in Kayenta Anasazi Prehistory. *Plateau* 35(3): 86–92.

Lindsay, Alexander J., Jr., J. Richard Ambler, Mary Anne Stein, and Philip M. Hobler

1969 *Survey and Excavations North and East of Navajo Mountain, Utah, 1959–1962.* Museum of Northern Arizona Bulletin no. 45, Glen Canyon Series no. 8, Flagstaff.

Lingenfelter, Richard E.

1958 *First Through the Grand Canyon*. Glen Dawson Pubs., Los Angeles.

1978 *Steamboats on the Colorado River, 1852–1916.* University of Arizona Press, Tucson.

Lipe, William D.

1958–1960 Weekly Reports and Correspondence, Glen Canyon Project. University of Utah Archives, Accession 499, Box 25/8. Salt Lake City.

1960 *[The] 1958 Excavations, Glen Canyon Area.* University of Utah Anthropological Papers 44, Glen Canyon Series 11. Salt Lake City.

1967 Anasazi Culture and Its Relationships to the Environment in the Red Rock Plateau Region, Southeastern Utah. Ph.D. dissertation, Yale University.

1976 Human History and the Plateau: An Archaeologist's View. *Plateau* 49(1): 1–17. (Reprinted 2004 in *Plateau: The Land and People of the Colorado Plateau* 1[1]: 47–54 [Flagstaff].)

Lipe, William D., William J. Breed, James West, and George Batchelder

1975 Lake Pahgarit, Southeastern Utah. A Preliminary Research Report. In *Canyonlands Country: A Guidebook of the Four Corners Geological Society*, edited by James E. Fassett, pp. 103–10. Four Corners Geological Society.

Lipe, William D., and Alexander J. Lindsay, Jr. (editors)

1974 *Proceedings of the 1974 Cultural Resources Management Conference* (Federal Center, Denver). Museum of Northern Arizona Technical Series 14. Flagstaff.

Lipe, William D., et al.

1960 *[The] 1959 Excavations, Glen Canyon Area.* University of Utah Anthropological Papers 49, Glen Canyon Series 13. Salt Lake City.

Lister, Florence C.

1964 *Kaiparowits Plateau and Glen Canyon Prehistory: An Interpretation Based on Ceramics.* University of Utah Anthropological Papers 71, Glen Canyon Series 23. Salt Lake City.

Lister, Robert H.

1957–60 Field Reports and Correspondence, Glen Canyon Project. University of Utah Archives, Accession 499, Boxes 24/25. Salt Lake City.

1958 *The Glen Canyon Survey in 1957.* University of Utah Anthropological Papers no. 38, Glen Canyon Series no. 1. Salt Lake City.

1959a The Glen Canyon Right Bank Survey. In *The Glen Canyon Archaeological Survey, Part I,* by Don D. Fowler et al. University of Utah Anthropological Papers no. 39, Glen Canyon Series no. 6, pp. 27–162.

1959b The Waterpocket Fold: A Distributional Problem. In *The Glen Canyon Archaeological Survey, Part I,* by Don D. Fowler et al. University of Utah Anthropological Papers no. 39, Glen Canyon Series no. 6, pp. 285–317.

Lister, Robert H., J. Richard Ambler, and Florence C. Lister

1959–61 *The Coombs Site, Pts. I–III.* University of Utah Anthropological Papers 41, Glen Canyon Series 8. Salt Lake City.

Lockett, H. Claiborne

1933 The Prehistoric Hopi. Master's thesis, University of Arizona, Tucson.

1934 Northern Arizona's First Farmers. *Museum of Northern Arizona, Museum Notes* 7(4): 14–16.

Lockett, H. Claiborne, and Lyndon L. Hargrave

1953 *Woodchuck Cave: A Basketmaker II Site in Tsegi Canyon, Arizona.* Museum of Northern Arizona Bulletin 26. Flagstaff.

Long, Paul V., Jr.

1966 *Archaeological Excavations in Lower Glen Canyon, Utah, 1959–1960*. Museum of Northern Arizona Bulletin no. 42. Flagstaff.

n.d. Excerpts from San Juan/Colorado River 1959/1960 San Juan River Float Excavation Project. Manuscript in author's possession.

Longwell, C. R, H. D. Miser, R. C. Moore, Kirk Bryan, and Sydney Paige

1925 *Rock Formations in the Colorado Plateau of Southeastern Utah and Northern Arizona*. U.S. Geological Survey Professional Paper 132. Washington, D.C.

Luckert, Karl W.

1977 *Navajo Mountain and Rainbow Bridge Religion*. American Tribal Religion Series 1. Museum of Northern Arizona, Flagstaff.

Lyon, Edwin A.

1996 *A New Deal for Southeastern Archaeology*. University of Alabama Press, Tuscaloosa.

MacKinnon, William P. (editor)

2008 *At Sword's Point,* Part I: *A Documentary History of the Utah War to 1858*. Arthur H. Clark Co., Norman.

MacNeish, Richard S.

1974 Reflections on My Search for the Beginnings of Agriculture in Mexico. In *Archaeological Researches in Retrospect*, edited by G. R. Willey, pp.207–34. Winthrop Pubs., Cambridge, MA.

Madsen, David M.

1989 *Exploring the Fremont*. Utah Museum of Natural History Occasional Publication 8. Salt Lake City.

Madsen, David B., and Steven R. Simms

1998 The Fremont Complex: A Behavioral Perspective. *Journal of World Prehistory* 12(3): 255–336.

Malotki, Ekkhart

2000 *Kokopelli: The Making of an Icon*. University of Nebraska Press, Lincoln.

Mange, Juan M.

1954 *Unknown Arizona and Sonora, 1693–1721, from the Francisco Fernández del Castillo Version of Luz de tierra incógnita*. Translated by H. J. Karns et al. Arizona Silhouettes, Tucson.

Marquis Who's Who

1954–98 *Who Was Who in America*. 10 vols. Marquis Who's Who, Chicago.

Marston, Otis

1960 River Runners: Fast Water Navigation. *Utah Historical Quarterly* 28: 291–308.

1969 The Lost Journal of John Colton Sumner. *Utah Historical Quarterly* 37: 173–89.

Martin, Russell

1989 *A Story that Stands Like a Dam: Glen Canyon and the Struggle for the Soul of the West*. Henry Holt and Co., New York.

Martineau, Lavan

1973 *The Rocks Begin to Speak*. K. C. Publications, Las Vegas.

1992 *The Southern Paiutes: Legends, Lore, Language and Lineage*. K. C. Publications, Las Vegas.

Mason, J. Alden

1945 Archaeological Explorations in the Neighborhood of Navajo Mountain, Northeastern Arizona. Manuscript on file, University of Pennsylvania Museum Archives, Philadelphia.

Mathews, Tom

1958 Field Reports and Correspondence, Glen Canyon Project. University of Utah Archives. Accession 499, Box 24. Salt Lake City.

Maugh, Thomas

2009 The Mystery of Everett Ruess's Disappearance Is Solved. *Los Angeles Times,* Science Section, May 2.

May, Stephen J.

1997 *Zane Grey: Romancing the West*. Ohio University Press, Athens.

McCourt, Tom

2003 *White Canyon: Remembering the Little Town at the Bottom of Lake Powell.* Southpaw Publications, Price, UT.

McGimsey, Charles M.

1985 "This, Too, Will Pass": Moss-Bennett in Perspective. *American Antiquity* 50(2): 326–31.

McGivney, Annette

2009 *Resurrection: Glen Canyon and a New Vision for the American West.* Glen Canyon Institute, Salt Lake City.

McGregor, John

1941 *Southwest Archaeology*. John Wiley and Sons, New York.

McKinney, Kevin C. (editor)

2000 Introduction. Digital Archive. Geological Report by J. S. Newberry and Map by J. N. Macomb from *The Exploring Expedition from Santa Fe, New Mexico, to the Junction of the Grand and Green Rivers of the Great Colorado of the West.* Open File Report 00–368. Version 1.0. CD. U.S. Geological Survey, Washington, D.C.

2002 Digital Archive. *Report upon the Colorado River of the West Explored in 1857 and 1858 by Lt. Joseph C. Ives, Geology Report with Maps by John S. Newberry.* Open File Report 02–25. Version 1.0. CD. U.S. Geological Survey, Washington, D.C.

McNitt, Frank

1966 *Richard Wetherill, Anasazi*. University of New Mexico Press, Albuquerque. 2nd ed. (Originally published 1957.)

McPhee, John
1971 *Encounters with the Archdruid.* Farrer, Straus and Giroux, New York.
McPherson, Robert S.
1988 *The Northern Navajo Frontier, 1860–1900: Expansion Through Adversity.* University of New Mexico Press, Albuquerque. (Reprinted 2001, Utah State University Press, Logan.)
1992 *Sacred Land, Sacred View: Navajo Perceptions of the Four Corners Region.* Signature Books, Salt Lake City.
1999 *A History of San Juan County.* Utah Historical Society, Salt Lake City.
2001 *Navajo Land, Navajo Culture: The Utah Experience in the Twentieth Century.* University of Oklahoma Press, Norman.
McPherson, Robert S., and Richard Kitchen
1999 Much Ado About Nothing: The San Juan River Gold Rush, 1892–93. *Utah Historical Quarterly* 67(1): 68–87.
McVickar, Janet L.
2001 *An Archaeological Survey of Natural Bridges National Monument, Southeastern Utah.* Intermountain Cultural Resources Management Anthropology Program, Professional Paper 64. National Park Service, Santa Fe.
Measeles, Evelyn B.
1981 *Lee's Ferry: A Crossing on the Colorado.* Pruett Publishing Co., Boulder, CO.
Meltzer, David J.
2009 *First Peoples in a New World: Colonizing Ice Age America.* University of California Press, Berkeley.
Meyer, William B.
2000 Gannett, Henry. *American National Biography Online,* http://www.anb.org/articles/13/13-00582.html.
Miller, David E.
1966 *Hole-in-the-Rock: An Epic in the Colonization of the American West.* 2nd ed. University of Utah Press, Salt Lake City.
Miller, Wick R.
1986 Numic Languages. *Smithsonian Handbook of North American Indians,* vol. 11, *Great Basin,* pp. 98–106.
Miller, William C. and David A. Breternitz
1958a [The] 1957 Navajo Canyon Survey Preliminary Report. *Plateau* 30(3): 72–74.
1958b [The] 1958 Navajo Canyon Survey Preliminary Report. *Plateau* 31(1): 3–7.
Miser, Hugh D.
1924 *The San Juan Canyon, Southeastern Utah: A Geographic and Hydrographic Reconnaissance.* U.S. Geological Survey Water Supply Paper 538. Washington, D.C.
1925 Geologic Structure of San Juan Canyon and Adjacent Country, Utah. *U.S. Geological Survey Bulletin* 751: 115–55. Washington, D.C.
Miser, Hugh D., K. W. Trimble, and Sidney Paige
1923 The Rainbow Bridge, Utah. *Geographical Review* (October): 518–31.
Moffat, Riley M.
1985 *Map Index to Topographic Quadrangles of the United States, 1882–1940.* Western Association of Map Libraries Occasional Paper 10. Santa Cruz, CA.
Moore, W. R.
1955 Escalante: Utah's River of Arches. *National Geographic Magazine* 108(3): 299–425.
Morgan, Dale M.
1964 *The West of William Ashley.* Old West Pub. Co., Denver.
Morley, Sylvanus G.
1908 The Excavation of the Cannonball Ruins in Southwestern Colorado. *American Anthropologist* 10(4): 596–610.
Morris, Earl H.
1919 *The Aztec Ruin.* American Museum of Natural History Anthropological Papers 26(1): 1–108.
1929 Field Notes, Bernheimer Expeditions, 1929. Library Archives, American Museum of Natural History, New York City.
1939 *Archaeological Studies in the La Plata District, Southwestern Colorado and Northwestern New Mexico.* Carnegie Institution of Washington Publications 519.
Morss, Noel
1927 *Archaeological Explorations on the Middle Chinlee, 1925.* American Anthropological Association Memoir 34.
1931a *Notes on the Archaeology of the Kaibito and Rainbow Plateaus in Arizona.* Papers of the Peabody Museum of American Archaeology and Ethnology, vol. 12, no. 2. Harvard University, Cambridge.
1931b *The Ancient Culture of the Fremont River in Utah: Report of the Explorations under the Claflin-Emerson Fund, 1928–29.* Papers of the Peabody Museum of Archaeology and Ethnology, vol. 12, no. 3. Harvard University, Cambridge.

1954 *Clay Figurines of the American Southwest*. Papers of the Peabody Museum of Archaeology and Ethnology, vol. 49, no. 1. Harvard University, Cambridge.

Moseley, Michael E.

1975 *The Maritime Foundation of Andean Civilization.* Cummings Publishers, Menlo Park, CA.

1993 *The Incas and Their Ancestors: The Archaeology of Peru.* Thames and Hudson, New York and London.

Mulder, William

1959 The Mormons in American History. *Utah Historical Quarterly* 27(1): 59–77.

Munthe, Jens

2002 *Arches of the Canyons and Kaiparowits Plateau, Grand Staircase–Escalante National Monument.* Arch Hunter Books, Thompson Springs, UT.

Murphy, Miriam B.

1996 *A History of Wayne County*. Utah Historical Society, Salt Lake City.

Myers, Tom

2008 Why James White's 1867 Raft Trip Doesn't Float—at Least through Grand Canyon. In *Reflections of Grand Canyon Historians: Ideas, Arguments and First Person Accounts*, edited by Todd R. Berger, pp. 125–30. Grand Canyon Association, Grand Canyon, AZ.

Nash, Stephen E.

1999 *Time, Trees, and Prehistory: Tree-Ring Dating and the Development of North American Archaeology, 1914–1950.* University of Utah Press, Salt Lake City.

National Geographic Magazine

1904 Colossal Natural Bridges of Utah. *National Geographic Magazine* 15(9): 367–69.

National Park Service

1950 *A Survey of the Recreational Resources of the Colorado River Basin*. U.S. Dept. of the Interior, Washington, D.C.

Nelson, Lowry

1952 *The Mormon Village: A Pattern and Technique of Land Settlement*. University of Utah Press, Salt Lake City.

1954 *American Farm Life.* Harvard University Press, Cambridge.

1969 *Rural Sociology: Its Origin and Growth in the United States.* University of Minnesota Press, Minneapolis.

Nelson, Nancy

1991 *Any Time Any Place Any River: The Nevills of Mexican Hat*. Red Lake Books, Flagstaff, AZ.

Newberry, John S.

1857 *Reports of the Geology, Botany and Zoölogy of California and Oregon*. Pacific Railroad Survey Reports vol. 6. U.S. Gov't. Printing Office, Washington, D.C.

1861 Geology of the Colorado Exploring Expedition. In *Report upon the Colorado River of the West* by Joseph C. Ives, Part III. U.S. Gov't. Printing Office, Washington, D.C. (See also McKinney 2002.)

1876 *Geological Report: Report of the Exploring Expedition from Santa Fé, New Mexico to the Junction of the Grand and Green Rivers of the Great Colorado of the West, in 1859*. U.S. Gov't. Printing Office, Washington, D.C. (See also McKinney 2000.)

Newcomer, Joseph

2008 The Annotated "It's a Long Way From Amphioxus." http://www.flounders.com/amphioxus.htm.

Newell, Frederick

1902 Testimony of Frederick Newell. *Hearings before the Committee on the Irrigation of Arid Lands of the House of Representatives, Jan 28–Feb 9, 1901*, pp. 8–88. U.S. Gov't. Printing Office, Washington, D.C.

Nichols, James

1958 Field Reports and Correspondence, Glen Canyon Project. University of Utah Archives. Accession 499, Box 24/10.

Nichols, Tad

1999 *Glen Canyon: Images of a Lost World.* Museum of New Mexico Press, Santa Fe.

2000 Interview with Tad Nichols. *Boatman's Quarterly Review* 13(2): 1–35, http://www.gcrg.org/bqr/13-2/nichols.htm.

Nims, Franklin A.

1967 *The Photographer and the River, 1889–1890. The Colorado Cañon Diary of Franklin A. Nims with the Brown-Stanton Railroad Survey Expedition.* Edited by D. L. Smith. Stagecoach Press, Santa Fe.

Noble, David G.

2004 *In Search of Chaco: New Approaches to an Archaeological Enigma.* School of American Research Press, Santa Fe.

Nordenskiöld, Gustavo

1893 *The Cliff Dwellers of the Mesa Verde. . . .* Translated by D. L. Morgan. Nordstedt and Söner, Stockholm and Chicago.

Novak, Shannon

2009 *House of Mourning: A Biocultural History of the Mountain Meadows Massacre.* University of Utah Press, Salt Lake City.

Novak, Shannon A., and Lars Rodseth
2006 Remembering Mountain Meadows: Collective Violence and the Manipulation of Social Boundaries. *Journal of Anthropological Research* 62(1): 1–25.

Olson, Ronald W., Jr.
1969 The Powell Survey Kanab Baseline. *Utah Historical Quarterly* 32: 261–68.

Oregon Historical Society. n.d. *Guide to Amos Burg Photographs, 1889–1986*. Oregon Historical Society, Portland.

Orr, Diane (writer and director)
2000 *Lost Forever: Everett Ruess*. DVD. W. Beecher Films, Salt Lake City.

Ortiz, Alfonso (editor)
1983 *Southwest*. Vol. 10 of *Handbook of North American Indians*. Smithsonian Institution, Washington, D.C.

Osborne, Carolyn M.
2004 *The Wetherill Collections and Perishable Items from Mesa Verde*. Lulu.com Publishing, n.p.

Osborne, Douglas
1957 *Excavations in the McNary Reservoir Basin near Umatilla, Oregon*. Bureau of American Ethnology Bulletin 166, River Basin Surveys Papers 8. Washington, D.C.

Pace, Paul S.
2004 Joseph C. Ives—Soldier-Surveyor: A Life in Conflict. Paper presented at CSLA/NALS Joint Conference, Las Vegas, NV, April 14, 2004. Copy in author's possession.

Palmer, William J. 1869 *Report of Surveys across the Continent, in 1867–'68 on the Thirty Second and Thirty Fifth Parallels for a Route extending the Kansas Pacific Railway to the Pacific Ocean at San Francisco and San Diego*. W. B. Selheiner, Printer, Philadelphia.

Parry, C. C. 1868 Account of the Passage through the Great Cañon of the West by James White. *St. Louis Academy of Science Transactions* 2: 499–503.

Parsons, Elsie C.
1938 The Humpbacked Flute Player of the Southwest. *American Anthropologist* 40(3): 337–38.

Parsons, Talcott, and Evon Z. Vogt
1962 Clyde Kay Maben Kluckhohn, 1905–1960. *American Anthropologist* 64: 140–61.

Pattie, James O.
1962 *The Personal Narrative of James O. Pattie, of Kentucky*. Edited by William Goetzmann. J. B. Lippincott, Philadelphia and New York. (Originally published 1831.)

Pearce, T. M.
1972 *Oliver La Farge*. Twayne Pubs., New York.

Peckinpah, Sam (writer) and Arnold Laven (director)
1965 *The Glory Guys*. Film. United Artists, Hollywood.

Pepper, George
1902 *The Ancient Basket Makers of Southeastern Utah*. Supplement to the *American Museum Journal* 2(4), Guide Leaflet no. 6.

Peterson, Charles S.
1995 In Memorium: C. Gregory Crampton. *Utah Historical Quarterly* 63(4): 370–74.

Phoenix, David A.
1963 *Geology of the Lee's Ferry Area, Coconino County, Arizona*. U.S. Geological Survey Bulletin 1137. Washington, D.C.

Pierce, R. C.
1916 *The Measurement of Silt-laden Streams*. U.S. Geological Survey Water Supply Paper 400. Washington, D.C.

Pierson, Lloyd M.
1998 Lloyd M. Pierson Papers, UU-Accn 1706, Special Collections, Marriott Library, University of Utah, Salt Lake City.

Pike, Zebulon M.
1925 *The Southwestern Expedition of Zebulon M. Pike*. Edited by Milo M. Quaife. R. R. Donnelly, Chicago.

Pisani, Donald J.
1992 *To Reclaim a Divided West: Water, Law, and Public Policy, 1848–1902*. University of New Mexico Press, Albuquerque.
2002 *Water and American Government: The Reclamation Bureau, Water Policy, and the West, 1902–1935*. University of California Press, Berkeley.
2004 Floyd E. Dominy, http://www.waterhistory.org/histories/dominy/html, accessed March 7, 2004.

Pogue, Joseph F.
1911 The Great Rainbow Natural Bridge of Southern Utah. *National Geographic Magazine* 22(11): 1048–56.

Pond, Alonzo W.
1965 *Deserts: Silent Lands of the World*. Norton Pubs., New York.

Porter, Eliot
1963 *The Place No One Knew: Glen Canyon on the Colorado*. Sierra Club, San Francisco.

1969 The Canyons of the Colorado—Past and Present. In *Down the Colorado: John Wesley Powell—Diary of the First Trip Through the Grand Canyon*, pp. 149–63. E. P. Dutton, New York.

Powell, James L.

2008 *Dead Pool: Lake Powell, Global Warming, and the Future of Water in the West.* University of California Press, Berkeley.

Powell, John Wesley

1867 *Scientific Expedition to the Rocky Mountains: Preliminary Report to the Illinois State Board of Education.* Illinois State Board of Education, Normal.

1869 Major J. W. Powell's Report on his Exploration of the Rio Colorado in 1869. In *New Tracks in North America,* by W. A. Bell, pp. 559–64. London. (Reprinted 1947 in *Utah Historical Quarterly* 15: 21–27.)

1873 Some Remarks on the Geological Structure of a District of Country Lying to the North of the Grand Cañon of the Colorado. *American Journal of Science and Arts,* 3rd Series 5: 456–65.

1874 *Professor Powell's Report on the Survey of the Colorado of the West. . . .* 43rd Congress, First Session, House of Representatives Miscellaneous Document no. 265, Serial 621. U.S. Gov't. Printing Office, Washington, D.C.

1875a *Exploration of the Colorado River of the West and its Tributaries: Explored in 1869, 1870, 1871, and 1872, under the direction of the Secretary of the Smithsonian Institution.* U.S. Gov't. Printing Office, Washington, D.C.

1875b The Cañons of the Colorado. *Scribner's Monthly* 9: 293–310, 523–37.

1875c An Overland trip to the Grand Cañon. *Scribner's Monthly* 10: 659–78.

1875d Ancient Province of Tusayan. *Scribner's Monthly* 11: 193–213.

1876 *Report on the Geology of the Eastern Portion of the Uinta Mountains and a Region of the Country Adjacent Thereto.* U.S. Geological and Geographical Survey of the Territories, 2nd Division, Washington, D.C.

1878 *Report on the Lands of the Arid Regions of the United States, with a More Detailed Account of the Lands of Utah.* 45th Congress, 2nd Session, Executive Document 73, Serial 1805. Washington, D.C.

1879 *Report on the Lands of the Arid Regions of the United States, with a More Detailed Account of the Lands of Utah.* 2nd ed. U.S. Gov't. Printing Office, Washington, D.C.

1881 Report of the Director. *First Annual Report of the U.S. Geological Survey, 1879–1880,* pp. iv–xxi.

1882a Report of the Director. *Second Annual Report of the U.S. Geological Survey, 1880–81*, pp. v–xxii.

1882b Sur la nomenclature générale, sur la coloriage et les signes conventionnels des Cartes Géologiques. *Congres Géologique Internationale, Compte Rendu de la 2me Session, Bologne, 1881*, pp. 627–42.

1884 Report of the Director. *Fourth Annual Report of the U.S. Geological Survey, 1882–83*, pp. iii–xxxii.

1885 Report of the Director. *Sixth Annual Report of the U.S. Geological Survey, 1884–85*, pp. xv–xxix.

1886 Letter. *The Work of the International Congress of Geologists, and of its Committees.* International Congress of Geologists, American Committee, Berlin.

1888 Methods of Geologic Cartography in Use by the United States Geological Survey. *Congres Géologique Internationale, Compte Rendu de la 3me Session, Berlin, 1885*, pp. 627–642.

1890a United States Irrigation Survey. Abstract of First Annual Report, 1888–1889. *Tenth Annual Report of the U.S. Geological Survey, 1888–89, Part II: Irrigation*, pp. vii–xxx.

1890b J. W. Powell Testimony to Congress. In *Eleventh Annual Report of the U.S. Geological Survey, 1889–90.* Part II, *Irrigation Survey*, pp. 355–57.

1891 Discussion sur le Coloriage des Cartes Géologiques. *Congres Géologique Internationale, Compte Rendu de la 5me Session, Washington, 1891*, pp. 79–80, 208–11.

1895 *Canyons of the Colorado.* Flood and Vincent, Meadsville, PA.

1896a Physiographic Regions of the United States. In *Physiography of the United States*, pp. 65–100. National Geographic Society, Washington, D.C.

1896b Certitudes and Illusions, Chuar's Illusion. *Science* 3: 426–33.

1947 Major Powell's Journal July 2–August 28, 1869. Edited by W. C. Darrah. *Utah Historical Quarterly* 15: 125–31.

1902 The Scientific Explorer. In *The Grand Canyon of Arizona: Being a Book of Words from many pens about the Grand Canyon of the Colorado River in Arizona* (Passenger Department, Santa Fe Railway System, Chicago), pp. 18–32.

1964 *Canyons of the Colorado.* Argosy-Antiquarian Ltd., New York. (Originally published 1895.)

1968 John Wesley Powell's Journal: Colorado River Exploration 1871–1872 (edited by D. D. Fowler and C. S. Fowler). *The Smithsonian Journal of History* 3(2): 1–44. (Reprinted 1990 in *Canyon Legacy* 5: 1–12, Moab, UT.)

1987 *The Exploration of the Colorado River and Its Canyons.* Penguin Books, New York. Reprint of Powell 1895, 1964.

Powell, Walter C.

1948–49 Journal of W. C. Powell, April 21, 1871–December 7, 1872. Edited by C. Kelly. *Utah Historical Quarterly* 16–17: 257–478.

Preuss, Charles

1958 *Exploring with Fremont: The Private Diaries of Charles Preuss.* University of Oklahoma Press, Norman.

Priestley, J. B.

1990 Rainbow in the Desert. In *Rainbow Trails: Early-Day Adventures in Rainbow Bridge Country.* Edited by J. E. Babbitt, pp. 97–111. Glen Canyon Natural History Association, Page, AZ. (Originally published in *Saturday Evening Post*, June 18, 1938.)

Prudden, Lillian (editor)

1927 *Biographical Sketches and Letters of T. Mitchell Prudden, M.D.* Yale University Press, New Haven.

Prudden, T. Mitchell

1897 An Elder Brother to the Cliff Dweller. *Harper's New Monthly Magazine* 93: 545–61.

1903 The Prehistoric Ruins of the San Juan Watershed of Utah, Arizona, Colorado and New Mexico. *American Anthropologist* 5: 224–88.

1906 *On the Great American Plateau. . . .* G. P. Putnam's Sons, New York and London.

1914 The Circular Kivas of Small Ruins in the San Juan Watershed. *American Anthropologist* 16: 33–58.

1918 A Further Study of Prehistoric Small House Ruins in the San Juan Watershed. *American Anthropological Association Memoirs* 5(1).

Pyne, Stephen J.

1994 *Grove Karl Gilbert: A Great Engine of Research.* University of Texas Press, Austin.

2000 Clarence Edward Dutton. *American National Biography Online,* http://www.anb.org/articles 13/13-0457.html.

Quartaroli, Richard D.

2008 John Wesley Powell's Cartography of the Colorado Plateau: Grand Canyon's "Great Unknown" and the West's Arid Lands. In *Reflections of Grand Canyon Historians: Ideas, Arguments and First Person Accounts*, edited by Todd R. Berger, pp. 11–18. Grand Canyon Association, Grand Canyon, AZ.

Rabbitt, Mary

1979 *Minerals, Lands and Geology for the Common Defence* [sic] *and General Welfare.* 3 vols. U.S. Geological Survey, Washington, D.C.

Redd, Charles

1950 "Short Cut to the San Juan." *1949 Brand Book.* Westerners International, Denver.

Redford, Robert

1978 *The Outlaw Trail: A Journey Through Time.* Grossett and Dunlap, New York.

Reilly, P. T.

1987 Norman Nevills: Whitewater Man of the West. *Utah Historical Quarterly* 55(2): 181–200.

1999 *Lee's Ferry: From Mormon Crossing to National Park.* Utah State University Press, Logan.

Rettie, Dwight F.

1995 *Our National Park System.* University of Illinois Press, Urbana.

Rinaldo, John B.

1935 *An Archaeological Reconnaissance of the San Juan and Colorado Rivers.* Rainbow Bridge–Monument Valley Expedition, Preliminary Bulletins, Archaeological Series 5. Mimeographed.

Ringholz, Raye C.

2002 *Uranium Frenzy: Saga of the Nuclear West.* Rev. ed. Utah State University Press, Logan.

Roberts, David

1999 The Legend of Everett Ruess. *National Geographic Adventure* 1: 136–45.

2009 Finding Everett Ruess. *National Geographic Adventure* 11(3): 74–81, 101–4.

Roessel, Robert A., Jr.

1983 Navajo History, 1850–1923. *Handbook of North American Indians*, vol. 10, *Southwest*, pp. 506–23. Smithsonian Institution, Washington, D.C.

Roessel, Ruth (editor)

1973 *Navajo Stories of the Long Walk Period.* Navajo Community College Press, Tsaile, AZ.

Ronald, Ann

1975 *Zane Grey.* Boise State University, Boise, ID.

1982 *The New West of Edward Abbey.* University of New Mexico Press, Albuquerque. (Reprinted 1988, University of Nevada Press, Reno and Las Vegas.)

Roosevelt, Theodore
1913 Across the Navajo Desert. *The Outlook,* October 4. (Reprinted in Babbitt 1990.)
Rothman, Hal K.
1991 *Navajo National Monument: A Place and Its People—An Administrative History*. Southwest Cultural Resources Center Professional Papers 40. Santa Fe.
1993 Ruins, Reputations, and Regulations: Byron Cummings, William B. Douglass, John Wetherill, and the Summer of 1909. *Journal of the Southwest* 35(3): 318–40.
Roundy, Jerry C.
2000 *"Advised Them to Call the Place Escalante."* Art City Publishing, Springville, UT.
Rudy, Jack
1955 *Archaeological Excavations in Beef Basin, Utah*. University of Utah Anthropological Papers no. 20.
Ruess, Everett
1940 *On Desert Trails with Everett Ruess.* Desert Magazine Press, El Centro, CA. (Reprinted with additional materials 2000, Gibbs Smith, Salt Lake City.)
Rusho, W. L.
1969a *Powell's Canyon Voyage*. Filter Press, Palmer Lake, CO.
1969b River Running in 1921. The Diary of Ellsworth L. Kolb. *Utah Historical Quarterly* 37(2): 269–75.
2010 *The Mystery of Everett Ruess.* Gibbs Smith, Salt Lake City.
Rusho, W. L. (editor)
1969c Francis Bishop's 1871 River Maps. *Utah Historical Quarterly* 37: 207–13.
Rusho, W. L., and C. Gregory Crampton
1992 *Lee's Ferry: Desert River Crossing*. Rev. ed. Cricket Productions, Salt Lake City.
Sahagún, Bernardino de
1950–1982 *General History of the Things of New Spain—The Florentine Codex.* Translated and edited by Arthur J. O. Anderson and Charles E. Dibble. School of American Research Monograph Series 14, pts. 1–13. Santa Fe.
Salmon, Doris F.
2009 Enos A. Wall, http://www.media.utah.edu/UHE/w/WALL,ENOS.html.
Sapir, Edward
1930–31 *The Southern Paiute Language.* Proceedings of the American Academy of Arts and Sciences 65(1-3). Boston.
1931 Southern Paiute Dictionary. In *The Southern Paiute Language*, Proceedings of the American Academy of Arts and Sciences 65(3): 538–730. Boston.
Schaafsma, Polly
1994 *The Rock Art of Utah.* University of Utah Press, Salt Lake City.
Schmeckebier, L. F.
1904 *Catalogue and Index of the Publications of the Hayden, King, Powell and Wheeler Surveys.* U.S. Geological Survey Bulletin 222 (Series G, Misc. 26). U.S. Gov't. Printing Office, Washington, D.C. (Facsimile reprint 1970, Northwest Books, Portland, OR.)
Scientific American
1878 The Cañons of the Colorado. Compiled from Sources of the Professor J.W. Powell Expedition. *Scientific American Supplement* 5, no. 118, pp. 1869–71.
Scott, Hugh L.
1928 *Some Memories of a Soldier.* Century Co., New York.
Service, Robert
1968 *Collected Poems of Robert Service.* Dodd, Mead and Co., New York.
Sharrock, Floyd W.
1959–62 Field Reports and Correspondence, Glen Canyon Project. University of Utah Archives. Accession 499, Box 25. Salt Lake City.
1964 *[The] 1962 Excavations, Glen Canyon Area.* University of Utah Anthropological Papers 73, Glen Canyon Series 25. Salt Lake City.
Sharrock, Floyd W., Kent C. Day, and David S. Dibble
1963 *[The] 1961 Excavations, Glen Canyon Area.* University of Utah Anthropological Papers 63, Glen Canyon Series 18. Salt Lake City.
Sharrock, Floyd W., David S. Dibble, and Keith M. Anderson
1961 The Creeping Dune Irrigation Site in Glen Canyon, Utah. *American Antiquity* 27(2): 188–202.
Sharrock, Floyd W., and Edward G. Keane
1962 *Carnegie Museum Collection from Southeast Utah*. University of Utah Anthropological Papers 57, Glen Canyon Series 16. Salt Lake City.
Sharrock, Floyd W., et al.
1961 *[The] 1960 Excavations, Glen Canyon Area.* University of Utah Anthropological Papers 52, Glen Canyon Series 14. Salt Lake City.
Shepardson, Mary
1963 Navajo Way in Government. *American Anthropological Association Memoir* 96(65), pt. 2.

1995 The Gender Status of Navajo Women. In *Women and Power in Native North America*, edited by L. F. Klein and L. A. Ackerman, pp. 158–76. University of Oklahoma Press, Norman.

Shepardson, Mary, and Blodwen Hammond

1970 *The Navajo Mountain Community: Social Organization and Kinship Terminology*. University of California Press, Berkeley.

Short, Vaughn

1978 *Raging River, Lonely Trail: Tales Told by the Campfire's Glow*. Two Horses Press, Tucson.

Silverstein, Elliott (director), and Walter Newman (writer)

1965 *Cat Ballou.* Columbia Pictures.

Smith, Beatrice S.

1994 The 1872 Diary and Plant Collection of Ellen Powell Thompson. *Utah Historical Quarterly* 62(2): 104–31.

Smith, Dwight L.

1960 The Engineer and the Canyon. *Utah Historical Quarterly* 28(3): 263–73.

Smith, Dwight L. (editor)

1962 Robert B. Stanton's Plan for the Far Southwest. *Arizona and the West* 4: 369–80.

Smith, Dwight L., and C. Gregory Crampton.

1987 Introduction to *The Colorado River Survey. . . .*, by R. B. Stanton, pp. iv–xiii. Howe Brothers, Salt Lake City.

Smith, Watson

1956 George Walton Brainerd 1909–1956. *American Antiquity* 22: 165–68.

1963 Ansel Franklin Hall, 1894–1962. *American Antiquity* 28: 228–29.

1992 One Man's Archaeology. *Kiva* 57(2): 103–91.

Spamer, Earle E. (compiler and editor)

2010 *A Bibliography of the Grand Canyon and Lower Colorado River,* http://www.grandcanyonbiblio.org, accessed numerous times, 2000–2010.

Spense, Mary L. (editor)

1984 *The Expeditions of John Charles Frémont,* vol. 3*: Travels from 1848 to 1854*. University of Illinois Press, Urbana.

Spicer, Edward H.

1962 *Cycles of Conquest: The Impact of Spain, Mexico, and the United States on the Indians of the Southwest, 1533–1960.* University of Arizona Press, Tucson.

Sprang, Elizabeth

1992 *Good-Bye River.* Kiva Press, Las Cruces, NM.

Squier, E. G., and Edwin H. Davis

1848 *Ancient Monuments of the Mississippi Valley.* Smithsonian Contributions to Knowledge no. 1. Smithsonian Institution, Washington, D.C.

Stansbury, Howard

1988 *Exploration of the Valley of the Great Salt Lake.* Smithsonian Institution Press, Washington, D.C. (Originally published 1851.)

Stanton, Robert Brewster

1851–1960 The Robert Brewster Stanton Papers, Collection w89–a633, New York Public Library, http://nypl.org/research/chss.

1890 Through the Grand Canyon of the Colorado. *Scribner's Magazine* 7: 591–613.

1892 Availability of the Canyons of the Colorado River of the West for Railroad Purposes. *American Society of Civil Engineers Transactions* 24: 351–62.

1893 Engineering with a Camera in the Canyons of the Colorado. *Cosmopolitan Magazine* 15 (3): 294–303.

1908 *Diagram Showing the History of the Exploration and Navigation and Survey of the Grand and Other Cañons of the Colorado River of the West from 1540 to 1908.* Library of Congress Maps Archives, http://lccn.loc.gov/99446133.

1919 The Alleged Journey, and the Real Journey of James White, on the Colorado River in 1861 [*sic*]. *The Trail* 12(4): 5–26.

1932 *Colorado River Controversies.* Edited by J. M. Chalfant. Dodd, Mead, New York.

1965 *Down the Colorado*. Edited by D. L. Smith. University of Oklahoma Press, Norman.

1987 *The Colorado River Survey: Robert Brewster Stanton and the Denver, Colorado Canyon and Pacific Railroad.* Edited by Dwight L. Smith and C. Gregory Crampton. Howe Brothers, Salt Lake City.

Stearns, Frederic A.

1931 Rainbow Bridge Exploration Trip via the Colorado River. *Pacific Mutual Life Insurance Co. of California News* (October): 378–83.

Stedman, Raymond W.

1982 *Shadows of the Indian: Stereotypes in American Culture*. University of Oklahoma Press, Norman.

Steen, Charlie R.

1981 Erik Kellerman Reed: A Brief Biography. In *Collected Papers in Honor of Erik Kellerman Reed,* edited by Albert R. Schroeder. Papers of the Archaeological Society of New Mexico 6: 1–14.

Stegner, Wallace

1962 *Beyond the Hundredth Meridian: John Wesley Powell and the Second Opening of the American West*. Houghton, Mifflin, Boston. (Originally published 1954.)

2006 *Clarence Edward Dutton: An Appraisal.* University of Utah Press, Salt Lake City. (Originally published 1936.)

Stein, Mary Anne

1966 An Archaeological Survey of Paiute Mesa, Arizona. Master's thesis, University of Oklahoma, Norman.

1984 Pottery Pueblo: A Tsegi Phase Village on Paiute Mesa, Utah. Doctoral dissertation in anthropology, Southern Methodist University, Dallas.

2009 Recollections from the Glen Canyon Project, Museum of Northern Arizona, 1961 and 1962. Manuscript in author's possession.

Sterling, Keir B., et al. (editors)

1997 *Biographical Dictionary of American and Canadian Naturalists and Environmentalists*. Greenwood Press, Westport, CT.

Steward, John H.

1948–49 Journal of John H. Steward. edited by W.C. Darrah. *Utah Historical Quarterly* 16–17: 181–252.

Steward, Julian H.

1931 The Ceremonial Buffoon of the American Indian. *Papers of the Michigan Academy of Science, Arts and Letters* 14: 187–207. (Reprinted in Julian H. Steward 1977, *Evolution and Ecology: Essays on Social Transformation*, edited by J. C. Steward and R. F. Murphy, pp. 347–65, University of Illinois Press, Urbana.)

1936 Pueblo Material Culture in Western Utah. *University of New Mexico Bulletin* 287: 1–64.

1937 *Ancient Caves of the Great Salt Lake Region.* Bureau of American Ethnology Bulletin no. 116. Washington, D.C.

1938 *Basin-Plateau Aboriginal Sociopolitical Groups.* Bureau of American Ethnology Bulletin no. 120. Washington, D.C.

1940 Native Cultures of the Intermontane (Great Basin) Area. *Smithsonian Miscellaneous Collections* 100: 445–502.

1941 Archaeological Reconnaissance of Southern Utah. *Bureau of American Ethnology Bulletin* 128: 281–356. Washington, D.C.

1977 *Evolution and Ecology: Essays on Social Transformations,* edited by J. C. Steward and R. F. Murphy. University of Illinois Press, Urbana.

Stewart, Omer C.

1987 *Peyote Religion: A History.* University of Oklahoma Press, Norman.

1998 *Cannibalism Is an Acquired Taste; and Other Notes from Conversations with Anthropologist Omer C. Stewart.* University Press of Colorado, Boulder.

Stiles, Jim

1999 Ken Sleight: For Seldom Seen, Tilting Windmills Has Been a Way of Life. *Canyon Zephyr* (August–September). Moab, UT.

Stokes, William L.

1986 *Geology of Utah*. Utah Museum of Natural History Occasional Paper no. 6. Salt Lake City.

Stone, Julius F.

1932 *Canyon Country: The Romance of a Drop of Water and a Grain of Sand.* G. P Putnam's Sons, New York.

Suhm, Dee Ann

1959 Extended Survey of the Right Bank of the Glen Canyon. In *The Glen Canyon Archaeological Survey, Part I,* by Don D. Fowler et al. University of Utah Anthropological Papers no. 39, Glen Canyon Series no. 6, pp. 163–284.

Sumner, John C.

1947 J. C. Sumner's Journal, July 6–August 31, 1869. Edited by W. C. Darrah. *Utah Historical Quarterly* 15: 113–24.

Suran, William C. (editor and transcriber)

2003 *The Brave Ones: The Journals and Letters of the 1911–1912 Expedition Down the Green and Colorado Rivers by Ellsworth L. Kolb and Emery C. Kolb.* Fretwater Press, Flagstaff, AZ.

Swanson, Frederick H.

2007 *Dave Rust: A Life in the Canyons.* University of Utah Press, Salt Lake City.

Sweeney, Catherine L.

1961 Ethnohistoric Study in the Glen Canyon. *Utah Archaeology: A Newsletter* 9(3): 9–13.

1961–62 Weekly Field Reports and Correspondence, Glen Canyon Project. University of Utah Archives. Accession 499, Box 25/12.

Sweeney, Catherine L., and Robert C. Euler

1963 Southern Paiute Archaeology in the Glen Canyon Drainage. *Nevada State Museum Anthropological Papers* 9: 5–9.

Taylor, Walter W.
1945 Letter from 1st Lt. W. W. Taylor, USMC, U.S. Naval Hospital, St Albans, New York. In *Gleanings from the First Fifty Years of Teocentli,* edited by C. R. McGimsey, p. 54. Bulletin of the History of Archaeology, Occasional Papers no. 1.
1948 *A Study of Archaeology.* American Anthropological Association Memoir no. 69.
1949 [Field Notebook] Survey in Tsegi Area, Oct. 6–7, 1949. W. W. Taylor Papers, Box 20, National Anthropological Archives, Smithsonian Institution, Washington, D.C.
1958 *Two Archaeological Studies in Northern Arizona, The Pueblo Ecology Study: Hail and Farewell, and a Brief Survey through the Grand Canyon of the Colorado River.* Museum of Northern Arizona Bulletin 20. Flagstaff.
1988 *Contributions to Coahuila Archaeology: With an Introduction to the Coahuila Project.* Southern Illinois at Carbondale Center for Archaeological Investigations Research Paper no. 52.
2003 *Sandals from Coahuila Caves.* Dumbarton Oaks Studies in Pre-Columbian Art and Archaeology no. 35. Washington, D.C.

Taylor, Walter W., and William Y. Adams
1951 Pueblo Ecology Survey. Permanent Site Record. Unpublished field notes. W. W. Taylor Papers, Box 20. National Anthropological Archives, Smithsonian Institution, Washington, D.C.

Taylor, Walter W., and Robert C. Euler
1980 Obituary: Lyndon Lane Hargrave, 1896–1978. *American Antiquity* 45(3): 477–82.

Thomas, Marcia L.
2004 *John Wesley Powell: An Annotated Bibliography.* Praeger, Westport, CT.

Thompson, A. H.
1875 Report on a Trip to the Mouth of the Dirty Devil River, dated July 30, 1872. In *Explorations of the Colorado River of the West. . . .* by J. W. Powell, pp. 139–145.
1939 *Diary of Almon Harris Thompson, Geographer, Explorations of the Colorado River of the West and Its Tributaries, 1871–1875,* edited by H. E. Gregory. Utah Historical Quarterly 7, nos. 1–3.

Thompson, Gerald
1976 *The Army and the Navajo: The Bosque Redondo Reservation Experiment.* University of Arizona Press, Tucson.

Thompson, Gilbert 1883 Report of Mr. Gilbert Thompson. *U.S. Geological Survey Second Annual Report, 1881–82,* pp. 32–41. U.S. Gov't. Printing Office, Washington, D.C.

Thompson, Raymond H.
2000 An Old and Reliable Authority: An Act for the Preservation of American Antiquities. *Journal of the Southwest* 42(2).
2001 Edward Bridge Danson (1916–2001). *American Anthropologist* 103(4): 1136–38.

Thompson, Raymond H., and Benjamin W. Smith
1996 Samuel Watson Smith 1897–1993. *Kiva* 61(3): 317–31.

Thrapp, Dan (editor)
1990 *Encyclopedia of Frontier Biography.* 3 vols. Arthur H. Clark Co., Spokane.

Tippets, Ruby Noyes
1961 *A Song in Her Heart.* Privately printed, Salt Lake City.

Titiev, Mischa
1939 The Story of Kokopele. *American Anthropologist* 41(1): 91–98.

Tocqueville, Alexis de
1945 *Democracy in America.* 2 vols. Alfred A. Knopf, New York. (Originally published 1835–40.)

Topping, Gary
1984 Harry Aleson and the Place No One Knew. *Utah Historical Quarterly* 52(2): 165–78.
1997 *Glen Canyon and the San Juan Country.* University of Idaho Press, Moscow.

Turner, Christy G., II
1960 Mystery Canyon Survey: San Juan County, Utah, 1959. *Plateau* 32(4): 73–80.
1962a *A Summary of the Archaeological Explorations of Dr. Byron Cummings in the Anasazi Culture Area.* Museum of Northern Arizona Technical Series 5, Glen Canyon Series 32. Flagstaff.
1962b Further Baldrock Crescent Explorations: San Juan County, Utah, 1960. *Plateau* 34(4): 101–12.
1963 *Petrographs of the Glen Canyon Region.* Museum of Northern Arizona Bulletin no. 38, Glen Canyon Series no. 4. Flagstaff.

Turner, Christy G., II, and Maurice E. Cooley
1960 Prehistoric Use of Stone from the Glen Canyon Region. *Plateau* 33(2): 46–53.

Turner, Christy G., II, and William C. Miller
1961 [The] 1960 Northeast Navajo Mountain Survey. *Plateau* 33(3): 57–68.

Tyler, Daniel
2003 *Silver Fox of the Rockies: Delphus E. Carpenter and Western Water Compacts.* University of Oklahoma Press, Norman.

Utah State Historical Society

1980 Register of David E. Miller Papers, 1948–1978. Utah State Historical Society, Salt Lake City.

2000 *The Utah History Suite, Edition 3.* CD. Utah State Historical Society, Salt Lake City.

Utah State University

2010 Guide to the Lowry Nelson Collection, 1918–1974. COLL MSS 17. Utah State University Library, Logan.

Utley, Robert M.

2004 *After Lewis and Clark; Mountain Men and the Paths to the Pacific.* University of Nebraska Press, Lincoln.

Verdoia, Ken

1997 *The Frontier Photographers: The Eyes of the Nation.* KUED Public Television, Salt Lake City/PBS Television, New York.

1999a *Glen Canyon: A Dam, Water and the West.* Documentary film. KUED Public Television, Salt Lake City/PBS Television, New York.

1999b Interview with Ken Sleight. Background to *Glen Canyon: A Dam, Water and the West.* Documentary film. KUED Public Television, Salt Lake City, www.kued.org/productions/GlenCanyon/interview/sleight.html.

Wallace, Edward S.

1955 *The Great Reconnaissance: Soldiers, Artists and Scientists on the Frontier, 1848–1861.* Little, Brown and Co., Boston.

Ward, Albert E.

1999 Charles L. Bernheimer: The Tenderfoot and Cliff Dweller from Manhattan. Introduction to *Rainbow Bridge,* by C. L. Bernheimer. Center for Anthropological Studies Reprint, Albuquerque, pp. 1–52.

Waters, Frank

1946 *The Colorado.* Rinehart and Co., New York.

Webb, Robert H., Jayne Belnap, and John S. Weisheit

2004 *Cataract Canyon: A Human and Environmental History of the Rivers in Canyonlands.* University of Utah Press, Salt Lake City.

Webb, Roy

1989 *Riverman: The Story of Bus Hatch.* Labyrinth Pubs., Rock Springs, WY.

1993 Never Was Anything So Heavenly. *Blue Mountain Shadows: The Magazine of San Juan County History* 12 (Summer): 35–50.

1994 *Call of the Colorado.* University of Idaho Press, Moscow.

2004 "Set My Spirit Free": A History of SOCOTWA. *Confluence 2004*: 1–11.

Webb, Roy (editor)

2005 *High, Wide and Handsome: The River Journals of Norman D. Nevills.* Utah State University Press, Logan.

Webb, Roy, and Brad Dimock

2000 *Galloway to G-Rig: The Evolution of Watercraft on the Green and Colorado.* N.p.

Weber, David J.

1971 *The Taos Trappers: The Fur Trade in the Far Southwest, 1540–1846.* University of Oklahoma Press, Norman.

Weisheit, John

1993 Harry Aleson, River Pioneer. *Boatman Quarterly Review* 6(2), http://www.gcrg.org/bqr/6-2/aleson.htm.

Weller, Ted

1959 San Juan Triangle Survey. In *The Glen Canyon Archaeological Survey, Part II,* by Don D. Fowler et al. University of Utah Anthropological Papers no. 39, Glen Canyon Series no. 6, pp. 543–675.

Welsh, Vince, Cort Conley, and Brad Dimock

1998 *The Doing of the Thing: The Brief Brilliant Whitewater Career of Buzz Holstrom.* Fretwater Press, Flagstaff, AZ.

Wellington, Arthur M.

1889a The Denver, Colorado Canyon and Pacific Railroad Project. *Engineering News and American Railway Journal* 22: 278–79.

1889b Canyons and Railway Lines. *Engineering News and American Railway Journal* 22: 813–14.

Wendorf, Fred

2008 *Desert Days: My Life as a Field Archaeologist.* Southern Methodist University Press, Dallas.

Wendorf, Fred, and Raymond H. Thompson

2002 The Committee for the Recovery of Archaeological Remains: Three Decades of Service to the Archaeological Profession. *American Antiquity* 67(2): 317–30.

Westwood, Richard E.

1992 *Rough-Water Man: Elwyn Blake's Colorado River Expeditions.* University of Nevada Press, Reno and Las Vegas.

1997 *Woman of the River: Georgie White Clark, White-Water Pioneer.* Utah State University Press, Logan.

Wetherill, Benjamin A.

1977 *The Wetherills of Mesa Verde: Autobiography of Benjamin A. Wetherill.* Edited by Maurine S. Fletcher. University of Nebraska Press, Lincoln.

Wetherill, John, Pat M. Flattum, and Frederic A. Stearns
1961 Early Trip up the Colorado from Lee's Ferry to Rainbow Bridge, January 1931, from Wetherill-Flattum-Stearns MS. *Plateau* 34(2): 33–49.

Wetherill, Louisa W., and Byron C. Cummings
1922 A Navaho Folktale of Pueblo Bonito. *Art and Archaeology* 14(3): 132–36.

Wetherill, Marietta
1992 *Marietta Wetherill: Life with the Navajos in Chaco Canyon.* Edited by Kathryn Gabriel. University of New Mexico Press, Albuquerque,

White, Charles A.
1909 John Strong Newberry. *National Academy of Sciences Biographical Memoirs* 6: 1–25.

Whitehall
2004 Whitehall Rowing and Sail—History of the Whitehall, http://www.whitehall.com/legacy, accessed January 15, 2004.

Wickham, Paul
2005–9 Irish McCalla http://terrorstaralis.com/sheena/irish/films/river.htm.

Widtsoe, John
1911 *Dry-Farming: A System of Agriculture for Countries Under A Low Rainfall.* Macmillan Co., New York.
1914 *The Principles of Irrigation Practice.* Macmillan, New York.
1952 *In a Sunlit Land: The Autobiography of John A. Widtsoe.* Deseret News Press, Salt Lake City.
1955 A Journal of the John A. Widtsoe Colorado River Party, Sept. 3–19, 1922 (edited by A. R. Mortensen). *Utah Historical Quarterly* 23(3): 195–231.

Wilkins, Thurman
1958 *Clarence King: A Biography.* Macmillan, New York.

Williams, William F.
1929 Statement of W.F. Williams, 05/22/1929. Rainbow Bridge Collection, Manuscript 239, folder 12. Special Collections, Cline Library, Northern Arizona University, Flagstaff.

Winship, George P. 1896 The Coronado Expedition, 1540–1542. *Fourteenth Annual Report of the Bureau of Ethnology for 1892–93,* pp. 329–613.

Witkind, Irving J.
1975 The Abajo Mountains: An Example of the Laccolithic Groups on the Colorado Plateau. *Four Corners Geological Society Guidebook, 8th Field Conference, Canyonlands,* pp. 245–52.

Witkind, I. J., R. E. Thaden, and C. F. Lough
1952 File Report on the Archaeological Sites in the Monument Valley Area, Arizona. Submitted to Bureau of American Ethnology, Smithsonian Institution. Copy in Taylor Papers, National Anthropological Archives, Smithsonian Institution, Washington, D.C.

Woodbury, Angus M.
1944 A History of Southern Utah and Its National Parks. *Utah Historical Quarterly* 12(3–4): 111–209. (Reprinted 1950 by the author, Salt Lake City.)
1954 *Principles of General Ecology.* Blakiston, New York.
1965 *Notes on the Human Ecology of Glen Canyon.* University of Utah Anthropological Papers 74, Glen Canyon Series 26. Salt Lake City.

Woodbury, Angus M., Stephen D. Durrant, and Seville Flowers
1959 *A Survey of Vegetation in Glen Canyon Reservoir Basin.* University of Utah Anthropological Papers 36, Glen Canyon Series 5. Salt Lake City.

Woodbury, Angus M., et al.
1958 *Preliminary Report of Biological Resources of the Glen Canyon Reservoir.* University of Utah Anthropological Papers 31, Glen Canyon Series 2. Salt Lake City.
1959 *Ecological Studies of Flora and Fauna in Glen Canyon.* University of Utah Anthropological Papers 40, Glen Canyon Series 7. Salt Lake City.

Worster, Donald
1985 *Rivers of Empire: Water, Aridity, and the Growth of the American West.* Oxford University Press, New York and Oxford.
2001 *A River Running West: The Life of John Wesley Powell.* Oxford University Press, New York.

Yochelson, Ellis (editor)
1980 *The Scientific Ideas of Grove Karl Gilbert.* Geological Society of America, Special Paper 183. Boulder, CO.

Young, Robert W., and William Morgan
1980 *The Navajo Language: A Grammar and Colloquial Dictionary.* University of New Mexico Press, Albuquerque.

INDEX

Abbey, Edward, 180, 355
Adams, A. P., 146
Adams, Eileen, 48
Adams, Nettie Kessler, 310, 318–20
Adams, William Y., 229–31, 244, 273, 318
Agassiz, George Russell, 154, 367n49
"Age of Museums," 243
agriculture, and Ancestral Puebloan cultures, 329–30, 333
Aikens, C. Melvin, 264, 265, 294, 306, 307, 312
Alarcón, Hernando de, 14–15
Albright, Horace M., 161, 221–22
Aleson, Harry, 147, 177, 234–37
Alexander, Herbert, 264
Allen, H. Jennings, 138
Allen, Robert N., 190–91
Alvey, Edson, 139, 253, 312
Alvey site, 6
Ambler, J. Richard, 262, 323, 324, 326, 329
American Anthropological Association, 229
American Anthropologist (journal), 202
American Association for the Advancement of Science, 244
American Exploration Society, 221–25
American Journal of Science, 60, 75
American Museum of Natural History (New York), 212
American Placer Corporation, 110
Anasazi, 210, 306, 328. *See also* Ancestral Puebloans; Chaco Canyon
Anasazi Heritage Center, 360n20
Anasazi State Park Museum, 262
Ancestral Puebloans, 210, *329*, 333. *See also* Anasazi; Basketmaker cultures
Anderson, Keith M., 208, 266
Anderson, Robert, 5, 247
Anderson, Roy, 132
Andrews, Amy H., 222
Andrus, James, 63
Animas River, 17
Anthony, De Leon, 170
anthropology, and culture history approach, 308
anticlines, 92
Antiquities Act (1906), 120, 206–7, 244, 245, 353
Anza, Juan Bautista de, 18
Apaches, 334
Archaeological Institute of America (AIA), 203–4, 244
archaeology: author's early training in, 1–2, 5–10; early history of in Glen Canyon Country, 200–31. *See also* Anasazi; Basketmaker cultures; "conjunctive" approach; Glen Canyon Project; historic archaeology; looting; petroglyphs; salvage archaeology; *specific sites*
Archaic cultures, 329
Arches National Park, 118
Arid Lands Report (Powell 1878), 181, 182
Arizona State Museum, 208
Armijo, Antonio, 23
Army Topographical Engineers, 243
Arnold, Thursa, 232

Ary, Janet, 286, 292–93
Ashley, William H., 25–26
Atkinson, Eugene, 164, 165
atlatl, 330
Atomic Energy Commission, 347
Aton, James, 108
Atwood, Wallace, 222
Augusta Bridge, 118–19
Aztec Ruins, 213

Baars, Donald, 100
Babington, Suren H., 223–24
Baird, Spencer, 76
Baker, Charles, 48, 49
Baker, Mildred, 166, 168
Baker, Pearl, 137
Bakker, Gerhard, 177
Bald Rock Crescent, *16*, 322
Barnes, Becky, 178
Barrette, T. J., 294, 306
Bartlett, Katherine, 316
"Basin Province," 75
Basketmaker cultures, 202, 209–10, 213, 303–4, 329–33. *See also* Ancestral Puebloans
Bass, William Wallace, 47–48, 49, 126
Bates, Walter G., 185
Beals, Ralph L., 222, 225, 228
Beaman, E. O., 55–56, 67, 157
Beard, Merle "Peaches," 269
Beauchamp, Bayne, 227
Beaver Creek site, 320, *332*
Beckwith, E. G., 29
Bedonie, La Mar, 336
Begay, Nasja, 123, 126
Behunin, Amanda Monettie, 2
Behunin, Elijah Cutlar, 2, 3, 136
Behunin, Isaac, 2
Behunin, Nettie, 3
Behunin, Tabatha Jane, 136
Bell, Lorin, 166, 167
Bell, William A., 46
Benchmark Cave, 270, 305–6, 329
Bennett, Anne Mariah, 2
Bennett, John W., 223
Benton, Thomas Hart, 25
Berger, Bruce, 349, 351
Bernheimer, Charles L., 155–56, 211–12, 213–14, 322
Bernheimer Alcove, 215, 330
Best, J. D., 110
Betatakin site, 206, 207, 208
Biddlecome, Joe & Millie, 137
biography, of place, 10
Bird, Charles Sumner, 154
Birdseye, Claude, 165, 193, 196
Birney, Herman Hoffman, Jr., 134, 135, 217, 218, 296
Bishop, Francis Marion, 55
Bitsinnies, Fannie, 326
Black, Jim, 109
Black Hawk War (1866–1871), 63
Blake, Henry Elwyn, 191, 192
Bliss, Joe, 117
Blossom, Rose, 159
Bluff City (Utah), 342
boats: and Brown expedition, 105–6; and canoes, 174, 280–81; and early exploration of Colorado River, 25–26; and ferries, 344, *345, 346*; Flavell's design of, 141–42; Galloway's design of, 143, 160, 172; Glen Canyon Project and "San Juan boats," 259–60; and inflatables, 161, 176; and kayaks, 171–72; mining and steamboats, 115–17; Hydes and sweepboats, 159; Nevills and experimental designs for, 164, 165; and Oregon drift boat, 172; and Powell expedition, 40, 41–42, 57, 66, 67, 68; rubber rafts and triple rigs, 178–79; types used by Russell and Monett, 145
Bodenheimer, Peter, 266, 267
Bodfish, Sumner H., 81
Boles, John, 159
Bolton, Herbert Eugene, 255, 359n12
Bonanza Dune, 307
Bonnemort, John, 107
Bonneville, Lake, 93
Borderlands Studies, 255
Boulder Dam, 199
Boulder Mound, 216

Bourke, John Gregory, 80
bow and arrow, 330
Bowles, George, 202
Boyer, Diane E., 190, 194, 196
Boy Scouts, 174–75, 180
Bradbury, Norris, 259
Brady, Matthew, 56
Bradley, George Y., 38–39, 42, 44
Brainerd, George W., 222, 225, 228
Bray, Joseph Randolph, 158
Breasted, James Henry, 309
Breternitz, David, 270, 273, 317
Brew, John Otis, 216–17, 315
Briggs, Henry, 27–28
Bright Angel Trail, 146
Bronson, Fletcher, 346
Brooks, Frank S., 110
Brower, David, 9, 354
Brown, Eliza, 152
Brown, Elizabeth, 186
Brown, Frank, 41, 105
Brugge, David, 317
Buckles, William, 262
Bullard, Benny, 259
Bureau of American Ethnology (BAE), 246
Bureau of Ethnology, 72, 76, 82, 182, 243
Bureau of Reclamation, 186, 245, 250, 269, 335, 337, 354
Burg, Amos, 173, 174
Bush, W. H., 106
Buss, Walter R., 224
Buzenbark, Blaine, 179–80
Byers, William N., 37, 44

Cachupín, Tomás Vélez, 16
Cahn, Charles, 109
Caldwell, R. E., 193
Calhoun, A. R., 46
California: early maps of, 27–28; and Geological Survey of California, 35; and Spanish explorers, 17; U.S. annexation of in 1846, 243. *See also* San Francisco earthquake
Cameron, Ralph, 154
Campbell, Richard, 23
Cannon, George Q., 217
Cannon, Jane, 217
Canyoneers, Inc., 170–71
Canyonlands National Park, 354
Canyon Surveys trio, 232–37
Capitol Reef National Park, 136, 354
Carmel formation, 101
Carnegie Museum (Pittsburgh), 228
Carpenter, Delphus E., 196
Carson, Kit, 334
Cassidy, Butch (George Leroy Parker), 135–37
Cataract Canyon: description of by fur trappers, 23–24; description of by Powell, 53–54; and inscriptions by early explorers, 26
Cedar Mesa sandstone, 99
Central Numic languages, 68
Century Magazine, 118, 121
Cha Canyon, 331–32
Chaco Canyon, 120, 203, 210, 214, 332. *See also* Anasazi
Chaffin, Arthur, 169, 346
chain and compass method, of surveying, 78
Chalfant, James M., 361n33, 364–65n40
Chama River valley, 16
Chapman, Carl, 250
Charles H. Spencer (steamboat), *116*, 117, 152
Chasm of the Colorado (painting), 71
Chemehuevi Indians, 68, 309
Chenowith, William R., 191
Chicago World's Fair (1893), 201
Chinle formation, 99, 100, 115
Christensen, Heber, 191
Christiansen, Rose, 2
chronology: for Ancestral Pueblo cultures, *329*; relative versus absolute for culture history of Southwest, 327
Chu, Lee Moi, 178
Chuarumpeak (Kaibab Paiute), 68–69
Civil Works Administration (CWA), 245
Claflin, William F., Jr., 215–17, 261
Claflin-Emerson expeditions, 215–17
Clark, Georgie. *See* White, Georgie

Clegg, Edith, 173
Cliff Palace, 200
climate: and Ancestral Puebloan cultures, 333; Glen Canyon Project and description of, 254; and possibility of future natural draining of Lake Powell, 357. *See also* flash floods
Clinton, Bill, 353
Clogston, John, 191
Clover, Elzada U., 164–68
coal, and mining, 115, 117
coccidioidomycosis, 210, 289
Cogswell, Raymond A., 148
Colburn, Justin E., 70
Collett, Reuben, 340–41
Collier, Donald, 222
Collier, John, 222, 225
Collier, Malcolm Carr, 335
Colorado Canyon Railroad, 114
Colorado River: early exploration of by watercraft, 25–26; early maps of, 27–28; formation of system, 102; plans for harnessing of, 181–99; and Powell expedition, 41–44; and railroads, 103–7; and Spanish explorers, 14–22. *See also* Glen Canyon Dam; river running; water resources
Colorado River Aqueduct, 199
Colorado River Compact (1922), 193–97, 354
Colton, Harold S., 222, 306, 316, 328
Colton, Mary Russell Ferrel, 316
Comanche language, 68
Comb Monocline, 92
Committee for the Recovery of Archaeological Remains (CRAR), 246, 249
conflict, and Ancestral Puebloan cultures, 333
Congressional Record, 188
"conjunctive" approach, to archaeology, 229
Conley, Cort, 173
Conroy, Maurice, 4
conservation movement, and protections for public lands, 120
contour intervals, and mapping, 78, 362n15
controversies, about Powell expedition, 44–52
Conway, Johnny, 301, 303
Cooley, Maurice, 9, 259, 273, 333
Coombs, Ephraim, 261
Coombs site, 261–63
Coon, Wayne, 266, 267–68
Cooper, Joe, 346
copper, and mining, 109
Corbett, John M., 248, 249
Coronado, Francisco Vásquez de, 14–16
corrasion, and erosion as land-shaping force, 93
cosmology, and Navajo, 336–37
Cosmopolitan Magazine, 103
Cousins, Peter, 264
Crampton, C. Gregory, 9, 249, 255, 280, 343
Creeping Dune site, 276, 292, 331
Creer, Leland H., 257
Cressman, Luther, 248
Cretaceous period, 101, 102
Cross, John, 147, 175
Crossing of the Fathers, 20, 344
cultural history school, of anthropology, 308
cultural resources management, 249
Cummings, Byron, 119–20, 121, 122, 203–6, 316
Cummings, Calvin R., 320
Cummings, Malcolm, 205–8
Cummings Mesa, 101, 321, 323
Cutler Group, 99
Cutler, Hugh, 168, 306
Cutter, Victor M., Jr., 168

dams: Congressional hearings on, 199; and hydroelectric power, 185–86; plans for on Colorado River, 187–93. *See also* Glen Canyon Dam
Dana, James Dwight, 363n31
Dance Hall Rock, *340*, 341
Danson, Edward B., Jr., 249, 317, 325
Dark Canyon, 197
Darrah, William Culp, 39, 48
Davis, Arthur Powell, 36, 81, 186–87, 192–93, 194, 195, 196, 197–99
Davis, D. W., 196
Davis, E. S., 242
Davis, Jefferson, 32

Davis, Millard, 264
Davis Dam, 199
Day, Kent, 312
Dead Sea, 352
Dean, Emma, 36, 38
DeBuys, William, 192
De Chelly sandstone, 99
De Colmont, Bernard & Genevieve, 171–72
defensive structures, and Ancestral Puebloan cultures, 333
Defiance House, 283, *285*, *287*, 328, 333, *353*
Dellenbaugh, Frederick S., 47–48, 52, 55, 56, 59, 61, 63–64, 91
Dennis, H. W., 193
Department of the Interior, 188
Desert Culture, 248, 329
De Seyne, Antoine, 171–72
Desha Complex, 329
Díaz, Melchior, 15
Dibble, Charles, 247
Dibble, David, 275, 276, 287, 301
Dice of God, The (Birney 1952), 217–18
Dickinson, Alf, 109
Diehl, Dorothy, 325, 326
Dimmock, C. H., 35
Dimock, Brad, 160, 171, 173
Dinosaur National Monument, 354
dinosaur tracks, 101
Dirty Devil River, 34, 62–67. *See also* Fremont River
Disaster Falls, 42
Dittert, Alfred E., Jr., 273
Dodds, Pardon, 63, 65, 107
Dodge, Homer Levi, 174
Dodge, Richard Elwood, 94
Dogi (Navajo guide), 133
Dolores River, 17
Domínguez, Francisco Atanasio, 17–22, 42, 255, 307, 343, 359n12
Dominy, Floyd E., 199, 355
Douglass, A. E., 226
Douglass, William B., 120–21, 122–23, 206–8
downcutting, and erosional forces, 102, 333
Doyle, Al, 126
Dubendorff, Seymour S., 148, 149–50
Dunn, William, 38, 39, 40, 43, 45, 49–52
Durrant, Stephen David, 257–58
Dust Devil Cave, 325, 329
Dutton, Bertha, 310
Dutton, Clarence E., 80–81, 84, 85–89, 149, 184
Dyar, W. W., 118

Earl, Tabatha Jane, 2
Eaton, Theodore H., Jr., 223
Echo Park dam, 354
ecological surveys, and Glen Canyon Project, 257–58
Eddy, Clyde, 158–59, 161
Edison Company, 150
education, of author, 4–5
Egloffstein, Friedrich, 25, 29, 31, 34–35, 360n22
Egypt, and salvage archaeology, 244
Ellingson, Malcolm, 175
Ellsworth, Elmer Ephraim, 65–66
Emerson, Raymond, 215–17, 261
Emmett, Bill, 146
Enger, Walter M., 223
Englemann, George, 29
erosion, and geology of Glen Canyon, 93, 102
Escalante, Silvestre Vélez de, 17–22, 42, 255, 307, 343, 359n12
Escalante River, 60, 62
Escalante Ruin, 360n20
Escalante, town of (Utah), 297–300, 337–38
ethnoarchaeology, and Glen Canyon Project, 9, 307–13
ethnography: and author's research on Shoshone of Wind River Indian Reservation, 304; and Powell expedition, 69, 72
Euler, Robert C., 49, 270, 309–10, 312
Evans, Larry, 5
Explorer (steamboat), 28–29, 30–31

Facing Your Danger (movie), 170
Fagen, James, 150
Fall, Albert, 196
falling dunes, 49, *98*, 291, *292*

family, biographical information on author's, 2–4
Faraday, Michael, 186
Farquhar, Francis P., 221, 370–71n118
faults, and geology, 74
Federal Power Commission, 199
Fennemore, James, 56, 63, 67, 344
Ferris, Charles, 23
Ferris, Warren A., 23–24, 359n28
Fewkes, Jesse Walter, 155, 207, 208
Field, Eugene, 317
field directors, of Rainbow Bridge-Monument Valley Expedition, 225–27
"field houses," 305
field labs, and Glen Canyon Project, 325–26
Firebrand River (Río del Tizón), 15
"fire pits," 305
Flaming Gorge Dam, 199
Flaming Gorge Project, 249
flash floods, 168, 278
Flattum, Pat, 161, 162, 221
Flavell, George F., 141–43
Flavell, Roland, 141
Fletcher, John Gould, 205, 208
Flowers, Seville, 258
Floyd, John B., 32
Flute Player House, 209
Ford Motor Company, 222
Forgotten Cañon (Birney 1934), 217
Forgotten Canyon, 280–81, 283, *285*
"Fort Moqui" (Watch Tower), 276, *277*, 333
Foster, Gene, 317
Fowke, Gerard, 244
Fowler, Catherine. *See* Sweeney, Catherine
Fowler, Eldon C., 2, 4
Fowler, James, 2
Fowler, Mark Charles, 293
Fowler, Vance, 4, 303, 306
Fowler, William, 2
Franklin, Ansel, 220–25
Fraser, George Corning, 154–55, 156
Fraser, George Corning, Jr., 154
Fraser, Jane, 155
Fraser, Sarah, 156
Frazier, Russell, 68, 160–61
Freeman, Lewis, 193
Frémont, Jessie Benton, 25
Frémont, John Charles, 21, 24–25, 27, 28
Fremont culture, 210, 216, 333
Fremont River, 25, 54. *See also* Dirty Devil River
Frost, Jack, 164
Frost, Kent, 170
fur trappers, and fur trade, 22–24, 25–26. *See also* mountain men

Gallatin, Albert, 28
Galligan, Elizabeth, 325
Galloway, Nathaniel, 112, 143–44, 148, 153
Galloway, Parley, 143, 158, 160
Gambee, Martin, 224
Gannett, Henry, 77, 81–82, 187
Garcés, Francisco Hermenegildo, 18
Garfield, James, 50, 76, 182
Garlick, Charles, 36, 81
Garlick, Eliza, 36
Gates, Loyd, 6, 7, 139, 253, 264, 295, 312, 326
Gates Roost site, 7, 251, 333
Geib, Phil, 305, 329
General Land Office (GLO), 120–21, 181
Geographical Review, 122
Geological Survey of California, 35
geology: and Powell's descriptions of Glen Canyon Country, 74–75; and research of Dutton and Gilbert, 84–93; status of in twentieth century, 94–102. *See also* anticlines; falling dunes; gold mining and gold rush; laccoliths; natural bridges and arches
geophysics, 93
Ghiglieri, Michael, 360n1
Gibbons, Fred, 149
Gibson, Gordon, 247
Gibson, Wilbur (Bill), 165
Gignoux, Natalie, 349, 351
Gilbert, Grove Karl, 13–14, 34, 62, 65, 84, 89–93, 363n31
Girl Scouts, 310
Glen Canyon: and Holmstrom's Colorado River trips, 174; Lake Powell and disappearance of, 352–54; mourning of disappearance, 354–57; and

photography by river runners, 149–50; Powell and naming of, 60; sites considered for dams in, 197–98; Steward's description of, 219. *See also* Glen Canyon Country; Glen Canyon Dam; Glen Canyon National Recreational Area; Glen Canyon Project

Glen Canyon Country: and biography of place, 10; definition of, 11, *12*; early archaeology in, 200–31; early explorers of, 11–26; and ecological surveys, 257–58; geology of in twentieth century, 94–102; geology of and work of Dutton and Gilbert, 84–93; and gold mining, 107–17; and harnessing of Colorado River, 181–99; images of in popular culture, 118–39; and imagination, 348–57; knowledge about precontact societies of in 1968–69, 327–47; and mapping of, *12*, 27–35, 61–62, 76–83, 190–92; Powell and exploration of, 36–72; Powell and U.S. Geological Survey, 73–83; river running and recreational exploration of, 140–80, 232–41. *See also* Glen Canyon; Glen Canyon Dam; Glen Canyon Project

Glen Canyon Dam, 10, 199, 348, *350*. *See also* Powell (Lake)

Glen Canyon Group, 99

Glen Canyon Institute, 356, 357

Glen Canyon National Recreational Area, 353, 354

Glen Canyon Project: author's early involvement with, 8–9; beginnings of, 242–58; and ecological surveys, 257–58; and fieldwork in 1958, 251–55; and fieldwork in 1959 and 1960, 275–93; and fieldwork in 1961 and 1962, 294–326; and historical surveys, 255; implementation of, 259–74; and Museum of Northern Arizona, 316–26

Glory Guys, The (movie 1965), 218

gold mining and gold rush, in Glen Canyon Country, 107–17, 346

Goldwater, Barry, 168–70

Goodman, Frank Valentine, 39, 42

Goodman, Paul, 336

Gothic Arch, *120*

Gould, Richard, 287, 294

Graham, Charles, 201

Graham, Dick, 6

Grand Canyon: and Dave Rust, 153–57; erosion and downcutting in formation of, 102; first published descriptions of, 31, 32

Grand Canyon of the Yellowstone (painting), 71

Grand Gulch, 201

Grand Staircase–Escalante National Monument, 83, 87, 102, 353

Graves, W. H., 91

"Great American Desert," concept of, 26

Great Basin Anthropological Conference, 312

Great Depression (1930s): and gold rush, 117; and salvage archaeology, 245

Greatest Story Ever Told, The (movie), 348–49, 351–52

"Great Gambler, The" (Navajo), 124–25

great houses, and Chaco Canyon, 332

"Great Surveys," 73

Green River, 24, 197

Gregory, Herbert Ernest, 92, 94–98, 121, 133, 169, 222

Grey, Zane, 123, 125–32, 136–37, 154, 365n20, 365n26, 365n28, 366n29, 366n39

Griffin, Cecil, 295

Griffin, Claren, 297

Griffith, John, 135

Grimm, Dick, 266

"ground truthing," and historical surveys, 255

Grover, Nathan Clinton, 189–90

Guernsey, Samuel, 208–9, 210

"gumshoe survey," 263

Gunnerson, James, 5–8, 251, 261, 264–66, 273, 300

Gunnison, James, 42

Gunsight Butte, 8, 20, 59

Hall, Andrew, 40

Hall, Ansel, 228

Hall, Charles, 340, 341

Hall, Edward T., Jr., 222, 225

Hall, E. Raymond, 257

Hall, James, 29, 44, 85

Hall's Creek, 262–63

Hamblin, Jacob, 50, 52, 62, 63, 65, 343–44

Hammond, Blodwen, 335

Hanks, James, 132, 366n47

Happy Jack Mine, 346

Hardy, Vilate, 311
Hargrave, Lyndon L., 221, 222, 225–27, 229, 316–17
Harper, S. S., 105
Harrington, Jean Carl, 256
Harrington, Mark R., 245, 306
Harris, LaPhene (Don), 147, 165, 170
Harris-Brennan River Expeditions, 170
Harris Wash, 294
Hartan, Andrew J., 55, 56
Harvard University. *See* Peabody Museum
Hatch, Ada, 325, 326
Hatch, Don, 161
Hatch, Ira, 344
Hatch, Robert Rafael (Bus), 160–61, 354
Hatch, Ted, 161
Hatch Expeditions, 161
Haury, Emil, 248
Havasupai people, 334
Hawkins, William Rhodes, 38, 39, 43, 44, 51
Hay, Billy, 174
Hayden, Ferdinand Vandeveer, 29, 73, 76
Hayden, Julian, 270
Heald, K. C., 94, 121
heliograph station, on Navajo Mountain, 82, 132–33
Heltagito Rockshelter, 317
Henry, Joseph, 57, 89, 186
Henry Mountains, *15*, 60, 65, 89–92
Heritage of the Desert (Grey 1910), 126–27, 130
Hermitage, 329
Hettinga, Irene, 178
Hewett, Edgar Lee, 203, 204
Hillers, John K., 56–57, 63, 65, 66, 67, 68, 70, 71–72, 79–80, 91, 157
Hislop, John, 141
historical surveys, and Glen Canyon Project, 255
historic archaeology, 256
Historic Sites Act (1935), 246
Hite, Cass, 106, 108, 110, 118, 146, 149, 345–47
Hite, John, 151
Hobler, Philip, 324, 326
Hodge, Frederick Webb, 214–15
Hohokam culture, 210, 327–28
Hole-in-the-Rock, 338–43
Holgate, Eugene, 323
Holmes, William Henry, 66, 88–89, 200
Holmstrom, Haldane (Buzz), 166, 172–74
Homer, Winslow, 41
Homestead Act of 1862, 181
Honaker brothers, 145
Honaker Trail formation, 99
Hoover, Grace E., 222
Hoover, Herbert, 199
Hopi, 18, 22, 68
Horsefly Hollow Site, 289, *290*
Hoskininni (Navajo), 107, 108, 334
Hoskininni Mining Company, 110, 111, 113, 114, 115, 148
Hough, Walter, 121
Howells, James, 135
Howland, Oramel G., 38, 39, 40, 43, 45, 50–52, 55
Howland, Seneca, 38, 39, 43, 45, 50–52, 55
Hoyt, John Clayton, 189
Hubbell, Lorenzo, 225
Humboldt, Alexander von, 21, 28, 29
Hunt, Charles, 13–14
Hunt, Charles Butler, 91–92
Hunt, Ernest, 164
Hunt, Leigh, 191
Hunter, Jane, 180
Husted, Wilfred, 262, 278
Hyde, Frederick A., Frederick Jr., and Talbot, 201
Hyde, Glen & Bessie, 159
Hyde, Hugh, 191
hydroelectric power, and dam building, 185–86

Illustrated American, The (magazine), 201
Imperial Valley (California), 192
Indian Joe, 118
Ingalls, George, 69
Inscription House, 205–6, 208
International Congress of Geologists, 78, 362n15
irrigation systems, 182, 183. *See also* water resources
Ives, Joseph Christmas, 29, 30–31, 32

Jacka, Robert, 306
Jackson, Helen Hunt, 127
Jackson, James W., 66

Jackson, William Henry, 71, 88, 200
Jaeger, Oscar, 158
Jake, Carl & Minnie, 310–11
Jameson, Rachel, 147
Jayne, Fred, 161
Jean, Jim, 179–80
Jeffers, Le Roy, 155
Jennings, David, 253, 306
Jennings, Herbert, 253
Jennings, Jesse D.: author's first meetings with, 1, 5, 6; and Depression-era archaeology projects, 245; and Glen Canyon Project, 8, 242, 246–48, 249–50, 253, 254, 256–57, 259–60, 268, 270, 271–73, 275, 289, 291, 309; and pottery classification, 328
Johnson, Ezekiel (Zeke), 96, 156, 211, 213–14
Johnson, Joel H., 211
Johnson, Warren, 103, 344
Johnson, Willis, 173
Johnson Canyon, 307
Jones, Charles, 215
Jones, Charles Jesse "Buffalo," 125–26, 154
Jones, Kevin, 139
Jones, Stephen Vandiver, 55, 57, 107
Jorgensen, Joe, 266
Jotter, Lois, 164, 165, 167, 168
Judd, Neil M., 119, 121, 123, 125, 205, 208, 214–15, 244–45, 272
Julien, Denis, 26
Julien, Etienne, 26
Jurassic era, 100–101, 102

Kaibab Indians, 68–69
Kaibab Plateau, 75
Kaiparowits Plateau, *17*: and Clyde Kluckhohn, 132–35; and early archaeological expeditions, 216; and Glen Canyon Project, 8, 264–66, 295–97; and pueblos, 330–31; and Zane Grey's novels, 129
Kanab (Utah), 269
Kane Creek, 59
Kawaiisu language, 68
Kayenta formation, 99–100
Kayenta region, 210
Kayenta subdivision, of Anasazi, 328
Keane, Ed, 301, 303
Kearns, Charles, 324
Keet Seel, 202, 208, 369n15
Kelley, Tracy Randall, 82
Kelly, Charles, 26, 68, 135–36, 137, 217, 218
Kelly, Isabel T., 308–9
Kent, William, 5
Keplinger, Lewis W., 51
Kerns, Virginia, 218
Kidder, Alfred Vincent, 202, 205, 208–9, 210, 225, 229, 328
Kincaid Act, 192
King, Clarence, 35, 38, 73, 76, 78, 182
King, Willie, 326
Kino, Eusebio, 255
kinship, and Navajo, 335
Kiste, Bob, 278
kivas, 208
Kleinerman, Isaac, 313
Kluckhohn, Clyde, 124, 128, 132–35, 228, 297, 366n41
Knipmeyer, James, 136
Knowles, Emery, 118
Knox, F. S., 113
Koehler, Arnold, Jr., 155
Kokopelli, 209
Kolb, Ellsworth, 150–52, 154, 157, 191
Kolb, Emery, 150–52, 154, 156, 157, 160, 166, 191
Koloseike, Alan D., 294
Kosse, Alan, 306
Kroeber, A. L., 222, 255, 308

Labrum, Dale, 175
laccoliths, 91, 101, 363n31
La Farge, Oliver, 209
Lago, Don, 39, 51
La Harpe, Bernard de, 28
Lake Canyon, 284, 288–89, 291, 292, *293*
Lamb, Sydney, 304
Lance, John, 333
Land Act of 1804, 181
Lang, Charles, 201
Langbein, Walter B., 199
languages, Numic family of, 68, 334

Lankin, Gus, 38
La Plata River, 17
Larabee, Charles, 168
La Rue, Eugene C., 156, 158, 188–89, 190, 191, 193, 194–95, 197–99
Lasky, Jesse L., 126, 130
Laughter, Floyd, 318, 323, 336
Lauzon, Bert, 152
Lava Falls, 43
Lavender, David, 143
Leche-e Rock, 59
Ledbetter, Jeri, 160
Lee, Emma, 344
Lee, John D., 51, 56, 67, 83, 344
Lee, Kathryn (Katie), 237–41, 354–55, 357, 372n12
Lee, Ronald, 247
Lee's Ferry (Utah), 343–45
Levy, Jerrold, 335
Libby, Willard, 248
Lincoln, Abraham, 66
Lindsay, Alexander J., Jr., 208, 242, 273, 319, 320–21, 322, 323, 324, 325, 328
Lindsay, Jane, 325
lining, of boats through rapids, 42
Lint, Leigh, 192
Lipe, William D., 266, 273, 276, 277, 283, 285, 287, 288, 301, 328
Lister, Florence, 262
Lister, Robert, 139, 251–55, 260, 261–63, 273, 283–84
literature, and structure of Zane Grey's novels and stories, 127
Lizard Alcove, 329
Lobo Arch, *252*
Lockett, Hattie Greene, 371n148
Lockett, Henry Claiborne, 137, 227–28
Lone Star Ranger, The (movie), 130
Long, Horace J., 118
Long, Paul, 324
Long-Salt, Robert, 336
Long's Peak (Colorado), 26, 38
Long Walk (Navajo), 334
looting, of archaeological sites, 206–7, 244
Loper, Bert, 108, 144–48, 149, 151, 156, 174, 175, 190–91, 192, 345
Loper, Jehail, 144
Loper Ruin, 271, 276
"lost mine" stories, 107
Lost Pueblo (Grey 1954), 129–30
Luckert, Karl, 336, 337
Lynch, Thomas, 294, 314

MacNeish, Richard S., 223
Macomb, John Navarre, 32–34
Mance, Henry Christopher, 82
mapping, of Glen Canyon Country, *12*, 27–35, 61–62, 76–83, 190–92. *See also* surveying
Marble Canyon, 54, 106
Marston, Otis (Dock), 140, 322
Martin, Paul S., 224
Martin, Russell, 249, 348, 354
Martineau, Lavan, 311
Mason, Charlie, 200–201, 202
Mather, Stephen, 156
Mathews, Thomas, 261, 263–64, 271, 273
Matley, John, 72
Matthews, Washington, 335
McCalla, Irish, 178
McCormick, George, 109
McCourt, Tom, 347
McDuffie, Duncan, 221
McGimsey, Charles R., 250
McGregor, John C., 316, 328
McLoyd, Charles, 201
McMurrin, Sterling, 5
McNitt, Frank, 203
McPherson, Robert, 108
Mead, Elwood, 196–97
"meander method," of surveying, 77
Meek, Fielding B., 32
"Mericats," 337
Merrick, James, 107
Mesa Verde area, 210
Mesken, Edward, 110
Mettler, America, 144

Mexican Hat Expeditions, 238
Mexico: independence of and opening of Santa Fe Trail, 22; U.S. invasion of in 1846 and annexation of New Mexico and California, 243
Meyers, Joan, 192
Middle Park country, 37
Miera y Pacheco, Bernardo, 18, 21
Mikkelsen, Norma, 273
Mikkelsen, Robert, 5
Miller, David E., 337, 339, 343, 375n42
Miller, William C., 318, 324
Mills, W. R., 110
mining. *See* coal; copper; gold mining and gold rush; silver; uranium
Miser, Hugh D., 190–91
Mitchell, Earnest, 107
Mix, Tom, 311–12
Moenkopi formation, 99, 100
Mogollon cultures, 210, 328
Moki-Mac river-running company, 175, 357
Möllhausen, Heinrich Balduin, 29, 31
Monett, Edwin R., 145, 146
monoclines, 92
Mono language, 68
Monterey (ship), 28
Monument Valley, 209, 219–28
Moody, Martha, 178
Moore, Raymond, 92, 155
Moorehead, Warren, 201
Moqui Canyon, 285, 291–92, 294, 301–4, 330
Moran, Thomas, 70–72, 88
Morgan, Dale, 25, 304
Morley, Sylvanus Griswold, 205, 208
Mormons: and Boy Scouts, 175; and Hole-in-the-Rock, 338–43; and militia companies, 63; Navajo and missionaries, 326; and Powell expedition, 50–51; and settlements in Glen Canyon Country, 337–38; and water allocation, 183; youth groups and Colorado River trips, 175–76; and Zane Grey, 126
"Mormon War" (1858), 30, 50
Morris, Earl Halstead, 208, 212–14
Morris, Jon, 294
Morrison formation, 101
Morss, Noel, 216, 261, 322
Mosely, Michael F., 320
Moss, John, 200
motion-picture cameras, 150
"Mound Builders," 242–43
Mountain Meadows Massacre (1857), 50, 51, 344
mountain men, 39. *See also* fur trappers
movies: and Glen Canyon Country as setting for *The Greatest Story Ever Told*, 348–49, 351–52; and images of outlaws in Glen Canyon Country, 137; and river running, 157–59; of Zane Grey novels, 130–32. *See also* motion-picture cameras
Mud Hole Spring, 296, 300
Mukuntuweap National Monument, 367n50
Mulder, William, 275, 285
mules, and Glen Canyon Project, 296
Mulroy, Mary, 262, 311
Muñiz, Andrés, 18
Murphy, Robert, 304
Murphy, Roger, 175
museum(s), and collection of ethnographic and archaeological materials in nineteenth century, 243–44
Museum of New Mexico, 249
Museum of Northern Arizona, 242, 249, 316–26, 327. *See also* Glen Canyon Project
Music Temple, 59, *67*, 285
Mystery Canyon, 106, 322
mythology: and Navajo, 124–25; and Powell's work with Southern Paiutes, 57, 61
myths, about Powell expedition, 44–52

Nasja Mesa, 322
National Defense Education Act (NDEA), 275
National Environmental Policy Act (1969), 250–51
National Geographic Magazine, 118, 119, 121, 122, 139, 214, 215
National Geographic Society, 214
National Historic Preservation Act (1966), 250
national monuments, 120, 207, 244
national parks, 120
National Park Service, 242, 246, 249, 322, 326, 337

National Research Council (NRC), 245
National Science Foundation, 250, 294
natural bridges and arches, 118–23. *See also* Rainbow Bridge
Natural Bridges National Monument, *119*, 121, 211
Navajo: arrival of in Southwest, 334–35; and Clyde Kluckhohn, 132; and early archaeology in Glen Canyon Country, 205, 208; and Glen Canyon Project, 324, 325–26; and Rainbow Bridge, 124; and silver working, 107; society and ideology of, 335–37
Navajo Dam, 199
Navajo formation, 101
Navajo Mountain, *16*: and Bernheimer expeditions, 212; and Clyde Kluckhohn, 132–33; and myth of heliograph station, 82, 132–33; and Navajo, 335; and Powell expedition, 58, 60; and Spanish explorers, 20
Navajo National Monument, 207–8
Navajo Nation Monument Valley Park, 354
Navajo Reservoir Project, 249
Navajo Sandstone, 100, 241
Nelson, Ernest, 336
Nelson, Lowry, 337, 338
Nelson, Nels, 208
"Nemo" inscriptions, 138–39
Nevills, Doris Drown, 163, 164, 168, 170
Nevills, Mary (Mae) Davies, 163
Nevills, Norm, 163–71
Nevills, William A., 163
Nevills, William (Billy) E., 163
Newberry, John Strong, 24, 28, 29–30, 31–34, 89–90, 93
Newell, Frederick H., 185, 188
Newhall, Frederick, 187
Newlands, Francis, 187
Nez, Buster Hastiin, 336
Nichols, Edward Tatnall (Tad), 237–41
Nichols, James, 260–61, 263, 273
Nims, Franklin L., 103–4, 106, 157, 344
Nixon, Richard, 251
Nordenskiöld, Gustaf, 201
Northern Arizona Society of Science and Art, 316
Northern Periphery, 210
North Fork ("Secret Canyon"), 301
Noyes, Fred, 3, 136
Noyes, John Humphrey, 3
Noyes, Nettie, 117, 136
Noyes, Ruby, 4
Numic language family, 68, 333–34
Nusbaum, Jesse, 218, 222, 372n24
Nyswander, Dorothy, 217

Oastler, Frank & Maude, 156
O'Brien, John, 82
O'Dea, Thomas, 5
Old Spanish Trail, 22, 32, 339, 340
"Old Ute" trail, 63
Oliver, Wesley, 191
Olsen, Chet, 264
Olsen, Jennings, 5
Ortelius, Abraham, 27
Osborn, Henry Fairfield, 149
Osborn, S. E., 200
O'Sullivan, Timothy, 38, 56, 90, 157
outlaws, and popular images of Glen Canyon Country, 135–37
"Outlaw Trail," 137
Owens, Jim, 154

Pace, Eli, 51
Pacific Railroad, and surveys in 1850s, 35
Pack Creek Ranch, 180
Pahgahrit, Lake, 291, 333, 341
Paige, Sidney, 191
Paiute Mesa, 321, 325
Paiutes: and Rainbow Bridge, 124; and Spanish explorers, 19, 22. *See also* Southern Paiutes
Paleo-Archaic peoples, 329
Palmer, Lyle, 291
Palmer, William Jackson, 31
Panamint language, 68
Paramount Pictures, 130
Paria Canyon, 20
Parker Dam, 199
"Park Province," 75

Parry, C. C., 46
Parunuweap Canyon, 307
Pathé-Bray Company, 158–59
Pattie, James Ohio, 23
Paviotso language, 68
Peabody Museum (Harvard University), 208, 209, 215–17
Pecos Classification, 210, 327
Pecos Conference, 270–71
Pecos Ruin, 209
Pectol, E. P., 216
Pendergast, David & Esther, 314
Pennington, Leslie, 294
Petrified Forest National Monument, 99
Petrified National Forest, 120
petroglyphs, 149, 209, 241, *286*, 333. *See also* rock art
Philadelphia Centennial Exposition of 1876, 72, 76
photographs and photography: and Glen Canyon Project, 267–68; and Powell expedition, 55–56, 67–68, 70–72; and river running groups, 145, 149, 150, 152, 240. *See also* motion-picture cameras
Pierson, Lloyd, 259
Pisani, Donald, 182, 197
pit houses, 330
Pitot, James, 28
place, biography of, 10
Plateau Province, geology of, *85*, 88, 92–93, 98–100
plate tectonics, 101
Pogue, Joseph E., 94–95, 121, 122, 123
politics, and establishment of Glen Canyon Project, 249–51
Pollock, Joe, 312
Pond, Alonzo W., 224
popular culture, and images of Glen Canyon Country, 118–39
portaging, of boats around rapids, 42
Porter, Calvin, 49, 294
Porter, Eliot, 9, 11, 240, 354
Pottery Pueblo, 326
pottery "types," and index artifacts in southwestern Pueblo archaeology, 328
Powell, Lake, 10, 335, 347, 348, *350*, 352–54
Powell, Clem, 67
Powell, Ellen, 36
Powell, John Davis, 186
Powell, John Wesley: and *Arid Lands Report* of 1878, 181, 182; author's interest in, 9; biographical materials on, 360n1; and Bureau of Ethnology, 182, 243; and early descriptions of Cataract Canyon, 24; and exploration of Glen Canyon Country, 36–72; and G. K. Gilbert, 90; on gold mining, 107; and Music Temple, 285; and Public Lands Commission, 182; on Stanton's plan for railroad, 106; U.S. Geological Survey and geology of Glen Canyon Country, 73–84, 85, 86; and water resources, 182–84
Powell, Joseph, 36
Powell, Martha Ann, 186
Powell, Walter Clement, 56, 59
Powell, Walter Henry, 40
Preemption Act of 1841, 181
Preuss, Charles, 28
Price, John, 263
Priestley, J. B., 123–24
Proctor, J. P. and Elizabeth, 156
Prudden, Theophilus Mitchell, 202, 330
publication, of reports from Glen Canyon Project, 254, 258, 271–73, 327
Public Lands Commission, 182
pueblo(s), and Kaiparowits Plateau, 330–31. *See also* Ancestral Puebloans; Hopis; Zuni
Pueblo Ecology Project (1951–52), 228–31
Purdy, William, 262
Purtymun, Elmer, 233
Pyramid Lake (Nevada), 352

quad sheets, and mapping, 78
Quartaroli, Richard, 171
Quist, Albert, 175
Quist, Bob, 175, 357
Quist, Clair, 175, 357
Quist, Goddard, 147
Quist, Richard, 175, 357

Raibourne, Downey, 6, 263–64
railroads, 35, 103–7

Rainbow Bridge, *17*, 121–25, 206–8, 335–37, 365n26, 365n28
Rainbow Bridge National Monument, 354
Rainbow Bridge-Monument Valley Expedition (RBMVE), 219–28
Rainbow Trail, The (Grey 1915), 127–28, 130
Randolph, Edward, 118
Rasmussen, Stan, 259
Rattlesnake Point, 8
Reclamation Act (Newlands Act 1902), 187–88, 193
Reclamation Service, 188, 192, 196, 245
Redford, H. E. D., 5
Reed, Erik Kellerman, 248, 249, 270, 273
Reed, William & James, 26
Reeder, Bill, 147
Rehab Center, 330
Reid, Dell, 166, 168
Reilly, P. T., 343
Reisner, George, 244
reservation, and Navajo, 334. *See also* Wind River Indian Reservation
Reservoir Salvage Act (1969), 250
Richardson, Frank, 55
Richardson, Hubert, 134
Richmond, William, 143
Riders of the Purple Sage (Grey 1912), 126, 130
Rigg, Jim, 170
Riley, George, 107
Rinaldo, John B., 222
Rio Grande, and Spanish settlement, 16
Ritchie, Norman, 262, 264, 266
Rivera, Juan María Antonio, 16–17, 18
River Basins Surveys program, 246
River Goddesses (film 1950), 177–79
rivers and river running: and Canyon Surveys trio, 232–37; definition of "navigable," 246; during years of Glen Canyon Project, 140; early history of, 141–57; and filming of canyons, 157–59; and Georgie White, 176–79; and Hatch Expeditions, 160–61; and historical surveys for Glen Canyon Project, 256; and Hyde family, 159–60; and implementation of Glen Canyon Project, 259–60; in post-World War II period, 174–75; and Rainbow Bridge, 161–62; and Rainbow Bridge-Monument Valley Expedition, 227–28; and SOCOTWA organization, 175–76; sources of information on, 366n2; and trips in 1937 and 1938, 162–74; by Wright, Lee, and Nichols in 1952, 237–41. *See also* boats; Powell, John Wesley
Roads to Ruin (Birney 1930), 217
Robber's Roost, 135–37
Robbins, Lynn, 266
Robbins, Sterling, 264
Roberts, David, 139
Roberts, Frank H. H., Jr., 246
Roberts, Henry, 216
rock art, *104*, *282*. *See also* petroglyphs
Rockwood, Florence, 135
Rocky Mountain Scientific Exploring Expedition, 38
Rogers, Clarence, 288
Rogers, Keith, 49, 288, 291, 301
Rogers, Urban, 259
Rogue River (Oregon), 172
Roosevelt, Nicholas, 123
Roosevelt, Theodore, 3, 120, 121, 123, 185, 187, 207
Rosner, Anne, 168
Ross, Richard, 262, 263, 276, 278, 283
Ross, Scotty, 118
Roth, Lina Elise (Dolly), 125
Roundy, Jerry C., 337, 338
Ruess, Everett, 137–39, 227, 253, 366n66
Rusho, Bud, 343
Russell, Charles Silver, 145, 146, 147
Rust, Dave, 126, 134, 152–57, 215, 216, 261, 367n52
Rust, Emma, 156
Rust, George S., 152
Rust, Jordan, 155
Rust, Orion, 153
Rust, Ruth Snow, 154, 156
Rust, Will, 153

St. George, Utah, 306–7
Salton Sea (California), 192
Salt River, 185
salvage archaeology, 206, 243, 244–47, 249, 372n24

San Benito de Salsipuedes, 19
Sand Dune Cave, 325, 329
Sanderson, Robert, 216
San Francisco earthquake of 1906, 93
San Juan gold rush (1892–93), 108–10
San Juan Mission, 342
San Juan River, 65
San Juan Triangle survey, 263–64
San Juan Valley, 16
San Rafael Group, 100, 101
Santa Fe Railway, 105
Santa Fe Trail, 22
San Xavier del Bac (mission), 18
Sapir, Edward, 99, 311
Sauer, Carl, 255
Savage, Charles R., 56
scale, of mapping, 78
Schirra, Wally, 175, 313, 357
School of American Archaeology, 205
Schow, Andrew P., 340–41
Schumsky, Walter, 306
Scorup, James A., 118, 119, 291
Scott, Donald C., 134, 155, 215, 216
Scott, Hugh L., 205, 369n29
Scott, Louise, 216
Scott, Walt, 176
Scribner's Magazine, 185
Sears, Robert, 324
Segazlin Mesa (Lost Mesa), 324–25
Semmes, Cora, 32
Separation Rapids, 43, 47
Service, Robert, 107
Setzler, Frank, 228
Shaffer, Lulu Blanch, 143
Sharp, Alexander, 287–88
Sharp, Charles C., 148, 149
Sharp, Lauriston, 132, 288
Sharrock, Floyd, 283, 287, 292, 301, 304, 305, 306
Shaw, Merlin, 175, 176
Shepardson, Mary, 335
Shinarump Group, 99, 100
Shivwit Indians, 50, 51, 52, 68
Short, Vaughan, 355
Shoshone, 68, 304
Sibley, Robert, 221
Sierra Club, 354, 371n118
silver mines, 107
Sipapu Bridge, *119*
Sitgreaves, Lorenzo, 30
Sleight, Ken, 179–80
Slickrock Canyon, 284, 305
sluicing, and gold mining, 109, 115–17
Smith, Charles, 144
Smith, Dwight, 365n40
Smith, Elmer, 247
Smith, George Otis, 199
Smith, Jesse Raymond, 126
Smith, Joseph, 338
Smith, Tom (Pegleg), 23
Smith, Watson, 220, 222, 224, 228
Smith Fork Bar, 280–81, *282*
Smithsonian Institution, 72, 207, 242–43, 246, 313
Smokis (lodge or fraternity), 168–69
Snyder, Karl, 109
social organization, of Navajo, 335
SOCOTWA, 175–76
Southern California Edison, 191
Southern Numic language, 68, 334
Southern Paiutes: and ethnoarchaeology, 307–13; and Numic language group, 334; and Powell expedition, 38, 50, 57, 61, 68–70, 362n5. *See also* Paiutes
Southwest Manufacturing Company (Arkansas), 260
Southworth, John, 168
Spanish: and early explorers of Glen Canyon Country, 14–22; and Navajos, 334
Spencer, Charles H., 115
Sprang, Elizabeth, 237
Sprang, Richard W., 233–37, 371–72n10
Spruce Tree House, 201
Squier, E. G., 242
Stabler, Herman, 193
Stanton, Elizabeth Cady, 105
Stanton, Henry Brewster, 105
Stanton, J. R., 113

Stanton, Robert Brewster, 26, 46–47, 103–7, 110–12, 144, 153, 157, 161, 257, 342, 361n33, 364n3, 364–65n40
Stanton, Robert Livingston, 105
Staveley, Gaylord & Joan, 170
steamboats. *See* boats
Stearns, Frederic A., 161–62
Steen, Charles R., 248–49, 273, 346
Stegner, Wallace, 48, 76, 88, 175
Stein, Mary Anne, 310, 325, 326, 328
stereographs, 72
Stetson, Clarence, 193
Stevens, Brigham, 288, 301
Stevens, George, 349
Steward, Jane, 219
Steward, John F., 55, 75
Steward, Julian H., 217, 218–19, 248, 308
Stewart, Kilton, 217
Stewart, Omer C., 217, 222, 224
Stone, Julius F., 110, 114, 148–50, 157, 173, 361n33
Story, Dee Ann, 273, 275–76
Stout, Carol J., 273
Straight Cliffs formation, 101
Stranger from the Tonto (Grey 1956), 128–29
Strole, George, 48, 49
Suhm, Dee Ann. *See* Story, Dee Ann
Summerville formation, 101
Sumner, John Colton, 37, 38, 40, 43–44, 51, 54, 110
Surprise Pueblo, 324
Surprise Valley, 322
surveying: early history of in Glen Canyon Country, 62; and plans for dams on Colorado River, 190–92. *See also* mapping
Sutton, Dave, 177–78
Swanson, Frederick, 152
Sweeney, Catherine (Kay), 8, 9, 10, 72, 263, 273, 293, 309, 310–13, 357
synclines, 92

Tadje, August, 147
Tallsalt, Robert, 230
Talus Ruin, 269, 370n110
Taos, and fur trade, 23
Taylor, Elmina, 2
Taylor, Walter W., 228–31, 270
Tennessee Valley Authority (TVA), 245, 372n12
Tennessee Valley Historical Society, 244
Teocentli (newsletter), 254–55
Tertiary era, 101, 102
Thomas, Dudy, 233, 237
Thomas, Franklin, 193, 194
Thomas, Oliver, 294
Thomas, Wylie, 294
Thompson, Almon Harris, 36, 55, 61, 62, 63, 64, 65, 66–67, 71, 79, 80, 81, 83, 91, 184, 337
Thompson, Ellen, 40, 67
Thompson, Gilbert, 79, 81
Thomson, John, 113
Three Mile Ruin, 307
Tillohash, Tony, 311
Timmican, Jimmy, 312
Topping, Gary, 237
Torrey, Jay Linn, 3
tourism, and interest in archaeology of Southwest, 244
Tower Butte, 59
Trasker, Harry, 191
triangulation system, of surveying, 78, 79, 80, 82
Triassic era, 100, 102
Trimble, Kelly W., 190–91, 192
Trinity Church (New York), 33
Turner, Christy G., II, 273, 319, 322
Twain, Mark, 285
Twenty Five Mile Gulch, 6–7

Uden, George, 112
Uinkaret Indians, 68
Uinta Basin, 42
Ukwatsi-ngwi, 337
Ulloa, Francisco de, 14
U.S. Army Corps of Engineers, 246
U.S. Coast and Geodetic Survey, 78, 306
U.S. Department of Agriculture, 183
U.S. General Land Office, 78
U.S. Geographical and Geological Survey of the Rocky Mountain Region, 73

U.S. Geographical and Geological Surveys West of the One Hundredth Meridian, 73
U.S. Geological and Geographical Survey of the Territories, 73
U.S. Geological Survey (USGS), 61, 62, 72, 73–83, *84*, 187, 188, 190, 192, 362n15
U.S. Irrigation Survey, 183–84
unit pueblos, 330
University of Utah, 5, 242, 247–48, 249
University of Utah Press, 273, 283
Upper Trail, and Kaiparowits Plateau, 295
uranium, and mining industry, 346
Utah: and irrigation systems, 183; and liquor laws, 269. *See also* Escalante; Kanab; St. George; Utah State Parks
Utah Power and Light Company, 192
Utah Archaeological Society, 307
Utah Natural History Museum, 327
Utah State Parks, 262
Ute Indians: conflict with Spanish and Navajos, 334; and ethnoarchaeology, 307; and Numic language group, 68; and Powell expedition, 38, 57, 61, 71; and Southern Paiutes, 69
Utley, Robert, 24

Vanadium Corporation, 346–47
Van der Elst, Dirk, 264
Vanishing American, The (movie), 130–32
Verdoia, Ken, 357
Vermilion Cliffs National Monument, 354
Violet Marie (steamboat), 115, 117
Virgin Kayenta Branch, of Anasazi culture, 210, 306, 328
Virgin River area, 306–7
Vitruvius (Roman), 77

Wade, Vent, 135
Walcott, Charles, 184, 188
Walker, Don, 285
Wall, Enos A., 204
Ward, Henry A., 89
Warm Creek, 115, *116*
Warner Brothers, 170
Wasp House, 292, *293*
Watch Tower. *See* "Fort Moqui"
watercraft. *See* boats
Water Hole, The (movie 1928), 130
Waterpocket Fold, 263
water resources: and Colorado River Compact, 196; and history of irrigation systems, 182, 183; and Powell, 182–84. *See also* Colorado River
Webb, Robert H., 190, 194, 196
Webb, Roy, 114, 160, 171
Weber, Frank, 136
Weber State University, 4
Wellington, Arthur M., 106–7
Welsh, Vince, 173
Wendorf, Fred, 249, 372n24
Wenner-Gren Foundation for Anthropological Research, 250, 294
Western Literary Messenger (magazine), 23–24
Western Archaic, 329
Western Numic languages, 68
Westinghouse, George, 186
Westwood, Richard, 178
Wetherill, Al, 200, 202
Wetherill, Benjamin Kite, 133, 200
Wetherill, Clayton, 202
Wetherill, John, 49, 82, 94, 96, 121, 123, 126, 132, 161, 162, 201, 203, 208, 212, 213–15, 221, 365n15, 369n6
Wetherill, Louisa Wade, 121, 203, 205
Wetherill, Marietta, 203
Wetherill, Richard, 94, 200–203
Wheeler, George M., 73, 90
Whipple, Amiel W., 29, 30
White, Georgie, 140, 176–79, 233
White, James, 45–49, 291
White Canyon, 118, 345–47
White Canyon Mining District, 109
Whitfield, Robert P., 85
Whitmore, C. E., 202
Whitney, Josiah D., 35, 78
Widtsoe, John D., 193–94, 195–96, 365n15
Wild Horse Mesa (Grey 1928), 129, 130, 133
Wilhelm, Lillian, 126

William, Hanner Mariah, 3
Williams, Jonathan P., 109
Williams, William Franklyn, 109
Wilson, Bates, 263–64
Wilson, Bill, 123, 162, 170
Wilson, J. W., 112
Wilson, Jack, 142
Wilson, Lindsey, 254
Wilson, Wylie, 294
Wilson Canyon, 284
Wilson Dam (Muscle Shoals, Alabama), 244
Wilson Fold-Flat Company, 164
Wimmer, Tom, 191, 193
Wind River Indian Reservation, 304
Wingate, Benjamin, 99
Wingate formation, 99, 100–101
Winn, Bertha, 347
Wisherd, E. L., 214, 215
Wissler, Clark, 244–45
Wittgenstein, Ludwig, 10
Wolcott, Charles W., 187
Wonderland Expeditions, 180
Wood, Floyd B., 223
Wood, John Taylor, 40–41
Woodbury, Angus M., 224, 257
Woodchuck Cave, 137–38
Woolley, Edwin D., 153
Woolley, Franklin B., 63, 153
Woolley, Royal, 153, 154
Work, Hubert, 196
Works Progress Administration (WPA), 245
Wormuth, Francis, 5
Worster, Donald, 48, 76, 182
Worth, Conrad, 161
Wright, J. Frank, 140, 170, 237–41, 259, 318, 320
Wright, Otis, 259

Yellowstone National Park, 120, 243
Young, Brigham, 43, 50, 344
Young, Robert D., 193
Young, Stuart, 205
Yuma Indians, 18

Zion Canyon, 307, 367n50
Zion National Park, 2
Zuni, 18, 22